D0402675

JAY
WINIK

SIMON & SCHUSTER

New York London Toronto
Sydney Tokyo Singapore

ON THE BRINK

The Dramatic, Behind-the-Scenes Saga of the Reagan Era and the Men and Women Who Won the Cold War

NATIONAL UNIVERSITY
LIBRARY   SAN DIEGO

SIMON & SCHUSTER

ROCKEFELLER CENTER

1230 AVENUE OF THE AMERICAS

NEW YORK, NY 10020

COPYRIGHT © 1996 BY JAY WINIK

ALL RIGHTS RESERVED,

INCLUDING THE RIGHT OF REPRODUCTION

IN WHOLE OR IN PART IN ANY FORM.

SIMON & SCHUSTER AND COLOPHON ARE REGISTERED TRADEMARKS OF SIMON & SCHUSTER INC.

DESIGNED BY BARBARA M. BACHMAN

MANUFACTURED IN THE UNITED STATES OF AMERICA

10 9 8 7 6 5 4 3 2 1

LIBRARY OF CONGRESS CATALOGING-IN-PUBLICATION DATA

WINIK, JAY

ON THE BRINK : THE DRAMATIC, BEHIND-THE-SCENES SAGA OF THE REAGAN ERA AND THE

MEN AND WOMEN WHO WON THE COLD WAR / JAY WINIK.

P.   CM.

INCLUDES INDEX.

1. UNITED STATES—FOREIGN RELATIONS—1981–1989.   2. UNITED STATES—FOREIGN RELATIONS—

SOVIET UNION.   3. SOVIET UNION—FOREIGN RELATIONS—UNITED STATES.   4. COLD WAR.

5. REAGAN, RONALD.

I. TITLE.

E876.W59   1996

327.73—DC20   95-25775

                                                                    CIP

ISBN 0-684-80982-6

TO LYRIC—

WHO MAKES MY LIFE COMPLETE,

WITH LOVE

CONTENTS

Only politics and perhaps an accident of geography, the luxury of being bounded by two oceans, prevent us from recognizing the historical enormity of the Cold War's final decade and stunning end. Yet not since the Allied and American triumphs in World Wars I and II has a period so singularly shaped our destiny and changed our lives, infinitely for the better. As with those previous conflicts, America's Cold War victory is a heroic story of triumph and will, an accomplishment that we must not only know and celebrate but, more importantly, understand.

This book is that story, a portrait of the Reagan era. It is a complex, riveting, and as yet untold tale: of a visionary president and the men and women who served him; of the great and divisive debates over how to deal with the Soviet Union; of shifting political loyalties and the rebirth of one political party and the floundering of another; of personal anxieties and untold hopes; and of a tumultuous time that gripped the nation at home, stirred the imagination abroad, forced unprecedented change upon the Soviet Union, and forever altered the world.

As the 1980s began, no issue more intimately or powerfully dominated American lives and governed the fate of the nation as did the Cold War, and no issue mattered more than its resolution. Since 1945, the United States and the Soviet Union had been locked in a brutal contest between two diametrically opposed political systems, liberal democracy and Soviet Communism, which together for four decades had carved up the globe. But, by 1980, the two sides seemed headed for a final showdown.

Soviet troops were brutally setting siege to Afghanistan; from the dusty roads of Nicaragua to the bushlands of Angola, regional conflicts were exploding with ferocious intensity; America was routinely under attack at the United Nations; and the policies of containment and détente, or U.S.-Soviet co-existence, lay in tatters. As the Carter administration drew to a close, a U.S.-Soviet confrontation loomed in Europe over the deployment of nuclear missiles. For a dispirited America, which was then doubting itself militarily, politically, and economically, these events had ominous portents—as they did for the world at large.

Thoughtful men and women, in America and Europe, now openly feared that democracy itself could perish. Others, only a little less darkly, instead foresaw the Cold War lurching on indefinitely: two heavily armed camps, East and West, forever teetering at the brink. And still others, hawks and doves alike, contemplated the dreadful specter of war.

To be sure, for the new Reagan administration, the stakes could not have been higher. One misstep could be cataclysmic; one wrong decision could spell the difference between a cold peace or nuclear Armageddon. And the freedom of countless millions hung in the balance.

In a defiant act of boldness, upon entering office, Ronald Reagan and his administration decided to break radically with the past. Where preceding administrations had believed military confrontation and brinksmanship were a costly precursor to war, the Reagan administration believed they were a necessary component to secure peace; where preceding administrations had sought diminished tensions with the Soviets, the Reagan administration vocally championed democracy and human rights. And in the most audacious break of all, the Reagan administration decided that the Cold War must be not simply "managed," but that it was a contest to be decisively won.

In itself, this break is a remarkable story of leadership and vision. But it is also a dramatic story. Abroad, behind the thick, confident walls of the Kremlin, an old Soviet order wrestled with an adversary it could no longer predict or recognize, and found itself inexorably under siege. At home, in the nation's capital, Reagan's policies plunged hard-liners and doves into virtual civil war. An old liberal establishment was eclipsed by a new conservative counterestablishment, careers were made or broken over policy differences, clashes were bitter, and each side stopped at nothing to get its own way. It has been said that the essence of history is human drama. Indeed, the personal passions, the political struggles, the contest of individual wills, and the divisive domestic conflicts were as integral to the outcome of the Cold War as the U.S.-Soviet dimension itself.

This book thus weaves together both stories at the heart of the Reagan era and the Cold War's end: the U.S.-Soviet relationship, and the world of Washington. It is told as a narrative, largely through the eyes of the key players on various sides, from their rise in the late 1970s through the white-hot 1980s, to the conflict's denouement. Many of these individuals were exemplars of the era; in each case, through their stories and their concerns, we can see the larger issues unfold—with the awesome reality that there was no benefit of hindsight for their actions, no luxury of picking and choosing one's battles, and no escaping the punishing choices imposed by history.

Throughout, the Reagan era was marked by great urgency and even greater cause—and in every sense of the word, it was a saga. It was a time when greatness was gained for some and lost for others; a decisive period that gave rise to heroes on one side and mistaken judgments on the other. And it was the crucial chapter in the most important world event of the last half century. In conveying this history, I have sought to do justice to its sweeping qualities and its human elements, as well as to the blistering intensity that defined those years.

This is that story.

JAY WINIK
CHEVY CHASE, MARYLAND
1996

This was how it began.

In the early hours of April 24, 1980, just north of the Aswan Dam, three hundred miles south of bustling Cairo, and not far from the majestic pyramids of Egypt, at a place called Wadi Kena, Colonel Charles Beckwith, commander of the super-secret antiterrorist squad Delta Force, was roused from a fretful sleep by an aide. A big gruff man and former Green Beret, the fifty-one-year-old Beckwith had spent most of his life in the shadowy world of "special warfare." Up until that morning, his identity was so secret that even his middle name was classified.

Beckwith prided himself on being able to endure just about any environment. In the mid-1960s, he had commanded a special group of irregular forces in Vietnam, comprised of Vietnamese, Cambodian, and Chinese ethnic mercenaries. At the time, he drew up a flyer to inspire new recruits that read: "WANTED: Volunteers for Project DELTA. Will guarantee you a medal, a body bag, or both." Before his tour was over, Beckwith almost got his wish. In January of 1966, while he was flying in a helicopter low over the An Loa Valley, a Vietcong bullet ripped through his abdomen. On the verge of death in an army triage hospital, Beckwith yelled and cursed to be taken into surgery. The doctors hadn't wanted to waste their limited resources and time on Beckwith. He had lost too much blood. But after his screams, they relented, and waited for him to die on the table. He didn't, instead using up twenty-three pints of blood. Within another year, he was back on the front lines, serving another tour.

So it was telling that even the battle-hardened Beckwith was unhappy with the makeshift Delta Force base at Wadi Kena, originally a Russian-built facility consisting of ramshackle huts and reinforced concrete hangars. Some of his men attributed his restlessness to the blistering heat, others to the constant hum of the flies, but in all likelihood it was the waiting.

Beckwith was not a man patient with the nuances of diplomacy or the niceties of the military chain of command; he liked action, and even now, he was afraid the politicians would pull the plug on his rescue mission. But the aide who awakened him brought good news. The CIA had just learned that all fifty-three Americans held hostage by the Iranians were in the chancellery of the U.S. embassy compound. This would simplify his operation to free the hostages. Beckwith, who would personally head the rescue party on the ground in Iran, was delighted. Using the latest piece of intelligence, he quickly modified the assault plans. A smile crossed over his face, and he thought, "History is going to be made."

The mission to rescue the fifty-three American hostages would be difficult, if not unorthodox. Some thought it was simply crazy. It required a complex series of rendezvous, moving men and machinery by land, sea, and air. The first phase would begin the next afternoon, when Beckwith and his handpicked, specially trained, 132-man rescue force would be airlifted by six large-bellied C-130 transport planes to the island of Masirah—Beckwith's men had dubbed it "Misery"—off the coast of the Gulf nation of Oman.

From there, their initial destination would be Desert One, a staging ground at abandoned salt flats in Iran's Dasht-e-Kavir desert six hundred miles north of the coast and two hundred miles from Teheran. At Desert One, they would rendezvous with eight RH-53D Sea Stallion helicopters from the nuclear-powered aircraft carrier USS *Nimitz*, now steaming in the coastal waters off the Gulf of Oman.

After a grueling 570-mile flight, protected by the cover of darkness, the Sea Stallion choppers would then refuel at Desert One for the next leg of their journey, a 135-mile dash to a mountain hideout code-named "Figbar," about sixty-five miles southeast of Teheran. The helicopters and the men would arrive before dawn and hunker down for the day. Then after nightfall, nearly two days into the operation, the assault team would travel to Teheran in trucks provided by four undercover agents recently placed inside Iran, disguised as European businessmen. The actual rescue mission would occur just before midnight, in the heart of Teheran. It would be carried out in under an hour.

Once the American hostages were freed, the entire party would speed in the trucks to a pickup point, either in the courtyard of the embassy compound or to an adjacent soccer stadium. The six Sea Stallion helicopters would swoop in from their hideout near Figbar, pick up the men, and fly them to an abandoned airfield thirty-five miles southwest of Teheran, which would have been secured by Ranger ground commandos. From there, transport planes would airlift the hostages to safety. If all went according to plan, the long ordeal of the Americans held captive by the Iranian Revolutionary Guards and the Ayatollah Khomeini would be over.

In Washington, the mission had been dubbed a strictly humanitarian operation, even in planning sessions. But critics felt the plan was too lean and spare, with far too few men to overwhelm the militants holding the embassy in crowded downtown Teheran (a city of five million people, nine thousand miles from the U.S.), pick up the hostages, and escape to safety. One early plan had called for at least six hundred men and thirty helicopters in the assault force. Force would be necessary, the military planners had argued, a lot of it—to make an omelet, you had to break a few eggs. But for President Jimmy Carter and his more dovish advisers, a smaller strike was considered less bloody, less provocative to Iran's Arab neighbors, and more politically acceptable at home.

Some of the president's men, like Secretary of State Cyrus Vance, were against the use of force altogether. Vance's chief deputy, Warren Christopher, was horrified that Delta Force was planning to shoot the Iranian guards. When Beckwith had briefed Carter's top advisers on the operation in a White House Situation Room meeting, Christopher exclaimed, "You mean you're really going to shoot to kill? You really are?" Beckwith almost smiled in disbelief. His men were trained to shoot an enemy assailant not once but twice, through the middle of the head. He knew force would have to be used.

The operation's risks were considerable, and casualties, both among hostages and the Delta Force, could not be ruled out—it was estimated that thirty men would die. All in all, it was a highly complicated plan, designed to hit the Iranians from the ground instead of the air, from the east instead of the west, out of the line of flight from friendly bases in Turkey and Egypt. Surprise and speed were essential. With so many staging points and opportunities for detection, there was almost no room for error. It would be messy, but the Carterites felt it could be done.

That night on his ramshackle cot in Egypt, as he drifted back to sleep, Beckwith rehearsed the details of the raid over and over in his mind. He was drenched in sweat from the Egyptian heat. The plans had been six months in the making, and he had come a long way since the Joint Chiefs of Staff, responding to pressure from the White House for options, tasked him with putting together a rescue mission, virtually from scratch. Remarkably, when he began designing the operation in the fall of 1979, Beckwith had to rely primarily on old documents and intuition. On November 12, he had been officially informed that the U.S. no longer had any intelligence agents in place in Teheran. Not one.

From planning, Beckwith had shifted rapidly into training his elite group. Beckwith's men were headquartered at Fort Bragg, North Carolina, in an isolated compound originally built as a prison. It was just the right cover for his secret operation. Informally known among themselves as "Charlie's Angels," Beckwith's men underwent rigorous training in preparation to respond to just about any contingency, any hostage situation, any highjacking around the world.

Even so, the Iran mission was different. In moments of levity, Beckwith would joke about the difficulties of Desert One, "The difference between this and the Alamo is that Davy Crockett didn't have to fight his way in."

Access to Delta's personnel was so highly restricted that they didn't even show up on the personnel roster of the military computer. The existence of Beckwith and his men was available only on a need to know basis—and few people out of government, or in, needed to know. Only half in jest, Beckwith once asked a superior, "What if any of my men get stopped by a policeman for speeding?" When one enterprising reporter looking to write a story about a possible American hostage rescue attempt checked with army records for information about Beckwith, he found the following:

Charles Beckwith
Born: June 27, 1929
Attended College: 1952
Assignment: Classified
Serial Number: 258364046

The story was never written. The *New York Times* summed it up, later, after the pain and humiliation, with a front-page headline: "Who Is Charles Beckwith?"

It would be for the Iranians to find out.

To protect security, the training site was moved from Fort Bragg to the remote woods of North Carolina. There, at Camp Smokey, the men of Delta Force underwent a crash course for the Iran rescue attempt. They learned about Iranian customs, and memorized Farsi phrases, such as "*Ma baradar has team*"—We are brothers. A large-scale eight-by-twelve model of the U.S. embassy compound and surrounding streets, fourteen separate buildings on thirty-seven acres of walled-in real estate, was built, and meticulously updated as new intelligence reports and new photographs were acquired. Without any agents in place in Iran, one crucial daily ritual was watching the evening television coverage. The men would crowd around the TV to look at Peter Jennings reporting live from Teheran. No soldier sitting in that room liked Jennings. "Pretty boy" was the kindest name they called him. Raucously shouting, they taunted him as he spoke, free, while other Americans were still hostages. But for Beckwith, these nightly newscasts contained valuable clues that he made sure not to miss.

While other viewers grimaced at the humiliating scenes of a scruffy band of Islamic fundamentalists shouting "Death to the Great Satan" and "Death to America," Beckwith dispassionately watched for details about the enemy his men would face. Were the gates at the embassy secured? (The motor pool gate was chained and padlocked.) What type of weapons did they have? (The Revolutionary Guards outside carried G-3 assault rifles, the military guards inside carried Uzi submachine guns, M3 carbines, and handguns.) How well were the guards and the paramilitary forces trained? (They carried their guns like amateurs.) Each night, these segments were taped, screened, and pored over by Beckwith and intelligence analysts.

Step by step, Beckwith pieced together a portrait of the Iranian captors, their habits, their routine. Thick workbooks were filled, detailing which way doors opened, the locations of the keys, and idiosyncrasies of the guards. The veil of mystery surrounding the Islamic militants was slowly but surely lifted. Beckwith knew this: your enemy was different, very different, but you had to know him, you had to understand his thinking, his unique psychology.

And in time, they would know who Charlie Beckwith was.

In March, Beckwith and his men packed their bags and headed west to Yuma, Arizona, for a full dress rehearsal of the Desert One rescue operation. The 1.5 million acres of training desert at the Marine Corps Training Station, Yuma, where the temperatures reached a scalding 110 degrees by day and dipped sharply to near freezing at night, made it ideal practice territory. Even the Israelis came to train here, blazing across the skies with their Kfir fighter planes. Beckwith's men trained at night and slept by day. In the afternoons, discussion classes were held, and, like athletes preparing for the Olympics, each man's performance was critiqued. The group slept in prefab housing and ate one hot meal a day: C-rations spiced up with jalapeño peppers and hot sauce.

One contingent of the Desert One force had been training at Yuma since late November: the helicopter pilots. As a general practice, night helicopter flying was rare, and there were few pilots in the U.S. armed forces with any experience in night flying, even fewer with practice in flying without lights. The roughly six-hundred-mile flight that would have to be made by the helicopters into Iranian airspace, without breaking radio silence, hovering in and out of canyons at one hundred to two hundred feet to escape detection by Iranian radar, was without precedent in military operations. Thus, the air wing of Desert One, the men who would shuttle Delta Force in Iranian territory, refuel at an unspecified location in the desert, and bring the ground commandos and hostages to freedom, was slowly but inexorably born.

Each night, the pilots at Yuma would fly through the vast desert canyons, first for an hour, steadily building up to four hours. Many otherwise competent pilots couldn't handle it. The blackness of the night, the absence of sensory stimuli, gave an eerie feeling of being in space, like plummeting into a black hole with no return. The silence was acute, and perception enormously exaggerated. One mistake, and a helicopter could easily career into a cliff. Navigating with night vision goggles was a new, still untested art. It was uncomfortable to the flyers, "like wearing two roles of toilet paper around your eyes," explained Major James H. Schaefer, one of the tactical flight trainers at Yuma. For even the most fearless man, the "pucker factor was high," marine slang for a nervous tightening in the stomach and the bowels, like a kiss.

Beckwith himself was proof of this. Despite being shot down three times in Vietnam, after a night run out at Yuma he grimaced, slightly under his breath, "I have to admit, it sure as hell scared me to death flying out there."

Yet, slowly, steadily, a cadre of able pilots was put together.

It was on the seventh full trial run in the desert of the southwestern U.S., on March 25 to 27, that Delta Force and the pilots made their breakthrough. They flew accurate distances, made the ride by truck to the mock embassy compound built to scale, climbed the wall, neutralized role-playing guards without incident, and made a successful helicopter rendezvous while an airstrip was held. The exercise was flawless, like a Broadway dress rehearsal on the eve of an opening, when everything finally comes together.

Army Chief of Staff General Edward "Shy" Meyer told Beckwith, "If you don't think you have the edge, say so and you won't go."

But at that point, it wasn't even a toss-up. Beckwith didn't have to skip a beat: "Delta has the edge." Charlie's Angels were tough and ready. The time was now. On the morning of April 21, Beckwith and his men touched down at the staging base in Wadi Kena, Egypt.

As scheduled, on the morning of April 24, they boarded two C-141s in Egypt for the trip to Masirah Island. They landed at 2 P.M. By 4:30, Beckwith was airborne once again, this time in a C-130 transport plane. His destination: Desert One, Iran.

Five other transport planes would follow, two carrying the rest of Beckwith's commandos, and three bearing fuel for the Sea Stallion helicopters to refuel at the Desert One staging ground. Inside the hull of the C-130, his men sat shoulder-to-shoulder, their equipment and weapons strapped in the webbing overhead. The cabin interior was lit only by small red lights. As the plane crossed out of the Gulf of Oman and straddled the Iranian coast, it spiraled downward, dipping abruptly from three thousand to four hundred feet to evade Iranian radar. Few men spoke. The day before, in Egypt, they had been so high strung that they spontaneously burst into singing "God Bless America." At that moment, Beckwith was touched and proud. But this night, there was only silence and anxious anticipation.

They were a special team, a brotherhood of men who would fight and die for their country, an elite commando squad that few would ever know. Clad in jeans, unpolished army boots, and field jackets specially dyed black, they passed the time by checking the fresh edges on their knives and fiddling with their newly reassembled guns. The American flag stitched into the jacket of each man's right shoulder was covered with tape. Upon reaching the embassy, the tape would be ripped off.

Halfway through the trip, Major General James Vaught, the overall task force commander and Beckwith's interlocutor with the Washington policy makers, right up to the president, relayed that the eight Sea Stallion helicopters had just taken off from the *Nimitz.*

"Operation Eagle Claw," the designated name for the rescue mission at Desert One, was now fully under way.

GROUPED IN A loose diamond formation, the helicopters, resembling huge beetles, their legs hugging their wide bodies, briefly hovered at four hundred feet before racing north at more than 140 miles per hour to meet Beckwith and his Delta Forces. The largest helicopters in the U.S. armed forces (they could normally carry thirty-seven men comfortably, and up to fifty if packed tightly), these Sea Stallions were specially refitted with additional fuel for the long trip to Desert One. Seats had been removed to make room for special equipment that the Delta Forces would use, including ladders to scale the embassy walls in Teheran.

The Sea Stallions flew in pairs, under a prearranged buddy system. Without secure lines, in-flight radio contact would only be made in an emergency. From their helicopters, as they swung north, the pilots saw a light red haze resting over the Gulf of Oman.

Flying one of the lead helicopters was Major James Schaefer. For the six-foot-three, thirty-four-year-old Schaefer, this mission was an opportunity of a lifetime. As far back as he could remember, he had always wanted to fly.

He didn't do particularly well at Pierce Junior College in California, and transferred to St. Martin's College in Washington state on a basketball scholarship, a diversion from an otherwise unspectacular academic career. But the laconic Schaefer, the oldest of six kids from a family of moderate means and traditional values, was hardworking and looking for his niche in life. In 1966, he returned home to a draft notice, and seized the opportunity to enlist in officer candidate school in the marines. "If I were going to go, I might as well decide which force I'm going to be in," Schaefer would later say. After a tour in Vietnam, he returned to the U.S. as a member of Project 19, a marine program that specialized in tactical development; he trained with Israeli and British forces and soon made a name for himself as a skilled helicopter pilot.

When the American hostages were seized, rumors swept through the military like a prairie fire that a daring rescue mission was in the works. "A great opportunity," Schaefer thought. He wanted in. He got it.

In Yuma, where he was stationed, Schaefer became one of the more respected pilot instructors. As a sign of how valuable he was, in March, when the joint task force overseeing the Delta Force operation sent a pilot out to the *Nimitz* aircraft carrier, cruising in the Gulf of Aden, to test the Sea Stallions, Schaefer was the man they picked.

Lest his cover be blown, he was ordered not to wear a name tag when he boarded the *Nimitz*. Instead, on a ship in the middle of the Indian Ocean, the missing name tag made Schaefer stick out like a sore thumb. Even though more than five thousand men were stationed aboard the *Nimitz*, on the ship everybody knew everybody. For twelve long days, Schaefer was the mystery man, fending off questions like "Are you part of the rescue mission we keep hearing about?" "Do you need an extra man?" "When do we start?" The sailors swarmed around Schaefer, and all he could think of were the words "Don't wear your name tag." Lamely, Schaefer replied to each question, "I'm doing ship surveys for the navy yard."

Now Schaefer was back on the *Nimitz* for real. The morning of April 24, the day Desert One began, had started out tensely for him. One of the marine pilots had accidentally set off a firefighting system, and Helicopter No. 5 was doused in a foam-and-saltwater solution. A Catholic, Schaefer couldn't remember when he last went to church. But that morning, he solemnly bowed his head and prayed, for himself, his mission, and his country. After all the excitement, the reality had dawned. Training was over, this was the real thing. "Some of us may not come back," he commented to his co-pilot. But Schaefer was not without a sense of humor, and optimism. He stowed away a few unlikely items in his helicopter: three bottles of whiskey and a number of cowboy hats marked "Lute's," from his favorite beer-and-burger joint, "to be broken out when we had picked up the hostages, to celebrate our return."

But as dusk settled over the Gulf, Schaefer and his fellow pilots were not thinking about endings. The mission had swung into high gear. They were heading away from the water and into the skies above the vast deserts of Iran.

AT 10 P.M., Iranian time, Beckwith's transport plane touched down at Desert One. It was a smooth landing, even smoother than the one rehearsed in March at Yuma, Arizona. Bingo.

His adrenaline was racing.

The Desert One staging area was relatively remote, traveled mainly by entrepreneurial Iranian rug merchants, drug smugglers, and elderly Persians who came out of the mountains to make a religious pilgrimage, as they had for over a thousand years. The closest city was Tabas, thirty miles away. A once bustling place, nineteen months earlier it had been decimated by an earthquake and was now a virtual ghost town. Since then, a new Iranian curse had been coined: "Go to Tabas."

Shortly after the force had landed, a Mercedes bus filled with forty-five Iranians came lumbering down a packed dirt road that cut into the Delta Force landing strip. The problem had been anticipated. Beckwith fired a single shot into the bus's tires, bringing it to a grinding halt. His men then unloaded the confused passengers. They would be held temporarily in one of the C-130 transport planes, attended to by a guard and accompanied by one of Beckwith's Farsi-speaking men, an Iranian general who had fled to the U.S. when the shah was overthrown and was now used by the American military and intelligence services.

Just moments later, an Iranian fuel truck abruptly appeared, followed by a smaller pickup truck. Not taking any chances, one of Beckwith's men carefully aimed a shoulder-held, light antitank weapon. The soldier scored a direct hit; the vehicle exploded, and three-hundred-foot flames crackled into the sky. The driver scrambled out of the truck and, though dazed, managed to spot the pickup truck behind him and jumped in. A Delta commando anxiously shouted in Farsi, "*Bija enja, Bija enja*" (Come here, come here), but to no avail. The smaller truck made a hard U-turn, and successfully sped away across the flats.

Could the mission continue?

By secure voice communication, this information was relayed to General Vaught in Egypt. He in turn relayed the information to Washington, where he had a direct link only to the secretary of defense and the chairman of the Joint Chiefs of Staff. The Desert One mission was so secret that even the watch team at the Pentagon Command Center had no idea of the operation. Their attention was focused on another event in the Middle East, Israeli gunboats operating close to shore near Palestinian camps in Beirut, Lebanon, flashing lights and firing flares to harass terrorists in their strongholds.

A nervous voice in Washington asked if the operation's cover had been blown. Via Vaught, Beckwith responded that he believed not. And if it were, he felt it was a small risk. Having come this far, Beckwith didn't want to turn back. Washington asked for confirmation of Beckwith's recommendation.

Beckwith advised they continue.

Smoke continued to darken the sky, and some minutes later, when the second of the five transport planes landed and Beckwith's men filed out, the commandos shot a quizzical look at the flaming truck. Beckwith jauntly bellowed, "Welcome to World War III."

Using a prearranged code, Beckwith had his radio operator contact the two agents waiting to meet them at Figbar, their hideout southeast of Teheran, to see if everything was okay.

"All the groceries are on the shelf" was the response. In other words, no hitches there.

But as the Delta Force sat on the desert flats, the operation hit yet another snag. The Sea Stallion helicopters were supposed to arrive at 11:30. By midnight there was still no sign of the helicopters. Unable to communicate directly with them (their scrambler phones were only linked to General Vaught in Egypt and their open lines were shortwave radios), all Beckwith and his men could do was wait.

Daylight would break in just five and a half hours, 5:30 local time. As each minute elapsed, their margin of error diminished, and Beckwith increasingly feared he and his men wouldn't make it to their hideaway, a three-hour flight, until after dawn.

That would be a big problem.

A MINIMUM OF six helicopters would be needed to carry out the rescue mission; two more were added as spares in case of emergency. The military actuaries in charge of statistical analysis calculated that if there were eight helicopters, there was a 96.5 percent probability that at least six would make it to Figbar. Sending ten would have raised the probability to 99.2 percent. But only eight Sea Stallions would fit in the hangar deck of the *Nimitz*. More would be picked up by Soviet photo reconnaissance, raising suspicions. The Carter White House, which had the final say, opted for caution. They went with eight. It would prove to be a fateful decision.

One hour into the flight off the *Nimitz*, the eight helicopters hit their first string of bad luck. Helicopter No. 6 was disabled by a loss of pressure in its rotor blades, and was forced into an emergency landing. As planned, Helicopter No. 8 landed too. The crew and classified matériel were transferred to No. 8, but No. 6 had to be abandoned. The remaining helicopters continued on, unaware of the malfunction in No. 6. As they hugged the ground at an altitude of one hundred to two hundred feet, Schaefer turned to his co-pilot, Les Petty, and remarked "how clear and vivid everything is," just like what they had marked on their maps. "A piece of cake," he said.

Below them, they could see Iranian camel farms dotting the landscape—populated by ambling herdsmen, hunchbacked women, and loud children playing with the livestock. It was a timeless world, like something out of T. E. Lawrence, largely unchanged for more than a thousand years.

Two hours passed. The helicopters approached the town of Bam, an isolated Iranian village where the local police numbered a handful and had to watch over no more than fifty people. Still, the helicopters were not about to take chances. They turned off their lights, and spread out in formation across the sky in a straight line, from east to west, stretching six miles across: this way, the unsuspecting locals below would hear only one, fleeting loud noise, rather than a series of seven different noises. In the fading twilight, it was likely that the local gendarmerie didn't even pay attention to the droning sound.

Once past the town of Bam, the helicopters regrouped again in pairs, as they approached the Zagros mountains to the west, and would soon be climbing over two steep ridges to the north that separated them from Desert One. The first ridge was six thousand feet, and the second stretched nine thousand feet. Schaefer was relaxed nonetheless. No pucker factor this time. From his standpoint, everything was proceeding like clockwork; he even joked to his men that he was hungry and would like a snack.

Then, in an instant, two helicopters, a half mile in front of him, were swallowed into the sky. Suddenly, a chill went up his spine. It was as if they had fallen into the Bermuda Triangle, Schaefer thought. Just like that, gone.

"Where are Helicopters 1 and 2?" Schaefer cried out in his deep, baritone voice. "They've totally disappeared."

He struggled to keep his composure. "Check the maps, check the maps! Maybe there's a lake below us, that would account for a heavy fog."

"There's none on here, sir," co-pilot Les Petty said plaintively.

Schaefer was frantic. "The ground's disappeared now, I can't even see the ground; slow this aircraft down!"

"We're down to a hundred knots, sir, down from one thirty."

Fighting off panic, Schaefer, now feeling the heat of his flight suit, said: "We're at a hundred feet now, approaching the six-thousand-foot ridge, and we're limited to a cockpit and a window. Hold on tight for this one."

Then a terrible thought struck him: this was how helicopters crashed.

Within minutes, the temperature inside the cockpit soared to an intolerable ninety-five degrees. But what was worse, everything, the pilots' lips, their night vision goggles, their flight suits, their instrument panels, everything was coated with a fine dust, the consistency of talcum powder. Schaefer and his men couldn't make out anything except the feel of the dust, which floated in the air like a heavy cloud and stuck to them liked melted wax.

"God, what the hell is this?" Schaefer thought.

This dust storm was different from anything they had ever encountered in their training back at Yuma, nor was it anything they had been warned about. Normally, a sandstorm is filled with swirling sand and strong winds. But these helicopters had flown into a meteorological phenomenon known as a *haboob,* rare in the U.S., but common in the Middle East.

The *haboob* hung in the air, obscuring both the pilots' vision and their senses. Totally unprepared for this fine dust, the pilots flew through it for two hours, in a state of confusion and anxiety. Their now sweaty flight suits clung to their skin like Saran wrap.

Then, suddenly, Helicopter No. 5, the one that had been doused with firefighting liquid that morning, lost its gyroscope. Dizzied by vertigo, the pilot could not negotiate the six-thousand-foot and nine-thousand-foot ridges that were approaching.

In a state of panic, he broke radio silence and, speaking in a one-word code to General Vaught in Egypt, relayed his intention to turn back, even though he didn't have enough fuel to reach the *Nimitz.* General Vaught passed this on to the *Nimitz,* which reversed course and raced back to the Iranian coast to meet the ailing helicopter. It was a close call. Moments after touching down on the deck, the helicopter ran out of fuel.

The six remaining helicopters continued on, with the last one finally landing at Desert One at 1:10 A.M., an hour and forty minutes late. Major Schaefer was the first to touch down.

Beckwith, who knew nothing about the sandstorm, was upbeat in greeting Schaefer. "Are we glad to see you. How are you doing?" he grinned.

"It's been a hell of a trip," Schaefer said, shaking his head. Looking visibly riled, the normally unflappable Schaefer added: "If you had any sense, you'd move the helos out, put everyone on the C-130s, and go home." As soon as he uttered the words, Schaefer was sorry. He passed them off as a joke or momentary lapse. Deep down, he still wanted to go on.

In a routine check of the six helicopters, it was discovered that No. 2 had lost the use of its hydraulic pump, and would be unable to take off again. Now Beckwith was rankled. This meant three helicopters were out of operation, leaving only five to carry out the rescue. According to long-agreed-upon plans, this would trigger an automatic cancellation of the mission. There was no longer any margin of safety, none whatsoever, as far as Beckwith was concerned.

Beckwith and his men quickly ran some calculations. They could leave behind six thousand pounds of matériel, including men, or they could try to load everything into the already overloaded five remaining helicopters.

From Egypt, General Vaught asked Beckwith: "Would Eagle [Beckwith's code name] consider going on with five?"

Beckwith, the man who for six months, day in, day out, had toiled to put together the rescue mission, who all his life had built up to this moment, made the most painful decision of his life.

"No."

Beckwith paused. The heat was terrible. Sucking in his breath, it was as though his life were coming to an end, a horrible grisly end. Vaught was listening.

"I recommend abort."

GENERAL VAUGHT PASSED the word on to Washington, to General David Jones, the chairman of the Joint Chiefs of Staff, and Secretary of Defense Harold Brown. Brown picked up his secure phone to call Zbigniew Brzezinski, the president's national security adviser. The message was tersely put: "I think we have an abort situation."

Brzezinski rushed to notify the president, who was in conference in the Oval Office. The two men walked into Carter's adjacent hideaway, a small study linked to the Oval Office by a short corridor. Upon hearing the news, Carter muttered, "Damn, damn."

He called Secretary of Defense Brown for confirmation, and asked:

"What's Beckwith's recommendation?" Brown relayed that it was unchanged; Beckwith's view was that the operation, as planned, couldn't proceed with only five helicopters. There was no discussion or inquiry into alternative options. Ultimately, the final decision was up to the president. The president mulled it over for five minutes, each of which seemed like an eternity. It all came down to Jimmy Carter.

Carter cradled his head in his hands, then sat up and managed a single sentence: "Let's go with his recommendation."

IN IRAN, A frustrated, almost heartbroken Delta Force prepared their evacuation—the one contingency that they had never rehearsed in training. As sixteen C-130 engines roared and the steady whop whop of the Sea Stallions droned on, the sound on the ground was deafening. The refueling hoses were picked up, and two of the six C-130s took off. For their part, the Delta commandos, unclear about the next step, were getting on and off the remaining Sea Stallion helicopters. The entire situation was chaotic.

Inside Schaefer's helicopter, Marine Corporal George N. Holmes, Jr., a deeply patriotic twenty-two-year-old from a sleepy town called Pine Bluff in Arkansas, was fidgeting. Ten days earlier, he had packed all his personal belongings, along with his last paycheck, and mailed the package to his parents. He dashed off a handwritten note: "I won't be needing them for a while." He was tight-lipped about where his next assignment was, but his parents read between the lines. Like so many of the others involved in this secret mission, the hope was that the world would read about the stunning raid after its success—just as it had when the Israelis rescued their hostages at Entebbe in Uganda. A dejected Holmes and his fellow soldiers in the helicopter pondered the fact that after half a year of intensive training, after endless days of waiting for the go signal, after having traveled halfway around the world, this was now not to be. They were going to return empty-handed, humiliated by a series of technical mishaps, bad weather, and a reluctance to have used more than eight helicopters and ninety commandos against the Iranians. He heaved a sigh, and, hearing Schaefer's instructions, prepared to take off.

A ground crewman was directing traffic with a small frequency radio and by waving his arms. Schaefer was ordered to veer left and taxi around a C-130. He lifted the helicopter twenty feet in the air, where it hung suspended like a houseplant. Time seemed frozen.

Les Petty, Schaefer's co-pilot, was reading off a stream of flight data: altitude, power, maximum pressure. Dust was everywhere. The ground crewman seemed to be motioning to them to change direction. Schaefer fought the chaos and fought the heartbreak. Dust sifted into his eyes, and all he could make out of the swirl of blackness was the ground crewman, now walking in the direction of the C-130, signaling Schaefer to follow him. Schaefer, who could see nothing else in the darkness, reversed course and banked right. Then came a noise and a plume of flame that reached almost instantaneously into the sky.

"It was a loud thud. Like a baseball bat slamming the plane," Schaefer later remembered. At that moment, the rotor blade of Schaefer's helicopter had cut through the C-130's fuselage, neatly slicing it into two. Schaefer's helicopter burst into flame; fire spewed from the nose and poured into the window and the belly of the aircraft. Scrambling frantically, Les Petty managed to escape out of his window, but two of the three crew members in the working bay area died on impact with the C-130. George Holmes never even knew what hit him.

Then Schaefer heard the screams of Marine Sergeant Dewey Johnson, who was sitting behind him on the right. He reached back with his arm, and pushed his glove covered hand through the fire to pull Johnson to safety. Just a little closer, he thought . . . one more moment . . . "Dewey had my hand for a second. And then he stopped screaming."

Johnson, a thirty-one-year-old native of Jacksonville, North Carolina, died, amid three burning bottles of whiskey and charred cowboy hats.

Schaefer's final moments of consciousness were frenzied. He shut his aircraft down, and, almost passively accepting death, started to curl up into a fetal position. But as the molten heat from the flames drew closer, Schaefer, with only seconds remaining, began to struggle. "If I'm going to die," he thought, "I don't want the last image that my parents and kids have of me to be of a still, burning body. At least I ought to be running."

Schaefer pushed himself up and crawled out the window, fell to the ground, and furiously rolled around in the dirt to smother the flames already engulfing his back and his hand. His final sight, before he blacked out, to awaken later at the army's burn center near San Antonio, Texas, was of Beckwith's Redeye ground-to-air missiles. They were to be used by the Delta Forces against Iranian aircraft to secure the safe passage for the escaping hostages, but now they lit up the Iranian sky, somewhere in the godforsaken desert, like fireworks on the Fourth of July.

Beckwith ordered the crewmen to evacuate the five remaining helicopters, which were brimming with fuel and liable to explode at any moment. The Delta team piled into the remaining C-130 transport planes and took off, leaving the abandoned helicopters and their classified contents behind. Beckwith's last recommendation to General Vaught in Egypt was to send in an air strike to destroy the remains of the wreckage. Washington denied the request on the grounds that if any Iranians were killed in the process, improbable as this might have been, the military in Teheran might initiate reprisals against the hostages.

A dirty, dazed Beckwith, who had seen so much that he thought he could never quite see more, leaned his head against the window of the C-130. Desert One was a mission intended to bring Americans home. It succeeded only in leaving eight more behind, never to return. They had spirit, guts, the right stuff. Who back home in Washington would understand that? Jimmy Carter, a man he didn't vote for, and the Congress, what did they know about special operations? Once they started asking questions and started second-guessing the operation, then the search for a scapegoat would begin. The press would get wind of his name and hold him up beneath the hot glare of television lights and cameras, or the cool accusations of headlines.

But that would be tomorrow. Beckwith looked out the window of his C-130, thinking of what might have been, of the hostages still in Teheran, of the broken hopes and the humiliation of his country, and of the eight brave young men who were charred ruins, and he, Colonel Charles Beckwith, special forces commander, cried.

CHARLIE BECKWITH WAS right. Recriminations would follow. But this dismal failure in the desert was more than a single mission gone awry. As the Carter years drew to a close, the Desert One debacle was to become emblematic of the decade that had preceded it, a decade marked by the slow, relentless erosion of American power and prestige around the globe.

American foreign policy seemed to have reached a nadir. The unease that had afflicted the country since the last helicopters lifted off the rooftop of the Saigon embassy in ignominy now appeared to have sapped the national will. And, for perhaps the first time in the postwar era, as the 1980s began, even the very outcome of the Cold War was in doubt.

With Soviet military power on the rise, the nuclear arms race accelerating, and regional wars festering, a crucial historical moment had been reached. The overarching question for all Americans was again what to do about the Soviets. Should the U.S. be soft or tough, confrontational or conciliatory? And these questions were not only immediate, but urgent and very real. The decisions, small and large, to be made in the coming months and years would decisively affect the future of the U.S. and of the world. But with each day that passed, the road to be taken looked ever more uncertain, the solutions even less so.

Yet this turbulent time would give rise to a new force in America, a unique coalition of conservatives and neo-conservatives, Republicans and Democrats, men and women. Galvanized by Ronald Reagan, this new counterestablishment shared one overriding bond: to reverse the national decline abroad.

Ronald Reagan and his administration had their roots not simply in a single election, but in an entire decade of international turmoil, in a prolonged period of American soul-searching, and in the détente years of Richard Nixon, Gerald Ford, and Jimmy Carter. But this new counterestablishment and the president they would serve had a dramatic and often fiercely debated vision. They were singularly dedicated to redrawing the lines of conflict. They did not shrink from confrontation, East versus West. They would countenance negotiations, but not at any cost. And they rejected the time-honored foreign policy establishment verities of "stability" and of passively managing the Cold War to a stalemate. Instead, their ultimate target was the Soviet Union; their goal was no less than to reshape the world.

Their arguments were complicated and often misunderstood. Indeed, to many, their goals seemed not just unattainable and unrealistic, but downright dangerous. Throughout the following decade, the wisdom of their policies was hotly contested by the establishment that they would supplant. From the moment they took power, Ronald Reagan and his administration found their tenure marked by pitfalls and obstacles; by escalating tensions and an opposition as fierce at home as abroad; and most of all, by the raised stakes of the two superpowers engaged in looming conflict and desperate proxy battles around the globe.

But the story of the Reagan era, of the historic reversal of America's fortunes and the end of the Cold War, begins not at countdown, but at inception, in the years that brought these men and women of the counterestablishment together and formed their élan. Their route to the corridors of power in Washington was winding and circuitous. And the years leading up to Desert One were their time to rise.

RISE

It was a steamy July morning in 1979, a sweltering haze hung over Washington, and Richard Perle was late. Jacket off, shirt drenched, he dashed the six blocks from his cramped Capitol Hill town house to the majestic vaulted ceilings and glistening floors of the Russell Senate Office Building. He wound his way through the narrow streets, past the quaint row houses, with their big windows and bright shutters. He heard the drone of perilously perched air conditioners, and the steady drip, drip as they wrang water from the air. Washington in the summer was humid. It sat, heavy and fermenting, like an old dishrag. The city had been built on a swamp, and in July, beneath the brick and marble and asphalt, the swamp showed.

Perle arrived, rumpled and damp, and a bit pudgy at the age of thirty-seven. He had already missed the morning staff meeting, and was close to missing his luncheon appointment. But in his office at the Permanent Subcommittee on Investigations, chaired by influential Washington Senator Henry M. "Scoop" Jackson, no one raised an eyebrow. Perle was known for working odd hours, laboring at his desk until 2 or 3 A.M., making phone calls in the morning from the privacy of his home, and eventually rolling into the office sometime before noon. Already, he was a bit of a legend in Washington, hailed as a folk hero and brilliant conceptualizer by his admirers, and as a genius, an evil genius, by his detractors, who would come to call him "the Prince of Darkness."

In a town where many changed their views with each prevailing political fashion, Richard Perle stuck to his ideas and convictions. He had brains, purpose, tenacity, and charm, a powerful combination in a hyperbolic, ever-more combative city. He was not patrician, pedigreed, or affably Ivy League. He was a middle-class kid from the Hollywood Hills in California who was making it big.

. . .

EVIDENT TO ALL sides, he clearly relished his pressure-filled job as one of the nation's most influential voices on nuclear arms control and as a relentless critic of détente in U.S.-Soviet relations.

Perle stayed a moment to go over the morning's phone messages and papers. Then he exited the office, a little less breathlessly than he had arrived. Lunch was waiting. Peter Wilson, a State Department spokesman for SALT II, the recently signed U.S.-Soviet Strategic Arms Limitation Treaty designed to cap the nuclear arms race, would be early for his appointment, as he always was, and Perle would be on time, at least for Perle, only ten, maybe fifteen minutes late.

Peter Wilson and Richard Perle went way back, to their first days in Washington, ten summers before. Then, they were both bright young men, roommates, youthful Cold War Democrats brimming with ambition and energy, supported by the same powerful mentors, men whose names already resonated as among the titans of modern history, Dean Acheson, Albert Wohlstetter, Paul Nitze. In those heady days, they had been locked together as allies in political combat to strengthen America's defenses against the growing military power of the Soviet Union.

A decade later, the urgency of this crusade had only grown—the Soviet Union was stronger than ever, while the U.S. increasingly looked like a hapless paper tiger in world affairs. For the Carter administration, the danger of a catastrophic nuclear war seemed a little too perilously close. So Wilson, now working for President Carter, would draw on his friendship with Perle, the golden boy on Senator Henry Jackson's staff, the senator who increasingly loomed as a key figure in the Senate debate on ratification of the SALT treaty, a debate that the whole world would be watching.

Wilson would seek to enlist Perle's support for the treaty. Their meeting was scheduled to occur over lunch, in the Senate Dining Room.

IN THE SOMBER halls of the Russell Building, where every footfall echoed down the long corridors, the rumpled Perle looked vaguely out of place amid the moldings, marble, and mahogany. Portraits of statesmen, painted in thick oils and somber tones, of men like Daniel Webster and Arthur Vandenberg, who stood for loyalty to the Senate as an idea and an institution, sternly surveyed the meeting rooms lining the corridor. In serving their president and their country, these were congressional giants who, as in Bismarck's memorable words, "heard the footsteps of God as they marched through history."

But they were also men from a different era, from a time when the Senate was still a club, a slow and deliberative body reflecting the folkways of a nineteenth-century institution, where its work was punctuated by rich meals, good gossip, and long retreats back to home states. From World War II through the early years of the Cold War, Congress either deferred to the executive on foreign and military matters, or a chosen few worked with the president and his men, hand in hand.

It was in the suite of rooms at the Wardman Park Hotel, occupied by Senate Foreign Relations Committee Chairman Arthur Vandenberg, where the senator and President Truman's hand-picked emissaries, Bob Lovett and George Marshall, labored together to craft the bipartisan principles of the NATO Western alliance to contain Soviet Communism, often meeting during the cocktail hour. Then, a small band of men controlled foreign policy, that is, until the disillusionment and pain of Vietnam, and the Vietcong's Tet Offensive exploded in living rooms across America. The failure of intervention in Vietnam stirred the old isolationist leanings that had tugged at the American psyche since the founding of the republic, and congressional liberals and conservatives alike pushed to pull back on America's commitments abroad.

Smarting from its acquiescence in Vietnam, believing that all those much-decorated generals and East Coast establishment intellectuals from Harvard had it wrong, that the war was a disaster, a stunned Congress was no longer willing to be used as a passive instrument. Congress had been a willing partner in waging the Cold War, but it flexed its muscles on Vietnam, with senators talking about "the limits of intervention." No longer could a small group of like-minded men sit down and quietly decide policy for the country. Congressional committees hounded the administration, and, aided by the bright lights of television, eventually forced the end of American involvement in South Vietnam.

Spurred by Vietnam, Congress also undertook a number of reforms, and increased its staff, from 9,400 in 1972 to 20,000 in 1979. This new army of experts behind the senators and congressmen, the nameless and faceless figures, the "shadow lawmakers," brought a new expertise and new grit to the legislators. Richard Perle was one of them. But he was also different.

Throughout the 1970s, as the U.S.-Soviet relationship once again moved center stage, Congress continued to play a role in international affairs, although in the arcane and delicate matters of nuclear arms control and negotiations that were so pivotal in East-West relations, Congress generally preferred to comment more on broad themes than on minute details. That at least was true of most senators and their staffs, with the exception of Richard Perle and the man he served, Senator Henry "Scoop" Jackson.

Jackson, a liberal on domestic and social affairs, a self-styled Truman Democrat and a man of enormous integrity, was unshakably hard-line on issues of national security, and was regarded as one of the most thoughtful cold warriors in the Senate. Jackson's implacable anti-Communism was not of the same stripe as that of the Republican far right. Rather, it was similar to the thinking of many European socialists and the American trade union movement at the height of the Cold War, fiercely anti-Soviet in its fight against Communist infiltration of its ranks. He deeply believed in the American experiment and the benefits of democracy. He was a passionate defender of human rights. And Jackson was, by every measure of character and public service, a remarkable man.

He had come within a hair of being picked by John F. Kennedy to be his running mate in 1960, and twice made a bid for the presidency himself, in 1972 and 1976. Even as his own party increasingly moved to the left on foreign affairs, inspired by George McGovern's isolationist, anti-defense message, Jackson never strayed from his fundamental positions. And despite the foundering of his presidential hopes, and the leftward drift of his party, he remained one of the most influential senators in the United States. Indeed, twice presidents from both parties offered to make him secretary of defense.

In the Senate, on defense issues Jackson was without peer, and colleagues regularly deferred to his expertise and leadership role. His devotion to the subject, his good contacts, his strong power base deriving from senior positions on the Armed Services Committee and as chairman of the Permanent Investigations Subcommittee gave him a natural edge over his colleagues and with the administration. And while the uncharismatic Jackson was not destined to be president, and would become only a minority voice among the Democrats, he still acquired a small but tenaciously loyal following. These men and women proudly dubbed themselves "Jackson Democrats."

Since 1969, Richard Perle had been not just a Jackson Democrat, but also almost constantly at the senator's side. "I have complete confidence in Richard," Jackson would repeat, time and again over the course of a decade. When Perle had been on Jackson's staff for all of six months, Jackson, during a meeting with Yitzhak Rabin, then the Israeli ambassador to the U.S., said: "I want you to meet my right-hand man on national security issues," and marched Ambassador Rabin into Perle's office next door.

Jackson and Perle were a natural match. Perle's parents had both died of cancer the year Perle joined Jackson's staff, and Jackson, who was paternalistic by temperament and remarkably unpretentious for a senator (constituents walking into his office would be surprised to see the senator down on his hands and knees on the floor, poring over defense charts, while his staff sat comfortably in chairs), became a surrogate father to Perle, whose keen mind and evolving charm masked an inner shyness. Jackson was protective of Perle in every sense of the word. He taught Perle legislative strategy. He made sure Perle filed his income tax returns and paid his parking tickets and would exhort him to please, please balance your checkbook. When Jackson had early morning breakfast meetings, Jackson's secretary would prod the hopelessly late-rising Perle with a call, to ensure that he would be on time.

But Jackson was drawn to Perle out of far more than concern. In Perle, he found a brilliant intellect, someone able to simultaneously grasp nuance and details, and grand ideas. And in Perle, Jackson also saw more, not just mind, but soul. Perle could be rough in political combat, but he had a generous heart, forever offering his help, opening his small home and table. Russian émigrés slept on his couch, not because Perle found it fashionable, but because he believed it was right. Perle also quietly supported and looked after his retarded younger brother, who was still living in California. And there lay perhaps the greatest connection between the Washington state senator and the former Californian: principle. Perle was a young man of principle, with an unswerving belief in and loyalty to his country and a complete willingness to subsume his life to what was right. Jackson believed in principles, fought for them, and Richard Perle was the person he wanted beside him in that fight. Politically, Jackson and Perle agreed on virtually every issue. They talked every day, though they didn't have to. The two were so in sync that Perle rarely had to check with Jackson to see where his boss stood on an issue.

In the Senate, a staffer's ability to deliver his member on an issue is the final source of his power, much in the way a union negotiator will be successful only if he genuinely represents his membership. "I always knew just how far I could go, instinctively, without putting Scoop out on a limb he didn't want to be on," Perle said. The result was to give Perle a powerful combination: a broad mandate and a long leash. And he used it to push his and Jackson's ideas and ideals, a philosophy of meeting the Soviets at every step of the Cold War, with convictions that shocked the more timid in Washington.

Thus, it wasn't Perle, the Senate staffer, who was making the pilgrimage to the State Department to see Peter Wilson, the administration official, but the other way around.

SUNLIGHT STRUCK THE bushes outside the upper windows of the Senate Dining Room, casting a thicket of light on the pressed linens, polished silver, and lunching senators, along with a few select staffers, often scribbling furiously on steno pads. Those at each table spoke in hushed tones of serious business. The only audible disturbance was a third cup of coffee being poured, or a satisfied senator splurging on ripe strawberries with a side of cream.

Perle and Wilson asked to be seated at a corner table, where it was less likely that they would be overheard, or that the two of them, Perle and an administration official, would be noticed. The latter was improbable. As Paul Friedenberg, another Senate aide, noted, Perle stood above most staffers. "He was one of those staffers who was like a hundred-and-first senator," Friedenberg said, "always a presence."

Wilson was anxious. These were bright years in his life. He had been a crack analyst at the CIA, and was now in a prized slot in the administration in the State Department's policy planning shop, the same office where such giants as George Kennan and Paul Nitze had made their early mark. It was just the right place for a young talent on the rise. It was, he said, "his day in the sun." If President Carter was reelected, Wilson would surely advance into more prestigious jobs. Yet as he and Perle took their seats at the table, Wilson felt a gnawing doubt.

In late May, Wilson had called Perle to get on Perle's calendar. Perle had hemmed and hawed, and explained he knew how busy Wilson must be. He didn't want to take up his valuable time, but of course, he'd love to get together with Wilson when they were both free. Wilson sensed that Perle was blowing him off. So he told Perle he'd make the time, whatever was convenient for Richard. July was good. So July it was.

Perle was one of the leading critics of the administration's SALT treaty, the treaty that the Carter administration argued was designed to bring the enormous U.S.-Soviet nuclear arsenals under control. In his capacity as a State Department official, the White House had already sent Peter Wilson around the country to explain to elected officials, local leaders, and newspaper editors the necessity of ratifying the SALT treaty. Lately, Wilson felt his travels appeared to be bearing fruit. Public support for the treaty had risen, not dramatically, but at least moderately.

But today, Wilson was not here at the White House's behest, but on his own initiative. Where so many others had tried, and failed, Wilson would make one last attempt to get Richard Perle on board. Having spoken to opinion makers across the country, he would now lobby his old roommate.

He knew it would be anything but easy.

THE WHITE HOUSE had been making arguments for an arms control treaty for the last two years. And from the moment it had taken office, the

Carter administration had paid enormous personal attention to Perle, treating him as though he were a foreign country. Staffers in the administration were alternatively appalled and jealous as word traveled that Richard Perle could be seen at the White House "every day."

Walter Slocombe, the principal aide to the secretary of defense on arms control issues, and William Hyland of the CIA, both considered two of the more hard-line types in the administration, were regularly dispatched to address Perle's concerns, and lunched frequently with him. "It was good fun," Perle said with a touch of modesty. "They tried to persuade me, and I tried to persuade them."

Slocombe personally liked Perle, but he called dealing with him tough sledding. "Perle had strong convictions," Slocombe recounted, "and stuck to his guns."

Peter Wilson's immediate boss, Anthony Lake, the director of the State Department's Policy Planning Staff, was equally solicitous of Perle. On January 28, 1977, just after moving into his new post, Lake sent a letter to Perle's home, rather than to his work address, inquiring about "lunch" in "the last week of February." Lake also penned a note at the bottom, "Please do send me possible Policy Planning names. I really am interested." And hoping to influence Perle's next chat with the powerful Washington political columnists Roland Evans and Robert Novak, he penned a final line: "pace E. and Novak."

Most policy makers, and certainly most Senate staffers, would have buckled in the face of this attention and flattery, or at the least would have become more pliant, more accommodating. But Perle seemed impervious to the attention, and the administration was slow to realize he couldn't be bought off.

Carter's national security adviser, Zbigniew Brzezinski, thought of hiring Perle on the National Security Council, and asked Barry Blechman, a deputy director at the Arms Control and Disarmament Agency and a well-known arms control liberal, what he thought of the idea. Blechman, not known in Washington for his buoyancy, perked up, speaking with surprisingly colorful language. "It would be a great idea," he said, "a lot better for us to have him inside the tent pissing out, than outside of the tent pissing in." But Brzezinski didn't hire Perle, and in fact never even asked to speak to him. Ultimately, in the quest to win over Perle, the administration always had to retreat from the trappings of its office and return to its arguments, the only language to which Perle would respond.

The arguments over arms control on both sides were anything but academic. The threat of a superpower confrontation was too great not to try to wrestle the nuclear genie back into the bottle, as was the horrifying possibility that the U.S.'s defenses against the Soviets would be dangerously weakened, and it could end up on the losing side of the Cold War. The issue became even more heated once President Carter and his Soviet counterpart, Leonid Brezhnev, signed the SALT II treaty at a special summit in Vienna on June 18, 1979. It was a momentous occasion, the climax of seven years of Soviet-American negotiations.

As the signing ended, the two men stood up, shook hands, and, captured by the moment, fell into a spontaneous embrace. Brezhnev, the aging Communist leader, his burly arms outstretched, his hands still clasped on Carter's arms, lapsed into a rare flight away from his atheistic faith. "If we fail," Brezhnev said, "God will not forgive us." Feeling the drumbeats of history, Carter replied, "I, as President, am entrusted with the security of the United States of America, I would never take any action that would jeopardize that sacred trust. President Brezhnev, you and I both have children and grandchildren and we want them to live, and to live in peace."

The summit was hailed by its supporters as a giant step for the human race, away from the abyss of nuclear annihilation. But in the offices of Senator Henry Jackson and Richard Perle, it received a very different response. Jackson and Perle did not believe evil should be accommodated. And to them, the Soviet Union was evil. It was a ruthlessly expansionist system. It jailed its citizens indiscriminately, killed them if it wished. It denied free speech, suppressed immigration, declared dissidents psychotic. Moreover, it callously wore down its citizens in long lines and frigid rooms. It was a system that ravaged dreams. And it had power. Had nothing been learned from two world wars and the Holocaust? wondered Jackson and Perle. For them, the overriding lesson of the twentieth century was that evil with power could not be indulged, except at a terrible price.

On the eve of Carter's departure to Vienna, Jackson had warned: "Against overwhelming evidence of a continuing Soviet strategic and conventional military buildup, there has been a flow of official administration explanations, extenuations, excuses. It is all ominously reminiscent of Great Britain in the 1930s, when one government pronouncement after another was issued to assure the British public that Hitler's Germany would never achieve military equality—let alone superiority. The failure to face reality today, like the failure to do so then—that is the mark of appeasement." His view did not change once Vienna was over.

For all the rhetorical flourish of the signing, the fine print was disheartening. The actual treaty did shockingly little, in Jackson's estimations, to curb the most lethal of Soviet weapons, while time and again it tied America's military hand. This was a bad treaty, and Jackson would not back down.

The administration quickly fired back its own salvo. The SALT treaty would mitigate the threat of the giant land-based Soviet nuclear missiles, the SS-18s. To those like Perle and Jackson who said the treaty could be improved upon, the response was equally sharp. When asked if the treaty could be amended by the Senate, Carter's secretary of state, Cyrus Vance, fired back an uncharacteristically sharp answer, no, it could not. Andrei Gromyko, the Soviet foreign minister, agreed. SALT supporters argued that a treaty that blunted the threat of Soviet power, even if not perfectly, was better than no treaty at all. Nothing, it was said, nothing, was more dangerous than the two nuclear powers not talking about controlling these horrible weapons of mass destruction.

Perle was troubled by the treaty, and contemptuous of the terms in which it was being discussed. He felt the apocalyptic talk was nonsense, and that it would be a grave mistake to ratify the treaty in its present form. It was not that Perle did not believe in treaties, only that he did not believe in bad ones.

After the signing of SALT II, he broke his silence and went public with his reservations. In early June, *Time* magazine convened a panel of experts in New York for a high-profile all-day conference to discuss the upcoming Senate debate on the treaty. Although it was his wife's birthday, Perle went up to New York. He was all but a lone voice in his criticisms of the treaty. "I simply refuse to believe this treaty is beyond improvement," he maintained.

Watching Perle, *Time*'s Strobe Talbott thought he conducted himself with a remarkable degree of civility, even as he said things other panelists found outrageous.

Perle stood his ground. In *Time*'s coverage of the symposium, he was featured prominently as the pivotal figure in the debate. The magazine emphasized Perle's determination to see the SALT II negotiations reopened with the Soviets. Underneath a picture of Perle in shirtsleeves, he was quoted as saying: "The Administration will become an apologist for the Soviets."

To the administration, this statement was a shot across the bow. Peter Wilson took note. If Perle was not satisfied, his boss, Scoop Jackson, would not be satisfied. Wilson's calculations were simple. If Jackson sided with the administration, treaty ratification would be assured. If he sought to amend the treaty fundamentally, requiring renegotiation with the Soviets, then the treaty was sunk. The two sides had already been at it for seven years. The Soviets had already said they wouldn't accept such amendments. It was that clear-cut.

.   .   .

NOT EVERYONE IN the administration shared Wilson's views. The administration vote-counters in congressional relations, "the SALT salesmen," were cautiously optimistic that the Senate would eventually ratify the treaty. They predicted that they would do it with Jackson and Perle—or without them. Every Monday, the White House convened a SALT working group to discuss strategy. But when it became more and more uncertain that the White House would get the necessary sixty-six votes in the Senate to pass an unamended treaty, the administration hired Lloyd Cutler to coordinate the SALT selling campaign.

Cutler, a soft-spoken New Dealer, moved with ease among Washington's establishment. With the likes of Henry Kissinger, he might talk about "kibitzing," but Cutler had long since shed the trappings of his Jewish immigrant family, and had emerged as one of the capital's principal power brokers, a veteran Washington insider who specialized in behind-the-scenes fixing.

Cutler had honed his skills when his law firm, Wilmer, Cutler and Pickering, represented industrial giants in their battles with the government. When the Pharmaceutical Manufacturers' Association clashed with the Hill over drug pricing, and the American Automobile Manufacturer's Association jousted with Ralph Nader over the issue of automobile safety, Cutler was the man on the side of big business. In the same breath Cutler's firm represented J.P. Morgan & Co. in its fight against banking reform.

Now Cutler, as White House chief legal counsel, hustled between the White House and Capitol Hill, conducting discussions with the Senate that were, observers felt, every bit as delicate as those the White House had so painstakingly negotiated with Moscow. Cutler believed progress was being made, and at the critical moment he felt convinced that the administration would have the votes to ratify the treaty. While in private Cutler acknowledged that getting Perle's, and thus Jackson's, endorsement was "enormously important," in a public burst of confidence, Cutler upped the ante for would-be dissenters. The master fixer and compromiser put treaty skeptics in the Senate on notice. "The Senate critics of the treaty," Cutler declared, "have failed to lay a glove on it."

Perle, taking Cutler's comments as a direct challenge, baldly dismissed Cutler out of hand, not in private, but in the pages of the *Washington Post*, labeling Cutler "self-serving." As though speaking to a novice, Perle continued, "I commend the record of hearings before the Armed Services Committee, wherein it becomes clear that the treaty failed to lay a glove on the continuing Soviet buildup."

"Perle was," Cutler said afterward, choosing his words with the utmost diplomacy, "one of the very key intellectual influences behind the criticisms of the treaty."

. . .

It SEEMED TO Peter Wilson that Perle had always been key, always been influential. In the ten years he had known Perle and watched him, from his CIA office in Langley and State Department perch at Foggy Bottom, Wilson marveled at how Perle had established himself as a major figure in every controversy over America's nuclear policy, the issue that dominated the newspaper headlines and concerns of so many Americans. As Perle's star rose, so, too, it seemed, did his reach, his network of allies in the capital, and his standards for being satisfied.

Perle's imprint was seen in virtually every one of Senator Jackson's legislative maneuvers on U.S.-Soviet relations. And Perle's criticism was bipartisan: before Carter and the Democrats, his arrows were directed at the détente polices of Nixon, Ford, and the Republicans.

Wilson had seen it so many times before. Perle's calm and charming persona effectively hid his deadly serious agenda: he was ferociously anti-Soviet, fiercely hard-line, driven by seemingly implacable convictions. He believed in democracy. He believed in human rights. And he believed that the only way to guarantee both was through strength, not weakness. No other nation, in Perle's eyes, has U.S. interests at heart. He disliked American officials who were soft on the Soviets, and was equally scornful of the Western allies willing to accommodate their Soviet neighbor. Perle was a fighter, honed in the trenches of the Senate, the quintessential guerrilla on the inside who would stop at nothing to achieve his goals.

Wilson wondered if he had been naive in setting up this lunch.

"It's GOOD TO see you, Peter, long time no see," Perle said, his smile inviting, his tone warm. Wilson, the Princeton graduate, with his perpetually clean-cut looks, appeared every bit the model Boy Scout. Today was no exception. Wilson flashed a nervous smile, and explained he was seeing Perle on his own initiative. The administration had not formally asked him to come by. Wilson wanted to talk about arms control. SALT would help put a cap on Soviet programs. It was a modest start, but a start nonetheless.

The lunch seemed to go on forever, like a grueling five-set tennis match, with a constant barrage of volleys, back and forth. The two talked specifics and details of the treaty for over an hour. Wilson said the treaty will restrict the limits beyond which the Soviets will not be able to go. Yes, Perle said, but it does nothing to restrict the most feared missiles in the Soviet arsenal, the Soviet SS-18s.

The treaty will improve our verification capabilities, Wilson said. Yes, said Perle, but with the loss of Iran and our listening posts there, verification is limited, and the Soviets, who have increased their nuclear arsenals with undiminished fury since SALT I, have held out for and gotten a treaty replete with loopholes that they will exploit. They did this with their new SS-19s, and they will certainly do this with the highly accurate cruise missiles, which, given their small size, mobility, and their ability to carry nuclear or conventional warheads, are almost impossible to verify, Perle added.

But, Wilson said, the treaty doesn't restrict the U.S. options in key weapons categories, such as the submarine-launched Trident nuclear missile, and the ten-warhead MX missile. An adequate defense effort will be possible. We can do whatever we deem necessary.

Perle was annoyed by this, and it showed to Wilson. For Perle, this was the nub of the matter—how democracies negotiate with a totalitarian country like the Soviet Union. At the first sign of a Soviet balk, too many men, who had built too much of their careers on the shifting foundations of compromise, rushed to be accommodating. If they could produce a piece of paper, national security be damned. Perle was disgusted.

"Let's face it," Perle argued, "this administration came to town with no experience in foreign affairs. It drew its policies from people who love arms control, hate the military, and dread even the slightest confrontation with the Soviet Union."

Neither Wilson nor Perle had touched much of the food. There were few people left in the dining room.

If the Soviets cheat, Perle continued, the U.S. will never do anything about it, certainly not under this administration "Let's be frank," Perle said, "the last thing this administration will want to do is complain about any Soviet behavior."

Wilson feared he was losing the argument, but he couldn't sense why. He too had always felt that détente was oversold—but unlike Perle, he believed there were still merits to a less-than-perfect arms treaty.

Perle showed no signs of relenting. He pulled out a plastic model comparing U.S. and Soviet nuclear missiles. On the left side were the U.S. missiles, in gray—four altogether; on the right were the Soviet missiles, six, in black. The large Soviet missiles dwarfed the American ones. Wilson, his face flushed with the implication that he didn't understand Soviet power, angrily called it "a plastic dildo," and said that the size of the missiles said very little about their ability and accuracy.

Perle returned to the fundamentals. "Carter's not a serious person. He's no commander in chief, and his people can't be trusted," he said.

"They'll sell out our security—look at how Carter reversed himself on the B-1 bomber, and canceled the neutron bomb."

This was difficult for Wilson to rebut. Perle did have a point about a commander in chief standing firm against the Soviets. Soviet aggression was on the rise. Communists were now in power in Cambodia, Angola, Ethiopia. And perhaps most chilling of all, there appeared to be indications of Soviet interest outside of its normal sphere of influence—in Afghanistan.

Perle discussed another thesis of his: the U.S. and the Soviets were in a prewar stage leading to World War III, not completely dissimilar from the Germans and the British before World War II. The Soviet buildup will produce military superiority in the 1980s—but their long-term future is clouded by economic stagnation. This will lead the Soviet leadership to find itself under powerful pressure to "exploit its window of military advantage in the 1980s in order to avert the bleak future awaiting it in the 1990s."

It was not that Perle thought a nuclear war was imminent, or even likely. But he worried that the Soviets would exploit this military advantage, and the fear of nuclear war in the U.S., for imperial gain. Senator Daniel Patrick Moynihan, a disciple of Perle's boss, Scoop Jackson, agreed. On the floor of the Senate and in various articles, Moynihan, taking a cue from Scoop, also likened the foreign policy debate in the U.S. to the debate in Britain in the 1930s.

Wilson was unable to persuade Perle, so certain was Perle of his arguments. Perle had really learned these street skills up on the Hill, Wilson thought to himself. He was not the same young kid he had first met ten years earlier. In 1961, a British journalist described the defense intellectuals who pondered nuclear strategy as men who "move freely through the corridors of the Pentagon and the State Department rather as Jesuits through the courts of Madrid and Vienna, three centuries ago, when we in Europe were having our own little difficulties." From his position in his Senate office, Perle had attained the status of a modern-day Jesuit. And, in Perle's eyes, Wilson had committed the ultimate heresy, for which there seemed to be no absolution. "I defended SALT publicly," Wilson said.

Since the start of the Carter administration, Wilson and Perle's disagreements over SALT had already led to a steady drifting apart. But this time it was different. There was a finality to the tone. Wilson had given it his last stab, and had failed. He concluded there was no administration arms control agreement that Perle would accept. Perle was beyond his reach, and probably anybody else's in the Carter administration.

. . .

ON THAT SUNNY day in July, Wilson couldn't have known how fast and dramatically the international landscape would change in just one year. The events that followed that lunch would confirm Richard Perle's grim view of the world and the changing equation between the United States and the Soviet Union. Over 150,000 Soviet troops would invade Afghanistan. Soviet violations of human rights would rise. The U.S. would apply too little power in attempting to rescue the American hostages languishing in Iran. And as a result of these failures abroad, Senate consideration of the SALT II treaty would be shelved—permanently.

Newspapers and magazines would headline stories with the words: "America in Retreat." In capitals around the globe, suggestions would be made that the U.S. was slipping behind the Soviet Union. The specter was raised that democracy would turn out to be nothing more than a bold experiment, an experiment that had failed.

And by the following July, Richard Perle would have left the staff of Senator Scoop Jackson.

But as Wilson and Perle stood up from the table, neither knew exactly what was coming. And as they shook hands and parted in the hallway, Wilson did not know that he and Perle would never joust again over arms control, or anything else for that matter.

"After that last lunch, we never, never spoke again," a dejected Wilson said. "For those who fell out of favor with Richard Perle, his motto was: 'take no prisoners.'"

For Perle, it seemed, the sides were clear. There was now nothing more to say.

When Richard Perle arrived on Capitol Hill in November of 1969, he was the proud owner of two suits and several hundred books. Neither born into the establishment nor bred into wealth, Perle had spent nearly all of his twenty-seven years as a student. Now he was to become a staff member for Scoop Jackson, and be paid what seemed to him a princely sum, more than he had dreamed of or, for that matter, could spend, $18,000.

From that position on Jackson's staff, Perle would emerge as one of the leading conceptual—and creative—thinkers on defense in the capital. He would publicly spar with Henry Kissinger, become a valued source for Washington columnists, and an indomitable foe of the Carter administration. He would also go on to be, as *Time* magazine diplomatic correspondent Strobe Talbott put it, "a watchdog, then a critic, and ultimately the single most effective opponent" of arms control. It was an unlikely end for someone from Perle's beginnings.

Richard Perle came to Washington as an opponent of the Vietnam War. Politically, he considered himself a social democrat, which is to say he was liberal on domestic issues, anti-Communist on foreign policy, and believed in the centrality of democratic governance. The thought of voting for Republican Richard Nixon over any Democratic candidate, let alone Bobby Kennedy, "was beyond comprehension." He was a middle-class Jewish boy from California who had once dreamed of being a literature professor in the quiet confines of a small liberal arts college. For him, the well-bred establishment world of Washington was a most unlikely place to be.

For years, Washington was a city that measured success by good lineage, handsome breeding, and family connections, not by ideas and arguments. In Washington, intellectuals were awkward outsiders, continuously eased out by smooth establishment insiders who could wage clean bureaucratic wars. The ultimate prize was power. And intellectuals knew little about bureaucratic battle in pursuit of power. Henry Kissinger, the deft national security adviser, was the exception, not the rule. Most intellectuals fared badly. The noted historian Arthur Schlesinger, Jr., gained his reputation not from his work for Jack Kennedy (Washington columnist Joseph Kraft tartly quipped: "Therein lies . . . the famous Washington mystery: What did Arthur Schlesinger do in the White House?"), but from his time in academia. Ted Sorensen, Kennedy's brilliant speechwriter, watched Washington's rumor mill shred his reputation, and was publicly humiliated when Jimmy Carter withdrew his name for CIA director. Even George Kennan, the father of containment, was more at home as a Princeton scholar than as an insecure policy maker in the State Department.

In Washington, it wasn't enough to have powerful sponsors; one needed a tolerance for endless bureaucratic battles and the Washington whisper mill, an open line to the press, and, as the journalist David Halberstam once noted, the ability to run with the pack, not clumsily, but with a special feel for the rules of the game, the sort that they taught in refined prep schools like Groton or Choate and honed at Yale and Harvard. Intellectual arguments and ideas alone didn't cut it, which made a career in Washington seem anathema for Richard Perle.

Perle grew up in Los Angeles, the elder son of a businessman and a housewife. His father, a high school dropout and the child of Russian Jewish émigrés, was a textile merchant and gambler who, like many Jews, brought his family west from New York to Los Angeles after World War II. The Perles lived in a solidly middle-class area, in an art deco apartment complex. The elder Perle was earthy and bubbled with enthusiasm. He relished golf, playing cards, and "the good life." He had no pretensions, no cultural airs or affectations, and handily displayed the signs of an immigrant family having scrapped its way to middle-class achievement. Perle never felt he had much in common with his father, and even less with the trappings of glitter that were L.A. When given the chance, he would quickly gravitate elsewhere.

Perle's mother radiated a formal, stately quality. Friends were struck by her beauty and grace. She could be "a little bit cool," but there was no doubting that she was classy. She loved to entertain but didn't like to cook, and the family ate out often, four or five nights a week, frequently at the neighborhood delicatessen. Perle and his mother were close; he adopted her charm and attraction to beauty and style.

Growing up, Perle was both an intellect and a cutup. His parents sent their precocious son to a private high school, where, despite being elected class president, his mediocre grades and irreverent behavior were too much for the school administrators. He was asked to leave. "A bad role model," the school said. At Hollywood High School, however, he thrived. Considered there to be shy and bright, he stood out for dressing formally, in shirts, sweaters, and ties. He also became part of the budding literary bohemian set, which included the sons and daughters of the well-to-do Hollywood crowd. Some of them had been dragged before the House Un-American Activities Committee. Their children called these hearings "the witch hunts." Politically left-wing, Perle was personally appalled by the government's intrusion on the exercise of free speech and its suppression of personal liberties.

Perle continued to run with a similar crowd in college at the University of Southern California, where he quickly became popular among the small pocket of academically minded students. At USC in the 1950s, Perle was considered a bit of a radical. He was energetic, liberal, and ebullient. "Always a bit of an imp," his close college friend Harvey Waterman said.

But in his junior year, Perle stumbled into an introductory political science class taught by Ross Berkes. He was enchanted. In the course of lecturing, Berkes paced back and forth, tugging on his eyebrows and wrinkled forehead as if he were squeezing out ideas. Perle was transformed.

The main text for the course was Hans Morgenthau's *Politics Among Nations: The Struggle for Power and Peace*, the bible for the "realist school" of international relations. Morgenthau espoused the theory of power politics, or social Darwinism writ large, stipulating that the strong nations survive, and the weak are plundered. Morgenthau wrote: "Human nature, in which the laws of politics have their roots, has not changed since the classic philosophies of China, India, and Greece endeavored to discover these laws. . . . We assume that statesmen think and act in terms of interest defined as power, and the evidence of history bears this assumption out." Perle changed his major to international relations. More than two decades later, he would still say, recalling Morgenthau, "the world hasn't changed one bit, it's about power politics, and always will be."

Perle then dashed off an application to the London School of Economics and Political Science, a prominent English university that boasted such distinguished alumni as John F. Kennedy and Daniel Patrick Moynihan. To his father's surprise, Perle was accepted. His bags packed, in 1962, Perle saw Europe for the first time.

THE LONDON SCHOOL of Economics was another world for Perle. Its redbrick buildings and cobblestone alleyways were nestled in the heart of London, just a few minutes' walk from the glistening Thames, bustling Fleet Street, and the Parliament. Just down the street was the famous

British Museum, where Karl Marx had spent thirty-four years of his life penning *Das Kapital.*

Academically, the LSE was comparable to Oxford and Cambridge, although its student population was drawn from a more diverse cross-section of England. Twenty percent of the students came from abroad. Occasionally, the LSE took chances and admitted American students whose records were a little spotty. Richard Perle was one of them.

Under the tutelage of Professor Hedley Bull, Perle took advantage of the LSE curriculum and read strategic studies, a discipline in political science designed to understand the perils of the nuclear era. There was a heady feeling in the Political Science Department, where, from its cramped fourth-floor quarters, faculty and students pondered the awesome meaning of the atomic bomb and the likely turns of the Cold War. They felt they were on the crest of a new profession, pioneers of a new age.

Perle came to this field with a bit of an edge. Back in L.A., during high school, he had dated a girl named Joanie Wohlstetter. She had told him her father was "a mathematician." But Albert Wohlstetter was in fact one of America's leading theoreticians of nuclear war at the Rand Corporation, an air force–sponsored think tank based in Los Angeles. Wohlstetter was flamboyant and eccentric, worldly and suave, and spoke as easily about food and wine as he did the threat of Russian bombers and missiles.

When Perle and Wohlstetter first met, they talked briefly about the intricate world of nuclear weapons and international affairs. Wohlstetter later gave Perle his article on strategy, "The Delicate Balance of Terror," from *Foreign Affairs*, to read. In questioning the security of America's nuclear forces against a surprise Soviet atomic attack, this influential article had already created quite a stir in the upper reaches of government. Ultimately, it would form the foundation for efforts to reduce the vulnerability of American nuclear power, for the need for a "second-strike capability," and for Kennedy's declaration that there was a "missile gap" between the United States and the Soviet Union. It was anything but an easy read, and hardly standard fare for a high school student. But an excited Perle read the article, and read it again, "so dense were the ideas in the pages."

He and Wohlstetter, the high school student and the master strategist, then had a long conversation about the "nuclear balance of terror," the first of many conversations about the esoterica of nuclear strategy that the two would have over a lifetime. Even after Joanie and Perle split, he and Wohlstetter stayed in touch, the strategist becoming an intellectual mentor and eventually a friend. By the time Perle went to London, Wohlstetter had already been a significant influence on him. Wohlstetter saw in Perle what Jackson would later see, a young man with an uncommon sense of principle and of right and wrong, with an intellect and a determination not only to think, but to do. Perle knew about European wines, and he learned to think like a Rand analyst: that when it came to nuclear weapons, there was no substitute for rationality and cool-headed thinking, no place for excessive sentimentality or emotion. In the struggle to preserve the peace, the unthinkable, nuclear war, did have to be thought about. Richard Perle, the middle-class kid from a mediocre school who looked rather lackluster on paper, fit in quite well at the London School of Economics.

IN OCTOBER, THE Cuban Missile Crisis disturbed the academic calm of the LSE. On Monday, October 22, a week into the crisis, as Soviet missiles sat in Cuba, while American forces went on alert and prepared for a naval blockade, Perle lay on his bed in his small London flat and flicked on the radio. His roommate, a Romanian Jew who first tried to pass himself off as an Italian, Edward Luttwak, had already gone to sleep. Perle rotated the dial, trying to get the latest news.

Suddenly, he heard the voice of President Kennedy, in a recording from his television appearance in the U.S. Kennedy proclaimed to the United States and the world: "It shall be the policy of this nation to regard any nuclear missile launched from Cuba against any nation in the Western Hemisphere as an attack by the Soviet Union on the United States requiring a full retaliatory response upon the Soviet Union."

The U.S. and the Soviet Union were on the brink of a nuclear war, and Kennedy was calling Soviet Premier Nikita Khrushchev's bluff. Textbook Morgenthau, textbook Wohlstetter, Perle thought.

In London, there was panic. Corner markets quickly ran out of food. "It's that Cuban Missile Crisis," Perle's grocer explained, "the housewives are stocking up." Classes were canceled at the LSE. In their place, an "Emergency Debate" on Kennedy's response to Khrushchev was held.

The LSE auditorium was packed. Student after student stood to denounce the actions of the brash young American president. Anti-Americanism hovered in the air. One student, echoing the sentiments of those before him, declared it was the "beginning of the immediate destruction of the planet." Perle, pipe in hand, decided he had enough, and made his way to the podium, amid hisses and catcalls. He spoke in measured tones, but gave a rigorous defense of the United States. The United States was protecting the most important principle, freedom, Perle said. It was the Soviet Union that had provoked the crisis, and, he finished, "The Russians will back down."

The whole room quieted. Perle and his defense of freedom had won them over. His roommate, Luttwak, said afterward, "It was a colossal thing for him to do."

This moment would become vintage Perle: keeping his cool, arguing broad principles, playing to the crowd against the odds.

RICHARD PERLE RETURNED to the U.S., and in 1964 was accepted to Princeton's prestigious Ph.D. program in political science, where he rejoined his old friend Harvey Waterman, then working on his dissertation as an associate at Princeton's Center for International Studies.

Among the graduate students, Perle was the most conservative. He spoke endlessly of *realpolitik*, the need for a strong military to counter Soviet aggression and defend democracy. He was the resident "hawk" among his friends, but as even Waterman conceded, he was never knee-jerk in his views, and took the time to understand the issues. "Perle took the problems seriously, did his homework, and genuinely bore a sense of responsibility for his positions."

At Princeton, Perle also fell in love, and married a young Danish woman, Lisa. She was blond, very Nordic, and fragile. Their friends felt they were a "strikingly good-looking couple."

But one week after the marriage, Lisa Perle suffered a nervous breakdown. Her prognosis was poor, and Perle was devastated. He took Lisa back to Denmark, hoping she would be able to put her life together. He even constructed a dissertation topic that would enable him to continue his studies abroad and stay with her.

Two years passed. Perle had done only minimal research on his thesis. And Lisa, still not fully recovered, couldn't face returning to the U.S. Perle couldn't remain in Denmark forever, nor did Lisa want him to. So Perle returned home to pick up the pieces of his life. Yet he continued to stay in touch with Lisa, long after his second marriage, always a loyal friend.

When he returned, Perle took a job in Massachusetts with Westinghouse's in-house think tank in Waltham. By day, he analyzed U.S. defense posture. Unwilling to forgo his handsome Ford Fellowship of $3,000, Perle intended to work on his thesis by night. But he didn't stay long. Albert Wohlstetter was on the phone.

IN THE SPRING of 1969, Wohlstetter offered Perle a job in Washington with a newly formed group called the Committee to Maintain a Prudent Defense Policy. The outfit had been formed by Wohlstetter and Paul Nitze, former head of the State Department's Policy Planning Staff and a deputy secretary of defense. Its other supporters included the legendary Dean Acheson. Wohlstetter asked Perle to become the committee's chief researcher. There would be no salary, only expense money, but the work was enormously important. It would be a good experience. Would he take it?

The answer was yes. But Perle would only take a sabbatical from his job at Westinghouse. He would return. And he intended to finish his thesis.

Along with Perle, two other young men, Peter Wilson and Paul Wolfowitz, were enlisted by the committee to do battle on behalf of the anti–ballistic missile (ABM) defense system, capable of destroying incoming enemy missiles in midair. Wilson and Wolfowitz were protégés of Wohlstetter's at the University of Chicago, where he taught political science when not working with Rand. Edward Luttwak, Perle's former roommate from the LSE who was now in Israel, told Perle he was interested. The brilliant Luttwak had turned his attention from economics to military analysis. With a helpful word from Perle to Wohlstetter, Luttwak also joined the fray. A proud Acheson called them "our four musketeers."

These four scrappy but deeply serious kids were tasked to work like a shadow Pentagon, drafting position papers for senators and their staff, doing background analyses, and providing quick-response answers to press questions. Fifteen thousand dollars had been raised to support the organization. Half of it was personally put up by Nitze. A White House aide, Bill Casey, was personally responsible for taking care of the other half of the committee's funds.

On the committee, it was Dean Acheson who most dazzled Perle. Acheson, Truman's secretary of state, was as responsible for the Truman Doctrine as President Truman and as responsible for the Marshall Plan as General Marshall. At the age of seventy-five, his health marred by a thyroid condition, he had to strain to hear others speak. But Perle marveled as he watched Acheson who, by force of intellect and sheer presence, shaped the attitude of the committee board members around the table, guiding the logic, the strategy, the urgency. Watching the statesman, the young Perle suddenly realized the impact one could make in public life.

His opportunity would come, after the critical vote on the ABM system. Following a long struggle, at summer's end, with Senator Jackson managing the debate on the floor of the Senate, the Safeguard ABM system was approved. A jubilant Nitze, recalling the little two-room operation, said of his four Young Turks, Perle, Wilson, Wolfowitz, and Luttwak: "With these fellows and only fifteen thousand dollars . . . we ran circles around all the big-name experts."

. . .

PERLE HIMSELF HAD done a bit of impressing, developing a mentor-protégé relationship with Nitze. Nitze, at the age of sixty-two, had advised every president since Franklin Roosevelt, and was one of the country's consummate public servants. He had succeeded George Kennan as head of the State Department's Policy Planning Staff, and had been in and out of government ever since. A Cold War Democrat, Nitze was the model of Yankee noblesse oblige. The silver-haired Wall Street investment banker had amassed a small personal fortune at the prestigious Dillon, Read and Co., and had married even greater money. His wife, Phyllis Pratt, was heir to the Standard Oil fortune, and her uncle, Harold Pratt, had donated a stately Park Avenue mansion in New York to be the home of the Council on Foreign Relations, the informal headquarters of the foreign policy establishment.

Nitze saw the Soviet Union as a compulsively hostile power, bent on world domination, and felt that U.S. cooperation with the Soviets could only be achieved from a position of strength. This suited Perle, the hardline Wohlstetter disciple, just fine. That fall, when President Nixon asked Nitze to join his nuclear arms negotiating team in Geneva, Nitze, who thought Perle was "brighter than hell, scrappy and dedicated," wanted the young analyst to accompany him to Europe.

But Perle already had an offer, from Senator Jackson, who asked him to take a job on the staff of his Permanent Subcommittee on Investigations. This committee had almost unlimited power in the Senate, and was a marvelous opportunity for Perle. Perle, the young cold warrior dazzling his elders about him, helped Nitze during the transition period as a full-time consultant at the Department of Defense in the fall. Then, it was on to Senator Jackson.

JACKSON HAD AN exceptionally good staff. His staff director on the permanent subcommittee was Dorothy Fosdick, called "Dickie" by friends, but affectionately referred to by colleagues as "the Bubbie," Yiddish for grandmother. Fosdick, just over five two, with short graying curly hair and a broad smile, was an institution in Washington in her own right. Her father was the well-known liberal cleric Harry Emerson Fosdick, for whom the philanthropist Andrew Carnegie had built New York's Riverside Church. She was the first woman to hold a senior position in the State Department, working on Kennan's Policy Planning Staff and assisting in devising the Marshall Plan, but she rejected an offer to be the first woman admitted to the Council on Foreign Relations, scoffing, "I don't want to be a token." Even her widely known affair with the far more liberal former presidential candidate Adlai Stevenson did little to diminish her hard-line views. When Stevenson went on to become U.S. Ambassador to the United Nations, only to be called "soft" by Jackson, he was stung by the charges, and called up Fosdick. "Can't you get the Senator to go a little easier on me?" he pleaded.

The Jackson foreign policy shop was known as "the Bunker," which captured the spirit that bound the team together in their crusade. On the one hand was a small band of Wohlstetter-taught strategists, recruited by Perle and Jackson, such as Charles Horner, an expert on China. Then there were the labor types and Social Democrats, who hung around the Bunker or joined the staff for a stint before moving on, including young talents such as civil rights activist Tom Kahn, later an assistant to AFL-CIO head Lane Kirkland, or Carl Gershman, a young Social Democrat, who would become director of the National Endowment for Democracy. Professionals unhappy in the private sector, looking for an entrée into the policy world, would get their start at the Bunker, like Elliott Abrams. Conservative academics like Richard Pipes, a Harvard historian, and Robert Conquest, a Harvard political scientist, would likewise enter the Washington policy world through their affiliation with the Bunker.

The Bunker even had de facto members in the administration. Paul Wolfowitz, while at the Arms Control and Disarmament Agency (ACDA), would come by the office and collaborate with Perle, as did John Lehman, who was at the NSC. One of the more notable occasions was in February of 1977, when Wolfowitz and Perle spent all night writing a twenty-three-page single-spaced memo on SALT II for the newly elected president, Jimmy Carter. It called for deep cuts in the Soviet and U.S. missile forces and would serve as the opening stance Carter used with the Soviets on SALT II.

Unlike most Senate offices, where there was a chain of command, and memos would have to be signed off by layers of staff before they reached the senator, the Bunker was a free-flowing one-room operation, with little bureaucracy and little backbiting. There was not enough time in the day as it was, and the circumstances of Jackson's good fight didn't allow for the sort of bureaucratic impediments found elsewhere on the Hill and in the executive branch. In their eyes, the inhabitants of the Bunker were a beleaguered few, fighting the lonely war against the left-wing forces of darkness, always on the precipice, about to be overwhelmed.

Perle constantly talked about the lonely battles, the isolation, the attacks on himself and his colleagues. He had mastered the smallest details of nuclear weapons and treaties, even while maintaining a clear philosophical distaste for compromise with a system that directly challenged democracy. For this, he was hated by the growing New Left ranks within his own party. But he believed in his country, and was not going to be ashamed of it, or apologize for it by giving its security away. And there, ultimately, were the lines drawn.

The men and women of the Bunker were Democrats, but their own party now rejected their ideas; they collaborated with the Republicans, but they weren't in the same party, and certainly didn't belong to the same clubs. They were intellectuals, but only a handful of universities would countenance their ideas, and then only with grudging disdain. But they had Scoop Jackson, whose office provided a home, and Richard Perle, the ringleader, who brought them together, creating a network of friends and followers that stretched throughout all reaches of government, from the lower echelons where staff work was being done, up to cabinet secretaries such as Defense Secretary James Schlesinger.

Perle, Jackson, and most everyone in the Bunker despised détente, the theory that the U.S. could limit competition with the Soviets, and that the two superpowers should seek to diminish tensions between each other. While speaking the language of peace, in Perle's view, détente gave a hunting license to the Russians to pursue nuclear superiority and export aggression. Perle's brief, as Senator Jackson's chief aide, was to deny the Soviets this license.

Henry Kissinger, one of the towering giants of American foreign policy, as the intellectual architect of détente was the chief villain, and, for the better part of Kissinger's tenure in government, first as President Nixon's national security adviser, then as secretary of state under both Nixon and Gerald Ford, he and Perle clashed. That Kissinger was widely revered did little to mitigate the irreverent Perle's sting.

THE CENTERPIECE OF détente was arms control. In 1972, Jackson had reluctantly voted for the first nuclear arms treaty, SALT I, negotiated by Henry Kissinger, but only after attaching the Jackson Amendment, which stipulated that no future agreements could limit the U.S. to an inferior number of weapons in any category. To secure the amendment's passage, Perle, briefing books in hand, worked around the clock, often pulling all-nighters out of his home. He collaborated with twenty-five senators in this effort. The Senate vote in favor of the Perle-drafted amendment, insisting that all future treaties must be based on parity, had a profoundly far-reaching affect on the climate of all future arms negotiations.

Jackson was also deeply unhappy with the U.S. negotiating team. After the election, in 1973, Nixon and Kissinger attempted to mollify the powerful Jackson and a displeased Perle. The White House fired a quarter of the Arms Control and Disarmament Agency staff, including a dozen of the principal negotiators. One of the very few to survive was Paul Nitze.

The dismissal of the arms control team rang through Washington like an unmistakable warning shot, a domestic declaration of war against those who sided with Kissinger, the arms controllers, or the "détentists." It was quickly labeled throughout the administration and on the Hill as "the purge," and became a stark symbol of the fate that awaited those who ran afoul of Perle and Jackson. President Nixon even went as far as telling Jackson that he could name the new head of the Arms Control and Disarmament Agency. Perle wasted no time recommending names of his allies for the available slots.

After the firings, Perle's reputation grew, and as is so often the case in Washington, so did his influence.

Perle and Jackson continued to extend their reach into the heart of U.S.-Soviet relations, not just in weapons, but on basic principles. Together, they struck a blow for human rights. In 1974, they devised legislation to deny trade benefits to any Communist country that did not permit its citizens to emigrate freely. Dubbed the Jackson-Vanik Amendment, its principal target was the Soviet Union, which harshly restricted attempts by Jews and other religious believers to leave the country. Jackson-Vanik directly linked human rights for Soviet Jews with U.S. trade benefits for the Russians. It was the first major piece of international human rights legislation ever passed in the U.S.

The Soviet Union was furious over the provision, and Kissinger himself minced no words in blaming the amendment for the breakdown of détente. It "blighted U.S.-Soviet relations ever after," he angrily commented.

While the Soviets claimed the amendment unduly interfered in their internal affairs, a leading Soviet dissident and father of the Soviet H-bomb, Andrei Sakharov, disagreed. At great personal risk, Sakharov sent a letter to the Congress endorsing the Jackson-Vanik Amendment.

After the amendment passed, a shaken Henry Kissinger, seething with frustration over this crippling blow, fumed: "If that son of a bitch Richard Perle ever gets into an administration, after six months he'll be pursuing exactly the same policies I've been attempting and that he's been sabotaging."

This was not the last time that Perle and Kissinger would clash. Indeed, few people in Washington were ever able to irritate and inflame Henry Kissinger in the way Richard Perle did. A man of enormous historic accomplishment and deserved stature—and without question, with one of the thickest skins and strongest egos in Washington—as Presidents Nixon's and Ford's secretary of state, Kissinger was one of the most powerful men in the world. Kissinger held court at the White House and the State Department, and heads of state, presidents, kings, and princes came calling at his door to pay obeisance. Yet Henry Kissinger, the cabinet secretary, became obsessed with Richard Perle, the Senate staffer.

In May of 1976, when Kissinger was returning from a trip to Africa, he happened to pick up *The Christian Science Monitor*. In the paper, Perle had accused Kissinger of silencing an official protest to Turkey for allowing Soviet aircraft to fly over the country during the 1973 Arab-Israeli War. A fuming Kissinger promptly wrote to Senator Jackson demanding further information about Perle's charge. Perle, not Jackson, responded with his explanation. Kissinger replied with a passionate two-page defense, this time written directly to Perle. Clearly exasperated, Kissinger wrote, "We have reached an amazing state of affairs when a Senate staff member can accuse the Secretary of State in writing not only of having acquiesced in but conniving in the transit of Soviet arms across the territory of a NATO ally. . . ."

KISSINGER WAS ALREADY smarting from another run-in with Perle, the result of a single piece in the *Washington Post* in late 1975.

Perle actively cultivated press contacts. One journalist said that Perle was "unquestionably one of our town's greatest leakers." Perle, however, always denied leaking—that is, revealing top secret details of sensitive national security secrets, including the arms negotiations. "Absurd," Perle would counter. "There's a McCarthyite quality to the accusation on leaks."

His secret? "Reporters need help in figuring out the arcane details of arms negotiations. I never hesitated to help them with that." Shrewdly, he could also find just the right person, scattered somewhere in the national security bureaucracy, to talk with a reporter or writer. And Perle never hesitated to marshal his resources in the press, including columnists Roland Evans and Robert Novak.

It was one particular Evans and Novak column that enraged Kissinger.

In December of 1975, Kissinger was readying himself to fly to Vladivostok to put the final touches on the SALT II arms agreement with the Soviets. The document was in the last stages of being reviewed by the national security bureaucracy, and Kissinger felt he was close to achieving a firm agreement. It would be a crowning touch on Kissinger's contribution to détente with the Soviets, capping his career as the master negotiator, the man who ended the Vietnam War, and would have presided over not one but two nuclear arms control agreements.

Then, Evans and Novak published a column in the *Post*, charging that concessions to Moscow were going to be made by Secretary of State Kissinger, to "save a SALT II agreement at any cost." Only Secretary of Defense Donald Rumsfeld could prevent Kissinger from making dangerous concessions, Evans and Novak wrote, which could "decide the fate of SALT II and influence the country." Rumsfeld, a friend of Perle's, subsequently intervened privately with President Ford, and Kissinger's mission to Moscow was blocked that month. By the time Kissinger got to the Soviet Union in January of 1976, Ford was reeling from accusations by his challenger in the Republican presidential primary, Ronald Reagan, of selling out to the Russians. Ford was no longer interested in a Kissinger-written SALT II, particularly one his own secretary of defense opposed. The treaty was never signed.

Robert Kaiser, writing in the *Washington Post*, referred to the Perle-inspired Evans and Novak column as a piece that "may have changed the course of history." It took three more years and most of the Carter administration to get a formal SALT II treaty signed.

"I never regretted the issues I fought over with Kissinger," Perle maintained. "I believe we were right and he was wrong."

PERLE GOT UNDER Kissinger's skin partly through his mastery of sources and facts. But Perle and the Bunker also needed allies. Thus, Perle set about to erect a shadow empire, a network of friends and sources throughout the government, providing him with the ultimate currency in Washington: information. The Bunker operated on the principle that there are people inside the bureaucracy who can't get a good hearing from their superiors, disaffected officials who shared Jackson's and Perle's hard-line view. "We let the word out," Perle would say, "that these people could always work with us, that we had an open-door policy."

Specialists throughout the executive branch, from the State Department and the CIA to the Pentagon and its intelligence branches, found that Richard Perle was always a friendly voice and ear. As Walter Slocombe, one of Carter's top defense aides, commented, "Perle always had exceptionally good contacts in the government." Some officials groaned, "He would know more about what was happening in negotiations than we did." Others took it more personally. Senator Gary Hart's dovish administrative assistant, Larry Smith, himself an expert on arms control, said, "Richard was always waving some paper or cable to underscore he knew something, usually some negotiating snag or problem, that we didn't have access to." Using a crucial fact, at a crucial moment, and making it widely known, gave Perle enormous clout.

And just as Scoop Jackson cast a protective net around Perle, Perle in turn sought to do the same with others who came to him with information—often at great personal risk. But in the contact sport of Cold War politics, lives and careers were broken as quickly as they were made. If lining up against Perle and the Bunker had its price, lining up with the Bunker sometimes would have even greater consequences, often dire, even shattering.

This was never more evident than in the hidden trenches of the SALT battle—as Perle and his allies would find out.

CHAPTER 3

David Sullivan had spent four years toiling at the CIA to write a single intelligence study. Day in, day out, he torturously examined every shred of evidence from human intelligence, Agency jargon for spies, and communication intelligence, information picked up from satellites, covering Soviet negotiating behavior during the nuclear arms talks with the U.S. He assiduously devoured every cable, every report he could get his hands on, going to great lengths to be included on the distribution lists for the most super-secret papers, including blue-stripe reports, which were given out exclusively on a need to know basis.

The more Sullivan sifted through the evidence, the more clearly patterns began to take shape. He wanted to finish the report, to be done, to move on, but then, each day, the more he dug, the more he was drawn in. It was the curse of professionalism and an excessively compulsive nature. He wanted to produce an irrefutable study, in part because he was convinced that his conclusions were so startling.

He found that the Soviets had exploited a number of loopholes in SALT I, which Henry Kissinger was apparently aware of but chose to overlook, enabling the Russians to begin developing a whole new class of nuclear missiles. "The Soviets have used the SALT II negotiating process as a smoke screen behind which to conceal their increasing strategic superiority from a complacent U.S.," he wrote. But more than simply taking advantage of loopholes, Sullivan found evidence that the Soviets were blatantly violating the terms of the SALT I accords. Item one was the new Soviet SS-19 nuclear intercontinental ballistic missile, which, based on its design, was a willful treaty exploitation. Item two was even more serious. A careful reading of his report foreshadowed the systematic Soviet efforts to build a new ABM missile site, which would later occur in the little-known town of Krasnoyarsk. This was also prohibited by the 1972 treaty, though the Soviets would claim that the Krasnoyarsk facility was a radar station. Since the site was shielded from America's satellites by thick cloud cover, official satellite confirmation would not be made until four and a half years later, in July 1983—and then it would be denied by the Soviets.

Overall, an implication of the Sullivan report was stark and unmistakable: in the current climate, the U.S. SALT II agreement would seriously weaken the U.S. national security posture.

To Sullivan, this was exactly the kind of analysis the president and his advisers, including the delegation negotiating the SALT II treaty, needed to have before a summit meeting was scheduled. There was no reason to suspect that his top bosses at the CIA would feel otherwise. Sullivan had already garnered some impressive reviews during his career as an analyst. "A number of views which he helped to pioneer have in fact now found more general acceptance in the intelligence community," David Sullivan's supervisor wrote in his January 11, 1978, CIA performance evaluation.

The review went on to cite Sullivan's nearly completed study on Soviet violations, singling it out for praise. "Now that it is almost done, his study must be recognized as a most important research achievement— one which is likely to have significant impact on policymakers for a long time to come." Thus, Sullivan's immediate superiors agreed with his dramatic conclusions—his work was now bearing fruit.

The study, *The Soviet Strategic Planning Process and SALT*, was slated to be published in both a long and short version, the long one for government analysts, the short one containing mainly conclusions for high-level policy makers in the administration and members of Congress. The report was expected to be so significant that its distribution list was expanded. It was classified as top secret, NOFORN (no foreign nationals could read it), WINTEL (warning—intelligence methods, including spies, provided data for the report), and had no less than eight code words, making it one of the most highly classified reports ever written in the CIA.

As the paper neared completion, not long after his glowing performance review, Sullivan met with his superiors and all the agency office chiefs and NIOs, or national intelligence officers. Sullivan believed it would be a pro forma meeting, a chance for him to outline the case being made in his paper. He was excited. He expected that this group would enthusiastically embrace the report, just as his immediate supervisors were doing. He also looked forward to the meeting's intellectual give-and-take that could produce helpful feedback for the final version. But, inexplicably, the meeting did not go according to plan.

The agency chiefs were displeased and wanted major revisions. Sullivan heatedly argued that the proposed changes "will alter the paper's substance and mask its conclusions," and were "suppression of evidence." But his protestations fell on deaf ears.

To the outside world, the CIA presented itself as an unbiased, rational animal. But this was pure fiction. The Agency was no less immune to the prevailing political whims and views of the current president and Agency director than was the State Department, or Housing and Urban Development for that matter. And David Sullivan's paper went sharply against those prevailing views of the pro-SALT Jimmy Carter. (Later, when the report was in galley proofs, Agency chiefs even took the action of asking that a disclaimer be included with the report indicating that Sullivan's view was not shared by other Agency analysts.)

Sullivan was outraged: he felt the content of the paper was being watered down to the point of unrecognizability. His analysis was being slowly strangled. The paper was dying a bureaucratic death. Slowly, Sullivan made a fateful decision: he would fight back.

The decision would change his life, pitting him against powerful and at times unknown forces that he often barely understood. The ramifications would reach into the highest echelons of the policy community.

But the die was cast.

DAVID SULLIVAN WAS an intense man who appeared chronically on the edge. Even in the CIA, he stood out as unusually driven. Friends affectionately called him "mad dog." Others thought he exhibited signs of paranoia. In truth, Sullivan was a loyal, conscientious, if often overzealous patriot, reared in a military family (his father assisted General Curtis LeMay with atomic targeting strategies in World War II), who wanted little more than, as he would tell his friends, to "do right."

After graduating from Harvard and receiving a master's degree from Columbia, Sullivan had joined the marines and fought in Vietnam. Serving was a matter of conscience. He was a decorated war hero, and his medals hung proudly in his home. When he returned to the U.S., he joined the CIA as an intelligence analyst—an appropriate way to serve one's country at the height of the Cold War. With his marine-style crew cut, an amiable smile, incessant gum chewing, broad shoulders, and a neck that looked like a tree trunk, Sullivan struck people as more like a football linebacker than a Harvard graduate. He was, however, a thorough analyst. But in the politically charged environment of the CIA in the late 1970s, the straight-shooting but bureaucratically naive Sullivan was out of his political depth.

As Agency resistance to his report mounted, Sullivan grew concerned, then flat-out worried. He hinted to his wife, who also worked at the CIA, about his problems at work, but she was unable to comfort him. As the months dragged on, he lost faith in his Agency colleagues. His frustration grew. It was politics, he thought, sheer politics—they didn't want to upset the SALT negotiations. Then another, darker thought entered his mind. "I didn't have any particularly great ambitions for fame," Sullivan remarked, "but I feared that if something happened to me, if I died, my report would be suppressed by the Agency."

He thought of other mysterious instances of "accidents" in the CIA. He would not be the first.

Sullivan started putting out feelers for another job, which by pure chance led him to a meeting with Admiral Elmo "Bud" Zumwalt, the former chief of naval operations and a highly respected cold warrior.

It was an unusually brisk day in September 1977 when Sullivan went to meet Zumwalt at the Systems Planning Corporation in Rosslyn, Virginia. Suddenly, in Zumwalt's office, Sullivan unburdened himself, and told the admiral that he feared his important study would never see the light of day. Taking a deep breath, Sullivan asked Zumwalt what he should do.

"Go see Richard Perle in Senator Jackson's office," Zumwalt told him. "He's trustworthy, has the appropriate clearances, and understands the importance of this kind of material—and so does the senator." Zumwalt offered to broker an introduction and set up a meeting between Perle and Sullivan. Sullivan said no, he didn't want to go outside of CIA channels. He knew that such freelancing actions, while not illegal, would certainly be frowned upon. "My paper's publication by the CIA is my objective," he told Zumwalt. "I don't feel it would be proper for me to make contact with someone on Capitol Hill." The meeting ended on that note.

But as weeks and months went by, his paper was no closer to publication. Zumwalt's suggestion stuck in Sullivan's mind.

In February 1978, an increasingly distraught Sullivan sought distraction by attending a top secret CIA seminar on Soviet conduct and the Cold War, held at one of the Agency's leased buildings, the Broyhill, in Arlington, Virginia. One speaker's smooth grace and calm demeanor particularly impressed Sullivan. This man delivered a chilling message to the Agency analysts: the Soviets couldn't be trusted, and the U.S. had to be particularly careful in the SALT talks. On impulse, Sullivan mustered up his nerve and approached the speaker. He mentioned his paper.

After Sullivan spoke, Richard Perle carefully eyed him and replied, "It sounds very interesting. I'll order a copy once it's published.

"By the way," Perle added, as Sullivan looked nervously about to see if anyone had seen the two speaking, "let's keep in touch."

. . .

FEBRUARY DRAGGED ON, as did March. Sullivan continued to prepare his paper for publication. Should he tell Perle? Should he take Zumwalt's advice? Should he give Perle and the senator his paper? On the evening of April 10, after dinner, he got into his car, drove down the winding road past Spout Run, well beyond the Lincoln Memorial, and went back to the Agency. Few cars were out at this time of night.

Sullivan inserted his magnetic card to get into his office cell. The clock clicked him in. It was 10:50 P.M.

Sullivan moved as quickly as possible. He got a copy of his paper. All of the copies were numbered, so that once released, distribution could be controlled and monitored. All copies, that is, except the original.

Sullivan took the original paper, unnumbered, and went to a Xerox machine—not the one near his desk, but a machine in a different office altogether. At 11:54, his Xeroxing finished, he logged out of the Agency, and despite the cool night air, he was sweating. The next day, on his own initiative, he called Perle and invited him to his home, for dinner and to talk.

Perle drove to Sullivan's house in suburban Virginia. They chatted politely for a few minutes and then cut to the chase. Sullivan pulled out the short version of his report, stressing that it had to be stored in a secure place. "I'm afraid they'll never release it," he said in a pained voice, "so I'm giving it to you."

Perle reassured Sullivan about its safekeeping, saying he would first put it in his safe at his office, and then transfer it to an appropriate storage facility in the Office of Senate Security. Sullivan was visibly worried. Perle attempted to soothe Sullivan further—he reminded him that, as a Senate aide with the appropriate clearances, he had a "need to know" this information. Besides, he and the senator would formally request the paper from the CIA. It would take time to get it through the bureaucratic channels, but he would eventually get it. With that, he opened the trunk to his car, put the paper underneath a clutter of books and papers, and drove immediately to his office.

Once inside the Russell Senate Office Building, Perle read the report. He found it a "marvelous piece of work." Perle had long been concerned about going ahead with new weapons treaties if the Soviets indiscriminately violated existing ones. The debate over SALT II would entail some real hardball. Now he had serious reason to be more than concerned. This paper suggested what he feared: the Americans were disarming. The Soviets were not.

. . .

SEVERAL WEEKS AFTER Perle and Sullivan met, George Murphy, an old CIA hand, was browsing through the vaults at Senate Security. Now retired from the Agency, he was able to keep in contact with the intelligence world by working at the Office of Senate Security. Inconspicuously labeled Room S-407 on the fourth floor of the Capitol, this room maintained a complete catalogue of all classified material stored in the Congress. If a senator or an aide had to be briefed, and didn't want to go through the trouble of having a room debugged, it was handled here. The office also advised staffers on how to conduct themselves when traveling abroad, giving them strict guidelines for avoiding terrorists or foreign agents working for the KGB. But mostly, the office stored classified papers being read by Senate staff.

From this job, Murphy could see exactly which senator or Senate aide was working on what, by seeing what classified material they had secured in the Office of Senate Security vault. It was a great place for an old Agency guy to be. With a bit of satisfaction, he could twist the dials on the safes after checking if they were fully closed, almost as if caressing them.

One day, Murphy's curiosity was piqued when he saw the double-enveloped report by Sullivan checked out to Richard Perle. It had the appropriate red stamp of top secret on the outside, but the report inside was unnumbered. That's odd, he thought.

Murphy picked up the phone to call a friend in the Office of Security at the CIA, just to make sure everything was okay.

PERLE FELT THE Sullivan report was "first-rate," an "absolutely first-class work." He briefed Scoop on it, and Scoop agreed. They could make use of it in the Senate ratification debate of SALT. During the remainder of April and on into May, at his own initiative, Sullivan continued to feed information to Perle, including handwritten notes. To ensure that no piece of paper would fall into the wrong hands, the security-conscious Sullivan personally brought everything directly to Perle at his office. But as May progressed, Sullivan grew worried. Perle had yet to receive the first paper through official channels.

Unexpectedly, the Agency informed Sullivan that he was scheduled for his five-year polygraph. The polygraph was supposed to be routine but, in truth, most CIA employees were checked only every seven to ten years. There was no explanation as to why Sullivan was being called now. Sullivan did not know about George Murphy's phone call from Senate Security or that it had triggered a widespread probe into the possibility of Agency channels being breached—if not worse.

The polygraph was normally a routine examination, consisting of roughly ten primary questions. One of the questions was: "Have you passed any classified documents to unauthorized people in the last five years?" Sullivan felt he would have to say yes.

The thought of the polygraph panicked Sullivan. He went to call Perle. Perhaps Richard would have some idea, he thought. He reached for his desk phone, picked up the receiver, only to slam it down abruptly. He was afraid the phone was bugged. He looked around at his colleagues and muttered under his breath about having an appointment, the dentist or something—they couldn't understand his words, or why he dashed out in such a hurry.

A few minutes later, standing outside a small group of shops, Sullivan reached into his suit pocket for change. He was out of breath. He looked around to see if he had been followed. It wouldn't be the first time an analyst was trailed by its own, he thought. Satisfying himself that he wasn't being watched, he stepped into a phone booth, put in a dime, and called Perle.

Perle saw no need to further excite an already upset Sullivan. He told him not to worry about the polygraph. Sullivan's infraction was minor. It did not violate any laws, and Perle was entitled—that is, authorized—to see the material. The only violation was not transmitting the paper through the normal procedural channels, in this case, the office of CIA Legislative Affairs. And of course, as Sullivan had felt, once Scoop had the paper, the whole issue would be moot. "Just keep calm," Perle reassured him.

"What do I do?" a still agitated Sullivan asked, his tone slightly frantic, "I know I won't be able to bluff them."

There was a pause at the other end of the line.

"Do what you have to do," Perle said.

IN THE FOLLOWING days, Sullivan pressed Perle to try to get a copy of the paper before the test, and Perle redoubled his efforts. He had his colleague Dickie Fosdick request the short and long versions of the paper. He also called Colonel Bill Odom, one of Brzezinski's aides on the National Security Council, to see if the NSC would authorize or ask for the paper to be released to Jackson. Odom was sympathetic, a hawk, and, like Perle, a skeptic of SALT. Also like Perle, he had faced accusations within his own party of being "insufficiently pro-détente." Odom said he would look into it.

July 21, Senator Jackson was finally given access to both versions of Sullivan's paper. But to the senator's surprise, they were not brought by courier, as was standard practice. Curiously, CIA Director Stansfield Turner personally took them to Jackson. This action left little doubt how important the CIA felt Sullivan's paper was, even as it sought to mute its potentially far-reaching impact. On the 23rd, Perle had dinner again at Sullivan's. Perle could see how agitated Sullivan had become. He tried to calm him down. Cooperate with the polygraph, and don't worry about the outcome, Perle told him.

But Sullivan was less sanguine, and was again on the verge of panic. Perle was unsure Sullivan could weather the strain. At a time when the Agency was closing ranks, Perle refused to turn his back on Sullivan. He set about trying to find a safety net for Sullivan should the polygraph not go well. Perle told Sullivan he would look into what he could do "in case there were problems."

On the 26th of July, Sullivan drove to work. His mind was racing, until he felt almost dizzy. He believed he had been fully justified in giving the material to Perle. The CIA was clearly suppressing his work. His paper was vital to national security. But the consequences of going around CIA channels could mean dismissal, perhaps even a legal suit. If he had been smarter, he thought, he would have gotten a lawyer. Frank Snepp, an antiwar liberal who wrote a book about his experiences in Vietnam without prior CIA clearance, had to endure a civil suit raised by the Agency. Sullivan could be subjected to the same fate. He saw his life flashing before his eyes.

The examiner strapped Sullivan in and routinely went over the polygraph procedure. Then he told Sullivan what questions would be covered during the test. It wouldn't take more than an hour.

Sullivan didn't wait for the formal exam to begin. Sweating, he broke down immediately. He didn't try to beat the test. He told the examiner about giving the material to Perle. He was met by a startled look, and the examiner rushed to a phone to make a call. After a flurry of activity, Sullivan's routine five-year, one-hour polygraph turned into a marathon three-day polygraph about the nature and content of the documents and notes he had passed on to Perle.

It was strangely cathartic for Sullivan. He felt a mixture of anxiety and relief—it was all coming out now. He was finally unburdened, his conscience cleared. Sullivan cooperated fully with the examiners, making only a simple request. He asked to meet with Director Turner, whether he was relieved or retained. He had decided to carry a letter of resignation tucked in his suit pocket, in the event that Turner's body language indicated Sullivan's services were no longer required.

The CIA apparatus swung into action. Sullivan might be a bigger fish than he had appeared. On August 14, he was interviewed at great length again. This time, the CIA probe focused on his passing of cables to Perle that mentioned "Trigon," the code name for Aleksandr Ogorodnik, a high-ranking Russian official whom the U.S. had successfully recruited from the Soviet Ministry of Foreign Affairs.

The CIA's implication was that Sullivan's freelancing had led to Trigon's death. Few offenses within the Agency were considered more serious. It was a rare thing for the CIA to successfully penetrate the inner sanctums of Soviet decision making, and every spy was a highly valued asset. Literally, no intelligence source was better than a well-placed, reliable mole. And Trigon, who provided information on Soviet intentions in the nuclear arms talks, on grand strategy, and Soviet foreign ministry material, had been a fountain of the most sensitive secrets. He was considered the best intelligence asset since Oleg Penkovsky, a highly placed Soviet agent who had been crucial to the U.S. in resolving the Cuban Missile Crisis.

Yet unexpectedly, in Moscow in July 1977, when Trigon was preparing to make a dead-drop in a prearranged spot with Martha Peterson, his CIA case officer, Peterson was rounded up by the KGB, declared persona non grata, and expelled from Moscow. Simultaneously, Trigon was arrested by the KGB, and subjected to a brutal interrogation and torture. That same month, unable to withstand the intense beatings, Trigon committed suicide with a CIA-supplied cyanide pill stored in his fountain pen. Thus, the U.S. lost one of its most valuable intelligence sources.

A variety of explanations were offered, leading to heated accusations and vehement denials, vigorous charges and blistering countercharges. Rumor had it that Vernon Walters, then deputy director of the CIA, offered one explanation: Trigon had been compromised by an injudicious comment made by David Aaron, Brzezinski's deputy at the NSC, at a cocktail party brimming with foreign diplomats and overheard by a Romanian official. Aaron, in turn, later blamed Richard Perle for spreading the unsubstantiated rumor that he was responsible for the death of this agent. Perle, in turn, blamed it on comments made by the television reporter Leslie Stahl. It would later turn out that neither Aaron nor any other of these outsiders was responsible for compromising Trigon. It was someone in the CIA.

"SULLIVAN WAS COOPERATIVE throughout the session," his CIA interviewer wrote in a memo summing up the day's worth of additional questioning on the fourteenth. The CIA interviewer additionally noted: "Perle's advice [to Sullivan] has been consistently to remain calm, to continue to cooperate with the investigative procedure, and not to worry about the outcome."

Sullivan, still unclear about what Perle could actually do for him, felt the need to clear his own name. He sat down at his desk at work and pondered his future. He would shortly be meeting with Stansfield Turner, the Agency's director. He took out a yellow legal pad, and in longhand wrote a twenty-three-page explanation of what he had done. At the top of page one, he wrote simply: "Statement of David S. Sullivan, analyst, CIA."

He began, "I disclosed information to Richard Perle on my own initiative because I exhausted Agency command channels, and I believed it was vital to protect national security." Two hours later, he sat there, emotionally drained, and concluded: "I was upholding the Agency's motto: Ye shall know the truth . . . the CIA was suppressing the truth." His fate was now out of his hands. Sullivan's twenty-three-page scrawled handwritten statement was slapped onto a formal CIA routing sheet and passed up the line.

CIA Director Turner was outraged by Sullivan's insubordination. Sullivan's study on Soviet violations contained some of the government's most closely held information on sources and methods of obtaining intelligence about the Soviet Union. On August 24, Turner called Sullivan into the director's conference room.

"David, you have done much good work for the Central Intelligence Agency, and you are to be commended for this," he told Sullivan. Turner paused, looking Sullivan straight in the eye, his broad face squinting intensely. "However," he started.

Sullivan, standing erect, like a marine at attention, broke his composure and pulled out a letter from his jacket. It contained his resignation, effective immediately, and he handed it to Turner. The director felt cheated. It was, as he would later write to Sullivan, "a resignation made in full anticipation that firing was only minutes away."

Turner looked icily at Sullivan, and wagged his finger, "I will see to it that you will never work in the national security field again." But Sullivan now had other thoughts on his mind: his parachute.

Four hours later, Sullivan met with Senator Lloyd Bentsen. Perle had arranged it. David Sullivan was hired that same day to work as the Texas senator's legislative assistant for defense and arms control.

The next day, Turner issued a letter of reprimand to Sullivan. It criticized Sullivan for the discredit he had brought upon himself and the Agency. And it made one particularly damning charge. Turner said Sullivan's release of highly classified documents, including information from "a very sensitive source . . . ha[d] deleterious consequences to national security." Sullivan felt that Turner had implied he might have caused the downfall of Trigon. It was a devastating charge for Sullivan, now employed by the U.S. Congress. All of Sullivan's reports that had been distributed throughout the government were hurriedly collected by the CIA and placed in Agency safes.

While others were rumored to have caused Trigon's demise, now the official paper trail appeared to lead to David Sullivan. He was shut out of the executive branch. He would be denied security clearances in future jobs. The CIA, in a fit of institutional rage at its lower levels, tracked Sullivan's whereabouts for the next four years. His wife, reeling under the pressure, suffered two heart attacks.

"My career was ruined," Sullivan recounted. "I'm not blaming anyone, certainly not Richard Perle. But I lost more than ten years of my life seeking to clear my name."

TURNER DID NOT stop with Sullivan. He requested a meeting with Scoop Jackson, where he planned to ask for Perle's dismissal. Jackson, who had little love for Turner, included Perle in the meeting. A stunned Turner was thrown off guard. Unsure how to play it, he beat around the bush, and then finally indicated that he had dismissed a CIA employee, David Sullivan, who had leaked material to Perle. Looking momentarily befuddled, Turner then authoritatively said, "I've done what I had to do."

Jackson decided that he had heard enough, and cut Turner off midsentence, ending the meeting with a single verbal stroke: "I have complete faith in Richard."

When a somewhat shaken Turner left the room, both Perle and Jackson looked at each other with a smile and laughed.

IN HIS LAST act while still inside the CIA, David Sullivan left a list of names with the Agency of people he feared were double agents working for the Soviet Union. "One of these was a mole," he insisted. The implication was chilling. Sullivan contended that not one but several people might have burrowed their way in, penetrating the inner sanctum of American intelligence.

Five weeks later, in late September, the CIA followed up on one of Sullivan's tips, calling John Paisley in for a "technical interview." Paisley had been decorated with an intelligence medal, and as a former deputy director of the Office of Strategic Resources was in a key position to have access to virtually all CIA activities. He had retired in 1976, but still remained deeply involved as a consultant to the CIA, and continued to enjoy extraordinarily high security clearances. By all accounts, he was the most unlikely of moles. He also had not had a polygraph since 1953.

Paisley never made it to his CIA interview. Sometime in the early morning hours of September 25, 1978, he disappeared.

Shortly before 10 that morning, his sailboat ran aground on the shore of the Chesapeake Bay. Scattered throughout the boat were sophisticated electronic gear and highly classified code-word CIA papers, which had been smuggled out of the Agency. A 9mm bullet was found underneath a broken galley table. Equally ominous, Paisley's boat also had a powerful short-wave radio, capable of making burst transmissions, which meant it could relay whole batches of data, quickly and efficiently, to Soviet satellites without being detected by the U.S.

Paisley himself was found six days later, a bloated, decomposing corpse floating facedown in the Bay. A bullet hole was visible in the back of his head, rope marks around his neck indicated a struggle, and two nineteen-pound diver's weight belts were fastened across his chest and abdomen. Soon thereafter, some Agency hands privately speculated that Paisley could have been the worst mole ever inside the CIA. Yet a denial reflex in the Agency quickly took over. Rather than get to the bottom of matters, the CIA swept these potentially vast problems under the rug and coasted along.

The Paisley case would remain forever unsolved, the full scope of the damage unknown. Meanwhile, the paper trail to Trigon's downfall continued to point in one direction: David Sullivan.

THE TRIGON CASE was finally unraveled in 1984, six years later, during a joint FBI-CIA interrogation of two CIA agents, both defectors from Czechoslovakia, who had for years professed to be staunch anti-Communists. They had been placed on the CIA payroll eleven years earlier, in 1973.

In a suite of the Barbizon Plaza Hotel in Manhattan, FBI and CIA agents kept Karl Koecher, a tall, athletic Columbia Ph.D., and his wife, Hanna, a gorgeous blonde, locked in two separate rooms. For three harrowing days, the agents questioned the pair.

In the U.S., after defecting, the Koechers had led an exciting, unconventional double life. In the mid-1970s, while Karl had meticulously translated documents for the CIA, the Koechers as a couple had been at the center of a Washington–New York group that practiced swinging, or wife swapping. In a town house just three blocks from the White House, the Koechers would engage in freewheeling sex with other professionals: doctors, journalists, government officials with high security clearances, and professors. But aside from their sexual practices, the Koechers led a second secret life, as spies for the Czech and Soviet intelligence services.

While working for the Agency, Koecher had passed on material to the Czech secret service and the KGB that led to the death of Trigon. No one in the Agency had known about this breach or about how many others had taken place. And they certainly didn't know about the Koechers' swinging and their myriad Washington sex partners, which had left many high-level American officials open to intelligence blackmail. Nor did they know that in 1976 Koecher had even traveled to Czechoslovakia, where he met in a cloistered estate on the outskirts of Prague with the Chief of the K Directorate of the KGB, Oleg Kalugin. All those years, Koecher had easily passed the Agency's polygraph test.

Koecher was deemed so significant by both the Americans and the Soviets that after pleading guilty in the New York Circuit Court to espionage charges, he was exchanged for the famous Soviet Jewish dissident Anatoly Shcharansky in February 1986. Jerry Brown, a CIA agent who wrote up the internal classified case, concluded: "We will never know the full story of Koecher's espionage activities." To this day, the full extent of the damage caused by the Koechers remains undetermined. No one was ever reprimanded for either the Trigon or Koecher fiascoes.

But for David Sullivan, the story wasn't over. Finally, in 1990, the CIA, speaking through its counsel, wrote a perfunctory letter to Sullivan's lawyer. In it was the sentence: "We have reviewed CIA records and they contain no evidence that Mr. Sullivan was responsible for the death of an Agent."

CHAPTER 4

Almost in a trance, President Jimmy Carter stared out of his Oval Office window onto the South Lawn of the White House. He barely noticed the soft traces of snow that lay on the ground. Three years earlier, he had said to the American people that they could be "free of an inordinate fear of Communism." Yet now, on this chilly January day in 1980, the cover of *Newsweek* magazine told a very different story. In bold letters, it brandished the headline "A New Cold War" and pictured Soviet tanks ominously perched in the hills of Afghanistan.

In the wake of the Soviet invasion of Afghanistan, Carter was anything but eager to return to the brinkmanship and hair-raising U.S.-Soviet confrontations of the Truman and Kennedy years. Privately, he hoped that cool heads would prevail. To demonstrate that, for now, there would not be business as usual, Carter ordered a set of reprisals against the Soviet Union: a grain embargo, a halt of new sales of high technology to the Russians. But this was, he felt, still a measured response.

No fingers were poised on the nuclear triggers, as they were during the Cuban Missile Crisis. Nor was he sending troops to Afghanistan, as the U.S. had done two decades earlier in Korea. On the advice of the Senate majority leader, Robert Byrd, the president had reluctantly shelved congressional consideration of the SALT II arms treaty. In Jimmy Carter's eyes, the threat of a spiraling arms race was as great as any Soviet atrocity, and the arms treaty was not meant as a favor to the Russians. In time, he hoped the Senate would see fit to ratify the treaty. In time, he hoped that U.S.-Soviet relations would be back on track.

But Afghanistan was only one problem. Just south, in Iran, was another indication that Carter's well-ordered, moralistic view of the world seemed to be coming apart. The Ayatollah Khomeini had called the U.S. "a defeated and wounded snake," and the American people, losing patience with the scruffy band of Islamic fundamentalists holding the Americans hostage, were starting to clamor for action. But this did not dim Carter's hope that Cy Vance, his secretary of state, would secure their negotiated release.

Carter's dream upon becoming president was that he would preside over a new era of peace and disarmament. His critics accused him of pipe dreams, of being a naive sentimentalist. Now, as a new decade opened, the winds of war were blowing.

CARTER HIMSELF WAS stunned by the Soviet invasion of Afghanistan, and even took the invasion as a personal affront. In a television interview with ABC on New Year's Eve, he snapped, "My opinion of the Russians and their ultimate goals has changed drastically in the last week—[more] than ever in the previous two and a half years." The president especially felt betrayed by Leonid Brezhnev, the Soviet Communist party chief. When the two leaders spoke on the Washington-Moscow hot line, communication reserved for only the most dire situations, Brezhnev claimed his armies were invited into Afghanistan—a bald-faced lie. And to complicate matters for Carter, recriminations and alarm bells were being sounded throughout Washington, and not just by the hard-liners in the Republican party but by members of his own party, particularly the Scoop Jackson Democrats.

Carter didn't particularly care for the "neoconservative wing" of the Democratic party, the Scoop Jackson Democrats. They were, he felt, too hawkish, too uncompromising, too mired in the old Cold War mentality of the past. Shortly after his election, he had met with the core of leading Jackson Democrats, members of the Coalition for a Democratic Majority, or CDM. Through CDM, they sought to persuade the Democratic party to take a stronger stand on national security issues. The meeting was a failure, and ended in mutual, albeit private, recriminations.

Where Carter fervently believed in arms control, the CDM adherents railed against the dangers of declining defense budgets. Carter wanted to deal with long-ignored problems of global poverty, ignorance, and illiteracy; they were, he felt, obsessed with Soviet and Cuban adventurism in the Third World. Carter had entertained the idea of appointing some of the neoconservatives to positions in his administration—but not after meeting with them. Their dire assessment of the Soviet Union and worst-case analyses had little place in Jimmy Carter's dovish White House. He put it to them bluntly early on: "I don't need your advice, I need your support."

As Carter was fond of pointing out, contrary to what Scoop Jackson's followers seemed to think, he, Carter, had been elected president, not the senator whose star they followed. As Carter saw it, he didn't owe them anything. During the transition period, he made his point by stating publicly, "I beat Jackson in the primaries." Carter felt strongly that it was the job of all Democrats to support their president, not the other way around. Besides, Carter reasoned, it was not as though the Scoop Jackson Democrats had anywhere else to go.

But that was 1976. Many things had since changed, and U.S. foreign policy seemed to be in tatters. Carter was annoyed by the accusations of weakness, but in an election season, he could no longer ignore them, not as his poll ratings dropped precipitously.

The Republicans were nipping at his heels, charging he was soft on the Russians. The criticisms from conservative Democrats were damaging him further, and he was facing a primary challenge from Ted Kennedy and the liberal wing of his party. So upon the advice of his aides, including Vice President Walter Mondale, who had been lobbying for Carter to hold a second meeting with CDM, he consented to another session. To win the election, he would need the support of the entire party, which meant making peace with the Jackson wing. Carter hadn't lost sight of the fact that now, more than ever, he needed them. Their endorsement could insulate him from the ongoing Republican attacks, especially those by former radio announcer, actor, and governor of California Ronald Reagan.

Carter's strategy for dealing with the coalition would be simple. Flatter them, address their concerns in broad strokes, let them vent their grievances. And at a minimum, ensure that they didn't actively oppose him— keep them loyal.

After all, he was the president. It was rare for the commander in chief to slot out a chunk of time in the middle of an international crisis to consult with a group of outside policy experts. A beleaguered LBJ did this especially in the waning days of his administration when he specifically sought the counsel of the Wise Men, the bastion of the establishment. But Johnson made the mistake of actively consulting with this group, which eventually opposed him on the Vietnam War. Carter wouldn't make the same mistake. He would address CDM's concerns—but not ask their advice, at least not in a serious way. He also knew that Scoop Jackson, the spiritual head of CDM, and his staffer, Richard Perle, would be absent this morning.

Zbigniew Brzezinski, his national security adviser, would be in the meeting. As his administration hawk, Zbig would be a reassuring presence. Fritz Mondale, who had ties to several in the group, would be there too. At the very least, Mondale believed common ground could be found with these cold-warrior Democrats, or that, in an election year, a truce could be forged. In the final analysis, Mondale wanted Carter and CDM to agree that they were all Democrats, all in the same tent, working toward the same goal.

But, goodwill efforts aside, one problem gnawed at Carter's White House aides. The public attacks by CDM on Carter's policies were far more blistering than those levied by the Republicans, and made them, White House staffers thought, an unpredictable lot. Nothing Carter did seemed to please them. As far as his aides could tell, Scoop Jackson, not Carter, commanded their loyalty, and he had been waging a relentless war on the president's most treasured goal: the SALT II nuclear arms control treaty. Just to play it safe, the White House didn't put the CDM meeting on Carter's public schedule. No sense in advertising it to the press. No reason to take any chances.

Little did Carter know it, but this meeting, on the final day of January 1980, would help change the course of history, with ramifications for the Democratic party and the conduct of the Cold War throughout the rest of the decade.

JUST THREE BLOCKS from the White House, with little fanfare, a handful of men and women, briefcases in hand, swept into the Hay Adams Hotel for breakfast—and to discuss their ten o'clock appointment with the President of the United States.

Relatively unknown outside of the New York–Washington corridor, this small group, the leadership of CDM, consisted of some of the most formidable and enigmatic intellectuals brought together in decades.

In sheer scholarship and rigor of thought, though not necessarily government experience, they resembled the prestigious study groups convened by the elders of the Council on Foreign Relations a week after the U.S. entered World War II. Back then, as the American people steeled themselves to confront Hitler and Japan, these men, meeting at the old council headquarters on East 65th Street, next door to the mansion FDR had occupied when he was governor of New York, called on their country to accept the awesome task of winning the war and to take up the burden of global responsibility. After the war, the establishment came together again, as these Wise Men gathered in Georgetown salons on P Street and contemplated the reconstruction of a war-torn Europe.

In the Kennedy era, an Olympic age where brains and intellectuals were harnessed to run the nation, the establishment reached a pinnacle. These were action-intellectuals, tough men who understood power and were comfortable wielding it. But the Vietnam War broke the golden men of Camelot. As the 1970s rolled around, the Kennedy intellectuals and the hardheaded elites, the establishment, who had helped govern the country with a clarity of purpose and sense of American destiny, were swept from power. They were no longer a pharaonic cult devoted to the promotion of freedom over totalitarianism; instead they prophesied and even accepted the decline of American power. As early as 1970, Admiral Bud Zumwalt recalled Henry Kissinger, a great statesman and the most sober of the lot, heaving a sigh of despair: "The U.S. has passed its historic high point, like so many other civilizations, and cannot be roused to the political challenge. We must persuade the Russians to give us the best deal we can get."

But if the Kennedy intellectuals and the establishment were backing off, if the bipartisan consensus for an activist foreign policy had broken down, the neoconservatives, this small collection of men and women, old-fashioned liberals bound together by an affiliation with Scoop Jackson and CDM, would pick up the gauntlet and fill the void. Strategically poised in the marketplace of ideas, their political connections assured through Jackson, these intellectuals were ready to become the new brain trusters, the new shapers of Washington policies and agendas. And they actively sought the task of charting the nation's destiny in the coming decade.

Yet the CDM group was profoundly different from the establishment. While the establishment frequently was comprised of moderate Republicans, and a healthy smattering of Democrats, political parties were of little consequence to them. The establishment frowned upon ideological fervor, and embraced pragmatism as a way of life. They were part of a class that rose above populism, and most certainly above partisan politics. They served the president. More to the point, they served the office of the presidency, less the man than the institution. Indeed, though a respected former New York governor and longtime diplomat who served as FDR's special envoy to Churchill and Stalin, Averell Harriman's open partisanship nevertheless frequently grated on other establishmentarians. John McCloy, the Wall Street lawyer and confidant of many presidents, was more the model. When McCloy reminded FDR that he was a mainstream Republican, FDR muttered, "Damn it, I always forget."

By contrast, these neoconservatives took their roots as lifelong Democrats very seriously. They came from families that revered the Democratic party. Few of them had grown up with Republicans, few knew Republicans. FDR, JFK, and LBJ were acronyms, less of names than a place for them: these presidents were the standard-bearers of a political party that took in immigrants, provided a home for Jews and Catholics, worked for social progress, were opposed to discrimination. For the neoconservatives, whose parents came streaming into this country on packed boats and were crammed in at Ellis Island, the Democratic party enabled the sons and daughters of clothing merchants and grocers to become writers, professors, lawyers, and labor organizers. The Democratic party was their key to advancement. For these immigrants and children of immigrants, some of them former socialists, many of them Jews or Catholics, who prized education as the highest virtue, individual liberty and merit were what mattered. And it was the Democratic party that rewarded merit, not the country club Republicans, so often stuck on hiring and admissions quotas.

They also felt the Democratic party prized freedom abroad. FDR took on Hitler, and Truman, later to be followed by Kennedy, would articulate sweeping doctrines to support those struggling for freedom around the world. Kennedy put it well, writing shortly before his death, "We are the watchmen of the walls of world freedom." For those who had lost family in the fires of the Holocaust, or whose families were the victims of oppression in czarist and then Communist Russia, and in Eastern Europe, freedom mattered. This is what the liberalism of the Democratic party meant to them: merit and equal opportunity at home, freedom abroad. Thus, it was no surprise that, unlike the establishment, their own background led them to feel strongly about being Democrats. On a deeper level, liberalism and the Democratic party were about more than ideology, they were a part of their very identity. That's how it had always been.

IN 1972, ONE month after George McGovern's forty-nine-state election loss to Richard Nixon, CDM assembled with a breathless sense of urgency. In his bid for the presidency, McGovern, a former political science professor and the son of a preacher, locked horns with the backroom bosses and boardroom figures of the mainstream Democratic party and gave voice to the reformers and the college-educated, antiwar movement. This new movement, quickly dubbed the New Left, or McGovernism, rebuffed the traditions of the Democratic party center, which had long adhered to internationalist ideals and supported containing Soviet power.

Many party elders had bristled at McGovern's embrace of the strident, antiwar, and often anti-American message of the New Left. This was, as Harvard professor Steven Kelman noted, a movement that derided America, not celebrated it. The young reformers cheered, not for American soldiers but for Mao, Ho Chi Minh, and the Vietcong. The New Left praised the Arab Liberation Movement, criticized the Czech reformers for opening up contacts with Western imperialism, and glorified the brave North Vietnamese infantryman heading off to battle.

George McGovern shared these views and dreams of an idealistic universe where America carried out its foreign policy with spades and shovels, not guns. At an antiwar rally on the Boston Common on October 15, 1969, McGovern, his smooth forehead glistening in the sun, earnestly told 100,000 protesters, a number of them taking the day off from their studies at Harvard, that "America must withdraw to save her honor."

Three years later, upon receiving the presidential nod from the Democratic party delegates, just two minutes short of midnight, from his penthouse suite at the Doral Hotel overlooking the Miami Beach skyline, McGovern could note with satisfaction that his philosophy had paid off. With the support of the increasingly powerful New Left, to whom he gave a greater voice within the party, and the same kind of young people who had turned out in Boston on that October day, McGovern was propelled to his party's nomination for the highest office in the land.

During the campaign, McGovern took his antiwar, anti-interventionist message to the country like a road show, addressing both highbrow black-tie Democratic party fund-raising events and campus protests, where the speakers wore jeans and tie-dye shirts and chanted for revolution. His campaign slogan was "Come home, America"; his underlying message was that world problems existed not because America didn't have enough power, but because it had too much power. America's "interventionist ways" were, to McGovern, the source of the problems, not their solutions.

As if taking their cue from the inimitable words of the cartoon strip Pogo, the New Left seemed to be saying, "We have met the enemy, and he is us."

So in 1972, CDM was founded to wrest the party back to center, away from the isolationism of the New Left and back to the muscular foreign policy of Franklin Roosevelt, Truman, Kennedy, and even Johnson. Smarting from the takeover of the Democratic party, Norman Podhoretz, the influential editor of *Commentary* magazine, his wife and noted author, Midge Decter, and Ben Wattenberg, a former Johnson White House speechwriter and political scientist who had penned some of Johnson's most fiery rhetoric, wrestled with a draft paper for this fledgling organization.

Amid Podhoretz's book-strewn apartment on the Upper West Side of Manhattan and over cups of rich black coffee, they talked about their mission as dusk fell over the New York skyline. The Democratic party had deserted them, ousted them and their ideas, told them that people of their views "need not apply." But they had not left the party, the party had left them. They were determined to reclaim its core. Like European intellectuals plotting revolution in the salons and coffee houses of a bygone era, these New York intellectuals spoke with passion and fervor about their cause, a passion for the intellectual center of the party and the country, and fervor for its traditional ideas of social compassion at home and the promotion of freedom abroad. They decided they would issue a manifesto. Working on a draft already scribbled by Decter, they massaged it until it was in final form. To counter McGovern's theme of "Come home, America," they wrote "Come home, Democrats," and called for "progress, freedom and security."

Scoop Jackson became the group's honorary co-chairman. For Jackson, the group would become an intellectual clearinghouse outside of government that would promote his views and his agenda in the domain of ideas. Hubert Humphrey was slated to be the other co-chairman.

Meeting in Humphrey's private chamber in his Senate office in Washington, Wattenberg explained the group's purpose, liberalism at home, vigilance abroad. Humphrey, always full of energy, a committed Democrat who came within a hair of becoming president in 1968, was just about to sign on; "I like it, Ben," he declared, with his usual buoyancy. But then Humphrey's administrative assistant, new to the job and watchful of Humphrey's position within the party, intervened. "Senator, perhaps you should sleep on this."

Humphrey looked puzzled. His aide went on to talk about the perils of this group making Humphrey look like a conservative, which wouldn't sit very well with the growing liberal wing of the party. Much to Wattenberg's chagrin, and Jackson's disappointment, Humphrey declined to join. So Jackson, as was so often the case, went it alone, even offering his fund-raising lists, which included such Democratic party heavy hitters as Alexander's Robin Farkus; Harriet Zimmerman of the United Jewish Appeal; Sonny Dogole, the Philadelphia businessman; Walter Shorenstein, the San Francisco business magnate; and Washington lawyer Vic Raiser. With seed money kicked in by Al Barkin from the AFL-CIO, the Coalition for a Democratic Majority was born.

CDM operated less as a formal organization than as a clearinghouse of ideas and as a haven for hard-line intellectuals, whose view of the world saw halting Soviet expansionism and reversing the decline in American power as their first priority. One member, Jeane Kirkpatrick, would often say, "We are a state of mind." The group lived by the words "Ideas have consequences."

In bringing together like-minded individuals, many of them former radicals and ex-socialists, most of them Jewish, through its conferences, published articles, and relentless political action, CDM rapidly established itself as a formidable Washington presence and as a counterweight to the New Left. Meanwhile, the more refined establishment, scarred by the lessons of the Vietnam War, increasingly merged with the New Left and preached that the U.S. had to accept restraints on its foreign policy. But in the end, this brand of pragmatism failed them. Without philosophical moorings, treating the Americans and Soviets as simply overarmed mirror images of each other, the establishmentarians began to lose their way, and, in turn, the neoconservatives derided them in the most sweeping of terms. The establishment was experiencing, they declared, "a failure of nerve."

Alexis de Tocqueville was the first to note that it was the political theorists, not the princes, ministers, or lords, who were the shapers of events leading to the French Revolution, and it was the neoconservatives loosely clustered around Jackson who were now seeking a new revolution in foreign policy. By the midpoint of the decade, *Newsweek* reported a seismic shift in the intellectual climate of the country: "In intellectual circles, the social thinkers who were once the driving force of Democratic liberalism—men like Arthur Schlesinger, Jr., and John Kenneth Galbraith—have been upstaged by a group of 'neoconservative' academics, many of them refugees from the liberal left."

They fought their battles mostly in the corridors of public opinion, and, to a lesser extent, in the offices of Capitol Hill and the bureaucracies of Foggy Bottom and the Potomac. As some of the brightest, most provocative and eloquent people in America, they became a shadow party, a counterestablishment, and perhaps most important, they were in a position to legitimize the ideas of U.S. policy makers.

But to be successful, they needed a dog in the chase—a president to rally behind.

CDM SUPPORTED JACKSON'S bid for the presidency in 1976. After skipping the Iowa and New Hampshire primaries, the well-financed campaign got off to a good start. Jackson won the Massachusetts primary and made a strong showing in Florida. In a burst of excitement, Jackson told his people, "We now go on to a landslide in New York." Jackson did win New York, courting pro-Israel Jewish supporters and getting 38 percent of the vote, but it was not a landslide, and his campaign fell victim to the media expectations game. Scoop all but ceased campaigning for the nomination after being drubbed in Pennsylvania, eventually tossing his support to the governor from Georgia. He refused to join in the "stop Carter" attempts by the McGovernites, Representative Mo Udall and Senator Frank Church, who bitterly contested Carter to the very end.

At first, the neoconservatives thought Carter, a former naval officer who went before the platform committee of the Democratic party and declared that détente had been "exploited by the Soviet Union," would be an improvement over the policies of weakness that they felt had characterized Nixon's and Ford's administrations. But their hopes were soon dashed as Carter began assembling his foreign policy team.

During the transition, CDM met with one of the men in charge of the personnel search for the president-elect. The conversation shifted to a discussion of Lane Kirkland, the secretary-treasurer of the AFL-CIO, who would go on to become labor's president in 1983. The Carter transition aide looked blankly at the neoconservatives, and said, "Lane Kirkland?"

"Yes, Lane Kirkland," they said. "He's very sound on foreign policy."

The president's man persisted, asking quizzically, "But does the AFL-CIO have anything to do with foreign policy?"

The CDM delegation was shocked. Here was one of the top personnel officials staffing the White House for Carter, and he seemed completely unaware that the labor movement had operated major international programs, stretching back to the dark days at the end of World War II, when they fought Communist infiltration of the West European political parties.

The Carter transition team did invite CDM to send a list of people from the Jackson wing of the party to be considered for foreign policy positions in Carter's administration. After a considerable amount of deliberation and consultation, and questions about who the right people would be, who shared Scoop Jackson's ideological orientation, who had sufficient expertise, CDM passed on a list of fifty-three names for senior administration jobs. Only one appointment was made, and it only modestly touched on serious foreign policy.

Peter Rosenblatt, a Yale College man and a graduate of Yale Law School, formerly a young aide in the Johnson White House, was designated to be the president's personal envoy to the negotiations on the political status of Micronesia, an archipelago of tiny islands in the Pacific where the U.S. once conducted nuclear tests. It was less of a defense or foreign policy issue than an Interior Department issue, leading some to quip that Micronesia's status was regarded as more of a waste disposal problem than a diplomatic matter.

Rosenblatt took the job. With his horn-rimmed glasses and quiet demeanor, he was a sound man, very meticulous, his words always weighed with care. In his bearing, he was somewhat unusual among the neoconservatives. He spoke with a voice that suggested authority, and his demeanor was that of the WASP establishment—very Yale, more Wall Street than ivory tower, the word "rather" pronounced "rahh-ther"—distinguishing him from many of the more intellectually scrappy neoconservatives, who still carried vestiges of their New York accents and spoke as much with their hands as with their voices.

Rarely did Rosenblatt openly venture the sort of bold-sounding opinions that characterized other Scoop Jacksonites, though he certainly was as tough on the Soviets as the rest of them. He too felt the New Left and the McGovernites were anti-American. He had little sympathy for the new Third World agenda sweeping liberal university departments. He bemoaned what was going on at Yale, as one department after another turned on the Vietnam War and the Cold War consensus. But his lawyerly demeanor gave his pronouncements an air of compromise and moderation. One friend later remembered him saying of Carter's foreign policy aide, "Tony Lake and I may have disagreements, but he is [pause], an honorable man."

This made Rosenblatt more palatable to Jimmy Carter's people, including an old friend of his and an ally on the inside, Dick Holbrooke, the incoming assistant secretary of state for East Asia. But the offer to Rosenblatt scarcely assuaged CDM, which took the appointment as an insult.

Elliott Abrams, then an aide to Senator Pat Moynihan, remarked, "They froze us out completely. We got one unbelievably minor job. It was a special negotiator position. Not for Polynesia. Not even for Macronesia. But for Micronesia." Moynihan himself fumed, "A conservative governor came to town and the people he appointed regarded the ideas of the coalition as far more a threat to the republic than the ideas of the Republican National Committee."

One member of the coalition summed up the entire process, saying succinctly, "What we put forth as an appointments list was treated as a purge list."

On the eve of the Carter inauguration, relations between CDM and Carter turned from bad to worse. At a public foreign policy forum in Washington to discuss the likely agenda for the new president, Ben Wattenberg sat on the speakers' dais, feeling disgusted. Wattenberg was always a unique figure in Washington. A man of boundless energy, when he got fired up, his hands would be in perpetual motion. He never walked into a room, he swept into it like a whirlwind, immediately capturing the attention of everyone present.

His hard-line ideas made him a favorite of Senator Jackson's; indeed, Jackson had chosen him to run his 1976 presidential campaign. But Wattenberg's genial personality and good humor also made him a darling of the Washington press corps, and he skillfully straddled the world of punditry in his lively books and newspaper columns, and the world of politics as chairman of CDM and a confidant to Jackson. He also had a tough side to him, a willingness to roll up his sleeves for a good political fight. He rarely fought personally, it wasn't in his nature, but when he fought, he fought hard. And when his turn came to speak, he discarded his notes, and, no longer able to contain his energy, he whipped his glasses off his head, twirled them, put them back on the bridge of his nose, and then whipped them off once more.

Wattenberg minced no words. "It is customary to wait a hundred days to see how the president is doing, but considering what Jimmy Carter has done by appointing a bunch of Johnny-one-notes to his foreign policy team, liberals who clapped for Jimmy Carter with one hand, I will wait only a hundred hours to make my pronouncement about his foreign policy."

CHAPTER 5

That January morning at the Hay Adams, one by one the members of CDM sat down. Not every member of the delegation slated to attend the presidential meeting was present. In attendance now were the most active and dedicated members, many of whom did not simply work together but were also friends. Breakfast was ordered. Not since the nomination of George McGovern in 1972 had they gathered together with such a sense of historic mission.

Now, as then, they were about to contemplate bold decisions—depending upon what Carter would say to them. They were coming to Carter not just as defenders of hard-line policies, but as members of the same political family—which like most families often underwent periods of difficulty before reconciliation. They expected that today would be the same. A peace meeting. After years of being in exile within the Democratic party, they would be brought back into the fold.

As those present helped themselves to black coffee, eggs, warm Danish, and bagels and lox, the mood was light, almost frivolous. Midge Decter and Norman Podhoretz were there, along with Elliott Abrams, Pat Moynihan's former chief of staff, who was now engaged to Midge Decter's daughter Rachel. Also at the table were Austin Ranney, a political scientist, Jeane Kirkpatrick, Ben Wattenberg, and lawyer Max Kampelman.

Wattenberg, CDM's chairman, began the breakfast with some chitchat—he recounted his role on Jimmy Carter's Presidential Commission on Ambassadorial Appointments.

Wattenberg explained, "Along with former Secretary of State Dean Rusk and Governor Reubin Askew, once a month I would trudge over to the commission offices and thrash out lists of ambassadorial recommendations for the president. When we first met with Carter at the outset to receive our marching instructions, the president said he wanted more than the typical foreign service types. 'The State Department isn't wiring my appointments,' Carter told us. He wanted diversity, 'diversity among men, diversity among women, diversity among blacks and Hispanics.' "

Wattenberg recalled how he piped up, much to Carter's surprise: "I said, meekly, but not too meekly, 'Mr. President, we need ideological diversity too.' Carter searched for this on his cue cards, and not finding it, he nodded his head, 'Right, that's good, let's also get ideological diversity.'

"So as post after post opened up—ambassador to Chile, ambassador to Argentina, ambassador to Israel—I proposed a brilliant scholar, Jeane Kirkpatrick. Jeane always made the short list, the handful of three or four names, but this recommendation was never accepted by the administration."

Looking over at Kirkpatrick, a grinning Wattenberg unleashed his punch line, "The President probably read something you wrote, Jeane—and fainted."

Everyone at the table laughed, including Kirkpatrick, and then the atmosphere turned much more earnest. Max Kampelman, his eyes surveying the room, sizing up everyone's mood, motioned. It was time to get down to business.

Kampelman was the elder statesman of the group. At sixty-eight, he was hardly glamorous or flashy. He moved in a slightly awkward way. But his small elfin frame would fill up a room whenever he spoke. His soft but firm voice had the effect of being almost thunderous, reflecting the unwavering confidence of his words. Kampelman had the air of a religious man, a rabbi, or even a preacher. Even when he engaged in a rare moment of idle chatter, every word was negotiated with the same care as a legal document.

He was rigorously disciplined. He kept not one but two secretaries, and they could barely keep up with him. Kampelman crossed every t and dotted every i. It was not simply that he did four things at once, he didn't; instead, he did one thing at a time, with relentless efficiency. Max Kampelman was meticulous, driven, and very good at what he did.

In 1968, he came very close to becoming secretary of state, only to watch his fortunes go up in smoke as Hubert Humphrey was defeated by a last-minute Nixon surge. Months earlier, after the convention, when Humphrey's fortunes had looked brighter, Humphrey had called on Kampelman to draw up a list of names for his potential cabinet, and Kampelman later noted that Humphrey decided that Henry Kissinger or Zbigniew Brzezinski would have been his national security adviser. Of course, the unstated implication was that someone else would have been Humphrey's secretary of state. Many believed the job would have gone to Kampelman.

But of course, Kampelman said nothing about who would have been secretary of state, which made his list of the top choices for national security adviser all the more intriguing. This was Kampelman's style. Give credit to others. Artfully flatter them. Let it be known, discreetly, that you keep only the best company, that you have gravitas. And the supremely confident Kampelman had gravitas. Despite humble beginnings, he moved among the power brokers and Washington establishment with ease and confidence.

Ben Wattenberg often referred to Kampelman as the "grand old man." Others said that "when Max spoke, it was as if he were talking to God." Growing up in the Bronx, he attended yeshivas as a boy, and he had long been motivated by religious and philosophical questions about good and evil. Under the influence of a Reform rabbi, and a number of Quakers whom he met during college at New York University, the strongly religious Kampelman became a rarity in World War II: a Jewish conscientious objector. But Hiroshima and Nagasaki, and the Holocaust, dispelled his notions that pacifism was viable in the modern world; there was no choice but to be strong against the likes of Hitler and Stalin, and their successors. Kampelman became an ardent cold warrior, but one driven by moral considerations, to whom politics and God were not that far apart.

Those who typically held Kampelman's hard-line views, notably the other Scoop Jackson Democrats, had their share of Washington enemies, but not Max, as friends and colleagues called him; he had few enemies in this town. Even his detractors always hastened to add that they disagreed with Kampelman "respectfully." (Elliott Abrams would later say about Kampelman: "He should have been a member of the establishment. He's a lawyer, he's rich, he's always careful.")

Kampelman's hard-line agenda and his ability to straddle the political middle without sacrificing his hawkish principles made him wickedly deceptive, a hard-nosed wolf in establishment sheep's clothing. He was helped by an uncommon sense of decency, and a reluctance to get personal in a political fight. Kampelman was supremely considerate; he rarely ever uttered an unkind or embarrassing word about anyone.

But Kampelman also had power. He liked to look people straight in the eye when he spoke, an intimidating prospect to many who did not know him. Kampelman was a fox, a master of the political game, and in the practical world of Washington, few wanted to be on his wrong side. Former Nixon speechwriter turned sage *New York Times* columnist William Safire praised Kampelman as a Democrat to be considered for secretary of state in an incoming Republican administration. Morton Kondracke, *The New Republic*'s senior editor, would later rave that Kampelman should be made secretary of state—"for the Democrats." Another columnist, Cord Meyer, a silver-maned old CIA hand, when asked who his candidate for secretary of state was, said tersely, "Max, it should be Max."

In Washington, it was a clear measure of Kampelman's stature that he was always on someone's short list to be secretary of state. And in truth, were it not for the Democratic party's drift to the left, Kampelman would have been just about everyone's choice for secretary of state.

After Carter was elected, CDM had expected that at least Kampelman would be appointed to a significant position in the administration. But there wasn't even a nibble. Had Kampelman been given a high post, their elder would have been a voice on the inside, the CDM perspective would have been represented. They would have been not just mollified, but content. But the call never came, and, as the CDM people used to say, "we were forced to wander in the wilderness."

Recently, however, a quiet overture had been made. As a disciple of Hubert Humphrey, Walter Mondale knew and respected Max Kampelman, a former legislative aide to Humphrey. The previous month, Mondale had summoned Kampelman to his office, and floated the idea of making him the ambassador to the Conference on Security and Cooperation in Europe's (CSCE) "Helsinki Review" talks on human rights and security issues, set to take place in Madrid. Mondale explained that it was anything but a done deal, but it gave Kampelman a palpable stake in Carter's political fortunes. Mondale also asked Kampelman not to go public with the ambassadorial offer until it was firmed up.

Mondale felt duty-bound to tell Kampelman that Vance had already offered the job to his man, Bill Scranton, the former governor of Pennsylvania and U.S. ambassador to the United Nations. Unspoken, however, was the suggestion that this dangling appointment should neutralize the participation of Kampelman as a critic of the president. Mondale also knew that if Kampelman were given a key post, it could help keep CDM on the Carter bandwagon; indeed, he had felt it was a mistake not bringing them into the administration early on.

So the January 1980 meeting between the president and CDM was a risky proposition for Kampelman, even if shrewdly calculated and personally heartfelt. The meeting would burnish Kampelman's hard-line credentials with Carter at a time when Carter's own views were shaken by Soviet aggression. In addition, Kampelman had long personal and professional ties to the vice president. Brzezinski too was a kindred spirit and a friend. However, Kampelman ran the risk that if CDM came on too strong with Carter, or if the chemistry was poor, the thin-skinned president could be offended. This could sink Kampelman's own chances of becoming ambassador to the Helsinki talks. Kampelman wanted the position. He told his wife, Maggie, about it, saying it was a job where he felt he could make a difference by holding the Soviets accountable for their systematic oppression of human rights. It was a risk he was willing to take.

That morning, Kampelman began to frame the tone for the meeting.

Kampelman had severe doubts about Carter's seriousness as a leader. Nonetheless, he said, "A president is a busy man, it's no easy matter to get his ear. We shouldn't bicker with him, his time doesn't come lightly."

Midge Decter, as she recalled it, felt she had seen this so many times before. Kampelman, the smooth insider. Always speaking in conciliatory terms. Always keeping his cards close to his vest, his words carefully weighed.

Kampelman, waving his hand, instructed, "We should build bridges with the president."

Decter privately disagreed. True, she was a writer, not a lawyer, an ideologue from New York, not a Washington consensus builder, though Kampelman was not the type to cook up a consensus that was pure mush. She didn't need a job in the administration, and didn't lust for a position. But she felt that Kampelman's thinking was symptomatic of CDM's larger problem: the Humphrey wing of CDM was too willing to compromise and cut a deal. That stance had gotten them nowhere. She felt what was needed now was not bridges, but a few bombs.

Elliott Abrams, by far the youngest of the delegation, countered, "The president has ignored us since he became president, and only now that he needs us for reelection is he coming to us."

Wattenberg, an inveterate optimist, sided with Kampelman, and agreed that bridges should be built. He spewed out a list of ideas that sounded to some as if they could have come off a Chinese menu, so sweeping was their range. As one of Wattenberg's close friends and admirers would say, Wattenberg had a new idea every minute. Among his suggestions, Wattenberg said the group should consider recommending a "Freedom Olympics" to Carter, to take the place of U.S. participation in the Moscow Olympics.

But the CDM people were feeling feisty, and that day such ideas didn't fly. Moreover, it quickly was decided that this was the wrong way to approach a meeting with the president. If they just kicked around ideas, with no beginning, middle, and end, a high-powered version of the boys shooting the breeze, the meeting would be a waste—perhaps not for the president, but most certainly for CDM.

We can't give him a laundry list, Kampelman said. We need to make use of our time. Decter nodded her head in agreement. So did the others.

Kampelman, his head leaning back, his eyes half closed, said to his colleagues, "The president should be given the benefit of the doubt. We should stress our agreement with his new, firmer policies toward the Soviets." The group all agreed that the president seemed to have turned over a new leaf with his strong response to the Soviet invasion of Afghanistan. They decided they would focus on reinforcing the president's tough-nosed, post-Afghanistan policy, not his instinctive dovishness, and not his version of détente that had prevailed until Afghanistan.

Austin Ranney, an owlish-looking and low-key political scientist at the American Enterprise Institute, looked over in Kampelman's direction. Ranney was no fire-breathing conservative. Indeed, when he first came to the AEI, with the help of Jeane Kirkpatrick's husband, Kirk, he had been "a little nervous" about working among so many high-profile conservatives. Ranney, however, felt he fit in comfortably with the CDM people, even though he was at the left of their spectrum.

As the breakfast progressed, Ranney thought to himself that if Carter had had the initial foresight to appoint Kampelman White House counselor, or deputy secretary of state, CDM wouldn't even be here today to offer its advice or try to make peace with the president.

Now, after Afghanistan, with Carter's team in disarray, his political fortunes looking tenuous, Ranney believed they could at least expect the president to agree to their view of the world, and openly indicate that there would be a role for the CDM people—certainly, for heaven's sake, as he had confided to friends, for Max and Jeane Kirkpatrick—in a second Carter administration. The perpetually modest Ranney took a sip of coffee and thought to himself, "We should expect at least this much."

Kampelman continued: "We should appoint a spokesman for different issue areas, and keep the meeting directed." But Kampelman did not offer to be the group's lead spokesman. Instead, he turned to Ranney and said, Austin, will you lead off and talk about U.S. policy toward the Soviets? It wasn't meant as a question.

"Certainly," Ranney said. "I'd be glad to."

"After Austin's comments," Kampelman explained, "we can then each contribute. But we'll play it by ear as we see fit."

Jeane Kirkpatrick, her lips pursed, cradled her black horn-rimmed glasses. Kirkpatrick was surprisingly subdued that day at the Hay Adams. She had been listening intently. Her perpetually raised eyebrows gave her an air of sustained skepticism. Today, that skepticism ran deep. Far from being enthusiastic about meeting with the commander in chief, she sat with mixed emotions.

She was already peeved at the president. Carter, she had learned, hadn't even put the meeting on his official White House schedule, as though they weren't even trustworthy Democrats. These things didn't happen by accident. Kirkpatrick had been quite vocal that she felt Carter had treated the Scoop Jackson Democrats like "pariahs." And now this.

It also hadn't escaped many people's attention, including Kirkpatrick's, that she was never asked to join the Carter administration. Indeed, some members of the Carter White House were going around town bragging that they had kept her out. Early in 1977, Anthony Lake, Carter's principal representative to the foreign policy community, told a group of assembled guests at a Georgetown dinner party that he had "done a good day's work." The guests edged closer, anxious to hear Lake's every word. "I managed to veto Jeane Kirkpatrick as ambassador to Israel," he said proudly.

The stories and bad-mouthing continued. Kirkpatrick was too prickly, too ideological, too strong-willed, they said. "Besides," one official added, twisting the knife, "she's just an academic."

Kirkpatrick was never one to suffer in silence, and her enforced political exile was no different. Of late, Kirkpatrick, more so than an Austin Ranney or a Ben Wattenberg, had taken to wrestling with her identity as a Democrat. In an unusual, almost impassioned piece written in the fall of 1979 for *Common Sense* magazine, the journal of the Republican party, she chose the provocative title, "Why We Don't Become Republicans." Changing parties, she wrote, "is like denying part of one's self and one's heritage." Even though the Democratic party is "a far cry from the party of my parents and grandparents," and even though her party had produced presidential candidates whose policies and commitments were very far from her own, she added, "the problem is that the Republican Party has not articulated any inclusive vision for the well-being of the whole community." To drive home the point, she concluded, "one is not only part of one's party, but more crucially one's party is part of one's self."

"To understand Jeane Kirkpatrick," said Walter Beach, an old family friend, "you have to understand how this Midwestern girl gone east took her roots as a Democrat very seriously." Jeane Kirkpatrick, the daughter of a Duncan, Oklahoma, oil wildcatter and a secretarial-school graduate mother, had come a long way from small-town Oklahoma. From the time she learned to read, she devoured books with a passion. By fourth grade, she was, by her own account, "into Stevenson and Dumas," and had bought herself a thesaurus. She took elocution lessons, and as her father followed the oil boom north out of post-Depression Oklahoma into Illinois, she developed into an unabashed socialist. As she moved from Stephens College in Columbia, Missouri, in 1946, to Barnard College in New York City, where she got her B.A. in 1948, and further study at the University of Paris in the early 1950s, and then finally a Ph.D. in political science from Columbia in 1968, she had made an impressive journey from her early days on Main Street.

Kirkpatrick had risen to the status of a cerebral political comer, dealing in the commodities of ideas and language, freely horse-traded among the new elite known as the neoconservatives. From her prestigious position at Georgetown University's Department of Government, and as the first woman resident scholar at the American Enterprise Institute, she had literally written herself from a suburban Washington kitchen into the inner sanctum of one of America's leading policy think tanks. Her views were sought by the readers of *Commentary* magazine and *The New Republic*, she was respected by the likes of Max Kampelman, and courted by members of the glittering New York political literati such as Norman Podhoretz and Midge Decter. And she had cachet among such political intellectuals as Ben Wattenberg and Senator Pat Moynihan. Yet as Jeane Kirkpatrick's friends suspected, the stirrings of ambition were hardly quiet. She wanted more.

Kirkpatrick's desire to move beyond academia had been growing since the Johnson administration, when she saw that she was not just a professor—but that she knew, actually knew well, Hubert Humphrey, the vice president of the United States. Kirkpatrick's husband, also a highly respected academic (he had been Max Kampelman's Ph.D. thesis adviser at the University of Minnesota), had taught Humphrey and been a close confidant throughout Humphrey's political career. That close relationship had also extended to Jeane.

Within the Democratic party itself, Kirkpatrick was long an active participant. From 1972 to 1974, she was a member of the Democratic National Committee and a vice chairman of the committee's Vice Presidential Selection Commission. She then moved on to sit on the Democratic National Convention's National Commission on Party Structure and Presidential Nomination from 1975 to 1978. When Humphrey declined to run in 1976, she backed Scoop Jackson, and that year served on the Credentials Committee for the Democratic National Convention.

This was a natural evolution for Kirkpatrick. Having distinguished herself as a rising star in the academic world, she now was increasingly moved to seek a position where she could influence events more directly, not restricted by the confines of the ivory tower, but actually to make policy inside government itself. Her old friend Austin Ranney called Kirkpatrick's growing desire to move beyond theory into practice a reflection of her "citizenly motives."

However, Kirkpatrick was increasingly disgusted with the rise of the 1960s New Left, the growing counterculture, and the antiwar movement. It had helped cost her old friend Humphrey the election, and even worse, dishonored America. (In 1975, when the U.S. pulled out of South Vietnam, Kirkpatrick wrote to Humphrey in a state of self-proclaimed anguish: "I regard the U.S. refusal to provide material aid to South Vietnam today, in its hour of greatest need, as the most shameful display of irresponsibility and inhumanity in our history.") The forces of the New Left were, she was convinced, fundamentally hostile to American culture and institutions. They perceived the U.S. as a sick society surfeited by materialism and technology, and advocated unrealistic, utopian reforms. The McGovern movement of 1972 had prompted her to run, unsuccessfully, in the Maryland state primary on a slate of delegates committed to former Vice President Humphrey.

Yet although McGovern's nomination represented for Kirkpatrick the triumph of the counterculture and the antiwar movement within the party, she continued to support such traditional liberal causes as the welfare state and the labor movement, even as her anti-Communist, pro-Israel views drew her further away from the center of a party that was moving ever more to the left. She turned to CDM to help reduce the antiwar, dovish, antilabor, McGovernite influence in the party. Midge Decter would say, over and over, that she "adored Jeane. She was just brilliant, and very striking."

Renewing the Democratic party in the 1970s was almost like a religion for Kirkpatrick. While she had been raised a Southern Baptist, and her husband a Methodist, their three children had no formal religious upbringing. They were not confirmed, nor were they baptized. Some years earlier, when her son Doug was in elementary school, he came home one day, flushed with excitement and pride. As Kirkpatrick poured him a glass of milk, she asked, "What happened in school today?" Doug, smiling proudly, replied, "Today, we talked about what we are. Jimmy said he was a Catholic. Then Annie said she was a Jew. My friend Timmy said he's Episcopalian."

"Well, what did you say?" Jeane asked.

Her son, all of seven years old, beamed. "I said we're Democrats."

When Carter became the Democrats' nominee in 1976, Kirkpatrick gave him her support. But that support was short-lived, and Kirkpatrick had become a persistent critic of Carter's policies since he came into office.

Increasingly, she despaired over the twists and turns of Carter's foreign policy, lurching usually to the left, with little regard for American security and the promotion of freedom. She despaired at the tide of events running against America, the failure of American leaders to come to grips with the moral complexities of world leadership. As the presidential election approached, she talked incessantly to colleagues about the failures of U.S. policy, batting ideas back and forth about the appropriate course Democrats should pursue. Her famous dinner parties and monthly wine-tasting get-togethers also took on an increasingly intense tone.

Old friends would gather for the French food and the wine, reminiscent of the European salons of a previous time. One of her more distinguished guests, whose family boasted no fewer than three secretaries of state, loved to go to Jeane's as much for the conversation as for Jeane's fine food. "She's fantastic," said the eighty-two-year-old Eleanor Lansing Dulles, taking time off from summering at the Dulles estate in Henderson Harbor off Lake Ontario in upstate New York. "Simply fantastic." But, as the 1970s were drawing to a close, conversation always came back to old questions of geopolitics: what to do about the Soviets?

"She was going through a prolonged mental process of sorting things out," one friend, watching the inner workings of Kirkpatrick, noted.

Some of that sorting had become clear two months earlier, when she fired off a withering blast at Carter in the November issue of *Commentary*. The *Commentary* article was a watershed piece for Kirkpatrick, professionally and personally. It reflected her own struggle with her identity as a Democrat, and her increasingly gloomy assessment of world events.

In the tightly reasoned essay, called "Dictatorships and Double Standards," Kirkpatrick argued that there was a distinction between totalitarian and authoritarian regimes. Moderate autocratic regimes of the right tend to be less repressive than Communist regimes of the left, she wrote, and "more compatible with U.S. security interests." For example, she asked rhetorically: "How can an administration committed to nonintervention in Cambodia and Vietnam announce that it 'will not be deterred' from righting wrongs in South Africa?" To this she added, "A realistic policy which aims at protecting our own interests and assisting the capacity for self-determination of less-developed nations will need to face the unpleasant fact that, if victorious, violent insurgency headed by Marxist revolutionaries is unlikely to lead to anything but totalitarian tyranny."

Boiled down to its essence, the message was fairly straightforward and accurate. Jimmy Carter was, in Kirkpatrick's view, no less than a willing accomplice, if not a midwife, to efforts that brought to power the Sandinista Communists in Nicaragua and the fundamentalist Khomeini regime in Iran. Both were more hostile to America than their unruly predecessors. They were, she contended, even more dictatorial than the pro-American regimes of Anastasio Somoza and the shah, and, under the shadow of the Soviet Union, not as likely to democratize.

Finally, in a slap at the reluctance of the Carter administration to use sufficient force abroad, she warned against U.S. administrations that

"forswear unilaterally the use of military force to counter military force."
Kirpatrick concluded by saying that the failure of the Carter administration's foreign policy was now "clear to everyone except its architects."

This article in *Commentary*, like the piece she wrote in *Common Sense*,
attracted an unusual amount of attention, and had caught the eye of a
number of well-placed Republicans. Richard Allen, Ronald Reagan's foreign policy guru and watchful talent scout for his presidential campaign,
was just one of the people impressed by Kirkpatrick's ability to articulate
the very conceptual approach to foreign policy Republicans had been
searching for. Not unsurprisingly, the Carter White House was less than
happy, and let it be known that they were outraged by her philippic
against the president during a campaign season.

BUT SITTING DOWN together that January morning, what mattered now was
how Carter treated them, and what he said. After Afghanistan, he appeared to have seen the light, and was finally ready to take a tougher
stand in foreign affairs. Like everyone else at the CDM breakfast, Kirkpatrick believed Carter would surely indicate that they, CDM, had been
right from the start about Soviet intentions—and, just perhaps, he would
reach out to CDM for guidance. And if Carter reached out to CDM, despite her misgivings, she would be receptive. So, when her turn came to
speak, Kirkpatrick's face showed little of her distaste for Carter, revealing
instead a contemplative guise. She said simply, responding to Kampelman's prodding, "I'll be happy to talk about Central America policy."

ELLIOTT ABRAMS WAS unusually quiet at this breakfast. He was thirty-two
years old, which made him a generation younger than everyone else. He
was smart, ambitious, hungry. That Abrams was present at this meeting
was also a clear indication he was a young man on his way up.

In the company of the CDM elders, however, he frequently chose to say
less and listen more, though Abrams was hardly shy about expressing
his views. Austin Ranney, after listening to Abrams at one of Kirkpatrick's dinner parties, had turned to his wife, Nancy, and said, "Now
there is a very bright young man."

This was also a time of enormous change in Abrams's life. He was engaged to Rachel Decter, Norman Podhoretz's step-daughter and Midge
Decter's daughter. He had left Senator Moynihan's office as chief of Staff,
and for the last year had been practicing law with the prestigious firm of
Verner, Lipfert, Bernhard and McPherson. Harry McPherson, Democratic

party elder extraordinaire, former counsel to LBJ, an establishment member if ever there was one, had brought Abrams to the firm. "Let's do it," McPherson said, and hired the Harvard-trained Abrams. Among the oak-paneled law firms of the nation's capital, Abrams could scarcely have found himself a more lucrative position to be in—financially and professionally.

A relationship with McPherson alone was a ticket into the inner circle of the establishment, if Abrams only stuck it out and did the requisite grunt work on the path to becoming partner. The route was safe and secure. Everything he had dreamed of as a kid was now within his grasp—money, security, the prospects of a good family life, a solidly upward career. But despite outward appearances, and the fact that Elliott Abrams was not one to engage in excessive introspection and suffer from bouts of self-doubt, things just weren't right.

Abrams found the law tedious and hopelessly boring, with little intrinsic merit. He wanted to be part of the policy world—even if the Democrats, under President Carter's leadership, didn't want him. Looking for a start in the executive branch, Abrams would have liked a job in the Carter administration, but he was forced to labor instead as, in effect, a member of the loyal opposition from his slot in Senator Moynihan's office. Indeed, he still held out a faint hope that a second-term Carter presidency would include more than the McGovern spectrum of the party, and make room for him. He yearned to get back into government.

Throughout the steamy Washington summer of 1979, Abrams had been breakfasting once a week with Ben Wattenberg and Penn Kemble, to discuss what was next for the Scoop Jackson Democrats. Kemble, like Wattenberg, was a tireless Democrat, a talented politico, and CDM's first executive director. Kemble was also Wattenberg's alter ego, and Wattenberg was forever bouncing ideas off him.

As a young civil rights activist, Kemble had chained himself to the Brooklyn Bridge to protest the lagging progress on civil rights in America. But he broke with the New Left when it started occupying buildings and chanting anti-American slogans. Along with Wattenberg, the two became the heart and soul of the day-to-day workings of CDM. But Abrams increasingly didn't share Wattenberg's and Kemble's views that the Democratic party would, in time, return to its pro-defense, anti-Communist traditions. Nor did he buy their contention that it was important for CDM to do what it could, at any price, to strengthen the Democratic party.

Abrams was ready for greater status and power. Unless Carter signaled a clear change, Abrams saw little point in hanging on to a political party that he no longer identified with and that no longer wanted him.

Unlike the other Scoop Jackson Democrats, he didn't feel bound by tradition or party affiliation—not unless Jimmy Carter gave him a reason to think otherwise.

BREAKFAST WAS FINISHED. The CDM members made the short walk from the Hay Adams past Lafayette Park to the iron gate by the corner of 18th Street and Pennsylvania Avenue. Before them stood the White House. At 9:45, they were cleared by the White House guard for entrance to the West Wing, and were then led into the Roosevelt room, dominated by the heavy inlay table where the president's top advisers usually met. They all stood as the president, looking drawn and tense, walked into the room, with Vice President Mondale and Zbigniew Brzezinski, his national security adviser, trailing behind. Not since 1972 had a meeting taken on so much gravity. The next hour and a half would determine the fate of these CDM members for decades to come.

CHAPTER 6

"I'm glad you could all come and join me today," Jimmy Carter said in his Georgia drawl, as he took his place at the center of the massive oblong table in the Roosevelt Room of the West Wing in the White House.

Mondale was already sitting across from the president's chair on the other side of the table. Brzezinski, sitting at the table's end to the left of Carter, sat up straight, snapping to attention when the president entered. Stu Eizenstat, the president's trusted domestic policy adviser, who had helped play a major role in Carter's victorious 1976 campaign, quietly took a seat against the wall, behind the president. He cradled a pad on his lap, ready to take notes. Wattenberg, Decter, and Kirkpatrick sat to one side of the president, Admiral Bud Zumwalt and Sonny Dogole on the other. Austin Ranney sat next to Mondale on one side, flanked by Maria Thomas and Joshua Muravchik (two CDM staffers); Abrams, Podhoretz, and Kampelman were on the other.

The sense of anticipation was high.

The president looked tired. His hair was considerably grayer, his deep blue eyes lacked the strength they had just a few years before. He seemed weary. Wattenberg crossed his hands on the table, and thanked the president for taking the time to see them. As planned, Ranney spoke first.

"Mr. President, as you know, all of us voted for you. While we have had disagreements, we have strongly supported your policies since Afghanistan."

The president sat poker-faced.

Ranney continued. "Sir, it strikes us that there are two views of U.S.-Soviet policy. One holds that the Soviet Union is a mature superpower, with interests that sometimes conflict with ours and at other times allow for cooperation, but it can be dealt with in good faith. The other view is that the Soviet Union is fundamentally a totalitarian power, is dangerous and expansionist, and is fundamentally hostile to the United States. It seems to us that pre-Afghanistan, you have held the first view. But events in Afghanistan and Iran seem to have caused you to now hold that the second view is correct. This is a change we support and applaud."

Ranney added, "If this is the case, it may be good to add some officials to your administration who are more in tune with the second policy."

Two red spots welled up on Carter's cheeks, his face became flushed. He flashed an icy smile, but his forced grin did little to mask his displeasure.

Clearly rankled, Carter intoned, "Your analysis is not true. There has been no change in my policy. I have always held a consistent view of the Soviet Union.

"For the record, I did not say that I have learned more about the Soviets since the invasion of Afghanistan, as is alleged in the press. My policy is my policy, and has been my policy. It has not changed, and will not change."

Carter did not address the personnel issue.

Abrams slumped in his chair, ever so slightly. "Say it ain't so, Joe," he thought, stunned at Carter's vehement response, his dismissal of their offer to come to the president's assistance, his reluctance to distance himself from earlier policies that clearly hadn't worked.

Decter thought to herself that a similar look by the head of state in a less democratic country would mean that they were about to be carted out to be shot by a firing squad.

Walter Mondale fidgeted slightly, and craned his head to the right. He knew Carter's answer was insufficient, and wanted to gauge both Kirkpatrick's and Kampelman's response. Kirkpatrick and Kampelman looked completely inscrutable. Both were jotting down notes on notepads. Neither was looking at the president. Neither was looking up.

Bud Zumwalt, the retired chief of naval operations, wheeled around in his chair to face Carter. Zumwalt had heard through the grapevine from Averell Harriman that the president had said there were two men he didn't want in his administration. Zumwalt was one, and Paul Nitze was the other. Zumwalt was no fan of Carter's; indeed, he frequently told others that he feared for his children's future if Carter continued as president. But he was a military man, and showed the president his due respect.

Zumwalt said, "I have heard your recent statements that we need to defend the Indian Ocean and Persian Gulf oil routes. My concern, sir, is that we don't have sufficient military capability for this task, a fact which could be disastrous."

There was a long pause.

Carter stared at Zumwalt, and said, "I want to thank you for the statement, and thank you for the support of my efforts."

Austin Ranney, for one, was horrified by Carter's answer. Carter had responded as though Zumwalt had praised the state of American readiness. It was a complete nonresponse, a brush-off of a serious military question posed by someone who had been one of the highest ranking military men in the land, and formerly the most senior naval officer in the country. "My God, what a disaster this is," Ranney thought.

Podhoretz then spoke, urging the president to mount a vigorous human rights offensive against the Soviet Union, among both the American people and in the world community. Carter said, "Yes, I know how interested you all are in human rights. So am I, as you know. And I need help in ginning up support for a very dire problem."

Carter added, "I would like your help with Uruguay."

Wattenberg's mouth dropped. He was stunned. It was an utterly incoherent answer. The president didn't even know how to lie to them well, he thought.

The unflappable Eizenstat partially covered his face with his hand. Brzezinski, not normally known for his reticence, said nothing. Kampelman pushed his glasses down to the bridge of his nose, and continued to take notes. Mondale, Ranney thought, was visibly disturbed by Carter's performance.

A half hour slipped by, a fairly long time for the president to spend with a group. Carter stood up, thanked them all again, and excused himself. He had another meeting to attend.

Before everyone else packed their materials to leave, Mondale interjected, "As a favor to me, if you could, please stay for a few more minutes, I'd like to speak with you a bit more."

MONDALE PROCEEDED TO explain how good, how tough on the Soviets, how sober a commander in chief the president really was. He spoke for an hour, giving his view of the world, a view he said that was shared throughout the administration, including by Jimmy Carter. It was a hard-nosed speech. We have to be tough with the Soviets. Afghanistan is yet another manifestation of a new phase in Soviet aggressive behavior. There could be no business as usual. Now, more than ever, it is important to stand up to the Soviets.

Wattenberg was delighted. For us, he thought, Fritz had "hit every string on the guitar, every chord on the piano."

Kampelman, never quick to rush to judgment, felt the situation was potentially salvageable. He took Mondale's discussion as a good sign as well. He hadn't taken the lead in the meeting; he had listened. He felt that Mondale's speech was a demonstration that the president had overcome the weaknesses that saddled his administration pre-Afghanistan. This was an administration he could work for, if Mondale's offer turned out to be genuine.

The CDM delegation walked out of the White House after the meeting, straggling, exchanging notes, talking. It was, all in all, a bizarre meeting, like nothing they could ever have expected. They all knew Zbigniew Brzezinski, Carter's national security adviser. Yet Brzezinski had said nothing the whole meeting. Most of the group felt that Carter had made little attempt to embrace them, and even less of an attempt to understand their views. Some believed they couldn't have scripted a meeting designed to alienate them more.

Whatever hopes these members had had for Carter were clearly dashed.

Austin Ranney was more liberal than the rest of the group. As he ambled along, his head slightly bowed, he thought to himself, "I'll vote for Carter, but holding my nose." (Many years later, at a cocktail reception at the University of Minnesota, Mondale shared a drink with Ranney. He walked up to Ranney, now at the University of California at Berkeley, and said, "Austin, my gosh—do you remember that meeting in the cabinet room in 1980. What a disaster Carter was. But there was not much more I could do about it.")

Abrams was more vocal. "The meeting was a disaster, the straw that breaks the camel's back. Carter told us he will continue to pursue a leftist McGovernite–Andy Young foreign policy." Abrams left little doubt that the meeting was crucial for him, but didn't elaborate further.

Wattenberg, who saw a silver lining in just about everything, was less pessimistic. Even if Carter was horrible, Fritz was outstanding. The meeting had been a disappointment, to be sure. But wasn't that the way the Democratic party has been since 1972?

Kirkpatrick and Decter walked side by side. They had all hoped to see a change in the president. Instead, the ideological divide was as great as ever, as was, it seemed, the rancor between their wing of the party and the McGovern wing. It was thoroughly disconcerting. "What did you think?" Decter asked. Kirkpatrick told her, in a firm voice and clearly annoyed, "I am not going to support *that* man."

Kirkpatrick had echoed the views of the others, except for Wattenberg and Ranney. For his part, the lawyerly Kampelman revealed nothing, his reaction undisclosed.

But, as discontented as the CDM people were, their one major problem, as the Carter White House had correctly calculated, was that these renegade Democrats, lifelong party activists, had nowhere else to go. In a second-term Carter administration, it was clear, their enforced exile would not change.

Yet on the other side of the political aisle, things hardly looked any better. George Bush, a middle-of-the-road, country club Republican, had been the surprise front runner in the Republican primaries after New Hampshire. And while the other top candidate, Ronald Reagan, was a former Democrat, it was unclear from the press coverage if he had the depth to be president. So far, he certainly hadn't surrounded himself with serious people, not the way Kennedy or LBJ had. Moreover, it was not clear, standing there on that chill January morning, that anyone in CDM was included in Ronald Reagan's vision of America.

CHAPTER 7

It was April 1 in Washington, three and half weeks before the Desert One debacle but well into the presidential primary season. Ronald Reagan, in his third try and final run for the office, was winning.

Sitting in his office, Richard Allen was savvy enough to realize that, as a former governor, Reagan had little actual experience in foreign affairs. The press was already saying Reagan lacked a well-defined or subtle view of U.S. national security policies. It was an image that had to be counteracted.

Allen, at forty-four, had already worked on the National Security Council staff in the Nixon administration. Sometimes acerbic, occasionally gruff, and frequently controversial, he had collided bitterly with Henry Kissinger—whose job he coveted but didn't get—almost from the outset. The contest proved not to be a clash of giants but an unmitigated rout. Within a year, Kissinger had elbowed Allen out. Allen retreated from government into private business. His commercial dealings, through the international consulting firm Potomac International Corp., reportedly with the likes of the well-known mobster Robert Vesco, had colored his public patina in the eyes of an already skeptical press.

But Allen had a well-developed and scholarly view of American foreign policy, forged among Republicans at the prominent conservative think tank in Stanford, California, the Hoover Institution. His views were consistent with Reagan's hard-line instincts, which for the last two years had earned him the role of Reagan's resident intellectual on national security issues. Once the campaign was in full swing, he moved up to the privileged position of directing all foreign and defense policy input to Reagan, much the same post that Anthony Lake had held four years earlier for Jimmy Carter. Allen also occupied a hallowed slot in Reagan's inner circle, along with Edwin Meese, Bill Casey, Lyn Nofziger, and Richard Wirthlin.

Allen's philosophy was simple. He believed, acutely, that a candidate is known by the company he keeps. The quality and prominence of the advisers a candidate can attract reflect his political philosophy, directly bear on his leadership ability, and provide a measure of credibility to his campaign. A star-studded cast of advisers could go a long way toward dispelling this image that Reagan was a lightweight in foreign affairs, and would give the candidate the luster of a man ready to lead America during turbulent times.

Allen was determined to provide such a star-studded cast for Reagan.

This task was made all the more urgent by the virtual exclusion of Henry Kissinger from Reagan's inner circle. Kissinger, whose views were regarded as anathema to the Republican right, was also regarded by many of Reagan's top advisers as having a reputation and ego that wouldn't permit him to play on the team without being its captain. For Richard Allen in particular, there was little incentive to resuscitate Kissinger from a political graveyard and bring him into the Reagan ranks. Thus, while Kissinger had some telephone contact with candidate Reagan, he was kept largely at arm's length.

But on its face, there was a downside to shutting Kissinger out. Kissinger was the intellectual godfather of détente, the centerpiece of foreign policy in the Nixon, Ford, and even Carter administrations. Détente was a symbol of continuity in U.S. foreign policy. Kissinger's noticeable absence from the campaign indicated that a Reagan presidency would be more openly confrontational with the Soviets and that there would be a sharp break with the past.

This was exactly the message that Allen was content to send. However, he also had to demonstrate that Reagan would staff his government with experienced advisers, serious people who had been in government before, men and women of vision and strength, people who knew how to get policies through a recalcitrant Congress, who could soothe the perpetually nervous allies, who had the stature to sit down across the table from experienced Soviet negotiators.

This wasn't the case at first. Reagan, a bedrock conservative, whose views were already being painted (however wrongly so) as overly simplistic, ringing with the ruffles and flourishes of Cold War rhetoric, was facing an uphill battle in establishment circles. Many condemned his ideas as a throwback to the 1950s, possibly igniting a new world war. As it stood, Reagan's inchoate brain trust of advisers had yet to convey the view of subtlety and nuance that soothed worried pundits and foreign leaders.

It was at this point that Allen seriously sought to court hard-liners with intellectual stature. There was one problem though: many were members of the other party.

· · ·

"WHO IS IT on the phone?" Jeane Kirkpatrick asked her secretary.

"Richard Allen."

Despite the reservations being expressed about Ronald Reagan, Allen's stock had risen in Washington. Kirkpatrick took the call immediately, even if Richard Allen was a Republican talent scout, and even if she only knew Allen in the most perfunctory way. Richard Allen was now not a man to be ignored. Nor, as it would turn out, was it a complete surprise.

In late February, Kirkpatrick had received a three-page, single-spaced letter on personal stationery from Ronald Reagan, the handiwork of Richard Allen. Allen had passed on Kirkpatrick's "Dictatorships and Double Standards" to Reagan, highlighting in bold yellow marker its key sections and conclusions. Reagan was so impressed that he wrote her almost immediately—but only after calling up Allen and asking: "I want to borrow her elegant phraseology—but who is she?"

Reagan liked what he saw. In his letter, he praised the article and proposed that he and Kirkpatrick meet at some point to discuss it. (Reagan later told her that no fewer than three people had passed on her article to him.)

At the time, Kirkpatrick was consumed with her place in the Democratic party, and not with, as she told her husband, Kirk, "this conservative Republican governor whom I have no interest in." She folded the letter, the name Ronald Reagan emblazoned at the top, and tucked it away, barely giving it a second thought—until Allen's call.

"In principle, would you like to meet with Ronald Reagan?" Allen asked Kirkpatrick. "I'm setting up a meeting with a small select group of policy people."

"No commitments if I do."

"Of course not," Allen said.

Kirkpatrick was ambivalent. She had little interest in helping out a Republican. She had never done so before, and she couldn't help but wonder what her old friend and mentor Hubert Humphrey would think. On a personal level, she knew and liked Gerald Ford. But she didn't regard him as an attractive or charismatic political figure.

Beyond that, this new crop of Republican candidates interested her even less. When Republican presidential candidates had come to a symposium at the American Enterprise Institute and met with the senior scholars, Kirkpatrick was unimpressed. After talking with Phil Crane, Howard Baker, John Connally, Robert Dole, John Anderson, and George Bush, she flatly told colleagues, "Not for me, they're just not my kind of people."

"Besides," she confided gingerly, "they are so, well, Re-pu-bli-can."

One of Allen's aides called back with a meeting date, and Kirkpatrick decided she'd better prepare, not to brief Reagan, but to find out more about him.

And what she found surprised—and attracted—her.

In Reagan's first term as governor of California, he became divorced from the romance of politics and learned about the harsh realities of governing. He approved a notably liberal abortion law. In his second term, he effectively dealt, and compromised, with a hostile Democratic legislature, launching a first-class mental health program and pushing through a comprehensive reform of California's welfare system. When Reagan was first elected, the state budget ran a deficit. When he left, there was a surplus, stimulated in part by increased taxes. And an added plus: at least early on, Reagan had been a Democrat. The standard rap on Reagan was that he was simplistic, a conservative troglodyte. Kirkpatrick's research suggested otherwise.

But Kirkpatrick had been around enough politicians to know a record wasn't enough. Beyond the public record, what was he like?

She contacted an old friend, Jesse "Big Daddy" Unruh, a Democrat and former speaker of the California State Legislature who had challenged Reagan for the governorship in 1970. "How was Reagan on women?" she asked. Much better than reported, Unruh said. He's not a male chauvinistic pig. "Can he govern?" Yes, much better than the press has made it out. "What about his style?" You won't hear it from the press, but he can compromise when necessary, Unruh said.

By the time Kirkpatrick made the trip around the corner from AEI to the Madison Hotel to meet with Reagan, she was somewhat more positively disposed.

Reagan arrived with his two most senior aides, Edwin Meese, his former chief of staff and confidant of fifteen years, and Bill Casey, the former Nixon aide and chairman of the Securities and Exchange Commission, and Reagan's new presidential campaign manager. Kirkpatrick was in good company when she arrived. Richard Perle's old mentor Paul Nitze was there, joined by Eugene Rostow, President Johnson's undersecretary of state for policy and a Yale Law School professor—and like Kirkpatrick and Nitze, a social liberal and a hard-line Democrat. Admiral Thomas Moorer, the portly former chairman of the Joint Chiefs of Staff under Nixon, was also there. Reagan was alternately charming, bubbly, and, after the introductions, thoroughly engaged.

The group talked national security issues through the afternoon. Reagan may not have been an expert, but he asked serious questions and displayed an impressive intuitive grasp of the salient issues. Like Kirkpatrick, he was worried about the decline of U.S. power and prestige in the world; like Kirkpatrick, he wanted to check the continued probes of the Soviets into the Third World; like Kirkpatrick, he wanted to redress the shifting nuclear balance of power. Moorer and this group of conservative Democrats saw the world as Reagan saw it. On his end, Reagan was impressed. From her perspective, so was Kirkpatrick.

That night, Kirkpatrick had been invited to George Will's house in Chevy Chase for dinner, in honor of an out-of-town guest, Ronald Reagan. Will, the brilliant columnist for the *Washington Post* and *Newsweek*, was a passionate supporter of Reagan's. At the former governor's request, Reagan was seated next to Kirkpatrick. Here, Reagan showed a different side, his charm, his self-deprecating wit, and a sincerity that wooed and soothed his dinner companions. Reagan was the star that evening, not simply because he was the guest of honor, nor because he was the leading Republican candidate, although these things mattered, but because of his masterful wit and his ability to connect with others.

At first, Kirkpatrick felt awkward, even a little shy. She had never before been around so *many* Republicans in a partisan context. She felt embarrassed at cavorting with "the other side." Reagan sensed this, and kidded Kirkpatrick.

"I was a Democrat once, you know," he teased. After pausing for dramatic effect, he added, "I felt a little funny when I first started associating with Republicans."

The ice was broken.

Kirkpatrick looked at Reagan and saw that Ronald Reagan, not his entourage, not his handlers, but the candidate himself, understood. "It gets better, you know," Reagan said, his eyes gleaming.

Kirkpatrick returned home, having spent six full hours with Reagan. Her husband, Kirk, peppered her with questions. "Well, what do you think?"

"He's an attractive person, very likable."

"What about his view of foreign affairs?"

"Generally correct and very realistic."

"Well?" Kirk pressed.

"It's too early, Kirk, I just don't know. Reagan kidded me about being a Democrat."

"They'll certainly be asking for a commitment after today."

Kirkpatrick nodded her head, and glanced at her hands. "It looks that way."

WHILE KIRKPATRICK'S SLOW dance with the Republicans was picking up speed and rhythm, the groundwork for a new coalition between Reagan's

California Republicans and the Jackson Democrats had actually been laid some years before. The seeds for discussion between the two sides were planted in 1976, with the founding of the Committee on the Present Danger. Eugene Rostow, another attendant at the Madison Hotel meeting with Reagan and a friend of Kirkpatrick's, was the catalyst.

An undersecretary of state under Lyndon Johnson, Eugene V. Rostow reinserted himself into the public debate in the early 1970s by associating himself with the Coalition for a Democratic Majority. Rostow, like Kirkpatrick and the other members of the coalition, was at once turned off by the liberal McGovernites who had seized control of the Democratic party, while also opposing the lunge toward détente promulgated by Nixon. A professor by training and temperament, Rostow was a quintessential man of the old establishment—support the Atlantic alliance, maintain the balance of power, be prepared to use force, back it up with a formidable nuclear deterrent, don't shirk from thinking the unthinkable, fighting and winning a nuclear war. When the Democrats largely abandoned the Truman-Kennedy tradition, Rostow thought CDM could be a vehicle to successfully prod the party back to its traditionally muscular ways.

In 1974, he headed up CDM's Defense Task Force, which blasted détente as a one-way street. The report urged the U.S. to respond to the Soviets' bid for military superiority, and sounded alarms about declaring the Cold War over, the effect of which would only lure Western opinion into dangerous complacency. But the report's warnings went unheeded, and Democrats and Kissinger cavalierly rejected its findings out of hand.

But by 1975, Rostow began to conclude he was wrong. "We just weren't getting anywhere," he said. "The Democratic party doesn't want to hear from us anymore."

Later, he penned in a letter, "We need more than a solo voice, we need a chorus." To Rostow, that meant a group with a broader base. In contrast to CDM, it would be bipartisan, an organization composed of heavyweights—not just intellectuals but former government officials and top executives. In short, it would be a nonpartisan citizens committee of distinguished Americans to awaken the American people to the Soviet threat before it was too late. Between the Scylla of a dovish Democratic Congress and the Charybdis of Henry Kissinger and détente, he felt this group would fill the void.

Rostow sounded out former Assistant Treasury Secretary Charls Walker and Defense Secretary Jim Schlesinger. With prodding from Schlesinger, Paul Nitze was also brought in. Rostow also met with Max Kampelman. Finally, the shape of the group crystallized.

On March 12, 1976, the first organizational meeting was held in Washington, at the Metropolitan Club. Rostow was appointed the group's chairman. David Packard, a former deputy secretary of defense; Fowler; and the AFL-CIO's Lane Kirkland became co-chairmen. Nitze was tapped as chairman of policy studies; Max Kampelman was the group's counsel. Joining the executive committee was a former Nixon official searching for a way to rejuvenate his clout and his name in Washington policy circles: Richard Allen. By late spring, another member had joined the group: Ronald Reagan. "He needed credentials," his national campaign manager in 1976, John Sears, would later say. "And the Committee on the Present Danger served as an alternative group of respectable advisers to brief Reagan."

Two other names would subsequently also appear on the group's roster: Jeane Kirkpatrick and Richard Perle.

But, as it came together in 1976, the group lacked a name. More than thirty were considered until Rostow suggested: why not borrow the name of another prominent committee that had been established by eminent men during the Korean War to urge higher defense spending and a return to the draft, the Committee on the Present Danger?

Some members thought the name overly alarmist. They feared being dismissed by the liberal press or being written off as fearmongers. Max Kampelman had a different take. "If there is a present danger, and we all agree there is, there's no sense in pussyfooting about it." The name stuck, and the committee was born.

By the time the roster of the Committee on the Present Danger was nearing completion, the group had developed stature and clout in Washington. Even the Nobel Prize–winning novelist Saul Bellow joined, remarking that he was "appalled by the self-hypnosis of intellectuals," unable to comprehend the nature of the Cold War. Because the committee was comprised of Republicans and Democrats, and thus wanted to avoid getting entangled in partisan election-year politics, it held off making a public announcement of its formation until after the 1976 election, focusing instead on its first policy statement.

Released as a slim book, it portrayed the U.S.-Soviet relationship in dark and ghoulish tones. Entitled *Common Sense and Common Danger*, the report starkly noted, "The principal threat to our nation, to world peace and to the cause of human freedom is the Soviet drive for dominance based upon an unparalleled military build-up." The coming decade, the report contended, would be a struggle against growing Soviet power, with national survival and the cause of freedom the ultimate prize. "Higher levels of defense spending" was the prescription. Otherwise, the report warned, "We shall become second best to the Soviet Union in overall military strength . . . isolated in a hostile world, facing the unremitting pressures of Soviet policy backed by an overwhelming preponderance of power."

By mid-1977, there was little doubting that this group, individuals who knew force, rational strategists who could think the unthinkable, had shifted the climate of the debate and made opposition to arms control and détente intellectually acceptable. Like CDM, the committee held the seeds of a new counterestablishment—and a dramatic new force in American policy making.

To the incoming Carter administration, the committee's view of the world smacked of right-wing extremism, the worst-case analysis. And like the Coalition for a Democratic Majority, members of the committee were excluded from the ranks of the new Carter government. Not a single member was offered a job. Carter's administration was staffed with liberals seared by the Vietnam experience, men who didn't like the use of force and reflexively shrank from it, exclusively preferring the tidy sterilities of diplomacy. To the Committee on the Present Danger, however, it was precisely "the Vietnam syndrome" that had prevented realistic policies, and had created what Jeane Kirkpatrick termed "a culture of appeasement, which finds reasons not only against the use of force, but denies its place in the world." And to the Committee on the Present Danger, the men in the Carter administration who believed otherwise were dangerous individuals, in power at a dangerous time, at a turning point in history that, as the Cold War heated up anew, was still being written.

Early in 1977, President Carter met with a delegation of eight members of the committee. The White House referred to the meeting as a "stroking session," and Carter was joined by Harold Brown and Zbigniew Brzezinski, officials who were more hawkish than Secretary of State Cyrus Vance or Paul Warnke, the arms control agency head. But the meeting started off poorly as Rostow and Paul Nitze gave opening presentations, and culminated in rancorous words between Carter and Nitze. Nitze, shaking his head at Carter, murmuring under his breath, was actually hushed up by the president. The meeting was a disaster. As Rostow would later capture the feelings of the committee: "We were stunned, just stunned. The notion that that fellow was president was just frightening."

While the committee was a nonpartisan group, it quickly evolved into an anti-Carter organization, spewing out its disgust at the president's policies of appeasement and naïveté. In its assault on the U.S. posture in the SALT negotiations, the group mustered its considerable resources. Its members printed dozens of pamphlets, gave speeches, issued press statements, and unrelentingly assaulted the weak U.S. posture in the arms talks. Employing Nitze's contacts in the administration, and pointed to the right people by Richard Perle—his legion of quiet dissidents—the committee often was privy to the most up-to-date intelligence information, even before it crossed the desks of senior State Department officials.

Columnists were treated to flip chart presentations and learned seminars by Paul Nitze and other committee members, and regularly took their information, and their cue, from the committee. The savvy journalist Morton Kondracke, himself a convert to the committee position, would note: "Right now, the hawks have more ergs of brainpower focused on SALT than even the Carter administration does, and vastly more than their arch-foes in the arms control community."

Once the SALT II treaty was signed, the committee went on the warpath to block its ratification. Nitze and others passionately testified against the treaty, lambasting it in talk shows and debates across the nation, and eventually before congressional committees. Soon, the administration found itself arguing in public about the esoterica of single-shot probabilities, throw-weight ratios, and blood-curdling nuclear exchange ratios. Operating out of the same seedy suite on Connecticut Avenue that was once the home to Adlai Stevenson and Eleanor Roosevelt's Democratic Policy Committee, the liberal conscience of the Democratic party during its years out of power in the 1950s, the Committee on the Present Danger emerged as a shadow government to challenge Carter. And it was winning the debate.

To combat the committee, the American Committee on East-West Accord, co-chaired by George Kennan, John Kenneth Galbraith, and Donald Kendall, the head of PepsiCo, was hastily formed. "U.S.-Soviet relations should be put on a businesslike basis" became its slogan. The American Committee sought to capture the moral high ground with the growing list of those worried about nuclear war, but its credibility was tainted by its funding sources. About half of the new committee's $145,000 income came from companies doing business with the Soviet Union.

But as one spokesman for the American Committee, Carl Macy, sighed, "Sorry to say, Jackson's experts are having a greater impact than Carter's experts."

Indeed, the committee began to appear as if it were serving as a shadow government in waiting. And, in the present climate, that would be for the Republicans.

By 1980, Jackson's experts were being looked to again, this time by Richard Allen and Ronald Reagan.

. . .

Early in 1966, Reagan, then a candidate for governor of California, received the endorsement of the John Birch Society. One of his first political mentors and most trusted advisers, Lyn Nofziger, hurriedly went to inform Reagan about this development, what he felt was clearly a problem in the making.

Reagan was barely fazed. He shook his head and smiled. "Lyn, let me tell you something," Reagan said. "If they endorse me, they are accepting my philosophy, and not the other way around." This statement was to become a hallmark of Reagan's thinking and his politics.

As Nofziger learned, Reagan believed in a big tent and in expanding the Republican party. Jews, Catholics, the Irish and the Italians, blue-collar workers and intellectuals, Democrats as well as Republicans—all were welcome. The one condition: accept Ronald Reagan's general views. As Nofziger put it, "If they want to help us get a job done, great. And we needed Democrats."

Nofziger was well aware that the Scoop Jackson Democrats had been treated badly by Carter and were disaffected. They were ripe for the taking. For candidate Reagan, hawkish Democrats were welcome not just for their support, but also for their advice. Thus, while Nofziger didn't actively seek to peel the Democrats away from Carter and a party that had deserted them, he welcomed Reagan's strategy of including them.

The task of wooing them more directly fell to Richard Allen. The message he sent was clear: Jackson Democrats were welcome to apply.

So by May 22, 1980, Allen had trumped the skeptics in the foreign policy establishment as well as the Democrats. On the eve of the Pennsylvania primary, with the Reagan team looking as much to the general election as to the waning weeks of the nomination, Reagan announced he was establishing a twelve-member policy council, augmented by two groups of specialized advisers, one on foreign affairs, the other on defense. "Sixty-seven distinguished experts," Reagan said. He added, "Their experience will be of great assistance to me as the presidential campaign addresses issues of crucial importance to the future of our country."

Richard Allen hastened to tell the press that agreement to advise the candidate "did not necessarily constitute political endorsement." But this did little to mask the fact that most, if not all, of the members of the advisory committee could be presumed to be Reagan supporters—including the Democrats. Among the names on the list was Jeane Kirkpatrick.

Nicholas Lehmann, a staff reporter of the *Washington Post*, called Kirkpatrick to ask her, What was the deal? Was she supporting Reagan? Kirkpatrick didn't directly answer, instead replying, "We are really treated quite badly by the Democratic party, and meanwhile we are bombarded with friendly messages from Republicans. After a certain time it begins to seem irresistible."

Kirkpatrick paused, and added coyly: "Especially if the person seems likely to be the next president of the United States."

By September, William Safire, the often prescient *New York Times* columnist, would tellingly write about these names for a Reagan administration: "As a group, they are experienced, respectable, occasionally brilliant and often innovative—and they would hit the ground running."

ACTUALLY, KIRKPATRICK FELT she was on the slippery slope with the Republicans. Despite her protestations that "these were not my people, I was not their crowd," she increasingly relished her role as a senior foreign policy adviser in the campaign. Still, she was apprehensive. In the fall, she was invited to an all-day retreat in the rolling Virginia hills to prepare Reagan for his debate with Carter. All the heavy hitters were there: Dick Allen, Nixon cabinet officials George Shultz and Caspar Weinberger, former NATO commander Al Haig, and the campaign manager, Bill Casey. During past meetings, she had had little in common with these advisers. Most of the time, she looked out and saw not foreign policy types, but a sea of Republicans.

"I felt hesitant about it, uncomfortable, and a little embarrassed. It was an adventure, to be sure. But I didn't like changing sides." At the Virginia retreat, however, there was one Republican she immediately hit it off with, with whom she would develop a close relationship and political alliance, Bill Casey. Casey was a stooped figure, with a loose lower lip and sagging jowls, but his disheveled appearance was deceptive. Casey ran the show. He also put Kirkpatrick at ease that day. "Casey was the real intellectual of the group," Kirkpatrick noted. "I really liked him."

Still, the question lingered in the press, and even among some of Kirkpatrick's friends. Why Reagan?

Kirkpatrick liked Reagan, and she increasingly saw him as a vehicle to deal with the pressing problems assaulting the U.S. and the world. For the first time, Kirkpatrick the academic was seduced by the prospect of using power for change. But this was only part of the story. For Kirkpatrick, the key was Ronald Reagan himself, the fact that he was not part of the Washington scene, that he had little in common with the establishment, that his core philosophy made him a very different type of Republican.

Kirkpatrick heightened her public profile during the waning days of the election. By the time Reagan defeated Carter, she had become one of his most visible foreign policy advisers and articulate partisans on his behalf. Then, after Reagan's landslide victory, the task shifted from campaigning to governing. Among the more visible members of Reagan's foreign policy transition team was Jeane Kirkpatrick. The fact that Scoop Jackson was also an active member of the transition team made a vast difference to her. "He metaphorically held my hand," she would later note.

Almost from the start of the transition, a feeding frenzy and subtle jockeying for who would get what jobs in the incoming administration began. Names were circulated widely, often by job aspirants themselves. Among the rumors floating around Washington was that Jeane Kirkpatrick, a relative unknown, an academic with no previous government experience, and a woman in a field traditionally dominated by men, would be named to an important post in the administration.

Kirkpatrick maintained she wasn't seeking a job, but did not discourage the speculation about a high-level Kirkpatrick appointment. What made her candidacy for a post so intriguing was that she was a Democrat. And what made her appointment so unlikely, according to the conventional wisdom of how a political party rewards party loyalists, was that she was a Democrat.

It was an issue Kirkpatrick couldn't duck. Instead, she took it head-on. "To support Reagan," Kirkpatrick said, "represented a really big step for me." Lest she disqualify herself from consideration for a high post, she added a note of enthusiasm: "But I did it wholeheartedly. I just became totally dismayed with Jimmy Carter."

As a senior adviser and a member of the inner circle on foreign policy for the president-elect, Kirkpatrick had come a long way from the young academic who was told by the University of Maryland that they had no need for a woman on their political science faculty. For years, her focus was, as she frequently kidded, "her intense child bearing and rearing years." But now, as she turned fifty-three, opportunities abounded.

At first, nothing happened. Kirkpatrick worked on the transition team, continued her research at the American Enterprise Institute, and was one of the luminaries at a gala dinner held for Ronald Reagan at the Mayflower Hotel several weeks after the election. Still, no job offer came.

December rolled around. The new speculation in the intense jockeying for positions was that Kirkpatrick was under consideration for the post of deputy secretary of state. Her rival cited by the transition rumor mill was Bill Brock, the soft-spoken, Southern-drawling Republican national chairman. For the United Nations post, Senator Jacob Javits of New

York, one of the quintessential party moderates, was suggested, along with Rita Hauser, a New York lawyer and one of Reagan's Middle East advisers. The days seemed to move very slowly. By December 6, Reagan had yet to name a single cabinet choice.

The race in public changed yet again by the next week. Kirkpatrick was dropped from consideration for a job in the State Department, instead being informed that she was in the running for the U.N. post. But Reagan transition sources made it clear that Rita Hauser was also still in the running, and the press wryly noted that the "wildly ambitious" Hauser had maintained top-level contacts with Reagan's inner circle, where she was highly regarded. With her party contacts, Hauser appeared to be the likely choice.

Kirkpatrick sought distractions by going on with life essentially as normal. She felt it was important to keep busy; she wasn't one to actively lobby for the job, and, as she informed one colleague, she "didn't know how to anyway."

At the invitation of an old associate, Mark Siegel, she was asked to address a fund-raiser in Miami for the American Friends of the Hebrew University. A longtime supporter of Israel, she told Siegel she'd be delighted. Siegel was an up-and-coming young mover and shaker in the world of Washington lobbying. In 1977, he had been Carter's White House liaison to the Jewish community, but he resigned over the administration's sale of military aircraft to Saudi Arabia. Still an ardent Democratic party activist, Siegel also knew the importance of good contacts. Producing Kirkpatrick, a senior Reagan transition aide whose name was still being bandied about for a high-level job, was a good catch. Just how good, however, he would soon find out.

On December 22, Kirkpatrick gave her speech to rousing applause. Israel shares America's finest values, the two of us stand alone in the Middle East as friends of freedom, she said.

After the speech, Kirkpatrick and her husband went for a long, leisurely dinner, and took a stroll along the promenade in the warm Florida night air. When they returned to the hotel, the desk clerk was almost breathless.

"Dr. Kirkpatrick, there's a message for . . . from Ronald Reagan," he stammered.

Kirkpatrick looked at her husband. Maintaining her composure, she said to Kirk, "How interesting." Inside, however, she knew something was going on, something big. She and Kirk rushed to their phone.

She called the number, and the president-elect picked up. Making an awkward stab at polite conversation, she asked Ronald Reagan how he was.

The consummately genial Reagan said, "I'll be better if you agree to be our ambassador to the United Nations."

Kirkpatrick threw him off stride with her answer, one his aides hadn't prepared him for. "I'm not sure if I can do that job," she demurred.

Kirkpatrick had said just the right thing. Reagan's philosophy was that he wanted people who needed to be asked to take a job, even cajoled, not to have people who were simply looking for a job. He turned on the charm. "I'm sure you can do it and I'd very much like for you to," he said.

"Well, if you really feel sure that I can do it, I'll give it my best try," Kirkpatrick responded.

She was about to put the receiver down, when Reagan added, "One more thing, Jeane. I'd like you to be a member of my cabinet."

Thus, Jeane Kirkpatrick became the first woman in history to be named U.S. ambassador to the United Nations. William Safire was elated by her ascendance. He hailed her as "intellectual," "forceful," "articulate." With cabinet rank and direct access to the president, she was, Safire concluded, Reagan's "most inspired appointment." Norman Podhoretz, the editor of *Commentary*, called her a "Cinderella story." The myth stuck. She soon became known as "the ambassador from *Commentary* magazine."

CHAPTER 8

All through the grim summer and fall of 1979, the abrasions of government life were becoming less bearable for Richard Perle. Locked in constant combat with the Carter administration, his numerous policy battles increasingly took on a personal and vicious tone. On the Hill, the banter of Democratic staffers would fall to a hush when Perle walked into Senate meeting rooms. As one staffer, no friend of Perle's, would put it, "In the context of 'us' versus 'them,' Perle fell into the 'them' column." When he could snatch time to reflect, Perle was invariably surprised at the venom of his political enemies scattered throughout Washington.

Combined with a lifestyle dictated by the exigencies of an unforgiving Senate calendar, it had begun to take a toll. By the winter, as a new presidential season got under way and Carter's demise began to look inevitable, Perle eyed his future once again—this time, not in government, but in private life. Perle was ready for what Washingtonians refer to as "a more normal lifestyle."

But after a decade in Washington, Perle had also become a bit of a fixture in town. Never was that more evident than on a steamy summer day in July 1977, when Perle tied the knot with Leslie Barr in a friend's backyard. Scoop Jackson was his best man. The invitees looked like a Who's Who of the country's leading politicos and policy makers: Jim Schlesinger; Lane Kirkland; defense hands Fred Iklé, Paul Wolfowitz, Lt. Gen. Ed Rowny; and columnist Bob Novak; Middle East scholar Bernard Lewis; and Jamie Jamieson of the CIA. Les Aspin, a moderate Democrat and defense intellectual, and an up-and-coming congressman, spent most of the time hanging around the pool with fellow Yalie and Carter ambassador to Micronesia Peter Rosenblatt.

The music was provided by three Russian Jewish émigrés, strumming on guitars and singing merrily. Wine and champagne flowed freely; by nighttime, three die-hard anti-Communists, Jim Schlesinger, Ed Rowny, and Lane Kirkland, were amusing the guests by singing the socialist "Internationale." The next day, nursing a hangover, Perle was up—for work.

He joined Scoop at a breakfast meeting with Bernard Lewis, to discuss the progress of the peace talks in the Middle East. But by the time his second anniversary had passed, he would be gone.

THE HARROWING DAY of the Soviet invasion of Afghanistan, Perle marched into Scoop Jackson's office to discuss its implications and Scoop's response. He also wanted to discuss his own personal plans.

Perle and Jackson agreed that the SALT treaty was "dead in the water." "I think it's time to move on to a private-sector career, I've done all I can do up here," Perle added. Scoop urged him to find something suitable outside of government. In March, Perle joined Abington Corp., an international consulting firm headed by John Lehman, a friend since he had first come to Washington.

Lehman had been a deputy director of the Arms Control and Disarmament Agency under Perle's hand-picked director, Fred Iklé, and before that a staffer on the National Security Council under Henry Kissinger. Super-conservative, in the early part of the decade Lehman had assisted Perle by hiring hard-liners in the government and by working against the SALT I treaty. From 1977 to 1980, when Carter was in power, Lehman attacked Carter's vacillations from outside the government, chairing the Republican National Committee's Defense Advisory Committee, which shaped the defense section of the Republican party platform. He was also an active member of the Committee on the Present Danger.

Lehman was distinguished not just by his views, but his lineage, making him an unusual soulmate among the ranks of Jackson Democrats. His blood line was blue, from the social register of Philadelphia, not the aspiring middle class of New York. He was a Catholic, and far from making the intellectual sojourn from the left to a more conservative position, Lehman was, by family tradition, Republican. He was also well connected in social circles, something that he introduced Perle to on a grand scale. On one of their trips to Paris, Perle and Lehman went to dinner and were joined by Lehman's cousin, Princess Grace of Monaco. With his social and political connections, and business savvy, Perle's good friend Lehman was just the right business partner. With a handshake, Perle joined Abington.

Almost overnight, Perle's life changed. His salary quadrupled in just three months, soaring to a base of $100,000, with profit sharing of roughly $80,000 by the year's end. While he could no longer indulge in his student hours and arrive at the office close to noon, he now worked a "predictably bourgeois eight-hour day." Advising a host of domestic and international clients in the aerospace and defense industry, Perle tapped into his Senate expertise and helped them understand the arcane vocabulary and the labyrinth of government arms procurement and decision making.

One thing Perle didn't do was get involved in the presidential campaign. It wasn't that he was uninterested, but his priority was to build up his client base and solidify his family life. He and Leslie had bought a house, and had a child. However, as election day drew near, and Reagan fever swept Washington, Perle could not afford to divorce himself from the political arena wholesale. On election night, Abington Corp. held a large gala party—it was hosted at Richard Perle's new home.

His guests cheered the landslide Reagan victory, as did Perle. Earlier that day, he had voted for a Republican to be president for the first time in his life. The transfer of the Senate over to Republican hands was a different story. Perle had little affection for liberal Senate stalwarts such as Birch Bayh and Frank Church, with whom he frequently tangled. But at this point, he still generally shared their more progressive views on domestic issues. The Reagan victory was necessary—in a dangerous world, the U.S. needed strength in a commander in chief, not Carter's prudish moralism. It was good for the country. But Perle did not share the elation over the Senate change of hands.

Perle's sobriety about the Senate election was short-lived, as was his recalcitrance to rejoin the political arena. After the election, the well-connected Lehman burst into Perle's office and informed him, "Richard, you are on the State, Defense, and Export-Import Bank transition teams." That November, Perle threw himself into the transition team work.

The transition was a handy way to be brought up to speed on the issues. But Perle had something else in mind. He immediately resolved to use the transition for a specific purpose: not to lobby for himself, but to get his friends and favorite candidates prominent jobs in the new Reagan administration.

Perle concentrated on the Departments of Defense and State to scout out the important posts. Thousands of résumés were collected and logged into heavy black three-ring binders for only tens of slots. People who had been out of power for four years, some even longer, hungered to get back in on the new wave of Reaganism. And new people by the hundreds, previously reticent conservative academics and intellectuals, messianic movement conservatives, cowboy-booted California outsiders, saw a role for themselves. So did a younger generation of conservatives, their hair slicked back, and gray suits primly pressed. Ronald Reagan summoned a new breed of action intellectuals and outsiders just as Kennedy had done two decades earlier. Everyone wanted in. Reagan's era was to be a new time, a time of enormous energy and unparalleled potential, a chance to shape a new order and forge new possibilities, a historic time to roll back Communism.

At the heady beginnings of the transition, suddenly the establishment was out, the counterestablishment was in. Perle knew it would be unproductive if he pushed too many people. So systematically he put his bids in for a few people carefully targeted for a handful of slots.

Perle started by pushing his business partner and old friend, John Lehman. At one grand dinner held at the Mayflower Hotel, President-elect Reagan was the honored speaker. Scoop Jackson was there, as was Jeane Kirkpatrick. Geared up by Perle, Jackson readied himself to promote one name: John Lehman, to be secretary of the navy. Lehman himself had been tenacious in promoting himself around town for the position. He lobbied the president's staff, telling everyone he wanted to be navy secretary, and, not only that, he would accept *no* other job in the administration. At the dinner that night, Jackson buttonholed the president-elect. He said that in his view, Lehman was the man to head the navy, pure and simple. Reagan pondered Jackson's words for a second, smiled at Scoop, and then, on the spot, said if Scoop felt that strongly, he would make sure it was done. Shortly after the inauguration on January 24, Reagan announced Lehman as his choice to be navy secretary.

Perle then bored in on three other names. He spoke first to Richard Allen about his old friend from the Committee to Maintain a Prudent Defense Policy days, Paul Wolfowitz, to head Policy Planning in the State Department. Wolfowitz, quiet, cerebral, with a teddy bear smile, was eventually chosen, and moved into the suite of offices that had once been home to another former colleague, Peter Wilson.

Perle also assisted Elliott Abrams, and helped Mike Rashish to become undersecretary of state for economic affairs. Rashish, uncommonly stylish by Washington standards and a no-nonsense straight-talker with a razor-sharp mind, was, like Perle, a neoconservative and a hard-liner. Perle knew Rashish could be counted on.

As the new year rolled in, Perle had everything he wanted. His people were neatly placed in the government—good for the policies he had always worked for, good for his business. After a lifetime of living on a debilitating Senate staffer's salary, he was thriving in the private sector. Leslie was at home with their son, and his new schedule at Abington Corp. enabled him to have a predictable schedule; long nights and absences on weekends were no longer a problem. This was conducive to a good marriage and a new family. In a town filled with workaholics, Perle took his personal life more seriously than most.

In January, Perle's plans were unexpectedly shattered.

. . .

HE CAME IN TO work one day and received a call from a friend in government. The word in the State Department was that Alexander Haig intended to call Perle and offer him a job, possibly a big one. Perle sounded Leslie out about a position in the administration. She wasn't happy about the prospect of his returning to government; the hours and schedule would be long, the money awful, the fame fleeting. Everything was going so well. Richard agreed, in principle, that he wouldn't accept an offer from Haig.

Still, before he made a final decision, as he would do so many times throughout his life, he called on his mentor, Scoop Jackson.

Jackson wasted little time in sketching out Perle's options. You and Haig won't get along, he told Perle. Haig is too stiff, too rigid, too much a straitlaced military man to adjust to your idiosyncrasies, Jackson instructed. Perle listened attentively. He thought, in Scoop's usual inimitable manner, his uncommon good sense was worth its weight in gold.

Perle let the word out through friends of his intention to remain in the private sector. It was sure to get back to Haig. Perle still valued his relationship with Haig; he didn't want Haig to be blindsided when he turned down the position. When they met, it was clear Haig had appropriately been forewarned. The new secretary of state played it cool, and didn't offer Perle a position outright, only telling Perle that he wanted him to join his team. By putting it this way, he gave Perle, and himself, an easy out—unless Perle made it clear he did want to join the State Department.

But Perle didn't. The two parted amiably, neither losing face. Perle went back to plow his many new connections and service his clients at Abington Corp. Only later would he learn that Haig was disappointed, and outraged, that Perle didn't leap at his offer.

Unexpectedly, in February, Perle was offered another job. His old friend Fred Iklé, now in the number three slot at Defense, wanted him to be assistant secretary of international security affairs, or ISA, at the Defense Department. Perle demurred. He was then offered a third job—Walt Slocombe's old position in Defense, as deputy undersecretary for policy planning, responsible for strategic nuclear arms talks. Perle felt the position was too limited. Once again, he turned it down.

But then, suddenly, his relationship with Lehman took an abrupt turn for the worse. According to a friend of the two, Perle and Lehman fought bitterly over the terms of how to continue Abington. After a bruising business battle, the two finally settled. By then, they were no longer on speaking terms. For his part, Perle was deeply shaken by the incident. It taught him a lesson about business. It also meant that by mid-winter

1981, Perle's personal circumstances were radically altered and his re-fusal of the administration jobs premature.

Perle and Leslie had a heart-to-heart. Reluctantly, he felt he could no longer rule out an administration post. But it didn't seem like much would be in the offing anyway: Richard had turned down three jobs al-ready. Opportunities were increasingly scarce, and those who over-reached found themselves empty-handed.

Perle went to Iklé with a counterproposal. He didn't want any of the current jobs. Instead, he wanted a whole new job, one that didn't exist yet. Merge ISA and Slocombe's old job and I'll take it, he said. In short, expand and recast ISA so that it encompasses all arms control (nuclear and conventional) and procurement between the U.S. and Soviet bloc, including oversight on all technology transfers. Far from being upset, Iklé liked Perle's audaciousness, and liked the idea. He said he would get back to Perle shortly. If he could sell it to the new defense secretary, Cap Weinberger, and the Hill went along with creating a new bureau, then they would talk.

In the meantime, Perle spoke to Jackson again. What did Jackson think of Weinberger?

Jackson felt it would be a better match than Haig. Weinberger and Perle would be able to get along, Scoop said. If the right job were offered, take it.

Later that week, Iklé spoke to Perle. ISA was going to be recast along the lines Perle had suggested, and would be called International Security Policy, or, in DoD parlance, ISP. Perle's wish list fulfilled, with Scoop's blessing, he accepted. ISP, in its reconfigured form, was positioned to be-come the central point for dealing with the Soviet Union. On March 23, 1981, Perle officially began working at the Pentagon as assistant secre-tary of defense designate. Once confirmed, his salary would be $67,200. In March, he received his last check for four months work of consulting. It totaled $50,000.

But his sabbatical from government was over, and Perle threw himself into his new position.

ANOTHER FORMER Democratic Hill staffer was also looking for a job during that transition season in Washington, Elliott Abrams. The previous spring, after returning from their honeymoon, Rachel Abrams watched her husband undergo a slow and quiet process of political transforma-tion, from alienated Democrat to ardent Reagan supporter. The more Abrams heard about Reagan, the more he liked him. The nomination clinched it. He told his new in-laws, Norman Podhoretz and Midge

Decter, that he wanted to work for Ronald Reagan. Did they have any contacts who could bring him into the campaign?

Yes, they did, Frank Shakespeare, movie mogul, former director of the United States Information Agency under Nixon, and the head of RKO Theaters. Shakespeare was a rare animal among broadcasting executives. He combined an aura of show business pizzazz with a demonstrable hard-line anti-Communism. Shakespeare was involved in the campaign.

In late August, Abrams and his wife went to the Hamptons for a vacation; Norman and Midge had a house there. So did Frank Shakespeare, who owned a spacious, modern East Hampton residence on the water. Over dinner at Shakespeare's, Abrams confided that he wanted to join the Reagan campaign. "A wonderful idea," Shakespeare said, "let's get you involved."

With that commitment, Abrams effectively severed his ties with the Democrats, even if he was only volunteering.

When Abrams returned to Washington, he reported to the Reagan campaign headquarters. Located in a seedy building in Arlington, Virginia, it hummed with activity. The musty floors, open cubicles, and cracked paint gave the impression of an outsider camp—which is exactly what it was. Over the next couple of days, Abrams rattled around the campaign, until he finally met William Timmons, the consummate "old Washington hand" in the Reagan apparatus, and manager of the day-to-day operations. At forty-nine, the pudgy Timmons had already directed convention operations for Nixon and Ford in earlier campaigns. In exile during the Carter years, Timmons parlayed his contacts into a highly lucrative lobbying firm. Timmons gave the nod to Abrams to work on the campaign, but it was up to Abrams to find a niche for himself.

"Find someone who can use you," Timmons told Abrams.

Abrams obliged. There were fewer Jews in the campaign than in a Democratic operation, a fact that Abrams seized upon. Snatching all the free time he could at night and on the weekends, he was soon campaigning in D.C., Maryland, and Florida for Reagan among Jewish groups. He coordinated outreach with Jewish leaders and high rollers. Abrams also rapidly cultivated connections with the right people. He introduced Morris Abram, head of the influential American Jewish Committee, to Ed Meese. He actively attended strategy meetings at Fred Iklé's house, and helped organize a drive to enlist professors for Reagan, by providing names of academics who supported Scoop Jackson in the 1976 campaign.

Abrams suffered none of the cultural shock that afflicted Kirkpatrick when she mingled among Republicans for the first time. Where she was embarrassed and ill at ease, Abrams joyfully noted that there were no McGovernites, no left-wing extremists floating around.

Election day was depressing for most Democrats, but for the Reagan supporters, it was a day of wild glee, as a Reagan victory appeared a near certainty. Abrams was invited to one of Washington's many election eve parties, at the house of Walter Berns, a Kirkpatrick colleague at the American Enterprise Institute. Even before the special election coverage began, they knew the outcome. Prior to the party, Abrams had talked to the AEI pollster William Schneider. Schneider was helping CBS with its coverage, and by the time the polls closed at seven o'clock Eastern Standard Time, he was able to report to Abrams that Ronald Reagan would be the overwhelming winner. Abrams was not one to revel in the festivities long, however. Now he had to maneuver himself into a position where he would be offered a job.

Abrams was given a paid leave by McPherson's law firm to work on the campaign transition. The firm knew the value of its associates and partners providing inroads into the administration, no matter what its political stripe. They wished Abrams well and gave him time to join the Reagan transition team.

He managed to get a slot on the transition working group examining the Agency for International Development. Abrams plunged in the transition team work with determination and zeal. He set foot into the State Department for the first time in his life; remarkably, he was never invited to State for a briefing during the entire Carter administration, even though he was the chief of staff for Pat Moynihan.

Halfway into the transition, Abrams sought some sage advice on his job hunt, and had a drink with Senator Moynihan at the Man in the Green Hat, one of the new fern-bar restaurants becoming so popular on the Hill. They squirreled themselves in the corner, away from the window, where it would be less likely they would be spotted.

"I'd like to be a deputy assistant secretary of state," Abrams told his old boss. It was a big position for a guy who was still only thirty-three. He knew a job in the Defense Department was out of the question. That was for the big boys. But he felt this was realistic.

Moynihan sucked in his breath and leaned over to Abrams. "That's not good enough, Elliott," the senator said. "You should ask to be an assistant secretary of state." Moynihan was a shrewd survivor in Washington, steadily moving up and through the ranks of government, in Republican and Democratic administrations alike. His advice was not to be rejected lightly. They agreed he should try for the slot of International Organizations, known in the State Department as IO, the bureau that oversees all the activities of U.S. international organizations. The post would require Senate confirmation.

But Moynihan's logic was simple. Everyone wanted to be assistant secretary for Latin America, or for European affairs. Abrams knew he wouldn't stand a chance for these plum posts. If Abrams shot too high, he could end up with nothing. But if he worked the system, and got enough firepower behind his name, he would stand a chance at getting the IO slot. Moynihan agreed to make calls to push Abrams's name, and would stress that as a former U.N. ambassador himself, he knew what was needed for the IO slot.

In addition to Moynihan, Abrams got Fred Iklé, who was slated for the number two job at the Department of Defense; Dick Allen, the national security adviser designate; and Richard Perle to support him. His new association with Timmons also paid off. Timmons would weigh in. Abrams was optimistic. He was getting close.

Through the grapevine, Abrams heard that the short list had narrowed, and his primary competition was a legislative aide to Republican Senator Paul Laxalt, the former governor of Nevada and one of Reagan's closest friends and associates since 1966. Laxalt called Reagan himself to endorse his aide. Abrams, now calling the transition team headquarters virtually every day to promote his own candidacy, countered with some intentional sophistry to nip the Laxalt staffer in the bud. Abrams argued that he would do a better job, and added a novel bit of reasoning: Laxalt was trying to get his aide a job in the administration, Abrams said, not because he wanted to promote him, but because he wanted to get rid of him, and this was a graceful way to do it. The argument kept Abrams's name in the running.

Unexpectedly, another obstacle arose. Rumor had it that Abrams's longtime friend Jeane Kirkpatrick, now the U.N. ambassador designate, wanted someone else for the IO job, Pedro Sanjuan. Technically, IO actually had jurisdiction over the U.N. ambassador, and the ambassador was supposed to receive instructions from the assistant secretary. Given Kirkpatrick's new cabinet-level status, the arrangement made no sense. There were no clean lines of authority, and traditionally, the two roles were fraught with institutional tension, pitting the U.N. ambassador, who was a peer of the secretary of state, against the assistant secretary, a third-tier job. Under just about any circumstances, the situation was a ticking bomb ready to explode. And that's what happened.

Kirkpatrick called Abrams up, to chat about the IO job. What would he want to do if he got the job? What did he think the IO job should do?

Abrams gave a general overview. The conversation was polite, until Abrams indicated his view that "the assistant secretary should have a hand in policy." There was silence at the other end of the line. Abrams felt the word "policy" froze Kirkpatrick on the spot. Her voice cool, she made it very clear to Abrams that she thought it was her place as ambassador to oversee policy. That was the mandate she had been given. She would work in conjunction with the other cabinet members, including the secretary of state. Period.

Abrams, at a loss for words, stayed silent. The conversation ended abruptly. Abrams was shaken by the call, and didn't know what to make of it, nor what to do about it. But by that time, the decision was out of both Abrams's and Kirkpatrick's hands.

WHILE ABRAMS WAS lobbying for his job, Woody Goldberg, Haig's new executive assistant, was trying to solve a problem for his new boss, the secretary of state. Goldberg was a soft spoken, taciturn, squat Jewish guy with oval glasses. He had been Haig's research assistant at the Foreign Policy Institute in Philadelphia, where Haig was a visiting fellow in 1979. Goldberg was a small-town boy from Reading, Pennsylvania, with small-town manners, polite, courteous, oblivious to the rough-and-tumble folkways of Washington. He was anything but slick. He never heard of lobbying for a job, he thought perks were something only corporate bigwigs got, he sprinkled his language with homespun homilies and down-to-earth sayings. Oblivious to the campaign, the transition, the power breakfasts at the Madison Hotel, Goldberg had planned to practice law. Until suddenly, out of the blue, Haig called up Woody and asked him to be his right-hand man.

Goldberg was shocked. He asked for a couple of days to think it over. Haig wanted a decision by tomorrow. Goldberg asked his wife, who shrugged her shoulders. Stoically, she said what he was thinking. You have to do it, Woody, it's what public service is all about.

So Goldberg, a Vietnam vet, a graduate of Dickinson College, and a midcareer grad of Temple Law School, the small-town boy, trekked off to Washington. He marched into Haig's transition office on the first floor, threw all his papers and all his files onto Haig's conference desk, and told Haig, "If I'm going to be your right-hand man, I should be right here." Goldberg never even noticed the large unoccupied transition office waiting for him.

Security clearance, what's that? he asked innocently. Window office, who cares, he told one State Department employee, we need to put a team together for the secretary. When an aide handed him a stack of invitations to fancy dinner parties and embassy receptions, Goldberg laughed. "I'm not here to be a social butterfly."

In neatly assembled piles, Goldberg kept files of all the candidates for the upper-level jobs at State. He kept them short: résumés and bios, references, occasionally published articles. The transition team handed over an elaborate scheme of the State Department to Haig, lines crisscrossing in an upside-down pyramid, with boxes and titles filled in with potential candidates. Haig and Goldberg took one look at it and chucked it out.

"We need a clean slate," Haig said. "Let's cut through the bullshit." They took out a fresh piece of paper. Haig gave guidance. He wanted Georgetown University historian Chester Crocker for Africa, and veteran diplomats Walt Stoessel and Larry Eagleburger by his side. He took some names from the transition, Paul Wolfowitz and Richard Burt, a *New York Times* reporter, on security issues. Good on Europe, that's important, Haig barked.

Haig said the same thing, over and over: let's get the best guy for the job. Political affiliation didn't matter, nor did White House ties. The one notable exception was Bill Clark, the amiable judge from California, and an old friend of Reagan's, who was made Haig's deputy secretary.

One day, Haig told Woody about a problem. Jeane Kirkpatrick, the new ambassador to the U.N., was told by Ed Meese and senior Reagan aide Michael Deaver in the White House that she reported to the president, and didn't have to coordinate with State. Haig's blue eyes flashed. Goldberg listened dutifully. Haig respected Kirkpatrick, and thought she was a true intellectual with dazzling star quality. The secretary was glad she had been hired. But he felt it was important that she work with State, rather than just report to the president. That's no way to run foreign policy, Haig said. It had to have a unified voice.

Thus, Haig told Goldberg to give Kirkpatrick special treatment. Make sure her Washington office in the State Department would be on the same floor as his, the seventh floor. Make sure it's a good office. She needs better security in New York. Goldberg was told to expedite it. Then the two sat down around the conference table and talked about how to build a workable institutional link with Kirkpatrick.

The answer was in Goldberg's folder: Elliott Abrams's résumé and recommendations. Goldberg briefed the general. "Great recommendations. He's smart, savvy, works hard, super-credentials. He's also a neoconservative and a friend of Kirkpatrick's—in fact, they practically have the same political godfather, neoconservative dean Irving Kristol. The two could work together, it would smooth the impossible link between State and the U.N. mission."

They didn't bother to take into account that Abrams was just thirty-three, only that he was accomplished. It wasn't an issue that he had worked for Moynihan, Moynihan was a solid cold warrior. It was irrelevant that he was a Democrat, Haig wanted the best people. But Haig and Goldberg wanted also to clean up the mess they felt the White House had generated by discouraging Kirkpatrick from working with State. Haig didn't take more than a minute. Abrams was a solid candidate, smart, a good friend of Kirkpatrick's.

Give him a call, Woody, I'll see him today, Haig said as he moved on to another slot.

THAT AFTERNOON, ABRAMS returned to his law firm from a lunch and fingered an odd message from his secretary, logged in on a pink "While You Were Out" slip. "Please call a Mr. Hayge, you have the number."

Abrams ignored the message, as he didn't know a Mr. Hayge. Only the next day did it hit him. He realized his secretary misspelled the name: it was Mr. Haig.

Abrams called Goldberg at Haig's office. Goldberg said the secretary of state wanted to meet with Abrams, that day if possible. Abrams rushed to see Haig, and was offered the job on the spot. He accepted immediately, becoming the youngest assistant secretary of state thus far this century.

MAX KAMPELMAN WAS the quintessential Washingtonian, a successful lawyer, and like most of those of the establishment, he did not need a job in government. He had stature independent of formal titles, he could pick and choose his jobs, and his commitments were numerous, between charitable boards, high-rolling business ventures, and as an informal counsel to party political figures. But that did not mean that Kampelman did not want a government job. He was, however, from experience, a cautious man.

In 1963, the night after John F. Kennedy's funeral, Hubert Humphrey informed Max Kampelman that the new president, Lyndon Johnson, wanted Kampelman to become counselor to the White House. Kampelman turned the post down. He was a Humphrey man, not a Johnson man, and Johnson rode his staff hard, ate them right up. He didn't need that.

A year later, Johnson tried again. Humphrey called one morning, at exactly ten o'clock, and said the president wanted to announce Max's appointment as a judge for the Court of Claims. But that was not all. After that Johnson intended to appoint Kampelman to the D.C. Court of Appeals, and after that, an appointment to the Supreme Court could not be ruled out, Humphrey said. Kampelman again declined.

But Johnson was if anything persistent, and in 1965 the burly Texan summoned Kampelman to the White House to inform him personally that he, the president, was appointing Kampelman to be chairman of the City Council of the District of Columbia. In the electric early days of the Great Society, with the nation's capital inching toward home rule, this was an exciting job, at the cutting edge of the great wave of progressive programs sweeping the country. Kampelman could barely get a word in as Johnson spoke. Johnson wasn't going to have Kampelman wiggle his way out of this one, so when Kampelman protested that he had mouths to feed, he couldn't afford the steep decline in pay from leaving his law firm, that he could only work if the post was part-time, Johnson was very reassuring. He had checked with the attorney general, arrangements could be made and Kampelman didn't have to leave his law firm, at which time the media rushed in, the lights of the cameras flashed, and the appointment was announced.

Kampelman was hooked this time, and whatever doubts he had were dispelled by the rush of publicity, the instant clamor of colleagues to talk to him, reminding Kampelman just how much Washington thrived on power and beat to its pulse. Kampelman returned to his office, basking in the light of the new publicity, his colleagues suddenly treating him like an ascendant star. He wasted little time in working out the details of the new job, including a change of legislation with Nevada Senator Alan Bible, head of the District Committee, to enable him to stay at his firm and hold the presidential post at the same time.

But then, just as suddenly, Kampelman was rudely treated to another lesson about Washington, and the ease with which one can fall.

It started almost innocuously with a piece by Clark Mollenhoff, a Pulitzer Prize–winning reporter for the *Des Moines Register.* Mollenhoff wrote about Kampelman's involvement in a disputed sale of manufacturing tools by one of his clients, a manufacturing company called NAPCO, to its partner in Delhi, India. An Agency for International Development grant helped make the transaction possible. Hubert Humphrey even interceded when the paperwork was held up, the sort of routine constituent service performed by U.S. senators. But the deal soured: the Indians claimed the tools were not what they expected and cried fraud. NAPCO in turn said it was Indian incompetence, that the machinery rusted on the docks because of negligence. After a bitter slugfest in court, NAPCO was ultimately exonerated.

But this didn't stop Mollenhoff from replaying the case splashed across the front pages of his newspaper, portraying Kampelman as a willing partner in a fraudulent scheme. Mollenhoff was aided in this campaign by a reactionary Republican congressman, H. R. Gross, who took to the House floor daily to accuse Kampelman of being unfit for a presidential appointment. The accusations turned ugly, with Kampelman being called everything from a "draft-dodger" to a "criminal."

Coverage mushroomed, as Walter Pincus of the *Washington Post* aggressively joined the fray. Kampelman sought to limit the damage and met with *Post* publisher Katharine Graham and executive editor Ben Bradlee, along with two daily reporters, Richard Harwood and Pincus. After hearing Kampelman's explanation, Graham and Bradlee were upset with Pincus's overly zealous coverage, and his playing fast and loose with the facts. But the damage was done, and Kampelman's skill as the consummate Washingtonian was tested as never before.

In private, Kampelman felt demeaned and wounded by the hostile stories. The glow of his appointment became a chill; he felt embarrassed, angry, even depressed. It was worse for his wife, Maggie. Store clerks acted uncomfortable when she walked in. People suddenly appeared uneasy around her, reluctant to exchange even a few pleasantries. Good friends cooled, dinner invitations plummeted from an avalanche to a drought. Max and Maggie worried about their kids.

Overnight, Kampelman had become a pariah. Descending fast, he sought out Senator Alan Bible, the chair of the District Committee, for advice. Bible was reassuring. "Look Max, everybody knows Gross for what he is," Bible said. "Sure, the press is awful, but we have the votes." Kampelman said he would stick it out, weather the press, hold his head high.

But neither Bible nor Kampelman took into account LBJ's reaction. One of LBJ's White House aides, Joe Califano, was also busy poisoning the well. Califano reportedly had little love for Kampelman, and used the opportunity to warn the president that Kampelman had become a liability. Pull the plug, he told LBJ, before you, the president, are embarrassed. A suitable replacement could easily be found. Johnson told Califano to go see Kampelman instead. Ask him if it's all worth it, Johnson said, that should take care of things.

Kampelman got the message. He cut his losses and withdrew, waiting for the hostility toward him to stop. It didn't. "The damage to my reputation lingered," he said. The facts supported Kampelman, but the perception fueled by Mollenhoff, the *Post*, and the clatter of political gossip was very different. Kampelman grew bitter about the press, bitter about his enemies, disheartened by the reactions of so-called friends. He began to give other victims demeaned by the media the benefit of the doubt; he called for curbs on the press in an article about his experience in the *Columbia Journalism Review*. But Kampelman didn't retreat. Instead, he plunged back into the fray, tempered, cautious, but no less a presence in the city, and certainly a wiser one.

SPRING 1980 WAS a dark time for the Carterites, as the administration lurched from one disaster to the next, fending off opposition in their own party, blistering attacks from the other party, and dissension within their own ranks as Brzezinski and Vance fought repeatedly for Jimmy Carter's soul. But the Democratic party hadn't given up the fight, and in March, before the others from CDM had publicly drifted off to the other side, Fritz Mondale finally got back to Kampelman. Bill Scranton had taken the Helsinki job, after all. However, there was a new development.

Kampelman and Mondale had known each other for years, and had an up-and-down relationship. But by 1980, Kampelman was much more comfortable with Mondale than with Carter. Mondale told Kampelman that the president would like him to co-chair the U.S. delegation to the Helsinki Review with Scranton. Though not the high-profile administration post Kampelman might have hoped for, the Helsinki position was an attractive opening. In late 1975, in the spirit of détente, thirty-one European nations and the Soviet Union, the Vatican, Canada, and the U.S. concluded a two-year conference on security and human rights issues. The thirty-five delegations then gathered in Helsinki to sign what became known as "the Helsinki Final Act" of the Conference on Security and Co-operation in Europe (CSCE).

Though nonbinding and not formally a treaty, the Final Act laid out guidelines for international behavior between East and West, and also called for increased travel, cultural and technological exchanges, and family reunification. While some hailed the act, which was personally signed by both Gerald Ford and Leonid Brezhnev, as a positive step, others criticized it as a second Yalta. They argued that it effectively codified the Soviet borders established after World War II, as well as Soviet hegemony over Eastern Europe, while merely paying lip service to human rights.

Whatever the act's actual effects, it was hardly the final word on East-West relations. Indeed, the Helsinki Final Act document itself called for follow-up meetings to provide a continuing forum for public exchanges between East and West. The first follow-up meeting was held in Belgrade, Yugoslavia, in 1977, and was generally regarded as uneventful. The second follow-up was scheduled to begin in the city of Madrid in the fall of 1980.

Mondale told Kampelman the job would be part-time and consume only three months. Kampelman accepted and wasted little time in preparing. Besides an opportunity for Kampelman, the Madrid CSCE conference would provide a critical forum for America to discuss not just human rights violations in the U.S.S.R. and oppression in the Eastern bloc, but also Soviet aggression in Afghanistan. For his part, Kampelman knew many critics feared the conference would dwindle into nothing more than an arena for Soviet propaganda, but he was convinced Madrid could be "a bully pulpit for freedom and democracy." He was anxious to begin.

But Scranton's health was failing, and he eventually withdrew from the assignment. Carter then appointed his old friend and attorney general Griffin Bell. Kampelman knew it was important to get off to a good start with Bell, whose close relationship with the president elevated the importance of the Madrid negotiators. Kampelman immediately flew down to Atlanta to talk to the judge.

Kampelman and Bell couldn't have been more different. Bell was a Southerner and a good old boy from Georgia; Kampelman was an intellectual from New York. Bell was no longer looking for yet another job in government after having already voluntarily resigned from the Carter administration; barred from power for years, Kampelman was now keen for public service. Bell had been raked over the coals by the Senate for belonging to exclusive clubs and had little stomach for the intense scrutiny that came with the limelight; Kampelman couldn't belong to those clubs, and chatted happily, if still warily, with the press and Congress alike. But Bell could be painfully direct and refreshingly candid, which suited Kampelman just fine.

In their first few minutes together, Bell drawled rhetorically to Kampelman, "Why should I take this job?" "History," Kampelman stressed. "Some day historians will cite the president's commitment to advancing human rights as one achievement of the Carter administration." Bell listened carefully, and nodded in agreement. But he wanted little to do with all the advance work.

This was fine with Kampelman, who would spend the next several months positioning himself as a powerful voice, and a public one, on human rights. He served at the pleasure of President Carter, and the political forecasts were that Reagan would sweep in the election. The opening round of talks wasn't until November 11, 1980, a week after the election. Having little time, Kampelman set out to make his mark—and position himself as best he could with what would likely be the incoming administration. In the meantime, he was working for Jimmy Carter.

Kampelman touched all bases of institutional support, going straight to the top, first meeting with Secretary of State Vance, then with Congressman Dante Fascell and Senator Bob Dole, the chairs of the Commission on Security and Cooperation, the congressionally mandated watchdog committee to oversee the administration's negotiating efforts. Kampelman worried about too much congressional meddling, and the spectacle of a stream of senators on congressional junkets stopping off at Madrid wanting to make proclamations. Instead of reinforcing *his* message, a cacophony of congressional voices would likely undermine Western unity. Kampelman knew he couldn't shut the Congress out, it was just a question of how much he had to include them. He then struck a clever understanding with Fascell and Dole.

Come on as vice chairmen of the delegation, he urged Dole and Fascell. Attend the sessions when you can. But there is a problem, he continued, we need unity in our talks, the U.S. must not appear weak, divided, or listless, the Soviets must not be able to drive a wedge between the executive and the Congress. Kampelman was worried about other members of Congress showing up and making speeches without proper coordination, turning the U.S. negotiating team into a spectacle. It was one thing for Dole and Fascell to give speeches, Kampelman wanted their input. But Kampelman was worried about the others.

Dole and Fascell were hardly immune to the flattery, particularly when Kampelman put it in such stark policy terms. They indicated Kampelman was right, and they would take care of things. But more than that, Kampelman had made Dole and Fascell into allies, whose support he could draw on later.

Kampelman then turned his attention to elevating his new position, puffing up the post from a backwater ambassadorship into the high-profile, high-visibility bully pulpit he had conceived for the job. Shuttling to European capitals, he consulted with the British, the French, the Germans, the Italians, the neutrals. He spent the hot summer months of July and August on a whirlwind tour of two dozen American cities, building a domestic base among ethnic, religious, and human rights groups.

The Latvians, Estonians, and Poles took to Kampelman, and he earned respect as a serious diplomat with the Europeans. But not everyone was pleased with him. He was viewed with thinly veiled skepticism among a number of the full-time human rights professionals. The *Wall Street Journal* also unexpectedly opposed his appointment. So did the prominent Soviet dissident Vladimir Bukovsky. Kampelman did not want a repeat of the D.C. Council fiasco, and rallied support from Helsinki Watch, a citizens group chaired by Random House CEO Robert Bernstein. That Bernstein was a liberal actually helped Kampelman. Bernstein was also passionate about human rights in Eastern Europe, and able to run the necessary traps. Enlisting Bernstein's help, Kampelman laid his critics' reservations to rest.

Early in September, Kampelman arrived in Madrid for the preparatory talks. He had never engaged in formal diplomatic negotiations before, but he was a seasoned business and law negotiator, and he knew the Soviet Union and its tactics. He was aware of the burdens of past administration mistakes, the desire to reach agreements at almost any cost. While he sought consensus at home to maximize his own negotiation leverage, he believed talks with the Soviets had to be blunt, firm, confrontational. Carter and Vance were too willing to come to negotiations with fallback instructions readied, Kampelman believed. He would not. They felt negotiations could alleviate U.S.-Soviet tension, where Kampelman felt tension was a part of the negotiations. Kampelman was a believer in cutting a grand deal at high noon, but he was not prepared to pursue an agreement at all costs. He felt if he hung tough, the Soviets would take him more seriously, that if he were willing to debate on his terms, not on the Soviets', they would eventually come around. He would stay as long as necessary, but would be willing to go to the edge—and walk away if there were no results.

From the very beginning, the Soviets and Americans repeatedly sparred and the talks dragged. The Soviets wanted to limit the amount of time devoted to such embarrassing issues as Afghanistan and human rights violations. Rather than seeking early compromise Kampelman snapped back in October, "If they're going to play a waiting game, we'll play a waiting game."

However, time was running out for Kampelman. When Griffin Bell joined Kampelman in Madrid for the formal opening of the Helsinki Review Conference on November 11, the eyes of the world were on Washington. It was unlikely that Kampelman and Bell could accomplish much—the world was breathlessly waiting for a new foreign policy team to be named by President-elect Reagan. It was thought Bell and Kampelman were history.

Early signals of this came in October, when candidate Reagan, who had earlier questioned the value of even attending the Madrid conference, sharply criticized the Democrats' policy toward the Helsinki review process. "At the last Review conference in 1977, the Carter administration, while speaking boldly to the public, spoke timidly to the Soviets," Reagan said. As Carter appointees, Kampelman and Bell would by tradition soon be submitting their resignations. In short, they were lame ducks.

. . .

BUT THIS DIDN'T stop Kampelman, the hard-liner, from laying down his own markers with the Soviets. If it had the ancillary effect of demonstrating to the Reaganauts that he was no Carterite, that a man of his views could fit right in with the Reagan crowd, so much the better. In his November opening address to the thirty-five-nation East-West Madrid Conference, Kampelman declared that the two sides, East and West, "were moving precipitously toward confrontation." He riled the Soviets by criticizing détente as a one-way street for the Soviets, denounced the brutal invasion of Afghanistan, and even took the Russians to task for recently arresting Victor Brailovsky, a scientist and leader of the Jewish emigration movement.

To put the spotlight on the Soviets further, Kampelman released his speech to the press for international dissemination. Soon it became evident that Kampelman wasn't *just* staking out a tough posture with the Soviets. A Reuters reporter in Madrid thought it was the toughest speech he had heard from an official voice, and inquired whether the speech had been cleared ahead of time.

"Cleared ahead of time?" one of Kampelman's aides mused rhetorically. "Why, Ambassador Kampelman wrote it himself," the aide boasted.

Back in Washington, at the morning State Department briefing, State said yes, of course it had been cleared. Whereupon the D.C. Reuters reporter called Roz Ridgway, the State Department counselor, to discuss the speech with her. Ridgway was in a panic. She hadn't read the speech, and didn't know what was in it. She delayed taking the reporter's call. Instead, she first called Kampelman in Madrid.

Kampelman said slyly it had never occurred to him to clear the speech, that nobody had ever said he should. Ridgway listened intently. She knew that Kampelman was anything but an incautious man; he certainly never acted without premeditation.

"Everything I said was consistent with the president's policy on human rights," Kampelman told Ridgway. When the Reuters dispatch went out the next day, it noted that Kampelman's tough speech hadn't been cleared. The leak came from the State Department. But once again, Kampelman was able to muster the necessary support. Griffin Bell took the heat off of Kampelman by contacting the president. A few days later, Carter got in touch with Kampelman and praised the speech. Kampelman was home free.

At the conference itself, Kampelman shrewdly upped the ante. Despite the suspension of most major U.S. policy efforts, he kept the focus on the talks by drawing a link between Carter and Reagan, emphasizing continuity and the firmness that would guide *both* administrations in these talks. Kampelman was not hindered by the fact that he had no formal

contact with the Reagan campaign; he was sticking to old-fashioned foreign policy principles of bipartisanship.

JUST BEFORE CHRISTMAS, the first session of the review conference came to
a close. Figuring they had seen the last of Kampelman, the NATO allies
asked if they could throw a good-bye party for him. With little assurance
that his career in government would continue under the new administration, Kampelman agreed.

It was becoming demonstrably clear that Carter appointees were not
welcome in the Reagan administration. Kampelman's friend Peter Rosenblatt, the only CDM figure to get a job in the Carter administration in
1977, was wrapping up his negotiations for the final status of Micronesia
and also wanted to stay on. Rosenblatt had the benefit of being an old
friend of Dick Allen's, and privately was supporting Reagan. With the
incoming Reagan people, he scathingly criticized Carter's "policies of
weakness." Yet Rosenblatt's resignation was accepted, and he was un-
ceremoniously told at 5:10 on a Friday afternoon he had twenty-four
hours to clear out his office for his successor. "That's government life,"
he quipped stoically to a friend. But in truth, it was a shock, and his example gave little reason to believe that other Carter-affiliated Democrats
stood a chance with the Reagan team. Including Kampelman.

But once again, Kampelman was no passive participant in events. Bell
resigned as a delegation leader and returned to Atlanta. Kampelman
took an entirely different tack.

Rather than wait for Dick Allen to call him, Kampelman used his leverage as a sitting ambassador for what it was worth. He got in touch with
Allen himself to brief him on the Helsinki Review talks. Allen and Kampelman were friends from the Committee on the Present Danger. In
1979, at Allen's urging, Kampelman had arranged for Reagan to speak in
Palm Beach before a crowd of major Jewish fund-raisers. It was a good
forum for Reagan, giving him a high-powered audience of Jews who had
become disaffected with Carter's increasingly heavy-handed ways with
Israel. After a warm introduction, full of praise, Reagan took the podium
to speak as a heartfelt friend of Israel's. Kampelman had given the introduction.

During the campaign, Kampelman had also suggested to Dick Allen
that Reagan make Scoop Jackson secretary of state. Allen sounded out
Reagan about the idea. Reagan was intrigued; he liked Jackson. Although the idea was later shelved, Allen and Kampelman were clearly on
the same wavelength, which gave Kampelman a free hand when he
called on Allen to brief him.

It certainly wasn't necessary for Kampelman to update Allen on the talks; as national security adviser designate, Allen could draw on an extensive staff. But Kampelman was touching the important bases. (Unknown to Kampelman, Millicent Fenwick, the aristocratic New Jersey congresswoman, was also leading a bipartisan group in the Congress, asking the incoming president to keep Kampelman.) Allen didn't need this prodding. Already responsible for bringing Kirkpatrick to Reagan's attention, he did the same with Kampelman. So when Kampelman also offered to brief his successor to the talks, Allen said that wouldn't be necessary.

Kampelman, who early in life was taught he could learn more by listening than talking, perked up. He innocently asked Allen, Why not?

I expect the president will ask you to stay on, Allen said.

TO THE BRINK

On March 23, 1981, Richard Perle officially assumed the title of assistant secretary of defense designate. His supporters were thrilled, and even his detractors had to grudgingly acknowledge that his eleven years of experience on Scoop Jackson's Senate staff made him the right man for the job. But the appointment also meant that for the first time in his Washington career, as a member of the executive branch, Richard Perle was now on the inside. Indeed, the significant transition he would have to make was evident in the very architecture of the Pentagon itself, different not just in culture from the Hill, but in setting and spirit.

The five-sided Pentagon was actually not in Washington, but in Virginia, perched on the banks of the Potomac, looking out toward the city. Built to accommodate the American military machine that blossomed during the World War II, it was like a self-contained city, rising to the bright glass windows of the defense secretary's office, and descending into subbasement depths, where military and civilian personnel watched over each small nut and casing of the machinery of war and peace.

Unlike the older, more elaborate departments, the Pentagon announced that it was all business from the moment anyone stepped through its doors at the River Entrance. Here, there were no stone columns and sunken reception areas, like at the Department of Agriculture, or sleek glass walls and bright flags, like at the Department of State. The Pentagon was a rather dark, wood-paneled affair, adorned with photographs of the secretary and the joint chiefs, and watched over by military guards. The ceilings were low, the floors utilitarian. And in a now quaint touch of modernity, escalators connected the different levels. In fact, the even motion of those mechanical stairs was just the image the Pentagon wanted to project: a seamless, efficient movement of men and matériel.

And, unlike Capitol Hill across the river, where members and their staffs had the luxury to pick and choose their issues, at the Pentagon a world agenda just kept coming at you, like a fast-moving train in a long, dark tunnel.

Policy making itself in the Pentagon was an intricate process, with a myriad of issues scattered over a complex assortment of bureaucratic levels, defined by heavy-handed acronyms. At the top sat the new defense secretary. Caspar Weinberger was Ronald Reagan's pick for the post. Weinberger, sixty-four, was very much a man of the Reagan administration. He was a person of enormous accomplishment and, to be sure, a Reagan conservative and good Republican. But more than that, he was a can-do man for the new Reagan era: loyal, committed, deeply anti-Soviet. Given a cause, he would advocate it. If there was a job to be done, he would do it. If someone needed to take the heat, he would take it.

His credentials were not just establishment credentials, but downright impeccable: Harvard (Phi Beta Kappa undergrad, editor of the *Harvard Crimson*, LL.B. Harvard Law, 1941), U.S. Army captain and a member of Douglas MacArthur's intelligence staff, a blue-chip San Francisco lawyer and later counselor to the industrial giant Bechtel. His government service was no less impressive, secretary of health, education, and welfare; chairman of the Federal Trade Commission; and a director of the Office of Management and Budget in the Nixon administration.

Yet Weinberger was a study in paradoxes. For one thing, he was not East Coast establishment but Reagan counterestablishment. Just under six feet tall, his squat build actually made him look short; with his hair always perfectly neat, his clothes crisply starched, he appeared to embody the image of Herbert Hoover, the 1920s man and one of Weinberger's early heroes. But Weinberger also had a wry and self-deprecating wit. Proper, sometimes to a fault, he was suffused with an air of insouciant irreverence. While he was raised by his mother to love the arts, at age fifteen he wrote to his congressman requesting to receive copies of the *Congressional Record*, which he then read assiduously. Possessing a keen mind, he refused to be burdened by unnecessary clutter or complexity, but instead cut to the chase, and doggedly stayed there. Details were left to staff.

Fundamentally, he was a tough, uncompromising litigator, in profession and in spirit. So, just as he had zealously slashed budgets as Nixon's OMB director, earning himself the name "Cap the Knife," when Ronald Reagan asked him to rebuild U.S. defenses, he would work just as zealously to ensure that an underfunded and demoralized military would be revitalized. Indeed, here, with complete devotion and determination, Weinberger would make his greatest mark. And a historic one at that.

From the very start, Cap Weinberger had made it his personal priority to preside over rebuilding America's hollowed-out defenses and restoring the morale of the men and women in uniform. He rejected the frequent exhortation by defense experts and members of Congress that the military return to the draft, fearing it would tear too much at the nation's social fabric. Instead, he believed in an all-volunteer force, but he wanted them to have the best.

As secretary, he was often gripped by an image from his youth, when he trained for World War II with only a wooden rifle, because real guns were in too short a supply. Weinberger feared if war came again, the U.S. would not have the luxury of two years to gear up, as it had against Nazi Germany, and that America's armed forces would be caught woefully unprepared. Only when the U.S. had restored its military capabilities, not just through increased defense spending, but by modernizing its navy and neglected nuclear arsenal, did Weinberger think that America's European allies would feel able to stand with the U.S. through the tense upcoming Intermediate-Range Nuclear Force (INF) missile deployment. Only then would the Soviets take the U.S. seriously. Nor did he want another Afghanistan or Iran on his watch, which also meant rebuilding U.S. defenses as quickly as possible. From the first day he set foot in the Pentagon, this was Cap's mission.

As a longtime friend and confidant of the president's, Weinberger would also soon emerge as one of the most powerful defense secretaries in this century, like Truman's Robert Lovett and Kennedy's Robert Mc Namara. But he also had a blunt, impolitic side. To some, he could be inflexible and dogmatic, unwilling to adapt to changes in the international environment, to engage in meaningful negotiations, or to adequately recognize waste and inefficiency in the military. To his liberal critics, his tenacity could be off-putting, as was the fact that he was not a man who readily sought conciliation. But for Weinberger, accommodation and compromise most often spelled cop-out, and served only to delay the hard decisions that had to be made. He had seen the deadly patterns of succumbing to wishful thinking and appeasement all too often in the past. And if he was a man not overly prone to introspection, it was because the mission was what mattered most. At the risk of unduly provoking the Hill Democrats (his refusal to compromise drove them crazy), or forsaking diplomatic niceties with overly sensitive European allies, Weinberger sensed the politics of the moment, which was that, at this critical juncture of the Cold War, the U.S. had to be indisputably strong and prepared. Everything else was secondary.

Even in his personal life, Weinberger radiated preparedness, right down to the chin-up bar he installed in the tiny alcove off of his private office, where the Defense Department kept a spartan single bed and bathroom for late nights and catnaps during crises.

Weinberger was a leader, not a micromanager. Like a commander, he wanted key individuals who could oversee important areas and details. Most of all, he wanted the very best people, and from all accounts, he felt Richard Perle was one of the best. He was principled, creative, thoughtful, able to produce superbly reasoned papers and memos. So, he let Perle, seasoned in the mercurial ways of Washington and keenly knowledgeable in defense matters, have a rather free hand in Soviet and arms control policy, convinced that the final product from Perle's office would be one of quality, the type of thing a cabinet secretary could confidently take to a president.

PERLE'S OFFICE, ROOM 4E838, just down the hall and up a floor from Defense Secretary Caspar Weinberger's suite, was part of the E-Ring, the heavy paneled corridors where the nation's top national security leadership maintained their offices. There, upright and muscular colonels in crisply starched uniforms and black polished shoes rushed briskly about in the hallways, talking defensespeak and snapping out orders, popping to attention as a general walked by. Everyone and everything radiated the serious business of national security.

The door to Room 4E838 actually opened into an anteroom, where Perle's personal secretary and military assistants sat. Beyond that lay his huge private office, which was decorated with a hodgepodge of special items. On the wall hung mementos from his travels—French posters, Japanese silk screens, and Persian miniatures. A rich Turkish rug led to an oversized globe that sat on the far side of the room, astride a bulky wooden conference table. Perched alone in the corner was an expensive AMA Italian espresso machine. But the room's cozy, even eclectic feel was rudely punctuated by five-foot-high metal safes locked with secret combinations, which stood as a reminder that this was, after all, the office of an assistant secretary of defense, whose portfolio dealt principally with the Soviet Union.

From his first day in the office, Perle was busy putting together his team. He knew his nomination had been greeted warily by some career civil servants and nearly all Carter administration holdovers. But, in return, Perle did not rush to judge any names that appeared on his personnel roster. The Richard Perle who came to the Pentagon was not the young, brash Senate staffer who, with Scoop Jackson, was held responsible for the infamous purge, the wholesale firings in the Arms Control and Disarmament Agency in the early 1970s. This Richard Perle was older and wiser. He had serious business in front of him. He was determined to give everyone a chance to prove him- or herself.

What Perle asked in return from his staff was loyalty, and that they share his unshakable commitment to a cause: rebuilding American defenses, rethinking the American approach to arms control, and standing firm with the Soviets. Perle also wanted the best people. He led through ideas, inspiration, and by delegation. He knew he was most effective when concentrating on a few key issues, and that was his game plan, so he wanted a staff that could handle responsibility, people to whom he could broadly delegate other details with confidence. And he didn't want just anyone, but a special breed, hard-headed men and women who shared his sense of urgency and excitement for America's mission, the task not just of reversing the Cold War but of mustering the resources of the nation to nothing less than winning it.

Perle shared the view that the American people had elected Ronald Reagan because they wanted the United States to change its posture in the world and with the Soviet Union. That was their mandate. At the close of the Carter administration, and after Desert One and Afghanistan, the world verged on the edge of chaos. The democratic West appeared frail, listless, on the losing side of history. Now, many of the hard tasks and hard choices would fall to Richard Perle.

WHEN HE FIRST set foot in the Pentagon, Richard Perle never worried about his upcoming Senate confirmation. As a veteran Hill aide, it was virtually guaranteed to be uneventful. So he quickly turned his attention to other matters. One key slot he wanted to fill with care was that of his deputy. Perle knew that to be successful in the Pentagon's swirling labyrinth and impossible bureaucracy meant that he had to control the agenda, not the other way around. Which also meant he would need someone he could rely upon and trust, who could assume many of the burdens of day-to-day dealings with the bureaucracy and allow him to focus single-mindedly on arms control, technology transfer, and U.S.-Soviet relations. Perle thus began the burdensome but necessary task of finding himself an appropriate deputy.

After sorting through names in his Rolodex, Perle was convinced that an old friend and colleague, Stephen Bryen, was just the person he needed. Bryen was tough, loyal, knew defense, and was available. Perle immediately offered Bryen the job with the rather long-winded title of deputy assistant secretary of defense for international economic and trade policy. Bryen would have Perle's ear and enjoy his confidence. It was done with a handshake and a smile.

But, within days of the Bryen announcement, Perle came under fire, and his own confirmation began to appear to be in jeopardy. From the bitter beginning, he was thus faced with a crisis, which, as some saw it, meant Bryen would have to go—or Perle would.

THE ISSUE, AS framed by Perle's detractors, was not Perle himself, but his support of Bryen. In 1978, Bryen had been suspended from the Senate Foreign Relations Committee for allegedly spying for the Israelis. The charge was never proven, but the damage to his reputation was done. Senator James Exon, Democrat from Nebraska, let it be quietly known that he felt Perle would quickly have to make a choice: cut Bryen loose and pick another deputy, or slug it out from the start, and risk his new job.

It quickly became clear that the Bryen nomination had the potential to wound Perle, perhaps irrevocably. A decision had to be made. Cut his losses, or fight, and fight hard.

STEVE BRYEN WAS a dry-witted defense intellectual with a mane of cropped white hair, a dark mustache, and a sloping physique. A New Jersey native with a Ph.D. from Tulane, and a Republican, he had come to Washington in 1971 to be the foreign affairs staffer for liberal Republican senator Clifford Case, a former professor with a penchant for brown suits and old shoes. Bryen quickly emerged as Case's man on the Senate Foreign Relations Committee.

Bryen, like so many others of his generation, was attracted to the bipartisan tradition in foreign policy, and the mystique of the Wise Men who shepherded American policy in the dark days after World War II. But he soon became disillusioned by the antiwar movement that rudely shattered this unity, including the once collegial Senate Foreign Relations Committee. Staffers on different sides of the aisle became increasingly polarized between the anti-Communist cold warriors and a new breed of liberals, who called for greater accommodation with the Soviets. A hardliner himself, Bryen would work on a number of issues with Perle.

The Perle and Bryen axis was forged in the early battles against Nixon's détente. In 1974, Henry Kissinger and Commerce Secretary Peter Peterson negotiated a number of secret agreements with the Soviets, including a deal that called for the U.S. to extend $3 billion in Export-Import Bank credits to the Soviet Union. Frequently contemptuous in his dealings with the Congress, Kissinger sought to keep this agreement from Congress's purview. From his Senate perch, Bryen smelled a problem, and swung into action after reading the cables that Kissinger had turned over to the Hill. In the course of examining every cable, Bryen discovered that one cable was missing. The set was incomplete.

Bryen went to Case and urged him to invoke what was considered an esoteric and rarely used law, PL 92-403, which stipulated that all executive agreements negotiated by the administration shall be transferred to Congress for review. Ultimately, Kissinger was denied his agreement. Senators Case and Frank Church personally intervened, and to the State Department authorization bill that year attached amendments prohibiting this massive transfer of bank credits to the Soviet Union. In working on this issue and other efforts to stem the flow of technology to Communist bloc countries, Bryen earned cachet in the Senate with one of its most powerful staffers, Richard Perle. The two soon became close political allies. They also became good friends. Bryen first introduced Perle to Leslie Barr, the sparkling, vivacious woman Perle would marry.

ON A HAZY fall day in 1978, Bryen came to work at the committee only to be summoned to an urgent meeting by his boss, Senator Case, now in his final months in the Senate. The previous June, a young conservative named Jeff Bell had beaten Case in the Republican primary. Bell was now running hard against another political novice, basketball star Bill Bradley. For Bryen, however, their election outcome was moot. Either way, he was soon out of a job.

Case called Bryen into his personal office, and closed the door behind him. Something was clearly wrong. Case was visibly upset, and told Bryen he had a few questions.

Had Bryen recently had coffee at the Madison Hotel with an official from the Israeli embassy?

"Yes, but why?"

With the congressional liaison, Zfi Rafi?

"Yes," Bryen said, he "often did."

Was someone else along?

"Yes."

Finally, Bryen mustered up the nerve to ask his boss what all the "hush-hush was about." Case made it clear that a serious matter was afoot, one of "harsh consequences."

Case informed him that Michael Saba, a former head of the National Association of Arab Americans, had told the chairman of the Judiciary Committee, Senator James Abourezk, a longtime supporter of Arab causes, that he had been sitting one booth over from Bryen at the Madison Hotel. Saba claimed to have overheard Bryen offering to pass on classified information to the Israelis—there was also murky talk of giving reconnaissance photos of Hawk missiles to the Israelis.

Bryen was stunned by the charges, and denied them vehemently. "It's crap," he protested, "absolutely untrue."

The senator continued. "Saba also heard you talk about 'we' and 'they.'" The implication of his statement was clear.

"It's just crazy," Bryen said. " 'We' is the Congress, 'they' is the administration. It's a common figure of speech."

"Maybe so," Case said, shaking his head. He didn't disagree, knowing that Saba was hardly an unimpeachable source, one who might very much like to bring down Bryen. Case also knew that the Israelis didn't need American photos of Hawk missiles; they could fairly handily get the pictures from their own planes with side-mounted cameras. Still, egged on by Saba, Senator Abourezk was determined.

"He's not about to let this one drop," Case told Bryen darkly. "He has asked the Justice Department and the FBI to look into the alleged incident." Once the facts were known, Case reassured Bryen, the matter would be resolved.

But in the meantime, Case said, pausing to find just the right words, Bryen would have to sweat it out.

Which is exactly what happened.

AFTER A NUMBER of hushed meetings between the Foreign Relations Committee chairman, Senator John Sparkman, his top aide, Norville Jones, and other members, Bryen was suspended from work with pay. He was told to take "a leave from the Senate Foreign Relations Committee." To avoid a stigma while the jury was still out, the committee would "consider" the time off "vacation time." But there was no getting around it. This was an unorthodox, punitive measure, a sign of the explosive nature of the charge. Whispers of treason were the subtext.

Almost immediately after Bryen went on leave, other committee staffers leaked what had happened, making a mockery of the claim that Bryen was just taking a vacation.

The press got wind of the story, and it was carried in the papers. National Public Radio correspondent David Enson did a lengthy spot piece on Bryen, who now tottered on the verge of ruin.

THE FBI INITIATED a full-scale, prolonged investigation. As Bryen saw it, without a shred of proof that he had done anything, his reputation was being destroyed. Bryen retained a lawyer.

Sympathetic yet concerned, Senator Case himself decided to conduct his own internal investigation. Unknown to Bryen, the senator had Mike Kraft, his executive assistant, do a thorough assessment as to whether there was any basis to the charge. A former reporter for UPI and then Reuters, Kraft was just the right guy for the internal probe. After a week of sleuthing around, Kraft reported that he had found nothing to implicate Bryen. But he had found two other pieces of profoundly disturbing information, which pointed to a more insidious plot. He explained the whole affair to Case.

First, Kraft noted "staff tensions." On the committee, Bryen had, if not enemies, disgruntled opponents among his staff colleagues. They resented both Bryen's mastery of technical knowledge and his personal support for Israel. They blamed him for helping to quash a committee staff recommendation for sharp cuts in U.S. aid to Israel, and they wanted Bryen "to get his."

A second, and even more troubling point, Kraft explained, was that Bryen never even had access to the photos in question. No reconnaissance photos from either the CIA or the Defense Intelligence Agency (DIA) had been logged in with the Senate Foreign Relations Committee clerk until several days *after* Bryen had been officially suspended. Until that point, only the administration had copies of the photos. There was "no way" that Bryen could have gotten his hands on the material.

Kraft continued. There were other curious things he had uncovered, oddities that didn't add up. Bryen was one of the most effective opponents of arms sales to the Arabs, and before the charges of collusion with the Israelis exploded, he was leading the opposition to the latest round of Sidewinder and Hawk missile sales to Jordan. Kraft noted that when some Hill staffers had met after Bryen's suspension to discuss strategy for opposing the missiles, they were stumped by some of the technical details. One staffer blurted out, "Too bad Steve isn't here, he knows all the issues." And that was the point, Kraft said, Bryen was no longer there. To Kraft, it was too clean, too surgical, too much of a coincidence.

"It smacked of a campaign to knock Bryen out of the action," Kraft told Case. "Steve's one of the most outspoken opponents of arms sales. This is real hardball." Between the discrepancy with the photos, the upcoming arms sales, and the long-standing staff friction, "the whole issue was a little weird, too much of a setup," he said.

Kraft concluded that Bryen didn't do it.

Case appeared to agree with Kraft's assessment. In the politically charged environment of the Senate, where only a handful of members were willing to go out on a limb for their aides (most members wanted "to protect their skirts," one staffer wryly noted), the apparent sting against

Bryen had been executed perfectly. But Case was an exception to the rule. Case sought to take the bite off the lingering charge, demonstrating his faith in Bryen by taking him onto his personal staff. He also came forward as a character witness for Bryen, asking other senators to do likewise. In Case's office itself, the staff sought to rally around Bryen. Still, for Bryen, the charge stung. "He never wanted to talk about it," said one friend and committee colleague. "It was clearly painful to him."

WEEKS DRAGGED INTO months. While Bryen sought to carry on life as normal, the charge continued to be devastating. Every day the official investigation remained unresolved, it hung like a stench of guilt and cast a bitter pall over his head. Other staff members of the committee, such as Norville Jones, the staff director, and Michael Glennon, the committee counsel, were convinced Bryen was guilty, though they had no hard proof. They feared that the "pro-Israel lobby" would stave off the investigation, darkly ruminating that no one "had the backbone to take this one on."

But that was not the case. Some in the government saw this as a golden opportunity. They would bring down Bryen, bringing the Israelis a little bit more to heel in the process.

FOR FORMER COMMITTEE staff director Pat Holt, the Bryen charge seemed to have another component to it. While it was based on speculation, Holt believed that the FBI did have evidence of an intelligence leak to Israel, but that their information had been picked up not by a chance encounter at the Madison Hotel, but by well-placed wiretaps and bugs at the Israeli embassy in Washington and by National Security Agency satellite intercepts. "This was pretty routine at the time," Holt later recalled. Other staffers also agreed.

But because wiretapping and bugging an ally was illegal, and certainly impolitic, the FBI had to find corroborating evidence, or risk an explosive public spat between the two nations splashed on the front pages of the papers. In this instance, Saba's and Senator Abourezk's allegations were a convenient smoke screen for information that the government had already acquired through less savory means. Holt, who by the time of Bryen's suspension had left the Senate, but remained in touch with committee staffers, was increasingly convinced this was the case. It also explained why "the FBI was breaking its balls to come up with something," Holt said.

The FBI did resort to extreme measures. They rifled through old phone records kept by Bryen's secretary, but came up short. After some discussion, they hired a crack hypnotist from Philadelphia, who was reportedly even able to help subjects recall numbers and letters on license plates. Then the FBI agents summoned Bryen's office mate, Murella Hanson, and asked if she would consent to being hypnotized.

Hanson was timid, knew nothing, and wanted to stay out of the whole sorry mess. But the FBI leaned hard, and left little doubt that she had no alternative. Maybe in the cramped quarters of their Senate office, where she and Bryen sat practically cheek-to-jowl, she might have overheard Bryen say something, only to have forgotten it, they reasoned.

On a dreary day, two burly FBI agents in tattered tweed coats and felt hats spirited Murella Hanson down to the isolated, marshy confines of the Marine Corps base in Quantico, Virginia, where she was to be hypnotized. But the hypnotist came up with nothing.

Bryen struggled to go on with life as normal, as the government's investigation dragged on.

When Case left office at the end of 1978, Bryen left the committee, no longer having a sponsor and protector. In 1979, Bryen married. And all year, the FBI was still at it.

FOR BRYEN, RELIEF seemed to come finally in 1980, after a treacherous two years. He was sent a faceless letter written in the bland abstractions of bureaucratese, absolving him of the allegations.

But the investigation had taken its toll. His reputation was marred among many of the defense establishment in Washington, and his subsequent work for JINSA, the Jewish Institute for National Security Affairs, whose goal was to increases military ties between the U.S. and Israel, only confirmed the darkest suspicions of Bryen's enemies. But there was one saving grace to the relative anonymity of his new job at JINSA. No longer in a significant government position, Bryen could quietly blend into the background. At JINSA, he no longer merited the venom of his enemies; he simply wasn't important enough anymore. But all that changed when he accepted Perle's offer to come work at DoD.

WHEN PERLE CALLED at the start of the administration, Bryen hadn't been thinking about an administration job for himself. But as Perle's deputy, Bryen could tap into what he did so well on the Hill—prevent advanced Western technology and credits from bankrolling the Soviet war machine. Weinberger was ready to make the formal offer. Bryen said it was too good to turn down. He told Perle, "It would be good to get back into the swing of things."

At the end of March 1981, Bryen began work at the Pentagon as a consultant, pending his formal naming, which awaited only Perle's Senate confirmation. But then the Bryen charges were again hauled before the Senate.

The Armed Services Committee, which has jurisdiction over all Department of Defense presidential appointees, informed the Pentagon that there was a hold on Perle's nomination. Any senator is entitled to hold up a nomination for formal consideration without his or her name being revealed, for as long as he likes. Frequently, the hold is placed because a senator wants a favor from the administration, and uses the nominee as a hostage in an intricate bargaining process. In this case, however, it didn't seem to be a matter of a senator wanting a favor. The hold was for the other reason commonly employed: a senator apparently had a problem with the nominee's fitness to represent the U.S. in a position of authority.

Through his sources on the Hill, Perle learned that the hold on his nomination had been placed by a Democrat, James Exon of Nebraska. "What's the problem?" he asked. Senator Exon said he questioned Perle's judgment. He had reservations about Perle, given that his chosen deputy was alleged to be an agent for the Israelis. Bryen himself had warned Perle that this could happen, but Perle had told him not to worry, "everything would be taken care of."

Perle had miscalculated. Exon wanted Bryen checked out again. Still, Perle refused to be swayed.

On the Hill, pressure to have Bryen removed escalated. Letters poured into the Senate offices protesting his appointment. Bryen was looking more and more like damaged goods. The only question was when Perle would do the smart thing and induce him to bail out.

Perle moved instead in the opposite direction, trying to nip this one in the bud. This was one story he didn't want to hit the papers. If word of Exon's hold became public, it would potentially destroy Bryen's reputation. Bryen had already been badly bruised—and cleared—during the original investigation, and a second round, he feared, could be devastating to him. Perle also knew there were equally problematic implications for his own career. Mishandled, a dragged-out public fight could cause Weinberger to reconsider Perle as head of International Security Policy. And even if this didn't happen, Perle would enter the Pentagon bloodied, a weakened official who would have to use up public chits even before his first policy battle. It wouldn't look good for Weinberger either, if the media got wind of the issue and gave it sizable play.

Perle knew he had to move fast.

He went first to Weinberger. Weinberger gently sat Perle down. "God," Perle thought, "I haven't even formally started the job yet, and I'm going to the secretary of defense with a crisis."

Perle explained the circumstances. This was, he said, a settling of scores, nothing more, nothing less. He asked Weinberger to stick by Bryen, and leave it to him. "I know the Senate, and I'll be able to wrap things up fast," he reassured the secretary.

Weinberger had confidence in Perle, and told him to do what had to be done. "I have no intention of jettisoning Steve," he said reassuringly. Perle felt partially relieved. Weinberger was sticking by his team. For now.

Perle quickly touched bases with other key administration officials, and then turned his attention back to the Senate.

He made a quiet appointment to see Scoop Jackson.

Perle sat down with his Senate mentor and explained the game of cat and mouse that was under way. A rehash of old trumped-up charges was holding up the appointment of the assistant secretary of defense, threatening the secretary of defense himself. Without a shred of tangible proof after a two-year investigation, urgent business of government was being delayed.

Scoop said he would talk to Exon and get back to Perle. "Don't worry," he counseled.

Perle then went back to Bryen and updated him. Stay put, he said. Perle then took his own advice and began working, waiting for the denouement of the standoff. And as spring faded into summer, with little patience for the bureaucracy, he quietly burned.

Finally, Scoop called. He said that in the back rooms of the Senate, a deal had been worked out. The staff director and general counsel of the Armed Services Committee, Rhett Dawson, would read the raw FBI files on Bryen. Dawson was Texas Senator John Tower's guy, a Republican and a loyalist, but tough and fair-minded. He was not a guy to oversee a whitewash. If there was a problem, the investigation would continue. But if there was nothing there, Exon would release the hold on Perle.

Jackson said nothing more to Perle, but Perle knew this spelled victory. He was confident that the files would turn up nothing, and that Exon had been rolled by Jackson. "Scoop did it in his own inimitable way," Perle would later explain. Perle didn't even bother to tell Bryen about the deal. He told him it was cleared up, period.

At 10:05 A.M. in Room 212 of the Russell Senate Office Building on July 16, 1981, Richard Perle appeared before the Armed Services Committee for his confirmation hearing, as the ordeal came to an anticlimactic end. He was all smiles that day. Senator Exon did not attend. Perle was praised repeatedly for his integrity and courage, and uncommon expertise in defense. The hearing was over in a brief forty-five minutes. On August 3, he was overwhelmingly confirmed by the Senate.

THE DAY AFTER, now officially an assistant secretary of defense, Perle met with Bryen, flashed a satisfied smile, and chuckled, "Let's get to work."

In truth, though, they had already been at work, hard at work, for nearly half a year—on another crisis that was not just brewing but was ready to blow up.

CHAPTER 10

In his first months in the Pentagon, even before his confirmation, Richard Perle had far more than personnel issues weighing on his mind. A historic battle was looming over the emplacement of American missiles in Europe, one that would in time bring the U.S. and the Soviets to the brink of confrontation, and, for many, perilously close to the nuclear trigger.

The decision to put American missiles into Europe had actually been made under the Carter administration. Ronald Reagan and his Defense Department had inherited the policy from their predecessor.

In 1979, in what became known as a two-track decision, NATO, the Western alliance forged after World War II, voted to deploy 572 Intermediate-Range Nuclear Force (INF) Pershing II and ground-launched cruise missiles in five European countries, while at the same time proposing to negotiate a reduction in these deployments if the Soviet Union would scale back its own missiles now threatening Europe.

The NATO move was anything but rash. It was made as a response to what the Western alliance saw as a clear provocation by the Soviet Union. The Soviets had dramatically upset the East-West military balance of power by unveiling up to 220 SS-20s, mobile, triple-headed, highly accurate nuclear missiles, aimed like a dagger at the heart of Europe, menacing its capitals and its military alike. NATO lacked anything comparable in its arsenal on the ground in Europe, and the Soviet move gave the Russians the upper hand in the global game of domination, intimidation, nuclear blackmail, and the ultimate threat—war. By 1981, the crisis had escalated as the Soviets continued to steadily emplace several missiles each week. It was an untenable situation for the West.

In the early months of the Reagan administration, it rapidly became clear that the stakes for INF deployment were vast. No issue would have greater consequences for peace and for war during the early 1980s. It was a crucial hinge on which the fate of the Cold War would turn. And if the U.S. were unable to put in place its own missiles for NATO's defense, it would deal a crippling blow to the Western alliance. The actual deployment date itself was set for November 21, 1983, in what was dubbed "the year of the missile."

When Richard Perle came to the Pentagon, the moment of reckoning was more than two years off. Nevertheless, the Soviets had categorically opposed the proposed NATO deployment. Even a "single missile," they ominously declared, was "unacceptable." In the midst of a burgeoning peace movement in Europe, as well as a grassroots nuclear freeze movement sweeping across the U.S. like a prairie fire, the stage had been set for a prolonged test of wills, if not a cataclysmic U.S.-Soviet clash. In both real and symbolic terms, the struggle for deployment would prove to be one of the most decisive periods of the Cold War.

As the Pentagon's chief man on arms control, Perle soon hurled himself into this precarious breach—the INF missile deployments. A time of Soviet threats, he believed, was not the moment to abandon principle or sound policy. Instead, it was the time to stand ever more firmly, ever more resolved. History taught that, when met with counterforce, totalitarian empires were the ones to blink.

NUCLEAR ARMS CONTROL. No issue was so riddled with its own acronyms and arcane language, nor was so dominated by the experts, as arms control. The vocabulary alone was dizzying. There was SALT I and II, the Strategic Arms Limitations talks, and then START, the Strategic Arms Reduction Talks, the superpower negotiations designed to reduce the most menacing of all weapons systems, strategic nuclear missiles based at sea and on land in the U.S. and Soviet Union, each set targeted at the other side. Then there were the INF missiles, the issue of greatest importance in the early 1980s, which focused on the nuclear missiles sitting in the heart of the Soviet-Eurasian landmass, the weapon of choice for a European conflagration. Accompanying these acronyms was the macabre language of strategy and the arms control process itself: "throw-weight," "circular error probability," "fratricide," "MIRV," "fractionation," "heavies," "verification," "cross-targeting," and "forward-based systems."

Yet, in truth, if the issue of nuclear arms control was at once complicated, it was also surprisingly simple. The breakdown was thus: not just for the left, but for adherents of détente from Richard Nixon to Jimmy Carter, the steady view persisted that arms control was the reliable instrument by which the two superpowers charted their course. Especially for those on the left, but also for the establishment, their devotion remained constant: however deep and real U.S.-Soviet differences, however shocking Soviet human rights atrocities and foreign aggression might be, the evils of nuclear war, not of totalitarianism, were the greatest threat. The enduring faith persisted that arms talks were the best way to manage, if not quell altogether, such differences. Indeed, more than just a framework, at a much deeper, more profound level, to those who believed in the process, arms control was a way of life, a symbolic, even intangible means by which the U.S. found a sense of stability in an uncertain and menacing world.

In this worldview, the U.S. democratic system and the Communist Soviet Union were treated as moral equivalents, the omnipresent danger being the arms themselves, not the nature of the regimes possessing them. The mantra was always the same: the arms control process must never be disturbed.

But the Reagan administration saw it differently. It sought a radical break with the past to establish a higher standard in arms control, one in which the Soviets could not cheat, build up their own arsenal, or exploit agreement loopholes. Concerned less with the symbolism of the treaty process and more with the substance of a treaty outcome, the Reagan team sought not just caps but deep reductions in the number of weapons, including those Soviet systems deemed most dangerous. And the Reagan administration worried less about the "negotiability" of the proposals it tabled in well-appointed rooms in neutral European cities, and worried more about what would strengthen U.S. security and the stability of deterrence. Too often in the past, and most recently at the SALT II negotiations, the U.S. had put forward a proposal only to retreat from it at the first sign of Soviet unhappiness. Time and again, American negotiators were willing to give into Soviet demands and engage in premature concessions to keep the discussions and the process moving. This time around, however, the Reagan administration was boldly determined to stand its ground.

Yet in seeking to improve not just Western security but the very fabric of arms control itself, the Reagan administration was stepping on cherished shibboleths of arms control dogma. And on the scarred and bruised ideological battlefield of U.S.-Soviet relations, the left seized upon every opportunity to proclaim the administration "an enemy of arms control" and even of "peace itself." This was sophistry. But that such talk was both erroneous and undercut the administration's hand in the looming INF deployment were beside the point in the increasingly highly charged domestic political arena. Time and again, in staying the course, the administration would have to contend not simply with the

Soviets, but with a raging public debate, often angrily at odds with its policies.

The INF debate would be a long and difficult battle, a fact that was most immediately apparent in the rash of demonstrations protesting—and threatening—the new U.S. posture.

ON APRIL 4, 1981, over 150,000 angry and frustrated protesters took to the streets of Bonn, calling for the U.S. not to deploy its INF nuclear weapons in West Germany. Some cradled infants, others pushed strollers or held young children by the hand. Knots of teenagers and women formed, shouting, "No U.S. missiles, No U.S. missiles" and "This is not a theater, this is our home." Posters portraying Ronald Reagan as a reckless nuclear cowboy were brandished by the crowd.

To Perle, this was yet another indication that the INF decision was shaping up to be one big headache. He had never been crazy about it; it was a marginal military fix, and an expensive one at that. As he also saw it, the nuclear freeze and peace movements should be railing against the Soviet missiles, but instead, they blamed their allies, the Americans. Complicating matters, he thought, was the fact that however well intended many of the marchers were, much of the peace movement was largely financed by Soviet funds. Finally, negotiating a nuclear freeze would be every bit as complicated as negotiating any other arms deal. And its advocates were not calling for the elimination of all nuclear weapons on both sides, but instead for "freezing" the two arsenals at their current unequal levels, thus leaving Soviet superiority in place.

But there was no denying the growing strength of this swelling band of protesters, or that this German march was a sign of more to come. Unless countered, this turmoil could drive the same political parties in Europe that had voted for deploying the missiles to call for a unilateral halt to the American weapons—or for extended negotiations, which amounted to the same thing. Perle, like Weinberger, felt strongly that deployment must go forward if the U.S. were not only to be successful in rebuilding its strength, but eventually to get a good arms agreement that reduced the growing Soviet threat. Deployment would be the guarantor of peace, not the other way around.

But for the time being, Perle was up against seemingly insurmountable odds. The Soviets had all the leverage. They already had up to a thousand warheads deployed; the U.S. had zero. This, however, did not stop the Soviet leader, Leonid Brezhnev, from having the audacity to call for a moratorium on all medium-range missiles, labeled a "peace gesture," but which would only guarantee the Soviet military advantage already in place.

And if this weren't bad enough, Perle thought, the pressure to be railroaded prematurely into negotiations wasn't coming just from the Europeans, but from the U.S. State Department. He had always felt that the U.S. could not lose sight of its strategic goals; otherwise, once it got into negotiations, it would be ineluctably lulled into signing a piece of paper and would end up seeking an agreement for agreement's sake, whether or not it served the American national interest.

Yet in government, the best of strategic goals were often waylaid by day-to-day headlines and emergencies. As the days and months wore on, it was inevitable that the call for an agreement, some agreement, would eventually rise to a fevered pitch. Much the way Truman and his advisers had to overcome enormous domestic resistance to NATO and the policy of containment, so this administration would have to struggle, at home and abroad, for good arms control and meaningful change.

Indeed, on the night of April 4, as a restless Perle tossed in bed, after flicking off the late evening news, he thought about the meeting of the allied foreign ministers in Brussels on March 31, five days before. Predictably, the West Europeans, under pressure from their marching publics, had pressed the American leadership to resume negotiations on INF. The State Department, he thought, with its congenital mind-set for diplomacy, had stressed America's commitment to an "arms control approach" in the communiqué issued following the meeting. Perle worried about such statements, written and disseminated in the heat of the moment. Nothing would damage the U.S. negotiating posture so much as a precipitous rush, unprepared, into arms talks.

Perle planned to assess the situation firsthand when he accompanied Weinberger to a Nuclear Planning Group meeting of allied defense ministers, in Brussels on April 7. In the meantime, he would first have to deal with his State Department counterpart, Richard Burt, the director of the Political-Military Affairs Bureau, State's in-house mini-Pentagon. Burt, whom Perle had helped to get his current job, was co-chair, along with Perle, of the interagency committee charged with devising directions for INF, and he was fighting Perle for control of U.S. policy at every step of the way.

VERY SOON AFTER coming into the Pentagon, Perle had established himself as perhaps the single most influential voice in DoD—and in government at large—on arms control policy. Weinberger, principally concerned with rebuilding the military, virtually ceded the arms control portfolio to Perle. The two also personally clicked together and conferred regularly, and Perle earned Weinberger's near total confidence. Whatever Perle's idiosyncrasies, the secretary, like Scoop Jackson before him, overlooked them. To most people Weinberger was "Mr. Secretary." Perle called him simply "Cap."

But it was hardly a free ride. For one thing, the State Department, by tradition and institutional authority, would take the lead in setting arms control policy. And arrayed against Perle was Richard Burt, who was the principal arms control theorist in the State Department. In this sense, the two were fated to be locked in conflict, and the tugging over INF policy frequently came down not to the secretary of state and the secretary of defense, but to Burt and Perle, or the two Richards, as they became known.

The two were a study in contrasts. Burt came into office at the tender age of thirty-three. Unlike Perle, he had never been in government before. He was also single.

Burt had developed a reputation as a defense intellectual covering national security affairs for the *New York Times*, and attracted the attention of the incoming Reagan team by virtue of his record of articles critical of SALT. He had been a good and incisive reporter, even though, according to one Carter official, Barry Blechman, Burt was a little too obvious with his sources (he met semiclandestinely at a Dupont Circle hotel with Carter NSC aides, and word quickly got around that this was where Burt received his information). But, like Perle, he had a natural grasp of the bedeviling intricacies of arms control.

Burt's features and manner were characteristically Anglo-Saxon. He stood lean and upright, his thick, prematurely gray hair combed back. His bland black-and-gold-striped Brooks Brothers ties gave him the look of a Wall Street banker, his only distinguishing fashion statement a bright red handkerchief dangling like a freshly blossomed flower from his breast pocket. His speech was controlled, his words carefully calibrated. Despite a lack of government experience, his natural talent and hard-driving personality enabled him to quickly establish himself as a serious policy player. On the flip side, his smarts were often marked by a moodiness and arrogance. He was secretive, frequently kept his own staff in the dark, rarely smiled or gave credit to colleagues, and earned a number of lasting enemies for poaching on their turf. Some Burt watchers described him as immature, but the appellation coined by one member of the media, "Mr. Smoothy," fit just as well.

All told, Burt's greatest strengths were not his obvious smarts, but an ability to reinvent himself and deftly cater to his audience; one day he was an Atlanticist, preaching the virtues of alliance politics; another day, he was a hard-liner, warning against the dangers of Soviet power. Fundamentally, his instincts were Republican centrist, which is to say they were grounded in a philosophy partially conservative but served up with a generous dose of pragmatism, more characteristic of the old establishment than of the Reagan counterestablishment.

In politically charged Washington, where some members of the administration were painted as the black hats, others as the white hats, he actively cultivated the latter reputation. (Indeed, he mastered the art of the perfect Washington pander on the Hill, playing the victim of Jesse Helms: "I'm not worried about the Democrats," he would confide innocently to Democratic congressmen. "It's Jesse Helms and the far right we have to look out for.") And philosophically Burt differed from Perle. He believed in the inherent virtues of arms control, and felt that the diplomatic process was every bit as important as the result.

All this in itself would have not made Burt a match for Perle. What evened the score was the fact that Burt was a dogged bureaucratic infighter. He also was not above misleading Perle, State Department colleagues, and even the secretary of state to achieve his goals. By most accounts, he did this without shame or remorse. Noted one official, "If Burt were a tennis player, he would be the type who could call a close line call 'out.'"

Once, Burt mocked an administration colleague who talked to him about "fair play" and respect for the "chain of command" in the policy process.

"Who cares about that?" Burt laughed, throwing his head slightly back in a guffaw. "What matters is winning."

From the beginning, Perle and Burt would clash.

To THE OUTSIDE world, Perle and his office often radiated the confident appearance of a well-organized juggernaut. But inside the Pentagon, its reputation was initially the diametric opposite. Perle's slightly bohemian ways and distaste for organizational detail gave the appearance of haphazard sloppiness. But, consistently, the best ideas and the best proposals on defense and the Soviets came from Richard Perle's shop.

Perle inspired loyalty and dedication among those who worked with him and served under him. The office buzzed with activity seemingly at all hours, and the people who worked in it became every bit as closely knit and dedicated to the cause of winning the Cold War as the staffers who had labored back on the Hill in the Scoop Jackson Bunker. Like the Bunker, Perle's office was a freewheeling place, unbureaucratic, bound as much by a sense of friendship as a sense of mission. And just as "Scoop" had been the leader of his staff, so "Richard" was the leader of his. What made it work was Perle's low-key style combined with his big-picture thinking and relentless ability to focus. More often than not, when there were problems with other offices or areas, aides would say that it simply needed "PTT"—Perle's tender touch.

One of the initial challenges for Perle and ISP was simply containing the endless bureaucratic routings and paperwork. That job fell to Bill Hoehn, a former vice president of the Rand Corporation. Unlike Bryen, who was Perle's policy deputy, Hoehn's primary duty was to manage the day-to-day. When he arrived, Hoehn was appalled at what he saw, confiding that "everything was screwed up." The record of the paper flow was completely chaotic, and there seemed to be no logic to Perle's handling of the huge quantities of paperwork that passed through his office. Perle was constantly on the phone, made no notes, often didn't inform people of what he discussed, and was usually behind in his work ("I'll confess I'm guilty," Perle often joked).

On his very first day on the job, Hoehn was startled to receive a heads-up call from the military executive aide to Defense Secretary Weinberger himself.

"You've inherited a real mess down there, let me tell you. You'll really have to fix it," Colin Powell, Weinberger's military assistant, told Hoehn.

To bring some order to the giant system, Hoehn tried to develop a tracking system to monitor the paper flow to Perle. Every night, he would try to debrief Perle on the day's events. He also made sure at the day's end that Perle's briefcase would have the urgent documents requiring immediate attention. If necessary, he had a Pentagon car take documents to Perle's home in Chevy Chase.

But Hoehn also quickly learned there was a systematic routine to Perle's methods. His focus was single-minded. Unlike other government officials who invariably became prisoners of administrative detail, Perle never got bogged down, never strayed from his priorities. Early on, he set the highest standards for arms control proposals to be tabled and agreements to be negotiated. He wasn't willing to settle for second best, not in ideas, not in outcomes, and most certainly not in himself. Hoehn saw that it was the mysterious key to Perle's effectiveness.

Indeed, there were two levels to the office, what Perle and his inner circle did, and what the rest of the staff did. There were thus insiders and outsiders. While Perle engineered the strategy, often known only to his insiders, the others did everything else, from preparing briefing books, writing congressional reports, and decoding cables.

Perle was an extremely considerate boss, who cared about his subordinates. His low-key style reflected a generosity and grace rare in Washington. Bob Joseph, a disheveled professor who had come to the Pentagon under Carter brimming with ideals and idealism and was deeply disappointed by Carter's failure to secure an arms control agreement, was completely won over by Perle and his arguments, becoming an ardent staffer and supporter. Read Hammer, a retired army officer, whom colleagues deemed "your model upstanding citizen type" because of his high standards of integrity, became one of Perle's most trusted aides. John Woodworth, also low-key and a respected arms negotiator, became another Perle admirer and often praised his boss with glowing adjectives. In all, Perle's list of supporters was long.

And the spokes of Perle's reach extended far beyond his own office. Over the years, he had cultivated a wide network of allies, friends, and informants throughout the administration, the intelligence community, and Capitol Hill, who reported to Perle in the same breath that they reported back to their own offices. They were called "Perle's mafia."

But all this had a purpose: affecting the outcome of U.S. policy. And for all the outward chaos of Perle's office, on the big issues, it smoothly positioned Perle to dominate U.S. arms control decisions.

PERLE'S STEELY DETERMINATION on arms control and his high standards for any arms agreement were evident to Hoehn from the outset. At his first Interagency Group (IG) meeting, which included participants from Defense, State, ACDA, and other relevant government agencies, Hoehn made the mistake of offering what he thought was a routine concession to Burt. He felt it was nothing significant, and it could lay groundwork to establish that the two could work with each other.

That evening Hoehn mentioned it to Perle in his day-end debrief. Hoehn even spiced up the story, noting that "Burt gave up something in return as well."

Perle leaned forward and looked Hoehn in the eye. In his mellifluous voice, Perle said, "Bill, I don't want you ever to give anything up. If it deadlocks the entire policy process, that's fine. If we don't get agreement on our terms, we just don't do it."

Perle paused, and then firmly explained. "If DoD doesn't get its way, we'll kick it up to the highest level, to the SIG [Senior Interagency Group meeting] or to the NSC. Then Cap will have his way."

Chastened, Hoehn signaled his agreement and began to walk out. As he reached the door, Perle injected softly, speaking, it seemed, more in sorrow than anger, "No deviations of this policy will be tolerated."

Only in the coming months did other patterns of Perle's style become understandable to Hoehn. Perle held his priorities close to the vest, sharing them only with his intimates. Most of his instructions were oral, not written.

Perle was always careful how he treated his employees, but if they failed to earn his trust or confidence, they often got what Hoehn referred to as "the dog-work": cable traffic; responding to numerous congressional inquiries. And they were not sent to IG meetings.

When pressed, Perle could even be slightly more Machiavellian. On important, contentious issues, Perle would strengthen his hand by setting his staff to work on issues that were at odds with his own priorities. This strategic deception was a carefully calibrated attempt to ensure that his hand for bargaining in crucial interagency meetings wouldn't be accidentally revealed at lower levels.

In those raw, life-and-death early days, one of these highly important and contentious issues was the INF missile controversy.

IN THE LATE spring and early summer of 1981, with the momentum of public sentiment moving toward arms talks, the U.S. commitment to the NATO deployments was at risk. That was also the message of the peace marches dotting Europe's capitals. Tensions were escalating.

In an effort to diffuse the opposition, Secretary of State Haig, with the president's authorization, had already publicly announced that the U.S. intended to begin negotiations with the Soviets by year's end. Watching events unfold, Perle felt the solution to the stalemate would be found as much in a political answer as in a military one. And a political answer dictated a political strategy. But what?

Returning from a high-level NATO meeting in Brussels, Perle knew negotiations were a foregone conclusion. What was now needed was something startlingly new to bring to the table. The stakes had to be raised.

On the plane, he roused himself from a catnap, and pushed a briefcase of position papers aside. The sky was pitch black, and as the plane flew over the water below, he collected his aides around him like a football huddle.

"What if there's no deployment?" he asked Lou Finch. Finch was a graduate of the Air Force Academy, but his political instincts were liberal. A systems analyst who had done targeting for U.S. bomber runs during the Vietnam War, he remained a devoted arms controller. Hardworking, he was thin as a rail, with a jutting jaw, and a habit of repeatedly clearing his throat when he was nervous.

"It would be the end of the alliance," Finch said.

"But we need an arms control track to make deployment politically palatable?" Perle responded.

"Absolutely."

"So what are the options?"

For two hours they talked about INF negotiating possibilities, surveying "missile throw-weights," "nuclear equivalence," "stability at equal levels," "counting rules," and "global limits." Perle just kept shaking his head, no, no, no. Exhausted, one aide finally burst out, "Is there an agreement you can imagine that would be in our interest?"

"No," Perle said, leaning back in his seat. There was a long pause. Perle knew that this was not an acceptable answer. Governments need to be for things, not just against them.

The aide, flustered, was silent.

Suddenly, a smile crossed Perle's face. "That's it," Perle said, wagging his index finger in the air. It was then that he resolved to commission a study to assess the bottom line for U.S. security requirements, to see just how low both sides could go.

BACK IN WASHINGTON, Perle, unwilling to watch events overtake him, pondered the options. He thought DoD had to table a proposal that would be a real eye-opener, a real show-stopper. It would be his gambit to take control. Otherwise, he would be outmaneuvered by the State Department, which was peddling a plan that called for "reductions to the lowest possible equal level." Perle thought this was not nearly strong enough to curb the defeatist impulses gripping Europe like a vise, let alone to enhance U.S. chances for getting a good arms deal.

In late August, Burt made a presentation calling for exactly what Perle feared: "reductions" at "equal levels." To Perle, statements like this and bland NATO press releases looked weak and impoverished next to dire Soviet claims that the "U.S. is willing to fight to the last European." More than that, they sounded downright inhumane.

Something had to be done to radically alter the arms control mix, to change traditional thinking. Perle mentally reviewed nearly four decades of Soviet-American relations, starting from Averell Harriman's belief, from which he and others of his generation had often strayed, that the Soviets did not necessarily consider pliable negotiators to be friends— nor did they regard tough negotiators as enemies. But much had happened since Harriman had made that determination in Moscow in the middle of World War II. And negotiations had very much changed since Averell Harriman's days in Spasso House, working in his bathrobe and

Moroccan slippers, clipping shrubs and shoveling snow to get a bit of exercise in the grim Moscow cold.

There was the image of a smiling John McCloy, floating arm in arm in the water with Nikita Khrushchev at the Black Sea resort of Sochi, only one and a half years before the Cuban Missile Crisis threatened nuclear war. More recently, there was the image of Carter's arms negotiators, ambling naked into the sauna with their Russian counterparts, before the invasion of Afghanistan. To Perle, it was quite clear that idle talk, vodka, toasts, dips in the ocean, and steam baths had not done much to draw the Soviets and the Americans away from the edge of nuclear war.

What seemed to be needed was a complete realtering of U.S. arms control positions and posture. What was needed was something daring, something meaningful, something that would speak not just to parliamentarians and officials but to protesters, shop owners, school kids, and ordinary citizens, something straightforward that his late father, standing among fabric bolts, would have nodded his head at and understood. Powerful and clear, this would be something to push the Soviets and the Americans from their high-stakes confrontation over Europe.

That August night after Burt's proposal, as Washington lay enveloped in the heavy residue of summer's heat, Richard Perle sat at his desk in his house. Before him stood a stack of studies by Pentagon analysts. Sipping a mug of strong, dark-roast coffee, he pored over the papers.

The evening wore on. Leslie and his young son, Jonathan, had long since gone to bed. But Perle was working. He had found what he was looking for. One cogent analysis. It argued that there were only 150 truly important facilities—i.e., airfields, naval bases, operational headquarters, nuclear weapons storage sites—within the boundaries of the European NATO nations. With three warheads on each SS-20 missile, the Soviets needed only fifty missiles to wipe out these key targets. To be militarily significant, then, any reduction would have to go below fifty Soviet missiles.

That's it, Perle said to himself. Perle picked up the phone to call the study's authors. It was already well past midnight. Groggy, and somewhat annoyed at having been awoken, the authors were nonetheless able to support their analysis.

Sitting in the quiet of his house, Perle saw the answer: zero missiles on both sides. Propose that both the U.S. and the Soviets lower their missile levels in Europe to zero. For the Soviets, it would mean dismantling their SS-20s. In return, the U.S. would not deploy any INF missiles. It was bold and simple, and would solve the military and political problem at the same time. It would put the Soviets on the defensive; it would have staying power with the Europeans. It would be clear, straightforward, and dramatic; it would enhance U.S. security; and it could be verified. After all, he thought, if the Soviets, who had called for a missile moratorium, were serious about halting the arms race, why wouldn't they do away with the missiles that had forced NATO to make the INF decision in the first place? Just get rid of the whole lot, on both sides. This was principled, it was secure, it was right. And, Perle added to himself, no matter how strong the pressure, this time the U.S. had to be willing to stand at the brink, and not back down.

Working into the early hours of the morning, Perle wrote up the proposal into a memo, entitled "A Defense Proposal." He sent it to Weinberger via his immediate superior, Fred Iklé. He also made plans to introduce it into the IG meeting with Rick Burt.

How could Burt, or anyone else, possibly reject this? he thought, turning off his desk light before he retired to bed.

In early October on a Monday, Perle readied himself to present the proposal to the IG group, which would be meeting at the State Department. John Woodworth, the office of the secretary of defense's representative to the upcoming U.S.-Soviet missile talks in Geneva, was sitting in Perle's office, waiting to accompany Perle to the meeting.

With a satisfied smile, Perle told Woodworth, "I want to introduce this at today's meeting. Take a look."

"My God," Woodworth thought upon reading it. It was a brilliant document, revolutionary in scope. And, "all the politics are right." Woodworth also noticed that Perle had labeled it "A Defense Proposal." In the yin and yang of policy making, this was an audacious act. Only when the military side of the Pentagon, the Joint Chiefs of Staff, have signed off on a proposal, is it formally labeled a Department of Defense proposal; otherwise, it's called an OSD, or Office of the Secretary of Defense proposal. The chiefs had not yet signed off. Perle was clearly trying to speed this through the system, and wasn't willing to countenance any more bureaucratic delays.

At the meeting, Woodworth was convinced that Burt, the co-chair along with Perle, was in one of his more imperious moods. More than usual, he was dismissing colleagues' ideas with a haughty wave of the hand. And also as usual, the room was nosily packed, with almost twenty-five administration officials.

Perle plunked down his proposal and, speaking for the Pentagon, triumphantly announced, "This is our position." After a brief discussion, in which Burt said such a proposal "could never"—pause—"never be acceptable to the Soviets," he rejected it out of hand, even laughing it off.

Woodworth watched as Perle silently steamed. Perle was usually a soft-spoken, but eminently forceful, advocate for his positions. He knew the facts, frequently better than most people in the room. He could run with an idea and its logic, leaving everyone else behind. But today there was nothing he could do. It was clear that State was geared up to kill the proposal. Burt was firmly wedded to his "reductions at lowest possible levels." And, for now, Perle had no other hand to play.

TIME WAS RUNNING out if Perle was going to get his zero proposal accepted. From California to Vermont, the nuclear freeze movement was building at home, erupting into an unusually powerful, heartfelt, and vocal grassroots movement, which included everyone from college students to suburban homemakers to urban professionals among its ranks. It was a movement that could not be ignored. Increasingly worrisome, however, in Europe, the freeze movement was not just an influential democratic force, but showed signs of becoming unstable, with some protests taking on a violent tone. The previous March, a U.S. security headquarters outside of Frankfurt was attacked, and firebombs were thrown at an armed forces employment facility in the city itself. On August 18, small pipe bombs had exploded at an American garrison in West Berlin. Only minor damage was caused, but it shook everyone up.

But it was on August 31 that U.S. policy makers became clearly unnerved. At 7 A.M., as most of the staff members of the Ramstein Air Force Base, the headquarters of the NATO Air Command in Central Europe and the largest U.S. air base on the continent, were filing in for work, a powerful explosion occurred. Brigadier General Joseph D. Moore, walking by, shouted as the hood of a car was blown over the top of a four-story building and 580 windows were blown out of two other structures. Ambulances rushed twenty-two people to the nearest hospital.

The next day, protesters violently struck again. Seven cars belonging to U.S. military personnel in Wiesbaden were overturned and then set on fire, to continuous anti-American chants. As a sign of displeasure over the failure of the Social Democratic party to take a firmer stand against the missile deployments, its Frankfurt offices were gutted. Tables were smashed, typewriters thrown through windows, files spread out over the floor. Then the building was set on fire. Thick black smoke billowed into the sky. Before fleeing, the protesters had pulled out cans of spray paint and scrawled anti-American slogans on the brick walls outside the burning building.

. . .

BUT EVEN IN the face of such turmoil, Richard Perle was not going to give up on his zero-option proposal—especially not now. If Rick Burt was going to stonewall the plan at State, he, Perle, would go higher. One man, Cap Weinberger, could take the zero option straight to the president.

CHAPTER 11

No sooner had Perle tabled the "zero option" proposal than the State Department began calling its own position "zero plus." This formulation, crafted by Burt, sought to give the appearance of boldness, like Perle's plan. But it also indicated a clear willingness to agree to a number far higher than zero. Burt's contention was simple: the Soviets would never accept zero. To have negotiations, the U.S. had to be willing to give some ground.

Perle disagreed. If the administration let it be known that it would settle for something higher, that's what would happen. Perle believed the bottom line in any negotiation had to be U.S. national interests, rather than simply whatever the Soviets would accept. Tabling zero and then backing away from it would guarantee that the Soviets would reject zero. It would also likely embolden the Soviets to seek terms that would preserve their military superiority in Europe. Perle believed the U.S. should seek to prevent that at all costs.

But Perle's plan still faced tough obstacles. Burt's veto had made other officials in the administration wary, even hostile, toward zero. It also didn't help that the government was now losing control of the public INF debate at home.

In a speech about international trade before the Philadelphia World Affairs Council, the president himself was besieged by protesters. Off-the-cuff, a smiling Reagan told the antinuclear hecklers, "I spoke here in 1975 and there wasn't an echo."

The hecklers shot back, yelling before the crowd of seven hundred business and civic leaders: "Are nuclear weapons the key to peace?" They also unfurled a banner: "Nuclear Weapons Bring Death To All The World's Children."

In this increasingly charged atmosphere, the formal Soviet-American discussions, slated to open in Geneva on November 30, 1981, were on virtually everyone's mind. After the bristling anti-Soviet rhetoric of the earliest days of the Reagan administration, for the public at large, the talks had become an important symbol of a new push toward peacemaking.

IN TRUTH, NEGOTIATORS had already been in Geneva for several months, conducting preliminary discussions with the Soviets.

One member of the negotiating team was John Woodworth, the Department of Defense representative to the talks. A career civil servant, thin and square-jawed, Woodworth had moderate political instincts, a wry sense of humor, and was the consummate professional. He was a team player, and was well liked by his colleagues. Unflappable and conversant in the details of the INF issue, he was a model negotiator for the U.S.

When he returned to Washington at the start of fall to discuss the state of play, Woodworth was surprised by the vehemence of the State Department, "ranting and raving about the slow pace of tabling a proposal," as he later characterized it. State seemed to want a proposal at any cost, even if it was rash and incomplete. They were, he thought, seriously misreading the Soviets.

Woodworth told Perle as much in a debriefing. The Soviets are not interested in negotiations, Woodworth said. "They spend most of their time lying to us about their military assets. Their only interest is in blocking the deployments."

"We just need to hang tough," Perle told Woodworth.

He paused, and asked, "Tell me, what happens if we deploy?"

Woodworth could see Perle was grim. "They say they'll walk out. I think they mean it," he replied.

"That's all right," Perle said. The gravity in his voice was palpable. "Just keep repeating our position once it's tabled. That's the only way to get to an agreement." Woodworth knew exactly what Perle was saying. This time, too much was at stake, not simply U.S. security, but the NATO alliance, and the entire military balance in Europe. This time, the U.S. could not back down.

The two men continued, both deadly serious. Then Perle seized the moment. His eyes twinkling, he added, with a touch of levity, "You know, the talks should be held in Helsinki, not Geneva. We get better press there."

Woodworth chuckled to himself. Perle could be completely outrageous sometimes. But he could also be completely right.

.   .   .

WOODWORTH HAD MADE the transition from the Carter to the Reagan administration, and counted himself as one of Perle's mafia. But he was surprised at how uninterested Perle was in the actual talks themselves. He knew Perle felt the U.S. compromised itself by the mere act of sitting down with the Soviets. More than that, he was struck by Perle's unshakable, almost religious faith in his positions. The fact that the State Department considered Perle totally outlandish didn't bother him in the least. He wore it like a badge of honor. Talking to Perle, Woodworth couldn't help but think that Perle was ultimately a loner, single-handedly seeking answers to the problems bedeviling the alliance.

But Woodworth had the sense that Perle was on top of his game with his zero option. Despite the views at State, at Defense, many rumors about the plan were traveling through the grapevine, and key people felt Perle had an ace up his sleeve. Perle, however, knew exactly where the zero-option proposal stood. With Burt holding it up in the interagency process, it would have to go straight to the president, if it were ever going to get a hearing in the administration, let alone be accepted.

IN EARLY OCTOBER, Perle, Woodworth, and Colin Powell were slated to join Weinberger for an eleven-day tour through Europe, designed to counteract the unease sweeping the continent, as manifested relentlessly in the growing West German demonstrations. They would make stops in Paris, Sweden, then on to Scotland for a NATO meeting, the tour culminating with discussions in London.

Before leaving, Perle put the final touches on a follow-up memo for Weinberger elaborating the rationale for a zero option. Edwin Meese, the president's White House counselor, had been impressed by Weinberger's initial presentation of the zero option. He had asked the defense secretary for more. Could an additional paper be done? Weinberger asked Perle to do a draft.

If Weinberger liked Perle's exposition, the secretary would then present it directly to the president for a follow-up discussion.

In all likelihood, this was the last route left—and his last shot—at influencing the U.S.'s opening position before the INF talks officially began on November 30. Perle felt he had to make the most of it. He put the finishing touches on the redraft and waited impatiently.

AS SUNSET DESCENDED, the slivers of final light gave Andrews Air Force Base a soft glow. Before boarding, Perle helped himself to a complimentary black coffee in a Styrofoam cup off the bar in the VIP lounge. The military assistants stood on edge, awaiting the arrival of Weinberger's car. Off in the distance, the cargo was being loaded into the secretary's plane, a souped-up C-135 that had once served as President Johnson's Air Force One.

As they began ascending, the pilot turned off the PA system, which had been blaring Willie Nelson's "On the Road Again." The song was Powell's choice, used to kick off all foreign trips. Some Reagan aides thought it an odd choice; Willie Nelson was, after all, Carter's favorite singer. But Weinberger didn't mind, so the song stayed. Because the weather was now turning chilly, Perle slipped a parka over his jacket to fend off the first gusts of winter.

Once aloft, Weinberger shuffled to the front of the plane and motioned to Perle to join him in his private compartment.

Perle reached into his attaché for a set of three-ring binder briefing books, the latest cable traffic, a yellow legal pad, and felt-tip pens. After he had briefed the secretary on each leg of the trip, Weinberger said, "There's one more thing to discuss," and he flopped a paper on the table.

Perle's heart began to race. It was his zero-option paper, redrafted under Weinberger's name, to be submitted to the president from Stockholm, via Edwin Meese. Meese would see to it that the president got the proposal without Haig or Burt intercepting it. Bingo. Perle was elated.

"I'm going to send this from the plane overnight by cable," the secretary said. "I'd thought you might want to have a read first." Perle scanned the memo. There was one major change, a handwritten passage from Weinberger that read, "The President will certainly be nominated for, and very likely be rewarded with, the Nobel Peace Prize if this proposal is accepted."

Perle looked over to the secretary. Weinberger gave an almost imperceptible nod. "He's going to need this for when the going gets rough—and it will get rough," Weinberger said. "It's good work, Richard. I hope the president accepts your proposal."

Restless with excitement, Perle could barely sleep the rest of the night. Weinberger and Reagan were perfectly in sync on these issues. It was unlikely, barring some completely unforeseen act, that anything could derail the president from accepting zero now.

GLENEAGLES IS AN elegant, sprawling golf resort nestled among the rolling green countryside and mists of Scotland, the country that invented the game. On one end is a chalky white castle dating back to the late Middle Ages, when bands of highlanders still roamed the land.

For most of its modern existence, Gleneagles was more commonly known as a leg on the Professional Golf Tour, rather than as a site of a NATO ministerial meeting.

The responsibility for hosting the NATO Nuclear Planning Group's annual meeting of defense ministers rotated from country to country. The event, which was invariably held in lavish places, was typically exorbitant. Fine wines and foods were always served. In the Pentagon, the Nuclear Planning Group ministerials were more commonly known as the "Nuclear Party Group" meetings. And in this case, despite the grimly serious agenda of INF deployments and strategy, it was clear that the British had spared no expense.

Helicopters busily ferried the defense ministers and their aides to Gleneagles. The press came in by bus. Security was everywhere. Police sharpshooters, rifles visibly displayed, took their places on the ramparts of the castle; hundreds of police supported by army intelligence and antiterrorist specialists cordoned off the resort. The security was so tight that the British joked the meeting was being held behind "the tartan curtain." But, privately, British officials confided their fears that Britain could be disrupted by the kind of demonstrations or bombings by antinuclear protesters that had been wracking West Germany.

Within NATO, however, Britain remained America's strongest ally. The links between the two nations had been tightened by the deep and special bond emerging between Margaret Thatcher, the grocer's daughter who was now prime minister, and Ronald Reagan. The "Iron Lady" and her conservative soulmate across the Atlantic would form the bedrock of the NATO alliance.

On Tuesday, on the eve of the official meeting, twenty-five protesters showed up at Gleneagles, and security redoubled its precautions. One American official was reprimanded for taking pictures from his bedroom window. That same day, Perle and Woodworth went for a stroll. When they wandered off a marked path to speak without any chance of being overheard, they were promptly found and dressed down by the police. They were told they were lucky they weren't shot.

For the meeting each national delegation was assigned an office, as well as a secure telephone, typewriters, and copy machines. But the crux of the work at this ministerial would be the communiqué released at the end of the two days. A consensus document that often reads blandly, communiqué writing itself was often a rancorous battleground of debate. The world was waiting to see if the NATO defense ministers would ratify the decision to proceed with the INF deployments, or if they would call for accelerated arms control talks.

The American delegation hoped the meeting would be uneventful. An acrimonious public spat among the allies would only weaken NATO's position. Besides, the real action was now in Washington, where the zero-option cable awaited the president. Going into the meeting, Perle saw little reason to be concerned. Everything was on track.

THE CALM OF the meeting was shattered before it even began.

The previous Friday, President Reagan had met with regional newspaper editors in Washington, principally to discuss U.S. policy toward Saudi Arabia. But some questions deviated from the main subject. One editor asked whether a nuclear war in Europe would spread to the United States. The president responded, accurately but indelicately, if not unwisely. "I don't honestly know. I could see where you could have an exchange of tactical weapons against troops in the field without it bringing either one of the major powers to pushing the button."

The transcript of the session was released on Saturday, and virtually ignored in the American press. At the *New York Times*, the statement merited only an afterthought, two small paragraphs tacked onto the article. But when the quote was picked up by the European press, two days later, it was front-page, banner headline news. The American president, European coverage indicated, was suggesting that a nuclear war could be confined to Europe. This touched a raw nerve among the growing European opposition to the proposed missile deployments.

The furor overshadowed the first day of the ministerial, and Weinberger was forced to convene a hastily arranged meeting with European and American correspondents. To his dismay, British Defense Secretary John Nott and West German Defense Minister Hans Apel initially refused to respond to the reporters' questions. Weinberger was thus forced to walk up to the microphone and field the questions himself.

Standing erect and looking determined, Weinberger tried to downplay the story, saying, "The attempts to make this into some sort of very large news story I think are quite wrong."

But the reporters didn't let up. "Mr. Secretary, don't you think the planned deployment of medium-range nuclear missiles appears to have increased European fears of a nuclear war?" one reporter shouted.

To Weinberger, it sounded more like a conclusion than a question. Stone-faced, Weinberger was privately annoyed. At times, he tired of how unremittingly hostile the press could be. And this was the wrong way to begin the ministerial.

"I don't think those fears are justified," he responded.

Another reporter fired back, "But wouldn't the United States seek to escape a nuclear war that began in Europe?" He aimed his cassette recorder right at Weinberger's mouth.

"That question is based on an assumption that totally overlooks one of the essential points: the U.S. has in Europe some 375,000 troops, and, with the families, well over a half a million people here."

Another reporter pressed, "Mr. Weinberger, do you think a tactical nuclear exchange could be confined to a limited nuclear war?"

The secretary had had enough. "This is a hypothetical, and I can't answer that," he said, declaring that the press conference was over.

Nott then finally waded into the stream of reporters to lend his support. "There are groups that may not agree with the alliance strategy, but overwhelmingly people in my country believe in NATO, support it, and support its strategy. This is the case in most European countries."

The press frenzy quickly died down. They weren't interested in Nott's comments.

FOR DINNER ON that first evening, the British had outdone themselves. Long buffet tables were arrayed with thick red ham, creamy mousses, cheeses, and exotic French pâtés. There was also an assortment of salad greens, a concession to the Americans, who seemed to like their vegetables raw.

Perle, an insatiable lover of smoked salmon, piled it on his plate, along with lightly fried bread thins. Then he maneuvered himself into a seat at a corner table, next to representatives from the German and British delegations. Woodworth was impressed with Perle's small talk and schmoozing. "This was Perle at his best," he thought.

Perle, however, had a second agenda. He wanted to suggest to the allies that they undertake a strong public relations campaign to dampen the European protests. His colleagues signaled that they too thought this was a good idea. It looked like it would fly.

As the evening wore on, rigid formalities and diplomatic caution dissipated slightly. Talk and information flowed a bit more freely. And Perle caught a whiff of something that might undermine the entire zero option.

The acting Dutch defense secretary was circulating a paragraph for inclusion in the final ministerial communiqué. The paragraph called for scrapping the deployment of U.S. missiles in return for Soviet concessions, but not for the withdrawal of Soviet missiles. Secretary Hans van Mierlo had given this plan a name: "the zero-level option."

Perle was aghast. The plan had basically the same name, but it allowed the Soviets to keep their missiles. Presenting this plan as named in public would seriously threaten the real zero option, now waiting on the president's desk. In the next few hours, Perle's high-stakes arms control gambit would be undone—unless the Dutch were stopped. Anxious, Perle went looking for Mierlo.

What the Dutch minister told him did not reassure Perle. Perle decided to stake out tough territory. "We will categorically oppose your zero-level option," he said.

Mierlo did not back down. "If you must," he replied. "But you should know our reasons. We are supposed to respond to the wishes of the people. It is important that Europeans see that we are striving to reach their goal of disarmament."

The Dutch were a dead end.

PERLE SOUGHT OUT Mory Stewart of the British Ministry of Defense. The two huddled in an isolated conference room. "Can I speak to you in the strictest confidence?" Perle asked plaintively.

Stewart chuckled, hungrily eyeing his whiskey, and smiled. Perle knew that of course he could. The special relationship between the two governments had never been stronger. Perle explained everything.

"Any thoughts?" Perle asked. His eyes were pleading.

Stewart smiled again. He explained that Perle didn't have to worry about the Dutch because they rarely pushed very hard. This was all being done for show, to appease the peace movement in Holland. Not even the Dutch thought freezing the missiles at current levels was a good idea. Stewart suggested the real problem was not the Dutch but the Germans. And the way to deal with them was not to work around them, but to tell them everything. "They'll come around," he said.

"But," he added, "it would be better if someone other than an American spoke to them."

"So what next?" Perle responded.

"Let me be of some assistance here. I shall request that the NATO secretary general speak to the Germans. That should resolve the issue at hand."

A nervous Perle waited for Stewart to work his magic.

The next day, the Dutch paragraph was quietly whittled down to a single, innocuous sentence at the end of the communiqué, blandly referring to a long-term goal of the "zero level." There was no public fight. Nevertheless, the *New York Times* portrayed this lone sentence as a colossal Dutch victory, and a clear defeat for Weinberger. Perle snickered when he read the story. If only the editors knew what was to come.

. . .

PEACE MARCHES CONTINUED to spread across Europe, angrier, rowdier, more anti-American. On October 10, 250,000, young and old, jammed into public squares in West Germany to protest the missiles. On October 24, as Weinberger and Perle were in London, preparing to return home, 150,000 demonstrators descended upon Hyde Park, chanting.

In Washington, after Gleneagles and the protests, the mood was bleak. But Perle returned home privately optimistic.

BY NOVEMBER 12, President Reagan himself had decisively settled the debate. He liked Perle and Weinberger's zero option, and rejected the State Department's bid for zero plus. Perle had gone to the top and won.

It was decided that the formal announcement of the zero option would be made during a speech by Reagan at the National Press Club in Washington, the first-ever presidential address to be beamed live, via satellite, to Western Europe. The address was timed to have maximum impact on European television newscasts.

The initial reaction to the zero option was excited and positive. West Germany and Great Britain immediately embraced the proposal. But, with unusual speed, the Soviet Union rejected the zero option, rebuffing it as a "propaganda ploy." The ailing Brezhnev even gave an interview to the West German magazine *Der Spiegel*, in which he went out of his way to discredit the proposal.

With the Soviets appearing intractable, the euphoria and unity over zero began to crumble. The public protests and the threat of resolutions in West Germany rejecting the planned deployment of the missiles again dominated the headlines and the debate, as East-West politics played out mercilessly, like a brushfire engulfing Europe.

This was just the first salvo in the missile countdown. And the Soviets wanted the endgame to be clear from the start: if missiles were deployed, they would walk out. The stakes could not have been clearer. The risks could not have been higher.

CHAPTER 12

Cameras flashed as the black limousine drove out onto the airport runway to whisk away Paul Nitze and his wife. It was the end of November 1981 in Geneva. For the past several weeks, his jaw locked, his eyes peering, Nitze, the chief U.S. negotiator at the INF talks, had sat quietly through the debate over the zero-option. He made little comment about the announcement, opening his mouth only to note cautiously that the proposal was "a solid basis for continuing negotiations."

Nitze was trying to lie low. He believed that a negotiated agreement must be sought and could be attained, but he did not press his opinion openly. There would be time later.

For now, he was positioning himself. With the international community following every move at the INF talks, he would be in the spotlight as never before. He was determined to make the most of it—which meant securing an arms control deal. But in the afterglow of Reagan's zero option INF speech, it was better to keep his cards close to his vest.

The day before, he had stopped off in West Germany to confer with the German chancellor, Helmut Schmidt. As one of the architects of the NATO alliance in the 1940s, Nitze felt a special affinity for the Europeans. He was earnestly struck by what he was told. The mood in Bonn was dire. Schmidt, puffing on his pipe, warned Nitze sternly that there must be progress in the negotiations by the fall of 1982. "Otherwise," he said, "deployments would fail, and American policy would be doomed."

That night in Geneva, he conferred with the U.S. ambassador and members of his delegation. He and his wife, Phyllis, had a good hot meal, and set about turning their new apartment into a cozy home.

Reporters swarmed around him the next day. Geneva had become a circus. Was the zero-option negotiable? Did he have flexibility? He did, after all, have almost two years before deployment. Nitze waved the reporters aside, and he and the rest of his delegation slipped businesslike into the Soviet mission without saying anything substantive.

In his first meeting with the Soviets, a ninety-minute get-together, he proposed a news blackout that would preserve the confidentiality of the talks. The Soviets accepted. Even when the talks were at an impasse, the blackout could ensure that they would be able to continue discussions without the hot public lights fueling charge and countercharge, recrimination and counterrecrimination.

This, it could be said, was their first agreement.

Tipping his hand slightly, Nitze shuffled out before reporters that afternoon and held a news conference. Cameras clicked. He had announced to the Soviet delegation that he had come prepared "to leave no stone unturned," but he didn't say this to the reporters packing the room. Still, Nitze conveyed optimism, and it was an upbeat press conference.

Despite the blackout, news of Nitze's determined dedication soon became the talk of Geneva and then Washington. The phrase "no stone unturned" took on mythic qualities. This was the first leak. The talks under Paul Nitze had begun.

IT WAS AN impressive start for the seemingly ageless Paul Nitze. Lean, tanned, and with thick wavy white hair, he was in remarkable physical condition for a man of seventy-four. He still rode horseback on his spacious farm in Maryland and played back-to-back sets of tennis. Where younger, less spry members of the delegation were worn down by the rigors of the long hours and wearying days of negotiation, Nitze would seem to be just getting started.

During much of his career, he had pushed the U.S. to build a stronger defense against the Soviets. In this sense, he was both protégé and political son of Dean Acheson, his longtime mentor and dean of the establishment. Yet he was less of a hawk than he appeared, remaining ever willing to cut a deal with Moscow if it would enhance the balance of nuclear terror. His pragmatism was of the old establishment school, born out of an earlier era of the Wise Men, who solved problems outside of political consequences and parties.

His public service was also born very much out of the same milieu of wealth, privilege, and success. In the 1940s, he had already had a flourishing career as a banker on Wall Street, and then moved on to a series of high posts in State and Defense in every administration from Franklin Roosevelt's to Richard Nixon's. He was genuinely there at the creation, and steadily rose through the ranks. But he never realized his principal ambition, becoming secretary of state, perhaps because of his steely, often brusque and independent personality. Still, his distinguished record of bipartisan service gave him a rare aura in the Reagan administration as its elder statesman, the proud vestige of an earlier era that created NATO and the Marshall Plan.

He had thus entered the administration with a coveted status, providing him with an authoritative voice in the highest reaches of government, and enormous stature and influence with the press. He was the paragon of the smooth insider. Tough, an effective bureaucratic infighter, keenly knowledgeable, even a touch brilliant.

But curiously he was also by habit and temperament an outsider. He was always a cold warrior, even when it wasn't fashionable, and in this sense was most courageous. A negotiator in the SALT I delegation, he resigned over differences with Henry Kissinger. In the Carter administration, he was considered too hawkish, and did himself no favor by being rude and condescending to the presidential newcomer, Carter. Nitze was not offered a job. He subsequently opposed Paul Warnke, a dove and old colleague from the Johnson administration, as head of Carter's Arms Control and Disarmament Agency, and undertook the heresy of publicly questioning Warnke's very patriotism and fitness to look after American security interests. His attack on Warnke was so vehement that to many it reeked of McCarthyism. Such an outburst would not have been tolerated in most people. But Nitze was well connected and rich, and still a revered member of the establishment.

Passed over by the Democrats, he carefully positioned himself for a Republican White House. Within two years, Nitze the Democrat emerged as one of the leading theoreticians of the hard-line Committee on the Present Danger, and, along with Scoop Jackson and Richard Perle, became the leader of the crusade against SALT II. This was the ticket that landed him his job in the Reagan administration.

His enormous wealth and financial connections gave him a freedom and independence few other modern public servants could enjoy. Nitze could walk away from the job, or buck orthodoxy, without suffering the consequences. His public broodings, moody tirades, and occasional bursts of unseemly spite were given greater leeway, as if they were somehow quaint or little more than the charming idiosyncrasies of the rich and powerful.

If he wore the trademarks of the old establishment, Nitze also had its weaknesses. He was a cold man, uncommonly detached, with a bloodless quality, who inspired others more by his intellect and station in life, and less by his spirit or personal qualities.

Above all, he was vain. Members of the establishment traditionally owed their duty to the presidents who hired them, not to themselves. This was not just conviction, but credo. Nitze was not hampered by such doubts. At times, it seemed he was convinced that he alone, not the U.S. government, nor his president, understood the problems facing the Western alliance. From the outset of the INF negotiations, he insisted that he was not a mere vessel of negotiating instructions crafted in Washington, and that he be allowed to negotiate "seriously." By this, he meant that he felt any final INF agreement would have to favor the Soviets, given the massive advantage they already held in European nuclear deployments.

It is ironic that Nitze entered office to the great misgivings of liberals, who saw him as the devious arch-villain who opposed SALT, rather than as a hardheaded problem solver. But in time, it would become apparent that his credentials as a hawk would give way to these other stronger predilections, an insatiable desire to play to history, and, more immediately, to forge a compromise for an INF agreement.

THE ONE MAN who had great misgivings about Nitze was another anti-SALT democrat, and a protégé of Nitze's—Richard Perle. Ever since Perle first came to Washington in 1969 to work with Nitze on the Campaign to Save the ABM, he had admired him tremendously, both for his intellect, and his unquestionable, selfless service to his country. The two continued to keep in touch after Perle went to work for Scoop Jackson.

But doubts about Nitze lingered uneasily in Perle's mind as the INF talks were about to begin. Nitze, who had worked to secure funding for the ABM defense, then went on to negotiate tirelessly the 1972 treaty restricting ABMs. For all his hawkishness, Perle suspected that Nitze was, deep down, not just *a little too* pragmatic, but a man literally controlled by an abiding faith in logic, rather than a deep-seated philosophy or an appreciation of the illogic and complexity of international politics and ruthless foreign leaders. He tended to make the fatal error of imposing logic on situations ruled not by rationality but by predatory emotions and irreconcilable differences, and his political judgment was surprisingly superficial, if not downright naive. Both drawbacks could prove treacherous in arms negotiations. And if that were the case, it was destined that the two, Perle and Nitze, would eventually clash, however awkward such a confrontation might be.

Indeed, while official Washington seized upon the Perle-Burt rivalry, in truth, the Perle-Nitze rivalry would become far more profound, more intense, more complex, and ultimately of far greater historical significance.

But at the outset, their differences went largely unstated, and the two men, mentor and protégé, one destined to eclipse the other, circled each other warily, respectfully, carefully.

. . .

THE DAY AFTER the Geneva negotiations began, the newspapers carried stories hinting at flexibility in the U.S. position. The articles were based on unnamed State Department sources. Most people in Washington knew the principal source was Richard Burt. Testifying before the Senate Armed Services Committee, Perle sought to set the record straight.

Easing himself into the witness chair, he stated firmly that there was no middle ground between deployment of the INF missiles and the zero option. "We have gone to Geneva with a proposal that we can defend, and defend it we will. There has been much speculation in the press that Paul Nitze has left for Geneva with a fallback position to be tabled in the event that the Soviets do not embrace the president's proposal," Perle said.

He looked up at the senators, and with emphasis added, "I can assure you that these reports are false."

Perle's testimony was actually aimed at two audiences: the Congress and Paul Nitze. Perle had already confided to aides that one of the benefits of the zero option was its clarity; it was something that would fence in Nitze, and prevent creative freelancing. But stronger stuff was needed as insurance. With this testimony, Perle had publicly put Nitze on notice not to do anything rash.

It didn't come completely as a surprise to Nitze. Before he left for Geneva, he and Perle had talked frankly.

Perle told Nitze that he should "be prepared to tough it out for a long, long time," adding that "you must resist the temptation of an agreement for agreement's sake." This remained, as it had always been, a central Perle principle. Nitze mainly listened, scarcely venturing his own opinion. The talk made an impression on him. Some weeks later in Geneva, Nitze pulled John Woodworth aside, and dutifully confided, "You don't get anywhere in these talks without Richard." Woodworth later noted, "Perle was a hovering presence over Paul, and Nitze took Perle damn seriously."

Woodworth himself was given stern instructions by Perle. "Hold your position," he was told, "don't be afraid to keep repeating the same thing to the Soviets." Stuck between these two firmly encamped, almost opposing, parties, Woodworth felt caught. He knew he had to carry out his instructions and represent DoD, and in this sense, he was Perle's eyes and ears. He also agreed with Perle. But he had a responsibility to support Nitze as the leader of his delegation. Like Perle, he deeply respected Nitze. It was, at times, a miserable position. And by the next summer, it would, for Woodworth, only become more so.

Privately, Woodworth shared Perle's view that the Soviets were "not there to deal," but to stir the peace movement and block the deployments. And, here, Nitze had a troubling blind spot. He thought the Soviets might be bluffing and it was his job to smoke them out.

But Perle and Nitze did agree on one fundamental point: the talks had to be conducted in such a way as to help get a handle on restive public opinion in America and the explosive politics of Western Europe.

Deployment was not scheduled until almost two years later, leaving plenty of time for things to go wrong. Meanwhile, the informal deadline of progress by the fall of 1982, given to Nitze by Helmut Schmidt, was rapidly approaching.

WHATEVER ENTHUSIASTIC HOPES the start of the negotiations may have brought quickly dissipated once the two sides got down to business.

On February 2, 1982, the U.S. delegation formally presented a draft of the INF treaty based on the zero option. The Soviets tabled their own draft proposal two days later. The two sides weren't even close.

Disingenuously, the Soviets claimed there was parity in European nuclear forces. They proposed that both sides reduce their arsenals down to three hundred weapons, including bombers and missiles. The Soviets would get there by reducing some aged ground missiles and bombers, and they would be able to retain their SS-20s. NATO, by contrast, would not only have to forgo the INF deployment, but the French and British, whose independent arsenals were not a part of NATO's, would be prohibited from expanding their weapons. This one-sided offer was as unacceptable to the Europeans as to the Americans. It was an all but transparent effort by the Soviets to disarm the European arsenal while also preventing U.S. deployments.

Through the tense first rounds of the talks, a cool stalemate continued. Week after week, the U.S. negotiators slogged through the talks with little progress in sight.

Then, on March 16, Leonid Brezhnev raised the stakes for the negotiations. If NATO deployed the U.S. missiles in Europe, he said in a speech, the Soviets "would retaliate." Exactly what form the retaliation would take was not spelled out. It was left to the American imagination to divine. But the implication was that there would be a grim repeat of the Cuban Missile Crisis, with Soviet missiles stationed somewhere off the American coast, this time perhaps in Nicaragua, or Soviet subs prowling the shores.

· · ·

ON MAY 7, 1982, President Reagan sought to calm the heightened international tensions. In contrast to his earlier scathing rhetoric about the Soviet Union, Reagan sent a personal note to Brezhnev, calling for a mutual effort to wind down the arms race. But this had little effect on the INF talks.

The talks themselves quickly degenerated into a tiring monotony, with the same positions being rehashed over and over. At first, this didn't bother Nitze, who felt the climate of the opening discussion was as important as the substance. "They are negotiating, have been negotiating seriously from the very beginning," Nitze proclaimed after the first round. He and Yuli Kvitsinsky, the top Soviet negotiator, also developed a relationship that, if not warm, was certainly respectful and informal. The two even verbally jousted, often playfully, in informal talks and cozy meals with each other. But the opening feelers of the first round soon slid into the drudgery of the second round. May and June came and went. The talks were going nowhere.

After Brezhnev's announcement, Kvitsinsky had even blurted out to Nitze, "You Americans have no right to be in Europe at all." This was a direct affront to NATO, an alliance premised on a shared bond and indivisible interests between the West Europeans and the Americans. Now, with only a little over a year before the planned deployments, Nitze felt time was precipitously running out. So was his patience.

Nitze was also panicked. He was haunted by the specter of the alliance breaking up, much the way it almost had during the clawing days and nights of the 1961 Berlin Crisis. He continued to heed Schmidt's injunction that he must show progress by fall of 1982, only months away.

Nitze was convinced that the deadlock could be broken. But, for him, this meant not just creativity, but heresy: moving off of the zero option. But not yet.

Despite continuing missile protests in Europe, and the ever swelling nuclear freeze movement at home, the president, agreeing with Weinberger and Perle, insisted that the Soviets should and will eventually come around to zero. A year was still plenty of time in the chess game of negotiations.

But Nitze was not a chess player. He felt a change was necessary. He knew he had to be careful. But quietly, discreetly, just as Perle feared and even predicted, Nitze sought to take matters into his own hands, even at the risk of conducting vigilante diplomacy.

CHAPTER 13

Nowhere were peril and promise held in more tantalizing equilibrium than in introverted Geneva, which sat quietly in a cradle between the gray confines of the Communist East and the bustling fervor of the democratic West. Its very facade radiated serenity and discretion; trustworthy Swiss bankers with pince-nez; cosmopolitan vacationers from Italy and France in lounge chairs on the slopes of Lake Geneva; broad boulevards where slender women shopped, wrapped in Pierre Cardin silk scarves, pricey alligator shoes, and thick furs. But the undercurrent of the city teemed with a bristling tension, for it was the sparring ground where diplomats met and thrashed out the esoterica of nuclear arms control. And as the early anticipation of fall 1982 had given way first to disappointment, and then, by the summer of 1983, to worry, Paul Nitze made a risky decision: to open up secret, informal discussions with the Soviets—a back channel—and break the negotiating deadlock.

Yet Nitze lacked authorization to do so. President Reagan's policy was the zero option, and Nitze would be brazenly defying his negotiating instructions, unacceptable under any circumstances. Moreover, mishandling informal talks could dangerously backfire, sending the wrong signal to the Soviets, and dooming the prospects of any agreement. Floating a compromise in the wake of Soviet threats about walking out could reek of precipitous capitulation, not tough-minded negotiation. Handled wrong, this was dangerous stuff. The risks to the American side, as well as to Nitze personally, were enormous.

But Nitze felt the potential for a compromise agreement was there, and that the pressing challenge was to test the Soviets to assess where mutual interests might exist. Under current policy, he was convinced this would never happen. The zero option lacked flexibility, which is precisely what he felt he needed. His hands were shackled when they needed to be unleashed. So, however perilous, he decided to strike out on his own.

. . .

AT FIRST, NITZE kept his own counsel and moved slowly. He decided to rope Yuli Kvitsinsky, his Soviet counterpart, into private exploratory conversations. In doing so he would, he confided to Norman Clyne, a member of his delegation, open up a back channel in the front channel, his own negotiations. He convinced himself that this approach was neither inappropriate nor suspicious.

Nitze approached Kvitsinsky with a feeler, and asked him if the Kremlin were interested in a superpower summit between Brezhnev and Reagan in the fall. The answer was an obvious yes, as was the fact that only the INF accords could be a suitable basis for a get-together between the two great powers.

Then Nitze sought to draw his counterpart into the gambit. "Shouldn't we put our heads together to contribute to that possibility?" he queried. Kvitsinsky agreed. How to proceed—and how far—was still unclear. Only as one event led to another would this marionette dance of the diplomats unfold, becoming clearer—and more dangerous—only in bitter hindsight.

DAYS FOLLOWED. NITZE loosened the snare, and told Kvitsinsky of his negotiations a decade earlier in SALT I, when he and Alexander Shchukin had taken a private stroll in the woods in the attempt to break ground on the ABM negotiations. This anecdote, which ended happily with the ABM treaty, was meant not just as a symbolic tease, but to coax and reassure Kvitsinsky at the same time.

Kvitsinsky replied carefully. He invited Nitze and his wife, Phyllis, to dinner. Nitze took this as an important sign. He accepted.

The food was served in the Kvitsinskys' ambassadorial apartment in the Soviet mission. The two couples were joined at dinner by the Russians' teenage daughter. The mood was light, and the conversation stayed safely on a social level. The only sign of the undercurrent of tension was Kvitsinsky's wife, who nervously picked and pushed her food around. The wife and daughter then quietly excused themselves into the kitchen to prepare dessert and coffee. The rattling of dishes could be heard, but it was a long spell before they returned. They knew the drill, and so did Nitze.

Still sitting around the dinner table, Nitze plucked a crisp piece of plain white paper out of his coat pocket, unfolded it, and gave it to Kvitsinsky. He had written on it suggestions as to how the two could hash out an exploratory package. Kvitsinsky fingered it carefully and read intently.

Nitze asked if he had changes to make. Kvitsinsky shook his head no. But he didn't signal yes, let's go forward, either. He said he needed to sleep on it.

Several days later, the two delegations joined each other at a dinner. Kvitsinsky was fidgety and demonstrably nervous. Nitze felt he even looked depressed. This worried him. He suggested that they catch some fresh air after dinner.

Once dessert was served, and delegation members retreated to different corners of the room with snifters of textured brandy and a good cigar, the two men stole out to the patio for a chat.

"How confident are you," Kvitsinsky asked with awkward humor, "that everything we're saying isn't being overheard?"

"Pretty confident," Nitze said, and added, "but somebody may have put a listening device over there." He pointed to a rolled-up awning curled on the moist grass.

"Better to meet in the woods," Kvitsinsky said, alluding to Nitze's walk with his Soviet counterpart in SALT I. Nitze took this as the answer he needed. However anxious he appeared, Kvitsinsky was willing to deal.

ON JULY 11, Nitze was visited in Geneva by Eugene Rostow, the head of the Arms Control and Disarmament Agency and a close political ally. In fact, Rostow, also a hard-line Democrat and a leading light of the Committee on the Present Danger, a distinguished former dean of Yale Law School, and an undersecretary of state in the Johnson administration, was partially responsible for Nitze's appointment as negotiator. Haig had been against it, but Rostow had fought him tooth and nail in Nitze's behalf. It hurt his relations with Haig, but Rostow prevailed.

Bald and round-shouldered, with happy eyes, he had a generous spirit and large political vision, priding himself on being tough-minded in the nuclear age. Like Nitze, he too was descended from an earlier, more quaint generation of policy maker, raised on the idea of service to one's country. But unlike Nitze, he lacked smooth insider qualities, nor did he have the safety of a personal fortune to retreat to.

The two quickly became close political allies in the Reagan administration, each seeing himself as a steadying voice and a seasoned elder statesman. Rostow also agreed with Nitze that some flexibility on the INF talks was desirable, and in vague terms he and Nitze had already discussed this in Washington.

Now in Geneva, Nitze was more specific about his intentions. He told Rostow that a foundation for exploratory discussions with Kvitsinsky had been laid. Nitze had confided in no one else; he was operating, for all purposes, solo. Still, Rostow smiled at Nitze's intentions, and thought to himself, "This is vintage Nitze." He approved the plan, and even went further himself, seeking to coax along Kvitsinsky with flattery when the two met in their own discussions. Smiling playfully, he teased, "I've always had a special regard for ambassadors who have the foresight to propose changes in their own instructions."

The stage was set. For weeks, Nitze had privately scrapped the zero option and had been manipulating numbers and hypothetical agreements to assess where a U.S.-Soviet agreement might be found. Finally, he felt he had it, but he bided his time until the moment was right. Then he would spring it on Kvitsinsky.

One day, he and Kvitsinsky took a cruise aboard a tourist boat along Lake Geneva. There were too many other people around them, and a flock of birds hovered annoyingly above. It was pleasant, but things weren't quite ready. Another time, they walked in the botanical gardens across the street from the U.S. mission. Still, the magic moment wasn't there. The dance continued. They lunched together quietly in elegant Geneva restaurants, often bathed with classical music, and invited each other for dinner at their respective residences once again. It was an intricate mating process.

Finally, their chemistry—and the moment—clicked.

THE SWISS JURA Mountains near the French border were a favorite retreat for Soviet diplomats. The snow is powdery, the temperature rarely dips down to a bone-chilling cold, and cross-country skiing is world-class; it is also a place where Soviets clad in Vuarnet sunglasses and driving their own cars could meet their blond-haired mistresses, some notoriously foreign and from the West, for a tryst without fear of getting caught. In the summer, the pass turns loamy and lush, and young sightseers in backpacks and khaki shorts walk up the rugged mountains. On July 16, the serenity of this scene was punctuated by a long Soviet limousine crawling slowly up to the mouth of the mountains. It was carrying Nitze and Kvitsinsky.

They emerged from the car, and both paused briefly to see if they were being watched. They then took a long walk down a mountain. The car would meet them at the bottom.

They walked for an hour and discussed points they could agree on. They stopped to rest on a log, and as a drizzle splattered, the two negotiated on another piece of paper that Nitze presented, on which they scribbled an eleven-point package, a take-it-or-leave-it proposition. An INF deal was being hatched between the two men.

Nitze tried to allay Kvitsinsky's nervousness. "Maybe we'll both go to jail," he joked.

Kvitsinsky replied, "No American government would send Paul Nitze to jail, and I don't intend to go myself."

Kvitsinsky then took the initiative. "The next step is up to me," he said. "I must present this to my government." He asked Nitze where he would be on his return to the U.S. Nitze said he would go back to Washington, and then would be vacationing at his home in Bar Harbor, Maine. Kvitsinsky warned that the package might be rejected altogether or severely amended, and left it unclear as to when, if ever, there would be a reply from the Kremlin. Nitze, when he watched Kvitsinsky speed off in his limousine, took from the walk the impression that he would be contacted soon.

The deal was done.

Nitze had made a major departure from the official negotiating position without authorization or informing anyone in the State Department or the White House. It was unprecedented and potentially dangerous. Now it was just a question of waiting—and reaction.

IN WASHINGTON, ROSTOW went to the new secretary of state, George Shultz, who had taken over after Alexander Haig's forced resignation on June 25, and informed him in broad terms that Nitze had established the basis for what could be a breakthrough on INF. But Rostow only presented Shultz with a general idea of what actually had been worked out. The new secretary was still unfamiliar with many of the details of arms control, and was mired in his own frantic attempt to quell another impossible situation, the turmoil in Lebanon. Even so, he was taken aback. Shultz was annoyed at Rostow's report, but the fact was, the full story was still being withheld from the secretary of state. Even at this stage, the Nitze-Rostow partnership was engaging in bureaucratic deception.

The deceit continued when Nitze returned to Washington. Before giving full details to his colleagues in the government, Nitze waited for a Soviet response. He sat by the phone. It didn't ring. For the time being, it seemed that his personal diplomacy had failed.

Nitze knew he couldn't withhold information from his own government indefinitely. But he was also unwilling to subject his initiative and his methods to full criticism, so he devised a strategy. Nitze set out to bring it to the president's attention for action, while bypassing much of the rest of the government in the process. But this demanded an intricate plan, involving measured deception and covering his bureaucratic tracks.

He had already set this process into motion after his walk in the Swiss mountains, when he wrote two memcons, or memorandums of conversation. The first memo laid out his reasoning behind his initiative; it lacked specifics and gave no hint that he and Kvitsinsky had gone as far on their own as they had. The second memo was more specific, and included the full proposal that he and Kvitsinsky had negotiated and committed to paper. He sent only the first memo to Washington, pocketing the second until he felt the time was right.

At home, Nitze briefed the INF interagency group, but only went as far as the first memo. Then he called on Perle.

Perle had gotten wind that something was up, but only in the vaguest of terms. Perle and Nitze met in Perle's office. Nitze shrewdly—and tactfully—flattered Perle by debriefing him in the Pentagon, rather than on Nitze's home turf at the State Department or on neutral ground over a meal. As he spoke, Nitze was uncharacteristically subdued, not his usual forceful self. He was also cryptic, talking in the future tense, of how it might be necessary for both sides to move off their opening positions. This was hardly new information to Perle, and he didn't think much of the conversation. He already knew Nitze was jittery about the talks—that was, after all, why he warned him at the outset to be prepared "to tough it out."

At no point had Nitze mentioned anything out of the ordinary. To the extent Nitze suggested he and Kvitsinsky were exploring alternatives in theory, enough so that Kvitsinsky worried it "might jeopardize his career," Nitze was protecting himself. Even this was vague. When Nitze left, Perle regarded the meeting as a standard debrief. He wrote it off as just another example of Nitze's continued "angst."

So when Perle left Washington at the end of July for an arms control retreat sponsored by the Aspen Institute in Aspen, Colorado, he did so content in the knowledge that everything was on track for the zero option—or, barring that, for successful INF deployments.

EVENTS CONTINUED TO move fast in Washington. Nitze briefed Burt in far greater candor than he did Perle. He regarded Burt as a more sympathetic ally. But Burt smelled trouble, and upon hearing some of the story, ominously warned Nitze, "Watch your step." Nitze weighed Burt's reaction and came to a quick conclusion. Burt couldn't be relied on to go to bat for him. This left Nitze little choice. He would have to take the INF proposal straight to the White House.

By now, Nitze and Rostow had enlisted the help of James Timbie. Timbie, a committed arms controller and career aide at the Arms Control and Disarmament Agency, was more at home in the Carter than the Reagan administration. Perle, for one, had long watched Timbie skeptically, and worried that Nitze relied far too heavily on him for analysis.

The three prepared a presentation for the president. Timbie, who was more plugged in than Nitze's own delegation, was sworn to secrecy. Nitze and Rostow then met with Judge William Clark, the national security adviser, who had replaced Richard Allen at the White House. Clark was deeply conservative, but was an honest broker. Nitze felt he could be relied on to be fair.

Clark was flabbergasted at what he heard. He felt this "unauthorized departure" from administration policy was a flagrant breach of discipline on Nitze's part. Still, he said, what was done was done. To the extent that the Soviets may be willing to offer concessions, he agreed this had to be explored.

Clark said the issue had to be aired before the president. In the meantime, he warned Nitze to "stand down," and not to tell anyone. This, of course, presented a problem for Nitze. Rostow had already briefed Shultz, and Nitze was having lunch with the secretary the next day. He also was meeting with Weinberger, as well as with Fred Iklé over at the Pentagon. It was one thing to withhold information from Perle, quite another from the defense secretary and the secretary of state themselves. Nitze decided to ignore Clark's adjuration.

LIKE THE DEFENSE secretary himself, John Woodworth, the Office of the Secretary of Defense representative, was still in the dark about the walk in the woods. But when he saw that Paul Nitze was penciled in on the executive appointments calendar to meet with Weinberger, Woodworth decided to insinuate himself into the meeting. What the heck, he thought. Perle was away; the talks were getting nowhere; he felt he would be part of a routine debrief between the chief negotiator and the secretary. He got himself included in the meeting. But nothing had prepared him for how shocked—and deceived—he would feel about Nitze's actions.

Only the three were present—Weinberger, Nitze, and Woodworth—which was one too many for Nitze. Woodworth could see that Nitze was surprised to see him, it was written all over his face. It was only supposed to be Nitze and the secretary. He had come to the meeting intending to speak frankly, but Woodworth was a complicating factor. Woodworth was, after all, one of the members of his own delegation whom he had kept in the dark about the proposed deal. His presence suggested that Weinberger had gotten word of what had transpired. It also raised the disturbing possibility that Weinberger could use Woodworth's presence as a foil to embarrass Nitze. But this was Nitze's only meeting with the secretary, so he forged ahead.

Weinberger started out lightly, "Paul, I don't know how you have the patience to do this, to talk with the Soviets day after day."

Nitze smiled. Woodworth knew the old silver fox, as Nitze was sometimes called, loved the flattery.

Weinberger continued, "I really admire you for this, I know how hard this is."

Nitze played it cool, and stressed that the negotiations were challenging intellectually. He relished that part, he said.

Nitze then praised Kvitsinsky as a bright, careful negotiator, and capable of surprising. He was trying to build up to informing Weinberger about the events that had taken place.

Weinberger clearly thought there was little else of substance to discuss. He asked Nitze if he would be going to his summer home on the Maine coast. He also had a place there, and loved its crisp summers and rugged coast. They swapped Maine summer stories for a few minutes. Woodworth thought to himself, so this is what the rich talk about, their summer vacation retreats.

Finally, the conversation hit a lull. Nitze then slowly turned in his seat and looked over to Woodworth, squinting. His expression was sour. Woodworth averted his gaze, and just sat there sheepishly, with a deadpan look on his face. He pretended not to notice Nitze's expression.

Nitze then proceeded to tell Weinberger about the walk in the woods. Suddenly, it dawned on Woodworth that he wasn't supposed to be hearing this. As far as he knew, Perle still didn't know about it. Weinberger was evidently hearing about it for the first time. Jesus, Woodworth thought.

The secretary was far too careful to give an immediate response to Nitze without first analyzing the new information. He said very little.

The meeting came to a close. Measured solely by Weinberger's expression, it seemed uneventful, but Woodworth walked out of the office dazed. My God, he thought to himself. This is big stuff what Nitze did. He liked and respected Nitze, and considered him to be a distinguished public servant; he felt they got along well. But he had problems with some of the substance of the walk. And the bigger part of the problem was not what Nitze did, but the way he did it. This was serious.

"Holy shit," Woodworth thought, "Nitze just went off on his own, and putting aside all his elaborate explanations, essentially bypassed the entire government. He not only betrayed his own team, but concocted rules for himself. It's inexcusable."

Woodworth hung his head in thought. He knew there would be hell to pay for this. He was also convinced that Perle would not be happy when he heard the news—that is, once he did.

COOL AND COLLECTED, Nitze left and made his way to Fred Iklé's office. Perle was still out of town, and he felt that while Perle would only stonewall him, there was a chance he could bring Iklé around to his side. So where he had withheld information from Perle, he would lay it all out for Iklé. With a little bit of luck, Iklé could help bring Weinberger on board.

IN JULY, WASHINGTON is hot and frenetic. At a dizzying pace, Congress rushes to complete its work, so members can leave town to visit their districts and go on vacation. In August, the frantic rhythm of the capital shifts, and grinds to a near halt. This made the highly secretive meeting of the National Security Council that Clark convened in early August to review the Nitze proposal all the more extraordinary.

Neither Reagan nor Bush was there. But Shultz, Weinberger, Rostow, CIA chief William Casey, and General John Vessey, the chair of the joint chiefs, attended. Each participant was allowed to bring only a single deputy. To underline the importance of this meeting, Clark pointedly told the group "not to breathe a word of the meeting to anyone."

Rostow thought there would be problems with Weinberger. But Iklé, after hearing Nitze's brief, was cautiously supportive, and in advance of the NSC meeting urged Weinberger to keep an open mind. He said he would. In the NSC meeting, to virtually everyone's surprise, Weinberger indicated the proposal sounded interesting. It warranted further study.

With Weinberger at least temporarily on board, the group decided to explore the proposal in greater depth. Clark again cautioned everyone about secrecy. Only the participants and a designated deputy were to know. Weinberger indicated this was problematic. He and others in the room would need the technical help of staff. It was inevitable, he stressed. What he left unsaid was that he wanted to run the proposal by Perle, who was still in Colorado.

The stage was set for a meeting with the president, once further technical examination of the INF deal was undertaken. Despite the machinations and obstacles, Nitze felt his persistence was paying off, if not with the Soviets, as least with his own government.

· · ·

BACK AT THE Pentagon, as Weinberger predicted, secrecy eroded. Iklé tasked Bill Hoehn and Ronald Lehman, both on Perle's staff, to scrub the Nitze proposal for flaws.

Hoehn thought to himself, "Oh my God, this might be a serious flyer." He asked Iklé how the administration was going to play it. Iklé said there would be a meeting with the president in a matter of days, and the Pentagon had to be prepared to weigh in with its recommendation on the Nitze proposal. For now, he added, Weinberger was disposed to give the proposal consideration.

Hoehn was shocked. He rushed from Iklé's office to his own, closed the door, and asked not be disturbed. Things were moving fast. He played out the options. There was one option he knew he didn't have to mull over. Perle had to be informed. Rather than having his secretary dial the phone, Hoehn looked up the number and called Aspen, Colorado, himself.

CHAPTER 14

Richard Perle was happy to be away in Colorado. The unremitting pace of his job was affecting his family life. Unlike many senior government officials and others in Washington, he valued time with his wife, Leslie, and young son, Jonathan. But foreign trips, long-drawn-out weekdays at work, lonely weekends in the office, had taken a toll at home. Richard and Leslie rarely ate together, and he couldn't remember the last time they had seen a movie, as he had subsumed his personal life to the grueling exigencies of national defense. Before moving to his post in the Pentagon, he had cooked all the meals, even preparing rich French feasts served under cozy candlelight. In the two years since, he barely cooked at all. He didn't have time for it, or for much of anything else, for that matter. Marriages suffered in Washington. Many, in pursuit of power, were willing to pay that price. Perle wasn't, and it grated on him.

Perle knew he and his wife desperately needed some time together. So he had his secretary inform the Aspen Institute that he would accept their invitation to attend their weeklong seminar on arms control. Not that he thought he would learn anything at the conference. It would be a crowd of academics, pretentious types from vine-covered East Coast schools who, he often joked, could barely negotiate a year's sabbatical, let alone a treaty with the Soviet Union. In Colorado, they would be spewing out abstract theories that, he felt, bore virtually no relationship to the real world. "Game theory," "the prisoner's dilemma," "action-reaction." He never had much use for these arcane academic ideas, which he thought detracted from the central theme of international affairs: power politics. In these conferences, the participants often made straightforward subjects hopelessly complicated. Conversely, truly complicated issues, which could be discussed only at highly classified levels (for which they didn't have clearances), were hopelessly simplified, often missing the point altogether.

Many of the academic invitees were tenacious detractors of his hardline approach. They might be civil to him to his face, but he knew that behind his back most were harshly critical of him, even saying spiteful and bitterly personal things. A week with academics wrestling mightily to understand affairs of state was not Perle's idea of how to have a good time.

But he had his reasons. The setting for the conference was at a beautiful resort tucked away in the mountains. Mornings, he could attend the seminars. He could doodle, let his mind tune out and relax. Afternoons were free. This was time he could spend with Leslie.

For three days, it was bliss. They took long strolls along the cool footpaths of the mountains, curled up before the fireplace in his rustic suite, and snuck out for sumptuous meals in town. The conference was predictably superficial. But it was at least paying for the vacation. And he was with Leslie. He was finally relaxed, and Leslie was happy.

On the fourth day, he and Leslie planned to venture off to an afternoon concert. All throughout the morning session, Perle kept staring at his watch, waiting for the time when he would make his escape. Then, a tug on his elbow jarred him out of his quiet reverie. "Mr. Perle, I believe this is for you," said a lodge employee, thrusting a slip of folded paper into his hand. It said simply, "Call your office, ASAP."

Perle's first instinct was to ignore the message. But Perle had left careful instructions not to be disturbed. That the prohibition on contacting him had been broken meant it must be serious. He excused himself to go to the bathroom, and then found a pay phone down the stairs from the conference room. When he called his office collect, his personal secretary, Bobbi, accepted immediately and said, "Bill Hoehn insisted. He's been waiting all day for them to track you down. I think it's important. Let me connect you to him."

HOEHN SOUNDED OVERWROUGHT when he picked up the phone. He said he was worried because this was an open line. It would be relatively easy for the Soviets to intercept the call. "Richard, you need to figure out if you can get access to a secure phone, or, if not, for me to call you later from my home. It's harder for them to tap a private line."

"What's wrong, tell me what you can."

"I'm going to speak cryptically. There's been an event in the negotiations that you need to be aware of."

"Okay."

"It is a potentially new and strikingly different thing."

"Give me some details."

"I'll sketch out the rest tonight when we talk. It has to do with our white-haired gentleman."

Perle knew that had to mean Nitze. Something had broken in the talks, but what? Maybe they had made a breakthrough on zero, but Hoehn's tone clearly suggested something else.

"What's happened?" Perle was insistent, although calm.

"Come on, Richard, this is an open line."

"Damn it, Bill, give me the gist."

"Our friend has made a far-reaching proposal without any instructions. No one knew. Now he's gone to the NSC to get approval to propose it formally.

"Entirely on his own—a substantive proposal." Perle was horrified. Nitze had been pushing the limits already, but this had violated all the rules of negotiations. It was unforgivable.

He was no longer so calm.

"Look," Perle instructed Hoehn, "be home tonight at eight. If I don't get to a secure phone, you'll have to call me. It's difficult for the Soviets to intercept phones that are not in their line of sight. You should also check to see if there is a secure phone in the area that I can tap into. Let me know if there is."

If not, Perle added, he would give Hoehn the number of a pay phone, in code. He looked around for a few minutes, and then read off the scrambled numbers as Hoehn dutifully copied. The conversation complete, Perle hung up the receiver. Then he walked into the phone booth next to his, took out a large sheet of paper and scrawled "Out of Order" in big letters. He attached the sheet with a paper clip, and stood for a minute, wondering.

This was the last thing Perle needed. Depending upon how serious it was, he could be forced to return home. This was out of the question. He had promised Leslie two more days. He would have to wait and hear what Hoehn had to say, and then make a decision.

Damn, he thought to himself.

HOEHN CHECKED INTO finding a secure phone. Perle would have to drive at least two hours to a nearby military facility, and doing so would risk tipping everyone off at the conference that an incident was brewing. This was not desirable either. Which meant plan B. He would call Perle at the pay phone from his home.

By six o'clock, most people at the conference were preparing for dinner. Not Richard Perle. He was impatiently pacing by a deserted phone booth. It was eight o'clock in Washington.

This time, Perle asked for the essentials.

Hoehn again spoke cryptically, but Perle was able to get the basics. Nitze had panicked, gone off on his own, and cooked up a compromise with the Soviets. He proposed a package in which the U.S. and Soviets would be allowed 225 warheads on each side. The U.S. would have to give up deployment of all its Pershing II ballistic missiles slated for West Germany, the fast-flying missiles that could reach targets deep inside Soviet territory within six minutes. The Soviets would reserve the right to keep one hundred missiles, each with three warheads, in Asia, and the U.S. would have the theoretical right to match them, though as a practical matter it would not do so. Which would, in effect, codify Soviet superiority in missiles. It also meant scrapping zero.

"There will be a meeting of the NSC, and Nitze is pressing to make this proposal formal. Iklé thinks it's got merit. The secretary has kept an open mind. You need to come home."

Perle was making frantic calculations in his head.

Ironically perhaps, the uncompromising hard-liner was initially attracted to some of the substance of the offer. He felt it had potential. But the timing and presentation were awful. Perle was simultaneously intrigued and shocked, and then angry at Nitze. He also had a decision to make—should he go home immediately or could he handle this from afar? He decided he would stay.

"I can't."

"Well then I'll need some guidance."

"Look, what bothers me most is not the substance, but Nitze's end run. Nitze may have told Kvitsinsky that it was his own proposal, but they'll never believe this in Moscow. They'll conclude that we're abandoning parts of our position and, worse still, that we're collapsing before deployment. We've said all along that the principle of global equality is not negotiable. Now it'll be shown to be negotiable. That sends absolutely the wrong message at the wrong time."

Hoehn was scribbling away, taking notes.

"Politically it's dumb. Germany has gone to bat for these missiles against great domestic pressure. The chancellor's on a limb to deploy, and Nitze's in Geneva sawing it off."

"Just a sec," Hoehn said. "I want to get this all down. Okay, I'm with you. What do you want me to do?" he asked, plaintively.

"Do a detailed analysis of the military implications of giving up the Pershings and allowing the Soviets to keep SS-20s. Start out with a predisposition that it is conceivably interesting. I'm at least inclined to explore it more to see if it has merit. Before then, give Cap a memo in general terms outlining what I've told you."

"You got it."

"Oh, Bill, tell the secretary I'll be back on August 12, and will have something for him then. Let him know I'm working on this."

"Right."

"If there are any changes, call me. I need to know the secretary's thinking. In the meantime, tell the White House we need to resist being stampeded into a decision. There's got to be careful review first."

"See you soon, boss."

Damn again, Perle thought to himself, slamming the phone back into the wall, annoyed. So many people had put so much into crafting this policy. The president and the secretary had put themselves personally on the line—along with America's credibility as a leader—and Nitze had come along and treated it all as an errant ball of dust.

HOEHN WAS STRUCK by how displeased Perle sounded. It was clear he was furious about Nitze's freelancing. But he himself saw two problems that limited how much Perle could maneuver in this instance. Firing the patrician Nitze would be a public relations disaster. "You just couldn't take Nitze out and shoot him," Hoehn later commented. Moreover, half of the American public thought the U.S. was not negotiating seriously, and the perception was that the administration was opposed to arms control, intent only upon building up INF. They didn't catch nuances like the fact that sometimes you had to build up before you can reduce.

Second, Hoehn was worried about the far-right conservatives. They always said that if the Soviets played hardball, the U.S. would cave. This seemed to be exactly what Nitze had done, and would play directly into their hands. All told, he thought, it looked like a lose-lose situation, killing the chances for a good deal altogether. And Perle was boxed in.

The next two days were grueling and hectic. Hoehn and Ron Lehman put together the paper for Weinberger that Perle had requested. But it lacked Perle's big-picture touch. What was needed, Hoehn felt, was not Perle's guidance, but Perle himself. "He came back in the nick of time," a thankful Hoehn later said.

RESTLESSLY WALKING ABOUT in his hotel room, Perle grew red-hot. He turned over in his mind a bill of particulars against Nitze. Nitze had been deceptive in his actions, dishonest with his colleagues, and put the European allies in an impossible situation. He also substituted his personal judgment for that of the president of the United States. It was rogue diplomacy, Nitze stealing authority that was rightfully Ronald Reagan's. He sat down on the balcony of his suite and with a yellow legal pad wrote out a memo to Weinberger documenting his concerns.

The more Perle wrote, the angrier he got. This was a bad way to conduct arms control, and bad for sound negotiations. It was how nations, their knees buckling, gave up valued ground. Whatever the possible military merits of the plan's particulars—and they would come to be questioned—Perle believed the overall consequences of Nitze's actions were momentous: the NATO alliance could unravel and America could be seen as unable to stand firm against the Soviets. It could jeopardize everything.

Perle decided then and there that Nitze's plan had to be stopped.

AT THE PENTAGON, news quickly spread through ISP about the meeting in the woods. When Perle returned, he emphasized that there could be no leaks about the proposal. He didn't want it to get out to the press, not until a spike had been driven through it. Discussions of the proposal were marked on his schedule as simply "Project X." Remarkably, the secrecy held.

His first day back, Perle called Woodworth to his office. Woodworth was uncharacteristically nervous. He couldn't remember a time when he had seen Perle this viscerally agitated.

"How could this have happened?" Perle asked Woodworth. His voice was calm, but his eyes looked angry.

It suddenly occurred to Woodworth what Perle was getting at. He realized that Perle was trying to see if he knew about the walk, which would've been a real breach. "But I didn't know zilch about it when it happened," Woodworth confided. He told this to Perle.

This was a difficult time for Woodworth. He felt so betrayed by Nitze that he considered resigning. He also felt that anyone other than Nitze would be—and should be—fired. Only Nitze's prestige could save Nitze. Woodworth unburdened his feelings to Perle.

Perle was assuaged, and nodded that he understood. But in case there was any doubt, he said firmly to Woodworth, "Well, we're just going to have to kill this thing."

IT TURNED OUT that the White House was equally angry, and on August 24, President Reagan sent a memo to Secretary Shultz directly reprimanding the negotiator. Nitze was not named, but there was no mistaking the target of this dress-down. Henceforth, all arms control initiatives had to be cleared by the interagency system. Nitze had egregiously exceeded instructions. It was the sharpest reprimand Nitze had ever received in three decades of government service.

Yet as Nitze retreated to his summer estate in Maine, he was less concerned with the reprimand than he was with Perle's impending counteroffensive. Word of what Perle thought about his initiative got back to Nitze. "It was an act that signaled premature retreat, and of political and intellectual cowardice," Perle had said of his former mentor. The lines were now drawn, and the president would decide.

Over a sunny weekend at the beginning of September, the president went to Camp David to catch up on his work, carrying an interagency working group paper on Nitze's proposal. Reading the paper, Reagan was puzzled by why the U.S. would want to give away the Pershing missiles at all. They were fast and accurate, and they constituted powerful leverage over the Soviets in the negotiations; cruise missiles, by contrast, could be defended against with missile defenses. No such defense existed for ballistic missiles, including the Pershings. Upon returning to Washington that Monday, Reagan queried his White House aides about what effect giving up the Pershings would have on the strategic arms talks on offensive missiles, where the U.S. position was to *emphasize* the importance of ballistic missiles. It was a good question. He asked for the joint chiefs' response.

The chiefs largely agreed. They provided their response in a position paper that concluded it was questionable as to whether the U.S. would want to give up ballistic missiles while allowing the Soviets to keep their SS-20s. They didn't like the precedent it set, and they too felt valuable leverage in the INF talks could be lost. The bureaucratically deft Perle intercepted their paper and rewrote it into one representing the Department of Defense's position—making it sharper, crisper, and more pointed. In turn, he used these points to brief Weinberger.

Then, on September 13, the full NSC met to decide the fate of Nitze's proposal. Nitze was there to present his case directly to the president. This would be the critical meeting on the walk in the woods. Having thus far not heard from the Soviets, and dressed down by his own government, Nitze had one last shot to make his case, and was determined to make the most of it.

Nitze chose to emphasize that the Pershings were not militarily necessary. The U.S. would, therefore, be wiser to trade them for reductions in the Soviet SS-20s. Reagan listened attentively.

But this salvo about the Pershings was just the opening Weinberger needed, and which Perle's paper had prepared him for. Weinberger blasted away at Nitze's logic, following a script that Perle had put together for him in advance of the meeting. The president agreed with Weinberger. Speaking calmly, he asked Nitze if the U.S. could do without its new missiles, why couldn't the Soviets do without theirs?

This was the logic of the original INF zero option proposal; it was simple and final. Like Perle, the president saw no need to deviate from it.

This uncomplicated and straightforward question, more than any, went directly to the heart of the INF issue. Nitze had now retreated precisely to compromise and negotiability as the basis for his actions. In doing so, he was arguing for a more muscular variation of what some liberals and moderates had been calling for, even if dressed up more elegantly. He replied that it was "inconceivable" the Soviets would dismantle their modern missiles in exchange for an American promise to cancel missiles that it hadn't even yet deployed.

Reagan smiled, and leaned slightly in Nitze's direction. "Well, Paul," the president said, "you just tell them you're working for one tough son of a bitch."

The president had made up his mind, siding with Weinberger and Perle, not Nitze. The U.S. would stand firm.

It turned out that the president had actually gone easy on Nitze in the NSC meeting. Behind closed doors, when Reagan first met with Weinberger to discuss the walk in the woods, the president was furious, not just with the offer to give up the Pershing missiles, but also with Nitze's unauthorized actions. Indeed, Weinberger could hardly recall a time when he had seen Reagan so livid.

Weinberger met with Perle back at the Pentagon. "I think it's dead, he told his assistant secretary.

"Dead—or wounded?" Perle asked, looking concerned.

"My guess is dead."

Two days later, Weinberger proved to be right. The president issued a new national security directive that reiterated zero as the U.S. position, and made clear that any alternative would have to allow the U.S. to deploy Pershings.

News of the walk still had not publicly broken; the gag rule still held. The press still knew nothing about the walk in the woods. And at month's end, the repudiation of Nitze was total. When Nitze met with Yuli

Kvitsinsky in Geneva for a new round of talks, he was informed that Moscow had rejected the plan they had worked out months earlier. There was no more recourse this time. The walk was decisively defeated. The evidence, in fact, also pointed to another conclusion: the Soviets never seriously entertained it as anything but a ruse to probe how much the West and the Americans were willing to give up. The walk never stood a chance.

CHAPTER 15

The mild weather of December gave way to a relentless winter storm on January 16, 1983. The Northeast was pounded with up to eight inches of snow; Washington fared little better, being ground down by a blustery drizzle and icy white flakes that halted traffic.

That Sunday morning, Perle yawned, rubbed his tired eyes, and stooped down to retrieve the *New York Times*, then sank into his high-back oak breakfast chair for a leisurely cup of coffee with Leslie before the morning talk news shows began. Jonathan scampered playfully through the kitchen. Perle ripped off the thick rubber band, unraveled the folded paper, and was horrified to read the headline above the fold, anchoring the left column: "U.S. Aide Reached Arms Agreement—Later Ruled Out."

The cat was out of the bag. The article documented in vivid detail Nitze's private efforts to broker an INF accord. Perle's initial reaction was that this would create sympathy and adulation for Nitze, turning him into the proverbial white knight, the splendid gladiator fighting for arms control against the black hats, those stubborn conservatives pushing for deployment and holding out for zero. The spin was already there in the article. Perle's eyes widened. A senior State Department official was quoted as saying, "A mythology may be created in Europe about all this, that somehow Rostow and Nitze negotiated a breakthrough that the Neanderthals in Washington blocked."

There was nothing in the article that held Nitze accountable for violating both the basic rules of government and of diplomacy and effective negotiations.

Perle also saw other troubling signs, ones that could jeopardize adhering to the zero option and the scheduled NATO missile deployments in the fall. Nitze had signaled that NATO was willing to settle for less. Now, in another article, the *Times* was reporting that Bonn and Rome were willing to settle for less than the zero option, and were expressing interest in an "interim solution," which is to say, a variation of Nitze's proposal. With these cracks in the alliance, the pressure would grow to block the INF deployment altogether. This was yet another reason why Nitze's private adventure had been so disastrous. Divisions in the alliance would jeopardize the zero option, deployment, and Western security.

Failure to deploy meant a military and moral victory for the Soviets. It would be an unparalleled turning point in the Cold War. This spelled disaster.

Perle hoped that the damage could be contained. But there was little doubt about what the upcoming months held in store: things were only going to get tougher from here on in.

NITZE, HIS JAW locked tightly, was also upset by the headline. He felt the article revealed to the world that the administration kept him on a tight leash. It was humiliating.

The article also dealt with Eugene Rostow, who had been fired by Secretary of State Shultz four days earlier. The president had lost confidence in him, Shultz said at the time, leaving little room for a shocked Rostow to appeal his case. Yet the article pointedly indicated that Rostow's supporters and detractors cited the walk in the woods as part of the reason for Rostow's sudden dismissal. Nitze knew this impression was not completely accurate; Rostow had been feuding with other members of the administration from day one, making his removal almost inevitable. In Rostow's defense, he was a highly regarded and thoughtful public servant. But either way, one clear implication of the whole affair was that, unless Nitze fell into line, he could be next.

The loss of Rostow dealt a bureaucratic blow to Nitze. His anger at Rostow for leaking this story was temporary; but he would now have to reconcile himself to the bitter reality that his principal ally and supporter was no longer in the administration. The third round of talks in Geneva had gone badly. Dismally, he now felt there appeared to be little hope for a compromise.

IT WAS A difficult time for Rostow. He was still hobbling on crutches from a hip injury, and he had been ignominiously sacked by Shultz. But rather than give up on public service, he retreated to his old haunt, the winding Gothic towers and red and green lead windows of Yale Law School. From a quiet, oak-paneled study, he could write and speak freely on the pressing issues of arms control and the Cold War.

Curiously, it was at first bitter going. One would have expected the former chief arms controller to be welcomed warmly by his old university, and to be cherished as a valued resource. Yale was already furiously steeped in a search for arms control and conflict resolution, most notably in its weekly faculty arms control seminar held at Yale's interdisciplinary Center for International and Area Studies.

However, when Rostow offered to speak before the arms control seminar, a prominent faculty member protested about Rostow's having worked for Ronald Reagan. "If he comes here to speak, don't expect me to show up," he thundered. The invitation to Rostow was delayed. Instead of an academic quest for truth, the climate was chilling on open debate. It was also odd because Rostow had emerged as a dedicated arms controller, fighting a lonely battle with Paul Nitze against the Pentagon. But in the arena of charged debate in the 1980s, with regiments of the right and the left arguing across scarred ideological battlefields, the political center had been swept away. It would be months before Rostow would reestablish himself at his old university, dining at Yale's venerable eating club, Mory's, and regaling eager protégés with tales of public service.

In the meantime, after his firing, Rostow had come out swinging in defiance. Able to speak freely once again, this is exactly what he did. "The walk in the woods was vintage Nitze," he told his friends, and he "concurred all along." He told the *New York Times* that Nitze's accord was a good one, and should have been embraced. On the Tuesday after he was sacked, the *Times* quoted him as saying that the Nitze accord met the basic American goal of limiting "destabilizing weapons." Rostow apocalyptically cautioned further that "without arms control, the western alliance would be in grave peril."

The *Times* agreed with Rostow's assessment. And as Perle had feared, for three days running, it ran front-page articles about the agreement Nitze had tried to work out, only to be foiled by events out of his control. "He was," concluded the paper's editorialists, "negotiating in the real world," with the not so subtle implication that the likes of Richard Perle and Ronald Reagan were not.

Nitze joined Rostow in coming out with his own assault. The sympathy on his behalf was mounting, and supporters of arms control had conveniently overlooked the circumstances surrounding the walk and instead focused on the theoretical deal. Nitze immediately capitalized on this support. After stating that he "regretted the departure of my dear friend Gene Rostow from the administration," he defiantly told reporters that he was "not reprimanded" and "did not at any time exceed my instructions as a negotiator." This was, however, a preposterous and inaccurate inflation. But Nitze was shrewd enough to know that if further momentum in favor of a compromise could be whipped up, he could help force the administration away from zero. He could also make it politically impossible for the president to fire him, as he had done with Rostow.

Nitze met personally with Reagan to receive his instructions for the next round of negotiations, due to commence on January 26. That the president felt it necessary to send off the arms control negotiator, personally and visibly, was a sign that Nitze's political currency was again rising. After the meeting, Nitze ambled slowly out to the front lawn to brief reporters. He struck them as being cool as a cucumber.

Is there any give in the American position? a reporter asked.

Clad in a banker's dark gray suit, and speaking slowly and deliberately, Nitze emphasized, "The president's directive to me is to negotiate seriously, and he made that clear fourteen months ago at the beginning of these negotiations."

He continued, "If the Soviet side gives, then I'm sure we will give serious consideration to any serious proposal of theirs."

Reporters pressed closer to Nitze. In view of the recent events, this was a remarkable line that Nitze was audaciously articulating. "So we're not locked in on zero-zero?" another reporter shouted. Nitze refused to say no, and, virtually ignoring what the president had instructed him, added, "I won't answer that."

It was a stunning act of defiance, if not political drama. Overnight, the leak of the walk in the woods had made Nitze into the icon that the peace movement was looking for. The outcry was immediate. Even his own negotiating team saw it. "Paul became a hero," John Woodworth later remarked. "He single-handedly legitimized the arms control track. Before, it had belonged almost entirely to the freezers and their supporters."

And the effect of this would be felt almost immediately, casting the zero option and the actual INF deployment into serious doubt.

NITZE SOON FOUND an unlikely new ally in Rick Burt. The two had quarreled on and off, with Burt jealously guarding his State Department turf as Foggy Bottom's senior arms control theorist. But events, if only slowly, would inexorably push the two together into an alliance of convenience against Perle and Weinberger.

That January, Nitze sounded a dire note about the solidarity of NATO, repeatedly warning in private meetings, "Don't you know the house is burning down?" He felt rigid adherence to the zero option was a ticking time bomb for NATO. To Nitze, the alliance would crumble unless an arms control deal was made.

"Do you want to wait until it burns to the ground before you do anything?" he said, pressing this metaphor across the administration.

Burt watched with a combination of amusement and concern. The overwrought despair of a man forty-one years his senior led him to comment, "He's gone around the bend, he's panicking." He confided to aides that Nitze may be "falling apart."

But Burt shared Nitze's sense that an agreement had to be reached at virtually any price, though he expressed this view in far less apocalyptic terms. For some time Burt had been promoting what he called an "interim agreement," which amounted to his old zero plus. Burt's quest for an interim solution was assisted by the reports emanating out of virtually every bureau in the State Department.

In sober assessments to the secretary, the German specialists at State said the U.S. "would never" be able to get its missiles into Germany. The same was said about Holland. Even the Chinese specialists weighed in and cast doubt as to the possible success of the INF emplacement. The drumbeat was so constant, so uniform, that John Woodworth privately wondered if even Perle thought his very own plan could succeed.

Burt used these dire assessments as ammunition to prevail upon Shultz to urge the president to adopt a more compromising position. In the absence of a compromise, it was now argued, not only would there be no deal, but no deployment—and NATO would fall apart.

It worked. The decision was made to stick with the zero option as the stated negotiating goal, but the president would also send a signal that the U.S. would be willing to inject more give into the talks. On February 22, 1983, Reagan offered a first hint of this modified approach.

Speaking before the American Legion, the president announced that Nitze would be given greater latitude in the negotiations. "Ours is not a take-it-or-leave-it proposal," he told the legionnaires. Then, in March, the president went a step further, and while retaining the zero option as the overall goal, formally adopted the interim solution as the basis for the U.S. position. "When it comes to intermediate nuclear missiles in Europe, it would be better to have none than to have some. But if there must be some, it is better to have few than many," the president remarked.

But privately, some aides, on both sides of the zero option debate, worried that now the Soviets had little incentive to sign off on any modified arms deal. If they held out for a few more months, they might be able to block deployment altogether, thus precipitating a collapse within the NATO alliance.

FOR THE PEACE movement, however, the new administration position couldn't have come a moment too soon.

With seven months before a final showdown in November, the demonstrations increased in frequency and intensity. Several thousand determined protesters demonstrated passionately at a dozen sites throughout West Germany against the stationing of the INF missiles. They dressed in ghoulish outfits and paraded about as irradiated skeletons.

In England, thousands more linked arms and hands, forming a fourteen-mile human chain, spread across the countryside like the Great Wall of China. But there were ominous undercurrents to the protests, signs of lawlessness and violence. In one such raw signal of the movement's volatility, several hundred protesters broke the law and slithered under and over the perimeter wire fence surrounding the Greenham Common Air Base, due to receive the first of ninety-six cruise missiles in 1983.

Within months, the thousands would swell to hundreds of thousands, and in dusty plazas, open-air markets, and lush green fields, protesters across Europe would send the continent into convulsions.

The peace movement was given a major boost in May by a public pastoral letter released by the American Catholic bishops. Such priestly activism was rare, and more often than not, when it came to foreign policy, the pronouncements of the church were characterized more by careful temporizing than muscular declarations in the political arena. Not this time. After hearing testimony from over fifty witnesses, and an exchange of letters between National Security Adviser Judge William Clark and Cardinal Joseph Bernardin, the Conference of American Bishops released a letter that said nuclear deterrence is not a reliable instrument in the long run. As such, it posed an immediate challenge to the zero option.

Entitled *The Challenge of Peace: God's Promise and Our Response*, the pastoral document of the bishops committee urgently called for "accelerated work for arms control, reduction and disarmament," and to "develop nonviolent means of conflict resolution." In the church itself, there was hardly unanimity on this statement. Some of the younger priests saw it as a breath of fresh air, where others expressed dismay in unmistakable terms. European bishops and the Vatican in particular had urged greater moderation in the approach, incorporating a stronger foundation rooted in Catholic theology, not political fashion or temporary vexation.

But the American bishops, led by Cardinal Bernardin, were stubbornly defiant, and felt they were exercising their historic prerogative, the voice and conscience of a world that they hoped would emerge more peaceful than the present one, where the U.S. and Soviet Union were uneasily engaged in a tense standoff over the INF missiles.

Weinberger himself was furious over the bishops' letter, and, in a letter of his own, sharply rebuked them for meddling in the intricate debate over nuclear weapons and doctrine, when the government needed their support, not criticism. Their draft statement also was not, he charged, sufficiently critical of the Soviet arms buildup.

The bishops' policy prescriptions were a tad naive, and the timing problematic. But as the two superpowers raced toward a showdown, their fears about larger tensions were hardly unfounded.

The first disconcerting portents came in mid-February. Two Soviet warships, a guided-missile cruiser, the *Admiral Isakov,* and a surface frigate armed with antisubmarine depth charges, maneuvered visibly into the mouth of the Mississippi Delta, coming within fifty miles of American shores. Both ships were known to carry nuclear missiles.

The two ships had been cruising the Caribbean since November 25, when they arrived in Havana and Cienfuegos, Cuba, on "goodwill visits" as part of a flotilla of four. Their winter stay in these waters was the longest by Soviet ships since well before the invasion of Afghanistan. In the past, Soviet trawlers gathering intelligence on U.S. missile tests had lingered off the coast of Florida, and Soviet missile submarines had edged right up to the fifty-mile range. But this was the closest that Soviet warships had come to the U.S. since they began deploying to the Caribbean in 1969.

The symbolism of the Soviet vessels was hardly unintentional. The nuclear missiles they carried placed them theoretically within a fifteen-minute range of Washington, New York, Boston, and Philadelphia, twice as long as it would take for U.S. Pershings to hit command-and-control centers outside of Moscow, and half as long as it would take for American cruise missiles to fix on their targets.

The presence of the ships also called to mind a widely circulated threat made earlier by Vladimir Pavlichenko, an adviser to the Soviet arms delegation. Though he was listed under the auspices of the Academy of Sciences, he was a known senior KGB officer, and frequent attendant at international arms control conferences. Considered arrogant but candid, he had issued an ultimatum the previous summer, which he then elaborated on in February: If the INF missiles were emplaced in Europe, they would invite retaliation from the Soviets. If the U.S. insisted upon increasing the threat to the Soviets from Western Europe, he suggested rhetorically, it would have to contend with an increased Soviet threat from "Cuba and other Central American countries."

"How would you like to have missiles there?" Pavlichenko asked menacingly. It didn't take much for this threat to be interpreted. He was holding out the specter of a Cuban Missile Crisis in reverse. Whether the threat was bluster or real, it cut deeply into the American psyche. Nikita

Khrushchev, the U.S. had learned fatefully two decades earlier, had not been bluffing.

Soviet threats were also repeated in Europe. On the evening of January 19, 1983, as West German elections were about to get under way, Soviet Foreign Minister Andrei Gromyko was at a state dinner with his West German counterparts. Clad in his trademark dark suit, the seventy-three-year-old steadied his elderly frame, slowly rose to his feet, lifted his glass of red wine, and delivered a chilling toast.

"In the nuclear age, the Federal Republic of Germany and the Soviet Union are, figuratively, in the same boat."

He continued, "If there are gamblers and con men who state that they are ready to plunge humanity into a nuclear catastrophe for the sake of their ambition, who gave them the right to put the people who want to live down into the abyss with them?"

There was no mistaking Gromyko's words. It was a deliberate attempt to exercise nuclear blackmail over the West and the people of Germany. It was also a heavy-handed attempt to play on public fears and to meddle in the West German elections, urging the public to side with the Soviets against NATO and reject the deployment of the INF missiles. It also ignored the fact that the Soviets, not the U.S., had upset the nuclear balance of power.

But by whichever calculation, this was hardly reassuring to the peace movement. To them, the interim solution was clearly an improvement over the zero option. But as the fall and deployment inched closer, they hoped for more; their hope was that some arms deal could forestall any deployment whatsoever, and the possibility of impending calamity.

With little to hold on to, Nitze emerged as their hero, Perle, the Prince of Darkness, as their villain.

THAT SUMMER THE talks continued to drag on with no progress in sight. The Soviets were unmovable. They were peddling a new line called the "postponement option." In their most benign voice, they asked the U.S. to defer the INF deployment, and give the talks "an extra chance." They asked for "even a few months" rather than for an open-ended commitment.

It was no go from the American side, which sensed the Soviets were not negotiating, but stalling. If the U.S. let deployment slip for even a single day, it would be tantamount to cancellation. It would be a catastrophe for the West.

Meanwhile, West German opposition to deployment continued to grow. European protests continued to erupt. And at home in the U.S., the

State Department, Nitze and Burt primarily, began to search for variations of the interim agreement to salvage a deal, some kind of a deal, something, rather than risk a walkout.

BACK AT THE Pentagon, there was a sense of minor retreat. In the spring, Perle had weighed these events with a sense of foreboding and gloom. His zero option had come under repeated assault, and seemed constantly on the verge of unraveling altogether. He was also depressed about the constant bureaucratic infighting, the two-steps-forward, one-step-backward process of decision making.

He continued to worry about the effect that the job was having on his family life. "I'm thinking of leaving," he confided to aides and friends, "and going back to the real world."

One day, one of his aides, Doug Feith, burst into his office waving the latest news from Foggy Bottom. "Listening to them, you would think the U.S., and not the Soviets, was being obstructionist," he said. Another aide chimed in, "I wish we had a U.S. interest section in State."

Sadly shaking his head, Perle said, "So do I, so do I."

But Perle didn't leave. In the summer of 1983, with everyone preoccupied with the arms talks, the call for a deal could no longer be shrugged off as a noisy sideshow, an irritating nuisance. Like the country at large, he had to decide if he wanted to stand firm behind zero—and risk a certain breakdown in the talks—and, if the Soviets could be believed, even confrontation.

CHAPTER 16

In the middle of August, a tired Richard Perle readied himself for his yearly summer retreat to Provence, France. This was an indispensable part of his employment; his waistline bulging slightly, his hair a bit grayer, he especially needed it this year. Even the tense missile negotiations, the precariousness of the deployment, the crisis looming in the fall, could not impede his summer outing. He needed a break.

Before leaving, there was one immediate headache he had to clear up. His deputy with specific responsibility for overseeing the INF missiles, Ronald Lehman, was moving over to the National Security Council staff. With the Pentagon about to empty for the summer holiday, he had to have someone in place to oversee the operational aspects of the INF issue. The slot had to be filled before his departure. But with whom?

John Woodworth was just right in Geneva. Stephen Bryen was perfect doing technology transfer. Bill Hoehn was an administrative guy, with an expertise in conventional weapons, hardly what was needed here.

It was perhaps fortuitous that Perle learned Frank Gaffney, his old and trusted assistant on Scoop Jackson's staff, had announced he was intending to leave the Hill and move to New York. Gaffney was burned out by the long hours. The Senate was a young man's game, and he wanted to join his girlfriend, Anne, in New York. For several months, he had marketed himself for a position in the city. He was still looking.

I have a better idea, Perle told Gaffney. Come work for me as a deputy assistant secretary of defense, dealing with theater nuclear missiles and the INF deployment.

Gaffney had had little luck in finding a job in New York. At first, he thought investment firms or public relations agencies would jump at the chance to grab a young guy with his Washington experience and contacts. He quickly learned that Wall Street and Midtown moved to a different beat than the capital, which meant he didn't have a job to go to.

"Great," he told Perle, jumping at the new opportunity.

Perle asked Gaffney if he could start immediately. Once the defense authorization bill is over, I'm yours, Gaffney told him. In August, without taking a vacation, Frank Gaffney moved over to the Pentagon.

A graduate of Georgetown University with a neatly cropped beard and rounded shoulders, Gaffney was slender and wiry. In college he roguishly chased girls, and muddled thorough academically. But later, when he got the chance to work for Richard Perle on the staff of Jackson's Subcommittee on Investigations, he threw himself into the job with great relish.

Gaffney learned to think like Perle (hard-line), and even talked like him—emulating the silky, soft-spoken, and mellifluous voice that was Perle's trademark. His energy and devotion to Perle earned him the reputation as Perle's alter ego to friends, and as "Perle's pit bull" to detractors. But at thirty-two, despite his already significant position on the Hill, he was relatively inexperienced when it came to the culture of the Pentagon. Moreover, to his detractors, he lacked Perle's instinctive savvy. At first blush, he also had a youthful, cocky side to him, which in hostile company served to detract from his otherwise generous nature, his admirable loyalty to his colleagues, and his unmistakable, solid smarts.

This was all okay with Perle. Gaffney was not just competent, but extremely familiar with nuclear issues. He wouldn't take much breaking in. His loyalty was unquestionable. Better still, he would work night and day in Perle's behalf. Finally, Perle had great affection for Gaffney.

He would also be perfect in doing some of the rougher work, like keeping track of Rick Burt. There was some irony here, for at the outset of the administration, Burt had offered Gaffney the job as his special assistant at the State Department. Convinced he could have more influence on the Senate Armed Services Committee, Gaffney had turned it down.

One characteristic of Perle's management style was that he gave trusted deputies a lot of running room, providing only minimal and necessary supervision. Perle saw no reason why this should change for Gaffney when he left for France.

FOUR DAYS INTO the job, it was particularly sticky in Washington. Fred Iklé and Bill Hoehn were both on vacation, and Gaffney was left to his own devices. "It was a real flying handoff," he would later remark.

On the calendar that afternoon was an important meeting with Secretary Weinberger. Gaffney was told to attend and present Perle's views. The issue was SALT II compliance, exceedingly complex technologically and tricky politically. Perle had been relentlessly pushing to scrap compliance with the SALT II treaty from day one, but Shultz wanted to continue adherence. The joint chiefs were a critical swing vote. Thus far, they were against breaking out of SALT, preferring the "predictability" of the arms race as framed by the treaty. With the goal of working over the chiefs and enlisting their support, Weinberger convened a meeting of the top civilian and military brass in his spacious conference room.

Nervous about how best to go head-to-head with the uniformed heads, Gaffney put in a call to the vacationing Perle in France to ask for direction.

Do the best you can, Perle told him reassuringly. Gaffney saw that this was Perle in "his vacation mode." He would have to wing it.

They all sat around a long table. A flip chart was at the room's end. Weinberger led off the meeting with a short presentation, saying that he strongly objected to SALT. The navy representative made a case for SALT adherence. When it was his turn, Gaffney buried his nerves and argued his case strongly. The Soviets were violating the treaty, he said, and it should be scrapped. Gaffney glanced around the room, to assess the reaction. Everyone was listening attentively. He felt he was now on a roll.

General Jack Vessey, the chairman of the joint chiefs, then summarized the views of the military. Gaffney felt he had misrepresented a key fact, and interrupted the chairman.

"Jack, that's not right," he broke in, honestly.

Weinberger shot a furious look at Gaffney, and then stared. It was a stare that could kill. He himself called Vessey "Mr. Chairman." He certainly couldn't countenance Gaffney displaying such disrespect as to call Vessey "Jack." While Colin Powell could see the fury in his boss's expression, Gaffney, deep in thought, was oblivious. Two hours later, when the meeting broke up without resolution, he even felt he acquitted himself okay. He intended to debrief Perle when he returned to his office. He got a snack first.

To his surprise, there was an urgent phone call waiting for him. It was Perle, no longer in vacation mode.

"What did you say to General Vessey?" Perle asked.

"What do you mean? We discussed SALT." Gaffney could hear the sound of distress in Perle's voice.

"Colin Powell just called me in a lather. The secretary is evidently furious. Did you call Vessey 'Jack'?"

It dawned on Gaffney what had happened. He felt a rush of anxiety.

Let me patch things up, Perle said. He immediately called Powell, and explained that Gaffney meant no disrespect, that he had just come from the Hill, and that's the way things are done there. He insisted it was an error that wouldn't be repeated. He would see to it.

Powell relayed this to Weinberger, and the secretary accepted the explanation. And after that first bump, the usually well-mannered Gaffney began to thrive in his position.

. . .

Two months later, in October, relations between Burt and Gaffney became increasingly tense. As Gaffney saw it, one of his jobs was to keep "Burt honest." Burt had been carefully cultivating his image in the press, and was suspected of repeatedly leaking information to Strobe Talbott, the *Time* magazine correspondent chronicling the nuclear arms talks. As part of the bargain, Talbott was relatively uncritical of Burt, while portraying Perle as the arch villain in the INF drama. Thus Burt could position himself between Perle and Nitze, as both a hawk and a moderate, and get credit for it. Talbott's biased articles, invariably putting Perle in the crosshairs, were increasingly a source of irritation around the Pentagon. But to Gaffney, Burt's media posturing was less alarming than his behind-the-scene maneuvers to broker a last-second deal on INF.

Gaffney went to talk to Perle about it. Perle sat himself comfortably in his green leather wing chair, slightly slouched; Gaffney was poised like a wary cat on the edge of an adjacent sofa. He leaned his head toward Perle and warned, "Rick's persuaded catastrophe will happen if we don't have an arms control deal, and missile deployment takes place. He's assiduously whipping up ideas, initiatives, alternative strategies, to put a wrench in the process."

Gaffney continued. The latest idea was what Burt called "cosmetic concessions." However much Burt labeled this the "U.S. version of flexibility," Gaffney feared the effect would be the same: to halt deployment. The allies were already anxious. Vacillation by the U.S. would raise the alarms. Perle urged Gaffney to keep on top of things. Let's head this off if we can, he stressed.

At month's end, Gaffney and Burt met at the Dutch ambassador's residence in Brussels with the Dutch foreign minister, Hans van der Brooke. Along with the Germans, the Dutch were considered the weak link in the deployment. Earlier, in December 1982, the Danish Parliament had voted to freeze all funding to support the cruise missile emplacements, and the Danish prime minister would now have to overrule the Parliament. And if the Dutch also balked, the whole Western strategy could unravel. "They're in a position to euchre us if they decide to play tough," Gaffney had warned.

Burt, always smooth, was demonstrably furious at having Gaffney there as a de facto baby-sitter. Gaffney, for his part, was determined not to let Burt play upon Holland's vulnerabilities. When he raised the issue of public pressure, Gaffney countered and spoke of America's deep concern over the alliance. Burt rolled his eyes. The exchange continued throughout the meeting.

"He was never particularly pleasant to be with," Gaffney said later. "This night was no exception."

BUT, BY FALL, an even bigger development was afoot.

At CIA headquarters in Langley in September, an analyst was hunched over the most recent satellite photos of Eastern Europe. Where the day before he had seen a cluster of long prefabricated shelters that housed the Soviet SS-20s, something was now disturbingly different. A shelter had been taken down.

He took a magnifying glass to the photographs and stared at the white specks of light on the dark picture, which to an untrained eye would look like a bad negative of an arrangement of stars in space. But on these pictures, even the most minor discrete changes meant everything to the intelligence analyst.

This change was significant because the Agency didn't count missiles—it couldn't. Because the SS-20s were mobile, they could be wheeled from one location to another, hidden in airplane hangars, disguised in the dense forests of East Germany, and moved freely wherever else they could blend in with the scenery. Also, there was no way to tell a dummy missile, such as one filled with concrete, from an operational missile. But as a rule, all new missiles were accompanied by the prefab shelters; so from counting shelters the CIA would derive the number of Soviet missiles. In turn, these estimates were relayed to the U.S. government and then to the NATO allies.

For two years now, the CIA had attended monthly NATO meetings and briefed the allies. The CIA briefer would never show the actual photos, which could compromise vital intelligence sources and methods, but would flash overheads displaying lit-up drawings of new SS-20 deployments. NATO would then issue a press release announcing that the Soviets had once again put in place additional SS-20s, adding further substantiation to the NATO strategy of missile deployment.

Until now, this methodology had been commonly accepted. SS-20 deployment was cloaked in the greatest of secrecy. But where there were missile garages, there were technical support platoons, accessible roads, small buildings in familiar Soviet military arrangements, vehicle support centers, power supply lines, barracks, and also KGB warhead security battalions. And invariably, in the individual base areas located in deep forests and heavily fenced in by stringent security, there were SS-20s, even though the CIA never actually saw them in the satellite photos.

Over the course of the next two weeks, more garages were taken down. First one, then three, then five, then thirteen altogether. This would bring the number down, the first reduction of SS-20s since their deployment began in 1979.

At that point, the Agency resolved that this new information would have to be passed on to the administration. The analysts had no doubt that the information was explosive. It could signify a new trend that would inevitably give greater political force and urgency to the delay option for NATO missile deployments that the Soviets, some Europeans, and State Department officials were clamoring for.

But however delicate the information was, and even if these startling new revelations could hinder the deployment, the Agency analysts felt they had little choice. They reasoned that what the new data ultimately meant would be up to the policy makers in the executive branch to determine.

"What?" Gaffney exclaimed excitedly when he was first briefed on the apparent change in the missile numbers. "This is bullshit," he said. "Just months ago, you were telling us about KGB crews scraping off ice and snow on the garage roofs, and now this."

Gaffney was convinced, as he later put it, "the Soviets were fucking with our heads." Perle agreed with him that the suspicious timing recked of disinformation and manipulation. He told Gaffney that if this new set of numbers was presented to the allies, the Europeans could seize upon it as an excuse not to deploy. If leaked to the public, he feared there would also be a similar reaction.

This was only confirmed for Gaffney a few days later, when the Soviets pulled what he felt was another trick. They ominously slid open the roofs to some of the SS-20 garages, allowing a U.S. satellite to peer directly into the structures. They were empty.

This in itself didn't mean much. Ordinarily, the garages were believed to be empty while the SS-20s roamed about on maneuvers. But this latest tidbit of information only reconfirmed for the Agency analysts what they earlier concluded: SS-20 missile deployments in Eastern Europe were declining. But to Gaffney, the case looked very different. An already imperfect counting system was being manipulated and should hardly be the basis for so sweeping a conclusion. He worried that the CIA had gotten it very wrong.

A briefing was hurriedly prepared for the interagency group dealing with INF. Perle couldn't make it, and Gaffney went in his stead. Burt was already in the room when Gaffney walked in.

After hearing the presentation, Burt proclaimed that the U.S. must tell the allies "immediately." Gaffney fired back that the Soviets "were just turning the screws." Burt snorted.

Gaffney knew he had to do something. Ignoring Burt, he turned to the CIA briefer and bore down on the CIA's methodology. "Hold everything," he said, waving his hand. "Have you actually seen any SS-20s taken out of the field back to the Soviet Union?"

The Agency briefer was taken aback. Gaffney knew that they didn't count the SS-20s directly. What was he getting at? "No," the briefer said firmly.

"So can you be confident that taking down these shelters means that Soviet readiness has declined?"

"Put that way, no, but . . ."

Gaffney pressed further. "Is there any basis for assuming that the SS-20s have to be in those shelters?"

Angry and embarrassed, the CIA briefer shook his head.

"My point is," Gaffney added, "that there is no basis for passing this on to the allies. We cannot substantiate such wide assertions."

The CIA briefers protested vigorously. They said that these conclusions represented their best analytic judgment. Stifling this information would only compromise their independence, they said. This could not be allowed to happen.

Nobody is stifling anything, Gaffney said. If you could back up what you are claiming, that would be fine. But you can't.

Gaffney made it clear that he didn't plan to give in. Finally, the CIA relented, and the interpretations of the photographs were left out of their briefings to the NATO allies in Brussels.

The stage was now set for the final countdown, in the stormy months of November and December 1983.

CHAPTER 17

The morning of Sunday, June 7, 1981, Jeane Kirkpatrick was at home, still in her robe, relaxing with her husband, Kirk. Tea steeped slowly in the kitchen. This was a temporary refuge from the grinding exigencies of frantic activity at the U.S. mission to the United Nations. Today, aside from lurking tensions in Poland, and continued turbulence in Lebanon, all seemed quiet in the world. The only sounds outside were not the cacophony of U.N. delegates, but the shouts of children enjoying spring in suburban Bethesda yards and streets.

Kirkpatrick, the professor-turned-diplomat-and-cabinet-member, was still coming to terms with her new and slightly unfamiliar role in public life. She spent four days of a six-day workweek in New York at the U.N., reserving Saturday through Monday for cabinet and National Security Council meetings—she was a member of both—in Washington. It was a crushing schedule. A workaholic, she had come to relish the rare moments when she could just focus on one issue, rather than juggle her extensive portfolio of responsibilities. Spending a free morning with Kirk was an even greater pleasure. She didn't have to be in New York again until Tuesday.

But, shortly before noon, a call came in on her secure home line. A specially installed white phone, it was usually silent. But not this morning. She was needed immediately at the State Department. In her sixth-floor office, an urgent cable was waiting.

The report was grim, its implications far-reaching. Kirkpatrick felt a rush of adrenaline as she read the terse message. She picked up the phone to call her senior staff: "I'd like you to come to my office immediately," she said. "Last night the Israelis bombed Osirak, the French-made Iraqi nuclear reactor."

KIRKPATRICK WAS UNEASY. It wasn't that the raid was ill-timed—there was never a good time for events like this—but she knew shock waves from the attack would be felt immediately, rippling from the halls of the State Department right up to the U.N.

She was instinctively sympathetic to what Israel had done. Saddam Hussein, for some time, had been uttering grisly statements that the Arabs needed the bomb. Nor was his frantic effort to build the nuclear weapon, with the distressing complicity of the French, any secret. He was, at bottom, a ruthless dictator, a menace not to be dismissed lightly.

Yet, even this early on, she knew this incident would be a crucible of fire, a decisive challenge for the U.S. If she were successful in helping craft an effective U.S. response, it would vindicate not just the Reagan administration's new activist, pro-West foreign policy, but her own determination to show the world that the days of a temporizing America were now unmistakably over. But if she faltered, she would be cannon fodder for her critics, who would love nothing more than to see her publicly humiliated. "If she fails on this," chortled one official, "the White House will have her head on a platter."

Nor was it solely Kirkpatrick's call to make. This was the first crisis the administration had faced in the Middle East. How it was handled would be seen as defining American policy in the region, toward both Israel and the Arab world. It was Kirkpatrick's view that the Israelis probably had little choice in the matter, and that the world would one day thank them. But not now and, in the U.N., perhaps never. The rush to condemn Israel would be inevitable. She did not know how America's allies, even her own colleagues and her president, would react to the news. There were also considerations of international law and the legalities of Israel's preemptive strike that, as America's representative to the U.N., she would have to take into account. For one, the U.S. could not be seen as blessing the actual bombing per se. But until she had more answers, she could not proceed definitively.

By the time the sun set that day, there was no mistaking who would be on trial in the grim weeks ahead. On one hand, the Jewish state of Israel, trapped in the ruthless environs of a hostile Arab and Soviet-led bloc of nations, and on the other, the new U.S. ambassador, who but months earlier was conducting more or less polite exchanges over musty books and research papers with academic colleagues at Georgetown and the American Enterprise Institute, not negotiating with seasoned diplomats.

FROM THE FIRST day she walked into the U.N. corridors, Kirkpatrick was determined to make a sharp break from the past. Under Carter, the U.S. routinely accepted a barrage of anti-American attacks from the Communist and Third World nations in the U.N. Withering anti-American and anti-West criticisms were met with what she termed "silence and retreat" by previous American ambassadors. "It is easier to create an independent Namibia than to deal with the United Nations debate," Kirkpatrick had tartly told an interviewer. This was, perhaps, a slight exaggeration, but it was still an apt metaphor, reflecting her displeasure with a body increasingly at odds with the U.S.

Nor was such discontent with the international body the exclusive province of Republican activists fed up with the U.N., or anti-Carter partisans. As *New York Times* U.N. Bureau Chief Richard Bernstein would point out in an extensive *New York Times Magazine* article, by the time the 1970s came to a close, there was a growing sense that the U.N. had become excessively rhetorical, extremist, and antidemocratic, a place where the United States and its allies were attacked with relative impunity, even by countries with whom they maintained cordial relations. It had devolved into a rancorous body that served to fuel, rather than resolve, the angry flames of world conflict.

Not just in terms of formal votes, but in the tone and atmosphere of day-to-day U.N. proceedings, the chambers were filled with jargon inveighing against "Western" racism, colonialism, and fascism, while ignoring the sins of the Communist and Third World. Systematic Communist and Arab and Islamic fundamentalist atrocities, whether committed under the purview of Stalin or Brezhnev, or Saddam Hussein or Syria's Hafez al-Assad, or the Ayatollah Khomeini, were exempt from criticism. Not once had human rights violations in Communist countries been placed on the agenda of the General Assembly. The U.N. had become what one Western diplomat termed "a huge propaganda jamboree against the West."

The consequences were anything but academic. An organization whose charter repudiated the use of force showed an undisguised sympathy for "armed struggle" when carried out by Marxist national liberation movements or the Palestinian Liberation Organization. There, it repeatedly turned a blind eye to the most violent acts of terrorism.

All this had taken the U.N. far afield from its earliest years, when idealistic reformers harbored lofty and noble hopes of the U.N. as a nonaligned, independent body, bound neither to the whims of East or West, dedicated to the energizing principles of international law and conflict resolution. It never happened.

In its place, the U.N. had become a critical arena of the Cold War, an ideological extension of the U.S.-Soviet struggle. To be sure, the Cold War was a contest of hardened steel, sophisticated missiles and bullets.

But at its core, the Cold War was also a war of ideas, a struggle between political systems and dramatically different ideals about the relationship of man to man, and man to government. Communism's eschatological claim was to own history, with democracy fated to be a mere historical footnote. And this war of ideology had been waged with skill and tenacity at the U.N. by the Soviets. Kirkpatrick, fearing that democracy "was literally being overwhelmed," was determined to reverse this.

She summed up her goals this way: "It was a contest of ideas, and my view is not just that ideas have consequences, but that they have colossal consequences." As ambassador, she was thus determined that, in words and deeds, diplomacy at the U.N. would be ineluctably tied to the vigorous defense of American interests.

When Kirkpatrick first marched up to Capitol Hill for her confirmation hearings, she pronounced a terse warning. "If the U.N.," she said firmly, "engages in mischievous ideological struggle against fundamental principles of the U.S. and its friends, it should know that the patience of the American people has nearly run out." Administration watchers saw a deeper, more powerful message. Henceforth, U.N. diplomacy would be tied to power and national interest, and the Cold War competition with the Soviets would be extended to this forum in the international arena.

Indeed, as a professor and scholar, Kirkpatrick was supremely rational, but she also had an emotional, intuitive side, with a keen instinctive grasp of international politics and the broad forces that sweep nations and shaped the Cold War. Yet whether her new hard-line diplomacy, often characterized by blunt talk and sharp edges, would work, remained to be seen.

FROM THE START, Kirkpatrick had her work cut out for her. Her predecessors were sturdy models of the establishment, an eclectic but distinguished roster of insider public servants. A survey of names of previous ambassadors conveyed the staggering prominence of the job into which she was now cast. The scion of an old Brahmin family and a former U.S. senator, Henry Cabot Lodge, represented the U.S. as ambassador for most of the mid-1950s; then, former presidential candidate Adlai Stevenson, known for his bursting liberalism and erudition, presided in the glittering years of Kennedy's Camelot. Wanting his own man, President Johnson persuaded Arthur Goldberg, the brainy Supreme Court jurist, to leave his hallowed position for the U.N., but Goldberg was too independent and eventually fell out of favor with LBJ over the Vietnam War. Richard Nixon's ambassador, George Bush, was another contrast, a

model of insider rectitude, prim and proper, the quintessential play-by-
the-rules man. Afterward, the U.N. position was literally transformed by
Ford's envoy Daniel Patrick Moynihan, the flamboyant Irishman, a Harvard professor and neoconservative theoretician, intellectual yet defiantly populist. Moynihan wrote his own speeches and proved to be a
shrewd yet fiery activist. "This is a place of jackals," he angrily scowled
during one debate.

But the U.N. job was perhaps most immediately defined by Kirkpatrick's first Carter predecessor, Andrew Young. Young, like the president
he served, sharply reversed Moynihan's defiant stance and brought a
distinctly pro–Third World orientation to the U.N., coupled with a univer-
salist do-good idealism. He had a predilection for ongoing dialogue, but
critics felt he was too often more at home with criticisms of the West by
its adversaries than with a robust defense of America's policies. When
Young secretly met with the PLO's U.N. representative, in defiance of
U.S. assurances to the contrary, the public uproar was immediate. He
was promptly sacked.

But Young was quickly martyred by the political left, and came to typ-
ify the liberal establishment ethic, a standard against which Kirkpatrick
would be measured in the politically charged Reagan era. Young had met
frequently with Third World delegates, informally schmoozing with them
in the delegates lounge. He was sympathetic to their concerns, and as a
black man, many felt he would be more sensitive to the hurt caused by
the colonialist legacy of the West. He did not readily promote democracy
as a political model, and often sought compromise, to bridge and soothe
the distance between two points, no matter how contrary and opposite.

Kirkpatrick proved to be the very antithesis of Young. Where he was
solicitous of the Third World and Soviet Union, Kirkpatrick rarely hesitated to confront them with a bottom line; where Young was often a
bland diplomat rounding edges and smoothing feelings, Kirkpatrick was
bold and forthright, speaking not in diplomatic niceties but in precisely
crafted phrases that left little room for ambiguity; where Young saw
mutual culpability and moral equivalence in the Cold War, harboring a
vision not unsympathetic to socialism and its concerns, Kirkpatrick passionately believed there were moral differences between the democratic
("small d" she would stress) U.S. and Communist Soviet systems. All
told, she believed in the inherent goodness of democracy, and "sought
the preservation and expansion of individual freedom."

Early on, Kirkpatrick ran up against a U.N. culture viscerally inimical
to her ideas. She was nonetheless resolute. When Cuba sought to condemn Washington for "colonizing" Puerto Rico (a move that struck the

Puerto Ricans themselves as preposterous, but which found sympathy among American liberals and in the U.N. trusteeship council), Kirkpatrick met it with a tough stance. The Cuban effort failed.

In the same General Assembly term, in a paper directed by the Cuban foreign minister, ninety-three nonaligned Third World nations issued a twenty-one-page communiqué summarizing the state of the world. It charged the U.S. with "aggression" against Muammar al-Qaddafi's Libya, and with trying to "destabilize" Nicaragua and Grenada. To Kirkpatrick and others appalled at the communiqué, it was a one-sided, anti-American philippic. In a year when 85,000 Russian troops occupied Afghanistan, a Vietnamese- and Soviet-aligned puppet regime occupied Cambodia, and Libyan troops allied with the Soviets were hostilely stationed in Chad, the communiqué contained not a single word of criticism for the Soviet Union.

Kirkpatrick was disgusted when she read it, and promptly fired off what U.N. delegates referred to as a "letter bomb," which chided them for signing the communiqué.

She privately sent the letter to sixty-seven countries, asking them to explain their support for a document of "base lies and malicious attacks upon the good name of the United States." Prudently, she also gave them an opening to clarify their stand. "I do not believe these views are an accurate reflection of your government's outlook. And yet what are we to think when your government joins in such charges?" She asked for a reply.

Surprisingly, Kirkpatrick's gambit worked. A number of delegates quickly disassociated their countries from the letter, and others said they "would be more careful" the next time around. As one delegate wryly noted, "No one ever paid attention to such things before. We didn't know the U.S. cared."

Over time, Kirkpatrick expanded the scope of her efforts, and made it clear that the U.S. was keeping score of member nations' votes affecting American interests. With each session, the amount of anti-American invective decreased.

In U.N. discussions, Kirkpatrick was a brilliant speaker and debater, a masterful voice on American policy, striking even her passionate opponents as perhaps the most dazzling intellect in the world body. When she chose to speak at the U.N.—often she turned the floor of General Assembly debate over to her deputies—her speeches were events. Delegates surged to seats usually empty during routine debate.

Yet while Kirkpatrick quickly and successfully asserted her authority at the United Nations, other criticisms simmered and then surfaced. It was said that she had a reputation for being aloof and unavailable. She didn't socialize enough. Delegates charged that she didn't go to enough functions, parties, and dinners, where much of the work was actually done. She didn't engage in "give and take," and was too "confrontational." Her professorial style, searching for the exact word and phrase, often pausing to start over, seemed to some colleagues as if she were lecturing them, like students. A Kirkpatrick aide chuckled over the criticisms. "We don't need to be loved," she said. "Just respected."

Kirkpatrick herself defined her style. She didn't favor "quiet diplomacy so much as effective diplomacy," by which she meant not diplomatic manners, but the U.S. using its vast power to more effectively influence the conduct of business inside the United Nations. But if Kirkpatrick was succeeding at the U.N., she rapidly met stiff resistance in her own government, with the bureaucracy, the establishment, and her political adversaries.

At first, Kirkpatrick chalked this up to going against the grain of the liberal establishment, "for whom process," she noted, "not outcome and content, was far more important." Indeed, the pragmatism of the establishment, the yearning to reduce tension and foster stability in the U.S.-Soviet relationship, was itself an ideology, one that assumed a bloodless, genteel quality to global affairs, a belief that the Soviet *nomenklatura* or heavy-handed Third World dictators could be reasoned with, like opposing sides in a Wall Street leveraged buyout. For its part, liberal Democratic party orthodoxy had its own ideology, frequently seeing the U.S., as much as the Soviets, as the source of mischief in the world.

Like Richard Perle, Kirkpatrick felt that the establishment was wrong, deeply wrong, about the most basic issue of the era, dealing with the Soviets. She would say: "Everything is negotiable for them [the establishment], ideas and values are irrelevant. Thus, the establishment sees a symmetry in the superpower rivalry. That's nonsense. There is no such symmetry."

Her critics at home, however, did not let up. Kirkpatrick was routinely pilloried by named and unnamed sources in the press as a fanatic, as a zealous detached professor, as ideological. This irked her to no end. "If people agree with me, I'm idealistic," she once noted, "but if they disagree with me, I'm an ideologue."

Despite Kirkpatrick's dissection of her opposition, her skin could be thin. Asked about the hostility to her, she said, "The pain was real." And, while Kirkpatrick thought in big conceptual strokes, like a Richard Perle, the former professor lacked the prior Hill aide's well-honed bureaucratic savvy. Thus, as she sought to master the awkward governmental labyrinth, she at first approached it as a rational process, as it would be taught in a public policy school or political science course, not fully aware of her enemies and detractors at the White House and State Department, waiting like snakes in the tall grass to trip her up. Nor did she anticipate the depth of genuine hostility and the lengths to which political rivals could—and would—go.

This was all never more apparent than in the harried days when Kirkpatrick sought a resolution to the Osirak bombing crisis.

AFTER THE BOMBING, the National Security Council quickly met on Monday, June 8, and then again on Thursday morning. Kirkpatrick and the president were on the same wavelength. The Arab world, backed by the Soviet Union, was calling for a U.N. resolution, with economic sanctions and an arms embargo against Israel, which would condemn the act as "aggressive." This was unacceptable to Reagan and Haig, as well as to Kirkpatrick. Reagan instructed, "We can condemn the act, but not the actor."

Kirkpatrick knew what this meant. Reagan shared Israel's concerns that an Iraqi nuclear weapon threatened its very survival. Failing to attack would easily expose Israel to nuclear blackmail at the hands of a ruthless fanatic dedicated to its destruction. Future strikes, on Baghdad for example, would result in heavy civilian casualties. As it happened, the Israeli surgical strike had cost only one life, a French technician. Kirkpatrick watched Reagan. To her, it was clear that he showed "an empathetic feeling toward Israel."

But the U.S. had other considerations. Reagan indicated that while he didn't want a resolution injurious to Israel, he also didn't want the U.S. to have to vote against an Arab resolution. This could send a signal that the U.S. was implacably anti-Arab, endangering relations with more moderate regimes like Egypt and Saudi Arabia. He also didn't want to have to veto a resolution, because the Soviets would use this to drive a wedge between America and its moderate friends in the region. Finally, the U.S. envoy in the Middle East, Philip Habib, was hoping to cobble together a peace accord in Lebanon. When the meeting table cleared, the presidential marching orders had been laid out: it fell to Kirkpatrick to negotiate "an acceptable resolution" that the U.S. would "not have to veto."

Privately, Kirkpatrick hardly relished the task—neither negotiating with the Iraqi foreign minister, nor condemning Israel at all appealed to her—but she rose to the crisis. In public, when the Iraqi foreign minister, Sa'adoun Hammadi, insisted that the Security Council must punish Israel with sanctions, she bluntly fired back that the U.S. would veto such an action. But while the Security Council debate raged in public for more than a week, behind closed doors she and Hammadi cloistered themselves off in meetings, shuttling between the Security Council anterooms and U.N. Secretary General Kurt Waldheim's personal chambers.

Actually, Kirkpatrick had to undertake two sets of negotiations, one with the Iraqis, the other with her own legal people and the State Department. State and her career legal advisers insisted that the attack should be labeled "aggressive," meaning not in "self-defense." Kirkpatrick bitterly fought this, arguing that Israel's actions had to be understood not by the doctrinaire principles of international law, but "in their context," thus joining together procrustean exigencies of the law with the dynamic realities of international politics into a coherent framework. Eventually, she prevailed over her own bureaucracy, and used this victory as additional leverage to secure a better agreement with Hammadi.

For three days running, she constantly exchanged calls with the U.N. mission and State and the White House. When she felt it necessary, she spoke to Reagan directly. Finally, she got the president, Richard Allen, Ed Meese, the White House counselor, and Walter Stoessel, deputy secretary of state, behind her compromise resolution.

Then, on Thursday evening, June 18, the issue came to a head. Kirkpatrick and Hammadi finally nailed down language their respective governments could agree to. That same day, Reagan made a statement that Israel had "legitimate reason for concern" about Iraq's reactor, thus giving Kirkpatrick some wiggle room with the Israelis, themselves hoping that the U.S. would abstain from any vote condemning Israel.

The resolution's text was as notable for what it omitted as for what it said. Kirkpatrick felt that once the Iraqis agreed to omit language referring to the act as "aggressive," and any text about an arms embargo on Israel was deleted, she was then prepared to agree to it. Hammadi said he would give Kirkpatrick his final answer, which, loosely translated, meant he had to check with Saddam Hussein in Baghdad. Exhausted, Kirkpatrick returned to her residence, crawling into bed around 1:30 A.M.

She awoke at 6:30 to the blaring of two alarm clocks. After showering and groping to the kitchen for the tea kettle, she watched the early morning news, and rushed out before her usual departure hour of 8:45. After a final hour of back-and-forth, Hammadi, despite his personal reluctance, said he had the go-ahead. The deal was sealed.

Early that afternoon, awaiting the Security Council vote, Kirkpatrick looked tired and uncharacteristically strained as she sat at the large horseshoe-shaped table. When her turn came, flashing a slight grimace, she stiffly raised her right hand. Israel was condemned, 15–0. It was the first time that the U.S. had joined in condemning Israel since 1968, after an Israel commando raid on the Beirut airport.

While her vote was that of the diplomat, the action was belied by the expression on her face, one of disdain for the whole proceedings, and her subsequent explanation in which she insisted that the resolution did not "harm Israel's basic interests" and reaffirmed the "strength of the U.S. commitment and ties to Israel." As she later confided, the huge diplomatic triumph was a very Pyrrhic victory. "The whole affair," she said, "made me sick afterward."

She was not exaggerating. The purist in Kirkpatrick didn't like condemning Israel at all. But in the course of these intricate negotiations she came into her own, earning even grudging respect from the Third World and Communist diplomats. Reagan himself was genuinely pleased with the outcome, and the balance that had been struck. One of the biggest losers in the affair, everyone agreed, was the Soviets, who had hoped to isolate the U.S. and Israel, but failed.

Indeed, however much Kirkpatrick's detractors wanted to paint her as inflexible, she was widely given credit for delicately working out this important compromise resolution. Nor was it lost on the delegates that she added a gracious gesture to her statement, generously praising the "cooperative spirit, restrained positions, and good faith of the Iraqi foreign minister."

At the U.N., perhaps awkwardly, and certainly defiantly, Kirkpatrick had finally arrived as a major force.

ALEXANDER HAIG, THE secretary of state, hated to be out of the loop, and hated being overshadowed even more. As U.N. ambassador, Kirkpatrick reported to him. As he saw it, her job was not to make policy but to implement it. But as a member of the administration's top-level policy-making unit, the National Security Planning Group (NSPG), and as a cabinet member, she did have a hefty voice in the policy process, not as a subordinate, but on equal footing. Her direct access to Reagan only enhanced her standing. To Haig's consternation, when she came to the Oval Office, the president listened and usually agreed with her.

Nor was Kirkpatrick a wallflower. Lawrence Eagleburger, the undersecretary of state for political affairs, often watched in amazement at the substantial impact Kirkpatrick had in the NSPG meetings. As he pointed out, rarely did she shy away from expressing her views, even if she disagreed with the majority. "She would freely challenge the assumptions and proposals of the secretary of state—and no secretary of state likes that, especially from someone more or less subordinate," he noted. This was particularly true for Secretary Haig (or General Haig, as he was often called). Haig, extremely well informed in foreign policy, was the ultimate chain-of-command guy. The problem, as Haig saw it, was that he could not just issue orders to Kirkpatrick and have them blindly followed; she would talk back to him. Early on, the blood between the two went sour.

Less than a week after the vote on Osirak, Haig was on his plane, en route to Wellington, New Zealand. In flight, two of his aides spoke openly with reporters about the U.N. resolution, leaking a story that Haig had to intervene personally to rescue it from being too anti-Israel. Kirkpatrick, they alleged, was willing to accept a number of points that were unacceptable to the president, and Haig had to intercede with Hammadi to rescue the resolution from a disastrous outcome.

The next day, the *New York Times* ran a major story, "Mrs. Kirkpatrick Faulted on Iraq by Haig's Aides." This was a direct slap at Kirkpatrick. Hearing the criticism, she was furious and perplexed. "It was far-out stuff," she commented from her home in Provence, in southern France, where she was vacationing, "just sheer lies."

By her own acknowledgment, Kirkpatrick realized she was naive. She didn't fully understand the turf warfare that drove policy making, just as she often had difficulty making sense of the daily battles emanating out of the free-floating hostility in the government toward most of Reagan's conservative policies, even in his own State Department. Before coming to government, she believed that leaks from government sources always had a semblance of truth. Now she had come to see them as fabrications and efforts at disinformation, stealthily used to wage bureaucratic warfare. And, ironically, because Kirkpatrick was *not* a leaker, she was at a disadvantage. Her adversaries were able to attack her in the press with relative impunity. But, in the Osirak case, the leaks backfired.

If Kirkpatrick was furious, the White House was even more so—Haig's aides' comments had undercut it too. Moving with great speed, the White House sharply repudiated the statements. The president himself called Kirkpatrick at her French retreat to warmly congratulate her, and Haig thereafter disavowed the remarks.

But the gauntlet had been thrown down. Kirkpatrick came to government expecting her greatest challenge to be at the U.N. and with the Soviets. There she was making modest but demonstrable gains. Yet she didn't realize she would face a minefield at home, trying to contend with political rivals and civil servants wedded not to Reagan but to an agenda that belonged to the more enduring verities of the establishment bureaucracy. It shook up Kirkpatrick. As she put it, "I felt my world was being turned inside out.

"I could manage the U.S. United Nations mission successfully and defend us against two thirds of the world," she said, "but simultaneously defending the mission against the back stabbing from our own people, *that* was too much." And while her star was rising (she had already far eclipsed Richard Allen as the administration intellectual), Kirkpatrick could not shake a gnawing feeling of doubt, not that she couldn't survive, not that she couldn't have a major impact in the contest of ideas, but that it could come at a terrible personal price.

CHAPTER 18

In Kirkpatrick's eleventh-floor office at the United Nations, twenty-four hours a day, secret cables bearing news of upheaval, strife, and crisis poured in from American embassies around the world. They were meticulously logged into file folders, a carefully knit array of interlocking categories of conflict and trouble: the Iran-Iraq War, Disarmament, Central America, Poland, North-South Dialogue, the INF Arms Talks, Terrorism. But of these, one issue, holding particular importance to her, invariably caught her eye: the fate of Israel.

And as the thirty-fifth General Assembly session in 1981 gave way to the thirty-sixth in 1982, support for Israel, so symbolically vital to the precepts and philosophy of the Reagan administration's Cold War strategy, came under repeated and relentless assault in the U.N. The vote on the Osirak raid was just the beginning of a long and unnerving year. The Arab and Communist bloc sought no less than to accomplish in the diplomatic corridors what they had failed to do on the battlefield—to expel Israel from the world community. In this effort, they would seek to use a series of unrelated explosions in the Middle East cauldron as additional diplomatic ammunition, which in due course would frequently pit Kirkpatrick, and her president, at increasing odds with the establishment and the bureaucracy.

THE FIRST SIGNS that it would be a difficult period in the U.N. for Israel occurred quietly, more by institutional stealth than outright action. It began in January 1982, not in the somber workings of the U.N. Security Council but in the full glare of the entire General Assembly. The radical Arab states, working with the Soviet bloc and nonaligned nations, passed a resolution condemning Israel for annexing the Syrian Golan Heights. For years, Syrian rocket attacks had rained terror upon small Israeli villages in the north. They halted only after Israel conquered the Golan in its defensive war against the Arab world in 1967. After fifteen years, it had become ineluctably clear that Syria was still unwilling even to speak directly with Israel, let alone accept its existence or make peace with it. Thus, after heated internal debate in the Knesset, Israel made a major decision. With few other options, it chose peace through territorial security, and created a strategic buffer against its dreaded adversary, formally annexing vast stretches of fertile but largely unused Golan land. The U.N. reaction was swift, and Israel's actions were ominously deemed a demonstration that it was not a "peace-loving state."

In the beginning, the resolution was taken in stride at the U.S. mission, and the diplomatic phrase of art "peace-loving state" appeared to have no special meaning. Kirkpatrick didn't pay much attention to it, and her staff did not suggest immediate action. But gradually it dawned on the U.S. mission that the phrase had actually been chosen with meticulous care. Article 4 of the U.N. charter, its constitution, stipulates clearly that membership in the U.N. is open to all "peace-loving states." The implication was clear: the foundation was being laid for the expulsion of Israel.

That winter, Kirkpatrick knew this was the first blow of a long slugging match. But what form would the next punch take? What were the Arabs and Soviet bloc up to?

In the aftermath of the Osirak success, Kirkpatrick was no longer viewed solely as a lone voice in the wilderness. She became more confident in her role and, during the holiday season, shuttled back and forth to U.N. parties and social functions, more freely exchanging warm words with her colleagues (often in fluent Spanish and garrulous French), even relishing their cosmopolitan sophistication. Some colleagues still found her inaccessible, but she was clearly settling in. But Kirkpatrick was only just learning about the U.N.'s often harsh ways and was capable of being precipitously shocked by the undercurrent of bitter conflict that lay beneath the warm words and diplomatic socializing among U.N. delegates.

One fall afternoon, an important Arab ambassador pulled her aside, lowered his voice, and spoke to her in confidence. Kirkpatrick cocked her ear to listen. Israel, he whispered, was a "crusader remnant," a foreign body in alien territory. Like the crusaders, he stressed, it would one day "disappear." Kirkpatrick resisted the temptation to frown, holding her temper in diplomatic reserve. But she took this exchange as a lesson. The Arabs and Soviets freely sought to use the U.N. to hasten Israel's demise. To her shock, as months passed, she learned America's European allies weren't much different. Eager to explain the hidden norms and guildlike rhythms of the U.N.'s frequently freewheeling and chaotic culture, a number of European ambassadors routinely insisted that Israel was "a terrible embarrassment," "a nuisance," "stubborn and obstinate." You'll see, just watch the Israelis in action, the Europeans dutifully warned Kirkpatrick. They were fully convinced that out of the spotlight of public debate, she too would agree with them.

But she didn't.

Indeed, it was all ironic. Kirkpatrick, a woman in a man's world, a Democrat in a Republican administration, defied many labels. In the political parlance of the day, it was often commonly assumed that neoconservatives were not so much old-style liberals, now more in step with the conservative rhythms of the 1980s, as they were "Jewish conservatives."

But at the U.N., Kirkpatrick's colleagues assumed something rather different. Because she wasn't Jewish, they believed she wouldn't—couldn't—be really engaged with Israel's fate, but would be more like many of her predecessors, largely sympathetic to the Arabs, except when bowing to domestic political considerations and the incessant pressure of a loud Jewish lobby.

Kirkpatrick, though, was not of the old establishment school. Early in her scholarly life, she had worked with Professor Franz Neumann, poring through files filled with sordid revelations about the Nazi concentration camps (and later Stalin's gulags). She once said, years afterward, "It was, is, still all so fresh." The experience seared her deeply, and the shadows and stench of government-fostered death on a massive scale, politically inspired and cruelly implemented by totalitarian regimes, made her acutely sensitive to the evils of such regimes on one hand, and the terrible plight of the Jewish people on the other.

Moreover, by nature, temperament, and character, Kirkpatrick felt organically tied to the fate of the Jewish people, and just as deeply tied to the future of Israel. Indeed, like Ronald Reagan, when Kirkpatrick looked at Israel, she frequently saw a reflection of America, a young country of hard workers, pioneers ruggedly taming the land, a feisty and entrepreneurial people, a society rich in culture and the arts, a land as pluralistic in spirit as in law and practice, a rancorous, untameable democracy. Like America, it had its faults. But all told, she, and Reagan, admired the gritty little democracy.

On so many issues, but certainly when it came to Israel, Reagan and Kirkpatrick were one of history's more fascinating pairs. Reagan, the small-town boy, the man's man chopping wood at the ranch, a product of the glitz of California and the movie industry, was the soothing voice with the perfect political touch. A Eureka College B.A. thinking in broad verities, a former Democrat, he was also a dreamer. Kirkpatrick, the oil wildcatter's daughter, a scholar of high politics, a hungry consumer of philosophy, a Democrat, was Dr. Kirkpatrick, a rigorous social scientist, so very precise in her every utterance, garrulous but no instinctive glad-hander. Yet the two shared a sense of history, an impatience with moral waffling, an appreciation of courage, a desire not just to play but to win. To be sure, their links with Israel were intellectual, but they also sprang from the gut.

But Kirkpatrick was not one to be moved purely by sentiment, and Israel was, for larger reasons, an integral component of the Reagan foreign policy. Like the U.S., Israel was a democracy engaged in a great struggle for its way of life, a country where the people cherished political freedom, but were faced with mortal enemies seeking to destroy it. As such, Israel was an exemplar for other smaller countries, a model for the nascent democracies struggling to find their way, to throw off the yoke of dictatorial tyranny, whether of the Communist, fascist, or fundamentalist stripe. In her seminal *Commentary* article, "Dictatorships and Double Standards," she argued that the U.S. must stand up for its friends, not leave them helpless and vulnerable in a tough world. And of course, Israel was more than a friend and strategic ally; it too was stubbornly anti-Soviet. So perhaps no country fit the bill meriting support more than Israel. And passionate support in the Reagan administration for Israel was thus a natural outgrowth of the Kirkpatrick doctrine.

There was also a deeper component. As an embattled democracy, Israel was a palpable symbol of the democratic ideal, of a way of life to be enjoyed by all countries. For this reason too, Israel occupied a central spot in the weighty calculus of the Cold War. By standing shoulder-to-shoulder with this tiny nation, Kirkpatrick was asserting the legitimacy and primacy of democracy. To the Soviets, it sent a blunt message. Democracies *will* hang together. In the full force of time, they, not Communism, would lay claim to the future, and the democratic world, not the Communist world, would win the Cold War.

But Kirkpatrick's—or Reagan's—views were not universally shared. This too complicated her efforts over the difficult months of 1982.

THE ESTABLISHMENT HAD never felt very comfortable with Israel. When Britain jettisoned its empire and tossed Palestine to the U.N., President Harry Truman wanted to help create the new Jewish state. His most trusted foreign policy advisers, Acheson, Lovett, Marshall, Chip Bohlen, and Kennan, were dead set against it. Each of these men, scions of the establishment, claimed opposition on pragmatic grounds. Supporting Israel would jeopardize access to the Middle East oil pipeline and drive the Arabs inexorably into the hands of the Soviets. It would hurt U.S. national security in the region, from the Horn of Africa to the emirates in the Persian Gulf. And in any case, the Jews would never be able to make it on their own, and would need U.S. soldiers to salvage their Zionist cause. Truman, who knew something about the little guy standing up to the big guy, ignored his advisers, and the day the British Mandate expired, May 14, 1948, the U.S. promptly recognized the new state of Israel.

Yet even as Truman's advisers were proven wrong by history (Israel flourished, oil flowed, the entire Arab world did not rush headlong into Soviet arms), the establishment continued to argue Middle East policy on much the same grounds. Its long-standing views were probably best summed up by John McCloy, who as a Franklin Roosevelt aide had fervently argued against bombing the Nazi death camps (he invoked "technical difficulties" in attacking Auschwitz). He maintained for years that close relations with Arab rulers would guarantee regional stability, a steady access to cheap oil, and serve as a buffer against the Soviets. "It was," he said, "practical diplomacy."

As much as on any other issue, Kirkpatrick was weary of the establishment when it came to Israel. "With regard to Israel and the Middle East, the establishment has a reliable and steady bias against Israel, but they were wrong under Truman and they are wrong now," she stated.

One man in particular would take virulent objection to Kirkpatrick's pro-Israel stance, Reagan's White House chief of staff, and chief administration political pragmatist, James Baker. To Baker, Kirkpatrick's views were not a skillful assessment of historical forces and enduring international precepts, a principled policy of standing by good friends, but much like the rantings of a fanatic.

While this conflict did not openly come to a head until much later, it was carried on surreptitiously behind closed doors, fueled by leaks and harsh words fed to compliant reporters. Baker was a master of such moves, and invariably, when Kirkpatrick picked up the morning paper to read about White House meetings she and Baker had both attended, she could scarcely recognize the events described. While Baker, and Reagan's image man, Michael Deaver, were portrayed as forces of moderation and conciliation, Kirkpatrick always sounded, well, excessive. But the warning signs often came too late. "Nothing really prepared me for this," she later recounted, "for the knives in my back."

EASTER SUNDAY 1982 was a day of bedlam in the Middle East. A lone Israeli man, Alan Goodman, dressed in army fatigues, walked innocuously into the gold-leaf Dome of the Rock in the old city of Jerusalem, a Muslim mosque and a holy shrine to the Islamic world. Suddenly, he drew an

M-16 automatic rifle and, before anyone could act, sprayed gunfire around him. A frantic struggle ensued, and within minutes he was wrestled to the ground by Israeli police, but not until he had brutally killed an Arab youth, an unarmed Arab guard, and wounded forty other worshippers. It was a horrible scene, leaving pools of blood and screams in its wake. Goodman, an immigrant from Baltimore, was, like mostly every other Israeli under the age of fifty-five, a conscripted reservist in the army. He was also severely crazed.

The repercussions of the act spread wildly through a shocked and angry Arab world, from the unpaved roads of the West Bank, to the Arab kingdoms of Jordan and Saudi Arabia, and as far away as Muslim Indonesia. The Israeli people themselves were horrified by the incident, and the government promised to bring Goodman promptly to trial for murder. But this event, which in another context would have been chalked up to the pitiful actions of one deranged man, soon blew up into much larger proportions.

The Arab world quickly ascribed a much more nefarious design to the crime, blaming the Israeli authorities, even the army itself, for being directly complicit in the heinous act. Goodman's reservist status was held up as exhibit A. Within two days, the Arabs tabled a draft resolution in the U.N. condemning Israel. But the resolution went even further than that, stoutly referring to Jerusalem as "occupied territory."

From her experience over the previous year, Kirkpatrick felt it was important to handle this issue delicately. Twice before, on related matters she had been burned, once by State, the other in the U.N. itself. She didn't want a repeat incident. The Middle East was like a pot of water chronically on the verge of boil, always ready to spill over with seething steam. This time, she had to maneuver deftly.

The first time she had been burned was in the summer of 1981, when she had argued against the expansion of the PLO observer mission. Kirkpatrick was dead set against it. The PLO was a terrorist group, it did not need to double its size to fulfill its responsibilities at the U.N. PLO expansion was also aimed at undermining Israel. She made her views crystal clear in a pointed memo sent to Haig, but it was mousetrapped by pro-PLO bureaucrats and Arabists at State. As her draft made the rounds at State, they rewrote her views, *then* argued against them, and sent *this* memo up the line.

Haig, who was himself deeply pro-Israel, signed off on the memo, which had inexplicably metamorphosed from being against the expansion of the PLO mission when Kirkpatrick drafted it, to being for it (with her as the lone, dissenting voice) by the time it was recast as a "Decision Memorandum for the Secretary." The memorandum was so watered down that Haig had little idea why she was registering deep objections. The affair was a rude awakening for the former professor trying to figure out the maze called the policy process. She swore she wouldn't be snookered again.

The second case occurred in October of 1981, involving a Palestinian terrorist, Zihad Abu Eain. In 1979 he killed two Israeli schoolchildren and maimed thirty-six others, including adults, with a powerful bomb detonated near a sunny public garden and crowded bus stop in Israel. Abu Eain quickly fled, successfully slipping by Israeli authorities to safety in Jordan and then making his way to Chicago. Israel invoked a mutual extradition treaty with the U.S. and asked that he be returned. But the extradition was held up for more than a year as Abu Eain and his lawyer, Ramsey Clark, argued his case in American courts. They maintained that his act was a political offense, not a terrorist act, and hence was not extraditable.

His case eventually reached the U.S. Supreme Court, which declined to hear it. Abu Eain had come to the end of the line. Unable to find a haven in the U.S. legal system, he sought recourse in the international political process, and it was at this point that he appealed directly to the U.N. to oppose the extradition.

To Kirkpatrick, this was a matter of deep principle—and absolute rubbish. At stake was whether the U.S. was prepared to hold the line against terrorism. As it was, she felt Abu Eain had had his day in court, and lost. Not to be outdone this time, she paid greater attention to the bureaucratic process and the White House sided with her, overriding State's objections, and ordered that the extradition proceed apace. But her victory was partially tarnished by a vote in the U.N. General Assembly, which by a staggering two-to-one margin overwhelmingly condemned the extradition while ignoring the terrorist act.

After the Goodman incident at the Dome of the Rock, these two past events weighed on Kirkpatrick's mind, as did an urgent cable sent to her by Undersecretary of State Lawrence Eagleburger. Marked top secret, it pleaded with her to bear in mind how a U.S. veto over the Jerusalem language could prompt violence against U.S. personnel and American embassies in the Islamic world, indirectly recalling the Iran hostage crisis. Eagleburger further requested that Kirkpatrick try to work out a deal with the Islamic countries. Achieve a text the U.S. could agree to or, at least, from which it could abstain.

Kirkpatrick was not looking for a skirmish with Eagleburger, nor was she insensitive to the concerns he raised. But this issue was being blown out of proportion by the Arabs; moreover, by citing Jerusalem as occupied Arab territory they betrayed a deeper agenda, using this incident less to vent humanitarian outrage than to prejudge the holy city's status. Since the signing of the Camp David Peace Accords in 1979, the U.S. had stoutly rejected putting Jerusalem at the front of the agenda. This was a deal-breaker in the chronically brittle Arab-Israeli peace process. Moreover, Israel, for which Jerusalem was its holiest city and capital through the ages, was unyielding on this issue. Kirkpatrick knew that the nub of this matter were these opposing factors and her success would depend on skillfully juggling them.

But the incident had frayed her nerves. On the afternoon of April 14, one of her aides, Allan Gerson, mused aloud that it would be far better to tell the Arabs their efforts were bound to go nowhere than to engage in protracted negotiation with them. Kirkpatrick, perhaps worn out by too many meetings and too much travel back and forth between New York and D.C., was in no mood for what *ought* to be. She sharply snapped: "I don't want to hear another word about it, you've read my instructions on the subject."

Gerson, a trusted aide, shook his head sheepishly. However well he thought he knew her, there was always this impenetrable side, a repository of emotion and complexity that he never fully fathomed. He could also see the wear and tear of the job on her. After months at the U.N., Kirkpatrick the scholar was now Kirkpatrick the ambassador, seeking to harness an unwieldy system like a caboose that she could gently, but firmly, pull along.

Over the ensuing hectic days, as Kirkpatrick shuttled between meetings at the U.N. and NSC meetings, she gave every appearance of seeking to broker a deal. Publicly, she went through all the motions, as she and her staff alternately negotiated with State Department and Arab officials. Asked by Jordan's U.N. representative, Hazem Nuseibeh, about her disposition toward the vote, she put him on the speaker phone, so other officials in the room could hear the conversation.

"What's your government's thinking?" Nuseibeh probed. Kirkpatrick responded, "My government remains concerned." But she kept talks going. Her own bottom line continued to be that Jerusalem could not be in the resolution as "occupied Arab land." Still, her staff was often unclear exactly what she was up to, including two days later, when the Security Council commenced debate. She was keeping her options close to her vest.

It was a blistering debate, and the sniping and scathing remarks toward Israel that would have, in any other context or forum, been beyond the pale, touched frayed sensitivities, raw historical wounds, and exposed psyches. And it stood as striking proof that the contest of ideas and ideology between the U.S. and the Soviets, and the West and the

Third World, was a real war, a no-holds-barred animosity, bordering on violence, even if waged only with words.

Richard Ovinnikov, the Soviet deputy ambassador, snapped that the Goodman act was a result of "the complicity of the United States." Jordan's ambassador, Hazem Nuseibeh, cut deeper to the bone, comparing Israel's Zionist ideals "with Hitler's *Mein Kampf.*" The PLO's representative, Zehdi Terzi, chalked the rampage up "not to a solitary maniac," but to "state terrorism." And then Ambassador Farah Dirir of Djibouti, a small African nation at the mouth of the Red Sea, outdid the previous speakers and spoke about "trigger-happy Israeli soldiers" laughing with the "sadistic bouts of amusement of the Nazi Germans." It was too much for the American delegation, which alternately cringed and winced as they watched the Israel ambassador, Yehuda Blum, who had survived Bergen-Belsen, a Nazi death camp, turn shades of ashen white, then hot red.

For her part, Kirkpatrick had anticipated this circus, and stayed behind at her office in the U.S. mission, sending Chuck Lichenstein, her deputy, in her stead. When Lichenstein and the other aides returned dejected to the mission, they found Kirkpatrick in a surprisingly upbeat mood. She broke the news. Her views had prevailed in Washington, and the next day, when she cast her vote, it would be a veto if Jerusalem were labeled "occupied territory."

It was an object lesson for the Arabs. They thought she was bluffing, and that if they pressed her hard enough she would buckle.

Too often critics looked upon the struggle at the U.N. as a Greek tragedy, with fate having predetermined the end. Yet however much it often felt like that, that night, as the long New York shadows merged with dusk, and Kirkpatrick ate a quiet supper at her Waldorf residence, there was the dawning recognition that inch by bitter inch, the line could be drawn, the historical furniture could be moved, and that the weary struggle on behalf of the democratic ideal was worth the grief.

BUT HER RESPITE was momentary as crises continued. On June 6, a Sunday, only days after the Israeli ambassador to England was assassinated by a powerful PLO bomb, Israeli armored forces thrust into Lebanon, quickly raced past the barren hills in the south, and began to push north until they came into fateful contact with PLO guerrilla strongholds. Dubbed "Operation Peace for Galilee," the Israelis showed every intent of smashing the PLO guerrilla apparatus, which had been carrying out terrorist attacks from the Israeli-Lebanese border. That same morning, Kirkpatrick rushed to a hastily convened meeting of the NSPG, which had quickly formed a Crisis Management Group to deal with the invasion. Vice President George Bush was chairing the group.

Bush's body language was stiff and angry, and he was unusually animated. His geniality gone, his face flushed, he broke into a passionate attack on Israel's actions. It would radicalize the PLO, not break it, he maintained, and strain the precarious Israeli-Egyptian relationship to the breaking point. It would doom chances for advancing Ronald Reagan's Middle East peace process. Terrorism would rise. It was a disaster. Israel had to back down. Fast.

Others at the meeting could barely recall ever seeing the vice president so livid. It struck them as disproportionate to the event. Bush talked viscerally about the incident as though it were a personal affront directed *at* him *by* Menachem Begin, Israel's prime minister.

Watching Bush, Kirkpatrick was taken aback. The out-and-out hostility toward Israel wasn't even veiled. He was speaking as though Israel had suddenly launched a war against a neutral nation. Sitting in the room, Cap Weinberger was also outraged. He folded his arms across his chest and knit his brow.

To Kirkpatrick, Bush's torrent of dire warnings was far off the mark. Despite his intense views, Kirkpatrick saw her role as trying to persuade the group to "see the issue in its context," and "to take into account the facts on the ground." She explained that Israel had "very real security concerns." It wasn't accurate, she countered, to describe the Israeli operation as an invasion, "because PLO terrorists had been violating Lebanon's sovereignty, using its territory to shell and attack Israeli civilians and villages." Moreover, the incursion could strike a major blow against international terrorism. With the PLO dealt a bloody nose, Lebanon would have a chance of being repaired, and the U.S. would be in a position to advance the Camp David Accords. "Far from retreating," she argued, "the Israelis should continue their advance."

For a minute, her words hung there isolated. But they did not carry the day. With Bush leading the charge and unwilling to brook any dissent, the pressure to restrain the Israelis was acute.

In the ensuing round of high-level NSPG meetings, particularly those that Bush chaired, Kirkpatrick began to notice a strange tendency, a tendency for cabinet members not to debate issues, but often to stifle discussion, to lurch for consensus first, not last. While she was voicing loud dissent or illustrating a point with facts, others were often quietly fitting their views to conform with the emerging policy led by Bush. The meetings grew so emotionally charged that Kirkpatrick called them "awful."

Reagan himself was happy to listen to freewheeling debate, but his

White House advisers sought instead to narrow it. It was an ongoing struggle. To Kirkpatrick, Chief of Staff James Baker, who had earned her contempt, merited particular attention. He rarely tipped his hand or ventured an opinion in meetings. It was often hard to know where he stood on any issue. Peering through his intense, thin eyes, his powerful Texas frame seated bolt upright, he would be poised, like a gunfighter waiting to draw in a Wild West shoot-out. With one big difference. No one ever seemed to see the bureaucratically deft Baker fire his gun.

Kirkpatrick had learned her lesson with Baker early, and was at once bold in pressing her arguments, while a cautious team player. And as the round of tense cabinet and Crisis Management Group meetings progressed, and the very real differences of opinion between herself and Bush were openly exposed, like a wound, she sent a signal: she would hotly voice her views privately inside the meeting room, but show solidarity once a decision was made.

But the pressure was on not just at the White House but also at the U.N. That first Sunday afternoon of the crisis, Kirkpatrick raced back to New York for an emergency Security Council meeting. In the midst of an intense debate, the Soviet delegate, Oleg Troyanovsky, proposed splitting a draft resolution paragraph, "for clarity." But the effect would be far more. The split would effectively de-link a U.N. call for an unconditional withdrawal of Israeli forces from a PLO cease-fire and cessation of border attacks. The former would no longer depend upon the latter. Other delegates braced themselves for a stinging retort from Kirkpatrick. Instead, she stunned the room. Rather than indicating that the Soviet proposal would cause a U.S. veto, she simply muttered in a wan voice: "No objection."

Sitting nervously nearby, Kirkpatrick's bewildered aides, Chuck Lichenstein and Allan Gerson, were shocked. They knew she had been under siege, embroiled with Haig over the U.S. response to the recent British invasion of the Falklands. As the crisis unraveled, and Kirkpatrick had sided with the Argentineans and Haig with the British, he imperiously declared that generals don't speak directly to "company commanders." In the heat of the ten-week crisis, he refused even to communicate directly with her. Their quarrel was now out in the open and the immediate buzz in Washington was of a permanent Haig-Kirkpatrick rift. Calls for her resignation were now being openly aired. Kirkpatrick was fed up with Haig's machinations, and believed he had orchestrated a campaign aimed at her ouster. "I'm convinced he's tried to set me up," she had told her staff. The exhaustion showed on her face.

Her staff were also keenly aware that Bush had tried to lay down the line earlier in the day. For Gerson and other Kirkpatrick aides, perhaps she was simply succumbing to the inevitable. But Chuck Lichenstein, a good friend of Kirkpatrick's, was not one to hold his tongue. Unable to control himself over her surprising move, he blurted out a protest. "How could you do this?"

Kirkpatrick shot him an angry stare. "There are things I know that you don't know," she snapped. And indeed she did. What she had not told her staff was that far harsher alternatives toward Israel were being discussed back in Washington. There was talk of cutting aid, of other forms of censure, and she was seeking to head these moves off. But outside of top-level meetings, Kirkpatrick decided to keep mum. Like the foreign policy architects at the end of World War II, she believed that sensitive meetings about presidential policy should be kept private. So strong was that principle that she refused to "background" reporters with her version of events. At times, she also decided to keep her staff in the dark about the full content of the NSPG meetings, to prevent them from going to the press. To Kirkpatrick, leaking was a coward's game, and one that ultimately only undercut the president.

But Kirkpatrick also had another concern. Reagan himself was having doubts about Israel. Bush and Baker had furnished the president with a widely circulated UPI photo, printed on page one of the *Washington Post*, of a seven-month-old Palestinian baby girl, her arms bandaged from her hands to shoulders, purportedly as a result of an Israeli bombing raid in Lebanon. For a time, Reagan kept the photo on his desk, and asked, "Who would do such a thing to a child?" But the child was later located, and the photo was revealed as a hoax. (Indeed, she was actually the victim of a PLO gun battery in West Beirut, and had been only slightly injured.) Bush and Baker, however, never told Reagan. As Kirkpatrick quickly saw, all stops were being pulled out on this issue in the battle for the president's soul.

In the following days, the quagmire thickened, and in addition to the internal war over Israeli policy, the public anti-Kirkpatrick sentiment over the Falklands dispute continued. Kirkpatrick herself was particularly troubled by calls for her resignation in the *New York Times*. In a moment of weakness, she turned to her staff and pleaded for them "to turn the tide." At week's end, however, Kirkpatrick had no way of knowing that she would soon receive first one lift, then another, from most unlikely quarters, if not vindicating her initial instincts, at least strengthening them.

OVER THE NEXT week, the situation in the Middle East became increasingly tense. On the ground, Israeli tanks continued their push forward, marching into the outskirts of West Beirut; then, the Israelis boldly confronted the Syrians for domination over the skies of the Bekaa Valley, in Syrian-occupied Lebanon. In a series of screeching dogfights, they shot down two dozen Soviet MIGs. Not since 1970, when Israeli fighter planes downed Egyptian-piloted Soviet MIGs in similar hair-raising skirmishes, had the Soviets been so humiliated. Back then, they issued a stern warning to the Israelis: keep it up, and they would enter the fray. The Israelis backed down. But this time, the Israelis confidently pressed forward, turning their sights to Soviet-supplied surface-to-air missiles (SAMs).

At this dangerous juncture, the specter of a Soviet entry into the conflict could not be totally discounted, and Israel and Syria were murderously poised on the edge of battle. Official Washington was itself unsure how to play things. Philip Habib, the energetic presidential envoy, was busily shuttling between Jerusalem, Damascus, and Beirut to cobble together a solution, but with few results. Meanwhile, an unlikely Kirkpatrick-Haig axis continued to see merits to roughing up the PLO, and assuring Israel that border raids would not continue. In turn, they hoped this could lay the groundwork for a new semblance of order to be established in Lebanon. But the Bush mid-level State Department–led faction remained harshly skeptical, favoring an immediate Israeli withdrawal.

The two sides quarreled until the moderate elements of the Arab world sent an unexpected but decisive signal to tip the balance. However lamentable Israel's incursion was, emissaries of Egypt, Jordan, and others indicated in private that neither the PLO nor Syria should be allowed to control Lebanon. "Don't leave a vacuum," intoned one Arab ambassador. "Israel should not withdraw immediately," another hinted. Translated loosely, let Israel finish the job it had started, provided it didn't take Beirut itself.

Suddenly, Kirkpatrick's views looked like prescience. William Safire, of the *New York Times,* hailed Kirkpatrick's efforts. Ronald Reagan came down on her side. Official Washington followed suit, seeing "great possibilities" for a reordering of the chaotic Middle East patchwork quilt. Soon, a new plan was hatched. U.S. diplomacy should work to evacuate the PLO from Lebanon, removing them safely by sea.

Kirkpatrick was not consulted, and privately was not happy about a U.S. rescue of PLO terrorists. But she was a realist, and publicly appreciated the merits of this plan. It would remove the immediate danger to Israel, thus opening up possibilities for a more stable Lebanon, while being acceptable to the moderates in the Arab world. Buoyed by this turn of events vindicating her views, some of Kirkpatrick's fire returned. The morning Israeli Prime Minister Menachem Begin spoke to the U.N. General Assembly at a session on disarmament, all but roughly a hundred of the nine hundred delegates stood up and walked out when he took to the podium. Kirkpatrick was unfazed, and defiantly planted herself in a visible seat and clapped loudly when Begin finished. Before he entered his limousine for the airport, she rushed over to give him a warm embrace.

The next day, she promptly left for a two-week, five-nation trip to Central Africa. It was billed as a chance to consult with Francophile African nations on the upcoming "U.N. Decade for Women." To be sure, in view of the Lebanon crisis, it could have been delayed. But in truth, Kirkpatrick was beat. She wanted to cool off—and be away from Bush, Haig, and the incessant infighting.

She was in Togo five days later when the news came: Alexander Haig had lost the confidence of the president, and had abruptly resigned (she soon learned that he was fired). George Shultz would replace him. Kirkpatrick knew enough not to gloat, taking more solace than pleasure from Haig's unexpected ouster. Instead, it took another Kirkpatrick rival, the Soviet U.N. ambassador, Troyanovsky, to sum up the event. He quipped: "Mrs. Kirkpatrick is the first hunter on safari in Africa to bag her prey in Washington."

By mid-August, her persistence on Israel policy had paid off. The urgent throes of the Lebanon crisis had been defused. While Kirkpatrick was out of the policy-making loop on the Habib mission itself, in the critical final weeks she successfully staved off a French-Egyptian effort at the U.N. that would have all but doomed Habib's precarious diplomatic efforts. By month's end, Habib's labors reached fruition, and the PLO was emptied out of Lebanon. Yasir Arafat, over 8,500 PLO fighters, and the entire PLO guerrilla apparatus, retreated out of the musty alleys and crumbling hideaways of Beirut, eerily exploding their Russian Kalashnikovs into the sky and shouting hyperbolic statements of triumph and liberation, and left the port of Beirut on multinational-force ships. The ships were frequently escorted by the U.S. Navy, providing them safe but ignominious passage to Tunisia. (The French were left with the task of shipping Arafat's armored Mercedes-Benz to him.)

Yet even as she emerged stronger from this prolonged bout, Kirkpatrick would once more have to turn her attention to a U.N. whose sights were trained yet again on Israel.

THE FINAL ASSAULT came as the U.N. was beginning to wind up its business for the year. The U.N. Credentials Committee, a little-used body for rubber stamp resolutions, declared on October 6 that Israel's credentials were "out of order." This was an old ploy, used previously against South Africa, which was expelled from the General Assembly on the obscure procedural grounds that its credentials were deemed "wanting." The U.S. fought the move only halfheartedly, and South Africa was banned. The precedent had thus been set, and now it was Israel's turn. For Israel, and for American diplomacy, it was a nightmare about to come true.

The argument made in the committee was a contorted one, but it nonetheless held. Normally, the committee would adjudicate credentials between rival delegations claiming to represent a single country, like Cambodia, a country occupied by Vietnam and torturously wracked by infighting between dramatically opposed Communist and non-Communist government factions. But in Israel's case, the Credentials Committee was instead rendering a verdict on the legitimacy of its democratically elected government. When the final gavel came down, the committee denied Israel's legitimacy and the tiny nation was on the slippery slope to expulsion.

Hearing this, Kirkpatrick was incensed. Fresh from her victory in beating back the French over Israel and Lebanon, she was determined to take a stand. She had long been a tart critic of the U.N., asserting that it fanned rather than resolved conflict. But she felt ominous portents about this issue. It could not be allowed to drag out, not in view of the disastrous vote count on the Abu Eain resolution the year before. Plainly put, she felt it had to be stopped dead in its tracks. But how?

She was skeptical of the State Department taking the lead, and seized upon another plan. The year before, the U.N. Economic and Social Committee had voted to deny a seat to the U.S., prompting a feisty Oklahoma Republican congressman, Mickey Edwards, to promise to introduce legislation that required the U.S. to withhold 10 percent of its $90 million annual contribution to the committee until the U.S. was given a seat. The message was that opposition to the U.S. would come with a price, figuratively and literally. The U.N. acquiesced. So congressional action, she reasoned, was the place to start.

She furiously lobbied Congress to introduce legislation requiring a 25 percent reduction in the U.S. payments to the U.N. if the Credentials Committee's efforts to expel Israel were upheld. Members on both sides of the political aisle, Democrats Tom Lantos and Benjamin Gilman, Republicans Jack Kemp and Mickey Edwards, obliged. They also included in their resolutions that the U.S. would withdraw its membership in protest.

Having laid this groundwork, she then drafted a cable to be sent out under George Shultz's signature, to be delivered to every American envoy around the world, instructing them to warn their host country of how seriously America would take this vote. Shultz agreed to send it out, and a worldwide blitz commenced.

But Kirkpatrick still fretted. Drawing on her political science background, she had her staff do up a tally of the likely vote count on Israel's expulsion. It didn't look good. The African, nonaligned, and Communist bloc countries could be expected to vote in tandem. The U.S. could expect one third of the votes, but that was it. She worried that it was a debacle in the making. At a subsequent meeting with her staff, one of her aides quipped that this might be preferable. "The U.N.," he said, "was a cesspool, and this would provide an excuse for the U.S. to leave it too."

Kirkpatrick balked at this.

"No," she said, "that won't do," pointing out that the calculation was far more complicated. For one thing, Israel itself was jittery about the prospect. However much it was under fire in the international body, the U.N. had backed its birth, and Israel did not want to be expelled. Kirkpatrick argued that the Congress's efforts now had to be buttressed by vigorous support in the executive branch, starting with the president and secretary of state. Kirkpatrick did not intend to be unnecessarily alarmist, but she saw little alternative.

She decided to take this message straight to Reagan and Shultz.

ON OCTOBER 15, at a National Security Council meeting, she argued for a presidential declaration that the U.S. would withdraw from the U.N.—and withhold its payments—until Israel's rights were restored. This time she was totally prepared, bureaucratically adept, and persuasive. Reagan was moved by her urgent plea, and the next day, Shultz, on behalf of Reagan, made this unconditional declaration in a speech before the U.N. Shultz firmly delivered the proclamation. The U.S. mission then waited anxiously to assess the response.

Kirkpatrick's instincts were born out by the aftermath. Shultz's ultimatum, combined with the congressional legislation, spooked the Arab world. Within two weeks, the U.S. was able to muster the necessary support, and for the embattled Israelis, a crisis of enormous proportions had been averted.

As the 1982 U.N. session limped to a close, Kirkpatrick could finally relax a bit. She felt the U.S. had turned a corner in its U.N. diplomacy. The results were tangible. That December, she confidently told the press, "We are no longer as vulnerable as we felt." One of the reasons she cited: "We headed off the expulsion of Israel."

. . .

IN A SENSE, it was a fitting remark, a blend of understatement and confidence, and to the undiscriminating eye, totally contrary to the trend in world events. The world was still seesawing dangerously in the Cold War's demonic grip. The Soviets were still ensconced in Afghanistan, the INF missile negotiations were going nowhere fast, and the Western missile deployments were now seriously jeopardized by the wave of pessimism and isolationism that had seized the Democratic left like a bad flu. Menacing, ugly little conflicts of revolution and counterrevolution were festering in El Salvador and Nicaragua, and the CSCE Madrid review human rights talks, initially slated for only a few months, had no outcome in sight.

As the windows of her Bethesda house frosted in the late 1982 December chill, Kirkpatrick and her husband, Kirk, ever her most trusted adviser, engaged in a serious discussion about the future. She had made important advances, but problems remained. Yes, the horrible situation with Haig was gone, but Jim Baker, and his sleuthlike skill at manipulating the system, was an even more formidable adversary. Of course, there was still much work to be done. Especially in Central America, an area of great interest to her.

As they talked, Kirk told her that if she wanted to return to teaching, he would, it went without saying, support her. She smiled and reached for his hand, privately thinking that one reason to come back to Washington was to be, once again, with him.

CHAPTER 19

After one of the well-publicized and bruising battles between Jeane Kirkpatrick and Alexander Haig, Ronald Reagan stood up at the conclusion of a cabinet meeting, beat a long path around the polished wooden table past Haig, Judge William Clark, James Baker, and Edwin Meese, straight to Kirkpatrick. Then, with all eyes on the president, he reached out and gave Kirkpatrick a warm hug. As the rest of the room watched, Reagan chimed, loudly enough for all to hear, "You're doing a great job." Lest there be any remaining doubt about the point he wanted to make, Reagan then smiled broadly and said with a flourish, "You're my heroine."

It was a remarkable performance of both managerial virtue and political theater. Just when Reagan seemed disengaged, he would demonstrate his vast reservoir of instinct, an uncanny ability to cut through the fog of emotion and endless clutter right to the bottom line. Kirkpatrick was beleaguered, and the president wanted to make a sharp point—not just to her but the whole world. Kirkpatrick was a deeply valued member of the Reagan team.

To be sure, he did this in part because the two so often connected, intellectually as well as instinctually. The consoling arm he extended to her was as metaphorical as real. But Reagan was moved by another force as well. Kirkpatrick, a Democrat and woman, increasingly radiated star quality in the administration, and he wanted to keep her around. And there was a final reason. With refreshing regularity, she said what he thought, she asked him to consider doing what he wanted to do. When others decried "letting Reagan be Reagan," when his media-cautious advisers told him to pull back, she was right there, providing elegant but straightforward reasons why he should be proceeding full steam ahead.

The incident meant a great deal to Kirkpatrick. While others privately made excuses for Reagan, how he wasn't an intellectual, why he sometimes got facts wrong, how his attention span seemed to wane, she unabashedly believed in, and genuinely liked, Ronald Reagan. But 1983, it turned out, would test her role and her rise in the Reagan administration.

If, for Kirkpatrick, 1981 was the year of drawing the line with the Soviets and the U.N., and 1982 was the year of democracy and protecting Israel, then 1983 marked the start of a critical public discussion over U.S. policy toward Central America. It would be a heated, frequently searing debate across ideological lines, and Kirkpatrick, by force of her personality and training, was destined to play a leading role. With the U.S. and Soviets racing down to the wire over the missile deployments in Europe, with world tensions on edge, this arena promised still more division, more battle wounds, but, if the U.S. could stand firm, ultimately it also promised dividends in the Cold War.

CENTRAL AMERICA. In a moment of candor, the usually calm secretary of state, George Shultz, would heatedly note, "Central America is a swamp." He did not mean this pejoratively. It was a statement more about the bruising politics of Central America policy than about the region itself. But few doubted it was an apt metaphor for the quagmire bedeviling Reagan's policy makers.

Four of Central America's five major countries were, to varying degrees, lurching toward democracy. Three were secure or inchoate, the fourth one was embattled by Marxist rebels and a ruthlessly violent rightist fringe. The breakdown was thus: Costa Rica stood peacefully in the region, as an unarmed island, generally free of civil war and oligarchical or class conflict. It did not have an army, and it was a democracy, an example to its beleaguered neighbors like a Latin American Switzerland, or an early 1950s Lebanon (before that country, whatever its own internal contradictions, was swallowed by tumult from Syrian occupation, the PLO, and internecine warfare). Honduras, poor and dusty, was slowly and fitfully emerging out of a period of significant struggle, and with eventual success would soon move from authoritarian military rule to democratic governance. Its neighbor, Guatemala, after suffering under harsh military rule, would pledge to follow the same democratic course. It was a difficult and long road ahead, and the early signs were not immediately heartening; but, in due time, Guatemala would also follow its neighbors. Taken together, these three countries constituted the crest of a democratic wave that would come to prevail in America's hemisphere.

But then there were El Salvador and Nicaragua. For both left and right, it seemed every political slogan, every ghoulish fantasy, every political nightmare, could be applied to these tiny countries to the south. To those on the left, and many in the Democratic party, El Salvador was a symbol of oppression. It conjured up American-aided "right-wing death squads," a "repressive land-owning class," military goons holding down a "popular uprising" comprised of "peasant agrarian reformers," and "massive human rights violations" carried out with the "complicity of the U.S. government." To be sure, these gross excesses were not to be belittled. But, in turn, the left virtually ignored the excesses of the Salvadoran guerrillas. It was a fact that the Salvadoran guerrillas were self-proclaimed Marxists, aligned with the Cubans, Nicaraguans, and Soviets; but, inevitably, they were described as "embattled peasants with muskets." And rarely were they called Marxists. Instead, they were referred to by the establishment by the more delicate phrase "leftists," as though they were peasant versions of 1930s New York intellectuals.

To the Reagan administration and, for a time, many political moderates, El Salvador was considered a grossly imperfect country, but one in which a fragile democratic center could be nourished and cultivated. Although the newly elected government was often harshly repressive, it was fighting for its very life against traditional and often deadly extremist forces of the authoritarian right, on one hand, but also against a violent insurgency on the left, the FMLN (the Farabundo Martí National Liberation Front, in English translation). The FMLN's very credo was inimical to the rule of law and democracy, so brutally evidenced in 1982 when they sought to disrupt El Salvador's first elections. Having failed in their bloody "final offensive" to destroy the government in 1981, they retreated, resorting to terror and ambush. Then, during the election, the FMLN exploded out of the hills, destroying hundreds of buses and trucks designated to bring people to the polling places, spraying bullets and setting fire to buildings, proclaiming, "Vote today, die tonight."

But if U.S. policy could be subtle enough, over time, it could help control the forces of violence and repression on the right with the current, highly imperfect government and strengthen the democratic elements within El Salvador. The goal would be to promote continued democratic elections and the growth of democratic institutions, and to improve overall human rights practices, systematically rather than episodically. The Marxist FMLN, aligned with the Soviets, had shown no commitment to human rights, and the Americans could exercise no leverage over them. In a bad situation, policy makers opted for what they considered the best choice, supporting the current government and pressing for reforms. A Marxist El Salvador not only would have a dismal human rights record, but would be more likely to station Soviet MIGs, Soviet advisers, Soviet arms, and even Soviet nuclear missiles near American shores. This would be an unconscionable security risk, and, to the men and women of the Reagan administration, was unacceptable.

Kirkpatrick herself, restating the doctrine she had first laid out in *Commentary*, put the unenviable task of U.S. policy this way: "We live in an imperfect world. Most people are badly governed, and always have been. We wish we had only allies who were democratic and well-governed, but we still have to look after ourselves and freedom in the world. Sometimes we are going to support and associate with governments who do not meet our standards. The relationships between power and morality are often very complicated. I don't think they're so ambiguous, but I think they're very complicated."

Like El Salvador, the argument over Nicaragua ran along strikingly parallel lines, with a few twists. To the activist left, peace groups clamoring for the U.S. to get "out of El Salvador and Nicaragua," the Nicaraguan Sandinista regime had been "pushed into the hands of the Communists," and, like their FMLN brethren in Salvador, were "reformers." The Democrats in Congress were, on the whole, somewhat more sober in their assessments. It was largely agreed that the Sandinista government had emerged from a bloody civil war against Anastasio Somoza, promising "an independent, pluralist, and neutralist government," but then had reneged on its commitments. The Carter administration had initially rushed $118 million in emergency assistance to the Sandinistas when they came to power, undermining the claim that the Sandinistas were "pushed" into the arms of the Soviets. But within two years Carter cut off the aid.

As the Sandinista junta moved left, they revealed themselves as increasingly aggressive and menacing, casting off the mask of democracy and replacing a right-wing dictatorship with an equally repressive Marxist one. After one year, the pattern was clear: the Sandinistas engaged in massive political repression at home, closing down the unions, shutting down the popular press, routinely harassing the Catholic Church, squeezing out all democratic opposition from the government. They were militarily aggressive too, supporting the FMLN in El Salvador, building the largest army in all of Central America, introducing thousands of Cuban and Eastern bloc military advisers into the region, and openly aligning themselves with Marxist revolution ("Our political force is Sandinismo and our doctrine is Marxism-Leninism," declared one junta member) and the Soviet Union.

The effects were felt throughout Central America. The Sandinista regime bullied Honduras and threatened regional stability. Moreover, unrestrained, the Nicaraguan junta, in conjunction with the FMLN, was a dangerous bridgehead against American strategic interests. Guatemala and Honduras could eventually be endangered, and insurrection in Mexico could not be ruled out. Most ominously, in 1983 there was even open talk that the Sandinista junta would consider stationing Soviet nuclear missiles or nuclear-capable MIGs on Nicaraguan soil, virtually minutes from the U.S. border.

But as this debate was thrashed out politically in the U.S., it was any-thing but clear-cut. Indeed, even to mention Nicaragua and El Salvador in passing in the early 1980s was often the functional equivalent of a hostile act, threatening to bring the gaiety of a Washington dinner party to a strained hush, plunging dinner guests into accusation and counter-accusation about Reagan's policies and those of the Democrats. In the early 1980s, there was rarely a civilized discussion about Nicaragua and El Salvador; scarcely such a thing as bipartisanship. The lines and sides were sharply defined, more like rival governments than rival political parties in a divided government.

As a practical reality, the nuance of administration policy was thus hopelessly obscured. You couldn't be for *some* military aid and *some* eco-nomic aid. The issue had taken on a partisan divide, however much this created a climate of confusion and contradiction. Whereas many Rea-ganauts saw the issue principally and necessarily through a Cold War lens, their opponents chose to focus relentlessly on the political and moral failings of the Salvadoran government and the Nicaraguan rebels, while blatantly sidestepping the very same failings in the Sandinistas and FMLN rebels, and ignoring the Cold War dimension of the conflict al-together. This thinking, however well intentioned, was at best artless and at worst dangerous—for the fact remained, El Salvador and Nicaragua were an inextricable part of the great global game of Cold War geopolitics.

Contemplating all this, Jeane Kirkpatrick was in no position to engage in simple moral posturing. By 1983, she had emerged as a leading theo-retician of Central American policy in the administration. Then, in late January, President Reagan asked her to take a fact-finding trip to Cen-tral America to assess the situation and report back to him. Within weeks, as political animosities sharpened, the woman who had always regarded herself as a practical and careful social scientist would move beyond the strict confines of the U.N. into a new arena of political con-flict, giving her a chance to shine, to be sure, but also casting her into the center of an issue ripping the country at the seams.

FROM FEBRUARY 3 to 12, Kirkpatrick traveled through Latin America. It was an ambitious trip that came amid heated calls by congressional Democrats for a negotiated settlement, or power sharing, between the FMLN guerrillas and the Salvadoran government. The administration was considering an emergency request of an additional $61 million in military aid for the Salvadoran government. Congress had cut Reagan's earlier request for $82 million, authorizing only $26 million. Depending upon the outcome of the Kirkpatrick mission, the administration was now considering asking for the balance.

Kirkpatrick spent two days in El Salvador, in addition to stops in Panama, Costa Rica, Honduras, and Venezuela. She put in long hours, talking to a broad swath of people, from politicians and high-ranking government officials in their posh offices, to labor leaders in worn jeans and overalls, seasoned independent journalists, and educators.

Though she was traveling at the president's request, the trip itself had been opposed by the State Department. Thomas Enders, a foreign service officer, sent out a nine-page memo to the ambassadors of each country she visited registering the department's dissent. The message was "don't cooperate." To keep the cable from Kirkpatrick, Enders stamped a "No Dis"—"No Distribution"—classification on it. But early in her trip, one ambassador asked Kirkpatrick if she knew about "the long cable" and gave the startled U.N. ambassador a copy.

Far from being dissuaded from her mission, Kirkpatrick pressed on, from meeting to meeting.

Wednesday night, February 10, after meeting with the country's senior military and political leaders in El Salvador, she had a quiet dinner with José Napoleon Duarte, a political moderate in the Christian Democratic party, and likely to be the next president of El Salvador, following the national election in March 1984. Even as savage fighting raged in the countryside, and the streets were filled with constant tension, there was magic in San Salvador. The air was fresh in the evening and crickets chirped. That night, in the safe confines of the high, deep white walls surrounding the U.S. ambassador's residence, it was a time for frank talk. Kirkpatrick had known Duarte since the 1970s, and had great respect and admiration for him.

Congress was worried about the Salvadoran army's apparent inability to defeat the guerrillas. Kirkpatrick wanted to know how bad things were. She asked open-ended questions. How were things going?

Duarte, who was no warmonger and hated the use of force, delivered a blunt message to Kirkpatrick: the government did not intend to negotiate with the rebels, and would not countenance power sharing without elections. Power should be won through the ballot box. Only then would a legitimate government emerge.

Kirkpatrick understood what he was saying, and nodded her head. In the context of Salvadoran politics, negotiation would be interpreted as surrender, and the army could decide to take matters into its own hands. That outcome, which would lead to a wholesale American withdrawal, was just what the Communists wanted. She agreed it was important for power to be transferred through the electoral process, the essential ingredient for a budding democracy.

How were the guerrillas doing? she asked.

They were not winning, but they were well armed, Duarte said. The guerrillas had been receiving formidable amounts of military and other aid from the Soviet bloc, and the weapons greatly enhanced their capabilities. Kirkpatrick already knew this from intelligence reports, and indicated that she would relay his concerns to President Reagan. She didn't talk about specific military issues or military aid with Duarte. That she reserved for the Salvadoran army chief of staff. Duarte, like her, was not about weapons but politics.

Duarte also mused aloud, in distress, that the FMLN had propaganda allies in Washington, well-meaning lobbying groups who didn't know the first thing about the brutal nature of the guerrillas. But they're not reformers, he stressed, they're guerrillas. They've gotten "very skillful" at blowing up electrical grids and power lines, and attacking coffee plantations, he explained. He was also upset by bad press reports. It seemed to him that the press only focused on his government's internal problems, not on the formidable problems of reforming a society while in the midst of a war against the violent left. It was demoralizing and depressing, he said. Could she help?

She frowned. Of course she would do what she could. But the issue was so polarizing, it would be difficult. He knew that.

Then the talk turned to one of their favorite subjects, organizing elections. Both believed fair and open elections lay at the heart of a fledgling democracy. Into the wee hours of the night, they discussed election modalities, less like policy makers and more like social scientists.

Throughout the trip, one theme kept emerging to Kirkpatrick, a dramatic increase in the level of anxiety concerning ever-growing Soviet, Cuban, and Nicaraguan subversion of the region. The region's leaders perceived a long-range Soviet investment in Central America, while the U.S. stood by relatively passively. El Salvador was the immediate target. But Nicaragua had built up a formidable army, far beyond any defensive needs, and other leaders in the region were scared stiff. El Salvador was less threatened than the press reports suggested, as long as the U.S. continued to provide adequate levels of military assistance. Kirkpatrick, however, left feeling the Soviet's long-term goal was Mexico.

She was convinced that the Soviets wanted a Communist Central America. She saw ominous parallels with Western Europe after World War II, when the fear was that it would fall to the Communists, less because the Red Army could march across the border, and more because of incessant Soviet infiltration, subversion, and intimidation. Ultimately,

NATO and the Marshall Plan saved Western Europe. There was, of course, one big difference. The U.S. and Europe were separated by the Atlantic. Latin America stood at America's doorstep.

Indeed, the proximity was jarring to Kirkpatrick. El Salvador was closer to Texas than Texas was to Massachusetts. Nicaragua was as close to Miami, or San Diego and San Antonio, and Tucson, as each of those cities was to Washington, D.C. But there was another consideration. The old foreign policy establishment had a chronic bias against Central America. Its world focused rigidly on the protection of Europe, even if that meant ignoring the U.S.'s own backyard.

During this tense period, before and immediately after her trip, Kirkpatrick had a series of breakfasts, one on one, with Scoop Jackson. Kirkpatrick noted that there were staggering problems, the threat of Nicaragua's systematic subversion by terrorism and guerrilla activity, the FMLN, the frailty of the new democracies struggling to survive against these recurring stresses. But, she added, "there were important longer-range opportunities, particularly in the economic, cultural, and social fields." The U.S. should be giving generous doses of development and food aid, Kirkpatrick stressed. She felt that "these countries were like France, Greece, and Italy, facing unrest and disorder after World War II, until the U.S. came to their rescue."

They agreed that Vietnam was the wrong analogy for Central America, and that the right one was the Marshall Plan. That, Scoop said, was an effective use of American power, strength, and moral concern.

The two conceived of a comprehensive plan for confronting the threat of Communism, while at the same time addressing social and economic opportunities for the region in a broad framework. The U.S., they agreed, should initiate a major economic aid program for Central America, similar to the Marshall Plan. It would include military aid, not as an end in itself but for what Jackson called "a shield, for democratization, economic development, and diplomacy." It would be a marvelous act of generosity and vision, the best of America, he added.

Jackson said he too worried about Mexico. He told Kirkpatrick he had raised this with Shultz, and Shultz had agreed.

Kirkpatrick said she would take the idea of a Latin American Marshall Plan to the president. Indeed, she had written it into a three-page, single-spaced memo for him. For his part, Jackson said he would call for the idea from the Senate, in all likelihood for a bipartisan commission to formulate the details. Scoop, a big believer in bipartisanship (he never tired of saying, "In matters of national security, the best politics is no politics"), felt this issue needed the support of both parties—just as the Marshall Plan and NATO were given birth only because of Republican Senator

Arthur Vandenberg's willingness to abandon his isolationism and party politics to work with Harry Truman.

With that, Kirkpatrick readied to report to Reagan. The most immediate task, she knew, was emergency aid for El Salvador. If that bullet could be dodged, she felt there could be a bright future for the region—with America's generous assistance.

DAYS LATER, KIRKPATRICK reported to the NSPG. It was vintage Kirkpatrick. Her face that spoke of studied skepticism, her arched eyebrows, her softly knit suits and businesslike appearance, were arresting in the meeting room. It was always a showstopper when, during a discussion, she dramatically pulled her glasses off her head, paused for what seemed like an eternity, then in her clipped, perfect English issued a stern warning, invariably beginning, "Mr. President . . ."

Today was no exception. She told the president that the leaders and opposition groups alike in Latin America "feared that a guerrilla takeover of El Salvador would lead to stepped-up insurgent activity sweeping across all of Central America." Speaking with conviction and clarity, she minced no words. While even Shultz had previously made the point that the Salvadoran rebels "were creating hell with Soviet-supplied weapons," and wanted to "shoot their way" into the government, no one had talked this bluntly about the problem before with Reagan.

Observers at the meeting were immediately struck by how she had returned with a different story than had previously been presented to the president. And Reagan himself was rapt. It was no secret that he cared deeply about the Nicaraguan contras, and more broadly, the entire fate of democracy in Central America. But Kirkpatrick's own deep anxieties, and her stern message about the military situation, palpably touched him. His eyes widened as he listened.

Reagan said he intended to ask for more aid to El Salvador. He also liked the idea of a Latin American Marshall Plan, and intended to use some of the generic ideas in a speech to Congress.

The next week, on a Monday, Reagan called in a group of senior legislators from both parties to discuss the urgency of additional aid to El Salvador. While at this juncture Judge Clark at the National Security Council was handling Central America policy far more so than Shultz, Kirkpatrick, by dint of her personality, background in Latin America, and easy access to the president, was quickly carving out a role as the leading Central America policy maker. By summer, most agreed she was largely in the driver's seat. Although she modestly denied this as "grossly exaggerated," the facts were as revealing as her words. The first person

Reagan asked to brief the members of Congress was neither Shultz nor Clark, but Kirkpatrick.

To her supporters and disciples, in this period she acted with decisive conviction and clarity, balancing immediate interest—the Communist threat of Nicaragua and the FMLN—with big-hearted policy goals, a Latin American Marshall Plan. This plan was typical Kirkpatrick, combining the toughness of a conservative with the idealism of an older-style Democrat, and it enabled her to fill the yawning policy vacuum. State was always looking for a diplomatic angle, ignoring the military dimension, and Shultz, himself still being brought up to speed on the intricacies of Latin American politics, was delegating to his underlings rather than taking an active role. Clark, an able manager, lacked her grounding in foreign policy and appreciation for subtle diplomacy. Bill Casey, the CIA director and her friend and ally, was not in the direct policy loop, and White House policy makers James Baker and Michael Deaver fretted endlessly in private about upsetting the Congress, but brought no serious conceptual thinking to the table.

"Heroic," was how Richard Cheney, a Wyoming congressman, termed Kirkpatrick's performance, Illinois Congressman Henry Hyde called her "brilliant," and the conservative columnist William Buckley declared he was ready to sew her in as the fifty-first star on the American flag.

But to her detractors, she was politically inept and remarkably ideological. Indeed, she was particularly irritating to the liberal Democrats precisely because she had a way of spicing her opinions with pointed facts that many simply did not care to hear. "Very reluctantly, most serious observers have come to acknowledge that, yes, the area's location gives it a certain irreducible relevance to our national interest," she wrote in a scathing article that April in the *Washington Post*. And more pointedly, "We know by now what the government of Nicaragua is and what it intends. . . . We know who the guerrillas in El Salvador are, where and how they get their arms, what their plans are, who their friends are." And, leaving little doubt about who would be to blame in case of failure, she wagged her finger straight at the Democrats: "to deny any support to the democratic Nicaraguan insurgency against a repressive, aggressive Marxist government would have the clear effect . . . to make the United States the enforcer of Brezhnev's doctrine of irreversible revolution."

Over the next several months, in taking center stage on Central American policy, the more famous she became and the more she pointedly went after her adversaries, the more they hit her back. When Reagan went before the Congress on April 27, 1983, the speech he gave amplified the very themes Kirkpatrick had elucidated. Support democracy, support regional peace negotiations, provide a military shield for our friends, look to a long-term plan of development and aid. Building on Kirkpatrick's idea for a big Marshall-type plan, Reagan evoked Harry Truman in the glory days of 1947. Even House Speaker Tip O'Neill, a fervent opponent of Reagan's policies in the region, was moved. When Reagan declared, "It is the ultimate in hypocrisy for the unelected Nicaraguan government to charge that we seek their overthrow when they are doing everything they can to bring down the elected government of El Salvador," O'Neill, sitting on the dais with a scowl on his face, suddenly jumped to his feet and led the Congress in a standing ovation.

Yet the Democrats, increasingly isolationist and dovish, were largely obstructionist and in no mood to cooperate. They chose the charismatic Connecticut Senator Christopher Dodd to deliver the Democrats' response to Reagan's address. Dodd, with his prematurely graying hair and movie star looks, and a voice that sounded like Ted Kennedy's when he got riled, was genial and smart—but he was a fierce political partisan and an ideological dove. ("These guys see Commies everywhere, they don't understand indigenous movements," he once screamed to an interviewer. When pressed, "Well, what about the indigenous Marxists who've aligned themselves with the Soviets?" he did not answer and quickly changed the subject.) Dodd completely ignored the overall economic, diplomatic, and military package that Reagan was offering, and instead sharply decried Reagan's effort as "unleashing the dogs of war" and, in effect, bringing the Cold War to Latin America.

Kirkpatrick was appalled by Dodd's speech, and hurriedly consulted with several prominent Democrats, including Scoop Jackson, Texas Senator Lloyd Bentsen, and Representative Jim Wright, also of Texas, to see "if Dodd spoke for them." No, they said, and they added that they too felt Dodd had crossed the line, and the speech was "inappropriate." Two days later she decided to take her objections public, and blasted Dodd for being "demagogic" and "irresponsible," prompting the senator to issue his own heated, but defensive, denials.

This withering counterattack did not help the Reagan people with the Congress, nor did it help Kirkpatrick with the liberals, although the likelihood of any compromise was already very thin. Instead, political animosities increasingly sharpened in both the Congress and the press.

Eventually, Kirkpatrick and the administration prevailed on aid to El Salvador. When Duarte did win the presidency in March of 1984, his government stabilized the war with the guerrillas. Reform was in the air, and Congress would soon back down, following the administration's lead in bolstering the democratic center.

But the battleground at home was already shifting to Nicaragua.

.   .   .

THE REAGAN POLICY in Nicaragua was never as neat or tidy as it appeared. Portrayed by clamoring interest groups and the Washington press corps as bellicose and lurching inexorably toward invasion, it was actually at first hesitant in its efforts, even confused.

At the outset, Secretary of State Haig had wanted to deal with Central America by "going to the source," that is, "blockading Cuba." Determined to protect the well-being of the Pentagon, and wanting to concentrate on the defense buildup, Cap Weinberger was fixed on avoiding a military involvement. President Reagan was also disinclined to inject American troops, maintaining, "I'm just not going to do that," and calling the whole notion "lunacy." Baker and Deaver were firmly against any military action, wanting to concentrate on the president's economic program, and to keep him from looking trigger-happy. They argued for a more benign, hands-off strategy.

In the councils of the White House, this standoff left a vacuum. Bill Casey devised the initial answer, offering a way to square the circle with a discreet, more limited policy. A CIA program of aiding insurgent Nicaraguans, who would be dubbed the Nicaraguan resistance, or contras, would be cobbled together. Using Argentine generals to train them, roughly five hundred anti-Sandinista Nicaraguans, many of them former Somoza National Guardsmen (though this was not mentioned), would be trained and sent into the field to harass Sandinista targets, and interdict the flow of arms from Managua to the Marxist rebels in El Salvador. This latter rationale was how the program was sold to the congressional intelligence committees.

But the contra beginnings were modest, far short of anything like toppling the Soviet-supported Sandinistas, who were being bankrolled to the tune of up to a billion dollars a year. The CIA sought authorization of only $19 million for 1982 and 1983, with the Agency reprogramming $10 million more from its own discretionary accounts.

Even so, the CIA program was not sitting well with Congress. The first warning shot came in December of 1982. Edward Boland, a genial House liberal and head of the Intelligence Committee, pushed through an amendment that prohibited the CIA and Department of Defense from furnishing military equipment, training, or support to anyone "for the purpose of overthrowing the government of Nicaragua." The amendment soon passed the Senate and became law. Bill Casey immediately sent a long single-spaced cable of the amendment with explicit instructions about "dos" and "don'ts" down to CIA headquarters in a Tegucigalpa, Honduras, safe house, where it was posted in full sight on the bulletin board.

The Boland Amendment was congressional micromanaging at its worst—unwilling to make policy and take responsibility for its actions, but involving itself just enough to make the policy unworkable. One CIA agent noted the futility, if not surreal quality, to the amendment. "Jesus, what if the Sandinistas buckled to the contras? Would we be violating the law?" While internal Central Intelligence Agency assessments gave the contras little chance of overthrowing the Sandinistas at the time, the limits imposed by the Boland Amendment recalled the unrealistic restrictions that were at the heart of the dismal American strategy in Vietnam. By shackling the contras, it also inspired a desperate search for dramatic actions in the contra effort that were more sound than fury, leading in part to a rash of harebrained CIA schemes, like mining the harbors of Nicaragua, and a limited contra bombing raid on the Managua airport.

By the summer of 1983, that policy was clearly going nowhere. Congress refused to allocate further aid to the Nicaraguan contras, in part furious about the CIA's mining of the Nicaraguan harbors. Meanwhile, Kirkpatrick continued to support her idea for a Marshall Plan, and in July, President Reagan took her advice and appointed a bipartisan commission of distinguished Americans, led by Henry Kissinger, to devise a comprehensive political, economic, and diplomatic policy for the U.S. toward Central America.

KIRKPATRICK HERSELF WAS named as Reagan's personal representative to the commission, which included members representing a broad range of expertise, with such notables as Nicholas Brady, an expert on international banking; former Associate Justice Potter Stewart, to provide advice on judicial systems; Richard Scammon, a political scientist, appointed to make recommendations about elections; and Lane Kirkland, president of the AFL-CIO, to address labor problems.

Sensing an opportunity, Kirkpatrick, after being named to the Kissinger Commission, as it came to be known, gave a speech about Latin America, and ratcheted up the ideological campaign against the Soviet Union. "The Brezhnev Doctrine rests on the will and determination of some people," she said, adding, "it can be overturned by the will and determination of some other people." For Kirkpatrick, the battleground of ideas was not solely at the U.N.; as journalist Strobe Talbott would lament, "The U.S. was taking off the gloves in the back alleys of the Third World."

·   ·   ·

As Kirkpatrick gained ascendance in the administration, she was ridiculed on the establishment's news pages, like the *New York Times* (although it did acknowledge her as "the central intellectual force on Central America"), scorned on its editorial pages, and depicted in Congress as a bomb-throwing "Dr. Strangelovian character," a "conservative," and "reactionary." (Kirkpatrick often suspected James Baker of orchestrating the campaign against her, but she was equally reviled by political liberals.) Her every utterance was held up to microscopic examination. When she publicly ruminated that "in Central America, the United States is supporting the good guys in every sense of the word," a *Times* columnist chastised her for "whipping up a Soviet bogeyman to shore up a failing policy." Kirkpatrick, many detractors claimed, was unable to make fine moral distinctions, distressingly ignoring the excesses of right-wing regimes while showing concern only about the excesses of Communist ones.

But such views were as simplistic as the criticisms of Kirkpatrick. Her detractors ignored her repeated emphasis that a policy of morality must work hand in hand with America's larger strategic Cold War policy, and that national security was an intricate juggling act. Moreover, she remained one of the administration's staunchest defenders of building and nurturing democracy. To detached observers, these were serious positions and, indeed, nuanced ones—but in the battlefield at home, there was no middle ground, only trapdoors. What Kirkpatrick was often blind to was that her very visibility made her vulnerable, both to her enemies on the left and in the administration, each standing in the wings, seeking to push her into the abyss.

But she had her solid backers as well, and outpourings of support were frequent from various corners of the Republican party. She was the model Reaganaut, to Reagan what the action-intellectuals were to John F. Kennedy. She was part of the fierce intellectual energy on Reagan's side. Bill Casey loved her. "I'm going to run you for president," he repeatedly said. "Seriously, think about it, you can win." Cap Weinberger also was an ardent supporter. She and Judge Clark, the national security adviser and a close intimate for twenty years of the president, were key allies. Even the Republican rank and file thought of her not as a Democrat but as an astoundingly intelligent and brave icon, fighting a principled fight.

She also won an unusual, if not backhanded, compliment from George Shultz. On July 23, he marched into Reagan's office, boiling over with rage. Increasingly relegated by the NSC to a secondary slot in policy making on Latin America, and fed up, Shultz told Reagan he was ready to resign. Either he was "an errand boy," he said, or somebody the president could "have confidence in." He suggested Kirkpatrick or Weinberger as possible replacements. Unwilling to lose another secretary of state, and wanting to have a careful balance of opinions, Reagan prevailed upon Shultz to stay, promising greater authority and access. But it was notable that Shultz mentioned Kirkpatrick. Clearly, it was not just conservatives who felt she could assume the top foreign policy slot, but moderates as well. But whether they would actually embrace this idea was quite a different matter.

On October 13, the president unexpectedly announced that Judge Clark would leave his NSC post to succeed James Watt as secretary of the interior. Immediately, speculation began over who would fill this slot, and not without good reason. One conception of the NSC post was that the adviser would serve as a dispassionate broker, coordinating various viewpoints on policy throughout the government and faithfully representing them to the president. Yet, in practice, the NSC adviser often became directly mired in the policy fray, siding with Defense against State, or vice-versa, or attempting to stake out a position all his own. Under Nixon, then NSC adviser Henry Kissinger virtually eclipsed the secretary of state, thus proving the potential power of the NSC slot when in unusually intelligent, deftly skilled, and bureaucratically savvy hands. But Kissinger was unique among NSC advisers. So while Clark and Shultz had repeatedly clashed over policies and while the NSC post could be a powerful one, up to now the secretaries of state and defense ultimately had held more sway. Nevertheless, because an NSC adviser could emerge as a potent rival to a cabinet secretary, or as an indispensable ally, from the outset, it was a vicious struggle to name Clark's successor. Kirkpatrick's name was at the top of a possible appointment list, as moderates lined up against her and conservatives came out for her. But whatever Kirkpatrick's allies had in mind, James Baker had something else in mind. Himself.

BEFORE THE OCTOBER 13 announcement, the fix for the NSC job was already in the works. For some time, Baker, though he repeatedly denied an interest in foreign affairs in White House meetings, had been itching to move into foreign policy. Through a steady stream of policy backgrounders with favored reporters (especially with the *Washington Post* and *New York Times*), he had badmouthed not only Kirkpatrick but also Clark, which helped push Clark out of his job. For Baker, this was a golden opportunity.

Earlier, he had quietly approached Michael Deaver, telling him, "We've always made a great team, we still will." Baker's plan was that he would replace Clark, and Deaver would take his position as chief of staff. At first, Deaver was queasy about the deal. For one thing, he wasn't sure chief of staff was the right job for him. But Baker's smooth and persistent entreaties finally convinced him, and, with Baker leading the way, the two approached Reagan with the idea.

Reagan liked the plan's simplicity and quickly signed off. To codify the arrangement, Baker quickly prepared a draft statement announcing the changes. According to sources, it was Baker's intention to leak it after the NSPG meeting on October 14. Late that day, with howling rains swirling outside, Deaver called Shultz. He asked for his support for the move. The stage was set.

But the next day, on the morning of October 14, Bill Casey was pumped up. He had heard other rumors, that Bud McFarlane was going to be given Clark's position. He considered McFarlane a real lightweight, a plodder, everyone's staff man, someone who would be grossly out of his depth at the top. Alternatively, another rumor had been winding its way through the government: if the NSC job were to open up again, and Kirkpatrick didn't get it, she would resign. This, he felt, would be a disaster. Scribbling down a number of reasons why Kirkpatrick should get the position, he went to that afternoon's NSPG meeting fully prepared to make the case for her candidacy.

THAT DAY, REAGAN lunched with Shultz. They were to be meeting in the afternoon to discuss policy toward Lebanon, but the president was preoccupied with the pressing matter of Clark's replacement. Shultz had his own ideas too.

He respected Kirkpatrick, but didn't feel that her temperament was right for the job. Her strengths were her uncommon intelligence and her role as a vigorous advocate, not as a detached moderator, which was required of the national security adviser. Nor did he particularly favor Bud McFarlane, who he felt "got uptight under pressure."

Shultz told Reagan that he strongly favored Baker, who had a "deft touch," "would be good to work with," "sparkled," and was extremely "competent." Shultz left the lunch thinking that the president, while recognizing that the political right might have trouble with him, had settled on Baker.

AFTER THE NSPG meeting opened, Bill Casey eyed the room. Kirkpatrick, who was a regular attendant, was absent. It was terrible timing, although Casey was glad. Making the pitch for her would be easier without her being there. He was told she was at home with the flu.

Clark was still sitting in on NSPG meetings—until his replacement was officially named—and he took the opportunity to pass around a note announcing the new changes in the works. When Casey got it, he was stunned. Baker as national security adviser. The thought disgusted him. Casey thoroughly despised Baker. He couldn't stand his leaks, his constant manipulation for personal gain, his instincts that were far more political than conceptual. He felt that Baker, always touting his moderate credentials, had no vision, and was nothing but a deal-maker, *not* what Reagan needed; it would send the wrong message to Congress and the Soviets about the direction of administration policy.

Casey so loathed Baker that he had quietly told others, "The biggest mistake I have made in government was giving a foothold to Baker into the Reagan administration." He was desperate to stop this new move from happening.

As the Clark note slowly made its way around the table, Casey scanned the room, averted his gaze from Shultz, and eventually locked eyes with Weinberger and Meese. His eyes pleaded, "Can you believe this?" Ignoring the discussion about Lebanon, he shook his head in disgust, muttering under his breath, "Mindless, just mindless." Then turning to Ed Meese, the president's counselor, he mumbled angrily, "How the hell can you put the worst leaker in the administration in charge of the NSC?"

AFTER THE NSPG meeting, Clark invited Weinberger and Casey into his office. As the door closed, Shultz watched anxiously as he was obviously excluded.

Meanwhile, a flu-ridden Kirkpatrick had left her home and arrived late for the NSPG meeting. Looking around as she entered, she saw that the White House seemed tense that day. By the time she reached the NSPG room, all of the principals had gone, and the meeting, stacked with deputies, was moving on autopilot. Reagan was in the Oval Office, and, she was told, Weinberger, Casey, and Clark were "closeted off alone" down the hall from the NSPG. Evidently, they were discussing who the next national security adviser would be, and Kirkpatrick's name "was on the list." She was flattered that her name was being considered, but felt there was nothing she could do. It didn't occur to Kirkpatrick to do what every other candidate was doing—actively campaign for the job. Feverish, her nose rubbed red, she decided to go home and crawl back into bed.

. . .

LATER THAT AFTERNOON, Weinberger, Clark, and Casey emerged from Clark's office and buttonholed the president, arguing strenuously against the switch. They said it was "politically unwise," because the FBI was still investigating "Debategate," the case of the purloined Carter briefing books that inexplicably found their way into the Reagan camp. Baker was widely viewed as the culprit. They added that "substantively, Baker had no experience in foreign affairs" and "hadn't even showed interest." A strong and knowledgeable expert in national security affairs was what was needed at *this* critical time. Weinberger took the lead with Casey seconding him. They both recommended Kirkpatrick.

Reagan was taken aback, listening at first with bewilderment, then with resignation at the intensity of their argument. Finally, he said he would rethink his position.

The president marched back to the Oval Office, and at 3:30 picked up the phone to call Shultz. He said he was "holding off the announcement for a short time." Ten minutes later, he called Shultz again. Will you talk with Cap and Casey? he asked. Shultz knew what this meant. See if he could get Casey and Weinberger to reconsider their opposition to Baker. Otherwise, Baker was history.

When Reagan hung up the phone, he received a rash of calls supporting Kirkpatrick. Joseph Coors and other members of Reagan's "kitchen cabinet" of informal advisers called to push her name. So did two heavyweight intellectuals, leading conservative Bill Buckley and Irving Kristol, who had the distinction of being the godfather of neoconservativism.

AT FIVE, WEINBERGER and Casey met with Shultz. Shultz already had Reagan's and Bush's votes for Baker, but Casey was hell-bent against him. He was also lukewarm about the other candidates. Only one person had his and Weinberger's strong endorsement, Kirkpatrick. Shultz knew then that Baker was effectively dead in the water.

Shultz decided that he would rather work with McFarlane, and the next day told the president exactly that. He reportedly told Reagan that if Kirkpatrick were made national security adviser, he would feel forced to resign. He couldn't work with her in that position, he said.

AFTER MEETING WITH SHULTZ, Casey rushed to see Kirkpatrick at her Bethesda home. Oblivious to the fierce campaign on her behalf, she had quietly been reading Tocqueville.

She greeted Casey in her robe. She looked awful, but this was not a time for niceties. He exclaimed to her that he had strenuously fought to get her the NSC post.

Kirkpatrick liked Casey, had always liked him. She felt few men in the administration were as misunderstood by the establishment press as Casey, who was a "real intellectual," hardly the reckless cowboy they painted him to be. The two clicked.

As Casey shuffled out of the house, he paused briefly, looked over to Kirkpatrick with a big guffaw, and laughed. Hell, he said, if she didn't get the NSC post, there was a "fallback position"—he could run her for president.

ON MONDAY, October 17, the president hastily arranged a meeting with Kirkpatrick to discuss her plans. The two met in the Oval Office. Reagan intended to appoint McFarlane, but fearing the rumors that she intended to resign if not appointed, he was determined to convince her to stay. He offered to create a new White House position, adviser to the president for national security affairs. Its duties were still to be defined, but they could be worked out, he assured her.

Kirkpatrick listened attentively. She was puzzled and wondered who had been telling the president that she would resign if she didn't get the NSC position. Perhaps her enemies wanted her to resign, she thought, and were trying to box her in. But she "had no intention of doing so—and never had." She also wasn't interested in a new White House position. She thought that in such a position, without a solid institutional base, direct authority, or access to the president, she would repeatedly be outmaneuvered by Shultz and others. As U.N. ambassador, she already had cabinet status and was a member of the NSPG. It was a job she liked, and she felt honored to serve Reagan at this pivotal time in the Cold War. The discussion was unusually long, stretching for over an hour.

Reagan concluded, "It is important that you stay through the election cycle." Kirkpatrick told the president she had every intention of staying through the end of the General Assembly session, but "could not make promises after that."

THAT AFTERNOON, as the dust settled, Kirkpatrick was on the short end. The president formally announced he was picking McFarlane. The press portrayed it as a symbolic victory for the soul of Reagan's foreign policy, with the moderates prevailing over the conservatives. It was written that Kirkpatrick was "irritated," and the *Washington Post* even ran a prominent cartoon picturing her as an unappealing dragon lady with devious-looking eyebrows arched high and a cigarette dangling ominously from a cigarette holder. Kirkpatrick shook her head at the cartoons and at the headlines claiming that she would resign. "Pure fiction," she said. In turn, she sought to correct the record, announcing to the press that she "still had work to do at the U.N." But privately, she feared that she had reached the apex of her power, that McFarlane would be out of his depth and take a back seat to Shultz, the ultimate pragmatist. If so, she, the neoconservative-outsider-turned-insider, would end up an outsider once again.

THE FINAL MONTHS of the U.N. session in 1983 were especially tense. True enough, Kirkpatrick had devoted much of her attention to Central America, and was instrumental in moving the administration to a harder line against the FMLN and the Sandinistas, but she had increasingly been a force at the U.N. as well. "We take the United Nations very seriously," she told an interviewer at the time. This was evident in her every move.

When the Sandinistas sought propaganda victories at the U.N., she called their bluff, forcefully denying them an open forum with *her* extensive replies. She exchanged sharp barbs with Libya over terrorism, and jousted heatedly with the Soviets over their continued occupation of Afghanistan. She paid fastidious attention to details, driving home the point that the U.S. was willing to draw the line in defense of its policies, even eschewing otherwise routine, feel-good resolutions that were the bread and butter of the liberal establishment and the United Nations. Thus, when Resolution 83, "Prevention of an Arms Race in Outer Space," a pure Soviet propaganda effort, was voted on, the vote was 138–1–37, with her stoutly casting the lone negative vote; it was the same with Resolution 73, stating an urgent need for a comprehensive test ban treaty. The vote was 111–1–35.

But despite these accomplishments, it appeared she would never crack the wall to become a member of the president's innermost sanctum in the White House. Kirkpatrick had heard that even Ed Meese, a political ally, had said of her, "At the end of the day, she'll never be one of the guys."

William Safire, however, offered her his consolation and advice. "Run, Jeane, Run," he wrote, saying that, should President Reagan decide not to run for reelection, then not George Bush or Bob Dole, but she, "the hottest hawk on the Republican lecture trail," should.

CHAPTER 20

At the daily grind of the Helsinki Review talks in Madrid on human rights, Max Kampelman once told a colleague that he had a simple philosophy. There was one way, and only one way to really talk to the Soviets: head-on and bluntly. "Negotiation without confrontation," he noted, "was a charade."

Kampelman hated the standard State Department mush, the "diplomatic pussyfooting," and from early on this was dramatically reflected in his style of negotiations. If the Soviets wanted to talk "disarmament," he ignored them and focused on human rights. If they decried "American aggressiveness," he shot back in a feverish voice about their "brutality in Afghanistan." If they touted the glories of socialism, he pointed out that they "rule by fear," and that "fear does not produce loyalty." If they complained that the pointed language was "insulting" and would "poison relations," he hotly retorted with examples of their brutality in Afghanistan.

Carrying sheaves of documentation about Soviet abuses in his briefcase, no charge went unanswered. And as Ronald Reagan increasingly pushed his vision of East-West competition and confrontation, relentlessly exhausting and squeezing the Soviet system, Max Kampelman was in Madrid tending to the more protracted matter of locking the Soviets into a final Helsinki Review treaty document.

Kampelman was no cowboy, and he was not eagerly looking for a showdown. But he was more than willing to tiptoe right up to the edge.

Indeed, as the U.S. and the Soviets lurched to the brink over the INF missile controversy, the Cold War continued to be waged on other equally profound and vital fronts, regional conflicts in Central America and Afghanistan, but most significantly in 1982 and 1983 in the war of ideology, a heated contest not just between two superpowers but between two dramatically different political systems, democracy and Communism. In the full stare and hot lights of the world community, Jeane

Kirkpatrick was carrying out the offensive at the United Nations, while Kampelman, more quietly, was carrying the spear in Madrid. For the Soviets, it was like a pincer movement, facing not just a hardware challenge, but what became known as the software challenge, designed to delegitimize and ultimately to defeat the Soviet system.

To liberals who believed in détente and were fearful of the growing tensions arising out of the INF missile crisis, this was a lamentable set of events, carrying the risk of out-and-out conflict. Kampelman scoffed at this, feeling it was overly alarmist, and naive, talk. "I was convinced that there was too much concern in the West for Soviet sensitivities, coupled with far too much pre-accommodation," he said.

Yet, unlike Kirkpatrick, Kampelman was rarely ever dragged through the mud of partisan hostilities in Washington with the Congress and the press. In good measure, like Richard Perle, this was because Kirkpatrick was an administration star, which made her an inviting, and automatic, target. By contrast, the less-high-profile Kampelman labored patiently, in far greater anonymity.

But while she was a star, he was, in many ways, better suited for bureaucratic warfare than Kirkpatrick. She was urbane, and with a patrician lilt to her voice, professorial. He showed little of her thin skin, and though a hard-liner, he was by temperament and professional training more of a pragmatist than Kirkpatrick. She was the grand administration strategist, the brilliant administration conceptualizer, the Reagan theoretician who could deliver sweeping themes of action from jumbled, often contradictory, facts. By contrast, he was lawyerly, waving not themes of complexity and nuance, but an implementer. Calibrating his actions bureaucratically, he was, when the dust settled, first and foremost a doer.

One of Kampelman's first big decisions was how to handle the Helsinki Review talks upon their resumption in the spring of 1983. Broken off by an eighteen-month impasse over the imposition of martial law in Poland, they had resumed with full steam. The previous year, he had observed that the Soviets desperately wanted to cut a deal in Madrid. As he saw it, they wanted to wrap up these talks and move on to a Madrid-sanctioned disarmament meeting, to be in a better position to stop the INF missile deployments.

But while Kampelman's philosophy was never to concede, thus denying them an early agreement, it was also to keep talking. In due course, this eventually worked to the decisive advantage of the U.S. By March of 1983, talks that were supposed to have been locked up in three months had dragged on for almost three years. The U.S. had not compromised its ideals on human rights. And the Soviets had been denied the propaganda advantage of a disarmament conference before the slated missile deployments.

But now, after thirty-three grueling months of shuttling from Washington to Madrid, and hopping from European capital to European capital for consultations with the allies, Kampelman's energy and patience had run out. "There comes a time when negotiations must die or reach a conclusion," he grimly observed. It was, he felt, the time to cut a deal, or fold his cards and go home.

There were obstacles, however. The Soviets had failed to live up to their earlier human rights commitments, thus leading many to question the validity of these talks. Suppression of basic human rights of Soviet citizens had actually increased dramatically since the signing of the first Helsinki document in 1975. The Soviets had ruthlessly clamped down on Jewish emigration, harshly stifling family reunification. They continued to jam Western radio broadcasts. Fifty-one Russians, whose only sin was to believe in the Helsinki agreement and who organized to monitor their government's compliance with the 1975 accords, were thrown in jails, labor camps, psychiatric hospitals, or sent into internal exile. There, they languished in the cruelest of circumstances. More than five hundred Soviet citizens who had engaged in Helsinki Watch–related activities since the Madrid meetings began were similarly imprisoned for political or religious "crimes." And the talks were clouded by the suffocation of Poland through martial law and the armed occupation of Afghanistan.

George Will, the prominent conservative columnist, whose views were not lightly dismissed, was particularly perturbed. To Will, Kampelman was a tough, decent, able, and intellectual Democrat. But he feared that as the public became used to the sight of Western and Communist diplomats deliberating about freedom of expression, travel, trade unions, and other matters, the public would conclude that the people talking so earnestly, for so long, shared a political vocabulary and frame of reference. Thus, he feared that as the Soviets and the Eastern bloc violated virtually every particular of the agreement, the public would be given the soothing but misleading impression of moral equivalence between the liberal democracies and repressive Communist states.

In one of his tougher columns, Will, an insightful voice of Reagan conservatism, registered his fervent dissent. He wrote, "The purpose of the Helsinki process, [Kampelman] says, is to keep Moscow on the defensive and force it to pay a political and moral price," and "for teaching the educable, there is no better teacher than Kampelman. . . . But teaching civility to Moscow is like teaching golf to wolves."

Will had a strong point, and Kampelman was not unmindful of the criticism. "They talked reasonably, but behaved abominably," he himself lamented, in private.

But there were salutary effects to Kampelman's actions, many only clear in the benefit of hindsight. Through his persistent naming of individual and collective dissidents, the Helsinki process was invaluable to the few valiant persons laboring for freedom in the Soviet orbit, including many in prison. The brave Jewish dissident Anatoly Shcharansky was perhaps the most famous, but by no means only one in this category, repeatedly named by Kampelman at the talks.

And there was a larger purpose to Kampelman's actions—the struggle for "hearts and minds," as he called it, the "tarnishing of the Soviet image," which did ultimately begin to sting the Soviets. His continued verbal battering of Communist regimes, already under assault in the hardware arena, showed a systematic American willingness to question the legitimacy of their system that had hitherto been absent among the American establishment.

Indeed, in doing this, he was articulating the wishes of Ronald Reagan, who would himself raise the war of words and ideology at the highest levels to a harsher, unprecedented octave, one that had been off-bounds in the genteel give-and-take rhythms of previous administrations' diplomacy.

ONE OF THE HOTTEST authors in the early 1980s was Jean-François Revel, a Frenchman and former editor of L'Express, one of France's leading newsmagazines. In his powerful, best-selling books, The Totalitarian Temptation and, later, How Democracies Perish, Revel, a compelling intellectual, advanced the dire thesis that democratic civilization, the finest in the world, was in jeopardy. He wrote that the system of democracy "is the first in history to blame itself because another power is working to destroy it," and unless free people are willing to oppose totalitarianism, it may indeed, as Communism had predicted, perish.

President Reagan, for one, shared this fear, as did a number of his advisers. But he also detected cracks in the Soviet system, which if pressed could become deep fissures, and if pushed further could rupture the militarized but technologically backward Soviet regime. So, in a toughly worded speech before the British Parliament in June of 1982, Reagan launched a worldwide ideological offensive against the Soviets, calling for "a global campaign for democracy" and a "crusade for freedom that will engage the faith and fortitude of the next generation."

Echoing Winston Churchill at his famous Fulton, Missouri, "Iron Curtain" speech, Reagan charged, "The regimes planted by totalitarianism have had more than thirty years to establish their legitimacy," but have failed to do so. He talked of "the decay of the Soviet experiment" and a "great revolutionary crisis" within the Soviet bloc. Then, establishing a clear theme for American foreign policy, he concluded, "The ultimate determinant of the struggle in the world will not be bombs and rockets, but a test of wills and ideas." And he declared a new chapter unfolding in the Cold War. "The march of freedom and democracy . . . will leave Marxism-Leninism on the ash-heap of history as it has left other tyrannies which stifle freedom and muzzle the self-expression of people."

To liberals at home, like *Time* magazine's Strobe Talbott, who gulped and gasped at the speech, this was "dangerous bear-baiting," "extremist," and "militant." It was also an unprecedented break from the pragmatic policies of the establishment and the muted language of many past presidents, although its tough, plain talk recalled Harry Truman at his finest. But to those in prison camps, the murderous Soviet gulag, in struggling democracies, and among the ranks of Solidarity workers and underground Czech intellectuals in the stifling confines of the Eastern bloc, it was a breath of fresh air, a sign of American leadership, and a promise that one day they too could enjoy the same freedoms as their counterparts in the West. The force of these words was borne out not long after, when a dissident, released from the Soviet Union, met Kampelman. He first fell to his knees, and then stood up shaking, kissed the American negotiator, and exclaimed that while in prison he and others were sustained by Kampelman's relentless indictment of Soviet noncompliance with Helsinki's goals.

To the Soviets, from Brezhnev adviser Leonid Zamyatin up to Brezhnev himself, Reagan's speech had ominous portents as a "turning point, a self-unmasking of American policy as implacably anti-Soviet." True enough, it was only rhetoric, but it was a major departure from the past, not just a war of words, but signaling a new era in the U.S.-Soviet contest. They did not doubt that Reagan took the democracy crusade seriously, or that he envisaged dismantling the Soviet system. This was precisely what worried them.

By 1983, with Kampelman hammering these themes in Madrid, sometimes piecemeal, dissident by dissident, talking about Andrei Sakharov or anti-Semitism or Soviet imperialism or psychiatric hospitals, sometimes across the board, condemning the Soviet system wholesale, or supporting Solidarity in Poland, Reagan delivered an additional blow, turning up the rhetorical anti-Soviet heat from hot to scalding. Whatever ambiguity about his policies or the nature of the Cold War may have existed, he took this opportunity to definitively set its shape in a clearly defined framework. With the nuclear freeze sweeping the country, jeopardizing the INF missile deployments, he declared before a rapt audience of Christian Evangelicals in Orlando, Florida, "In your discussions of the nuclear freeze proposals, I urge you to beware the temptation of pride— the temptation of blithely declaring yourselves above it all and label both sides equally at fault, to ignore the facts of history and the aggressive impulses of an evil empire, to simply call the arms race a giant misunderstanding."

Toward the end of the address, he rallied the troops and added, "I believe we shall rise to the challenge. I believe that Communism is another sad, bizarre chapter in human history whose last pages even now are being written."

The speech, baldly calling the Soviets an "evil empire," prophesizing the end of their regime, was received poorly by the establishment. The old guard was particularly alarmed, even embarrassed, by Reagan's unabashedly pro-democracy, anti-Soviet vision, and circled the wagons of protest. Alarmed by the thought of a superpower confrontation, obsessed with an ideology of pragmatism, seared by Vietnam, the establishment had not just lost its will for global leadership, but was bereft of a moral compass, treating the U.S. and the Soviets as two versions of the same. Indeed, Averell Harriman, who that year visited Moscow to meet with the new Soviet leader, Yuri Andropov, made it known to anyone who would listen that he was completely disconsolate about "Reagan's fulminations" against the "evil empire."

George Kennan was even gloomier, viewing American actions as caught in the same kind of militarism and paranoia that inexorably sucked the Great Powers into World War I. To Kennan, Reagan and his administration were sacrificing the cool verities of realism to an alarming rhetoric of confrontation that, he snapped, "disqualifies the U.S. from active participation in the world." He gloomily predicted all this was leading to "a march toward war, that and nothing else." Kennan began leading a campaign against the "shrillness" of the Helsinki talks and "the confrontation" of the INF missile deployments, under the symbolic but simplistic banner of "a no-first use" for nuclear weapons campaign.

Indeed, nothing so dramatized the break from the old guard during the Reagan era as this war of ideology. As the establishment and the Reagan administration came to blows over their conflicting visions of the world, nothing could paper over their deep and abiding differences, the chasm between the paladins of détente and the post-containment Reaganauts. In Democratic party Georgetown salons at the Harrimans', coffee klatches of the mainstream liberal press, and the inner sanctum of the establishment Council on Foreign Relations, it was virtually impossible to find a single defender of Reagan's tough rhetoric. It was scoffed at on the Hill, apologized for by peace groups, and either dismissed as amateurish or reviled as dangerous on leading op-ed pages and in elite university research centers.

But this didn't fit with Kampelman's assessment. He, of all people, was acutely aware that the intelligentsia and establishment thought Reagan's undiplomatic words were ill-advised. But to Kampelman, the doer and realist, the lifelong anti-Communist, the Soviets were "evil," and they *certainly* were an "empire." He knew many of his liberal friends felt otherwise. But all his life he had not ducked unpopular and unfashionable causes, and in the chilly clime of the 1980s, none was more unfashionable among the establishment and liberals than anti-Communism.

One day, in a conversation with Kirkpatrick, the two talked about how prevalent "anti-anti-Communism" had become. Kampelman, who had been reviled earlier in his career and savaged by the press, had seen this all before. Nonetheless, he agreed with Kirkpatrick that civic obligation and the Cold War dictated that there was no alternative but to soldier on.

So in that March of 1983, when it became clear to Kampelman that the Soviets were ready to accept a draft document tabled by the neutral countries of the thirty-five member nations of the Conference on Security and Cooperation in Europe (CSCE), he wanted a concrete gesture of good faith, further proof of their sincerity. He sought from the president, and gained authorization, to add one more demand, to be discussed only in private with the Soviets. Before giving his blessing to an agreement, he would ask them to release a significant number of political prisoners and religious activists in the Soviet Union.

Privately, he harbored another hope, not just that a list of names would be released, but that this could lead to the release of the most important dissident in the Soviet Union, Anatoly Shcharansky.

It was then that he shifted his focus in his public talks with the Soviets to deeply private conversations, not with Soviet diplomats, but quietly in back rooms and over simple meals with the Soviet KGB.

It was almost ironic that 1983 marked the fiftieth anniversary of U.S.-Soviet diplomatic relations. It was the nineteenth-century French political theorist Alexis de Tocqueville, who in his classic *Democracy in America* had spoken of America's expansion via "freedom," and of Russia's through "servitude," and prophesied about the two colossus nations that "each seems marked by the will of Heaven to sway the destinies of half the globe."

But that was in a different century. For decades, Soviet leaders had sought to bully America, boasting of how their system would bury capitalism, and how the ideological struggle must continue by scientific doctrine, even in periods of détente. Their version of the Cold War was of two countries in the ring perhaps, but with only one fighter ultimately climbing out. The Soviets, however, did not take well to the Reagan counterpunch, in his "Campaign for Democracy" and "Evil Empire" speeches, repeated with tenacious perspicacity by Kampelman in Madrid. This became dramatically clear at a Washington celebration of the fiftieth anniversary of relations, a gala event attended by Americans and Soviets. Ambassador Anatoly Dobrynin gloomily made his way to the microphone, and then despaired in prepared remarks: "For us, words are deeds."

Indeed, the feeling in Moscow was almost uniform. Reagan's ideological campaign for democracy deeply shook them, leading them to question the stability of their ideological foundations as never before.

THAT SPRING, Kampelman met with Reagan in the Oval Office to report on the progress of the Helsinki talks, now nearing their end. He wanted also to inform him about his discussions on Anatoly Shcharansky. Immediately engaged, Reagan took the opportunity to inform him of a secret rendezvous he had had with Dobrynin a month earlier. Kampelman perked up in his wing chair, listening intently without interrupting.

Reagan indicated that while he was pushing the Soviets hard publicly, he had quietly encouraged keeping the doors of dialogue open. It had not gone unnoticed that he had called the Soviets an evil empire only once, sending more soothing signals through back channels. With Soviet cooperation, he indicated he was willing to move toward improved relations. But like Kampelman, he wanted a tangible symbol of Soviet willingness to work with the U.S. Sitting erect, Kampelman noticed an intensity in Reagan's speech, not usually associated with the more genial public persona of the president.

Reagan explained he was particularly concerned with the plight of seven Pentecostal Christians from Siberia, who had been holed up in the basement of the U.S. embassy in Moscow since 1978. These two families wanted permission from the Soviet authorities to leave the country, but the Soviets had repeatedly denied them the "right to leave."

Unsmiling, the president protested, "Why don't the Soviets let them go? Why is it that they won't let them practice their religion?"

His pique evident, he continued, saying such cases should be resolved quietly and quickly. If they would just let them go, the president emphasized, it would make it easier for him "to take positive steps" in other areas.

Kampelman was encouraged. For over a month he had been steadily working with Sergei Kondrashev, the head of the KGB at the Madrid talks, and the man in charge of the overall Soviet operation, to take on individual human rights cases. Shrewd and Machiavellian, Kondrashev had a direct pipeline to Andropov. Kampelman milked it for all he could, working out a deal for the release of Anatoly Shcharansky. There was one proviso, that Shcharansky write a letter to the Soviet authorities requesting "immediate release from prison on grounds of poor health." For Shcharansky, this acknowledgment smacked of capitulation to his Russian captors, and sounded an immediate dissonant note.

"I committed no crimes," he replied sharply. "The crimes were committed by the people who arrested me and are keeping me in prison." It was a very principled, as well as brave, stance, but his terms were unacceptable to the Soviets. For now, Shcharansky's release was a dead end.

Kampelman knew that he could continue to work for Shcharansky's release, but the fate of the Pentecostals presented a new opportunity to help the president and press the issue on another front. What was the current status of the president's request? Kampelman queried.

I haven't heard back, the president said with perceptible edginess. Kampelman could see the disappointment on the president's face. When Reagan asked him to tell Kondrashev directly that he had not received an answer to his earlier request, and "to make certain" Kondrashev knew of his concern, Kampelman needed little prodding.

In fact, the timing for the request was hardly perfect. The Soviets were bitterly apprehensive about the massive U.S. defense buildup, and furious about Reagan's and Kampelman's full-throated assault on socialism in their speeches. Soviet decision making was also stalled by the ailing Yuri Andropov, who had replaced Leonid Brezhnev as Soviet general secretary after Brezhnev's death, and who was now tethered to a dialysis machine several days a week.

But Kampelman pressed ahead. He contacted his old deputy at Madrid, Warren Zimmermann, who was now the deputy chief of mission at the U.S. embassy in Moscow. He inquired: What are the Pentecostals' circumstances? Who else is involved? How many family members are there? He also kept Secretary of State Shultz in the inner circle of the decision loop, even though his talks otherwise were a carefully guarded secret.

Zimmermann fished around for the information, soon determining that the extended families of the Pentecostals numbered up to sixty altogether. Not one to lightly capitulate, Kampelman took the whole list and gave it to Kondrashev, asking that they all be released.

He anticipated resistance, but gambled on the fact it was a small price to pay for securing a final deal on the Helsinki Accords. Kondrashev then paid a call on Kampelman with his reply. He could ensure their release, but there was one condition. They could all be released only if they went to Israel—not the U.S. He explained rather cryptically that if done this way, the decision could be made in "Moscow," without being held up by "less favorable quarters" of the Soviet structure.

Kampelman was not a cynic. He did not trust Kondrashev on everything, but felt he was sincere in his terms. He had also long felt that Kondrashev, and not his political counterparts, held the real power, so he accepted his explanation. By April 12, all the Pentecostals were allowed to leave for Siberia. By June's end, all but two were allowed to emigrate to Israel.

The hour was nearing to close the Madrid talks.

AT TIMES, the talks with the Soviets limped along with a calibrated monotony, and Kampelman had to look for signs, often subtle, often innocuous, that progress was being made. In this vein, Kampelman the realist was an inveterate optimist. When likewise there were depressing lulls, frustrating and often inexplicable holdups to an agreement, Kampelman sought to accentuate the positive. One such instance came in 1982, when he received a package smuggled out of the cold depths of a Soviet work camp in Kuchino, Perm Oblast, the tundra of the Soviet Union. Scrawled in barely legible, minuscule handwriting on ratty, thin toilet tissue was a message passionately urging Kampelman to continue the struggle for "basic human rights." In simple yet straightforward language, it called for the right to organize free trade unions, and for the end of religious persecution in the Soviet Union. It was signed by Balys Gajauskas, a Lithuanian political prisoner.

Kampelman was moved by the letter, and promptly framed and hung it on his office wall. The Shcharanskys and the Sakharovs, the historian and leading Solidarity intellectual Bronislaw Geremek, and people like Gajauskas, less well known, were what motivated him to confront the Soviets for yet another day. Such tokens of their appreciation were palpable symbols to Kampelman, not just of the indomitable strength of the human spirit, of the universal yearning for freedom, but of the weakness of the totalitarian face, unable to fully control all communication or to break the human soul or the human heart. Inspired by example, Kampelman persisted.

At the outset of the Madrid talks, the Soviets had largely rejected discussion of human rights as "interference in their internal affairs." On a number of occasions, they angrily retorted that they "would not change their practices to please the U.S." Yet after three years and logging over four hundred separate hours with the Soviets outside of the talks themselves, Kampelman was eventually able to present a united Western front to the Soviets. The Soviets had inched significantly toward accepting Western definitions of human rights.

For all their weaknesses, Kampelman was convinced the Madrid talks helped make human rights an indelible part of U.S.-Soviet relations. For Kampelman, they established a "moral tuning fork," a set of standards by which to responsibly judge international behavior.

In early September of 1983, the toiling and man-hours came to fruition, and the thirty-five nations signed a final agreement. It was not the millennium, nor peace in our time, and Kampelman knew this. Perhaps uncharacteristically Pollyannish, he still declared the Helsinki process "an accountability process." That was an overstatement. The Soviets had been violating the first Helsinki Accords with impunity, and there was little doubt they would continue to do so.

But the signing of the agreement did bolster the sagging spirits of the Western democracies. It further set down concrete markers about human rights, rejecting the Soviet view that human rights were about collective and economic rights decided by the *diktat* of the state, rather than about political and individual freedom. In the end, even critics of Helsinki could view it as an essential step in promoting human rights in the Soviet Union.

Despite the imperfections, Kampelman returned home able to present his efforts as a triumph of diplomacy. The Soviets themselves, thuggish in dealing with political prisoners, harsh in their treatment of Jews and other minorities, and xenophobic in clamping down on emigration, were in small but demonstrable ways stung by the outcome. Soviet ideology was increasingly hollow, its economic system had long since lost its attractiveness, and the allure of the "new Soviet man" was largely no more. Madrid contributed to this ebb. The sole Soviet claim to the future lay in military power, which drew allies not through persuasion and consent, but through aggression and force.

But with loose rocks do avalanches begin. Kampelman, like other Americans, now braced himself for the denouement of the missile controversy. The Cold War had once again shifted venue, its white-hot center no longer about human rights in Madrid, or choosing between the democratic U.S. and the totalitarian Communist world at the U.N. in New York, or in trouble spots in the barren streets of Managua, in the noisy chaos of San Salvador, or in the roughened hills of Afghanistan, but once again, in the quiet, misleading sterility of a pair of sturdy wooden tables in Geneva.

And with the missile countdown approaching, that, of course, was just the beginning.

CHAPTER 21

On August 31, at 2:21 P.M. Washington time, the huge Boeing 747, KAL flight 007, was coasting at 35,000 feet in the skies over Sakhalin Island, roughly equidistant between Japan and its final destination, South Korea. Despite the long flight, most of the 269 passengers were wide awake. It was an exhilarating trip. Crossing the International Date Line, the plane was chasing the soft rays of the receding sun. A few hours earlier, it had touched down for a refueling stop in Anchorage, Alaska. Arcing down from the sky, the passengers could see a magnificent sight, the first tinge of autumn, a hint of splendid reds among the deep dark greens of the thick Alaskan wildlands, the dark waters of Glacier Bay, and huge expanses of land.

In the airport, one could see laughing children recoiling and then smiling, greeted by a mighty seven-foot stuffed grizzly bear rearing up on its hind legs, teeth bared and arms outstretched. Before reboarding the plane, some of the passengers, including Larry McDonald, a Georgia congressman, thumbed through newspapers and magazines at the kiosks. Children nibbled on chocolate candy bars, and tourists purchased Eskimo artifacts and arts and crafts for souvenirs.

Now, unknown to the passengers or the crew, the plane had drifted three hundred miles off course and had accidentally flown into Soviet airspace. For two and a half hours, it was tracked by Soviet radar and followed by Soviet interceptors, flying under a bright half moon that lit up the night sky. For fifteen minutes, a Soviet interceptor pilot had watched the plane cruising calmly over the water. Then the command went out.

At 2:22, thirty-nine-year-old Soviet fighter pilot Lieutenant Colonel Genadi Osipovich, flying an SU-15 jet, received his orders: "Invader has violated state border. Destroy target."

Peering out of his plane, he could see the flashing navigation lights of the Boeing, and thought it was an odd shape for a reconnaissance plane. But any thought that it could be a civilian plane gave him little pause.

Osipovich, who bore a striking resemblance to Elvis Presley, was trained to carry out, not to question. He swung into action.

He fired a burst of warning shots. Had they hit anything, they would have sounded like the mad flapping of a giant bird trapped in a closet. Instead, they sped off into the distance, splashing into the sea, unseen and unacknowledged.

Under orders, the Soviet pilot did not try to make radio contact with the jet or escort the plane down. His mandate was clear: bring the plane down with force if necessary.

The Boeing neared the edge of the Soviet airspace into which it had accidentally strayed. In only 120 seconds, it would be back in international airspace. Osipovich received another message, coldly instructing: "Destroy invader." He visually inspected the plane one more time.

At 2:25, the commercial jet was making good time, and was to land in Seoul on schedule. But it would never get there.

Suddenly and inexplicably, at 2:26, two missiles blasted from the Soviet plane, and ripped through the Boeing. The jumbo jet blew into thousands of pieces, and all radio transmission came to an eerie and final halt. For twelve minutes, the mutilated passengers, the crew, and the remnants of the jet tumbled chaotically in a downward spiral before they disappeared into the black recesses of the Sea of Japan.

After the explosion, there was nothing but a stark naked silence over the water. Osipovich took a deep breath, and then relayed back to his Soviet command: "The target is destroyed."

He paused, and then added, "I am breaking off attack."

FROM A U.S.-JAPANESE listening post in northern Japan, the CIA obtained the radio transmissions of the Soviet pilot talking to his ground control. They were promptly passed on to Washington.

At 10:45 A.M. on Thursday, September 1, Secretary of State George Schultz convened a press conference at the State Department and made public the shocking news of the brutal shootdown of KAL 007. American outrage and sense of betrayal were immediate.

The White House reached Jeane Kirkpatrick in Marrakesh, Morocco, and asked her to return immediately to the United Nations. Reagan wanted her to take the lead in condemning Soviet behavior. Speaking before an emergency session of the U.N. Security Council, Kirkpatrick was resolute. Playing the two-minute audiotape of the shootdown that brought delegates to an audible gasp, she proceeded to condemn the Soviets in blistering terms. The downing of KAL 007, she declared, her tone forceful, was "characteristic" of the Soviets. "Violence and lies are regular instruments of Soviet policy," she added. And even more pointedly, "We are reminded once again that the Soviet Union is a state based on the dual principles of callousness and mendacity. It is dedicated to the rule of force." Delegates cringed at this harsh language, the strongest words Kirkpatrick ever spoke at the U.N., which stood in such sharp contrast to the more tepid statement released earlier by the State Department. But there was little doubt that the point got across. She mustered a successful effort to garner nine votes to condemn the Soviet Union. Even though the Soviets vetoed the resolution, it remained an important symbolic victory.

FOR FIVE BITTER DAYS, the Soviets continued to deny responsibility for the attack, despite evidence to the contrary presented to the world. Instead, they clung to a tired if not frightening propaganda statement made by the Soviet leadership and released by the Soviet news agency Tass. The paper claimed Soviet fighters had warned an "unidentified plane" that had flown in the direction of the Sea of Japan and was on an intelligence mission. The story was pure fabrication, but they stuck to it.

Finally, under international pressure, the Soviets buckled and acknowledged their role in the shootdown. But they denied all culpability. Speaking in Madrid, Spain, Soviet Foreign Minister Andrei Gromyko made the chilling statement: "We state: Soviet territory, the borders of the Soviet Union, are sacred." In short, Gromyko was saying, the Soviets would do it again.

For Paul Nitze, sitting in Geneva, this event was a vivid demonstration of the high stakes involved in the countdown to deployment—and why he felt a walkout must be avoided at all costs. Nitze thus sent an urgent cable to the administration. The Soviets would leave the talks by October 12. Time was running out.

On September 8, Shultz and Gromyko clashed bitterly in Madrid in one of the most acrimonious meetings ever held between the foreign ministers of the two superpowers. Deviating from initial plans, an aide, not Shultz, greeted Gromyko at the front door of the U.S. ambassador's residence. When the two met in the embassy library later in the day for their private one-on-one, Shultz brought up the KAL shootdown; Gromyko was irate, and said he didn't want to discuss it. He instead spoke about the arms race: "The world situation is now slipping toward a very dangerous precipice. It is plain that the great responsibility for not allowing a nuclear catastrophe to occur must be borne by the U.S.S.R. and the U.S.A. together."

Then, joined by a bevy of aides in another room, the tense meeting continued. When Shultz raised KAL again, Gromyko shuffled his papers and piled them into a neat stack, and slowly stood up. It appeared that he had had enough, and was about to declare the meeting over. He slowly surveyed the room. A sense of dread welled up among the aides.

Shultz stood up and, with an arm outstretched to guide Gromyko to the door, said firmly, his voice suffused with anger, "Fine, go!" The secretary's aide, Bill Krimer, cringed. It was the sharpest, and most dangerous exchange of foreign ministers, since the Cuban Missile Crisis. But Gromyko, reluctant to cut the meeting off, didn't leave. He paced slowly, gesturing and talking, and after a few minutes seated himself once again.

After two hours, the meeting came to a final, chilly end. The ministers departed uneasily from the room, only to be greeted by a sea of journalists. Gromyko waved aside the two-hundred-strong press corps milling around nervously with their cameras, photographer vests, and steno pads. Without saying a word, he was gone. It was obvious the meeting had gone badly. But how badly? They awaited the secretary.

Then Shultz emerged, grim-faced, unsmiling, his fist tightly clenched around meeting notes. He spoke of the "unprovoked Soviet destruction of a defenseless, unarmed Korean airliner," and "the preposterous explanation" that compromised the superpower relations.

He continued angrily, "Foreign Minister Gromyko's response to me today was even more unsatisfactory than the response he gave in public yesterday."

Observers of the meeting recoiled. That the superpowers were at a potential breaking point was undeniable. But would the arms talks continue? Could the U.S. now emplace the missiles, or would the allies seek more time rather than risk further escalation with the Soviets? How likely was a U.S.-Soviet confrontation?

THE AMERICANS did not write off the arms talks. Indeed, when Weinberger proposed that arms control negotiations be called off until there was a satisfactory resolution of the shootdown, the president rejected it. To be sure, Reagan had heatedly denounced the Soviet action in a major televised address from the Oval Office. That afternoon, he penned his own tough changes to his prepared remarks, rewriting most of the speech himself. He labeled the Soviet action a "massacre" no fewer than six times; his face radiating pique, he added that it was a "crime against humanity" and an "atrocity." But he was unwilling to call off the Shultz-Gromyko Madrid meeting. With what little precious time existed before deployment, he insisted the arms talks proceed.

Far from being the nuclear cowboy with his finger pressed to the button, in this crisis Reagan instinctively mixed toughness with flexibility, firm rhetoric and consistency of action with instinctive caution. This was never more apparent than later in the month as he spoke before the U.N. General Assembly and offered a more flexible version of the zero option. He called for global limits, with Perle's zero plan as a long-term—but not immediate—goal.

Two days later, the Soviets responded with a shrill and brutal voice. Yuri Andropov, the Soviet general secretary, issued a sweeping and unusually harsh (even by Soviet standards) denunciation of the American proposal. "All they do is prattle about some sort of flexibility at the Geneva talks," the statement said. But the proposal was nothing but "deception" that was "brazenly presented as something new."

Andropov then denounced the U.S. in language so sweeping as to dismiss any possibility of improved U.S.-Soviet relations under the Reagan administration. "Even if someone had any illusions about the possible evolution for the better in the policy of the present administration," he said, "the latest developments have dispelled them."

The lull in superpower relations was now rippling throughout the global arena, and, as the U.S. and the Soviets lurched from one crisis to the next, no less than Pope John Paul II was prompted to add his voice directly to the fray. He warned about the growing tensions poisoning the international atmosphere, and intoned fearfully that we are moving from a postwar era to a "prewar phase." It was a chilling use of words to describe the international climate. And as the run-up toward missile deployment approached, U.S.-Soviet tensions continued to heighten and the specter of a superpower conflict loomed, casting doubt not just on any last-second progress in the arms talks, but on the very missile deployment itself.

DURING THESE TENSE September days, Richard Perle was grieving. At the time of the KAL massacre, Perle was in Stockholm, debating Bruno Kreisky, the former chancellor of Austria, at an international conference on nuclear policy. It was generally viewed as a triumph for Perle, who acquitted himself well and spoke forcefully.

The next morning, he joined the American ambassador for a private breakfast at the embassy. Stockholm was hardly center stage on the front lines of the Cold War, and the ambassador treated Perle as a minor celebrity. This was a rare opportunity for him to play his part in the INF countdown, and he peppered Perle with questions and ideas about what steps the U.S. should undertake. He also wanted to gauge how the administration would handle KAL. Perle for his part was in a quiet mood.

During a lull, the ambassador asked, almost in passing, "Did you hear about Scoop Jackson?"

Perle perked up. His eyes brightened. He wondered what marvelous speech Scoop had given this time. "No," Perle replied. "What did he say?"

"He didn't say anything," the ambassador told Perle. "He's dead."

Perle froze. Then, in the next second, he wanted to scream or to run. Scoop, Scoop who had been like a father, who had been more than a father, Scoop could not be gone.

The ambassador, oblivious, has already moved on excitedly to another topic.

Perle heard words, a detached voice droning on, but he no longer heard the ambassador. Stuck in his ears, over and over, was that one sentence: "He didn't say anything, he's dead."

Perle felt like he was floating, slipping out of his body. All he could think was that he had to get out of there. "He's dead" echoed and echoed.

Briefly regaining his composure, Perle excused himself and headed for the bathroom. He had recently spoken with Scoop. Scoop had been fine. He stared at his face in the mirror. It was the color of ash. He bent over the sink. There's no Scoop Jackson, he thought.

For Perle, it was as if something deep inside him had been ripped out, a terrible, irrevocable personal loss. But it was more than his loss, he felt, standing there in an antiseptically clean bathroom in Stockholm. Scoop had been an unwavering voice of steadiness and reason in the debate on the Cold War. He was never partisan, and cared far less about parties than about the country. He also cared for people. Now, at one of the tensest moments in history, he was gone. Only his legacy remained.

Perle splashed cool water on his face. Inside, there was nothing but a void, a terrible, dark void.

ON OCTOBER 23, terrorists exploded a truck bomb in Lebanon, killing 263 U.S. marines. That same day, for forty-eight hours running, over two million Europeans once again linked arms, stormed national capitals with signs and placards, camped out overnight, and marched and sang against the INF deployment. Two days later, on October 25, the U.S. went ahead with an invasion and rescue mission (for American medical students) on the tiny Caribbean island of Grenada, where a Marxist, Soviet-aligned regime had seized control and was in the process of completing a militarily capable airfield. Shultz would later starkly describe the effect of the invasion: "It caused people to see that the U.S. would use its military power for strategic purpose." Indeed, it was the first time a Marxist government had been rolled back by Western force, and, however small,

Grenada was a symbolic blow to the Brezhnev doctrine of Communist irreversibility.

The Soviets reacted harshly. Soviet Vice President Vasily Kuznetsov, echoing the sentiments of the Kremlin, said the American leadership was "pushing mankind to the brink of disaster." The peace movement also denounced the American invasion, and busily declared a freeze was more urgent than ever.

All this news was occurring with a dizzying pace that threatened to overwhelm American and European policy circles. Nowhere was this more true than in the U.S. negotiating delegation, where even seasoned diplomats began to view each new piece of information in the same apocalyptic tones as the peace movement.

As the deadline for deployment approached, two great sentiments, the lust for peace, and the sober pursuit of the goal that the Soviets would only genuinely deal after the missiles were deployed, were drifting dangerously apart, with many last-second efforts foundering in the gulf between them.

The first cruise missiles were due to arrive in Great Britain on November 14. Now almost virtually obsessed with the harsh, potentially cataclysmic consequences of deployment, the American negotiating team felt this would be the day when the Soviets would walk out, with all the attendant consequences for the Cold War. That day, John Woodworth had an eerie feeling, one he couldn't quite explain and that he could only ascribe to the exigencies of the moment. When he was officially informed that Michael Heseltine, the British defense secretary, had announced to his Parliament that the first of sixteen missiles would indeed be arriving within the next twenty-four hours at Greenham Common Air Base outside of London, Woodworth feared war could be around the corner.

A half hour later, the Soviet delegation dropped off parting gifts with the Americans. Their faces were uncommonly glum. The Soviets believed they would now be summoned home, and Woodworth saw that they were getting ready to pack up and simply go. This could be the only interpretation of the customary end-of-the-round presents they had given. Fingering the generous supply of Soviet caviar and vodka, Russian folk art bowls lacquered in black and decorated with bright red flowers, and parting with a handshake, the Americans sucked in their stomachs, and waited.

Woodworth called his wife, Laura. "It looks like we're going home early," he said.

The cruise missiles arrived the following day, and there was pandemonium in England. Demonstrators pelted Heseltine with eggs and sprayed red paint on him; hundreds of other protesters were arrested outside of

Senator Henry "Scoop" Jackson, Democrat of Washington, one of the quiet giants in the Cold War struggle against the Soviet Union, fought against the détente policies of Republicans and Democrats alike. He never achieved his goal of becoming president, but his devoted following of "Scoop Jackson Democrats" would attain leading positions in the Reagan administration.

1

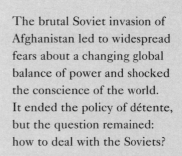

2

The brutal Soviet invasion of Afghanistan led to widespread fears about a changing global balance of power and shocked the conscience of the world. It ended the policy of détente, but the question remained: how to deal with the Soviets?

Best wishes
to Jeane Kirkpatrick
Jimmy Carter

In January of 1980, what was designed to be a critical peace meeting between the leaders of the Coalition for a Democratic Majority and President Jimmy Carter ended in bitter recriminations. "I will never vote for that man," Jeane Kirkpatrick would say to Midge Decter. Carter's performance at this meeting convinced a number of these Democrats that there was no place for them in their party, and led them to join with a former Democrat, Ronald Reagan.

Arch rivals Richard Perle ("the Prince of Darkness") and Richard Burt, sharing a rare moment of levity, fought bitterly over arms control policy. But it was Paul Nitze who would emerge as the principal adversary to Perle's zero option. "You have to be prepared to tough it out with the Russians," Perle direly warned Nitze.

Max Kampelman, a hard-liner and a close-to-the-vest negotiator, repeatedly upbraided the Soviets at the Madrid Review Conference for their systematic human rights violations and imperial behavior. He became a major player in the Reagan administration's war of ideology against the Soviets, and a favorite of the new secretary of state, George Shultz.

5

6

Ronald Reagan's "evil empire" and "global campaign for democracy" speeches were widely condemned by Western intellectuals and the establishment, but they helped sustain and nourish dissident groups like the trade union Solidarity, which was fighting for its life against the Polish Communist regime.

Jeane Kirkpatrick wasted little time in becoming a star in the Reagan administration. Early on, as U.S. ambassador to the United Nations, she put the Communist and Third World nations on notice that America's support of democracy was unshakable. After the Soviet shootdown of Korean Airlines flight 007, she denounced Soviet behavior in the strongest language used to date.

7

8

In Secretary of Defense Caspar Weinberger (left) and Secretary of State George Shultz (right), President Reagan had two extraordinarily talented and committed advocates for their respective departments, and the two men repeatedly fought to influence the president's Soviet policies. While Reagan often appeared to stand at arm's length above the fray, it was actually a hallmark of his shrewd management style. He benefited from this diversity of opinion, which gave him a variety of policy options before he made his final choices.

9

The widespread U.S. nuclear freeze and European protests were denounced by the Reagan administration as one-sided and a gimmick. But the protests had a profound effect, threatening to derail the INF missile deployment and deal a significant blow to the NATO alliance.

President Reagan always presented an upbeat, confident image to the outside world, but during the tense run-up to the INF deployment, and after the shootdown of KAL 007, he was deeply aware that the world had moved to the brink. Yet when Paul Nitze undertook his walk in the woods, and sought greater flexibility in the arms negotiations, Reagan felt it was crucial to stick to his convictions, and curtly told Nitze: "Paul, you just tell them you are negotiating for one tough son of a bitch."

10

11

When Jeane Kirkpatrick returned from an extensive fact-finding tour of Latin America in February 1983, she emerged as the administration's leading voice in shaping policy toward the Nicaraguan Sandinistas and the FMLN guerrillas in El Salvador. Along with Scoop Jackson, she feared that Mexico was the ultimate target. Her briefings to the president and the congressional leadership were so pointed that one administration official noted, "No one ever spoke to the president in such blunt terms about the problem."

12

In October of 1983, a bid by Caspar Weinberger and CIA Director William Casey to make Kirkpatrick the head of the National Security Council failed, but the president was determined to keep her as a leading adviser. "The chemistry between the two was extraordinary," one official said.

For ELLIOT ABRAMS
TRULY GUIDE, PHILOSOPHER
AND FRIEND. ~DM.
1979

13

After Jeane Kirkpatrick left the administration, Elliott Abrams emerged as the new administration point man on policy toward Nicaragua. He would have a bitter falling out with his former boss, Senator Daniel Patrick Moynihan (above). Described as the "contra commander in chief," he devoted his time to a broad array of issues, including El Salvador. Below, he confers with ailing Salvadoran President José Napoleón Duarte.

14

The president and George Shultz chose Max Kampelman to lead the U.S. negotiating team in Geneva once the high-profile arms talks resumed in 1985. Kampelman probed carefully, and internal bickering in the negotiations was often fierce. But the action soon moved from the day-to-day negotiating tables to the superpower summitry between Ronald Reagan and Mikhail Gorbachev.

16

Flanked only by interpreters and a crackling fire in the summerhouse of the U.S. villa at the November 1985 Geneva summit, Reagan and Gorbachev had an intimate conversation over arms control and U.S.-Soviet relations. Gorbachev was desperate to rein in SDI ("Star Wars"), but despite significant differences over policy, a personal, even warm, bond between the two leaders quickly developed.

On day two of the 1986 Reykjavik summit, Reagan and Gorbachev wrestled repeatedly over SDI in the most sweeping and dramatic U.S.-Soviet meeting ever. The two conferred outside Hofdi House before a spontaneous final session, in a last-second attempt to break the logjam. No formal agreements were reached, but this summit changed history. Shultz later noted, "Reagan dominated the meetings."

17

18

As the Reykjavik event came to a close, Reagan was uncharacteristically grim and angry. "I don't know what else I could have done," Gorbachev said. The president tersely responded, "You could have said yes."

Richard Perle, one of the administration's most creative policy makers, sought to craft a compromise at Reykjavik that would have enabled the U.S. to keep SDI. Gorbachev vetoed the proposal. Still exhausted from the round-the-clock meetings, Perle met with the press upon returning from Iceland, and sought to combat the impression that the summit was a failure.

19

Les Aspin, the powerful Democratic chairman of the House Armed Services Committee, often privately agreed with Reagan's stance on national security matters. In a concerted effort, he tried to move his party to the center on national security affairs, and warned Democrats: "We can't be the Dr. No of Defense." But his efforts failed as liberals sought to oust him as chairman for his pro-defense stands and his vote for contra aid. Aspin successfully regained his chairmanship in one of the most fascinating House struggles this century.

20

Reagan shaking hands with Richard Perle at a White House dinner on December 8, 1987, during the third Reagan-Gorbachev summit. This summit marked the unprecedented signing of the zero option treaty that the president had proposed six years earlier. But in this springtime for summitry, the treaty's principal author, Perle, worn down by the abrasions of government service, had already returned to private life.

21

22

In 1987, as the Cold War began to come to a close after Iceland, a new more moderate administration order prevailed in Washington. Jeane Kirkpatrick, long a favorite of the president's, had already left in 1985. Despite often being mentioned as a vice-presidential or senatorial candidate, she decided to exercise her influence as a leading conservative intellectual.

23

Where other members of the counterestablishment had since resigned, Elliott Abrams weathered the Iran-contra storm and stayed to the end of Reagan's second term. In August 1988, flanked by his family, he received the secretary of state's Distinguished Medal Award from George Shultz.

24

25

Soviet troops began leaving Afghanistan in 1988, an arms deal had been signed, and discussing human rights with the Soviets became commonplace. Under Reagan, the Cold War had all but come to a close. It was during President George Bush's tenure that the Cold War's end would be definitively marked, first by the ascendance of Solidarity in Poland, then the lighting of candles in Wenceslas Square in Prague, and the toppling of the Berlin Wall.

Ronald Reagan, under whose administration the Cold War was won, was as popular with the American people after his eight years as when he first took office. Though his presidency had given rise to a dynamic new conservative counter-establishment, Reagan himself returned home to his beloved ranch in California.

Parliament and Greenham Common. But the first missiles arrived without a hitch. And the Soviets, confounding the dire predictions of the peace movement, and simmering fears of the Americans in Geneva, agreed that they would continue to talk, despite the missiles in England.

But if the alarms were premature, it was only by a handful of days. The Soviets revised their statement on the sixteenth. They would walk out, they said, but only after the missiles arrived in West Germany. "Talks will be senseless," they stressed, "once missiles arrived in Western Europe." That meant November 23, 1983, a week later. In the meantime, both sides scrambled to undertake every last-ditch effort to forestall this possibility.

For his part, Nitze made one final push to prevent the deployment, which he actually felt would never ultimately be carried out. He and Kvitsinsky sought to revise a version of the walk in the woods, one which would have enabled the Soviets to keep 572 missiles, in return for the U.S. canceling deployment. The ostensible sweetener was that the Soviets would claim the French and British independent systems would not be an "immediate obstacle" to an agreement. It was clear Moscow was trying to capitalize upon last-minute Western jitters to bluff the U.S. into staving off deployment—the Soviet delay option. Nitze had bought into it, and openly so.

But it was too late. Washington didn't buy it.

The White House felt Nitze was being dangled on a string—once again—and instructed him to reject it. Incredibly, Nitze cabled back urgently that the U.S. should consider a "counterproposal" rather than a "black and white turndown." Again, the White House cabled that the answer was no. If Nitze was anything, he was stubborn. But this last rejection had broad and irreversible implications. The final round of the talks now teetered on the verge of collapse, and the countdown was quickly continuing.

Ironically, panic in the final days, already high from the U.S.-Soviet clashes of previous months, would be feverishly whipped up not by U.S. hard-line rhetoric, or even by ongoing Soviet intimidation and blandishments, though this remained a steady and worrisome factor, but by two seeming unrelated events that tugged at each other, one an ABC television special inauspiciously called *The Day After*, the other a fairly routine military simulation involving the use of nuclear weapons.

OVER TEN DAYS, from November 2 to November 11, the U.S. and its NATO allies carried out a highly classified war game, a nuclear release exercise dubbed "Able Archer." The secret exercise itself was not new, and was conducted yearly to test the command and control of nuclear weapons in the case of war. But with each passing year, nuclear arsenals and options changed, and the exercise became increasingly intricate. The task was to hone it with greater precision to the daunting chore of simulating a final resort to nuclear weapons in the fog and passion of protracted war.

Neither troops nor nuclear weapons were to be moved in the exercise; this would clearly have been too provocative to an already jittery Soviet Union. But the exercise did simulate the actual command procedures in a nuclear crisis.

The exercise was a mock scenario that involved an eventual decision to use nuclear weapons. The conflict was hypothetical, but entailed no less than what policy makers could actually encounter in the final stage before total war loomed. In theory, this meant employing the full American arsenal to wage all-out war; all told, this included covering fifty thousand targets in the Soviet Union, including the entire Red Army military, the country's sprawling industrial base, and the *nomenklatura,* the five thousand stony-faced men who comprised the elite Communist leadership.

However necessary, the exercise was by its very nature controversial. In 1956, when a comparable war game was held in Germany, the "Carte Blanche" games, there was a widespread public revolt against nuclear weapons. Further exercises were subsequently removed from the public eye, stamped with a top-secret classification, and held in the strictest of confidentiality.

In a word, Able Archer was about the doomsday scenario, the ultimate arena where only nuclear theologians and strategists, and reluctant warriors and military men tread. Originally, the plan was boldly going to include the participation of Weinberger, the joint chiefs, the supreme allied commander of NATO, and as the game got under way, the president and the vice president themselves.

But because of the growing international tensions, the war game was scaled down. The fear was real: conducting the game with the participation of the top civilian leadership for the first time could mistakenly signal to the Soviets that the exercise was a prelude to a future attack. Thus, the top-ranking civilian and military figures did not take part. Even so, the exercise sent shock waves rippling throughout the confines of the Warsaw Pact, from the flashpoint of tensions that was Checkpoint Charlie in Berlin, all the way to Moscow.

Midway through the exercise, the Kremlin reacted ominously and reportedly placed an estimated dozen nuclear-capable fighter aircraft forward-based in Poland and East Germany on a heightened-alert status. This precarious beginning was quickly ratcheted up, starting on the evening of the eighth. Moscow, fearing the worst, contacted its KGB stations scattered throughout NATO Europe, instructing them to collect all information about a possible surprise U.S. nuclear attack against the Soviet Union. The messages were sent as urgent. No delay would be countenanced.

In turn, Washington was unclear how to read the signals. White House advisers thought this was little more than a manifestation of an eleventh-hour Soviet scare campaign to ward off the INF missiles; the president himself later revealed that he was not so sure, saying, "It was something to think about." And it was against this backdrop, uneasily pervading the leadership of the two countries and their jittery populations, that the INF deployments were then placed in jeopardy by a combination of these Soviet machinations and an American movie.

THE DAY AFTER was scheduled to be aired at 8:00 Sunday night, November 20, virtually on the eve of the deployments. The movie graphically depicted a nuclear attack against Lawrence, Kansas, a sleepy university town of 49,000 outside of Kansas City. Overnight, publicity about the film thrust it prominently into the larger political debate about nuclear arms and the INF deployments.

The film started out lazily, portraying life in a small Midwest town for the first fifty minutes. Then, without explanation or warning, the bombs fall. The exact provocation and sequence of events are murky. For four minutes the scene is grisly. There is a bright white light in the sky over Lawrence, and then a blinding yellow light. There is a mushroom cloud, arching powerfully up into the sky, full of flame, followed by fierce firestorms and howling winds. A poplar forest bends. People, ordinary Kansans, are then vaporized, turning into images on X-ray film. A moment later, Jason Robards, the star, who survives, says it looked "like the sun exploded."

Successive scenes were a graphic rendering of the nuclear aftermath. Farmland was covered with ash and crops ceased to grow. Infants were born deformed. Robards's hair fell out, a facial wound grew larger and angrier, his complexion turned sallow. Life had been rudely arrested, and happiness snuffed out. Once-peaceful neighbors became bandits preying on their friends. A pregnant woman said sadly, "We knew all about the bombs. We knew all about the fallout. We knew all this could happen for forty years. Nobody was interested."

The movie engendered a feeling of hopelessness, a sense of passivity. Near the end, a printed message of white letters flashed across an eerie black background: "It is to be hoped that the images of this film will inspire the nations of this Earth, their people and leaders, to find the means to avert the fateful day."

As the *New York Times* TV reviewer put it in his Sunday article on the movie, the word "means" was code. The movie conditioned the audience to call for disarmament, or at the least for a nuclear freeze. Despite disclaimers by ABC executives that it made no political statement, according to the reviewer, it did precisely that. It said that deterrence, a political position, had failed. It also left the distinct impression, as the *Washington Post* later editorialized, that the deployment of the U.S. cruise and Pershing II missiles in Europe, not the Soviet missiles already stationed in the eastern U.S.S.R., were the provocation. The movie blithely ignored that the world was a more complicated place, that there could be a case for arming, that the success of deterrence, or arms control, took not one side, but two partners.

Yet however simplistic the movie was, it was graphic and powerful. Ronald Reagan, who previewed it at a private Camp David screening, found it "powerfully done" and "very effective." It left him "greatly depressed." Shultz himself worried that its timing could stir enough popular protest to block the deployment of missiles on German soil. The State Department put out a statement that seeking arms reductions was the best way to prevent nuclear war, and Shultz agreed to appear on a panel discussion for the show "Viewpoint" following the movie.

Millions of Americans gathered in churches, crowded into college lecture halls, or sat snugly in home living rooms to watch. That evening, it became the highest-rated TV movie of its time. Afterward, Shultz appeared on the panel discussion, moderated by ABC News's Ted Koppel, and seen by 100 million people. Other panelists included former Secretary of State Henry Kissinger; former Defense Secretary Robert McNamara, who, burned by the Vietnam War, was now devoting his later years to arms control; the conservative editor of *National Review*, William Buckley; Carl Sagan, the liberal scientist; and renowned author and international conscience Elie Wiesel.

McNamara, tense, driven, and hyper-rational, praised the show for stimulating a national debate. In his low, accented baritone, Kissinger fired back, "Are we supposed to make policies by scaring ourselves to death? To demonstrate by an orgy of pictures what we have known for three decades does not contribute to solving the problem." Kissinger, of course, had a point, but the passion of the moment drowned him out.

While Edward Markey, the Massachusetts Democrat who sponsored the nuclear freeze resolution in the House, called *The Day After* "the most powerful film in history," and said "that ABC was doing a $7 million advertising job for our issue," reaction was ultimately less fateful than expected. There was no mass panic in America. The people held firm behind Reagan.

In the earlier weeks, Weinberger and JCS Chairman Vessey had urgently briefed Reagan on U.S. war plans in case of a nuclear exchange. Now he was more convinced than ever that those who thought a nuclear war could be winnable "were crazy." He quietly sat down and penned how "sobering" the briefing was. Yet he was equally convinced the U.S. had to deploy the INF missiles and that only then would the Soviets genuinely "negotiate on arms reductions." With a subtle blend of resolve and caution, reminiscent of Harry Truman during the 1948 Berlin crisis and airlift, Reagan decided the West must stand firm in those remaining fateful hours, right up to deployment. It was one of his finest moments.

BACK IN GENEVA, the year of the missile was increasingly looking like the year of the walkout.

Then, on the eve of German debate about the missiles, Soviet Leader Yuri Andropov sent a letter to the recently elected German Chancellor, Helmut Kohl, warning West Germany that it must be prepared to face the consequences if it went through with the deployment. It was a last-ditch Soviet effort, another harsh and dangerously escalatory whiff of nuclear blackmail. It failed.

After two days of acrimonious, even angry debate, eclipsing virtually all other events on the world stage, on November 22 the German Bundestag approved the Pershing II deployments by a margin of 286–226. After three years of tough negotiations, bitter words, and ringing threats, the stage was set for deployment.

Shultz himself later recounted, "These were nervous times for the world," not because of "lack of conviction in the Reagan administration," but "because of the Kremlin threats."

The two sides were at the brink.

TWENTY-FOUR HOURS LATER, the first battery of U.S. Pershing II missiles was rushed to West Germany and promptly deployed. The American and Soviet delegations met that afternoon for a scant twenty-five-minute plenary session. At the end, the entire Soviet delegation simply stood up stiffly, thrust out their hands for a final handshake, and announced, "It is over." "It" was the talks. As they filed out, Woodworth could not help but think to himself, "They never thought we would stand up to them."

But this was precisely what had happened. His emotions were mixed, and he anxiously wondered what would happen next.

Looking drawn and angry, his words sagging, Kvitsinsky said the Soviets were discontinuing the present round of talks. No date for future resumption was offered. Soon after, the Soviets abruptly walked out of all other arms talks. For the first time in fourteen years, all U.S.-Soviet arms discussions had collapsed. The Soviets had made their view clear. As long as one INF missile remained in Europe, they would not be back.

REACTION IN THE U.S. government was somewhat tense, yet generally subdued. Not so in the journalistic community, which was quick to refer to the incident as a Cuban Missile Crisis in reverse. Others wondered aloud what the Soviet countermoves might be. Though partially qualified, critics noted that it was the end of arms control, perhaps bringing the two great superpowers to the precipice, or, as Strobe Talbott apocalyptically suggested, "the brink of nuclear war.

"The tone and substance of Soviet-American relations went from bad at the beginning of the year, to suddenly much worse in the fall, to absolutely awful at the end—the worst in more than two decades." But this time, Talbott bleakly predicted, the Soviets "would not blink."

REACHED IN HIS OFFICE with the news, Perle appeared to be unusually quiet, although he did little to conceal his smile signifying victory. One of his staffers popped a champagne cork to celebrate. Perle himself was not pained by the choices he had made over the previous two years, nor by the often relentless isolation. But he did not feel this was a time for open celebration. It was a time for serious policy making. He spent the waning hours of the afternoon working off the adrenaline, calling friendly journalists, monitoring for last-second developments. That night he would have a quiet supper.

Conventional wisdom had defiantly declared that the missiles would never make it. But, as Perle thought, and earlier predicted, the alliance had held, and the deployment was successful. The knock-down, drag-out fights, however unpleasant, had been necessary. His brainchild, the INF zero option, still remained a viable option—if and when the Soviets returned to the bargaining table. The "if" and the "when" were what was worrisome to many, but not to Perle. "We had to drive them hard on this," he reassuringly told his staff. "They'll come back eventually." Drowned out by alarmist rhetoric sweeping Europe and the U.S., Perle was part of a distinct minority in holding this view.

But Perle and his staff had been riding the buoyant crest of a wave for more than two years, secure in the knowledge that they were perfectly in tune with Ronald Reagan. At each harrowing step, every make-or-break decision, their instincts were pretty much Ronald Reagan's instincts. It was quite a roll.

With a little luck, standing firm, and pressing military competition, they could eventually spend the Soviets into the darkest reaches of oblivion. The U.S. had come a long way in addressing the alarming change in the U.S.-Soviet balance, from the dark days of Desert One and Afghanistan, to successfully deploying its missiles, defying Soviet bluster, threats, and outright nuclear intimidation. If others didn't see it that way, so be it, thought Perle. Time and, he believed, history would prove to be on the U.S. side.

Soon thereafter, Perle joined his wife, Leslie, and a couple of close friends for a low-key dinner at a nearby restaurant. After light banter and a hearty meal, Perle lowered his head and surveyed his wineglass, quietly lost in thought. He rendered a solemn verdict on the deployment. "It's not the end," he concluded soberly, "it's just the beginning."

And as history would have it, the Soviets would blink.

HOLDING THE LINE

The Oklahoma delegation pressed to the front, howling, hooting, and waving their signs wildly.

"Tell 'em, Jeane! Tell 'em, Jeane! Tell 'em, Jeane!" they shouted with enthusiastic relish.

It was like a big, brassy musical, fresh from a long run on Broadway. Her name echoed tumultuously throughout the massive Dallas hallway, as she strode up to the rostrum of the 1984 Republican National Convention in Dallas. Dressed in a vibrant green suit, with her thick glasses unostentatiously worn like a faithful neighborhood librarian, Jeane Kirkpatrick surveyed the auditorium, trying hard to contain the butterflies biting in her stomach.

"Tell 'em, Jeane, tell 'em, Jeane!"

The delegates were still on their feet, clapping, cheering, calling out her name. Kirkpatrick had never anticipated this wild demonstration and at first it unnerved her. Finally, the audience came to a prolonged hush, and with great deliberation and care, she launched into her speech. Each word was delivered with mellifluous articulation. Recalling the great Democrats of a previous era, she invoked the names of Harry Truman, John F. Kennedy, and others, the men who developed NATO, forged the Marshall Plan, devised the Alliance for Progress. These men, she said, "were resolute," not afraid to "speak of America as great," and "happily assumed the responsibilities of freedom."

But, she continued, the Democrats had abandoned this tradition at their convention, and "treated foreign affairs as an afterthought," behaving "less like a dove or a hawk than like an ostrich—convinced it could shut out the world by hiding its head in the sand."

Referring to the new party leaders as the "San Francisco Democrats," she chanted and taunted them as isolationist in world affairs, timid toward the Soviet Union, always ready "to blame America first."

"They said that saving Grenada from totalitarianism and terror were the wrong things to do—they didn't blame Cuba or the Communists for threatening American students . . . they blamed the United States instead. But then somehow, they always blame America first.

"When our marines, sent to Lebanon on a multinational peacekeeping mission with the consent of the United States Congress, were murdered in their sleep, the 'blame America first crowd' did not blame the terrorists, who murdered the marines, they blamed the United States. But then, they always blame America first."

By now, the pumped-up crowd had joined Kirkpatrick, waving flags and adding to the chorus, "No-o-o, they always blame America first!"

"When the Soviet Union walked out of the arms control negotiations, and refused even to discuss the issues, the San Francisco Democrats did not blame the Soviet intransigence. They blamed the United States. But then, they always blame America first."

"No-o-o, they always blame America first."

"When Marxist dictators shoot their way to power in Central America, the San Francisco Democrats do not blame the guerrillas and their Soviet allies, they blame United States policies of one hundred years ago. But then, they always blame America first."

As the speech ended, the entire audience rose to its feet, stomping and whistling, frantically waving signs emblazoned, "GOP Loves Jeane."

This was perhaps the biggest speech of her life, and Kirkpatrick had been nervous throughout. She had been preparing for days with a television-speech coach from the Republican National Committee convention organization. It was no easy feat speaking to fifteen thousand rambunctious delegates, while at the same time addressing the eighteen million Americans watching her on television. She soon learned it was critical that both audiences feel she was talking solely to them. During the speech she "tried to keep my wits about me" and "do it right." Dazed afterward, she had little idea of what a hit she had been.

But others knew immediately. Wyoming Congressman Dick Cheney pronounced the lifelong Democrat "the highlight of the convention" and "the de facto keynote speaker." Reagan Republican adviser Lyn Nofziger cooed, it was "the toughest foreign policy speech I've heard in twenty years." Indeed, no one listening to her that night doubted this was a historic speech that would be remembered decades later. By the following morning, Kirkpatrick was an overnight national sensation, and the talk of the party faithful was not just that she should be made national security adviser or secretary of state, but that she should be put on a future ticket as candidate for vice president. It was largely irrelevant that she was a Democrat and a woman. They simply wanted her.

Only some time after the speech did it dawn on Kirkpatrick how well it had gone. She drew a deep breath, as the cheering continued—and continued. Finally, she pushed her way through the crowd back to her hotel room, was hugged by her husband, and sat down with a tired thud. The speech, a hard-nosed political polemic, proud and patriotic, bold and vintage middle America, had been long in the making. It was also a hard-hitting analysis that raised serious questions about how the two political parties approached the Cold War. Written with verve and defiant flourish, she had rehearsed it alone and with colleagues over and over during the preceding weeks with a dedicated intensity.

She knew it was strong, controversial stuff. But the wheel of her personal history had inexorably turned—and, having faced four years of unremitting criticism from the Democratic party, *her* party, she was no longer willing to suffer in silence. Her mind finally made up, she would let it rip, speaking with conviction, perhaps not fully aware of the ramifications but willing to take the risk.

Kirkpatrick had not been to a political convention in over fifteen years, and *that* was as a Democratic Maryland delegate in 1968 in Chicago. Now, slumped with a giddy mix of excitement and exhaustion in her hotel chair, fingering a freshly poured glass of wine and chatting quietly with Kirk, she had crossed a Rubicon, never again to return to her original political party, but destined to be gloriously honored among conservative and Republican cohorts.

IRONICALLY, MANY LIBERAL Democrats didn't understand the phrase "San Francisco Democrats," taking it to refer simply to all Democrats, as an across-the-board philippic against a party that had just held its convention in San Francisco. But in her own way, for Kirkpatrick, "San Francisco Democrats" was a term of art, a phrase of precision. In fact, far from referring to all Democrats, she was emphasizing that she still very much cherished the memory of the Democratic internationalist tradition, albeit one that had more recently been rejected in its own party, only to find acceptance in the GOP. Thus stalwart anti-Communists and committed Democratic internationalists like a Harry Truman, or John Kennedy, or a Scoop Jackson were carefully exempted from criticism in her speech.

Much as the scathing speech irked Democrats, prompting angry calls and epithets like "she's a fascist," or "traitor," seasoned political observers saw the finely honed distinction she had made. More than that, the Democrats who were not San Francisco Democrats, however small in number in official Washington, disciples of Scoop Jackson or some from the Kennedy years, like columnists Cord Meyer and Ben Wattenberg, could watch this speech and not just agree with every word but even heatedly clap when she finished. Where new-line liberals felt that her phrase "blame America first" was an insult, impugning their patriotism, old-style liberals thought it was an apt diagnosis of new, doctrinaire liberal ideological canons.

There was one mistake in the speech, however, a line that as much as any other stirred the delegates, immediately bringing them to their feet howling. "It wasn't malaise we suffered from—it was Jimmy Carter—and Walter Mondale." Many years later Kirkpatrick would be sorry she had named Mondale. She admired and respected him as a proud Democrat, a good man, an important public servant. In the best of all worlds, he didn't deserve to be ridiculed. But in the throes of political combat, when he had taken out after *her* administration and *her* foreign policy ideas, she later acknowledged that she let sentiment get the better of her.

It was, without question, a momentous evening. Having crossed the threshold, however, Kirkpatrick had decisions to make, big decisions. Most significantly, whether or not to stay at the U.N., whether or not to stay in government.

KIRKPATRICK WAS "TRULY revolted" by the continued bureaucratic infighting, the unresolved—and perhaps unresolvable—tensions between hardliners and moderates in the administration. She felt that there was an establishment media, plugged in and wired to the Democrats in Congress, that she could not reach and that would never convey her message. Invariably, she felt the media printed what she said "out of context." She even took to calling the establishment press "the iron wall"—echoing the Iron Curtain dividing East and West—which "the Reaganauts were able to push slightly ajar, only to have it slam shut on them, time and time again." She once sputtered in pique that John Goshko and Thomas Friedman, both senior diplomatic correspondents for the *Washington Post* and *New York Times* respectively, ate out of Jim Baker's hands, "like lapdogs." To careful observers, even if this were meant pejoratively, and was perhaps impolitic to point out, it was not unfounded.

But what was she to do? She could take solace in the fact that she had made a difference at the United Nations. In 1984, the fights at the General Assembly were a tiresome repeat of years past. To be sure, they were not unimportant, but the American position in the world organization had steadily improved. The U.S. now confronted the world community with a stronger hand, and the vitriol of the Third World, the impunity of the Communist bloc, the steady chorus of anti-American sentiments, had waned significantly. To the extent that the U.N. did rant and rave, it did so with less energy and a diminished vitality.

Also dramatically reduced was the ritualistic humiliation and isolation of the U.S. and its allies. Yehuda Blum, the Israeli delegate, even joked that Kirkpatrick's effectiveness had "taken the fun out of the ritual condemnation of Israel."

So while she still looked at the U.N. with some distaste, for all its continued faults, Kirkpatrick was satisfied that the U.S. had significantly advanced its interests, and had made the U.N. as an international body a little more civil. "The festivals of hate have diminished," she pronounced to one interviewer.

But there were other disappointments that cut deeper. Her pet project, the Kissinger Commission report on Central America (redubbed the "Scoop Jackson Commission" by Reagan to honor Scoop), which called for an ambitious $8.4 billion in economic aid and increased military assistance, had received a tepid response when the White House sent it over to the Hill. The Democratic Congress, for all its talk of pursuing a comprehensive diplomatic and economic policy, refused to fund the program at meaningful levels. Driven by partisan politics, it quickly showed itself every bit as narrow-minded as the administration it was decrying. Focusing only on the military component of the overall package, at the expense of the rest of the recommendations, the Democrats virtually ignored the commission's ideas, and thus, rather than making history in Latin America, they became a footnote. In the summer of 1984, Congress also balked at continued aid for the contras. For Kirkpatrick, Central America was still unfinished business.

As the year progressed, she would remain a forceful voice for a strong American response to containing the Sandinistas and Salvadoran guerrillas, but, more often than not, hers was a voice in the wilderness, including in cabinet meetings, where she was often arrayed against the more pragmatically minded George Shultz.

While she got along far better with Shultz than with Haig, she and the bureaucracy continued to skirmish. Observers at the time noted that Shultz resented her influence with Reagan, feeling it was the duty of the U.N. ambassador to report to him, not to voice independent views. Predictably, a détente-minded career bureaucracy repeatedly sought to trim her sails and stifle her at every turn, resenting her sharp edges, tough talk, and candid anti-Soviet goals. At the same time, she was unwilling to play the role of "automatic team player," neatly falling in line behind Shultz. Wanting to continue her policy-making role that accrued from her cabinet status, but institutionally subservient to Shultz, she was fated in her job to be marred by ongoing conflict.

If Kirkpatrick was the intellectual star, forceful, classy, imposing, at times glittering, she still remained an awkward outsider. Terrible frustration welled up, and for a worn-out Kirkpatrick, the question began to loom, was it worth it?

There were other disappointments and abrasions. The open and unfettered discussion of ideas in the scholarly arena was always a cherished principle to Kirkpatrick, but that spring in a series of scheduled speeches she had fallen victim to an increasingly politicized academic environment. In appearance after appearance before university audiences, free speech and scholarly inquiry took a back seat to political ideology, and she was angrily shouted down by protesters. It happened first on February 15.

She was delivering an address at the University of California at Berkeley, and was heckled by an angry band of students protesting U.S. policy in El Salvador. Amid chants of "U.S. Out of El Salvador" and "Genocide in Guatemala," she was rudely driven from the lectern by the unceasing taunts of hostile students. She struggled to maintain her composure, eventually returning to finish her speech when order was restored, but angrily canceled an appearance the next day. On February 24, she also canceled plans to speak at Smith College, from which she was to receive an honorary degree, because a massive joint student-faculty protest was being planned, and Smith College could not assure her safety. Offended, but also cautious, she instead chose to receive the degree in absentia. In a later talk before four thousand people at the University of Minnesota on March 2, protesters rudely hurled epithets, equating her actions in Central America with "fascism" and "genocide," once again interrupting her repeatedly.

Then, that May, she was to receive an honorary doctorate at commencement from her alma mater, Barnard, only to have hundreds of students and faculty mount a campaign to have the college trustees withdraw the award. The Barnard faculty, though it had no formal say in the matter, pressed ahead, subsequently voting 48–18 to oppose the award. The resolution was drafted by Barry Jacobson, not a government professor or expert in foreign affairs, but a chemistry professor. "We feel we cannot separate her politics from her achievements," he declared. Over one thousand faculty and students met with Ellen Futter, the university president, to press their case. Futter stood her ground, but a disgusted Kirkpatrick, stung by the sequence of events, saved her the grief and turned down the award in advance.

In each instance, campus administrations apologized to Kirkpatrick. But Kirkpatrick was dismayed by the intolerance and myopia of the angry political left. She feared that their choice to fuse their political ideology with academic endeavors was a dismal sign of the times, a frightening precursor of a deeper and insidious erosion of academic freedoms. The left and its dogma now occupied the inner sanctum of the academy, and Kirkpatrick was in their crosshairs. It offended her, and rather than take it, she simply opted out.

She continued to be attacked from the liberal side of the political spectrum. It rankled her that the powerful, established feminist left was equally intolerant of her contributions. That she was the highest ranking female foreign policy official in history meant little to them. Taking the rather odd position that she did not really represent an advancement for women in a field once the sole domain of men, organized feminists were repeatedly cool to her. For Kirkpatrick, a woman who had demonstrated continuous pragmatism and compromise in raising three children, juggled with the relentless pressures of a career in academia and politics, these criticisms of her as an "ideologue" who was "moody" and "difficult" had been especially painful. Kirkpatrick herself had talked about the difficulties of being a woman in a man's world—even generously declaring Geraldine Ferraro's selection as Mondale's vice presidential candidate as "just marvelous," adding that "women all over the world would profit from her selection." But she received few words of encouragement or support from organized feminist groups, who were instead among her constant critics.

In the face of this, living in New York itself became a frustrating experience, and she particularly did not enjoy the separation from her family. Kirk had not been well, and was fighting an unnamed degenerative disease that had viciously attacked his muscles. Kirkpatrick yearned to return to Washington to be with him. She had done an effective job at the U.N. at a critical historical juncture, and was proud of her efforts. She was now a star in the Republican orbit, and a national figure. There was little left to keep her in government—that is, unless the position she had once coveted, national security adviser, which was also in Washington, was hers.

Kirkpatrick believed in public service, but not in a government job for its own sake. Having made her contributions, she was prepared to leave, to return to her family and to her teaching. If that view was out of step with political fashion, so be it. She had never before let political fashion collide with conviction. She would not do so now.

As 1985 approached, she let her intentions to resign be made known. But Ronald Reagan grew distraught at the idea of losing her. This, however, raised a vexing issue. Was there a job of sufficient stature to enable him to keep her?

FOR RONALD REAGAN, Kirkpatrick presented a dilemma. He desperately wanted to keep her in the administration. She was a fresh, articulate voice of his vigorous, anti-Soviet foreign policy, a centerpiece of the administration. No one else so deftly laid out a framework for confronting the Soviets in the Third World arena, particularly in Central America, as she had. And her spectacular popularity made her politically important, enjoying the firm backing of his ideological heartland. He fully knew that his conservative agenda was not shared by many of his advisers. She not only shared it, but eloquently championed it. It was important that he have serious moderate voices around him, like Shultz, but he equally needed thoughtful conservative voices in his stable. None shone quite like Kirkpatrick.

As William Safire put it, "She had the courage of the president's convictions," and was "the most thoughtful of the president's foreign policy advisors." Nor was it any secret that Reagan personally admired and liked her.

But there were few vacancies at the top. He liked Shultz just where he was at State, Weinberger was just right at Defense, Casey was his guy at the CIA. Shultz was still opposed to her at the NSC. This, of course, was inextricably linked to a rather new consideration. Having made significant progress in rebuilding America's defenses and staring down the Soviets over the INF missiles, Reagan was now committed to a policy of strength coupled with a policy of careful conciliation, including a possible summit and even an arms deal with the Soviets. But the bottom line was this: there were few vacancies at the top. He had to find her an equally or more powerful job, one she would be happy with, and one he could be happy with, or she would leave.

That outcome he had hoped to avert. But his options, as he found out, were painfully limited.

IN NOVEMBER OF 1984, just after celebrating her fifty-eighth birthday, Kirkpatrick formally announced she would resign, effective the following March. She wanted to return to D.C., to be with Kirk. She would return to foreign policy research at the American Enterprise Institute, to her endowed faculty chair at Georgetown where she would resume teaching, and engage in public speaking, lecturing, and writing once again. The announcement had instantaneous repercussions, and precipitated a flurry of speculation about whether she would actually leave, and attempts by Reagan to keep her on board.

Immediately, conservatives championed her for a top White House job. Fearing that the administration's goals would be hopelessly blurred and diminished by State Department officials and others like Baker who resented her aggressive role in the first four years, they touted keeping her as a necessity, to prevent a takeover by the moderates. They pointed out that the outcome of the Cold War still hung in a precarious balance. An important corner had been turned, but it was hardly irreversible.

Over the next several weeks, Kirkpatrick and her supporters, and the president, engaged in a rare display of public bargaining over her next assignment, a highly unusual minuet in full view. The implicit message: he was trying to find her an appropriate position. At first, it looked as though she would be offered the counselor's slot in the White House, being vacated by Edwin Meese, who was moving on to be attorney general.

But her supporters let the word out that this would not do. It had no day-to-day responsibility in the continuous flow of foreign policy decision making. In effect, it was vetoed.

Finally, by late January, Reagan announced in a press conference that he had an "unspecified post" for her, and speculation quickly had it that it would be the directorship of the Agency for International Development, an important job, although not with the clout she already had. It also lacked cabinet status. But the door was left open. Perhaps something else could be found, was the message.

When asked to comment, she snapped to a reporter through her spokesman: "I will have no comment on my future until the president and I have met again."

On January 30, she met for thirty-five minutes with Reagan in the Oval Office. She was wearing her trademark green, he was dressed in a brown suit. Summing up her feelings of the last four years, she told Reagan what "an honor" it had been to serve him, to be his voice during some of the difficult moments of the Cold War, to "champion the cause of democracy." It came time for the meeting to end, but Reagan continued chatting with her. He was truly sorry to see her go. At last, she rose to her feet, he stood, and the two faced each other. Seconds elapsed, and then Reagan gave her a most unusual presidential compliment. Clasping her with his outstretched arms, he thanked Kirkpatrick, not just with warm words, but with a spontaneous, warm presidential embrace.

When she emerged, Kirkpatrick quickly moved into a packed White House Press Room and calmly announced, "the time had come" to return to private life. It was clear that Reagan and Kirkpatrick were hamstrung by a law of physics. He wanted to keep her—but there was nothing suitable, and she was unwilling to take a lesser position.

Standing confidently before the throng of reporters, looking almost relieved, she gave a candid assessment of her tenure, explaining it had been an "extraordinary honor" to "serve the United States and the president" and "to speak for freedom in the world forum." She would continue to speak out clearly on behalf of shared foreign policy objectives, including "restoring and preserving American strength, supporting democracy and independence in our hemisphere, and defending our principles in the Middle East."

Kirkpatrick had always been an enigma in public life, stirring the imagination and strong passions in all who encountered her, inspiring her supporters, attracting the excoriations of her detractors. But she had always been an untiring voice of style, consistency, candor, principle.

Reflecting almost aloud, as though engaging in public introspection, she soon thereafter remarked, "I was a woman in a man's world, I was a Democrat in a Republican administration, I was an intellectual in a world of bureaucrats. I talked differently."

All this was quite true. When her book *Dictatorships and Double Standards* had come out in 1982, it revealed an uncommonly complex and supple intellectual, resisting easy pegs and static labels. Her essays showed her as almost just as uncomfortable with the New Right as with the New Left. She was most interested in working with institutions that embodied human habits as opposed to endlessly tinkering with programs of reform based on notions of what people ought to be, in carefully distinguishing between the allure of utopian ideas and the enduring reality of mankind's institutions. Cherishing liberty above all else, she sided with the authors of the American Constitution and the *Federalist Papers*, who believed in human fallibility, as opposed to thinkers like Plato and Rousseau, who believed in human perfectibility. No less than the *New York Times*'s long-time book critic Christopher Lehmann-Haupt was taken by the sway and gravity of her arguments, and wrote that she "draws a reader along by the sheer magnetism of [her] reasonableness. I for one am happy to have these essays."

For Kirkpatrick, though, even more had been at stake. Just as she believed that the conduct of war should not be left exclusively to the generals, she also believed that foreign policy should not be left solely to the establishment, which valued process over results, paper over content, and which had so dismally managed U.S.-Soviet relations in previous years. But as a rule, she was leery of intellectuals in politics, including herself. She believed power was a special temptation for intellectuals—

except, she would add, that their skills were not necessarily the skills of power. "I never thought intellectuals have a special calling," she once remarked, "or have a special qualification for politics." She harbored one exception to this rule. "In periods of great flux and challenge, when goals and pathways are not clear, and have to be found again, then intellectuals can play an especially valuable role."

After four years at the U.N., having carved out a role as the administration's leading foreign policy conceptualizer, not unlike Henry Kissinger in a previous era, she could safely say to herself that she had made an indelible mark on global affairs.

IN THE FRENETIC aftermath of her resignation announcement, there remained one last bit of unfinished business. She had served longer than any other U.S. ambassador to the U.N., with Henry Cabot Lodge and Adlai Stevenson the sole exceptions. She had had greater influence over the formulation and articulation of foreign policy than any of her predecessors. All this, as a Democrat.

Whatever her successes, the Cold War remained a fervid battleground, its outcome every bit as uncertain as perhaps the thrust of the administration she was now leaving. But whatever doubts bitterly gnawed at her soul, she had also come to a reluctant and painful conclusion. The internationalist spirit of the Democratic party that had once shaped and saved the world in the tense aftermath of World War II had been replaced by a spirit of defeatism, isolationism, and weakness.

On April 3, she announced, her voice fraught with palpable emotion, "I was born a Democrat, grew up a Democrat, and if Harry Truman were running today, I would vote for him." But, Kirkpatrick soberly added, she was "no longer willing to swim against the tide of my own party." On that day, she formally registered as a Republican.

Her supporters immediately said they wanted to run her for president in 1988, or induce her to make a Senate bid in her home state of Maryland. Few doubted she would be an exciting candidate, and the political oddsmakers hardly discounted her potential punch.

On April 9, when she received the Presidential Medal of Freedom, the nation's highest civilian award, for contributions to the security and national interests of the United States, there were cries to make her national security adviser or secretary of state. But it wasn't to be.

For Kirkpatrick, the honor was a small consolation for all that was bittersweet, and she was still deeply pained, even if philosophic, by the choices she had to make. But there was no alternative. In the grim business of the Cold War struggle, others would have to carry the flag from the inside. Her personal life beckoned. For Kirkpatrick, the rationalist had won out over the idealist, the exigencies of the Cold War over the inculcations of the better part of her adult political life, the lessons of Hamilton and Jefferson over Plato and Rousseau, the promise of the future over the teachings of her past.

CHAPTER 23

After eating a hearty breakfast and drinking a cup of thick black coffee, the old man ambled outside for a morning stroll. His expression was poker-faced but faintly sad, as it always was, with a slight pout around his lips. Gray clouds rumbled overhead, and the damp weather caused his joints to click as he walked. His shoulders stooped, he moved with a heavy gait down the steps to the yard, gripping the rail deliberately, as though ready to teeter over at any moment. But, for his age, he was in uncommonly good shape, and every day worked out with handweights to stay fit. This morning he was determined to get some rest on his first vacation in what seemed like ages, and strolled casually out into the yard. His wife and two grandchildren were still inside.

But he couldn't dispense with his sense of foreboding, his fixation with the current status of the Cold War, and the grim possibility that the Soviet Union was faced with a challenge that could escalate out of control.

The situation was the worst he had seen it since the Cuban Missile Crisis, and perhaps in his lifetime—he was nine years older than the Soviet Union itself, born in what now seemed a more peaceful, controllable era before the superpowers were dangerously locked in a deadly nuclear contest.

For seventy-five years, he had watched American administrations, presidents and advisers, come and go. They might have started out one way, talking tough, scowling about standing firm, but ultimately, all bended to the reality of great power coexistence. Yet this one was dramatically different. This one, from President Reagan to his conservative defense advisers, was seeking no less than to destroy the Soviet Union. He felt it was a dangerous orientation, and a rude break with the past. The American foreign policy built up painfully over two generations by the establishment now lay in tatters.

He felt this new administration was not seeking to wind down Cold War tensions, but to win the war altogether; it was not seeking peaceful coexistence with the Soviet Union, but Soviet retreat, retrenchment, even destruction. Rather than diminishing U.S.-Soviet tensions, it sought to escalate them, believing that the Soviet Union would blink. It did not want agreements, it wanted the appearance of negotiations. It wanted to bring down the Soviet Union.

Where would it end? he wondered.

In speeches, he had been railing unremittingly against American extremism for months now, but, he felt, to little avail. The whole gloomy situation was perhaps best summed up by his contemporary George Kennan, who aptly described the current confrontation. "The cards are lined up for a war," Kennan warned, "a dreadful final war."

Indeed, the facts alone were not reassuring. He knew that the Kremlin was in a heightened state of alarm. It was particularly panicked about the proposed Strategic Defense Initiative. And as a sign of the dismal times, the KGB was poised on alert. A month earlier, KGB residences scattered worldwide were alerted by confidential memo: "The deterioration in the international situation and the growing immediate threat of war on the part of the United States means that our service is confronted even more urgently."

He thought to himself, There has to be a way to climb down this ladder, at least to the way it was before Afghanistan.

That afternoon on Friday, July 27, 1984, he was meeting with George McGovern. Perhaps McGovern could talk some sense into the American people. McGovern was different. He was an old warrior for peace.

So, from the Crimean resort town of Yalta, which echoed with the footsteps of Roosevelt, Churchill, and Stalin, who here had once hashed out a controversial modus vivendi, the Soviet foreign minister, Andrei Gromyko, decided he would speak frankly about his fears with George McGovern, the former American presidential candidate.

McGOVERN'S SMILE WAS as gentle as always; his voice deeply earnest. He too was concerned about the tense world situation, and told the Soviet foreign minister so in no uncertain terms.

Gromyko blamed the breakdown of the INF talks on American intransigence. If the Western alliance had been more flexible, the talks might not have broken down, he said.

McGovern said he would relay this to the American people.

Gromyko asked McGovern if he expected Reagan to be reelected. McGovern said yes, he probably would. It looked as though Mondale was not mounting a strong campaign. There was still time, and he was cautiously optimistic, but the worst had to be prepared for.

Gromyko nodded, he understood. He said that he had also been predicting that Ronald Reagan would be reelected. The two men turned to the election aftermath itself.

If Reagan were to win, Gromyko said, he did not expect U.S.-Soviet relations to be "productive." McGovern recoiled briefly. He knew exactly what this meant: further tension, the risk of conflict, and, he felt, an unending arms race, arms piling on top of arms. Gromyko dropped the bombshell.

"They want to weaken the Soviet system," the foreign minister said ominously, his face looking pained. "They want to bring it down."

McGovern could see how stiff, how tense the usually steely Gromyko was.

"If the American position does not change, I do not see any prospects for serious negotiations," Gromyko continued. "This is the first administration that I have had to deal with that deliberately offers proposals to the other side that they know will be unacceptable. I am very pessimistic."

McGovern could see that the foreign minister was growing irritated, especially when he talked about American reluctance for talks on banning space weapons "of any kind."

They talked for three hours, and before either of them knew it, the time had come to leave. His car crawled up to the house, gently gunning its engine. A plane was waiting to take him back to Moscow, where he had been attending a conference sponsored by the left-wing Institute of Policy Studies in Washington and the Institute of the U.S.A. and Canada in Moscow.

As the former senator readied himself to depart, he warmly clasped the foreign minister's hand, and promised he would take Gromyko's message back to America.

THE EXCITEMENT OF the 1984 presidential campaign was punctuated by growing signs in private that the Soviet Union was obsessed by President Reagan's Strategic Defense Initiative, which it called "the militarization of outer space." Its benefits were felt early on, when in mid-September of 1984 the Soviets proposed starting a new round of talks on "space arms." SDI had brought the Soviets back to the table.

Secretary of State Shultz believed that the nuclear freeze movement, the intellectuals and academics, and the alarmists who said that arms control was dead, that the Soviet Union would never blink again, not this time, were completely wrong. The threat of a massive technological arms race, one the Soviets could neither afford nor win, would force them to exhaust their material resources trying to keep pace with the Americans, and had brought them back to the negotiations with a desperate, even frenetic sense of urgency. Soviet designs were apparent from early on: they may have failed to stop INF—and its successful deployment had already left the Soviet leadership deeply shaken—but with equal intensity the Soviets would now attempt to block SDI.

Which meant a slow but palpable thawing in U.S.-Soviet talks once again. And inexorably, like a coin tossed high in the air that drops loudly, bounces and spins wildly, then wobbles briefly before it falls to a gentle heads or tails, the two sides crawled back from the brink. Success or failure at this stage held out cataclysmic consequences.

In this critical interregnum, at stake was the outcome of the Cold War. And, in truth, it was not a coin toss but a stentorian contest, and history and fate would be determined not by odds or luck, but by the deliberate policies, decisions, and resolve of both great powers.

EVERY PRESIDENT PUTS his own unique stamp on his White House, and Ronald Reagan was no exception. He loved jelly beans, and gobbled them up almost as voraciously as he did politics. His buoyant enthusiasm was infectious. Virtually every staff office in the White House had a jar packed with presidential reds, whites, and blues, proudly displayed on coffee tables or White House desks.

Another Reagan stamp was his Strategic Defense Initiative. He had long nursed a deep revulsion to nuclear weapons, and never accepted the uneasy nuclear balance of terror that enforced deterrence by holding both sides at risk with the threat of complete annihilation. When told in a deeply classified code word briefing at the Pentagon that at least 150 million Americans would perish in a nuclear war, he shook his head in dismay. He felt this was morally and practicably unacceptable.

Earlier on, he had asked in one briefing, "What if radar detected that the Soviets attacked with a single missile, what would the options be?"

"Nothing," he was told—unless the U.S. retaliated and incinerated millions of Russians with its own nuclear attack.

Reagan thought this was simply crazy.

So the president harbored a deep dream that the world would someday rid itself of nuclear weapons. And this spawned a new initiative that he launched on his own: SDI. "Wouldn't it be better to save lives than avenge them?" Reagan said in a major televised address on March 13, 1983.

With these ten words, he was proposing nothing less than the neutering of nuclear weapons as guaranteed instruments of mass death, in effect, to revolutionize the nuclear balance of terror from mutually assured destruction to mutually assured survival. "Let us turn our great strengths in technology that spawned our great industrial base. . . . I call upon the scientific community in our country, those who gave us nuclear weapons, to turn their great talents now to the cause of mankind and world peace, to give us the means of rendering these nuclear weapons impotent and obsolete."

The speech was never staffed through the bureaucracy, and it took his own top aides by surprise, including Caspar Weinberger and Richard Perle, both of whom learned of it only the night before.

RICHARD PERLE WAS a quick convert to SDI. At the outset, Perle had been skeptical, but more because of how SDI surfaced—the allies and the Congress were not informed in advance, nuances and niceties that mattered—and less because he didn't see benefits to the policy.

He didn't fully agree with Reagan's sometimes larger-than-life rhetoric that SDI would be a *perfect* population shield and that we should get rid of *all* nuclear weapons. (Although, it should be noted that Reagan himself was fully aware of SDI's limitations and the fact that it would take up to two decades to fully develop the system, both of which he repeatedly acknowledged.) But, like Weinberger, Perle soon came to see a number of benefits to SDI. It would strengthen deterrence and protect against an accidental launch by the Soviets or a Third World madman. It was a counter against the massive air defense programs the Soviets had undertaken. He felt that critics who lampooned SDI, saying that a perfect defense was impossible, had it all wrong. They were setting up a strawman. The real standard was the desirability of a defense that, even if not 100 percent perfect, still could deflect a significant attack. He felt it was a powerful argument that was never adequately answerd by SDI's critics.

And finally, and just as important, SDI would be an important weapon in engaging the Soviets in a high-technology race they could not afford to lose, but did not have the capital to win. SDI could threaten to spend them into oblivion. That SDI had the Soviets looking to return to the talks after saying this would *never* happen while American INF missiles were deployed on NATO soil was, in Perle's mind and for many in the administration, vivid testimony to this fact.

SDI was bold and visionary, and quintessentially American. But it quickly aroused intense opposition, not just fierce rejection in the Soviet Union (which feared that American technology and know-how could make it work), but among liberals, academics, and much of the media (all of whom insisted it could *never* work, and derided it as a futuristic fantasy). There was a third, more sophisticated critique—one that accepted that the benefits of SDI could be enormous, but that the transition from offense to defense had to be made carefully. This critique was scarcely aired. Finally, it was said that once future U.S.-Soviet arms talks reached a critical point, SDI could function as a bargaining chip.

According to this reasoning, the U.S. could work "the arms control potential of SDI," offering to give it up in exchange for massive reductions of Soviet offensive missiles. Bud McFarlane, Reagan's new national security adviser, privately referred to this as "the greatest sting operation in history." Shultz also saw possibilities here. Though he was no great believer in it, Shultz felt SDI was a vivid symbol of American technological superiority, and, if the opportunity arose, it could be the ultimate bargaining chip, which the U.S. could play for all it was worth.

But Perle did not share this view. He was convinced if the U.S. hung tough, it could get deep reductions in the Soviet arsenal, accrue benefits of defensive technology, and wage a technological race to drive a nail through the heart of the already ailing Soviet economy. He had stood at the tumultuous center of the zero option debate. He had pushed for missile deployments when others cried apocalypse. And Armageddon hadn't happened. Indeed, the Soviets, who had believed that the U.S. would never successfully deploy the INF missiles, were so thoroughly shaken by the missile emplacement that they had begun to question their own doctrine of Marxist inevitability. Now, they were the ones making overtures to talk. Principle had triumphed, and so, it seemed, had Richard Perle.

Nor was Perle particularly troubled by the derisive term that the nuclear theologians and liberal elites used to brand SDI—Star Wars. In public circles he allied himself with Reagan's entrepreneurial spirit, his faith in the can-do spirit of American common sense and old-fashioned know-how. "Don't ever restrict technological innovation," he said to those who would prematurely seek to strangle SDI in its crib.

And for those who called SDI Star Wars, he once quipped to his staff, "Why not use it? It was a good movie. And besides, the good guys won."

But this tension, the seething tug between SDI as a program or as a wily bargaining chip, as impetus to drive the Soviets into the ash-heap of history or to resurrect them as a faithful partner in arms control, would sharpen in the months to come, permeating every discussion between the Americans and Soviets, the administration and its critics, the Pentagon and the State Department.

YET 1984 DID not start out as the easiest year for Richard Perle. For one thing, Ronald Reagan was now showing new signs of wanting to blaze a historic agreement with the Soviets. On its face, his fierce anti-Commu-

nism and the relentless military buildup he endorsed seemed wholly incompatible with a desire to reach out to the Soviets, to work with them
and to sign an arms agreement. But the strategy of first building up U.S.
military power and then negotiating from a position of strength had
sound logic, no matter how much it perplexed his detractors. Having uneasily weathered the apocalyptic months leading up to the INF deployment, Reagan was now eager to talk directly with the Soviets—and, in
his overall strategy, was far more nuanced than his detractors and even
some supporters gave him credit for.

On February 9, 1984, Soviet leader Yuri Andropov died, after only
sixteen months as general secretary, and was replaced by Konstantin
Chernenko. Like Andropov and Brezhnev before him, Chernenko was a
dogmatic Communist party elder, and was also sickly. Nonetheless, Reagan quietly exchanged a number of private letters with the new general
secretary to explore the possibility of a summit conference. Chernenko
was cool to the idea, but his letters and exchanges also revealed something else, that the aging Soviet leader was fixated on SDI—even demanding that the U.S. stop work on the system.

Reagan's feelers to the Soviets, however, raised a new question closer
to home: where did Richard Perle, the administration's most prominent
actor in arms control, fit in?

Initially, the picture did not look good. If Richard Perle had been an architect of the first term's policies, signs now indicated that his influence
could be on the wane, and even raised the distinct possibility that his
ouster was in the works.

THAT YEAR, *TIME* correspondent Strobe Talbott published an inside account of the arms talks, *Deadly Gambits*, that portrayed in relentless detail bitter administration infighting. Despite the alarmist tone (it spoke of
the end of arms control), demonstrable Soviet sympathy (it portrayed Soviet fears far more than American), and an unseemly condescending attitude (it sniffed huffily, and even mocked, that the zero option was
simplistic and *of course* could never happen), the book was seized upon
by Walter Mondale, the Democratic party's candidate, as evidence that
the administration was not committed to arms control.

And the book's unmistakable villain, the Rasputin systematically sabotaging arms control, even more than Caspar Weinberger, was Richard
Perle. So on October 14, 1984, in the Reagan-Mondale debate on foreign
policy, when Mondale cited the book before the television cameras, it was
a sign of trouble for Perle.

But in truth, some early signs existed that Perle was already being cut out of the process. On September 27–28, Gromyko visited the president and then the State Department. Perle was omitted from the meetings, and didn't even play a role in the preparations—unlike Richard Burt, who drew up many of the talking points for use by Secretary Shultz and the president. This was a direct slap at the Pentagon.

Over the next week, Perle's enemies circled and the anti-Perle rumor mill shifted into high gear, leaking that the White House would like to see Perle go. Leslie Gelb, writing in the *New York Times*, gave life to the story, speculating that Perle, "universally recognized as the intellectual and bureaucratic leader" of the "anti–arms control cabal," would have to be dumped.

Still, it was unlikely that Weinberger would ask Perle to go unless directly ordered to do so by the president. Thus, Perle could reason that he was safe as long as Weinberger was defense secretary. But this too, it briefly seemed, was tenuous.

On November 15, amid talk that Shultz was fed up feuding with the Pentagon, the secretary of state met with Jim Baker, the White House chief of staff. Tall, a ruthless pragmatist and remarkably effective, Baker was no fan of Weinberger's or Perle's; he was also masterful at manipulating the system. Even the squint of his eyes was imposing.

It thus came as significant news when Baker confidently assured Shultz: "The president will deal with the problem." Lowering his drawling voice just slightly, Baker's eyes darted about and he informed Shultz that two new ambassadorial appointments would be made: Jeane Kirkpatrick would go to Paris, and Weinberger to London.

Which meant that Perle would be a sitting duck.

That same day, Shultz also received assurances that he could bring Paul Nitze into the State Department, elevating him to be the czar of arms control, with the lofty title of special adviser to both the president and the secretary of state. He would inhabit a small suite of offices on the prestigious seventh floor of the State Department, a stone's throw away from the secretary's own spacious suite.

This was no ordinary promotion. Nitze had been intimately involved in nearly every major decision on U.S.-Soviet confrontation since the dawn of the Cold War; now he would be at Shultz's side for every critical negotiation, every interagency struggle, and every congressional debate. Far from paying a price for his disturbing lapse in the walk in the woods, Nitze was now being promoted to no less than Shultz's personal tutor and confidant on arms control. Once more, power appeared to be drawn like blood from the Pentagon.

Nitze's appointment was made formal days later. (In a compensatory move to assuage hard-liners, Shultz also made the hawkish Ed Rowny, who had been negotiating the Reagan-initiated Strategic Arms Reduction

Talks [START] until the Soviet walkout, a State Department and presidential arms adviser. But Shultz personally found Rowny "difficult," and thus Rowny's role in State was to be far less than Nitze's.)

On November 17, desperate to stop SDI, the Kremlin proposed a new round of arms talks, and on Thanksgiving, a year after the talks broke off over the INF deployments, Moscow and Washington agreed that Shultz and Gromyko would meet in Geneva on January 7 and 8 toward this end.

As word spread of the Nitze appointment, Perle, his gaze fixed, weighed the situation. The signs were demonstrably clear, and he knew that the balance of bureaucratic power was shifting in the government, away from him and Weinberger toward Shultz and Nitze. This was hardly good news, and, after nearly four years of holding his finger in the dike, he feared a precipitous rush toward concluding an abrupt arms deal. Once the talks got under way, they would, he worried, take on their own momentum—as had always happened in the past. Unlike others in government, he trusted Ronald Reagan's instincts completely. But it wasn't that simple. For one thing, he worried that Reagan was not always getting straight information.

He sat down with a yellow pad and pen and began to make some notes. He wanted to frame his thoughts for a memo to Weinberger.

He wrote:

SIGNIFICANT PRESSURE TO DO THE WRONG THING:

1. Fear of doctrinal change—especially among allies, also within/among Services

2. Budget Constraints—fear of another LTDP.

3. Paralysis regarding modernization of tacnucs following Pershing II/GLCM

4. Attack on "Warfighting"/"Prevail"/Sheer

ARMS CONTROL

A. Anticipatory self-constraint

B. Compromise conventional technology

C. FREEZE

And of course, protecting SDI.

Perle also knew that his detractors were gunning for his job. He had threatened to quit a number of times in the first term, and make some real money in the private sector. He thought this time that if he were to be cut out of the loop, or if Cap were to be fired, he should have an alternative.

AFTER THE ELECTION, Jeane Kirkpatrick did not get named ambassador to Paris, nor did she move to the White House. Instead, she tendered her resignation.

And Baker was also dead wrong about Weinberger. Reagan made it clear he wasn't going to remove Weinberger. For now, Perle could breathe easy.

Nor was Perle on the outs, certainly not yet, maybe not at all. Shultz himself soon indicated that Perle was still a force to be reckoned with. He invited all senior officials, a thirteen-member delegation total, to join him in his two-day talks with the Soviets, and Perle would be there as the Defense Department representative.

Weinberger, however, was excluded. He thus decided a decisive stroke was needed. Otherwise, he feared, Shultz would end up giving SDI away in Geneva. With the negotiating instructions for the U.S.-Soviet meeting still undecided, he felt he had to help determine their outlines—even if he wasn't going to be on the trip himself. Reagan, Shultz, and McFarlane were going to be meeting during the president's annual New Year's holiday at the Annenberg estate in Palm Springs, California, to finalize the program for Geneva. Weinberger insisted he be included. However stormy the meeting would be, he saw no other choice.

THE PRESIDENT WAS in a good mood. He liked festivities, and New Year's Eve was no exception; he was also glad to be out of Washington. Several hours before dinner, he met with Weinberger, Shultz, and McFarlane.

The president eased himself into a thick white sofa; McFarlane sat next to him. To one side, Weinberger sank into an overstuffed chair, Shultz into a matching one on the other side.

Weinberger carried with him a thick loose-leaf book of arguments and talking points that Perle had drawn up for the meeting. He was prepared for a scrap. Bud McFarlane opened the meeting by presenting the president with sixteen pages of draft negotiating instructions.

Weinberger heatedly argued that Shultz should not talk about SDI at all in Geneva, not even mention it; this way, nothing could be given away. He knew that Shultz and Nitze harbored hopes of exploring a grand trade, leveraging SDI for reductions in Soviet ballistic missiles.

Shultz countered that SDI was the primary interest for Moscow, and it was unrealistic to refuse even to discuss it.

Reagan indicated he was sympathetic to Weinberger's point, that SDI should be nonnegotiable, and the Soviets only wanted to get at SDI. But Shultz pressed further; it would be limiting him too much, he contended. He needed to be able to discuss it.

Reagan listened intently. The press frequently criticized him for having two warring cabinet secretaries, but the fact was, the final decisions were Reagan's. Finally, the president broke up the quarreling cabinet members and said: "Cap, we can't know where it will all come out, but we are going to engage the Russians. So George, go over there and get it started, without giving anything up."

WEINBERGER TOLD PERLE that the president said Shultz "couldn't give anything up." But he knew the Soviets would press hard. I'm counting on you to represent us, he told Perle.

Friday night on January 4, Perle packed his clothes for the three-day Geneva trip. Already, press expectations were high. A fever was mounting on behalf of the talks. Cap wouldn't be there, but he would do what he could to look out for SDI.

"Everyone's in a hurry for this one," Perle told his wife. "It's the same old story."

You wouldn't have it any other way, Leslie said, only half jokingly. "Twelve to one, I would say the odds are pretty even. Also, you can count on Ken Adelman." Adelman, the new head of the Arms Control and Disarmament Agency, was a brilliant thinker, a political soulmate, and most important, a close ally of Perle's.

"Yes," Richard said, "but don't forget—the Soviets will be there too."

CHAPTER 24

In the days before the January 7 Shultz-Gromyko Geneva meeting, the air was giddy with anxious anticipation and high hopes.

However much Richard Perle and Caspar Weinberger fretted about U.S.-Soviet talks and their seductive quality, which could cause the U.S. precipitately to relax its defenses, they were powerless to stop the new momentum toward negotiations. As Cold War tensions had intensified during the INF crisis, the prospect of a summit was invariably viewed, even if inaccurately, as the tranquil eye in the hurricane. Perle knew this was to be expected of the press, of much of the public, and of the Democratic party; but now there was a new and far more serious consideration, the president himself. To be sure, Reagan was tough-minded. But now even *he* felt summitry was what was called for.

Like it or not, Perle had to reconcile himself to a sobering reality. The prospect of summitry—the sight of signed documents carefully initialed by hostile parties, and large oak tables in wood-lined rooms that provided a haven where adversaries, regardless of viewpoint, could find temporary sanctuary and search for common ground—buoyed expectations and elevated hopes for the Geneva talks between Gromyko and Shultz.

Thus it came as no surprise that the Geneva meeting, though it was not at the head-of-state level, was billed as the most important get-together of the U.S. and the Soviet Union since 1979, when President Carter and Leonid Brezhnev clinked glasses and toasted peace, only months before these efforts were rudely shattered by the Soviet invasion of Afghanistan. Even Pope John Paul II, who helped keep opposition to the Polish Communist regime alive when it cracked down on Solidarity, blessed the meeting. On January 4, His Holiness weighed in to inspire the Geneva participants, grimly urging both nations to realize that they "share the same risk," and calling arms talks a "beam of hope."

Perle now had a choice to make. Would he represent the Pentagon down the line, risking the charge of being obstructionist, even if this put him on the side of the angels, even if he felt he were right? Or would he be a team player, seeking to control damage perhaps, but accepting the inevitable momentum of the slow but inexorable new direction of U.S. policy, and instead help shape it?

He kept a framed Winston Churchill quote on the wall of his Pentagon office, summarizing his approach to negotiations with the Soviets:

> *Never give in,*
> *never give in,*
> *never, never, never, never,*
> *in nothing great or small,*
> *large or petty,*
> *never give in.*

On January 5, as a ripple of anticipation washed over the thirteen members of the American delegation, briefcases in hand, darting up the stairs of Secretary Shultz's U.S. Air Force Boeing 707, Perle himself, determined as he was to remain faithful to Churchill's injunction and to DoD's interests, did not yet fully know the answer. Nor did he know how the meetings would play out.

EARLIER THAT DAY, Saturday morning, Shultz underscored the gravity with which he viewed the upcoming discussions. He convened a breakfast meeting at the State Department to hash out the ground rules. All the major departments were represented: State, the Pentagon, the NSC, the Arms Control and Disarmament Agency. He told them that the large delegation was a hallmark of the seriousness of their purpose; while only he, Bud McFarlane, Paul Nitze, Arthur Hartman, the U.S. ambassador to the Soviet Union, and the Russian-speaking Jack Matlock, as the notetaker, would be sitting in the room with Gromyko, everyone else would be on call for consultation—and they, he stressed firmly, would "be needed."

Normally Buddha-like, Shultz then turned unusually solemn. He didn't want the delegation demonstrating disunity, he said. Accordingly, he warned them against any press leaks.

"We have only one spokesman, Bernie Kalb," he lectured sternly. "No one is to talk to the press unless it is by my explicit decision."

On his notepad, Perle doodled a caricature, a smiling face with eyeglasses smoking a cigarette, and listened with amusement as Weinberger interrupted sarcastically, "It's a novel idea, to control press contact." Shultz pushed on, however, underscoring that his desire for a news blackout was real enough. Whether it was adhered to would be another story. Perle, for one, had his doubts; after all, he felt, more often than not, it was State, not the Pentagon, that leaked.

At 6:10 P.M., as the American plane arced upward into the velvety night sky toward this decisive set of discussions, his skepticism would prove to be fateful. And within hours, his very participation in the Geneva meeting would be in jeopardy.

NORMALLY, THE SECRETARY of state's plane would carry at least fifteen members of the press, but because of the unusually large number of senior government officials, staff, and security, only six members of the press were offered seats (although twelve were listed on the secretary's trip manifest). In Geneva, press interest bordered on mayhem. Over eight hundred reporters, national and international, crowded the steps of the Hotel Intercontinental, where the U.S. delegation was staying, and surrounded the U.S. and Soviet missions, ready to record the battle for posterity. The anchors of all three major television networks anxiously maneuvered for position.

The sight of intense rivals traveling side by side, Richard Perle on one hand, and Paul Nitze and Richard Burt on the other, fueled heated press speculation from the outset. The reporters on Shultz's plane busily drew a seating diagram of who was seated where to discern some pecking order in "officialdom," much as if they were CIA analysts trying to decipher the lineup of Kremlin officials presiding over the annual May Day parade. Then, sketching out the warring factions, Burt versus Perle, Nitze versus Perle, they labeled the plane, "the ship of feuds."

Unaware of the news blackout, the press was surprised at the barrier of restraint separating them from the normally more loquacious—and cooperative—policy makers. No one was chatting them up, spinning them, or feeding tidbits of information with which to write their stories. They instead were uncomfortably relegated to a sideline, watching the members of the delegation quietly pore over the secretary's talking points for the Geneva meeting. The atmosphere struck them as strangely tense. It wouldn't be until much later that they would learn about the blackout.

Finally, at one point over the darkened Atlantic, Shultz summoned the press corps for an on-the-record news conference. The media's questions were as long as Shultz's answers—and they ventured as many opinions as they asked for facts.

"This is a powerful delegation the United States is bringing . . . it's a star-studded delegation," one reporter briskly declared. Another boldly told the secretary, "People are anxious to see some result toward a better relationship of the two countries. Yet it seems to me that on both procedural and substantive grounds, going into it, the two sides are just about on totally different wavelengths."

Shultz remained poker-faced throughout.

The anxious mood of the press was best summed up by yet another reporter, who quizzed: "What would you tell the people who are going to be waiting now for the next three days for the result of this conference with baited breath, what kind of attitude do you think people of the world should have?"

Shultz paused, and speaking deliberately said, "I can't predict. People should wait and see what happens."

With a flattering smile, Shultz knew it was important to keep the press happy, he finally called the conference to an end and settled back into his chair—only to be disturbed some hours later by a vexing sight when he craned his head to the back of the plane. There, in full view, was Richard Perle standing in the aisle, openly talking to Don Oberdorfer of the *Washington Post*. This was clearly in stark defiance of his press ban. Earlier, Shultz had felt Perle made constructive comments about the talking points for the meeting he had worked out with Weinberger and the president in California, but this act of insolence was too much. There was little he could do there, but, he determined, this act could not go unpunished.

He quietly fumed and resolved that if Perle could not muster a satisfactory explanation, there would be no Geneva talks for him—only a quick and lonely flight back home to the United States.

He decided to speak to Bud McFarlane first, and then talk to Perle in Geneva.

ON THE PLANE, Richard Perle couldn't sleep, he was too wound up with adrenaline in anxious anticipation of the approaching meeting. His old friend Don Oberdorfer of the *Washington Post* was also restless. By happenstance, the two gravitated into the back of the plane to shoot the breeze. The flight was seven hours and fifty minutes, so there was plenty of time to kill. Mindful of the press ban, Perle steered away from talk of the summit, instead nudging the conversation to another important topic near and dear to his heart, the philosophical question about the relationship of the press to government. When was it acceptable for the government to withhold information from the press in the name of national security? When should the press exercise self-restraint and, in the name of the exigencies of national security, not print something?

That night he didn't get much sleep. His mind was racing.

•   •   •

THAT MORNING after arrival in Geneva, in Room 1602, Perle awoke to the rude jangling of his telephone.

His head was woozy. The worst thing about these trips abroad was the hours; the jet lag was one issue, but he had little choice but to wake up early, and despite the rush of adrenaline, it was always a bit of a shock to his system. Ignoring the seven-hour time difference that pushed the clock into daytime, he had stayed up for several extra hours preparing for the upcoming meetings, sorting through his files. Earlier in the week, Weinberger passed on to him what he called "Geneva-related" material, including a classified analysis of the Soviet views on Geneva. Stamped "FOR OFFICIAL USE ONLY," he noted the section that said: "The Soviet leadership has consistently underlined the importance of preventing the militarization of space and has stressed the 'interconnected' nature of limitations on offensive and defensive weapons." This, he was determined, was exactly what he wanted to prevent. He was also shocked to see how deftly written the Soviet propaganda was, perfect for U.S. reporters on a deadline, seeking quotes to fold neatly into stories.

Groggy, he thought the call might be his wife, Leslie, or a message from his office. It wasn't. It was a summons from the State Department secretariat to come immediately to Secretary Shultz's suite.

It's not that he was nervous as he made his way to Shultz's rooms. On God's green earth, he didn't have the foggiest clue what Shultz was calling him for.

WHEN PERLE ARRIVED at Shultz's suite, it was empty. He paced around gingerly, waiting for the secretary to show up. He stared at the wall hangings. Everything was meticulously in place. So neat. Twenty minutes later, he was still waiting.

Finally, Shultz arrived. Perle was surprised to see McFarlane with him as well. He knew this meant something serious was up, but what? Dour, Shultz looked like he had just returned from a funeral.

Shultz told Perle that he had expressly violated the instructions not to speak to the press. "If you don't like the rules," Shultz warned, "you can get on a plane and go home." Said this bluntly, his voice meant business.

This was hardly what Perle had expected. Initially taken aback, he fought off any feelings of being flustered. A cool, clearheaded explanation, the truth and the facts, were what was needed. Perle indicated to Shultz that Oberdorfer was an old social acquaintance. It was, he said, a *purely* social conversation. "I didn't talk to Oberdorfer at all about arms control," he calmly explained.

Shultz listened. It was an honest, straightforward, simple answer. It was also not what Shultz had expected. He was still not amused, and was slightly tempted to send Perle back, right then and there, to make an example to the rest of the delegation. But in the excruciating pause between Perle's answer and Shultz's reply, the secretary reassessed. The man standing before him seemed very different from the Richard Perle so often rumored about. In those long seconds, Shultz made his decision. He believed Perle.

"No contact" is the rule, "not at all," he stressed. "If you talk to the press again, you go home."

Perle nodded his head sheepishly in agreement, and said, "Okay, I understand."

Throughout the next two days, when Perle saw the press, he barely uttered a weak, "yeah, hi." Shultz was serious, and he didn't want to test the system twice.

Ironically, though, this face-to-face incident would ultimately bring Perle closer to Shultz than he had been in the past—which, given Nitze's new ascendant role, was not a bad thing after all.

THAT NIGHT SHULTZ watched his delegates, clad in jogging outfits or rumpled suits, climb on and off the elevators and roam the hotel lobby and wander aimlessly through the coffee shop and by store windows. Unable to speak to the press, they looked as though they had no purpose in life, except, perhaps, to declare the impending talks a disaster.

BUT WHO WAS the enigmatic George Shultz? That was the question asked as much by American administration officials as by the Soviets.

More often than not, in meetings with staff, even in public, Reagan's secretary of state comported himself like an ascetic Asian monk. He was inscrutable. For hours on end, Shultz simply sat, listened, watched, and said nothing. When he finally did speak, his speech was not mellifluous, but calibrated; words trailed out of his mouth not in a passionate staccato but like weary marchers in a protracted jungle war. He spoke with deliberation, less like a diplomat than perhaps a careful psychiatrist. His voice had not resonance, but modulation. It was as though his first word could be his last, so he made every word count. That was George Shultz.

Indeed, everything about Shultz seemed to radiate caution. To observers, the same words cropped up time and again to describe the secretary. "Patient," "careful," "reserved," "self-contained," "calm," "resolve," "a plugger," and "a born negotiator."

But this described process. What did Reagan's secretary believe in?

Was he passionate like Reagan? One got few easy clues from Shultz himself. More often than not, his only tell-all response in conversation would be an arched brow, a mild frown, an angry scowl or stare, or an occasional smile. But even these were rare.

His supporters were nevertheless adamant that Shultz was a man of strong beliefs. Though an intellectual (he saw himself this way as well), it was said that he was not a Henry Kissinger, a bold strategist, weaving disparate strands of thought into a coherent conceptual cloth. But, by his deeds and actions, it was clear Shultz was deeply committed to spreading democracy abroad and strongly anti-Communist, no less so than the president for whom he worked. And like Ronald Reagan, he was a man of vision, looking beyond the day-to-day to the more awesome task of harnessing the forces of history to the service of American security and the democratic peace.

As for regional conflicts, to Shultz, they mattered in the great global chess game against the Soviets: in Afghanistan, the mujahadeen were "freedom fighters"; in Nicaragua, democracy had to be reclaimed and the contras supported; in El Salvador, he wanted to strengthen the democratic center, which mean standing tough both against the radical right and against the Marxist left. Then there was the issue of human rights, the one area where the normally stoic Shultz showed a warm flicker of emotion, perhaps never more so than when talking with Jewish *refusniks* in the Soviet Union. As for the Soviets themselves, he felt they were an expansionist, cruel regime—even as he creatively sought ways to work with them, to tutor them in the benefits of open societies, to make them a little less dangerous, a little less Communist, a little more like the U.S.

By training and temperament, this Quaker descendant, reared as an Episcopalian, was a born negotiator. A graduate of Princeton, he had a doctorate in industrial economics from the Massachusetts Institute of Technology, specializing more in labor negotiations than economic theory per se. Besides teaching, one of his first passions and pursuits after graduation was as a labor–management negotiator. Since then, he had racked up a stunning array of credentials, spanning government, business, and academia, before becoming Reagan's secretary of state.

At one time or another, Shultz was a professor of management and public policy, the dean of the University of Chicago's business school, as well as secretary of labor, director of the Office of Management and Budget, treasury secretary, and president of Bechtel, a giant San Francisco–based corporation with global interests. (At OMB and again at Bechtel, Cap Weinberger had served under Shultz.) Before joining the Reagan administration, Shultz had comfortably settled down, a rich man from his business ventures and a tenured professor at Stanford, with a campus house he continued to call home.

All told, Shultz's four cabinet posts were an achievement virtually unequaled in American history. That he was extraordinarily capable was without question. But there was more to his success. He knew how to maneuver in Washington's bureaucratic labyrinth. Where others were chewed up, he steered his way carefully, distinguishing himself as a bureaucratic survivor of almost unequaled skill. He was a master at the insider's game. He knew when to speak up, when to keep his powder dry, when to draw the line, when to blur distinctions, when to confront the Congress, and when to hold out his hand.

Shultz also had a purist streak in him, making him a stickler on ethical issues. It was an admirable trait that nonetheless won him the opprobrium of Richard Nixon, who blithely dismissed Shultz as "a candy ass." Later, Nixon went so far as to oppose Shultz's appointment as Reagan's secretary of state. By contrast, Henry Kissinger was glowing in his praise: "If I could choose one American to whom I would entrust the nation's fate in a crisis, it would be George Shultz," Kissinger wrote in his memoirs.

But all this still begged the question: where did Shultz fit in with the bold counterestablishment Reagan team, which cared more about the destination than pleasing the crowd en route? Critics of Shultz saw him mainly as a Republican liberal, a little too comfortable with Washington insiders, too willing to cut a deal with Democratic committee chairmen or foreign adversaries. They contended he was too easily swayed by the mushy striped pants set at State, which was perhaps sometimes true.

But in fact, Shultz was a most complicated man, about whom appearances could deceive. If Dean Acheson, easily the greatest of the Wise Men, a man who could immodestly but justly speak about being "Present at the Creation," was the perfect secretary of state in his day, Shultz was just right for his. Indeed, he did fit in brilliantly in the Reagan era, not simply because of his own impressive talent, but, in the final analysis, because he was perfect as Reagan's secretary. This was a distinction that mattered.

Deliberately, if not instinctively, Reagan wanted both a George Shultz and a Cap Weinberger. To unknowing observers, this spelled random conflict and relentless infighting—State and Defense forever at each other's throats, literally like "two cats in an alley," some had observed. But for Reagan, the conflict was productive—and was just how he liked it.

It meant Reagan got the most out of both secretaries and both departments. The two men were the fiercest—and the best—advocates for their departments and their causes. Pitted against each other, each had to make his case and defend it, and in the process try to persuade Ronald Reagan. And ultimately, the president set the direction. If a softer Shultz line was what he felt was right, he went with that; if a more muscular Weinberger line appealed to him, he chose Cap; if he felt a compromise, a combination of the iron fist and the silk glove was necessary, he cobbled together a synthesis. This was the genius not just of Ronald Reagan, but of his approach.

Moreover, in their respective positions, the divisions between Shultz and Weinberger were often far different than portrayed. True, where Weinberger was tough, Shultz was comparatively softer; where Weinberger felt negotiations should be curtailed, or topics be out of bounds, Shultz wanted to keep talking, to give diplomacy another chance; where Weinberger was uncompromising, Shultz would stubbornly entertain a deal. Yet Shultz, the six-foot-three former marine, with a tiger tattoo on his rump, was no closet liberal: his running debate with Weinberger on the use of force was a classic example.

Seared by the post-Vietnam demoralization of the American military, Weinberger had great qualms about actually using American power. By contrast, Shultz felt the task of a great superpower was to exercise force when necessary. All told, Shultz was no mushy multilateralist or détentist like a Cyrus Vance, nor was he a do-gooder forever referring to international principles of law or the U.N., but instead he believed in the inherent justness of the American cause of democracy in the Cold War, and in the necessity of an American triumph in this historic struggle.

Indeed, it is telling that a relative of Shultz's, Peter Shultz, a Quaker living in Indiana at the time of the Civil War, chose to put aside his religion's pacifist teachings and enlist as a Union soldier when the North-South conflict erupted. More than a century later, another Shultz was again fighting on the front lines in behalf of freedom, not with a rifle, but as the senior diplomatic voice of the nation. And once George Shultz made up his mind, the normally introverted, reticent secretary had a way of making quite clear not just what he believed, but what he wanted done. And now, in the winter of 1985, he was determined to get the most out of these Geneva talks.

THE TALKS ALTERNATED sessions between the U.S. and Soviet missions over the next two days. Shultz, Nitze, McFarlane, and Matlock would meet with Gromyko and his staff, while the rest of the delegation was poised for consultation in an adjoining room. After each session, Shultz would walk next door and relate what had transpired, almost word for word.

When meeting in the Soviet mission, the delegation met afterword in secure quarters for the debrief.

On January 7 and 8, a blistering cold wave swept through Geneva and smoky light filtered briskly off the lake. The talks themselves had started out on a harsh note. Gromyko warned Shultz, "U.S.-Soviet relations are bad. If we do not find ways to end the arms race and the threat of nuclear war, it will be impossible to correct our relationship."

He added direly, "In fact, relations will heat up in this event."

Gromyko demanded a clear statement that the objectives of the new negotiations should be to "prevent an arms race in space"—their price for returning to the arms talks. Shultz stood his ground. He rejected this.

That afternoon, the dialogue took more concrete shape. Gromyko stressed that the three areas—European land-based missiles (INF); long-range offensive missiles based in the U.S. and the Soviet Union, as well as on planes and in submarines (START); and the new space technology of SDI—were all interrelated. Then, he launched into a diatribe against SDI. He said there was a need for a group on the "nonmilitarization of space."

"We see SDI not as defensive but as part of an offensive system. If you succeed, you could launch a first strike; we will have to do so too." He paused, and gestured with his hand. "Why go to all this trouble, why not eliminate the sword?"

Shultz fired back, citing existing Soviet treaty violations and Soviet efforts to mount a strong defensive weapons program, concluding that the American goal was to make deterrence "more stable."

Gromyko leaned forward and intoned a not-so-thinly-veiled threat. "If you will not stop your research program, we will have to lay it out for all the world to see. People don't want this. Neither blackmailer nor blackmailed be."

He then dramatically pointed to the sky, "Let's go up into a tower and think about the fate of the world."

The two, Gromyko and Shultz, continued down this path, speaking in the voluminous language of metaphor, of towers in the sky and aliens on earth. But however elaborately constructed, the message was clear. Gromyko insisted that all three weapons areas were interrelated. He wanted talks that would address all three simultaneously. "Let's establish three bilateral groups—one group, three task forces," he said.

Shultz agreed to the structure, but subtly changed the emphasis. "What we couldn't do is hold up progress in one area until all three were resolved. That," he recounted, "was a plan for inaction."

Shultz felt the U.S. had the upper hand. The Soviets accepted putting all three areas under one umbrella, which, he felt, would enable the U.S. to use the leverage on SDI to press the Soviets to reduce their offensive weapons.

The two men moved on to far less contentious details. Gromyko asked Shultz about naming special representatives for each of the three main areas of the negotiations. Shultz had no objection, but he averred that there could be one individual named as the overall boss of the three delegations.

Suddenly, Gromyko sharply interjected, "Yes, but no Wise Men."

The oblique reference to Nitze was not lost on Shultz or the American delegation. "That," Gromyko stated, "would not be wise."

During the day, enough progress had been made that the U.S. delegation working group proposed that the two sides release a joint communiqué, which would codify their agreement to establish the long-awaited resumption of talks. In turn, it could serve as a U.S.-Soviet statement to be released to the world.

At this early stage, hopes were running high, and final agreement to begin talks appeared, if not a foregone conclusion, then a good bet. But this all hinged on the success of the communiqué itself, which still had to be worked out. With only a day to do it, time was of the essence, and the impasse over the relationship of space and SDI to the two other areas had to be bridged.

The Soviets signed off on the principle of the communiqué, and on the second day, the two sides exchanged draft texts.

PERLE WAS DEAD set against the Soviet text, particularly its phrase designed singularly to kill SDI. It stated: "The objective of the talks [negotiations] will be to work out effective agreements aimed at preventing an arms race in space, limiting and reducing nuclear arms, and strengthening strategic stability." This was the phrase that Shultz had rejected—and, he felt, with good reason. It ignored the fact that Moscow had its own defensive programs, and that the Soviets had already deployed a number of weapons that could attack objects in space.

The statement sharply contrasted with the U.S. draft text, which emphasized the interrelationship of offensive and defensive systems and nuclear stability. It stated: "The objective of these negotiations shall be the reduction of nuclear arms and the enhancement of strategic stability, with the ultimate goal of the complete elimination of nuclear weapons."

But Shultz, McFarlane, and Nitze felt that the Soviet draft was an acceptable enough document to work off of, despite its convoluted language and brazen one-sided attempt to rein in SDI without reducing their own space-based weapons. Their view prevailed. Shultz's bottom line was that there be three interrelated—but independent—negotiating groups. So throughout the second day, from 9:30 to 2:45, the U.S. delegation wrestled with different draft texts while Shultz sought to negotiate Gromyko's agreement. Perle suggested blending the two drafts, and replacing the offending Soviet paragraph on objectives with the American statement of objectives. The delegation followed his suggestions. Shultz took it to Gromyko.

But time was running out. The statement would have to be released by day's end, and it now appeared that less progress had actually been made than they had hoped.

At 3:05, the two sides adjourned for a recess, without any agreement. Suddenly, the meeting appeared threatened with an impasse.

Richard Burt warned that if the meeting broke up without even setting a date for the resumption of talks, the member nations of the NATO alliance would be anxious—and overall, it would be a devastating setback to the prospects for arms control.

At 3:25, Gromyko handed an entirely new statement to the group stating simply that "the discussions were useful" and the two sides "agreed to continue the exchange of views" in "early March."

Danger signals immediately flared. Gromyko was, in effect, declaring there would *not* be a resumption of U.S.-Soviet talks, not unless the Soviets got assurances about reining in SDI. Once again, the Soviets were throwing out an ultimatum against a feverish deadline to get the U.S. to back down.

This was a hazardous gambit. With only hours left, the talks, the success of which had seemed so certain that morning, were now in jeopardy.

THE ENTIRE U.S. delegation was stunned. This was the typical Soviet tactic: threaten to walk out, and wait for an American concession.

Perle didn't like the smell of things. Once you've decided you can't fail, you raise the chances that you'll get a bad deal. He felt the Soviets were bluffing.

"This is nothing more than a negotiating ploy," Perle protested. But his scathing dissent placed him in the minority. As the press corps crowded the doors outside, the delegation was virtually unanimous in wanting a successful outcome to the talks. They urged Shultz to give it another try. Perle felt hopelessly outnumbered.

But this time, Shultz was impressed with Perle's argument; he agreed that the U.S. had to be prepared to walk out in order to get a good deal.

Amid the confusion and mounting tension of the meeting, Shultz was the steady oar of the group. Perle marveled at how he appeared calm and collected—it was, he thought, one of Shultz's great strengths.

Shultz then returned to talk with the Soviets, and for the next ninety minutes he and Gromyko jousted further. Shultz made it clear that the U.S. would not give up "the right" to conduct SDI research. But at 5:50 when he emerged from the room to enjoin his delegation to devise an agreeable text once more, he was working from the earlier Soviet draft as the basis.

THINGS WERE MOVING very fast now. Words were being penned in red ink, paragraphs moved around, and drafts passed back and forth; Burt, Nitze, Adelman were all scribbling. Shultz had told Gromyko that he wouldn't be rushed, but with hundreds of newsmen prepared to descend upon the delegation, time was running out.

Perle made the best of the situation. He suggested modifying the objectives with the wording "preventing an arms race in space and TERMINATING it on earth, BY limiting and reducing nuclear arms, and at strengthening strategic stability."

The "terminating" stayed in; the "by" was, after some debate, deleted. The Soviets will never accept this, one of the participants anxiously said.

At 8 P.M., a compromise was forged, and the two sides agreed upon the text. An amalgam of language from the two sides, it enabled SDI critics and proponents alike to claim a measure of victory.

The American delegation sped back to the Hotel Intercontinental in its motorcade. After Shultz telephoned the president from his suite to inform him that agreement on new negotiations had been reached, he then waded into the Grand Ballroom, the entire delegation bringing up his rear, to meet with the press horde. Like starved animals, ravenous from the news blackout, the huge throng of press massed, waiting to pounce. There were newspapermen scribbling on stenographer's pads, photographers festooned with cameras, television cameramen with Minicams strapped to their shoulders, soundmen with long black booms that they thrust forward, hoping to capture some telling murmur. Camera lights flashed hysterically, and the correspondents jostled to get close to the podium.

Shultz dramatically pulled out a sheet of paper. A huge clicking of camera shutters and a blinding flash of lights enveloped the room. "The agreement speaks for itself," he said, and then proceeded in his monotone voice to read the entire communiqué, word by word by word, to the world at large.

When he finished, he pushed aside his text from the dais, and looked out into the audience. "We are not euphoric," Shultz added, appearing on the verge of exhilaration and exhaustion. "We are hopeful." Pausing, he looked around him once again, captivating everyone, and injected emphatically, "This is a beginning."

THIS WAS NO idle exercise in wrangling over semantics. For the Soviets—and Western opponents of SDI—it would establish a clear linkage between reductions in strategic offense and restrictions on Soviet defense. For SDI proponents, it would constitute the basis for a transition from arsenals based on offensive to defensive systems.

Shultz was pleased with Perle's contributions. Perle singularly made the case to hang tough with Gromyko—and he was right. Shultz's respect shot up that day for the Weinberger aide. He filed it away that Perle was not an obstructionist as he was so often portrayed by the press, not to mention many of his own State Department people. He simply set different standards, higher standards, which in this case were correct.

Mulling over the two days' worth of events, he felt enormous effort was needed to bring about the agreement, but that a corner had been turned. The U.S.-Soviet talks would begin in Geneva on March 12, 1985. It was a big first step.

He instructed his delegation to fan out across the globe—to Brussels, Bonn, Tokyo, London, Beijing, Canberra, Eastern Europe—and brief the world on the momentous events, and the impending start of the new arms talks.

Perle demurred. Rather than travel, he felt a more effective use of his time was at home in Washington. There, he could work the media, brief Weinberger, return to the cozy confines of his house with Leslie and Jonathan. With the talks around the corner, the battle was far from over—it had just begun.

PERLE APPEARED WITH Bryant Gumbel the next day on the NBC *Today* show. He looked tired, but composed. Gumbel baited him from the outset: "Your reputation as a hard-liner is well documented. Nonetheless, are you pleased with the agreement?"

Perle knew that the fight—"the good fight"—was on. He had to address head-on the question on everyone's mind. Did the communiqué spell the end of SDI—or the beginning? So he emphasized, "We have important things to say to the Soviets about the potential over the long term for making the world safer through defensive forces."

When Gumbel, dressed in a designer suit and expensive tortoiseshell glasses, pressed the slightly disheveled assistant secretary further about "deep divisions within the administration," Perle bit his tongue, and demurred: "It was an extraordinary delegation that worked in close harmony to achieve a useful result. There were no significant disagreements."

But Perle sensed the disagreements would come. It was no secret that many in DoD and some members of the State Department thought that Shultz was often ill served by his subordinates, who tailored facts to suit agreements and who valued treaties at any price. Here, every word mattered, and here, Perle worried.

FROM HIS EARLIEST days as a Capitol Hill staffer, Perle was able to walk through the alleyways of Washington power and influence with an uncharacteristic ease.

Where others were sidetracked by secondary issues, Perle remained relentlessly fixed on his priorities. Where others were moved by fashionable political trends or derailed by fleeting newspaper headlines, Perle knew that the fog of political noise or momentary pressures could undo the most carefully laid policies. And much like the Wise Men of an earlier era, the handful of men who clung to their ideals, resisted the tug of isolationism, and crafted the Marshall Plan and the NATO alliance, Perle maintained an unshakable faith in the inherent strength of the U.S. and its ability to win the Cold War. But this meant a strategy for the long haul. And despite the initial opening with the Soviets, a genuine shift in superpower relations was a long way off. SDI remained critical. And the fight over SDI had now begun in earnest.

Perle wanted to brief Weinberger one-on-one. After the eleven o'clock press briefing in Geneva, his eyes tired and sunken, he had sat down with a grunt and immediately sent the defense secretary an "EYES ONLY TOP SECRET–SENSITIVE" memo that he had typed himself. It laid out, in his characteristically stark language, just how the communiqué could be used to blunt SDI, the system that had clearly brought the Soviets back to the table, and that they now feared enough to want to stop.

In part, he wrote: "You will see immediately that the text of the agreement reached here this evening is seriously deficient. The damage that the agreement does to our position, and especially to our ability to sustain congressional and allied support for SDI will emerge soon enough—if not immediately.

"The task ahead of us will be to define the relationship between space (we can call them defensive even if the agreement fails to do so) weapons and deep reductions in Soviet offensive forces. And while they will be parts of 'a delegation,' we can seek to accentuate the separateness of the three negotiating groups. . . .

"The great danger is that the theme the Soviets are certain to play— that we are violating today's agreement by continuing SDI while pledging to 'prevent an arms race in space'—will resonate on the Hill and abroad."

Perle went on to suggest that the Pentagon stress positive themes and minimize any talk about a "State-Defense disagreement." But he wanted any positions placed at risk by the agreement to be "shored up." He ended, "I will be back in Washington tomorrow and will give you a detailed account of the last two days. Best regards." Now he was back, and the real work was just beginning.

Things were moving at a breathless pace. During the three years of INF, Perle had eagerly shouldered the burdens of his job. Even his greatest opponents underestimated his gritty intensity, his sense of politics and possibilities, a willingness to play firm if a bit rough, and a defiant charm that made him unusually human and affable among the Washington policy gurus. Now there was a new momentum sweeping through the city and the world, a changing set of players, and progress would be measured less by bold strokes than by deft blocks, unexpected initiatives, and a willingness to limp along with modest results.

He had hard choices to make. With Ronald Reagan moving toward Shultz over Weinberger, State over Defense, talk over rearmament, change was inevitable. There was no way to maintain his current stance forever without sacrificing his effectiveness, his values, even his reputation. Choices would have to be made. The purist in Perle now wrestled with the pragmatist, Henry Jackson with a complex Ronald Reagan, his body with his spirit, destiny with exhaustion.

CHAPTER 25

One of the problems gnawing at Perle was that the policy process was a two-way street—and a difficult one at that. In power-sensitive Washington, his reputation for emerging victorious after the fiercest of turf battles increasingly gave him a near legendary standing—albeit not always flattering—among the opinion barons and Eastern establishment. His friends saw him as a hero, bravely standing up to the establishment, defiantly fighting the odds, and holding the line against brazen weakness and hasty decisions. His critics were less charitable. To them, he was the man who would start World War III.

Attacks against Perle became routine. He took them outwardly in stride, even relishing the sense of outrage his enemies felt. "Am I the Prince of Darkness, another Rasputin?" he said, joking with a *New York Times* reporter. "Of course not. There are no strings to be pulled. About all you can do is persuade people."

After years of scraps on the Hill, he felt his skin was thick. Yet each issue brought with it new scars, and a fresh set of problems. Too often, each fight was one step forward, one step backward.

His willingness to continue in his job depended on his assessment of his future influence. He had maintained his influence during the turbulent interregnum from the time when talks broke off after the INF deployment to the Shultz-Gromyko meeting in Geneva. Even then, there had been no respite from the bureaucratic guerrilla warfare—although, at times, he had desperately craved just such a respite.

During those months, one battle, like so many others, had unexpectedly popped up on his radar screen—over chemical weapons. At the heart of the fight was not just the issue itself, but turf, reputation, and principle, not just for him but also for his office. Lose one issue, and you look weak; others will then take you on. Which meant, in this unanticipated battle with Richard Burt, no matter how relatively innocuous the substance of the dispute may have been, at least by comparison to the great and more immediate issues dominating the stage, INF, SDI, technology transfer, this fight mattered far beyond its immediate significance.

It was, ultimately, about the perception of power, which in the various dialects and subtexts of Washington translated into power itself.

IN JANUARY OF 1984, Secretary Shultz was attending the Conference on Disarmament in Europe, a thirty-five-nation East-West forum on European security issues. Richard Burt was traveling with him.

More often than not, the forum was a babel of voices and talk, too large to accomplish anything of great substance. It lacked the inherent drama of U.S.-Soviet arms negotiations, and the electricity of a superpower summit. But with all the other talks still suspended, according to sources who spoke with Burt, Shultz wanted to make a splash.

Before deplaning, Shultz snapped his briefing book shut, squirmed uneasily in his chair, and turned to Burt. He said plaintively: Some of this stuff is so boring, so technical. Can't you do something that can get me press attention?

This was just the kind of opening Burt needed. Shultz had been deeply concerned about reports of Iraqi chemical weapons use on the battlefield during the Iran-Iraq war. According to the reports, West German companies had helped Iraq produce the weapons, and Shultz wanted tougher measures to control chemical transfers.

Burt responded quickly to Shultz: Why don't you make a bold announcement that the U.S. is going to put forward a draft chemical weapons treaty, to cover all the nations of the world?

Shultz liked the boldness of the idea. It was also a real attention-grabber, just what he wanted. But he felt there was one problem. "Am I even authorized to do that?" he asked Burt.

Yes, Burt said smartly, you sure are. I'll run it by the White House again, just to double-check its status.

The clear impression he left Shultz with was that the idea had been approved. But in fact it hadn't.

In the preceding weeks, Burt's office had floated the idea of a worldwide chemical weapons treaty to be presented at the disarmament conference, and the State Department had slipped in a paragraph with the announcement into a draft text for a presidential speech on arms control. But the treaty initiative was then rejected in interagency discussions, vetoed principally by the Pentagon, and edited out of ensuing speech drafts—although the earlier draft remained on file in the White House.

As the story was told, Burt immediately cabled John Poindexter, the deputy national security adviser in the White House, asking if he could find the speech drafted with the chemical weapons treaty language.

Poindexter was a career navy man who specialized in military operations and in promoting the use of limited force as a diplomatic tool. He knew little about the arcana of arms control; and while he had earned a reputation as a cool-headed and exceptionally organized manager, he was new to the deputy NSC position. He had only been there since October. Thus, it didn't occur to him to check whether the speech Burt was asking for had actually been delivered—or as to why Burt wanted it. Burt had presented it all as so very routine.

He reported back to Burt that the speech was indeed in the files.

Burt went to Shultz and pointed to the draft speech as confirmation of approval for the treaty. Shultz beamed. Good, he indicated, now he could table something positive.

Buoyed by Burt, Shultz told the delegates that the United States planned to offer a draft treaty "for the complete and verifiable elimination of chemical weapons on a global basis" at the forty-member disarmament conference in Geneva in April. While a year earlier, American officials had also indicated they would like a treaty banning such weapons, the administration was actually proceeding apace with building binary chemical weapons, which would have to be abolished if the treaty ever went into effect.

Burt's efforts were prophetic. The next day, the *New York Times* reported Shultz's announcement on the front page, above the fold. The subhead, in bold letters, proclaimed, "Chemical Weapons Treaty." Burt had successfully sidestepped the entire policy process with one clean, surgical stroke.

THAT MORNING WHEN Perle saw the announcement, he was aghast. (For very different reasons, the West Germans also responded coolly.) Perle's first reaction was that the joint chiefs, who had a vested interest in the chemical weapons program, would be furious about this announcement. His hunch was right. That afternoon, the chiefs got in touch with Perle. "How the hell did this get in there?" they asked.

Perle called Doug Feith, his deputy in charge of the chemical weapons negotiations, into his office.

Do you know what happened, he asked. Feith shook his head. "We killed this idea in the interagency meetings," he said. "I don't know how this happened." (It was only later that Burt himself, in a moment of boasting and candor, would tell an administration official the whole story.)

"It looks like a classic bootstrap operation. State somehow inserted it," he continued.

"Well, make it clear to the chiefs that we had nothing to do with it," Perle responded. Perle was irritated. He often felt the chiefs could—and should—be countered; indeed he did this during INF. But there was no reason to quarrel with them when they were on the same side. That was hardly smart.

That afternoon, Feith met with the chiefs. "Look," he announced, "the civilian side was also taken completely by surprise."

IN THE WHITE House, the announcement was regarded as a fait accompli. It would have been unthinkable for the president to repudiate his secretary of state, especially after this speech had been so prominently featured. Earlier on, after one of his knock-down-drag-out fights with Weinberger, Shultz had offered his resignation, saying that the president had to choose between the two. The president talked him out of it. But if the administration had backtracked on this major speech, it would have left Shultz no choice. To observers, he would be boxed in and have little choice but to leave. So Reagan told his staff, "Let's put forward a draft treaty then."

One unauthorized action led to another. The State Department promptly announced it would present a treaty within three months—which led to panic behind the scenes. The time frame was completely unrealistic. Virtually no serious preparatory work had been done for this treaty; and there was no hard, up-to-date analysis.

The administration scrambled to put something together, and finally the Arms Control and Disarmament Agency was able to produce a draft treaty that the negotiators could use. But it was fifteen years old, and participants pointed out the obvious: it was "hopelessly out of date."

AT THE PENTAGON, the chiefs and Perle were still deeply concerned. To be sure, the ACDA treaty was an arms controller's dream, but they didn't consider it a serious effort. Perle felt it was filled with holes wide enough for the Soviets to drive a truck through. They could easily cheat with impunity. But there wasn't enough time for DoD to present its own alternative. Perle asked Feith for his recommendation.

After a number of hurried meetings, Feith suggested to Perle that they instead concentrate on picking the most gaping error in the treaty and address that. They could kill the effort this way. "Great," Perle said, "go with it."

A lawyer by training, and fastidious by nature, Feith carefully inspected the draft document. There were gaping errors. Most prominently, it didn't provide for what was called "mandatory challenge inspections," anywhere anytime. Such inspections were common goals in multilateral treaties where verification and enforcement are invariably a concern. "That's it," Feith declared, feeling triumphant. He would contest the issue over verification. That's what he would use.

THE NEXT DAY, Richard Burt and Jonathan Howe, representing the European Affairs and Political-Military Affairs bureaus of the State Department respectively, chaired an interagency meeting at State to assess the ACDA draft text. The dingy, windowless room was unusually packed, filled with more than thirty representatives. Many expected a showdown. After his opening statement, Burt, looking self-confident and overly pleased with himself, turned to Feith.

"The Pentagon's position," Feith said authoritatively, "is that we will accept this text only if it contained mandatory anywhere-anytime challenge inspections."

The reaction was immediate, laughter, hilarious laughter. Burt grinned. *Ouch.* To listen from the guffawing, it would have seemed that Feith made a joke—but he was completely serious.

Feith huffed, "That's our position." His body tightened at the taunting, and Burt's reaction left him furious. He thought to himself, we're going to fight this one.

Burt stroked his silk tie confidently and bore in for the kill, this time looking more sober. This position will never be acceptable to the United States, he said. "Just ask the joint chiefs."

Feith knew Burt had a point. Much as the chiefs were sticklers about verification, they would be loath to give a green light for the Soviet inspectors to roam around at will looking at U.S. military facilities, with U.S. sanction no less.

The meeting ended with that. The key was now the chiefs—or defeat.

FEITH WENT BACK and confronted the chiefs. Sitting in the tank, the chiefs' super-secret, bug-proof meeting room, he presented them with two alternatives. "Look," he said, leaning his thin frame over, his index finger tapping *thud thud* on the meeting table, "if effective verification is necessary, then you must agree with this."

More taps with the index finger.

"If you feel such inspections are too high a price, then you'll have to write to the president in your options paper that you are not willing to 'pay the price for effective treaty verification.'

"And," he added, "if it is so important, shouldn't we be willing to pay the price?" Feith's logic was a lawyer's trick, neat on paper but a simplification of an issue that involved politics and diplomacy. In theory, it did not have to be either-or on the verification issue as Feith presented it; they had at least a third alternative—rejecting the treaty. Feith knew this. But he also felt the chiefs would be unwilling to go against prevailing sentiment for a draft treaty, particularly one that Reagan had signed off on, or to ignore verification altogether.

They said they'd get back to Feith on this one.

THE CHIEFS MET several more times with Feith. After agonizing over the decision, they eventually accepted his provision for mandatory challenge inspections. The draft treaty was modified.

This time it was Burt's opportunity to be outraged. He glared. He and State accused the Pentagon of cynically putting in this provision because the Soviets would never accept it, and, moreover, that at the end of the day, the U.S. wouldn't want them to. Feith bristled at the charge of cynicism, declaring this was an outcome the U.S. *could* live with.

"We played fair," Feith concluded, "and weren't nearly as cynical as State." Burt got the treaty proposed through a classic guerrilla operation, Feith felt. The Pentagon may have played rough, but it at least played by the rules.

IN MARCH, CIA Director Bill Casey also weighed in against the proposed treaty, but after listening to the arguments, Ronald Reagan sided with Shultz, while also stressing the deep importance of strong verification.

On April 18, at the Geneva Disarmament Conference, Vice President George Bush personally tabled a much-improved U.S. draft chemical weapons treaty, which provided for surprise on-site inspections. But after that, the chemical weapons issue moved to the back burner. Once again, larger, more immediate issues were gripping the U.S., especially nuclear arms control with the Soviets.

AFTER THE SHULTZ-GROMYKO Geneva meeting in January of 1985, Perle reviewed where things stood in U.S.-Soviet relations. He decided that the rush to arms control at any cost need not sail through unopposed. It was important at this juncture to hold the line. To start, his study on Soviet treaty violations was still in the works; he also felt the time had come to end adherence to the ABM treaty, if that could be accomplished.

There were, he concluded, still a *few* strings he could pull after all, and a full plate of work still left. And finally, there was Ronald Reagan. If Perle trusted one man's instincts in the clutch, it was the president's.

CHAPTER 26

Under three presidents, Richard Nixon, Gerald Ford, and Jimmy Carter, the belief persisted that the arms control process was the sturdy instrument by which the two superpowers so often charted their course. It was accepted that arms treaties were often imperfect, and even the most diehard of liberals usually acknowledged that the Soviets would take advantage of treaty loopholes and chisel away relentlessly at imprecisions. Yet among the more hard-headed establishment, the devoted scions of pragmatism, the steady consensus remained thus: U.S.-Soviet debate and differences were intense; the rivalry was, on the whole, very real; Soviet atrocities and prevarications were often unconscionable; but the faith persisted that the arms talks could quell such deep and abiding differences. Arms control was not just a framework, but at a different, even subliminal, level, a ritual, a way of life, and above all, a frequently intangible means by which the U.S. would divine a sense of stability in the truculent times of the Cold War.

Yet for Richard Perle, nothing was more of an anathema than the SALT II treaty, covering U.S. and Soviet strategic missiles, an unratified and therefore unbinding vestige of the Carter years, flawed in the first place, a dangerous shibboleth of the past, an obstacle to *real* arms control. More broadly, with summitry in the air, he was concerned about the integrity of the arms control process. Since his earliest days as a young staffer in the Senate, the evidence had overwhelmingly convinced him that the Soviets deliberately violated treaties, and that arms control without Soviet compliance was nothing more than an exercise in unilateral disarmament. He wanted the U.S. to stop adhering to SALT, the once unquestionable theological symbol of arms control.

For Perle, ruminating in his office, his dilemma was now a question of practicality, centering around one task: how best to kill the treaty.

. . .

UP TO THAT point, the United States had been complying with the SALT II treaty, despite the fact that Reagan himself had called it "fatally flawed" during the campaign ("never liked it at all," he would say). But at the time, no U.S. programs would push the U.S. beyond SALT II constraints. So, in part, the administration chose the path of least resistance. This was Ronald Reagan in his role not as revolutionary, but as pragmatist, biding his time.

During the final year of Reagan's first term, Perle had set about in earnest building the case for outright abrogation. Breaking out of SALT was fated to be a skirmish, but for Perle, it was a matter of principle and sound policy. SALT, shelved after the Soviet invasion of Afghanistan, had failed to reduce the actual stockpile of weapons on both sides; the Reagan administration could do better. A clean break with the past would send a strong signal to the Soviets that the U.S. wanted more than just cosmetic treaties, but genuine reductions that could be verified or would be adhered to. That was Richard Perle's goal: good, meaningful arms control—with teeth.

The drop-dead date for SALT was December 31, 1985. That was when the unratified treaty was set to expire. He had hoped to undo it even before.

PERLE FOCUSED HIS initial attention on a congressionally mandated annual administration report on Soviet violations of arms treaties. He had been instrumental in getting the Hill to request the report, but already the struggle had begun over what the report would actually say. Like sausage, it now had to be produced. It would be an interagency report, signed off government-wide. Which meant more fights, less control, and more headaches, and, he feared, the distinct possibility that it would be a whitewash.

Perle immediately put his deputy, Frank Gaffney, to work on it. They had a willing ally on the NSC, another former Senate staffer and a personal friend of Perle's, Sven Kraemer (a member of what *Times* columnist William Safire called the powerful "New Old Boy Network"). "He's doing marvelous work, heroic," Perle would later say of Kraemer. They also found an unlikely ally buried in, of all places, the offices of ACDA, the institutional voice for arms control.

But they were in the distinct minority. It was the interagency bickering of INF all over again, but worse. If any other agency disagreed about a violation, they could veto the Pentagon. Consensus ruled. And so back and forth the discussions went. In one meeting after another, the Pentagon and NSC would line up against the State Department, and heatedly debate the evidence like a talmudic dispute. Burt, reflecting the strong passion of George Shultz, was determined to prevent findings of Soviet violations. This was institutionally predictable, and Gaffney was also flustered by the CIA, which he felt was once again dragging its heels.

One day in the spring of 1984, Gaffney and an Agency analyst had just walked out of yet one more tendentious meeting. The analyst sidled up next to Gaffney, speaking in a near whisper. Gaffney briefly looked about to see if anyone could hear them, and then cupped his ear.

That day they had been discussing two new Soviet ballistic missiles, designated the SS-25 and SS-24. According to the SALT II accord, the Soviets were prohibited from having two new land-based nuclear missiles, although the Soviets had claimed one of the missiles, the SS-25, was not "new," but a "permissible successor" to an earlier missile. Seated around the table, Gaffney leaned over and instead insisted that this was a "clear" violation.

No, not so, said the others around the table. By meeting's end, the group demurred, opting to call it the less provocative and far less compelling "likely" violation.

Walking by his side now, the Agency analyst whispered: "It is almost certainly a conflict."

Gaffney agreed.

The analyst continued, "If it weren't for the fact that this would constitute an arms control violation, the Agency would call it a clear violation."

Gaffney recoiled at the admission. He knew it was futile to say anything more. He had long since decided that, despite the criticism heaped upon the Reagan CIA in the press, many of the analysts were, he felt, little more than liberal Ph.D.s with high security clearances; anyway, the Agency was every bit as adept at cozying up to the powerful Democratically controlled Hill committees that funded their massive budgets as the Department of Health and Human Services, or the Interior Department. He heaved a disgusted sigh and, this time, kept his mouth shut.

ONE THING ABOUT this whole exercise truly irked Perle. During the SALT I and SALT II debates, the treaty supporters insisted that if there were violations, this could constitute a material breach of the treaty. Yet now, when violations were detected, treaty supporters claimed they weren't militarily significant—or would poison the U.S.-Soviet atmosphere of relations. They had shifted the goalposts, thereby making the U.S. look weak and vascillating in the arms talks. He remarked to aides that a subjective interpretation of the data was inevitable, the evidence was often not black and white. They may look at the facts, and see the glass as half empty; the State Department may in turn see it as half full. Dis-agreements, he said, would develop along institutional lines.

"The problem," Perle explained, "was when 90 percent of the facts pointed to a violation, and the glass was almost completely empty—then the State Department would protest, 'it's not empty at all.' "

Perle had other concerns about the process, namely that there were multiple agendas underlying the violations report. There were some ana-lysts, determined to undo U.S.-Soviet relations at any cost, who found violations wherever they looked. He wanted a more intellectually honest approach. At one point, he was presented with a list of thirty violations. Many of the cases involved intricate and delicate sources of intelligence, and were classic gray area issues, the fifty-fifty split.

Be careful, Perle sternly warned. "If we overreach and get called on it," he cautioned, "the credibility of this entire exercise would be called into question." He said "to stick with the clear-cut violations," where, after a careful review of the evidence, there would be no dispute.

By year's end, the report on Soviet violations to Congress was finished and ready to go. It detailed seven areas of violations, including Krasno-yarsk. In 1984, super-secret American spy satellites gleaned a massive structure suspiciously lying beyond the thick Soviet cloud cover in cen-tral Siberia; it was the Krasnoyarsk phased array radar station. The So-viets claimed it was an "early warning radar," but such radars were permissible only on the periphery of a country's borders. Located deep in Soviet territory, some 4,000 kilometers from the Soviet Union's north-eastern border, and 750 kilometers from the nearest southern border, this giant station was a flagrant violation of the ABM provisions. As Perle had predicted though, even this was not called an outright violation at first; it was termed "almost certainly" a violation (the follow-up report was more definitive, stating that the radar station constituted an unam-biguous violation).

To Perle, however, Krasnoyarsk was a smoking gun in the American case against Soviet cheating. Moreover, the argument against continued American compliance was considerably strengthened by other findings in the report, notably that the Soviets weren't abiding by the terms of SALT themselves.

The report was slated to be released in November of 1984, in time for the congressional debate on defense appropriations.

NOVEMBER CAME AND went. The report was unexpectedly held up by the White House. Publicly, the White House denied the delay was motivated by the timing of the January 1985 meeting between Shultz and Gromyko in Geneva. But events revealed otherwise; no one wanted to sour the prospects of opening new talks.

On January 22, the report still had not been released. On that day, Reagan issued a written statement, saying that he viewed his arms control commitments with the Soviet Union in Geneva "with the utmost of seriousness." It added more definitively, "I have no more important goal than reducing, and ultimately eliminating, nuclear weapons."

The next day, the violations report was quietly issued to Congress. It received no press at the time. Reagan's statements the day before had overshadowed the report entirely.

For heaven's sake, Perle thought, shaking his head.

But now the issue was only just percolating to the surface, and a moment of truth would be around the corner. For one thing, a second report was due to Congress in February 1985; for another, a new American Trident submarine, sleek and almost as long as two football fields, and equipped with twenty-four multiwarhead nuclear missiles, was scheduled for deployment in 1985. If the U.S. did not retire an older Poseidon nuclear submarine, Perle's cherished dream of busting through SALT would be accomplished. A decision had to be made around June. Perle had five months to mount his assault.

SOON AFTERWARD, ON February 25, Perle testified before the Senate Foreign Relations Committee on Soviet violations. Three days earlier, he had testified before the House Armed Services Committee's new and powerful chairman, Les Aspin. This was part of Perle's plan to blitz the media and the Hill, and get the report out there himself to force the issue.

Today, he adopted a tone of "more in sorrow than in anger." But the battle lines had now been drawn. Earlier in the month, the Arms Control Association, a liberal interest group that was led by Spurgeon Keeny and other former Carter officials, had angrily denounced the report in a press conference. They criticized the administration for not having been tough enough on the Soviets in the Standing Consultative Commission, a forum set up to discuss and resolve disputes over compliance—suggesting that somehow Soviet violations were the U.S.'s fault. The group also contended that it was inappropriate to publicize the violations because it would spoil the climate for future arms control. Finally, they noted that even if the violations were violations—and they refused to grant this, even for Krasnoyarsk—they were not militarily significant.

This press event had special significance to Perle. He and the arms control groups had repeatedly clashed in the past while he was on Scoop's staff, long before he joined the administration. In their eyes, he could do no right; it also seemed the Soviets could do no wrong. To even the most casual observer, the contours of this fight were clear. It was not about facts per se, but ideology and philosophy—on both sides. "What do you expect from Spurgeon Keeny?" Perle would remark, in a combination of resignation and disgust.

Perle had anticipated the harsh reaction of the Arms Control Association, but this time, he was, as colleagues noted, "truly pissed." He went out of his way to issue a cautious, intellectually sound report that included only clear-cut violations. And then, he went the extra mile and took the unusual measure of inviting the Arms Control Association for a personal briefing on the report. They refused.

So he laid out all of this, and a rebuttal, in his Senate testimony. "The fact that the Soviets have cheated in the past does not rule out the possibility of mutually beneficial agreements in the future, but it does rule out the type of ineffective agreements based upon wishful thinking that we have negotiated in the past—and which some propose today," he said softly, his index finger and thumb clamped together in the air for emphasis.

Christopher Dodd took his glasses off his face, waved them in a circle, and asked: "Should the president break out of the unratified SALT II treaty, or should it dismantle the older Polaris submarine?"

Perle had been waiting for this, the question that would make the headline in the next day's papers. He stated that the president had not yet made a decision. But, he added, "It is a great mistake" for the U.S. to continue "honoring accords" while the Soviets were violating "quite important provisions." Looking sincere, he said further, it is time to end the "double standard" of having Washington adhere to "every crossed 't' and dotted 'i'" while letting the Soviets think they could play fast and loose with these accords."

When pointedly asked what the Reagan administration had decided, Perle said it was still assessing whether to continue to observe the unratified treaty when it expired at the year's end. He paused dramatically.

"But my personal view, Senator, is that the treaty limits should not be extended."

Upon hearing those words uttered, Democratic staffers rushed to the phones to call SALT supporters and muster a response. But when Perle's staff heard his statement, they smiled triumphantly. "That's it," said one of his aides, flashing an excited grin.

• • •

WHILE PERLE WAS testifying on the Senate side, the issue was being watched with the greatest of seriousness in the House, especially by Les Aspin.

Aspin was unquestionably the brainiest member of Congress on defense issues, and as the new Armed Services Committee chairman had vaulted past Senator Sam Nunn to the privileged perch as the most influential Democrat on arms control. What he would say on this issue, as on so many others, could be decisive.

Aspin, who attended Perle's wedding in 1977, had genuine respect for him. He knew that Perle was blithely dismissed by liberal members of Congress and the arms control groups; they vilified him as nefarious, dangerous, irresponsible. But that was not his view. He felt few people had mastered the intricacies of arms control and U.S.-Soviet relations the way Perle had. Aspin strongly believed it was important to carefully consider what Perle, who "had thought long and hard about these issues," said: mainly, Aspin contended, because Richard could be right. And he liked jousting with Perle; when the two sparred in the political arena, it was good-natured and with respect.

After Perle testified before his hearing, Aspin barked to his staff that he wanted some memos analyzing the Perle arguments. He loved reading memos, good, meaty extensive analysis. That Friday, he intended to bring in his senior aides for an extended brainstorming session, reminiscent of a college faculty seminar or a think-tank meeting, ideas being tossed around, one layer peeled away to reveal new sets of questions, which in turn were subjected to equally rigorous scrutiny.

Around 2 P.M., he bounded into his private conference room across the hall from his Cannon House Office Building office. Surrounded by bookshelves piled high with musty leather-bound volumes, Aspin, wearing a bulky ski sweater and brown cords (he had no other meetings today), sat himself down at the end of the conference table, and slouched his six-foot-three frame into the chair. His glasses askew on top of his head, he shuffled a stackful of memos and nodded to his three senior staff members, dressed primly in gray suits with red power ties and suspenders, to brief him.

"We've got to scope this thing out," Aspin said, "think it through." He then leaned back and listened.

One aide talked about the internal fight going on in the administration. "This is Cap's and Richard's war," he said. "There's a chance we could isolate them, if we weigh in against breaking out of SALT."

A second aide in the room had once worked for Perle, but left when he saw how far apart they were politically. Now he crunched numbers for

Aspin, working figures into charts and tables. Without SALT, he said, the Soviets could add thousands more warheads to their arsenal. A breakdown in SALT could lead to a massive breakout on the Soviet side, he said, fueling the arms race in favor of the Soviets. The numbers showed it. "They can fractionate their big heavies," he said, using the language of nuclear theorists, which meant simply that the Soviets could add warheads to their missiles.

Aspin's eyes opened wide. His interest was rising. "Ah hah, ah hah," he said, the emphasis on the "hah," shaking his head up and down. This was just the kind of stuff that he liked, good hard numbers, solid rational analysis, not soft emotional stuff. It also gave him ammunition to argue against breaking out of SALT, while still looking tough-minded. Aspin was pleased.

The third aide spoke, cautioning that he may be the skunk at the garden party. Aspin smiled. He had never been one to want unanimity, and carefully structured his senior staff to reflect the best minds on a variety of sides. His number cruncher was a liberal; this aide, a political moderate. He wanted to hear both sides.

Perle's arguments, the aide said, are compelling. In a business deal, you wouldn't allow one side to violate the terms of an agreement. Aspin, hearing this, leaned his head forward a bit. Hmm, yeah, he said.

The aide continued. I know we keep using the argument that the violations aren't militarily significant, but what is the standard for deciding when something is significant? If it's not the treaty itself, then we have no rational basis. We need at least to have a standard for ourselves. So, the aide continued, cautiously at this point, I think we want to be balanced in any criticism. Don't close the door on Perle's arguments. Politically, among the Democrats, you have to be for keeping SALT. But let's not forget that the Soviets are the ones violating these agreements, so you certainly ought to take them to task as well. This is right for the country, and will help us get better agreements. You can play a big role here. It's also good politics for the Democrats.

"Ah hah, ah hah, yup," Aspin said, leaning even further back in his chair. Lost briefly in thought, he agreed with this too. This argument was crafted not just to his political side but also to his high policy-maker side, the "not solely what's good for your party, but think of what's right for your country's national security argument" side.

"Right! We can't let the Soviets off the hook either," Aspin said firmly. But he still hadn't fully made up his mind.

At 5 P.M., Aspin lumbered out of the office, on his way to a dinner date outside of Georgetown. He carried with him the hefty memos his staff had written for him—along with his own long yellow pad, on which he had made extensive notes with thick black marker.

Aspin, while agreeing with Perle that SALT was imperfect, didn't fully buy Perle's SALT breakout argument. He felt that it was still better to keep the structure of SALT. In his own mind, Aspin had not decided when a violation was militarily significant, but, he believed, the strategic situation was currently stable enough that he could defer that decision for now. The numbers and charts his aide worked up on the SALT issue were good. Anyway, politically, he knew he was boxed in on this one. The issue had remained sacrosanct to the Democrats, as much religious theology as real analysis. Handled right, this issue endeared him to the liberals. But he also agreed that the principle of equity in arms control mattered; moreover, the Soviets were the ones cheating. They should be slammed, he couldn't forget that.

To his number cruncher, he wrote "See Me" in big bold letters on his memo. He also decided to use the other aide's argument, working off of his memo. But he wanted to take a look at the charts again. Then, a final decision: he would go public and oppose Perle's argument—as well as the Soviets.

On March 23, 1985, a private letter signed by twenty-three leading liberal and centrist Democratic representatives was sent to the new and energetic Soviet general secretary, Mikhail Gorbachev, who had replaced Chernenko, following his death after only thirteen months as party head. The letter warned that the Soviets must comply with existing arms control treaties or risk "serious consequences" for the future of arms control, specifically limits on space-based defense, which were the primary goal of the Soviets in the new Geneva arms talks. Krasnoyarsk, in particular, was singled out as a potential violation of the ABM treaty. The signatories included Les Aspin and Dante Fascell, the chairman of the House Foreign Affairs Committee.

And, these two powerful chairmen laid down their marker. No U.S. breakout of SALT. If the administration decided to undercut the expired treaty, the signal had been sent: congressional opposition would be fierce.

The Senate soon followed suit, adopting a compromise resolution to a military spending bill that urged President Reagan to continue adhering to SALT. The vote was 90–5.

ONE GROUP HAD still been conspicuously silent, The Joint Chiefs of Staff. In the final run-up to a decision, theirs could be a deciding vote.

. . .

UNEXPECTEDLY, PERLE GOT another chance to lobby for breaking out of SALT—at a dinner party on the quiet, leafy streets of Chevy Chase, Maryland. That spring, the columnist George Will had called him and asked if he could throw a party in Perle's honor. Of course, Perle said. Will asked him for the names of a few people he would like invited. Perle put down six names: two of them were his in-laws. He thought they would enjoy a grand Washington dinner party.

Will then issued the rest of the invitations to a blue-chip list of twenty-four for the party at his house, just around the corner from Perle's unlisted address. The acceptances soon piled in. Caspar Weinberger was coming, David Brinkley and Mrs. Douglas MacArthur said yes, and a senior aide to Margaret Thatcher and several sub-cabinet-level officials would also be in attendance. And then, unexpectedly, President Ronald Reagan indicated he too would be coming.

THE DINNER WAS held on a warm springlike evening in June. Reagan's arrival created some pandemonium in the neighborhood; the street had to be cordoned off for security reasons. This night, Perle would get his chance to talk in a casual atmosphere about SALT and Soviet violations with the president.

Before dinner, Reagan moved around like any other guest and chatted amiably with each of the invitees. It was Leslie Perle's fortieth birthday, and the president went over to her parents and talked with them for forty-five minutes. Leslie's father, a butcher in Baltimore, was thrilled. This was not just Ronald Reagan, his son-in-law's boss, but Ronald Reagan the citizen. Leslie beamed. Thatcher's aide later told people he had never seen a spectacle like that in his life. A dinner party with the prime minister and a butcher in England would be unthinkable. He called the party "a quintessential American experience."

Perle soon seized his opportunity and buttonholed the president. "You know, Mr. President, there's a serious problem in your government. At the assistant and deputy assistant secretary level, where much of the work is done, where your options papers are drawn up, the national security slots are filled with appointees, approved by the White House, who didn't vote for you, who can't stand you, who do everything they can to work against everything you stand for."

Reagan listened intently.

"I go into interagency meetings, and I'm invariably the only one who supports your positions. They don't have an ounce of loyalty to you, or to the presidency, only to themselves and the old way of doing things."

Reagan smiled his avuncular smile, and told Perle: "Richard, it was just like that in California too. You just have to get used to it."

Perle was disappointed. He felt Reagan didn't understand, but he had at least said his piece.

Over dinner, there were many toasts, and at one point, Perle and the president stood up at the table and swapped Soviet jokes, reflecting on the sad state of Gorbachev's Russia, for the dinner guests.

Perle related: "There's a fellow outside of Moscow who hears about a butcher shop in northern Moscow with meat. He takes a long subway ride, and then hops into a taxi to go and purchase the meat. He finally arrives at the shop and joins the line. Two and a half hours later, he gets to the counter.

" 'I'll have some beef,' the man says.

" 'We've run out of beef,' the butcher tells him.

" 'I'd like some veal then.'

" 'Sorry, all out.'

" 'Well, okay then, how about some sausage?'

" 'I just sold the last one to the man in front of you.'

" 'This *perestroika* is a complete farce,' the man shouts, and storms out of the store. Outside, a policeman grabs him by the collar.

" 'Twenty years ago, we would have shot you for this. Under Comrade Gorbachev, we are lenient. I'm just going to issue a warning. But don't let it happen again.' "

Perle continued: "When the man finally arrives home, his eager wife asks where the meat is.

"The man shakes his head and tells his wife, 'Hell, they're not only out of beef. Now they're out of ammunition.' "

Perle looked over to Reagan. He had the strong feeling that the president had heard this joke, although he laughed heartily nonetheless.

Before the president left, Perle, joined by George Will, pressed the president over SALT II. Once again, the old man smiled. Perle didn't know if his bid was successful—or if it had failed.

THE NEXT DAY, Don Regan, the new White House chief of staff, complained to George Shultz that Perle and George Will "had worked the president over" at a dinner party. Shultz remained expressionless. He had known nothing about this.

But, it turned out, the president had been swayed by an argument that had just been made to him by the Joint Chiefs of Staff.

The chiefs, in a split from the civilian side of the Pentagon, told the president that they feared the Soviet Union would be able to outbid the U.S. in an unrestrained nuclear arms race, while the U.S. military would be held back by domestic budget considerations and political restraints. They also said that the Poseidon submarines slated to be dismantled would be costly to maintain, and their military usefulness was now negligible. Thus, they asserted, there were economic reasons to abide by the treaty as well.

The chiefs' arguments held the day, and Reagan wrote out his decision by himself. On June 11, he announced that the U.S. would abide by the SALT II treaty for now. He said, "The U.S. will go the extra mile."

But, he noted, it would also reserve the right to prepare "proportionate and appropriate responses" to Soviet violations.

PERLE GOT THE news in his office. The Congress was gloating; State had prevailed. No matter what the spin, this was a defeat. He was dejected. To Perle, the other side had missed the nuance and the possibility in dismantling SALT II. They had chosen to remain shackled to the past, to an unratified shell that had no guarantees, no teeth.

Still, he saw a silver lining in the president's response mentioning "proportionate responses." The door was not closed entirely, but had been left open ever so slightly, if only just a crack. But a crack, he felt, meant another day, another opportunity. SALT II was flawed. And, if Richard Perle could wait, the issue of SALT would be back.

CHAPTER 27

It was a moment Richard Perle savored, the vegetables and dinner ingredients spread out before him in a tantalizing array: crunchy watercress, squeaky leaves of radicchio, slightly chilled mâche, a small but delicate goat cheese off to the side. From the sink rose the earthy smells of freshly rinsed lettuce, and all around him lay other intricate ingredients that would become engulfed in the clamor and fray of a busy kitchen, gearing up for a dinner that was only an hour away.

This kitchen, filled with high-tech cooking instruments and open spaces, its soft colors bathed in natural light, was for Richard Perle a sanctuary, cool, tranquil, consoling. It was his favorite spot, and cooking was his refuge from the stern and unrelenting pressures of government life.

He had recently spoken with an aide about the seeming collapse of civility in Washington. For this young man, going to work for Perle had been a quick ticket to social ostracism. The aide's friends had never thought of him as a Republican, and *certainly* not a Reaganite appointee, that was just so, so unthinkable. Some old friends had stopped calling completely. At cocktail parties, the ones he was still invited to, he would often look up to see a pair of angry eyes glaring at him; people in his neighborhood and casual acquaintances now turned their backs to him. The aide said that, outside of work, it was as though he were living among whispers, cruel sounds that echoed with unremitting hostility.

Perle had long since given up on the good graces and tolerance of the Washington liberal establishment; sure, there were some good people, civil in spirit and honest in debate, but these days they were rare. After his years on the Hill, he had had to learn to live in his own world, with his wife and son, socialize with his friends, and work with his colleagues.

But for younger staff, especially those new to Washington, he knew it could be tough, and in the Reagan years, often brutal. Personal, partisan attacks were commonplace and increasingly intense. He tried to make life easier for his more fragile colleagues by projecting an absolute sense of teamwork, loyalty, easy collegiality, and respect.

Of course, he had always been lucky himself. He had had powerful mentors and watchful sponsors. There were Paul Nitze and Albert Wohlstetter, but most of all Scoop and now Cap. He would try to be for his staff what his sponsors had been for him, and he tried to communicate this to his aide.

These daily frustrations were life in politically charged Washington. And when nothing seemed to work, there was the repose of kitchen, the easy movement of cutting, chopping, mixing, the rewards of creating.

TONIGHT, IN MARCH of 1985, he was entertaining Stephen Solarz, the increasingly influential congressman and New York Democrat, over dinner.

Perle liked Solarz. The boyish-looking congressman had a keen and probing mind, and a liberalism that stemmed from his personal roots in Jewish Brooklyn, nurtured by an antipathy to the Vietnam War, and tied to the procrustean exigencies of Democratic party politics. In the past few years, the congressman had been dispensing with some of the more utopian notions he had harbored when he first came to D.C., awaking to the nastier realities of the Soviet Union and global politics. The signs were all there. He had already bucked his party to support the INF missile deployments, even boldly authoring two op-eds on the subject. Solarz had been moving to the center, slowly but nonetheless demonstrably, much like Perle's other brainy friend, Les Aspin. And, just as Perle's friend columnist Charles Krauthammer had noted that Aspin could one day become secretary of defense in a Democratic administration, Solarz, experienced in foreign affairs and world-traveled, was a most logical candidate to become secretary of state.

Solarz was an engaging dinner guest. They boisterously talked defense, arms control, the Reagan Doctrine, the congressman unfurling his passionate views ("Yes, but Richard . . . ") in a staccato of facts and conceptual generalizations.

As Solarz considered his own bid to move to the political center—and slowly nudge his party along as well—Perle could not help but be taken back to the days when he worked in the Bunker with Scoop. Perhaps Solarz would be more successful than Scoop or he had been, but Perle had his doubts. Indeed, Solarz's engagement in a bitter contest to provide aid to anti-Communist guerrillas in Cambodia against fierce opposition, not just from the Democrats but from the administration, was but one palpable sign of Solarz's own difficult journey ahead.

For his part, Solarz thoroughly enjoyed the dinner. There were many things he didn't agree with Perle on, like SDI and the Nicaraguan contras, but they could disagree amicably—and there was much more common ground than had existed in the past. After he and his wife, Nina, drove off to their home in the seclusion of refined McLean, he made sure to send Perle a warm note, thanking him not just for the dinner, which he found delicious, but the conversation, which he told Perle he thought was "just as good." He also had a special request. He had been told that Perle had given a brilliant speech in London about SDI. Could he get a copy?

BUT FOR PERLE, in the next months, there would now be little time for friendly dinners. On July 1, the Soviet Union agreed to a summit in Geneva on November 19–20. Since the Gromyko-Shultz meeting, it was clear that SDI would be the central issue of contention. Just as Soviet sights were set on killing SDI, so the Pentagon's sights were set on saving it. And ever since the president's 1983 speech announcing a full-scale government effort behind SDI, a slow-motion collision course had been set uneasily in play between the president's dream of a missile defense and continued adherence to the ABM treaty.

The two were fundamentally incompatible, and at some point in the future it would be necessary to either push ahead with SDI or stay within the terms of the treaty. The collision could happen sooner or it could happen later. Shultz's view, despite the Soviet treaty violation at Krasnoyarsk, was later; for Perle, who had taken a dim view of the treaty since 1972, sooner was better.

For more than a decade, the ABM treaty was regarded as a steady bedrock of U.S.-Soviet relations, locked into place by unwavering domestic support from not just arms controllers, the academic community, and liberal interest groups, but from the moderate establishment. Yet in the summer of 1985, when Richard Perle ingeniously swiveled the barrel of a single Pentagon lawyer's legal gun and aimed it at the foundation of the treaty itself, he set off a battle that powerful senators bleakly would describe as no less than "the end of arms control abroad" and "a constitutional crisis" at home. The effects would be felt most dramatically within the Kremlin itself. But ironically, the spark for this conflict was ignited not by Perle or Ronald Reagan, or even the Soviets, but by a routine hearing in the Senate.

SENATOR CARL LEVIN, a liberal Michigan Democrat, frequently took on the role of committee prosecutor on the Armed Services Committee. His questions to witnesses frequently bore in on finely tuned legal questions concerning Pentagon waste, defense fraud, and procurement regulations. On July 25, 1985, he turned his razor-sharp mind to SDI.

It was a standard confirmation hearing for Donald Hicks, a former defense contractor who had been nominated to be undersecretary of defense for research and engineering; his portfolio would involve SDI experiments. Usually, such hearings were easygoing—senators asked a few questions, shuffled their papers and looked intensely interested, then, claiming other demands upon their time, declared that the candidate had their unyielding support and would be a credit to the country. Or, if opposed to the candidate, they thundered a few words of explanation and then left, their staff remaining behind dutifully scribbling notes. In a subsequent committee business meeting, the candidate would be voted through.

Other candidates were not so lucky. Sometimes they became unwitting elements in the viselike grip of a larger political struggle between the Congress and the executive. Otherwise uncontroversial, this was Hicks's fate that day.

Bearing a stack of questions about how—and whether—SDI could be pursued without violating the 1972 ABM treaty, Carl Levin, hunched over, reading glasses balanced on his nose, tenaciously questioned Hicks.

Hicks provided reassuring answers: SDI, in his opinion, could be conducted within the confines of the ABM treaty, he said. But that wasn't enough for Levin. The senator wanted a number of other, more detailed questions answered before he voted for Hicks's nomination.

The central question that dumbfounded Hicks pertained to restraints on "other physical principles," or future systems that might be created as an outgrowth of SDI research.

Hicks said he didn't have all the answers—but he would go back to the Defense Department, and return with authoritative responses in writing to the senator. With that, the committee adjourned.

In the meantime, across the river in the E-Ring of the Pentagon, there was a quickening buzz of activity. The Hicks exchange posed an opportunity to settle SDI once and for all.

SHORTLY AFTER THE hearing, Perle convened an interagency meeting in the Pentagon to supply answers to Levin. He surveyed the members of the committee to see just what was permitted or prohibited by the treaty. Six different people gave him six different answers, and surprisingly, not along the typical institutional biases of differing agencies. There was genuine confusion, and it was government-wide.

"This can't be," Perle said, astonished. "We've had this treaty since 1972. Yet none of you has the same answer."

The interagency committee agreed that more work should be done on the issue to get to the bottom of just what the treaty actually said. They would reconvene shortly, after consulting experts in their respective departments.

To formulate the Pentagon view, Perle had just the guy in mind: a new Pentagon lawyer recently hired by Fred Iklé, a former assistant district attorney named Philip Kunsberg. Perle felt Kunsberg, at the age of thirty-five, was bright as hell and just right to take a look at the treaty provisions. He was perfect: schooled in the law, yet virtually ignorant about the issue itself, he would thus not be overly prejudiced in one direction or another. Perle felt he was the one to make a fresh and honest legal finding.

PHILIP KUNSBERG HAD impressed a lot of people in a short time. After graduating law school, he eschewed the big white-shoe WASP law firms and joined the New York district attorney's office as an assistant DA. It was a prestigious assignment. Other well-known lawyers had hung their hats at the New York district attorney's office at one point, and like them, Kunsberg got stuck with some of the thorniest issues confronting the hard-boiled New York DAs: organized crime, gambling, and pornography. This was not a place where judicial reserve paid off; lawyers had to plunge into a boiling cauldron of prejudices, laundered money, fraud, violence, and passion.

Assistant New York DAs were the stuff of lore, notable for being hard-charging, roll-up-your-sleeves guys, street animals who got into the trenches, and were famous for being overworked, putting in long hours, and being underpaid problem-solvers. But Kunsberg did not plan on making a career in the DA's office. He found himself lured to government service on national security issues, first in the general counsel's office of the CIA, and then, working his way quickly up the ladder, for Fred Iklé in the Pentagon.

He almost never made it to his Pentagon position. On March 27, 1985, the Republican Senate Steering Committee sought to block his appointment. Eight powerful conservative senators, from Jim McClure to Strom Thurmond wrote to the Pentagon and the White House decrying Kunsberg. His sin was having weak conservative and Republican credentials. The senators wrote that he had "no record of support for President Reagan" and no "approval from the White House Presidential Personnel Office." Promoting another candidate for Iklé's shop, they declared that "the Presidential Personnel Office will not approve Mr. Kunsberg." But

Iklé stuck to his guns, and Kunsberg came on board. Four months later, Kunsberg was in Perle's office for a ride that would soon thrust him into the public eye on a scale he had never anticipated.

PERLE SAT KUNSBERG in his office. Kunsberg was well aware of Perle's far-reaching reputation as the driving force behind arms control policy in the Pentagon and the administration. Still, he was surprised at how low-key Perle was, how personable and charming, not at all like his reputation as the Prince of Darkness.

"Phil, I need your help," Perle said softly. "Will you take a look at this treaty, the public and secret negotiating record, and whatever else you may need, and give a fresh reading of it?

"Go away, work wherever you need to, and don't come back until you can tell us what it actually says."

How long should I take? Kunsberg asked.

"As much time as you need. Take a week, two weeks, just help us solve this problem authoritatively."

So Kunsberg immediately plunged into the tedious particulars of the evidence. That he hadn't spent his entire life doing arms control wasn't an impediment. Lawyers frequently had to—and did—learn new issues from scratch; there was a rich tradition whereby men and women of the bar were brought into government for special assignments in areas where they weren't experts. Besides, in this case, he thought, he only needed to make a legal finding, not a policy judgment. With this case as his sole assignment, he got to work, unfettered by outside distractions, constant meetings, and extraneous demands.

TEN DAYS LATER, Kunsberg had worked up a nineteen-page memo on the treaty, and brought it to Perle. He concluded that the Soviet Union had never accepted restrictions on space-based ABM systems if they employed "new physical principles," such as laser beams, directed energy systems, and other exotic technologies. Indeed, the record showed that while the U.S. sought to limit future systems in the 1972 ABM negotiations, the Soviets specifically were interested in keeping their options open. They made the case that you can't ban what you can't define, and this was laid out clearly in the treaty's "Agreed Statement D," which permitted testing and development of ABM systems based on these other physical principles.

The report continued to say any U.S. interpretation that restricted U.S.

research and development of future systems would be a unilateral American understanding, and was certainly not binding.

Presented with this report, Perle was stunned, later remarking that he "almost fell off his chair." He immediately set about taking action: convening another meeting of the interagency group on SDI to lock Kunsberg's legal view into government policy.

PERLE PRESENTED THE evidence, calling this the "broad interpretation," as opposed to the "narrow." The State Department officials went berserk; the meeting devolved into something close to a shouting match. Their criticism was scathing.

We can't agree on this, the State representative said. Your lawyer says this, but we need to have our lawyer look at it. Then we can reconvene.

As NEWS OF Perle's new ABM interpretation leaked out into the halls of the bureaucracy, it was bedlam. Career government attorneys at the Pentagon and the Arms Control and Disarmament Agency, who had spent their life's work addressing such issues, were apoplectic. The dispute immediately took on larger, even herculean proportions: sniping persisted between Foggy Bottom and the Pentagon, and a clash ensued between Perle and his young street-smart hired legal gun (or so it was alleged), and the career bureaucrats, lawyers who were keepers of the ancien régime.

The rap on Kunsberg by his detractors was that he was young; didn't know arms control; however good a *young* lawyer he was, he had dealt, after all, with organized crime, not the serious life-and-death issue of arms control; and he was suspect because of his connection to Perle. Critics also maintained that he spent only ten days on the issue, hardly enough time.

It fell to Shultz to break the deadlock. He decided not to turn the issue over to a career lawyer (in a fit of pique, at one point he would confide his own suspicions about the experts: "The problem is," he said, "they are too often mired in their own pet positions"). Instead, he chose the State Department's most senior lawyer, his new legal adviser, Judge Abraham Sofaer. A whispering campaign might work against Kunsberg, but most observers agreed that Sofaer's stature should make him an unimpeachable evaluator of the record. For Shultz, it also meant that he would not be handed the same old stale assessment from self-serving bureaucrats.

There is an old saying that a judge is just a lawyer who knew a governor. This held true even for Sofaer, a former member of the federal bench, whom New York Governor Mario Cuomo once praised, saying, "Abe Sofaer is a great New York lawyer." Certainly, Sofaer had some political connections and was a Republican loyalist, but he was no stooge. His scholarly writings on the Constitution and foreign policy were brilliant, serving as case law in the finest law and political science departments in the land. And unlike most career government lawyers, Sofaer was a talented scholar of the Congress, its rights, its privileges, its perpetual struggle for power with the executive branch.

His small innocuous frame belied a tenacious intellect and a steely legal resolve. The "Judge" to those who didn't know him, "Abe" to his friends, he was a classic lawyer's lawyer, as comfortable with the neutral principles of the law as with the booby traps and hazards of international policy.

After several months of persistently researching the record himself, Sofaer reached his own conclusion. He effectively agreed with Kunsberg. There were some differences and concerns about early deployment, but ultimately not ones that concerned the broad interpretation. On October 3, 1985, he told Shultz that the Soviets had insisted on flexibility in the 1972 treaty; the Americans had tried, but failed to persuade them to accept restrictive language on ABM development. Yet when the U.S. team explained the treaty to the Senate, they portrayed it as an American victory, as narrow and restrictive, consistent with preventing any resort to defense. The evidence was unmistakable. In short, Sofaer concluded, "We're justified in taking the broad approach now."

In his inquiry Sofaer even consulted with Paul Nitze, who had been directly involved in the negotiation of the ABM treaty. Confronted with the evidence, Nitze too had been convinced by Sofaer that whatever the American negotiators may have said a decade and a half earlier, there was no ban on the development and testing of new space defense. On only one point did Nitze disagree with Sofaer: actual deployment was another issue; he was not willing to concede that.

LATE FRIDAY THAT week, the Senior Interagency Arms Control Group met at the White House. The meeting was chaired by Bud McFarlane, the national security adviser. McFarlane, who had a burning interest in arms control, harbored many grand policy ideas and larger personal ambitions, even hoping to emerge as another Henry Kissinger. But others in the administration felt he was hopelessly in over his head. In either case, he was in a position to significantly affect the outcome of the ABM debate. He listened carefully as Perle and Iklé made an aggressive case for the broad interpretation. ACDA Director Ken Adelman, often a Perle ally, said he was "on the fifty-yard line." Nitze, carrying a memo that asserted it would be "politically unwise" to reopen the issue, played it cool, demurring in the face of Perle's and Iklé's passionate arguments. Instead of distributing his memo, he lent his considerable name to the broad interpretation as well. No one argued for the restrictive interpretation.

The issue was settled. The group agreed that its next step would be to prepare a strategy for consulting with the Congress and the allies, and for informing the Soviets. McFarlane said they would meet again in four days, on Tuesday, to hammer out the final issues.

Perle was delighted. A clean break with the past was at last at hand. Kunsberg had done good work, and would now be vindicated. The ABM treaty was an ill-considered and outdated document that had stood in relentless conflict with missile defense against foreign nuclear attack. Now SDI could be pursued unfettered; and the rigorous prosecution of competition with the Soviets would continue. Everything was now in place.

THAT SUNDAY, PERLE was lounging at home with his family, drinking strong coffee, reading the day's paper, talking to his son, Jonathan. He flicked on the TV at 10:30 to watch NBC's *Meet the Press*. McFarlane was the day's guest. Perle thought it would be uneventful, but it was important to see how the White House was making the case.

One of the questioners was Robert Kaiser, a *Washington Post* reporter who had written a long profile in the 1970s that portrayed Perle as a puppeteer, darkly manipulating anti-arms-control forces from behind the scenes. Even with Perle's current visible public profile, the same things were said. It was a no-win situation, he thought. He sipped his espresso.

Kaiser asked McFarlane how SDI could go forward without violating the ABM treaty. Perle lazily thought, now's the time for the standard government answer that says nothing substantive; issues always being under review, and all the rest. But to Perle's complete surprise, that was distinctly not what happened.

In his monotone voice, McFarlane proceeded to give a highly detailed answer, one that could only have been meticulously prepared in advance. "My God," Perle thought to himself, "what the hell is McFarlane doing? Can this guy be stopped?"

In fact, McFarlane had brazenly jumped the gun, on his own, without informing anyone in advance. He was, live on national television, going public with the new broad interpretation that had only just been decided two days earlier at the White House. Perle gulped. He couldn't believe what he was hearing. There was no staffing done; no preparation of the Congress; nothing had been said to the allies; no reasoning behind the conclusions. Perle feared that the press would be all over the issue.

He angrily thought to himself, Shit, this was no way to surface the announcement; it was SDI all over again. If he had to guess, he felt McFarlane was trying to sabotage SDI—because this was certainly no way to promote it. After having deftly maneuvered the situation to just where he wanted it, now he would have to engage in damage control. Again.

Perle's instincts were certainly correct; immediately after McFarlane's TV appearance, all hell broke loose.

IN GENEVA, MAX Kampelman, now the chief U.S. arms negotiator for the newly reopened arms talks with the Soviets, watched in horror as this episode slowly unfolded. He hadn't been privy to the decision making leading up to the frantic weekend, and was only getting his sea legs on the arcana of nuclear arms control, but he still got the drift pretty quickly.

His Soviet counterparts were furious. He felt the whole episode was unnecessary. Where Perle wanted to assert the new interpretation after laying the groundwork, the more cautious Kampelman thought the issue could wait. He remarked, "We're not at the point of doing research that required us to abandon the narrow definition. So why inject the issue? It soured the atmosphere terribly."

With each passing day, it seemed that Kampelman was speaking the language of the department he represented, State, rather than the hard-line dialect that had inextricably bound him with Perle in their earlier collaboration against SALT II via the Committee on the Present Danger. His mood was carefully noted by Perle's representatives to the Geneva delegation, John Woodworth and Dan Gallington. Gallington, considered abrasive, impetuous, and a rough-and-tumble bureaucratic infighter on the delegation, was suspicious of Kampelman from the start. He was consumed with a gnawing fear that Kampelman, a Democrat, and Shultz's appointee, would give away the store. Within weeks, this would sow the seeds of tumult in the delegation.

Two weeks later, Kampelman fired off an urgent cable to Shultz, saying that there were signs of private bickering and heated debate in the Soviet delegation. Of greater interest, Kampelman noted, the Soviets had indicated they would be interested in a U.S.-Soviet agreement not to break out of the ABM treaty while reductions in offensive missiles could take place. The implication was clear: SDI had the Soviets panicked. But

Kampelman was now worried about pushing the Soviets too hard and too fast.

Shultz's instincts were the same as Kampelman's. He too watched the uproar with a mounting sense of dread. Sam Nunn, the mighty congressional baron on defense in the Senate, immediately opposed the ABM reinterpretation; so did the House Foreign Affairs Committee chair Dante Fascell. Les Aspin also was not happy. The allies were registering their displeasure. Shultz felt corrective action was necessary.

Egged on by his new arms control adviser, Paul Nitze, the secretary was afraid that if the U.S. didn't say something, NATO could buckle. So after sounding these apocalyptic trumpets, he arranged to meet with the president. A hasty stopgap measure to stem the hemorrhaging was arranged. Shultz would announce that the broad interpretation was the legally correct one, but the U.S. would conduct SDI research in accordance with the traditional, narrow interpretation.

That Friday, Shultz reaffirmed this view in a major speech in San Francisco. Projecting a soothing demeanor, the whole troublesome issue, he said firmly, was now "moot."

PERLE WAS HARDLY jubilant at *this* outcome. He waded out into a pool of reporters the following Wednesday, confidently announcing: "With respect to the future elements of the SDI program, it remains to be seen which interpretation will apply." And, indeed, the ABM issue would return to center stage.

But for now, to be sure, he had been shrewdly mousetrapped by his rivals. It made no sense to retreat from what the U.S. had exerted as its legal right—particularly with the first U.S.-Soviet summit of the Reagan administration only weeks away, and no one who knew Perle doubted his intention to continue to press for the broad interpretation. But this time, no matter how skillful he had been, he was partially checked by his rivals and also by inexplicable events—at least for the time being.

This issue, however, would soon be overtaken by the ultimate challenge, the cold winds and prospects in Geneva, and a full-fledged summit rapidly approaching.

THAT WINTER, STARTLING intelligence reports trickled in indicating that beyond Moscow's panic about SDI, the Politburo was starting to rethink its occupation of Afghanistan. "Now was hardly the time to take the pressure off," Perle felt, "most certainly not now."

CHAPTER 28

After Max Kampelman was named to head the Geneva Nuclear and Space Talks, Bud McFarlane told the newly appointed chief negotiator that the president wanted to meet with him in full glare of the press. "Oh that's not needed," Kampelman said modestly. "I don't feel he has to see me."

"No, Max, you don't understand," McFarlane explained. "The president feels it's needed. He wants the whole world to see you with him, so they know he's serious about these talks, and that you have his full confidence as you get ready to move to Geneva."

It was a telling story about Ronald Reagan, who knew that simple touches mattered. But it was equally telling about Max Kampelman. Kampelman did not actively seek the spotlight; it sought him.

Indeed, in 1985, as the world geared up for the Geneva summit, Max Kampelman was a quintessential veteran of Washington—and now a key man on the inside.

KAMPELMAN MOVED AS freely among the titans of the establishment as he did in his world of the neoconservative counterestablishment; he was as at ease brokering deals with business and legal barons as hosting a gala charity event for the latest fashionable cause at the Woodrow Wilson Center for International Scholars that he had chaired; and he was courted by—and worked—both sides of the political fence. Where in the spiraling ups and downs of Washington politics careers were abruptly broken with the same meteoric speed as they were made, Kampelman, dubbed by insiders as "Mr. Bipartisan," was not just a survivor, he flourished.

But Kampelman succeeded not simply through his own considerable skill, but because he drew upon the strengths of both great political parties, strengths that Ronald Reagan, first and foremost, so powerfully combined: the compassion of liberals with the steely toughness of conservatives, idealism grafted onto strength, values upheld by power.

Above all, though, Reagan radiated a sense of destiny, the conviction that he could make a difference.

It was said that, as president, Jack Kennedy admired the cool toughness and unflinching pragmatism of such establishment Goliaths as Dean Acheson and Bob Lovett far more than his more liberal advisers, men like Chester Bowles and John Kenneth Galbraith, whom the young president considered overly idealistic and more than a bit mushy. Ronald Reagan, only six years older than Kennedy would have been, was not a cool pragmatist: he believed in the poetry of dreams, the soaring spirit of lofty democratic ideals, and was moved by a dogged sense of the American spirit, the view that with vision, America, the shining city on the hill, could change the world. He harbored deep reservations about the totalitarian nature of the Soviet Union, a system he felt was at once a danger to Western security and Western ideals, and cruel to its own people. In Ronald Reagan's world, America must be prepared to talk, but it must not let down its guard.

Reagan was scarcely like the ideological caricature portrayed by his detractors: committed to his core ideals, he could also, when necessary, be a ruthless pragmatist, albeit with a poetic side, who believed in a strong defense, but also in negotiations. His folksy manner and lax management style were hardly accidents; he wanted *both* a George Shultz and a Caspar Weinberger, thus ensuring that the president had quality advice reflecting the diplomatic and military dimensions of foreign policy; and he operated with an uncanny sense of timing and instinct, reacting to the incalculable rhythms of international politics, not to some academic script drafted in a haughty East Coast Ivy League school, or an artificial timetable whipped up by a cynical press corps or his partisan opposition on the Hill.

Jimmy Carter, who had an unfailing intellect, could, so the tale went, read the script for the song, but he didn't understand the words and was often painfully tone deaf to the rhythms of war and peace in global affairs. Reagan, by contrast, was directly wired into the music of history, unencumbered by the clutter of so-called complexity. He was not the trombone player in the orchestra, or the violinist, he was the conductor. Nuance, Reagan understood, was not being overwhelmed by information, but grasping the essence of the issue.

So while his first four years were a time of strength; his second term was, as the president confided to his advisers, "a time to capitalize on our defense investment"; the two terms, like a seamless web, running into each other, not Reagan I and Reagan II, but Reagan as Reagan Now. The Soviets were showing signs of buckling: they were running scared from SDI, the INF deployment had shaken them to their core, they were hopelessly entangled in the quagmire of Afghanistan, fighting the U.S.-supported mujahadeen, and gaining little from the messy little guerrilla wars of Latin America, and they truly feared that Reagan's prediction that they would one day be in the ash-heap of history was at hand. Reagan reasoned it was now time for the U.S. to act accordingly. Which meant not rolling over with the Soviets, as the far right feared, or negotiating at any price, though many conservatives and Reagan loyalists also feared this, but staying tough, engaging the Russians, securing a deal in U.S. interests.

Thus it was hardly surprising that the president told Shultz he was delighted with his new choice, Max Kampelman, a Democrat, as he himself once was, big-hearted but a hard-liner in foreign policy, a skilled and tough negotiator.

Kampelman's appointment was greeted by the press with an initial blush of skepticism. On January 18, when Shultz made the announcement from the White House Press Room, eyes opened wide, and he was asked, "Why Kampelman? He has no experience in the complicated field of arms control."

Shultz replied tartly, with a snap to his voice: "He's smart, he's a good negotiator, he's experienced. He did an outstanding job in his work in Madrid. And he's really first-class."

AND, AS WAS apparent from the start, Kampelman was his own man, not anyone's patsy. In one White House interagency meeting before the Geneva negotiations began, which included Perle, Kampelman was told that the Senate had created a bipartisan arms control observer group, comprised of ten members plus the majority and minority leaders. The question around the table: would this infringe on Kampelman's freedom as a negotiator?

Perle was concerned. Too many times in the past, he had seen the Hill send the wrong signals to the Soviets of a divided U.S. front.

Kampelman felt otherwise. He felt he could successfully woo and co-opt the Hill.

"Mr. President," Kampelman bluntly said, "I would like authorization to explore a workable solution with the Hill." The president agreed.

In the ensuing days, Kampelman shrewdly worked out a deal with Robert Byrd, the Senate majority leader. The senators would be observers, not negotiators, and they would be briefed on the sessions, but not sit in on them.

Many who watched the episode, reading the tea leaves of the administration's shifting alliances, were surprised. The expectation was that

Kampelman and Perle, friends, soul-mates from the Committee on the Present Danger and years of battle within the Democratic party, would eagerly line up together. Instead, they disagreed from the start. It was a subtle disagreement, partially but by no means exclusively along institutional lines, but revealing nonetheless.

Kampelman demonstrated that he intended to conduct negotiations his way.

PERLE RESPECTED AND liked Kampelman. He *knew* there would be differences in opinion. They had different styles, but Perle felt Kampelman had suitably twitted the Soviets in the Madrid conference, tying them down for four hundred hours until the Soviets finally caved, signing a document that could carry the label, as a colleague once said, "Proudly Made in the U.S.A."

Perle also understood that institutional lines invariably create friction. Much had been made in the press about Jeane Kirkpatrick's tensions with Elliott Abrams. This, he felt, was poppycock, an inevitable by-product of a hopeless institutional conflict in the lines of authority between the U.N. and the State Department. Kampelman now was in the State Department. Of course they would clash.

He wasn't worried that Kampelman might go off half-cocked the way Nitze had with the walk in the woods. Kampelman was a man of considerable discipline. Moreover, Kampelman was only as good as the leverage Washington gave him, which, if Perle had any say, would be not much, at least toward SDI. He felt Max would be "great" in overseeing the arms reduction side of the talks, where there was a glimmer of hope that equitable deals and deep cuts could eventually be secured.

And anyway, Perle had an ace in the hole: his DoD reps to the negotiations. If Kampelman were swept away by the State Department mind-set, or the lure of agreements, he would have forewarning from his guys in Geneva.

What he didn't realize was that fierce jockeying would happen so soon.

IF THE MATCH of Ronald Reagan and Max Kampelman seemed like it was staged in heaven, it had been a long, circuitous path to this elevated appointment.

After the successful conclusion of the Madrid conference on human rights, Kampelman returned to his spacious corner office at Fried, Frank, Harris, Shriver and Kampelman in the Watergate complex overlooking the Potomac River. He was once one of the leading rainmakers of this august firm, but now the reins of management responsibilities had passed on to newer, younger, more eager hands. Here, with his two loyal secretaries, he could settle into the comfortable routine of the well-heeled Washington lawyer: power lunches with members of Congress, stylish social events, legal cases here and there, and of course, special government duties for the president.

Quickly, the diversions of government assignments held sway. During 1984, he made six high-profile trips abroad on government business: they included a heartfelt mission to Europe on behalf of Soviet Jewry; a difficult trip to El Salvador as co-chairman of the American delegation to observe this tumultuous Latin American country's presidential elections; and a return visit, a celebration of democracy, for José Napoleon Duarte's inauguration as El Salvador's president. On this trip, he and Shultz struck up a lengthy conversation. The chemistry clicked. Shultz invited Kampelman specially to accompany him to Nicaragua. Kampelman accepted. It was there that an increasingly close relationship between the secretary and the negotiator was given its first brace of sturdy cement.

But Kampelman quietly nurtured another interest: the Democratic party and the 1984 elections. To be sure, he stayed above the fray of partisan politics, that would have been unbecoming of him at this stage. But he shrewdly made sure to keep his name in circulation.

When Ben Wattenberg, the columnist and ebullient former White House aide to LBJ, called Kampelman to enlist him as chairman of the Coalition for a Democratic Majority Task Force on Foreign Policy, he doubted whether Kampelman would sign up. After all, Wattenberg reasoned, CDM continued to count itself among the ranks of the politically disaffected in the Democratic party (though most of its original members had already bolted ranks, and were now well placed throughout the mid and upper echelons of the Reagan administration). He fired off a letter of invitation to Kampelman and waited.

"I'm not sure the grand old man will accept," Wattenberg fretted, privately fearing that Kampelman might feel CDM didn't help him with the Democrats, and could hurt him with the Republicans if its activity smacked of Democratic party politics.

To Wattenberg's pleasant surprise, Kampelman said "yes, of course." (Others noted that Max's desire to bring his party back to the political center was a labor of deep conviction, since McGovern's effective takeover of the party in 1972.) Handled deftly, this high-powered task force would have another benefit: keeping Kampelman's name in play.

That his co-chair of the task force was R. James Woolsey was also a plus. Woolsey, a defense expert who radiated a youthful vigor and a

Rhodes Scholar's smarts, was another high-powered neoconservative Democrat who felt more at ease with defense Republicans than most Democrats (his distaste for Carter was so great that his normally courteous and charming ways broke down at Carter's mention. Woolsey, his friends noted, derisively called the Georgian by his seldom used formal name, "James Earl Carter"). Woolsey palled around with Les Aspin, but also with Richard Perle and former Kissinger NSC deputy Brent Scowcroft, and freely lent his services to the Republicans. He let it be known he was available for further service. He was thus a good partner for Kampelman.

Together, Kampelman and Woolsey assembled a blue-chip list of serious foreign policy and defense experts to present an alternative platform to the Democrats. Their goal was to get the Democrats to say more about Soviet totalitarianism and to accept the need for a powerful military program to undergird U.S. policy.

In the late spring, Kampelman flew up to New York City and even testified on behalf of CDM before the Democratic Platform Committee. At first, the Democrats were in a quandary when Kampelman made his request. It was unthinkable to turn down such a vaunted member of the foreign policy establishment; yet he was a Reagan appointee, whose hard-line views didn't sit well with a party that still supported a nuclear freeze as policy, opposed SDI, and decried Reagan's hard-nosed stance with the Soviets. Eventually, the Democrats relented when CDM made a stink and threatened to take the whole story to the press.

With Democratic delegates clustered around him at a huge horseshoe table, Kampelman urged the party to call for a global program of rallying support for democracy, and to negotiate with the Soviets from strength, ending his statement with a line from Edmund Burke.

To say he didn't make a splash at the Democratic hearing would be an understatement. What Kampelman was saying, the Platform Committee, dominated by liberal Kennedy staff, including the famed Paul Tulley and a savvy young lawyer, Susan Estrich, and following the general tenor of the candidates in the campaign, wasn't buying. That day, the talk focused on "killing Star Wars" and "cutting needless defense spending."

Yet Kampelman's new activism stirred enthusiasm among his many admirers, and soon even his detractors had to take notice. Morton Kondracke, a middle-of-the-road, Scoop Jacksonesque writer for *The New Republic*, wrote that Kampelman was the best choice to be Walter Mondale's secretary of state if the Democrats won. That same season, Kampelman gave a talk at an intimate but high-powered event about the need for the Democrats to move to the political center. Thirty people jammed into the living room of former ambassador and New York socialite Angier Biddle Duke's stately River House residence in Manhattan.

As the late afternoon sun set, songs of praise were sung for Kampelman not just by the likes of New York's Mayor Ed Koch, Pat Moynihan, and real estate magnate Daniel Rose, but by the sage of American political life and Kennedy scribe, Teddy White, who stayed through the entire event to record it for posterity.

When Kampelman finished his pitch ("the Soviets are ravaging Afghanistan, trampling human rights, piling up arms, but still we must talk to them"), White, peering through his trademark round wire glasses, with a smile on his small face, was one of the first people to stand up, raise his Duke University–embroidered glass, and join a toast to a Democratic party that would once again return to its roots and traditions. "Here, here," the group cheered. Yet the party that they had lifted their glasses to sadly seemed no longer to exist, except, as Woolsey quipped, to a "handful who could be squeezed into a telephone booth."

In ensuing weeks, the talk among the political class began: Kampelman was advising Walter Mondale—or more accurately, it seemed, Mondale was reaching out to his old friend, Max Kampelman. Whatever tremors this may have created among liberals eagerly vying for top positions in the newly emerged Mondale camp, the old warrior from Minnesota was reaching out across the spectrum of his party. It was a reassuring gesture to those who wanted to know that Democrats could stand firm with the Soviets and be trusted with the nation's security in these perilous times.

But the question still lingered. Was the interest in Kampelman real, or was this just another symbolic gesture of the quest for diversity gripping the Democrats as they gathered to nominate their standard bearer in the summer of 1984 in San Francisco? Mondale, looking elegant but tired, his eyes pocketed with bags, said little about foreign policy in his acceptance speech for his party's nomination, and seemed strangely worn out, lacking the burning zeal needed by a candidate.

It was instead Mario Cuomo's rousing rhetoric that stood out. He thundered: "We give money to Latin American governments that murder nuns" to wild applause and cheering. "And then lie about it." More cheering and balloons flying. The Democrats implied that it was the U.S.'s fault that the arms talks had broken down, even though it was the Soviets who had walked out. Word among the delegates was that the speech was the handiwork of Tim Russert, a former Moynihan staffer. But surely there was something positive that could be said about American foreign policy, and something troubling about Soviet policy; what about the Soviet SS-20s, or their aid to the Salvadoran guerrillas, their brutal war in Afghanistan, the shootdown of KAL 007, the repression of Soviet

Jews and the Polish labor movement, Solidarity, the party's more moderate and conservative members asked. The convention platform document was largely silent, despite platform staffer Madeleine Albright's insistence that the document was tough. ("Look, I care about the Soviets too," she intoned, but she could only point to a clause here, a phrase there, that suggested any of these themes.) The conservative Democrats left San Francisco largely dispirited, little listened to, feeling frozen out.

Still, few of Mondale's old associates believed this inflammatory rhetoric actually reflected his views; he was not Alan Cranston, a California liberal—though his continuing embrace of a nuclear freeze on the campaign trail and his tactical abandonment of being a passionate voice for human rights in Eastern Europe and the Soviet Union were hardly cause for optimism. That was all politics, it was hoped, for Mondale inspired genuine affection and respect across the board, not the least among his more conservative Democratic Party admirers. "Fritz wouldn't forget his roots as a labor supporter and anti-Communist," Wattenberg noted. "His instincts are still sound in the clutch."

But what did Kampelman think? *That* was the question. One day shortly before the convention, Kampelman and Wattenberg lunched at the fashionable Jean-Louis Watergate restaurant. The CDM task force had finalized its report, which called for a powerful defense program, and criticized the Reagan administration, not from the left, but the right. In this sense it was tailored to Kampelman's unique position as a man for both parties. But it also picked up an influential moderate signatory, who personally added his own input: Democrat Les Aspin.

The sun was shining brightly that day, and the restaurant, resplendent with green plants, was bathed in white light. Wattenberg wanted to know if Kampelman could sign on to the Democratic document. And could he pass it on to his friend, presidential candidate Walter Mondale?

Kampelman looked almost somber. He formed his fingers into a tepee on the shiny tablecloth, leaned back, and closed his eyes. He looked almost pained. "Fritz doesn't seem to understand the Soviets anymore, but this is, after all, a campaign." Long pause. "I need to talk to Jeane," he said, meaning Kirkpatrick. More silence. Kampelman looked as though he were meditating, slowly drawing in his thoughts like a long drag on a cigarette. You could have heard a pin drop.

Wattenberg turned to the report. Kampelman opened his eyes, and took a bite of his salad, and perked up.

"I like it," he said. "It's tough. These things need to be said."

Wattenberg, whose colleagues had labored over the document, heaved a pleased sigh of relief. Kampelman gave it his backing.

"Just one change, Ben," Kampelman said in a sturdy tone. "Wherever the report criticizes Ronald Reagan, I suggest we take out his name and put in 'the administration.' "

An associate later remarked how wily Kampelman was; in his well-ordered universe, everything had a purpose.

The task force report received rave reviews from moderate quarters of the media as a sound and centrist document: journalists Mort Kondracke and Fred Barnes weighed in with glowing praise, *The New Republic* lead editorial hailed it, the *Wall Street Journal* wished these were the Democrats who ran the party, and the influential Suzanne Garment, in her *Journal* column, gave it her imprimatur. So did Cord Meyer, the old CIA hand and cold warrior Democrat, and a classic liberal of the old school. But the media also hammered away at another point: this document, reflecting the Scoop Jackson wing of the party, had all but been rejected, eclipsed by the Jesse Jackson wing of the party.

Here, though, Mondale showed where his interests lay.

Later in the campaign season, the time came for him to receive the customary daylong classified national security briefing from the administration; this briefing was a time-honored tradition in American democracy. Its goal was to give the candidate, who could be president, a greater feel for foreign policy, and to minimize partisan excesses. When McFarlane called Mondale, he informed him that he could invite three people to join him. It was understood that these people would occupy high positions in a Mondale administration.

For the coveted places, Mondale tapped David Aaron, his former staff aide on the Hill, and a deputy to Brzezinski under Carter; the brusque but brilliant James Schlesinger, a former CIA chief and secretary of both defense and energy, and Kampelman. The night before, Mondale and the three men sat around the table for dinner at the former vice president's home in Minnesota. It was a reassuring evening. Kampelman felt Mondale had grown as a vice president, had an impressive intellect and a feel for details, and a commendable vision of his own for American leadership.

"He's a fox," an old friend described Kampelman. "He almost had the brass ring, secretary of state, in 1968 under Humphrey. It was a blow. Now he was where he wanted to be. Disappointed as he was with the Democrats, he was positioned for a Mondale victory—on his terms—without having burned his bridges with the Republicans."

When Mondale was trounced in the election, Kampelman didn't let it slow him down. Rumors flew that he would be Jeane Kirkpatrick's replacement at the United Nations. Kampelman would have liked this post, but it never materialized. One day, the well-connected and old-establishment journalist Joseph Kraft called Kampelman and asked cagily: "When are you going to the Middle East?" Kraft had been told by a member of the Saudi royal family that Kampelman would be selected as the new presidential envoy for the Middle East. This too didn't materialize.

Kampelman himself was never satisfied with the comfortable life of the well-heeled Washington lawyer. He was forever making trips and serving as an emissary at the behest of State, or Shultz, or the president himself. But his apparent lack of desire to reenter the fevered pitch of full-time government life in anything but the most significant of positions served only to make him more indispensable to those who would eventually see that he did.

At FIVE O'CLOCK in the morning on January 9, 1985, Kampelman was startled by the loud ring of the telephone. It was CBS News. Dan Rather had cabled from Geneva with the scoop that Kampelman had been selected to head up the arms negotiating team. Could he confirm it?

"I don't have any comment," Kampelman barked, neither denying nor confirming anything (it was news to him), and hung up.

After shaving and eating breakfast, Kampelman had to push his way through TV cameras camped out on the lawn of his Victorian mansion. There were more cameras at his law firm. No comment again.

He spoke to his wife, Maggie, that afternoon. They didn't want to live overseas at this point. He was also slated to have cataract surgery. This was no time to be jetting off abroad.

Kampelman called Larry Eagleburger, former undersecretary of state and Kissinger's partner in his consulting firm, and asked Eagleburger to pass on the message that he was not looking for another government assignment. Eagleburger rang him back the next day: "Mission accomplished." He also mentioned that the U.N. job was a live possibility. Great, Kampelman thought, this was a job he would like. With that, on Friday, Kampelman and Maggie hopped on a plane for an engagement in Aspen, Colorado.

That was when the tide turned.

Kampelman was relaxing in his hotel suite before going out to give a speech to a group of young business leaders when he heard the jingle of the phone. It was a joint call, from George Shultz and Caspar Weinberger. They said the president was going to ring him in ten minutes. The president wanted him to head the arms negotiations; they said Kampelman could not say no.

As he put down the phone, his thoughts were racing, all the reasons why this was not the time to take this job. He barely had time even to talk to his wife before he gently put down the receiver for a second time, after having just promised: "Of course, Mr. President, I would be happy to head the negotiations."

So THAT DAY, on the eve of his departure for the talks, Reagan held a breakfast with Kampelman and a bipartisan delegation of congressional leaders. The mood was one of anxious anticipation.

"I won't produce an agreement for the empty satisfaction of saying we had one," Kampelman proclaimed. "But," he insisted, "I will explore all avenues that might open up."

AT THE OUTSET of the negotiations, Kampelman knew he would have to deal with the conflicting egos and agendas of his team. There was the question of three separate delegations to the Geneva Nuclear and Space Talks (NST). Former Senator John Tower would head up the strategic arms talks (START); Mike Glitman, a career Foreign Service officer, would oversee the INF talks; and Kampelman the defense and space talks (SDI). While the INF and START talks picked up in part from where the Soviets had walked out in 1983, the defense and space talks were new. And Kampelman, as overall chief of the delegation, was first among equals.

From the very first day, the Soviets sought to formalize the linkage of the three fora: harking back to Gromyko, they emphasized that progress could only be made in INF or START arms reductions if the U.S. cut a deal on SDI. In turn, within the U.S. delegation, there were subtle yet critical differences in approach and style, but also in substance: whether to keep SDI, or to leverage it. This discord percolated slowly at first, and then relentlessly fed suspicion and backbiting in the delegation, and eventually surfaced as outright conflict.

ONE OF THE first delegation differences was over a seemingly innocuous issue: the Senate Arms Control Observer Group. Bob Bell, a professional staff member on the Senate Armed Services Committee and Sam Nunn's top arms control adviser, accompanied the senator early on to Geneva. He was six feet tall, stood bolt upright, was soft-spoken with sandy hair, and mild-mannered. He was, in almost every way, the senator's alter ego, the man who could speak authoritatively for Nunn. He knew that Shultz was skeptical about the Senate observer group, as was Perle, but Kampelman had gone to bat for them. So he and his boss were determined to be helpful when in Geneva. And for his part, Kampelman was always quick to brief the Senate delegation, rapidly laying aside institutional and party lines.

This didn't fly, however, with John Tower, the chief START negotiator, who had little use for the observer group. Short, dapper, articulate, abrasive, the Texas conservative and former chairman of the Senate Armed Services Committee had left the Senate only weeks earlier in disgust, convinced that partisan members were tying the hand of the president in foreign affairs. When it was said he made a swift transition from the legislative to the executive branch, he drawled slowly, "The transition was made some time ago. That is why I made my departure from the Senate."

At one point, Tower became furious when Mike Glitman, the INF negotiator, told him that one senator, a Democrat and future presidential aspirant, had pulled Victor Karpov, the chief Soviet representative, aside at a cocktail reception and said that he need not worry about SDI. "Why do you say that?" Karpov asked.

"Congress will take care of the program," the senator boasted.

Tower was appalled by the senator's indiscretion. Traditionally, members of the legislative branch never criticize the administration on foreign soil. (Even the liberal Rhode Island Democrat Claiborne Pell once told Russian expert Jim Billington, before a trip to the U.S.S.R., "One never criticizes his country when abroad, it just isn't done.") This senator's indiscretion, Tower thought, only undercut the American position, and dangerously breached the trust between the Senate and the executive. And increasingly, from that point on, Tower was particularly wary of Kampelman's bipartisan overtures.

INITIALLY, Kampelman spent as much time mediating among his colleagues as negotiating with the Soviets. The Soviets nurtured the hope that the talks would be a creative free-for-all in which *their* version of a compromise would emerge—one that would kill SDI, or at least restrict it. They thus invoked the "interrelationship" of the three groups, the word that Perle was so dead set against in the Shultz-Gromyko January communiqué.

The Russians set the tone at the very first plenary session in March 1985, when Victor Karpov delivered a scathing opening statement, insisting that for there to be an agreement, any agreement, it must entail a trade-off between offensive and defensive arms.

Not long after this meeting, the U.S. delegation met in the bubble—the hot, cramped bug-proof chamber inside the American mission—and argued about the Soviet attempt for a trade-off. Kampelman finally waved his hand in disgust, as they hotly debated the relationship of the three groups, and the desirability of a trade. "Let's not argue about theoretical issues that are not yet before us," he said.

One of the State Department representatives buttonholed Kampelman in private and complained about the Pentagon "obstructionists."

"Look," Kampelman replied sternly, "learn to live with these guys. If you leave guys like that off, they'll knife you when you come up with something. Let them participate."

IN THE HIDEBOUND bitter opening months, Kampelman was skeptical of the Soviet sincerity to bargain in good faith. He resisted the constant drumbeat emanating out of the State Department, including from Shultz's adviser Paul Nitze, to explore ways to trade SDI for deep cuts in Soviet ballistic offensive missiles. In this sense, he agreed with Weinberger and Perle: a premature move could only lead to a bad deal.

Yet Kampelman was not a theoretician, but a negotiator. He harbored the notion that a trade-off could eventually be made. He decided he would bide his time. Often, once a week, he would assemble the entire delegation together to discuss the progress in each of the groups. He felt combining the sessions was both productive and therapeutic. He hoped that eventually he would get a sign, a debrief, a telling hint that a deal would be in hand.

JOHN WOODWORTH WAS back in Geneva, as part of the INF delegation in the talks. He was struck by how dispirited the Soviets seemed, how shocked they were by the fact that the Americans had stood up to them during the tense final months of the INF deployments, and by the fact that the Soviets, not the Americans, had blinked. He was convinced their confidence was shattered by the experience. It also reminded him of what Perle had told him back in 1982, when there were second thoughts, doubts, and self-recriminations in the delegation after the walk in the woods. "We just have to drive them hard."

Washington, he felt, now held all the cards.

Now, more than ever, he reasoned this was the time not to make unnecessary concessions. So it troubled him that the delegation was continually debating "how, when, and if" they should put limits on SDI.

As the early months went by, Woodworth became convinced that Kampelman was searching for a deal on SDI. He and Glitman, the head of the INF delegation, nurtured deep reservations about the way Kampelman was always combining the delegations, trying to foster one unified point of view. This, he felt, was a bid for an eventual giveaway of SDI.

He thought Kampelman should instead be emphasizing the separate quality of each delegation, and not play into Soviet hands—particularly with the Geneva summit approaching in November.

BEFORE SUMMER BROKE, Perle had one of his staffers report back to him on the progress of the talks. His aide flew to Geneva and spent a number of days meeting with the different delegations, mainly listening to members of all ranks. He found bitter internecine warfare, and feared that without Perle's intervention it would get worse.

He reported that the Defense Department representatives were "digging in for protracted battle," but were "catching shrapnel from the State tea sippers, the ACDA giveaway lawyers, the Joint Chiefs of Staff light charge—and the Soviets."

"I've just listened," he noted. "The need appears to stem from the jockeying by all three delegations and the different approaches to the talks within and between negotiations." The Pentagon guys were engaged in "barefisted fighting with State," and, he said, they feared "it's an uphill battle."

On the positive side, he noted that Kampelman "looks good, appears to be getting tough with the Soviets, and is learning to say *nyet* to 196 Soviet delegates."

Nothing was to be taken for granted, however. "The bottom line," he wrote, "is this place needs Perle's intervention and PTT: Perle's TENDER touch."

PERLE WAS PROUD of his staff. The arms negotiations were bound to be rough, with members of the delegation, representing their respective agencies and constituencies, coming into conflict. It would be particularly tough for the handful of Pentagon representatives, who were not charged with securing an agreement per se, but with faithfully representing America's defense needs.

Perle made a mental note to keep on top of the situation. But for now, he couldn't afford distractions. Weinberger had wanted to go to the summit, but Shultz had maneuvered successfully to cut him out of the loop. Instead, along with Fred Iklé, Perle would be the department's representative.

Through the grapevine, he also heard that Kampelman had suggested to Shultz that there be a joint communiqué as a centerpiece of the summit. Already, State was crafting countless agreements for signature with the Soviets, all smelling strongly of détente.

But Perle was consoled by one thought. His philosophy about Ronald Reagan was that if the president were given the straight facts and information, his actions and instincts would ineluctably bring him to the right conclusions. He mused that many at State, though not Shultz, were convinced that Reagan would invariably make the wrong decision—which is why they always sought to stack the deck with their presentations in briefings, talking points for the president, and draft communiqués.

As THE PACE quickened toward the summit, Kampelman returned to Washington to brief Shultz. "There's an almost plaintive effort by the Soviets to give an appearance of progress," he told the secretary. He then dropped the news. "The Soviets have tried hard to come up with words for a joint summit communiqué. At times they seem rather desperate: can't we find some words?"

Shultz told Kampelman that the Pentagon was violently opposed, but he had raised it with the president anyway. Reagan, when hearing of Weinberger's extreme dissent, snapped at Shultz that he too was opposed to this.

Instead of precooking a communiqué, Reagan told Shultz rather angrily that he had decided that he and the new, dynamic young leader of the Soviet Union, Mikhail Gorbachev, would produce an agreed-upon statement if they felt there was something worth saying.

Shultz felt this was "chancy," but if it was what the president wanted, then so be it. Still, it was unusual for a summit.

It was a gamble on Reagan's part. But before the summit even began, the intense jockeying to influence the outcome started in earnest—with a leaked letter from Weinberger to Reagan, which, in full glare of the public, had all the markings of Perle's fingerprints all over it.

With the Geneva summit less than a week away, Perle was working at a frenetic pace. His shop was a whirlwind of activity: position papers had to be firmed up, talking points massaged for the president, final meetings held. This cauldron of initiatives was leading up to the same goal: inserting the Pentagon back into the decision loop, ensuring that the views of the Defense Department would not be given short shrift once the summit was fully under way.

The early signs were not heartening. Perle was furious that DoD had been cut out of the pre-summit communiqué writing—hell, the Soviets had been given a copy even before *they* had; and it was a good thing that Weinberger had personally interceded with the president and helped put the kibosh on the communiqué. Now he had to make sure DoD was not similarly being cut out of writing the final talking points that would go to the president, although the scuttlebutt was that State had already outmaneuvered the Pentagon on this.

Anxiously stitching all possible loose ends together, he realized there was another thing he had to tend to. At one point, Perle buzzed over to the secretary of defense's office to see if the "Soviet arms violations letter" had been sent.

"Terrific," he exclaimed, when informed that the secretary had a final draft in hand.

The letter was a parting shot, a last-minute attempt to put the Pentagon's definitive stamp on the summit, to boldly influence the president's arms control positions and stiffen Reagan's resolve in his meetings with Gorbachev. In muscular language, Weinberger warned Reagan that at Geneva he would be buffeted by Soviet demands, and would "come under great pressure" to "limit SDI under the restrictive interpretation of the ABM treaty," and "to agree to continue to observe SALT II."

Drafted by Perle, the letter sounded alarms about agreeing to any "communiqué or other language that enables the Soviets to appear equally committed to full compliance—even as they continue to enlarge their pattern of violations." It spoke clearly and unambiguously (keep SDI, hold the Soviets accountable on cheating, don't be taken by warm words or promises, stick to U.S. interests), free of bureaucratic temporizing or the amorphous mush that so often composed the lexicon of diplomats. (One State Department paper for the summit indicated that after long years of "misunderstandings," "opportunities" had come and the president could perhaps "propose new guidelines" for the negotiators— the sort of warmed-over fluff that could have been written at virtually anytime, for any meeting.)

Even if Weinberger weren't there himself, the president would know exactly where *he* stood. But almost immediately, the letter touched off a firestorm of controversy about how tough and how firm the president should be in Geneva.

THE VIOLATIONS LETTER had been in the works for days, and was now ready to be finalized. After Caspar Weinberger personally signed his letter to the president on the thick cream paper bearing the red-and-blue-taloned seal of the secretary of defense, the ink barely dry, it was promptly clipped to an unclassified Department of Defense report on "Soviet Violations of Arms Control Treaties," photocopied, filed, and the original put into a double-sealed envelope. As a sign of the letter's importance, it was hand-delivered to the president's office by special courier. Reagan could read through it that evening.

The government courier quickly crossed the Memorial Bridge, pulled into the side entrance of the White House, and made his way past the guards manning the opulent lobby. From there, the letter was immediately delivered to the president's office, where it was meticulously logged in and put directly in the crisp pile reserved for his summit reading. As is customary practice, copies of the letter were then routed to the secretary of state, the White House chief of staff, the national security adviser, the director of Central Intelligence, and the head of the Arms Control and Disarmament Agency.

Inside the Pentagon itself, Weinberger was adamant that the contents of the letter remain under wraps, and warned his small circle of advisers familiar with the letter not to discuss it. As he never tired of repeating in morning staff meetings, he hated press leaks. The secretary's rigid discipline was maintained this time by the fact that less than a handful of his closest advisers even knew of the letter's existence, and only Weinberger himself and his trusted military assistant, Colin Powell, had seen the final version.

When the letter was logged into the Oval Office, it was Wednesday, November 13. Now what remained was to sit tight, and watch the results of the letter unfold.

FRANK GAFFNEY WASN'T going to the summit. But his team was working overtime, helping Perle get ready. In a brief moment of downtime, he kicked back and was chatting with some of his colleagues.

What's the best outcome for the summit?

Gaffney smiled intensely. "Nothing. One where nothing is given away."

PERLE AGREED WITH Gaffney's formulation, however starkly put or crude it might appear to critics. He felt the arms control and negotiations process too often lulled the U.S. into substituting hope and fear for the harsh realities of international conflict and for the verities of rational analysis. Since the Geneva meeting in January, he had come to respect and even admire Shultz, as a "thoroughly decent and admirable man." But he felt that the secretary had one blind spot: a greater commitment to the arms control process than he thought was wise.

Yet despite some intellectual differences, the relationship between the two men had continued to deepen. On the long flight home from Geneva the previous January, Shultz called Perle forward to his cabin in the plane. "I've heard a lot of negative things about you," Shultz said, "including from many of my own people in the State Department."

Perle said nothing. He wanted to make sure he knew where the conversation was going.

"You were extremely helpful, and I'm inclined to discount what I've heard."

Perle uttered a cautious, "Thank you, Mr. Secretary, I appreciate that."

Shultz continued, almost lightly: "I just want you to know that my door is open to you anytime, and I hope we can talk about the important issues, often."

What did this mean? What was the secretary really getting at? Perle was flattered, but he wasn't sure what to make of what the secretary had said. He didn't believe that he could just pick up the phone and initiate a one-on-one conversation with the secretary of state. That was rare for Shultz's own assistant secretaries, he thought. For Defense Department officials, it just wasn't done at all.

Later that week, however, Perle was stunned when his secretary, Bobbi, urgently buzzed him. "It's the secretary of state, he wants to talk to you."

Perle completely forgot about the conversation the two had had on the plane. The secretary of state didn't call assistant secretaries of defense every day—let alone ever. He wondered what was up.

Shultz cheerily got on the other end of the line: "I thought you'd have already come by to have a chat with me. Why, it's been almost a week already since my invitation."

That same afternoon, Perle rearranged his calendar and dashed over to talk with Shultz, the first of a number of private consultations. It was, to be sure, an unusual arrangement, but it served both their purposes. For Shultz, it enabled him to pick Perle's brain, to get a read on Pentagon thinking. It also enabled him to keep his own people honest, to ensure that he wasn't overlooking anything and that he was getting a balanced, enlarged picture. They never knew exactly what he and Perle discussed; this way, Shultz could use Perle as a hedge against his own people misleading him. He also genuinely enjoyed the give and take with Perle, and was thoroughly convinced that Perle had been vastly underestimated by his detractors.

For his part, Perle was warned by his staff that the arrangement was too suspicious, that Shultz was cleverly trying to drive a wedge between Perle and Weinberger. "Be careful," they exhorted.

Perle didn't disagree. He felt Shultz would have liked for nothing more than to undermine Weinberger. "I go into these meetings with my eyes wide open," he said. To make sure no wrong signals were sent, he kept Weinberger fully informed.

But he saw important bureaucratic benefits to these meetings. Direct access to the secretary of state was a tightly controlled privilege, "something that some twenty assistant secretaries of state heatedly vied for." So every time he went to see Shultz, Perle reasoned that it stiffened his clout in his ongoing contest with State. The perception of power magnified into actual power, outside his usual purview of the Pentagon. Now, more than ever, Perle was someone to be reckoned with.

It was also a fact that despite their deep disagreements over arms control issues, Shultz and Perle agreed on other matters. Perle had reservations about Weinberger's rigid criteria for the use of force, and privately agreed with Shultz (who was more willing to use force) in this running feud with Weinberger over the employment of American power abroad. He also admired Shultz's deep commitment to human rights. Shultz was, he thought, far more passionate about this issue than his own State Department aides. Finally, there was another benefit. Given their new relationship, Shultz was more receptive to including Perle in key decisions.

This was a card that Perle intended to play—at the Geneva summit if he had to.

. . .

SATURDAY MORNING, ALL hell broke loose; the Weinberger letter had been leaked to the *New York Times*. Reprinted in full, it immediately touched off a firestorm of controversy, crowding out other headlines, even threatening to cloud the mounting euphoria over the summit, just two days away.

Fingers immediately pointed to Perle for having leaked the letter. An angry Bud McFarlane told reporters that "someone was trying to sabotage the summit," leaving little doubt that he felt the culprit was Perle. That neither the letter nor the violations report was classified only invited a leak—an ingenious touch that was chalked up to Perle's Machiavellian handiwork.

On the eve of another major U.S.-Soviet meeting, Perle was, once again, in the eye of swirling controversy.

PERLE VEHEMENTLY DENIED that he was behind the leak. He was quick to note that the letter he sent to the secretary of defense's office was in draft form, with "Caspar W. Weinberger" auto-penned on the signature line— standard form for secretary of defense correspondence. The final copy that went out was different; the close read "Very respectively yours," and was signed simply "Cap." He hadn't even seen the final version; nor did he have a copy in his files, which only the secretary and Powell had.

Thus, it could only have been leaked by a recipient, which Perle reasoned was someone who objected to the substance of the letter. He didn't hide *his* contention that it could only have come from State.

GEORGI ARBATOV, SOVIET spokesman and director of the U.S.A. and Canada Institute (Shultz liked to refer to him as a "Soviet propagandist"), was outraged. He labeled the letter "a direct attempt to torpedo the whole arms control process." The issue continued to mushroom, and it was soon raised with the president himself.

A reporter shouted, "Are you going to fire Caspar Weinberger over this?" Reagan didn't rise to the bait. He fired back, "Hell, no!"

PERLE FELT IT was important to keep Weinberger closely informed as the summit unfolded.

So this time, in addition to the countless briefing papers stuffed into his bulging briefcase, he brought along a secure communication telephone, a portable briefcase-sized device that included a special classified system, complete with a crypto key that once removed would foil intruders seeking to access the phone. In a pinch, this device would enable Perle to speak directly to Weinberger without fear of being tapped by the Soviets. If necessary, he could sneak off and consult with Weinberger—and if an emergency were to arise, he felt Cap could put in a call directly to the president.

He also received a purloined advance copy of the extensive summit schedule, laid out in minute-by-minute detail in a book issued by the Presidential Advance Office. Entitled *The Trip of the President to Geneva, Switzerland, November 16–20, 1985,* this thick blue-covered trip book, bearing the seal of the president and affixed with a heavy industrial-size staple in the top left corner, was little bigger than a four-by-six index card. But the book was an indispensable piece of information, and for the summit participants it was known as the "bible."

In the bible, every move of the summit was detailed in meticulous diagrams, extensive charts, and lengthy scripts showing where the participants would sit in each meeting, which staff members would be included in the various briefings, who would ride with whom in the government limousines, and where communications and meeting facilities would be. Nothing was omitted or left to chance—which meant Perle could look through the book to see exactly the role he would be expected to play.

Understandably, summit participants pored over this book like anxious parents reading through catalogues from Yale or Princeton for their overachieving children. The book wasn't officially distributed until the summit participants on Air Force One and Flight 2600, the backup aircraft, had departed for Geneva, only heightening the suspense. Luckily, Perle had an advance copy.

Perle hungrily leafed through the pages, looking for his name. To his horror, he saw a number of meetings in which he wasn't included, labeled innocuously "operations meetings." There were a number of other "working lunches" where he was left out. He also was shocked to read for Thursday, the final day after the Summit: "Joint Event with General Secretary Gorbachev—Witnessing the Signing of Bilateral Agreements (if ready)"; it was clear that the State Department was looking to expand the scope of the summit as much as possible, and was gearing up for signed agreements.

It was also unclear if he would be part of any team that would negotiate a joint statement or communiqué that might emerge, let alone concrete bilateral agreements. He knew this spelled trouble.

Perle felt he had little choice. As soon as he had the opportunity, he would have to go directly to Shultz to clarify his role. It also meant he might be calling Weinberger sooner than he thought.

ONCE AIRBORNE, PERLE read through his copy of the master briefing book, a large, three-ring binder with talking points on virtually every subject that could arise with Gorbachev. Simple-looking on its face, the book was the product of repeated interagency fighting and guerrilla skirmishes. Every word, every comma and period, every sentence, had been picked apart, negotiated, dissected. In the end, the president could decide to chuck them all aside (given his lack of enthusiasm for large tomes and instinctive feel for the issues, this was a safe bet). But the dirty secret was that he would surely leaf through the book and, at times that *only* he would decide, follow its script to the letter.

Before leaving, Frank Gaffney had passed to Perle a handwritten note with some bureaucratic intelligence he had picked up: "The president's briefing book is a scandal. The talking points have been switched."

Leafing thorough the book, Perle's face flushed. The points hadn't exactly been switched, as Gaffney had been led to believe. But they had been so demonstrably altered, so watered down in the final version, as to be almost unrecognizable from what had been agreed upon in the interagency process. It was a sham.

But there was one insuperable problem. He was flying to Geneva on Flight 2600, while Shultz, and the president, were on Air Force One; the president was probably in his front compartment shuffling through his briefing books right now. And Perle was powerless to do anything about it.

This meant he had another problem to raise with Shultz. It was an endless, stinking battle, he thought to himself. And a hell of a way to start a summit.

BY THE TIME Air Force One and Flight 2600 touched down at Cointrin Airport in Geneva at 10:25 on the eve of November 16, the press was already camped out. Over three thousand journalists had registered to cover the summit, and a giant press plane carrying two hundred members of the American press corps alone had already pulled into Gate 17, a full hour in advance of the administration.

The weather was forecast to be "cold and clear," but instead a subfreezing chill swept menacingly across the city. This didn't stop the press. Double lines of Swiss security guards and police, each holding batons, formed an unbroken chain to protect the president when he emerged. Behind them, and scattered throughout in ominous reserve, were advance teams of Secret Service agents, prowling the grounds in their long trench coats for any conceivable irregularity, faces grim, miniature radios at the ready; concurrently, crack Swiss sharpshooters scanned surrounding buildings for possible trouble. Docked in formation was the president's escort: his Cadillac limousine, half a dozen motorcycle vehicles that roared above the din of the bitter cold wind, and two Secret Service chase cars.

The red lights of the motorcade flicked endlessly, brushing on and off the velvety asphalt and a light sheet of snow splayed across the runway. It was a hypnotic, almost dreamlike scene.

And then there was the press horde, shivering in heavy overcoats and crowding the runway on hastily erected viewing stands, ready to record for history the first words of the president. Live television crews furiously maneuvered for position. Stiff cold winds swirled women's skirts. The U.S. flag snapped and tossed in the cold.

The president, wrapped in a heavy jacket, emerged onto a specially built dais erected for Air Force One; after saluting the honor guard, he stepped to the microphone. Turning briefly to shake hands with Swiss president Kurt Furgler, he looked out over the crowd. This was the moment, the beginning, for which much of the world had hungered anxiously.

Yet the president appeared surprisingly gaunt and strangely tired. His voice was listless, lacking its usual verve.

"There are deep differences between the U.S. and the Soviet Union," he declared. But, he noted optimistically, he fervently hoped this would be a time for a fresh beginning.

"I hope this is the start of a new era that will open the way for peace that will endure beyond my presidency," he declared.

The summit would begin in earnest on Tuesday. But among the ranks of the staff, the jockeying relentlessly continued.

ON MONDAY, SHULTZ called Perle into his suite, and motioned him into an eight-foot-high box, the secure bubble in the secretary's room.

"I'd like to be part of the team that negotiates any joint statement," Perle said. He sucked in his breath. If Shultz nixed this, it would be a disaster.

Shultz, looking collected, repeated that he thought Perle did a great job in the January meeting. Perle nodded. Shultz then said, "There's no problem with you participating, but understand that Roz Ridgway (the assistant secretary of state for European affairs) will be in charge of the team."

Perle said that wouldn't be a problem, he had worked well with her before. Some people at the Pentagon thought she could be difficult, but he had few qualms about working with her, and respected her.

The two then discussed SDI. Shultz told Perle that he felt the Pentagon was misleading the president about what could be achieved in the SDI program operating within the ABM treaty restraints.

Perle sharply disagreed. He said, "The sort of restraints the Soviets were looking for would effectively kill SDI; you just can't confine it to the laboratory the way they want.

"Ultimately," Perle said, "you have to choose between SDI and the narrow interpretation of the ABM treaty; you can't have it both ways."

Now Shultz disagreed.

Perle was frustrated at his inability to convince Shultz. He thought his mind was made up, and he was listening to the wrong people on the issue. But as he left, Perle felt overall this meeting was a success: he and Shultz had reached that point where the two could disagree amiably. More important, he would now be included in the working group that would negotiate over the statement, which would enshrine any definitive policy that would emerge out of the Reagan-Gorbachev talks.

He didn't bother to raise the matter of the talking points. At this juncture, he felt it would have been futile.

MONDAY, PERLE SPOKE to Leslie. She asked how everything was going.

He thought to himself that the president had looked unusually tired and drawn, but he didn't want the Soviets to think there was a problem. He fibbed, and told Leslie everything was great, that the president looked fantastic, "in top form."

He hated not telling her the strict truth, but he felt this little deception was in the interest of national security. Leslie understood that Richard did this. If the Soviets were listening in on this call, he at least wouldn't be giving them any comfort in knowing that the president was nervous, and was not at his best. Perle took a small but pure delight in trying to foil the Soviets this way.

THE PRESIDENT WAS the official host for the first day of the talks at the Pometta Residence, Château Fleur d'Eau, an elegant nineteenth-century privately owned villa on the western shore of Lake Geneva.

At 10:05 on Tuesday morning, as Gorbachev's motorcade pulled up to the residence, the seventy-five-year-old Reagan made a snap decision. He shed his heavy coat and discarded his scarf, and bounded out energetically into the cold, hatless and coatless, to greet the fifty-four-year-old Gorbachev. The general secretary was tightly bundled in a thick topcoat and brown fedora, and, though two decades junior to the president, appeared older and more frail.

The two men tightly clenched hands and locked gazes, less like fighters in a ring than two old political pros, before the flash of the cameras, and then quickly moved inside.

Inside the Pometta house, despite countless hours of preplanning and scripting by advance teams, there was initial confusion: the awkward mingling of U.S. and Soviet officials, the clatter of different languages, and uncertainty over directions (notwithstanding the bible). Some officials moved into the spacious first-floor Petite Salon for coffee and an exchange of opening remarks between delegations, while others dutifully climbed the winding stairs to the second floor, where they would be held in reserve in the holding room.

Now things were moving at a rapid clip.

The president and a nervous Gorbachev were flanked only by their interpreters. Reagan guided the general secretary into the Blue Room. They were scheduled to talk for fifteen minutes. A fire was blazing and there was a scent of burning pine. As they entered, the heavy doors closed behind them. Their room remained guarded by stony-faced security guards.

After six tense years between the two superpowers, the two leaders were now together, alone, unencumbered by staff, nestled in a phantasmagoric outpost that had been a gathering point for adversaries since John Calvin and the Reformation in the sixteenth century, when Europe attracted refugees from religious persecution. Back then, Geneva had been dubbed "the city of causes."

The Geneva summit had begun.

Fixing himself in his chair, the president discarded his talking points on three-by-five cards and spoke extemporaneously. "There are all these people in the next room. They have given us fifteen minutes to meet in this one-on-one, and we can do that and spend the next three days doing what they have written for us. We can do that, or we can create history and do things that the world will remember in a positive way."

Reagan had already decided there was something about Gorbachev he liked, a certain warmth to his face, not the harsh coldness he associated with earlier Soviet leaders.

Listening to Reagan, Gorbachev had shaken his jitters. The day before, he told his staff that Reagan should be given the courtesy due an older man. For his part, Gorbachev was wrestling with his own political position at home. The new Soviet leader had sought to inject dynamism into the aging, decrepit Soviet Communist order, and had hinted to his Politburo that there could be changes in some of the basic foreign policy stances of the Soviet Union. At the same time, military competition with the U.S., SDI in particular, could cripple his country; he sought respite from this.

Later that morning, he would sharply tell the president: "Make no mistake, we can match you whatever you do, you should not have illusions about being able to bankrupt the Soviet Union."

He would also tell the president: "Our SDI will be cheaper and better than yours."

But the first tête-à-tête was an ice-breaker. The Soviet and American teams fretted nervously outside, waiting for the meeting to break after the designated fifteen minutes.

An hour later, the two men were still deep in conversation.

"Here we are," Reagan said wistfully, "two men in a room, and probably the only two in the world who could start World War III, or perhaps make peace and avoid the scourge of war."

Just as suddenly as the two men had withdrawn behind closed doors, a long ninety minutes later, the two leaders emerged, both radiating broad smiles. Whatever their political differences as leaders, as politicians, as men, they had connected.

But as the time came to translate this personal connection into concrete agreement during the waning hours of the summit, the rest would not be so easy.

THAT AFTERNOON, WHILE Reagan and Gorbachev sat across from each other at a long oval table, the president invited the general secretary once again to depart from the schedule. He asked Gorbachev to take a stroll in the fresh air. They could walk down to the heated summerhouse, along the winding pathway by the lake. Gorbachev immediately accepted.

Alone again, sitting in large overstuffed white chairs on rich Oriental rugs by a crackling fire, the two continued their discussion of arms control. Gorbachev stressed the "interrelationship" between cuts in offensive arms and halting weapons in space.

No, no, the president disagreed, "SDI would help rid the world of the scourge of nuclear weapons."

Gorbachev paused, and asked Reagan what he had in mind when he spoke earlier of complying with the ABM treaty.

"The laboratory theory simply isn't enough," Reagan said, indicating he was sticking with the broad interpretation. But then, to underscore the cooperative nature of the program that he envisioned, he made a remarkable offer: if the SDI research is successful, the United States could share the results of the work with the Soviet Union. The two could enjoy security together.

He continued, speaking directly and passionately: "The current doctrine is uncivilized. People want defense and they look at the sky and think what might happen if missiles suddenly appear and blow up everything in our country; people don't want that."

Gorbachev responded: "The missiles are not flying, and whether they would fly depends on how we conduct our respective policies. The Soviet Union wants to stop SDI before it is started."

The meeting was now deadlocked. After sixty-five minutes, the two men stood up, donned their overcoats, and strolled casually back to the château. Before they rejoined their teams, Reagan gestured that he wanted to say something. The two men paused.

"Why don't we have the next summit meeting next year in the United States?" This was a principal goal of the summit, and virtually every one of Reagan's aides had advised him not to broach this subject first. But he was the president. He forged ahead, acting on his instincts. They turned out to be accurate.

Without hesitation, Gorbachev, smiling, said, "I accept. But you've never seen the Soviet Union. Let's have the next one the following year in the Soviet Union."

This meant three summits in three years, more regular contact than had been made between U.S. and Soviet leaders since the difficult days of World War II. It was a spellbinding, even historic sight, right there, even then.

Reagan had repeatedly reminded his delegation, "this is our main adversary in the world, let's not forget that." But the personal rapport between Ronald Reagan, lifelong anti-establishment, small-town boy, populist cold warrior, and Mikhail Gorbachev, smart, with nerves of steel, a dreamy visionary in his own right, a moody and often long-winded KGB protégé of Yuri Andropov, whom Andrei Gromyko once described as "a man with a nice smile but iron teeth," had burgeoned almost immediately, forming an inextricable bond between that rarest brotherhood of men, the heads of state of the two most powerful countries in the world.

. . .

DINNER WAS A lighthearted affair. There was no real movement on any issues of substance during the day, but as evening broke, the mood was
defined by hearty laughter over shot glasses of vodka, fine Russian
caviar and jovial toasts, and rich food. Before dinner, the Soviets agreed
to begin work on an agreed-upon statement. So the real work, putting
conflicting ideas to common paper, translating policy rhetoric into definitive proclamation, would commence.

THE MORNING SESSION of the summit was hosted by the Soviets at their
mission, a large self-sufficient compound of a dozen buildings resembling a small city, tucked mysteriously behind foreboding heavy iron
gates. The stark utilitarian architecture of the gray buildings, jutting
out like a prison, was punctuated by the ornate nineteenth-century
Villa Rosa, the home of a former Reformed Church clergyman from St.
Petersburg. This was where Gorbachev slept, but the meetings themselves were held in the austere confines of the main administrative
building.

At the morning briefing, Roz Ridgway, the head of the American team
negotiating the communiqué, explained to Shultz that the Americans
were getting nowhere with the Soviets. "There is not a single formulation
of ours they can accept," she told the secretary in a state of exasperation.
"We have a lot of work ahead."

For Perle, groggy with too little sleep, but pumped up with adrenaline,
the summit had begun to resemble an air traffic control system: a swarm
of activity and lots of people rushing busily around, with something
bound to crash. In the holding room of the Soviet administrative building
he was joined by Ridgway; Robert Linhard, a National Security Council
staff member; and Mark Palmer, a deputy assistant secretary of state.
The Soviet delegation was headed by Alexander Bessmertnykh, chief of
the United States Department in the Soviet Foreign Ministry; Victor Karpov, the Soviet arms negotiator; and Oleg Sokolov, the second ranking
diplomat in the Soviet embassy in Washington.

When the Soviets indicated that they would not sign an accord on
broadened cultural exchanges unless the U.S. agreed to the Soviet terms
of arms control language, Perle was not surprised. This, he felt, was just
the beginning of a very long day.

And if the morning meeting between Reagan and Gorbachev was any
indication, it was going to be more than just a long day—but a potentially deadly exercise in frustration, disagreement, and deadlock.

• • •

REAGAN AND GORBACHEV were meeting once again.

"We must do better, and we can," Reagan said passionately, seeking to convey his abhorrence of having to rely "on the ability to wipe each other out" as a means of keeping the peace.

Gorbachev sat there, his eyes flaring like a leopard in the jungle, waiting to pounce at any second. He and Reagan agreed on the desirability of cutting offensive strategic arms by 50 percent; they danced around but discussed positively the possibility of an INF agreement. Again, they were back to SDI.

"I don't know what's at the bottom of the U.S. position," Gorbachev said, vehemence rising in his voice. He had suggested it was fueled by "illusions" that the U.S. could deploy SDI to achieve military and technological superiority over the Soviet Union. His formerly calm demeanor now reached a feverish pitch.

He said heatedly, "I am reluctant to inject tension into this discussion, but everything is coming to a halt if we can't find a way to prevent the arms race in space."

Suddenly, Shultz burst out of the plenary session, strode quickly past the security guards, and buttonholed Perle next door.

"They are saying something important. You should hear this discussion," he said sternly. "Come inside with me. I want you there."

The two raced past the security guards back into the room. The heavy doors slammed shut behind them.

PERLE POSITIONED HIMSELF by the side of the room. The rest of the participants were like ghostly apparitions, drifting around the room, as Reagan and Gorbachev heatedly debated each other with a passion rarely witnessed between heads of state.

REAGAN GLANCED DOWN to his index cards, but then put them aside, once again speaking extemporaneously, and clearly from the heart. "SDI isn't going to conduct war in space. There are nuclear missiles which if used will kill millions, on both sides. Never in history has the prospect of a war that would bring about the end of civilization been out there. Even if everybody reduces missiles by 50 percent, it's too many weapons.

"SDI gets around that. The U.S. is building a defensive system; it's not an offensive system. I'm talking about a shield, not a spear."

Gorbachev then launched into a staccato response. "I hear your arguments, but I'm not convinced. It's emotional, part of one man's dream. The reality is SDI would open a new arms race."

As Gorbachev spoke, Reagan scribbled some language on a yellow piece of paper, turned to Shultz and McFarlane and whispered, "Have a look at this and see if it makes sense. I've written down a possible compromise." With that, he began speaking again.

Meanwhile, Shultz and McFarlane energetically took the yellow paper, looked at it and motioned with hand signals to Perle to join them. Cupping his mouth to muffle his voice, Shultz asked Perle, "Do you think this helps?" Perle studied it quickly, deciphering the president's handwriting. He didn't want to get this wrong, there was too much at stake. He didn't, however, like what he read. "This is not right," he thought, "it's just not right."

REAGAN CONTINUED, "WE are at the point where the two sides are going to have to get beyond suspicions. We're trying, the United States, to see if there is a way to end the world's nightmare of nuclear weapons."

Gorbachev interrupted, "Why don't you believe me when I say the Soviet Union will never attack?"

Reagan started to speak, and Gorbachev interrupted again. "Please answer me, Mr. President, what is your answer?"

The president's eyes flared with energy, as he sought to respond. Again, Gorbachev, by now almost hysterical, interrupted.

"Just answer, just answer, just answer," Gorbachev said, seemingly in a senseless rage.

Reagan snapped back coldly, "I will if you let me."

PERLE FELT THAT the Reagan compromise on SDI, drafted in extreme haste, failed to square the circle; the issue was too technical, and understandably, this was the job for staff, not the president. He whispered to McFarlane and Shultz, "I don't think this is helpful."

Shultz nodded his head. "I didn't either."

Perle looked over to Reagan to see if he was expecting a response. Like an old warrior in the heat of battle, Reagan had long since moved on, clearly engrossed in his heated one-on-one with Gorbachev. This summit was moving very quickly.

He stuffed the yellow paper into his pocket. When he gave it to a colleague later on, he would wonder if one day it would show up at a Sotheby's auction.

. . .

GORBACHEV CONTINUED: "WE'RE prepared to compromise. We can talk about a separate INF agreement; we can talk about deep cuts in strategic weapons. But SDI has got to come to an end."

There was a long pause. Total silence. No one dared to speak, and Reagan sat there firmly. He too said nothing. He wanted to hear from Gorbachev.

Not even the creaking footfalls of security agents pacing about could be heard. It was Gorbachev's moment.

Finally, Gorbachev relented, "Mr. President, I don't agree with you, but I can see you really mean it. Maybe this has all grown a little bit heated."

Reagan noticed that Gorbachev was different in the plenary sessions from his one-on-one sessions. In private he was more persuasive, less rhetorical and bombastic; in public he was far more strident, and not nearly as effective.

TO THE PARTICIPANTS, it was clear that Gorbachev had given it virtually everything he had, employing every trick he could muster. But Reagan remained unyielding and sincere. Gorbachev now saw that he could not bully or lightly manipulate Reagan. Confronted with the conviction of the president, it appeared that, for the first time, Gorbachev accepted at a personal level the inevitability of SDI research.

The meeting ended. But the communiqué battle was now only just beginning in earnest.

BACK AT THE hotel that evening, Shultz told his working group, "You should be prepared to spend the night exploring areas where views are similar and might fit together. Roz is chairman. You'll have a rough night. The Soviets can call it anything they want. To us, it's an agreed-upon statement."

Perle was pumped up. The statement was important because it would serve as the authorizing policy document for the two governments in the weeks and months ahead. What it said would be crucial. Would it primarily reflect U.S. interests—or Soviet interests?

He was impressed with Bessmertnykh, finding him a worthy and admirable adversary. One goal was to ensure there were no references to the ABM treaty that could hamper SDI. Another was to avoid the Soviet generalities that would only provide them with loopholes to violate freely the very agreements they signed—like the ABM treaty of 1972.

Most of the U.S. team was working off of clouded senses, suffering from a debilitating combination of overwork, undernourishment, late-night wrangling over policy positions, and too little sleep. And the final night for them had barely begun. Their one bit of sustenance was a meager pittance: sandwiches grabbed on the fly as they huddled with their Soviet counterparts to draft a statement that the two great powers could agree to.

ELSEWHERE, FOR REAGAN and Gorbachev, now relaxed after a draining day, and the rest of their dinner party, an elegant supper at the Maison de Sausurre, an eighteenth-century gray stone château, awaited. Dinner was marked by warm toasts and levity. At one point, Gorbachev rose to describe a cartoon he had seen in a Western newspaper.

"It showed Mr. Reagan on one side of the abyss," he said, "and me on the other. In the caption Mr. Reagan was saying, 'We need a better relationship. You take the first step.'"

Reagan kicked his head back, broke into knee-slapping laughter, and then applauded heartily. The rest of the dinner party joined in clapping. Everyone smiled.

After dinner, they moved into the library, where Reagan and his wife, Nancy, seated themselves on a red couch, and Gorbachev and his wife, Raisa, and a handful of aides, sipped after-dinner drinks and coffee.

At 10:40, Shultz was called away from the room for an urgent phone call. It was Ridgway, telling him that the Soviets were "stonewalling," and the statement had run into difficulty.

It was Gromyko in Geneva all over again.

Shultz returned to the room, rose and pointed his finger at Georgi Kornienko, the first deputy foreign minister, and attacked him heatedly.

"You, you, you! You are holding it up, we cannot do business with you." He turned to Gorbachev and said vehemently, "Mr. General Secretary, we cannot do business with this man; he is not getting done what you want to get done."

Reagan was startled by the explosion, as was Gorbachev. The outburst prompted an appeal from Reagan to Gorbachev. "To hell with what they're doing," the president said. "You and I will say, 'We can work together to make it come about.' "

Reagan and Gorbachev then shook hands.

But in the negotiating session, precious little was happening, not until Gorbachev himself interceded with the Soviet team, and told them that he wanted a joint statement to conclude the summit. It was now past midnight.

．　．　．

PERLE FELT THE summit was on a roller-coaster ride, from confrontation to impasse to joint statement—maybe. Even the logistics of the meeting had been an effort. At one point, they had to leave the building they were in and move to another site, shivering in the freezing cold, slogging through the slush and ice, to go to the Soviet mission.

It was cold and dark as hell, he thought. And the Soviet mission struck him as foreboding.

He also didn't like where the discussion was going. The Soviets were digging in their heels on just about everything. Then, after Gorbachev called, he had a problem with his own delegation. Now that the Soviets were being more cooperative, Ridgway was too inclined to start making unnecessary concessions.

His philosophy was to press them hard wherever they could, and not give anything up. At one point, the Soviets said they couldn't accede to language referring to "human rights." Previously, they had maintained human rights was strictly an internal affair, not the business of the Americans or the world community. Bessmertnykh claimed there was no word for "human rights" in Russian, therefore they could only refer to "resolving humanitarian cases."

Even this would be a hugely important victory. Perle made a further suggestion. You can use " 'Humanitarian cases' in the Russian text, but 'human rights' in the English text." The two sides argued this, often bitterly.

Finally, the Soviets acceded to the demands.

Later in the evening, when Perle felt Ridgway was moving way too fast, he called for a recess.

What's this about, a frowning Ridgway asked, not entirely happy.

"I don't think we need to placate them so much," Perle said. "I say let's press them on every last point."

At 4:30 A.M., the negotiating session reached its climax, and a statement, so adamantly sought by Gorbachev, was agreed upon. It didn't mention SDI or the ABM treaty; it didn't hem in the Americans in future arms control efforts; it committed the Soviets to making human rights progress. It was, Perle felt, a good night's work; this was a document that reflected American considerations, not Soviet views, as was so often the case in the past.

Back at the Hotel Intercontinental, he drifted off into a long catnap, proud of the U.S. effort. He would have to be awake in one and a half hours.

．　．　．

Roz Ridgway later praised Perle for his participation in the all-night talks ("He sat at my right hand."), and Shultz also praised Perle, saying "he worked arm in arm with Ridgway." But in the closing ceremony, Gorbachev did not feel so charitable toward Perle. He blamed him for his obstructionism, and for holding up the negotiations that night.

The two delegations celebrated by secretly drinking champagne—secretly because the Soviet Union was in the midst of a stern anti-alcohol campaign—at a private reception concluding the summit ceremonies. In the reception line, Gorbachev exchanged warm greetings with all the senior aides in the American delegation, until he met Perle.

Staring Perle in the eye, Gorbachev said nothing. Seconds elapsed. Finally, Perle broke the ice. In his characteristically soft voice, he said, "Pleased to meet you, Mr. Secretary."

There was silence. At last, the Soviet leader extended his hand, gave a weak grip, and quickly moved to the next person.

Unknown however to many of the top participants, the final chapter on the summit had yet to be written. Somewhere in the State Department, the decision was made not to announce that two versions of the joint U.S.-Soviet communiqué had been agreed to, a Russian version that referred to "humanitarian cases," and an English version that referred explicitly to "human rights." Indeed, in its press guidance and in the official documentary record, State published only an English translation of the Russian statement, without any reference to the two versions—and thus effectively purged the unprecedented and hard-won phrase "human rights" from history. And this substitution was apparently made without the knowledge of George Shultz, Roz Ridgway—or Richard Perle.

But all told, the Geneva summit was still a big success. Four days later, Perle received a personal note from Shultz. "You especially have my gratitude and admiration for the skilled and determined way you performed at the center of the all-night negotiating struggle which produced the joint statement."

Not known for his informality, Shultz signed his note, "George."

CHAPTER 30

As the fourth round of the arms talks commenced with post-summit fanfare in January 1986, Max Kampelman sought to build upon the tenor of the new spirit of cooperation established between Ronald Reagan and Mikhail Gorbachev. With his Soviet counterpart, Victor Karpov, he quickly expressed a desire to speed up the talks.

In the heady early months of the talks in 1985, Kampelman was still unsure of the Soviets' seriousness. But a year later, the landscape had changed. Beyond the stale rhetoric and stony Soviet posturing, he now detected subtle but demonstrable signs of real movement in the Soviet positions, changes that reflected not just Gorbachev's apparent openness in Geneva, but indications that the Soviets actually were softening up; not just that an agreement was simply gestating beneath the surface, but that it was steadily evolving. He was determined to make the most of it.

This was not a change of position per se; it was Kampelman as the hardheaded negotiator and lawyer, probing for openings. But this push would soon come at some cost. His new orientation increasingly brought him into conflict with the Pentagon and his own often fractious delegation.

Still, the changes and possibilities in U.S.-Soviet relations appeared to heighten in the intoxicating but grim period after the Geneva summit. Hastened by U.S. pressure, the diurnal struggles of the Cold War increasingly looked like a contest the Soviets could no longer afford or win. The Soviet regime, which but seven years earlier had perilously tipped the global balance of power in its direction, was now foundering, and was frantically trying to get a grip on its own system.

This was never more dramatically evident than within hours of the Reagan-Gorbachev summit.

WHEN GORBACHEV LEFT Geneva, he deplaned in Moscow, was picked up by his black limousine, and sped off immediately to an urgent meeting of the Politburo. On the world stage, Gorbachev was a big hit. Britain's hard-line and sensible Margaret Thatcher felt he was a man the West "could do business with"; his distaste for SDI, his sweeping disarmament rhetoric, his talk of openness and desire to get Communism moving again radiated activism, giving him a bursting Kennedyesque aura that made him a darling of American liberals; and now, however modestly, he had clearly engaged Ronald Reagan.

But in Moscow, there was widespread disaffection and confusion. Gorbachev returned to a firestorm of criticism, and was immediately forced to defend his performance. He had gone to Geneva with one large goal, killing SDI, and he gave it his best shot; but after proclaiming space defense the major threat to peace and international stability, and after all the camera crews had packed their bags and gone home, after network newsmen and high-minded commentators had shuttled back to Washington, after the hype and spectacle had died down, the champagne had been secretly drunk, and the two delegations had parted ways, the glow of the moment was rudely punctured by a harsh assessment of the summit's results in the Politburo.

In a word, Gorbachev left Geneva empty-handed. More than that, he had buckled to the U.S. tactic of refusing to link progress in SDI with offensive arms cuts. In the Kremlin, it didn't escape notice that he had made the tacit concession of signing on to a 50 percent cut in offensive weapons and hinted that an INF agreement could not be ruled out, even as SDI was still going forward.

Old-line Stalinist officials like Vladimir Shcherbitsky bitterly denounced his performance, powerfully recalling more effective Soviet leaders, Russians who never let their country down; skepticism about the summit quietly seeped into the press; and, perhaps most ominously for Gorbachev, the Russian military, including no less than Marshal Sergei Akhromeyev, registered dissent. Taken together, the scathing criticism meant that at the next summit, a year from now, Gorbachev would have to produce.

But for now, the stormy Gorbachev had to get a fix on his country's current situation. It was bleak. American defense investments in the past five years had paid off handsomely—at the expense of the Soviet Union.

THE SOVIET UNION was an empire increasingly under duress: its thrusts in Central America were blunted by a growing band of Nicaragua rebels, and it was being thwarted by the rebellious, often savagely nationalistic mujahadeen clans in Afghanistan; Moscow's East European satellites were now under continued assault: restive populations were stirred by the cries not of Soviet Communism but of Ronald Reagan's global campaign for freedom, not by the stars of Marx and Lenin but the percolating defiance of Lech Walesa's Solidarity and Václav Havel's velvety movement of poets and writers, Charter 77. At home, the central control of Moscow could not rid itself of political prisoners, heroic images that haunted the very legitimacy of Soviet Communism: the celebrated face of an Anatoly Shcharansky, the silhouettes of anonymous men and women in Russian prison camps, smuggling scribbled notes of freedom on tattered papers; Russian Jews, smooth-faced children with large brown almond eyes and bearded grandparents in black hats bowing their heads rapidly in musty and tattered synagogues, where wooden pews were lit only by shafts of dusky light from rose windows; and a stream of boat people, jumping walls and fleeing in rickety crafts, going by foot and by train, always westward, all moved by Ronald Reagan's rhetoric of freedom.

As 1986 began, the ideology of Marxism was weakening. The Soviets had fewer soulmates. Their loyal outposts in North Korea and East Germany, Vietnam and Cuba, Nicaragua and North Yemen, and Angola and Afghanistan were increasingly isolated and strained. They still exercised leverage over a handful of radical revolutionary and terrorist movements, and enjoyed the sympathy of scattered university alcoves and idealistic peace movements. But more and more, on the global stage, only the magnitude of Soviet military power was real, and this too was now eroding in the face of the massive Reagan defense buildup. And SDI threatened to leave them dangerously behind in the one area where they had hitherto always excelled: military might.

Presiding over a system that was psychologically demoralized and under assault from the U.S., Gorbachev undertook dramatic reforms. He called for domestic restructuring, *perestroika*, and new political thinking in foreign policy, as well as *glasnost*, or openness in domestic matters. Then, from February 25 through March 6, 1986, he took his platform defiantly to the Twenty-seventh Party Congress of the Soviet Communist Party, the highest body in the Soviet Union, which met every five years. It was wracked by stormy debate and dramatic controversy.

In a long-winded six-hour address to the party congress, Gorbachev betrayed his dilemma: he wanted to reform and purify the Communist party, but was unwilling to do away with the corrupt and cruel system itself. Nor was he yet willing to give up the Soviet addiction to military growth—in his five-year defense plan, military expenditures were slated to rise almost 8 percent a year, and, all told, defense expenditures would increase an astonishing 45 percent over the next five years.

Gorbachev thus took his place before the Communist delegates as an almost tragic, even confused figure, neither fish nor fowl, not a dogmatic believer in the rigid shibboleths of the old Communist world, but unwilling to make a clean break and carve out a vision of the new world. He wanted respite for his economy, but pumped increasingly more rubles into the military. He spoke a language of peace, but still did not eradicate concrete signs that he was a man bent for conquest. And these dualities were all manifest at the party congress, where Gorbachev used language so harsh that it was reminiscent of the grossest ideology of traditional Marxists. But he also spoke boldly of the sins of the Brezhnev era, and laid out ideas for how to reinvigorate the Soviet Union.

Gorbachev was no democrat; he was still in many ways a traditional Communist party boss. But he was, as he demonstrated now, a realist. And impelled by the unremitting competition with the U.S., and a burst of his own vision, he showed signs that accommodation must mark Soviet relations with the West, the first time this was acknowledged among the dour ranks of the party faithful since the dawn of the Cold War, and for that matter, the Soviet Union.

Tucked away in his lengthy fulminations, he indicated that Soviet foreign policy was now in transition. Gorbachev stood before his assembled Communist comrades, thundering from his lectern, his hand chopping down in the air: "A turning point has arisen not only in external but international affairs. The changes in the development of the contemporary world are so profound and significant that they require a rethinking and comprehensive analysis of all its factors."

His speech was an exhausting one, and it created as much tumult with his comrades as national solace. The mere suggestion that the Communist party, nurtured on the belief in the inevitability of class struggle and founded on irreconcilable conflict in which socialism would one day inexorably sweep away a decrepit capitalism, might now have to co-exist with the Western world, dropped like an ideological bombshell. Eduard Shevardnadze, Gorbachev's slightly sad new foreign minister, and a visionary in his own right, winced at the speech, summing up the harsh aftermath this way: Gorbachev's actions "gave rise to a very stormy reaction."

But there was limited success. The twenty-seventh congress finally relented, and was willing to follow Gorbachev for the moment. In the end, it concluded, "without an acceleration of the country's economic and social development, it will be impossible to maintain our positions on the international scene." Thus, this was Gorbachev's mission.

His country was an elite under stress, politically, economically, militarily. Which meant Gorbachev desperately needed relief in the military arena, notably from the technological challenge of SDI, a program that Bessmertnykh, echoing the views of his party comrades, would later note, "looked like a horror to Gorbachev."

WHAT SHOULD THE U.S. response be? For Kampelman in Geneva, the calculation was anything but simple. Could he pry loose a separate deal on INF? On strategic arms? Or could he use the leverage of SDI to explore a larger, more sweeping nuclear arms reduction scheme? The answer was he would explore both. He knew full well that SDI was sacrosanct to the president, but without giving in on SDI research, he began to put out feelers. He sent out signals that a deal could be cut, with the unmistakable overtones that it could include SDI.

But Kampelman had only so much room. While he had significant input into the policy process, negotiating guidelines were ultimately drafted back in Washington and cleared by the interagency process.

One day, over a lunch break with his counterpart, Victor Karpov, Kampelman sought to use his dilemma to his advantage, and baited Karpov: "Look, Victor, I don't know if you know what wiggle room means." Kampelman dramatically pointed to his shoe.

"It means room for the toes to move in. At this movement, I have no wiggle room. None. That's because you are handling these negotiations badly. If you can come up with significant reductions, not promises but realities, I might get some wiggle room. But I can't even explore with you what is possible unless you show us more on the price you're willing to pay in reductions."

AS NEWS OF Kampelman's probing hit the Pentagon ranks, it touched off a minor furor. Kampelman felt that "discussing" and "agreeing" were two entirely different concepts. Squeezed between hard-liners and squishy liberals, between his own anti-Soviet animus and the dizzying prospects of a deal, Kampelman probed sharply—but cautiously. But the Pentagon representatives didn't believe that the Soviets understood Kampelman's fine, lawyerly distinctions. Nor were they wholly satisfied with his calculations. Institutionally, Kampelman was increasingly being drawn into the negotiation process, and taking on the State Department line, and with it the half decade of State-Pentagon rivalry. To most of State, SDI was negotiable. To most of the Pentagon, like the president, it was sacrosanct, and Kampelman's indications that he was looking for "wiggle room" in the talks were not reassuring.

Perle's aides feared that this was, once again, a slippery slope, another Nitze, the latest in a series of serious mistakes perpetrated by someone who should know better. (Indeed, Nitze was now promoting a "prohibited-permitted" plan for SDI, which would have preemptively placed restrictions on future SDI research.) Such acts from a Paul Nitze or Rick Burt were understandable, even expected by this point. But not from the fiercely anti-Communist Max Kampelman. To be sure, the differences in opinion were as much institutional as philosophical, a matter perhaps more of style than of substance. Kampelman himself maintained that he only offered the Soviets proposals on SDI that came directly from the president. But DoD representatives to the Geneva talks, who met daily with Kampelman, believed the ever so subtle signs were unmistakable: the president's chief negotiator wanted very much to cut a deal on SDI. That was the message they sent back to the Pentagon. And amidst the continuing tensions of the ongoing arms talks and day-to-day stresses that magnified the slightest disagreement (in negotiations, the placement of a comma could count for everything), these very real differences steadily escalated, and, as tempers flared, threatened to become personal, even ugly. They were largely played out over the fate of Dan Gallington, a Pentagon representative to Kampelman's group on the SDI talks.

The first precipitating event had come earlier in the year, and was unrelated to the talks themselves.

After the Soviets shot U.S. Army Major Arthur Nicholson in cold blood in East Germany, where he was cruelly allowed to bleed to death without help, Gallington, an air force colonel, informed Kampelman that in good conscience he, Gallington, couldn't accept a Soviet invitation to a reception. Kampelman took note of the incident, but at the time didn't think too much of Gallington's refusal. He shrugged it off, and told Gallington, who had been assigned by DoD to Kampelman's group on the SDI discussions, "It's your choice."

Shortly thereafter, Kampelman got word through the grapevine that Gallington had been "indiscreetly critical of John Tower," accusing him of excessively wining and dining the Soviets. This was too much for the proper Kampelman. He felt this came dangerously close to questioning Tower's patriotism. Tower himself was unmoved by such gossip, but Kampelman was outraged. He warned Gallington that any further evidence of such behavior would abruptly lead to his dismissal.

Later, Gallington had another run-in with a member of the delegation. Kampelman mulled it over. He finally decided to remove Gallington from the delegation. This was, he noted, not a decision he made lightly. He felt Gallington was talented, even if he were a little rigid in his views. It also meant he would effectively be removing one of Perle's representatives to the talks, raising the unpleasant specter of a conflict with Perle. But Gallington was a thorn in Kampelman's side, and seemed, to Kampelman, to be questioning his leadership. These were Kampelman's talks. He didn't want brash underlings making trouble.

BACK IN WASHINGTON, Perle had gotten a very different picture of Gallington, the talks, and his role.

In the new, rough policy environment of the 1980s, it was common for ambitious Washingtonians, looking to their next job and the next promotion, to distance themselves quickly from problems that did not directly affect them, which often meant personnel. Perle took the opposite approach. The harsher the criticism heaped upon his staff, the more he stuck by them.

Perle had kept himself informed throughout the negotiations, not just on the status of the talks, but the behind-the-scenes maneuvering and machinations within the delegation. Earlier in the year, one of his aides had warned Perle that the problem between Gallington and other delegation members was over policy, not personality matters or style.

"Regardless what you may have heard in Washington," the aide stressed, "it's about political views—and the brass ring, SDI."

From years of experience, Perle knew that there were always different sides to any conflict. But he also knew the easiest way to derail your political opponents was to call them "obstructionist" or "difficult." This also had the benefit of ignoring the actual substance of the disagreements. After all was said and done, Perle was not persuaded that the problem with Gallington was anything other than substance, and the substance was SDI. At the talks, Gallington was fighting any effort to soften the U.S. negotiating position on SDI, or any lapse into protracted discussions that would have the practical effect of hemming in SDI. And Perle couldn't help but notice that Gallington was glowingly described in internal reports as vigorous in defense of the Pentagon: one report concluded, "He has a big pair of brass balls and—along with his cohorts—is tenacious in close combat. . . . Gallington and his gang [should] stay in place."

But in April, Kampelman informed Perle that he would like Gallington to be moved to another assignment. "My patience has run out after a year," Kampelman told Perle, adding, "I have not taken this step lightly."

Perle balked. The answer was no.

He asked Kampelman to reconsider the decision, and then flatly informed Kampelman that he "would not recommend the change" to Secretary Weinberger. Kampelman countered with a compromise that would keep Gallington on the overall delegation, but not as a member of his group negotiating space and defense. That would be fine, Perle said. It was an acceptable alternative.

But the effort at compromise failed, and, after careful reflection, this time Kampelman put on an all-out press to get his way. He quickly ran smack into Fred Iklé, Richard Perle, and Cap Weinberger, who lined up united and determined behind Gallington.

IN LATE APRIL, Kampelman sent a memo to General James Abrahamson, the director of Strategic Defense Initiative Organization (SDIO), laying the groundwork for Gallington's removal. But back at DoD, Abrahamson routed a copy of the letter to Perle's deputy, Frank Gaffney. Gaffney nearly hit the ceiling. He immediately fired off a note to Defense Undersecretary Iklé: "The answer should be a clear 'NO.'" If that weren't clear enough, he wrote another huge "NO" in capital letters on the memo itself.

In Geneva, when Gallington heard rumors that Kampelman was seeking to shift staff around, he was determined to fight what he saw as an imperious move. Gallington sent an urgent cable to Perle and Gaffney, saying that Kampelman wanted to "use exploitable policy differences between ISP and SDIO which could be used to weaken DOD (read ISP) representation to the delegation." This was a message that had the benefit of a measure of truth (though it was self-serving), and it resonated with DoD.

Quickly thereafter, Iklé called Kampelman. His message was simple and stark. He said DoD wanted Gallington to stay, and Weinberger would be calling Kampelman himself to ask that Gallington be kept for the next round. Iklé added, "During this time you can judge whether his behavior would make him more acceptable to your part of the delegation."

On May 4, Kampelman got another phone call, this time from Perle. Perle was on his way to several European capitals, but upon hearing of the urgency over Gallington, swung into action. Calling from the car phone in his DoD sedan, he made the same proposal as Weinberger: accept Gallington for another round, see how it works out.

Max, I know the situation you're in, I understand your position, Perle said. But this is the position *we* have to take. You understand. Perle also had come to doubt whether changing representatives would actually resolve the issue. Personal conflicts aside, on SDI, DoD had one position. The State Department and Kampelman might have another.

Kampelman was upset, but he was boxed in. DoD was mobilized to stand up for Gallington, and Perle had helped defuse the situation, pointing out that these were not personal differences, but institutional ones. Gallington would stay, and trading away SDI would be that much harder.

LONG BEFORE HE came to Geneva, Max Kampelman was a deal-maker. He spoke in the confident tones of a man who was abundantly comfortable with himself; he listened attentively to others with the care of a shrewd poker player; he was always unfailingly courteous in personal relations, unless he felt some bluster served a purpose; and in negotiations, like everything else, he showed patient resolve, preferring to unfold his cards steadily and cautiously, rather than to lay them down in one impetuous showdown.

In almost every shape and form he was like his establishment predecessors, men like Lovett, McCloy, Bohlen—drawn instinctively to public service, motivated by noble goals, but pragmatic and ready to guilelessly deal when the opening was there. But in one major aspect he was different; he was not a cold realist, like a Kennan, or a Bismarckian adherent of realpolitick, like a McCloy. Ideas and ideals moved him. Kampelman did not see the Soviets as simply a mirror image of the U.S., haunted by historic fears and defensive xenophobia, but as an evil system, oppressive, cruel, and dangerous.

He was thus motivated and shaped by two conflicting impulses, the pragmatism of the establishment and the mind-set of a businessman searching for a realistic modus vivendi, and the bursting idealism and sense of destiny of the counterestablishment, the view that the Cold War was not to be managed but to be won. So, it was these two impulses, tugging and pulling uneasily at each other, that continued to shape Kampelman, first in the Madrid talks and now in the Geneva arms negotiations, and in his relationship with Shultz and then with Perle.

The whole Gallington incident had taxed his patience, and disgusted him. Kampelman, who on occasion could be prickly, nevertheless responded to the DoD in a letter saying that he did not wish to reject a "constructive proposal from the Secretary of Defense," adding that he "respects" Richard's loyalty.

But from then on in Geneva, he decided to draw in Ken Adelman and his arms control experts from ACDA, who had a greater institutional loyalty to the arms control process, as opposed to its content.

. . .

FOR PERLE, THE spat was nothing personal. He liked Max, and wasn't about to let the institutional differences separating them intrude on their friendship or mutual respect. But for all Gorbachev's talk about *glasnost* and *perestroika* in the Soviet Union, Perle preferred to deal in concrete facts and realities. The Soviets still kept political prisoners, still refused their citizens the right to travel freely, to change jobs and residences, and to emigrate. The Soviets had not yet reduced defense spending; they had not yet stopped bankrolling their Marxist guerrilla movements of national liberation; they had not yet rejected the Brezhnev Doctrine, the view that once a country was socialist, it was always socialist. And the idea of a wealthy, more efficient Communist Soviet Union didn't particularly appeal to him—rather than make the Russian bear more tranquil, it could make it more dangerous.

Perle was fond of telling the following joke about *glasnost,* which he delivered with verve:

"The Russians had decided to do away with corruption among the *nomenklatura,* the party officials. Which meant the law would be complied with and reforms would be real. But after one weekend at his dacha, Gorbachev was late for a meeting with the Politburo. He told his driver to speed up, but the driver, afraid of violating the speed limit, continued to drive slowly. The general secretary then said: 'You get in the back, and let me drive.'

"After fifteen minutes of speeding, they were picked up by the Russian police. The first policeman looked into the limo, and then waved it away without giving them a ticket.

" 'What happened?' asked the second policeman.

" 'It was a high government official,' said the first.

" 'But comrade, there are no exceptions.'

" 'You don't understand, comrade, this guy was really important.'

" 'Well, who was it then?'

" 'I don't know, but his driver was Gorbachev.' "

And for Perle, this was the vexing problem with Gorbachev: he, or for that matter, anyone else, couldn't be certain that Gorbachev wouldn't again decide to rewrite the rules. A more open and less aggressive Soviet Union was surely in the U.S. interest. But what if, as the Rand Corporation analyst and Sovietologist Harry Rowen had been asserting, Gorbachev used this period as little more than a strategic breathing pause, not just gaining respite from competition with the U.S., but creating a more efficient and technologically advanced Marxist empire that would again resume its international expansionism, and crack down harder and more ruthlessly on its civilians? That was hardly in the West's interests.

Perle was against giving the Soviets breathing room. More change was still necessary. He wanted to keep the pressure on.

DESPITE OBSTACLES IN unifying his delegation, Kampelman continued to forge ahead with arms control ideas that could yield tangible benefits for an eventual deal. In the spring, he returned to Washington, where he lunched with Fred Iklé. They discussed a seemingly sweeping proposal that Gorbachev had made to the U.S. in a letter on January 15, two months after the Geneva summit.

In this plan, Gorbachev called for eliminating all nuclear weapons worldwide by the year 2000. The plan was to be carried out in three phases, giving it an air of seriousness, rather than the fluff of universal disarmament schemes proposed by previous Soviet leaders. In the first phase, Gorbachev called for eliminating all INF missiles from Europe. This was a major shift that went a long way toward accepting, at least in principle, Perle's zero option, which since its announcement in 1981 had been rejected by Soviet negotiators and American liberals as unfairly "one-sided" and patently "nonnegotiable."

There was one major hitch: all the reductions were conditioned on American agreement to give up SDI.

When Shultz talked with Perle, Perle indicated that he was unhappy and even troubled by the proposal, worrying that it smacked of "propaganda." But, Shultz explained, Reagan liked it, even quipping, "Why wait until the year 2000?"

In a compromise, the White House publicly welcomed the plan, and without embracing any of its specific suggestions said the United States would give it "careful study."

In the ensuing months it became imperative for the U.S. to offer a counterproposal, one that would be equally dramatic, capable of capturing the world's imagination and hopes. Iklé had an idea that he had been kicking around for a while. Why not get rid of all ballistic missiles? He had long felt that ballistic missiles, with their rapid flight times that could destroy Washington and Moscow within a short thirty minutes, drove the fear of surprise attack and dangerously shortened the nuclear fuse. Even if it was impractical, Iklé said, it was no less so than the 50 percent reduction that was endorsed at the Geneva summit.

Kampelman grinned. He was positively enthusiastic about the idea. It would put the U.S. on the diplomatic offensive, and appeared to make sense from a nuclear strategic point of view. "Let's staff it through," he said. "Let's see what the Joint Chiefs think."

In the following weeks, Iklé discussed the zero ballistic missile idea with Perle and Weinberger. Perle was warm to the idea. Among other things, he felt this plan would "expose the theoretical basis for Soviet objections to SDI, thus putting them on the defensive." If the U.S. had no fast-flying offensive missiles, their objection that SDI would be used to launch a first strike would "smoke out the Soviets" and expose their objections to SDI as rhetoric.

A few weeks later, Iklé and Kampelman met again for a second lunch. For years these two men, like Perle and Iklé, had hobnobbed with many of the same friends, and shared the same social values and similar political commitments. They spoke a common language of strength, speckled with an appreciation for creative intellectual ideas. They agreed this time to press the idea with their respective bosses, Weinberger and Shultz.

In banding together around this idea, they were an uncommonly influential axis, poised to make a Washington power play, bringing a dramatic idea to their cabinet secretaries, and bypassing the bureaucracy in a lightning strike. It was vintage Kampelman.

On June 12 at the White House, it was Weinberger, not Shultz, who proposed the idea of calling for "zero ballistic missiles." Shultz sensed an opportunity and declared that Weinberger's idea should be seriously pursued. (When one participant objected, another chimed in: "Jesus, don't rock the boat. It's the only thing they've agreed on in years.") The senior administration arms control advisers then set about refining the idea.

On July 25, Reagan formally proposed the zero ballistic missile plan in a letter to Gorbachev. Even in a slightly watered-down form (the U.S. said it would not withdraw from the ABM treaty for at least five years— Moscow was asking for a fifteen- to twenty-year nondeployment—and if either side were to deploy SDI after that, it would submit a plan for sharing the benefits of strategic defense and eliminating all ballistic missiles), it still constituted a major new initiative.

Seven weeks later, Gorbachev replied, in a harsh, and almost unrelenting tone. He described the offer as a step backward, and didn't even bother to comment on the zero ballistic missiles proposal.

But despite the proposal's premature death, not just at the hands of the Soviets, but also from its critics in the U.S. bureaucracy who wrote it off as too utopian, there was another bit of resounding news to ponder. In the spring of 1986, Kampelman was able to step forward with a startling piece of information: despite the fact that the Geneva talks had appeared at a standstill, held captive to a whirlwind of tumult behind

Kremlin walls, there were now unmistakable indications that the Soviets might have unlinked SDI and INF.

"What we may be hearing," Kampelman remarked, "is the death rattle of an ailing regime." He fired off a cable to Shultz, marked urgent: "It is imperative that we not shut the door."

CHAPTER 31

Another area where the Reagan administration wanted to apply pressure on the Soviets was in regional conflicts, those nasty little guerrilla wars in obscure corners of the globe.

The target was Third World Communist countries aligned with the Soviet Union. This was a sharp break with the past, exposing deep fissures in the American psyche. Earlier administrations and the European-centered establishment chafed at proxy wars with the Soviets, fearing they would heighten Cold War tensions. John McCloy once complained to Dean Acheson, "Europe is, after all, the big leagues." In his view, hot spots were nothing but irritants, unseemly distractions to be avoided. Moreover, the establishment preferred the soothing predictability of dé-tente.

And of course there was the looming specter of America's failure in Vietnam. The very word, Vietnam, said it all. Vietnam spelled tarnished careers, battered U.S. prestige on the world stage, the fall of a president and the rise of the virulently anti-internationalist New Left, and it tarnished all those grand ideas about limited war concocted by Kennedy's best and brightest. By the early 1980s, Vietnam was not just a ubiquitous lesson, but for many passionate liberals, it was an unquestionable shibboleth. The flowering of 1960s idealism that had led to Vietnam, impelled by a combination of benevolent impulses and Harvard hubris, were expressions of the nation's conscience in an earlier time. But by the 1980s, liberal benevolence meant not a hands-on policy, but hands-off.

The Reaganaut counterestablishment, with its own sense of destiny and historic vision, saw it quite differently. It didn't buy into the liberal establishment view of the world. Just as the North Vietnamese and Viet-cong could wear down a powerful American-supported South Vietnam, pinning down the massive resources of the U.S. in the process, it felt the tables could be turned on the Soviets. Now, it reasoned, America could harness the forces of nationalism to its benefit. Indigenous anti-

Communist guerrilla movements, supported by the U.S., could exhaust Soviet-supported Marxist regimes.

This was the bold import of Reagan's British Parliament speech in 1982, when he declared a campaign for democracy and ideological war on the Soviet Union, and proclaimed support for anti-Communist movements. Convinced that Communism was a tired force, the president signed National Security Decision Directive 75 in 1983, designed to apply economic pressure and to bolster military competition with the Soviets. But not content to leave it at that, Reagan wanted to extend the competition with the Soviets further, to arenas of America's choosing in the Third World, the Soviets' Achilles heel. Soon, he blessed expanded CIA covert support for movements in the mountainous ranges of Afghanistan, Cambodian rice paddies, and the hills and pathways of Nicaragua.

Abroad, the dividends were slowly paying off. By 1985, the Soviets were spending anywhere from $8 to $20 billion a year in seeking to stanch these festering American-aided counterinsurgencies. Confronted with this counterpressure, there were inchoate signs that the Soviets had overreached in their aggressive rash of Third World military adventures during the 1970s. And unlike Vietnam, it wasn't American boys doing the fighting, but local, well-motivated recruits. Nor was it particularly expensive: it was a whole lot easier supporting an insurgency than resisting one.

If one issue, above all, stood atop the ramparts of trouble spots at the center of U.S. efforts, it was Nicaragua and aid to the contra resistance. But for Reagan, Nicaragua was more than an issue, it was a passionate crusade. The Sandinistas were to be thwarted. When Congress at one point denied military aid to the contras, Reagan countered angrily, "We'll just come back then, again and again and again." He was later asked at a press conference, on February 21, 1985, did that mean the Sandinistas must be overthrown?

Reagan thought for a moment, then replied elliptically that the goal was "to make them cry uncle."

The political reverberations of this statement were immediate. For the Democrats, it meant one thing: he wanted to remove the Sandinistas through the use of force. Far-right conservatives, who hoped this was the policy, actually feared a sell-out by Reagan. They smelled an eventual accommodation with the Sandinistas, reminiscent of the ill-fated Paris Peace Accords with the North Vietnamese.

As the debate on Central America policy wore on, public protests against Reagan's policies increased in fervor, becoming ever uglier, more personal, and bordering on the violent. And as the temper of liberal activists in the country grew more strident, the administration became more of a battered fortress, its goals and intentions seemingly locked inside, hidden from the sight of a watchful and partisan Democratic Congress, but often adrift in its own policy councils.

The line had been crossed. For four years, Reagan had been conducting a covert policy of CIA aid against the Sandinistas, fought at every twist and turn by the Democrats. In this earlier period, the policy guns were openly pointed primarily at El Salvador. But with Duarte's successful election, that issue increasingly stabilized and quieted down. The democratic center in El Salvador, although still buffeted by the forces of the right and the left, had begun to take hold.

It was only then, and after Reagan's reelection, that the guns of the administration began to swivel and the barrels of policy were publicly trained right at Nicaragua.

REAGAN HAD NEVER wanted to invade Central America. Bill Casey's early quick fix of forming a Nicaraguan resistance, the force that would come to be known as the contras, was supposed to be the answer. Yet in those earliest days, the rationale for the contras had actually been a perpetually moving target. For some, the policy was to interdict the flow of arms to El Salvador; others saw the contras as carrying out cross-border operations, lightning hit-and-run assaults that would curtail Sandinista export of Communism and revolution. The State Department increasingly adopted the view that the contras were to be traded away in an agreement, as bargaining chips in exchange for an end to Sandinista support for neighboring revolutionary activities. Bill Casey trudged before the intelligence committees to make the case that the contras could make the Sandinistas "more democratic," to keep their system "more pluralistic." (Although one State Department official, Thomas Enders, mocked this. "Sandinista Nicaragua will never democratize," he confidently said.) For their part, the CIA agents, the guys who ran the operation in the field, would have none of it. "These limited aims," they told the contras, "were for congressional consumption." This war was for keeps, and their goal was to overthrow the regime.

While contra beginnings were modest, unhappiness with Sandinista repression led their forces to balloon. During the first couple of years in the early 1980s, their numbers rose to more than five thousand, and eventually to seven thousand, as many men as the Sandinistas ever had in their rebellion against Somoza. Within four years, contra numbers shot up even further, fluctuating between fifteen thousand and eighteen thousand. They also began to operate deep in the interior of Nicaragua.

But for political reasons, the strategy of covert contra aid quickly back-fired. Reagan was effectively prohibited from making the case publicly for the program—all the details were highly classified. Questions that the Democrats scarcely asked about the Afghanistan operation, in which the U.S. covertly aided the Afghan mujahadeen, a disparate set of funda-mentalist splinter groups, themselves ruthless and undemocratic, some of them even anti-American, endlessly bedeviled the resistance program. For the Democrats, Afghanistan, halfway across the world in the Soviet orbit, was a good war; Nicaragua, in the recesses of the American back-yard, was a bad war. Moral considerations were suspended in supporting the mujahadeen. But they reigned when it came to the contras, while strategic considerations were suspended.

Among the most fervent of dissenters in the Democratic party was Speaker Tip O'Neill. He hated the contra operation, and was missionary in his opposition against it. O'Neill's aunt, Eunice Tolan, had been a Maryknoll nun. She died in 1981, at the age of ninety-one. But the Mary-knoll missionary order still exerted a profound and almost haunting in-fluence over the speaker. Another Maryknoller, Peggy Healy, who was based in Nicaragua, corresponded regularly with O'Neill. She painted a dark picture of a Nicaragua torn by civil war—an ugly war encouraged, supported, and masterminded by the CIA. O'Neill told his aides, "I be-lieve every word." His large whalelike frame wheeling around in his leather swivel chair behind his massive speaker's desk, he leaned for-ward and spoke with an ideological fervor, noting that politics was a world of shifting sands, loyalties, and values. "But nuns and priests spoke the truth."

On the issue of Central America, passion—and politics—clearly over-rode clearheaded geopolitics. However wrongheaded O'Neill thought the policy, he was driven almost exclusively by atavistic feelings of the Ugly American and visions of the U.S. as the neocolonialist exploiter. He looked at Latin America and saw a sea of poverty, discontent, and mili-tary repression run amok. American policy was not just risky, it was im-moral. In this calculus, much as far-right conservatives were seemingly insensitive to matters of poverty and corruption in the region, he fre-quently lost sight of what ultimately impelled the Reagan program in the first place: an expansionist and repressive Soviet-aligned regime in our hemisphere, increasingly looking more like a totalitarian Cuba than a democratic Costa Rica.

So as the speaker cast about for an alternative, he would come to grasp at the shifting edifice of negotiations, and would seek, if not an outright end to the contra war, at least to carefully circumscribe it. In time, the word was sent out among Democrats. For the Democratic

House leadership, the contra issue became a litmus test. Cross the line, and you crossed the speaker. Inspired by this mix of motives, Democrats took their cue, and began a steady assault against the administration.

The first warning shot came in December of 1982, with the Boland Amendment, prohibiting the CIA and Department of Defense from furnishing military equipment, training, or support to anyone "for the purpose of overthrowing the Government of Nicaragua." Within two years, in October 1984, the House had tried to reign in the entire military program altogether, taking it completely out of the CIA's hands, and upped the ante again. They passed a second Boland Amendment, prohibiting funds available to the CIA, DoD, and "any other agency involved in intelligence activities" to be used "to support any military or paramilitary activities" in Nicaragua. This amendment was far more sweeping than Boland I, allowing only humanitarian aid and, in effect, shackling the contra war. But fearing that they could be pegged with aiding a Marxist regime, Congress was unwilling to cut the contras off altogether.

When the amendment passed, Reagan was almost red-faced with disgust, and so angry he could barely speak. He left little doubt that he intended to revisit the issue. Nor was he about to let the contras dissipate due to lack of funding, or lose the leverage they gave him in dealing with the Sandinistas. The Congress had authorized only $24 million in humanitarian aid to the contras; the administration estimated that the funding would run out midyear. Reagan told Bush, Baker, and Bud McFarlane, we need to keep the contras together, "body and soul."

That fall and into 1985, the crisis intensified, and two factors wrestled uneasily with each other to bring about a resolution, an administration attempt to negotiate with the Sandinistas, and the brutal reality of the East-West conflict and the sordid nature of the Sandinista regime. As this cauldron of conflict played itself out, the administration would be wracked by further turmoil from the forces of the right and left.

IN 1981, THE administration had made a first stab at direct dialogue with the Sandinistas. The point man was Thomas Enders, assistant secretary of state for American Republics Affairs (ARA), the bureau overseeing Latin America. A hulking six-foot-six man, Yale educated, patrician, and haughty, he had a domineering style, but was brilliant and energetic. He also had a rogue cowboy streak, willing to take inordinate risks. That summer, before the contras formed, he hopped on a plane and took a quiet trip to Managua.

Meeting in cheap-paneled surroundings with the Nicaraguan Sandinista leadership, he proposed a grand deal. End your military support for

Communist insurgencies in neighboring countries, he proposed. In turn, the U.S. will accept the legitimacy of your revolution and normalize relations with you.

It was a bold overture, and was more characteristic of standard State Department diplomacy and establishment philosophy than the activism of a Ronald Reagan. In later years, many of Reagan's closest advisers, from Jeane Kirkpatrick and Cap Weinberger to Judge Clark, would warn about the pitfalls of negotiating with Communist regimes. ("It's like the Social Democrats in revolutionary Russia trying to talk Lenin into giving up totalitarian Bolshevism," snapped DoD's Fred Iklé.) But in the capital of Nicaragua, Enders put the deal on the table in no uncertain terms. He returned to Washington and waited for an answer.

It was, from many perspectives, a reasonable compromise. It would have represented a coup for the Sandinistas. In return for ending aid to other Marxist guerrillas, they could keep their political and economic system, maintain an alliance with the Soviets, and receive American diplomatic recognition. From the U.S. point of view, it was a significant concession. The U.S. had withdrawn recognition of the Somoza regime based on written Sandinista promises to follow policies of holding free elections, being nonaligned, having a mixed economy, and adhering to political pluralism. Now the U.S. would get none of this under the Enders proposal. Conservatives were livid, but the die was cast.

Enders didn't receive an answer. The Sandinistas wouldn't bite. Weeks went by, until, in early October, the deal was rejected at the United Nations by Daniel Ortega, the head Sandinista *comandante*.

Eventually, Enders's maneuvering cost him his job. He lost the faith of his superiors and was pushed out of his job by disgruntled conservatives. Conservatives also did not hesitate to point out that Tomás Borge, one of the *comandantes*, speaking at a military ceremony from slanted wooden bleachers before a crowd of followers in July of 1981, revealed the nature of the revolutionary fervor of the Sandinista regime. "This revolution goes beyond our borders," he boisterously declared. It was classic Leninism, and it was clear that the internal nature of the regime was inexorably bound up with its external actions. Yet by 1984, with Congress pulling the plug on the contras and congressional machinations under way to put in place the second Boland Amendment, George Shultz felt there was little alternative but to give negotiations another shot.

At a layover in El Salvador in June of 1984, Shultz asked Reagan's blessing to stop off unexpectedly in Managua for a dramatic, but private, airport meeting with Daniel Ortega. Reagan said yes. Shultz was ushered into an austere room, where he met a soft-spoken Ortega, clad in military gear. They talked for two hours. Acknowledging the contrast in temperaments, the two danced around each other, finally agreeing that Nicaragua and the U.S. would open up bilateral talks once more. At a stormy June 25 National Security Planning Group meeting, Shultz made the case for his decision. "If Nicaragua is halfway reasonable," he argued, "there could be a reasonable, negotiated solution." He cautioned that, otherwise, "our support on the Hill goes down."

Jeane Kirkpatrick had heard enough, and took the lead in arguing against these talks. She had spent years of her life pondering the mysteries and lurid dynamics of Communist regimes, and was well aware of how discussions at the table could be used by totalitarians to achieve what could not be won on the battlefield. She also fretted about the asymmetry in agreements signed by democratic and Marxist governments. Democracies were by nature constantly under pressure from a rancorous public to make concessions, as well as to honor their agreements. By contrast, totalitarian powers, unrestricted by domestic pressure, were not compelled to make concessions. Once agreements were signed, they could subvert them without penalty. She feared that any agreement without the leverage of the contras would lead to an ill-disguised diplomatic formula that permitted the Sandinistas to consolidate their power.

"It's vital for the administration to stand tough," she emphasized. By this she meant going back to the Hill and arguing for further support for contras. "We have not made the impression that, if the Congress cuts off funding for the contras, it is of major importance to the administration."

For a minute there was silence, as was often the case when Kirkpatrick was at her most forceful. She was directly challenging Shultz. Then Shultz weighed in once more, asserting that we have to demonstrate to Congress that "we are willing to negotiate."

Reagan himself had few illusions about diplomacy with the Sandinistas, but neither was he willing to prevent Shultz from giving it a try. He was interested in talking with the Soviets in Geneva from a position of strength, and felt the same principle could apply here. As was so often the case, Reagan instinctively sought nuance in his hard-line policies.

"It is far-fetched to imagine that a Communist government like the Sandinistas would make any reasonable deal with us," he responded, "but if it is to get Congress to support the anti-Sandinistas, then that can be helpful." He told Shultz to do it.

In the following days and weeks, a round of talks was initiated in Manzanillo, a stinking hot, flyblown place. The U.S. tabled a four-point plan that was a variation of the original Enders proposal. At the end of the process, the U.S. was proposing to terminate aid to the contras in return for free elections inside Nicaragua. As part of the bargain, the Sandinistas would cease support for outside Marxist revolutionaries.

For seven rounds, the talks dragged on with monotonous regularity. The U.S. team met with the Sandinistas eight times in Mexico, once in Atlanta, held over 120 meetings with allies in the region, and logged over 250,000 miles talking to assorted Latin American foreign ministers. But by mid-January of 1985, a despairing Shultz terminated the talks. Shultz realized that it was never a "serious effort" on the part of the Sandinistas. From Managua, they were watching the increasingly visible congressional votes more than they were dealing in good faith at the bargaining table. Never was this more evident than when Congress cut off funding to the contras in 1984. The Sandinistas promptly reversed many of their stances. By now, the talks were hopeless.

Even Shultz agreed that the U.S. was in a bind. Without the contras, they didn't have successful leverage with the Sandinistas. But without successful talks, an isolationist Congress was unwilling to fund the contras. Ultimately, this standoff forced the U.S., both the executive and the Congress, to focus increasingly on the nature of the Sandinistas themselves.

ALL THROUGH THE harrowing months of 1984 and early 1985, the Sandinistas revealed themselves as bent on building a dedicated Marxist-Leninist state, driven not by popular sentiment or the earthly needs of ordinary workers and campesinos, but by Communist elites, and the eschatological vision of the vanguard of history.

They brooked little opposition. One incident became legendary among the campesinos, sweeping the nation like a violent and deadly electric shock. It began April 10, 1982, in the once serene confines of Nueva Segovia. Seventeen evangelicals of the Assemblies of God were suddenly rounded up by the Sandinista secret police, disrupted in the middle of prayer. Their spiritual behavior was interpreted as civil disobedience, and, according to sources, "they were to be made an example." Shouting, the police took them out to a plot of land, handed them crude shovels, and ordered them to dig their own graves. Many dropped to their knees, tears in their eyes, and frantically prayed.

However much the evangelicals wept, knelt to beg forgiveness, or trembled in mortal fear, their actions were drowned out in the more powerful drama of the revolution. Their throats were slit and they were buried on the spot.

A year later, eleven people were massacred at a Sandinista army base

in the dark of the night, joining other mass graves that stood as warnings to "enemies of the revolution."

As the revolution continued, this ghoulish behavior was more the exception than the norm. The Sandinistas generally ruled not by outright
terrorism, but by oppression. Systematically, each independent pocket
of resistance was squeezed by the power of the state. In Managua, the
Sandinistas sought to hobble the powerful and stubbornly independent
energies of the Catholic church, shutting down Radio Católica and its
Commission for Justice and Peace, which monitored religious and civic
rights. They repeatedly harassed and eventually cracked down on the independent newspaper, *La Prensa*, published by the distinguished
Nicaraguan matriarch Violeta Chamorro. In the streets, despotic Sandinista mobs, the *turbas divinas*, and local blockwatchers acted as the menacing watchdogs of the state. Neighbor was set upon neighbor, children
upon children, block upon block, as they prowled the streets, instilling
fear and sowing dissent.

Disappearances were common. Young children were abducted against
their will into the army, and whole villages sympathetic to the contras
were forcibly resettled. Labor unions were smashed, and opposition political parties kept on a tight leash. People were thrown in prisons, and
the Sandinistas became known as masters of an eerie Cuban practice,
"torture without scars."

In 1984, under pressure from the U.S., the Sandinistas held an election, but it was marred by violence and intimidation. The opposition candidate, Arturo Cruz, a bespectacled and moody economist, pulled out
when it became clear that the election would not be fair. Even congressional liberals were stricken by the brownshirt tactics of the Sandinista
regime.

Yet what was perhaps most disturbing to Americans at all ends of the
political spectrum was the growing armed might of the state, surpassing
any defensive needs. The Sandinistas openly boasted that they had "the
largest military force in all of Central America," ten times what Somoza's
was, and nearly equaling the combined power of Honduras, El Salvador,
Guatemala, and Costa Rica. Shiploads of arms, carried in large crates
and containers, continuously poured in from Eastern bloc countries,
and in 1985 the Sandinistas had 340 tanks, advanced Soviet artillery
seen nowhere else in the region, and more than five MIG-25s, vintage
helicopter gunships of the sort used by the Soviets in their legendary
counterinsurgency sweeps against the mujahadeen in Afghanistan. By
1985 and in ensuing months, the Sandinistas would receive more than
$1 billion in Soviet aid.

Few also could detect any Sandinista willingness to moderate their revolutionary behavior. A secret speech delivered by one Sandinista *co-mandante*, Bayardo Arce, dismissed the loathsome eruptions of the opposition, and declared that revolution was the regime's internationalist duty. "We cannot cease being internationalists unless we cease being revolutionaries," he said. "We cannot discontinue strategic relationships unless we cease being revolutionaries. It is impossible even to consider this."

To the Sandinista followers, this was a rousing message. Liberals in the U.S. at first chose to whitewash the statement, dismissing its perorations as mere "rhetoric," until Congress defeated a vote for humanitarian aid on April 23, 1985, for the contras. The next day, however, Daniel Ortega flew to Moscow to ask for $200 million. It stung many who voted against the aid, and a number of legislators said it was so embarrassing that, had they known in advance, they would have voted yes rather than no.

The incident cast a potent shadow over the successive votes and the policy debate during the following year. Suddenly, no one but the extreme left wanted to abandon the contras entirely. That summer, it was comparatively easy for the administration to win approval for $27 million in humanitarian aid—food, clothing, medical supplies.

Modestly, a corner had been turned. But other changes were afoot in the administration. For one, Ronald Reagan wanted "to go all out" for military aid. But he would have to do so with a new lineup.

Jeane Kirkpatrick, the most articulate spokesman for the contras—so much so that the contras even named a guerrilla task force after her—was now gone.

Two months later, another casualty left, Thomas Enders's replacement, L. Anthony Motley, the former ambassador to Brazil and a happy-go-lucky forty-year-old. Before joining the administration, he had been a real estate entrepreneur and a Republican fund-raiser. He spoke Portuguese fluently and had a gutsy, cut-the-red-tape style. But caught in the crosswinds of the determined right and an implacable left and having to mend the CIA's covert fences while keeping a diplomatic line extended to the Nicaraguans, had proven to be too much.

Once, when Motley was riding up to the Hill with Bill Casey to testify behind closed doors on the Nicaragua operation, Casey began to rant and rave about Congress. "These fuckers," he said, their posturing was "bullshit." But Motley's own boss, Shultz, was not a buccaneer, but more of an establishment man. And no matter how difficult they could be, members had to be catered to and stroked. In time, no one, from the Hill to State to the CIA, was happy with Motley, and he was sniped at from all sides. That May, Motley resigned abruptly, with little public explanation.

Many felt that he too was forced out, and while he was perceived as a victim of favoring too much diplomacy at the expense of nurturing the contras, it was just as accurate to say that he tired of performing an impossible job.

Shultz had a decision to make. Whatever difficulties remained, the administration was making headway. It was time to pull disparate strands of the Central America policy together. But he didn't want a Wise Man establishment type, he wanted a doer. He had lost his two previous assistant secretaries, and didn't want to lose a third.

The job was a big position. It entailed overseeing the State Department bureau and U.S. embassies in more than thirty nations in Latin America and the Caribbean. It also meant day-to-day management of a staff of two hundred, and overseeing the highly charged contra policy. Shultz wanted someone with sufficient energy and thick skin who wouldn't be worn down, and a figure who could be insulated against—and would insulate him from—the conservative right. He also wanted someone who wasn't green, who could hit the ground running.

Only one candidate was considered. He asked his executive assistant, Charles Hill, to feel out thirty-seven-year-old Elliott Abrams. Make sure he'll accept the job before I offer it to him, Shultz instructed.

IF EVER ANYONE was suited to the needs of the assistant secretary of state for Latin American affairs in the Reagan administration, it was Elliott Abrams, the product of a fascinating political odyssey in which the diverse strains of America's great political traditions, conservatism and liberalism, were uneasily joined.

Elliott Abrams grew up in the Hollis Hills section of Queens, in a kosher household, with parents who believed deeply in the American dream. In the Abrams house, this meant that the grandchildren of immigrants should have a better life than their parents and grandparents. His father, Joseph, struggled, and succeeded, first through night school while working as a manual laborer by day, and then to build a successful immigration law practice. His mother, Mildred, worked as a public school teacher. Where other children rebelled against their parents, Abrams always got along well with them, and was especially close to his father.

The Abrams household was also very political, perhaps not as much as the more intellectually minded New York literary crowd, but dinner conversation frequently strayed into heated discussions that continued for hours. Abrams was the younger of two boys, and the more argumentative of the two, showing greater passion about ideas than his pragmatically minded brother and father. Like many of their neighbors, the

Abramses were liberal Democrats who revered Adlai Stevenson and were contemptuous of Joe McCarthy. They also believed strongly in education.

For high school, Abrams was sent to Elizabeth Irwin, a small progressive school in Greenwich Village. Its faculty was drawn largely from once blacklisted teachers. Among Abrams's classmates were a fiery young black woman named Angela Davis and another future radical, Kathy Boudin, as well as the orphaned children of convicted spies Ethel and Julius Rosenberg. The school proved to be an awkward fit for Abrams. Where most students went to school wearing the dress of the counterculture, ripped jeans, sandals, long hair, Abrams almost always sported a navy blue suit. The growing sentiment toward rebellion had almost an opposite effect on the quintessentially square Abrams, inuring him even further against the trends of the day.

From Irwin, Abrams went on to Harvard, entering with the class of '69. During the hurly-burly days of the campus activism that plunged the school into turmoil, Abrams developed a reputation as a conservative student. He refused to join the YPSL, or Young People's Socialist League, even though his roommate and future Harvard professor and Bill Clinton policy aide, Steven Kelman, in Adams House, was the organization's head, and another friend, Charles Schumer, who later became a prominent New York congressman, was also deeply involved. Abrams ardently defined himself as a liberal Democrat—pro-welfare, a believer in an activist government, against the Vietnam War, but not against a robust U.S. foreign policy abroad. He chaired the campus chapter of Americans for Democratic Action, ADA, the liberal lobbying group.

As in high school, Abrams looked old-line establishment. His sandy brown hair was short and neatly combed, and, with his crisp chinos and blue button-down shirts, he had a perpetually pressed look. He actually threw out worn jeans.

While Abrams didn't work spectacularly hard, he was captivated by his courses. He loved Government 180, a course on international affairs taught by an up-and-coming professor, Henry Kissinger, who would shortly move on to become Nixon's national security adviser. Another favorite was a course taught by Samuel Huntington, the brilliant political scientist, dealing with "Political Development and Political Order in Modernizing Societies." It was Sam Beard, however, who made one of the greatest impressions on Abrams. Beard, who regularly filled up the lecture hall with enthusiastic students, challenged the young Harvard students to think, considering six critical junctures in history. Beard's impassioned discussion of the Weimar Republic, in which he posed the question "When does a democratic society have the right, or duty, to defend itself by crushing antidemocratic movements by undemocratic means?" left a lasting impression on Abrams.

The student culture at Harvard also began to have a profound impact on Abrams. He came to thoroughly dislike the SDS, the Students for a Democratic Society, and its activists. Abrams, and many friends, believed the organization had taken on a totalitarian character. Abrams himself felt far apart from the group, culturally and politically. And, as his roommate Steven Kelman later recalled, "We talked a fair bit about the leaders of the SDS, who were spoiled WASPs, who went to elite prep schools." Abrams considered them "filthy leftists, acting with their parents' consent." Thus, while SDS radicals, the children of the elite, attempted to become a revolutionary vanguard in alliance with movements of national liberation in the Third World, Abrams and other children of East European immigrants, still dreaming of affluence, increasingly became defenders of the status quo. Abrams even helped form the Ad Hoc Committee to Keep Harvard Open when SDS members proposed a strike to close the university.

After Harvard, Abrams studied at the London School of Economics, and then got a degree from Harvard Law School. His brother, Franklin, five years his senior, who had gone to Harvard and Yale Law, had already joined their father's immigration law practice. The expectation was that Elliott would do so as well. But Abrams applied for a job with the U.S. attorney's office, and when he didn't hear from them, joined the New York City law firm of Breed, Abbott and Morgan in 1973, one of the city's white-shoe, WASP law firms. Founded in 1898, in 1973 it still had only eighty lawyers. The firm was very traditional, very corporate, its culture still Brahmin and staid—"like a family, filled with men of the old school," said the firm's librarian of more than forty years, Pat Lipari. Abrams was one of six recruited that year from Harvard, and he started out in the litigation department, a highly desirable place for a young, ambitious lawyer to be. He worked with Jim Zirin, an aggressive young litigator, fresh out of the U.S. attorney's office. With his salary of $18,000, Abrams rented a spacious apartment on East 86th Street, which he rarely saw.

From 7:30 A.M. to 9:30 P.M., Abrams put in long billable hours, churned out cogent draft briefs, and turned in favorable appearances in court. The firm's partners, including Zirin, were impressed by Abrams's strong writing skills and his hunger for responsibility. While Abrams didn't like the more mundane work that was the bread and butter for a new associate, he was moving swiftly along the partnership track. His father was extremely pleased. Elliott was fulfilling the advice given to him by his cousin Floyd Abrams, who would become the well-known First Amendment lawyer. "Cut your teeth in a large law firm," Abrams's cousin had told him.

After a year, Abrams mastered the musty instrumentalities of the law. But as the cases dragged on, he became tired of the long hours, the repetitious work, and the drudgery of writing appeals. He missed the heated political discussions and constant give-and-take that so engaged him as an undergraduate at Harvard. His paycheck didn't compensate for the tedium. There had to be a rational solution. He decided he had to talk to his bosses.

He set up a meeting with the two partners he worked for. He liked both, but neither seemed aware of the other's incredible demands. Almost sheepishly, he approached their secretaries to ask about a lunch. The two partners and Abrams met in the Wall Street Club, the dining room where each year senior partners wooed prospective associates. Abrams was sweating under his crisp pin-striped suit. Finally, he spoke, turning to one and saying, "You're giving me fifty hours a week of work." Then he repeated to the other, "You're giving me fifty hours of work."

There, Abrams thought to himself. He sat back in his chair, relieved. Now they would understand. The two partners looked at him, and almost at the same time, they responded dryly, "Yes, Elliott, go on. So what is it you want to tell us?"

Abrams was stunned. "The handwriting is on the wall," he thought. That afternoon, he shuffled off to his office to collect his thoughts. He was a Harvard Law School graduate working in one of the blue-chip Wall Street firms. And he didn't know what to do with his life. Abrams fiddled with his pencil, tapping it against his desk. He had no one else to talk to. He didn't know how to broach this with his parents or his brother. But he knew he wanted to leave the firm.

Weeks went by, and then, one afternoon, as Abrams aimlessly twirled his Rolodex, it stopped on a number, 202-224-3121. In his neat handwriting was the name Richard Perle, Professional Staff Member, Permanent Subcommittee on Investigations, Office of Senator Henry M. Jackson, 103 Russell Senate Office Building, Washington, D.C.

Abrams had first met Perle in 1971 while attending an Americans for Democratic Action convention in Washington, D.C. The two then had a drink at the Shoreham Hotel and hit it off. Perle, with his wit and charm, dazzled Abrams. Perle told Abrams that he and his boss, Senator Jackson, were "fighting the good fight—anti-Soviet, pro-Israel, pro-defense." He also said that Jackson might run for president someday. If he did, they'd be happy to have Abrams involved. Perle even took Abrams to meet the senator the next morning. Abrams had shaken hands with such luminaries as John Kenneth Galbraith, and even once met Professor Arthur Schlesinger, but never had he met an elected official. Perle told him to keep in touch.

Over the next couple of years, Abrams called Perle whenever he came to Washington. Perle's town house on Maryland Avenue, near the Senate, was a cross between a college group home and an international boarding hostel; it was always filled with guests, an array of exotic nationalities, often East European or Israeli. Perle would leave his front door open, or freely distribute his house keys.

As Abrams reached for the number again, he thought, Perle's work was hardly the boring stuff of Breed, Abbott and Morgan. Unsure of what to expect, Abrams found Perle was "still interested." Jackson was preparing to run for president. "Look, it's Friday," Perle said. "Get down here as soon as possible. You can stay at my place Sunday night, and I'll arrange for you to see Scoop first thing Monday morning." Then, pausing, he added: "Hold on, just a second—I see on his schedule that he's got a breakfast meeting at *The New Republic*."

"Does that mean I shouldn't come down?" Abrams asked, holding his breath.

"You bet it doesn't. I'll just bring you along with us."

It was music to Abrams's ears. Richard Perle had stuck to his word, and Abrams not only had a ticket out of the stifling world of the law, but a chance for the brass ring.

By Tuesday morning, Perle told Abrams, "Well, he's ready, it looks as though you have a job." Abrams was hired onto the Permanent Subcommittee on Investigations as an assistant counsel through the presidential campaign season. He took a pay cut of $3,000, and plunged right in. Working for Jackson, Abrams found a new lease on life, and when the presidential campaign fizzled, rather than returning to practice law in New York, Abrams found one excuse after another to stay in Washington. He didn't mind the long hours, and even relished work that was relatively boring by Capitol Hill standards, such as run-of-the-mill commencement speeches for Jackson.

In 1977, Abrams moved on to the staff of the new senator from New York, Pat Moynihan. He had met Moynihan during the Jackson campaign, and so impressed the former U.N. ambassador that Moynihan, readying himself for his own race for the Senate, asked Abrams to be his campaign manager. Jackson recommended against it because of Abrams's "lack of political experience," but when Moynihan won, Jackson wholeheartedly supported Abrams's move to Moynihan's staff as his special counsel and chief legislative aide.

Within a year, Abrams was promoted to chief of staff. The brilliant and quirky Moynihan was no ordinary senator, and as his chief of staff, Abrams was supervising some of the best and the brightest aides on Capitol Hill. As Dick Eaton, a subsequent Moynihan chief of staff, put it: the staffers were "ideologues, iconoclastic and idiosyncratic." Moynihan wooed the wildly funny and smart Charles Horner away from Scoop's staff, as well as Abe Shulski, a noted intelligence expert; Chester Finn, a bespectacled, Harvard-trained workaholic, who colleagues described as "quirky, but brilliant" (he dispensed with the office equipment and brought his own typewriter into the office); and an old laborite, Judy Bardacke.

For his press secretary, Moynihan hired a young Irish pol, Tim Russert, who started out first in the Buffalo, New York, office before being promoted to the Washington office. Abrams felt Russert had few real ideological or political convictions, aside from being "a committed Democrat." But Moynihan valued Russert's political instincts. Other staffers thought Russert a little "too ingratiating" with Moynihan, and more "left-wing" than the rest of the Moynihan team cared for. But Russert came to be liked partly through his humor. He was the office showman. He frequently did Moynihan imitations behind the senator's back, sending the staff spinning into belly laughs.

Initially, Abrams thrived as Moynihan's chief of staff, but there was inner turmoil about the political direction Moynihan would take. Barely palpable at first, simmering beneath the surface, the signs were nevertheless there almost at the outset. Moynihan's maiden speech on the floor of the Senate was a barnstorming philippic about why he was voting against President Carter's choice of the liberal Paul Warnke to be the chief arms negotiator. It was a bold act for a freshman senator, and a very Scoop Jackson thing to do—to vote against the president. And indeed, Moynihan collaborated with his Senate mentor, Jackson. Moynihan then amplified his stance, not in *Commentary*, the usual suspect, but in one of the dominant magazines of the New York well-to-do, *The New Yorker*. In a small way, the choice of *The New Yorker* over *Commentary* showed the direction that Moynihan, no longer the hard-charging U.N. ambassador but now the New York senator, was moving in.

IN 1978, *Commentary*'s editor, Norman Podhoretz, held one of his famous political parties, at least 150, if not more, crammed into his spacious apartment on the Upper West Side, between Broadway and West End Avenue. The area was dubbed "the Guilded Ghetto" because high-society Jews, unable to have an address on Park Avenue, could live here in grandeur equal to that of Park Avenue. In years past, when the Podhoretzes were mostly interested in talk about aesthetics and literature, Gloria Steinem, Jules Feiffer, and Norman Mailer were regulars at their parties, which were colorful affairs, brimming with bubbly drink and fluid talk. But as the Podhoretzes strayed into politics and foreign affairs, taking a hard line, they ended up breaking with many of their more liberal friends. Now the regulars were prominent political aficionados, Irving and Bea Kristol, Suzie Weaver (later *Wall Street Journal* columnist Suzie Garment), and publishing mogal Jason Epstein. And at this particular party, Elliott Abrams and Charles Horner, known principally for the simple fact that they were young Moynihan staffers, were invited too.

Abrams eyed the twenty-foot ceilings, the high windows overlooking the Hudson, richly stained parquet floors crafted with the care of an old French refectory table, the maid's quarters, and the hulking concert grand piano in the huge living room. He talked briefly to Midge Decter's grown daughter, Rachel, who had spent an entire summer at the Moynihans' farm in upstate New York when she was fifteen. Then, as Abrams began to mingle, there was a sudden hush. Podhoretz called upon him and Charles Horner to stand with their backs to the wall and face the assembled guests. It was a ritual known to everyone—except Abrams and Horner.

"Now Elliott and Charles will tell us about the progress of the senator, our old friend, Pat Moynihan," Norman Podhoretz informed the 150 gathered in the room.

For an hour, Abrams and Horner, pressed against the book-lined walls, were grilled. How is Pat doing? Is he holding up against the liberals? Is Scoop Jackson helping him out? What about the SALT talks, will he stand firm? Will he be doing anything about the Soviet probes in Southwest Asia? And of course, what about the oil fields in the Middle East? Abrams and Horner fielded each question, and dutifully reported that all was well in Senator Moynihan's office. But in fact, things weren't.

Cracks between Moynihan, the professor and senator, and his hard-line staff had started to appear. As the staff was increasingly estranged from the Democrats, Moynihan, the darling of the neoconservatives and heir apparent to Scoop Jackson, was moving in the other direction. By 1979, Moynihan had swung closer to the center of gravity in the Democratic party, toward the McGovern-Carter-Kennedy axis, while Abrams was a regular in the neoconservative camp. He was also dating Rachel Decter.

One weekend, Abrams came up from Washington to New York for a date. It was a pitch black evening, just right for a couple in love, and the two hopped in his new sporty lemon-yellow Mazda RX-7. Their previous dates had been standard fare—brunch at her place to honor their friend

Adam Myerson, the young editor of *The American Spectator*, a meeting at the Harvard Club, then off to dinner at one of New York's many fine restaurants. This was Elliott Abrams. He went to all the right schools, made all the right connections, planned his career carefully, was responsible, controlled, forward-looking. Rachel, on the other hand, was a New Yorker, already divorced from a failed marriage to an Israeli entrepreneur, and she had rebellious friends. Elliott was a little square, all neatly dressed, almost always in a suit or pressed khakis and a starched button-down shirt, nothing funky about him.

On this evening, Abrams announced they were going over to Brooklyn Heights for a romantic night to watch the glittering lights of the Manhattan skyline. Rachel expected a leisurely ride, when suddenly she found herself startled at Abrams's driving. He was racing the car madly, practically skidding along the corners and sharp curves of the road. He sped past everyone else along the West Side Highway, and not letting up, shifted into fourth gear, surpassing the speed limit as they careened across the Brooklyn Bridge and side streets along the river, leaving other cars to eat their dust. Rachel, her heart racing, looked at the man she thought she knew so well, Elliott Abrams, the steady, predictable conservative. She loved the ride.

Rachel Decter had known from the moment she met Elliott that she wanted to marry him. The first evening, she told her parents and sister in the kitchen that "he was it." When the two arrived at Podhoretz and Decter's apartment with a bottle of champagne in the fall of 1979 to announce their engagement, Midge Decter openly cried with joy, and even Podhoretz, not usually known for his sentimentality, got weepy. He, as the head of the neoconservatives' first royal family, would later boast that this was the closest thing to an arranged marriage among neoconservative elites.

The two were married in the apartment. Seymour Siegel, a professor at the Jewish Theological Seminary, who had given the benediction at Richard Nixon's second presidential inauguration, performed the ceremony. Rachel had met him while she was working at the religion page at *Newsweek*. Pat Moynihan and Scoop Jackson were also not just invited guests, but would sign the *ketuba*, the traditional Jewish wedding contract.

But by the time of the wedding Abrams was no longer with Moynihan. He had gone back to the law, working for Harry McPherson's law firm. It was from here, with Moynihan's help, and having actively campaigned for Ronald Reagan, that Elliott Abrams would move into the State Department and the new Republican administration.

. . .

AT THIRTY-THREE, Abrams had become the youngest assistant secretary of state in the twentieth century. But, in International Organizations, he had been placed in an unworkable situation, theoretically overseeing Jeane Kirkpatrick at the U.N. As was inevitable, the two neoconservatives skirmished. As soon as another opening in State appeared, the position for assistant secretary for human rights, Abrams heavily lobbied his friends in high places for the job. He went to see Reagan's confidant, Judge Clark, and said, "You asked me to think about candidates. I have figured out someone perfect for this job, I mean perfect! Me." Clark immediately responded, "Done."

Less than a year later, Abrams had emerged as a vocal, articulate, if not blunt force in administration foreign policy circles. As a former Democrat and disciple of Pat Moynihan, he was at first viewed with suspicion by conservatives. They feared this swaggering young man was a "liberal mole." For their part, human rights activists heaved a sigh of relief when he was named, precisely because he did come out of the Democratic party. The problems with conservatives soon faded. His honeymoon with the left turned out to be a courtship that never got off the ground.

In his first months, Abrams made his mark, authoring an influential memo that outlined the Reagan human rights policy. He called for the end of the "double standard" the famous term used by Kirkpatrick in her *Commentary* article—which he argued the Carter administration had applied to pro-American authoritarian regimes, while essentially going soft on adversarial, Communist regimes. This was the Kirkpatrick doctrine, with a human rights emphasis. He declared that for American foreign policy to have credibility, it must vigorously incorporate human rights into its spirit and its practice. He maintained that the U.S. must "neither coddle friends" nor simply "criticize foes," but instead must promote human rights everywhere, equally, which often meant "hard choices."

Setting his policy apart from what he saw as Carter's quixotic and often ineffective human rights crusading, Abrams injected a note of geopolitical pragmatism. "All pertinent interests will have to be balanced," he declared. As he saw it, sometimes quiet diplomacy was called for, other times, public diplomacy. "Human rights is not advanced by replacing a bad regime with a worse one, or a corrupt dictator with a Communist politburo," he wrote. He later added, "It is not enough to ask who is in power and what do we like, but what is the alternative, what are the prospects for change. Look at Vietnam and Iran. Bad situations can and do get worse."

Working from eight in the morning to seven at night, he relished the job and quickly thrived. Each year, he was responsible for compiling the annual human rights review, assessing the status of rights in 164 countries worldwide. In doing so, he walked a tightrope between activists who supported the vocal human rights policies of Jimmy Carter, and conservatives who felt it was more important to check Soviet power. While acknowledging that his reports provided the most "credible and comprehensive coverage of human rights conditions," the human rights lobby soon became harsh critics. Americas Watch and the Lawyers Committee for Human Rights accused him of whitewashing gross violations by friendly countries, like El Salvador and Guatemala, or exaggerating abuses in Nicaragua.

Aryeh Neier, vice chairman of Americas Watch, a human rights watchdog group for Latin America, was among the most vociferous of Abrams's critics. The two often sparred, and among the epithets for Abrams, Neier declared him to be a "prisoner of ideology," asserting that he "marshals facts to support his worldview," and sarcastically noting he was "vitriolic." Once, they appeared together on the *MacNeil/Lehrer NewsHour*, and Neier was so critical, Abrams said he wouldn't appear on a panel with him again.

This was all the more ironic because Abrams believed in the human rights community, and was especially supportive of their work in most areas of the world. In fact, when he started out, Abrams sought to work with the groups. He invited them to discuss their vision, and their grievances with him. But after one ill-fated, rancorous meeting in his office, the lines of discussion broke down, and henceforth he and the human rights community dueled across the ideologically charged camps of Republicans and Democrats.

In the murky and politically motivated debates around Central America, it did not escape Abrams's notice that virtually all criticisms like Neier's stemmed from groups comprised almost exclusively of liberal Democrats, many of whom were associated with the Carter administration. As for any indignities hurled at him, Abrams himself was aware "that they were using the veneer of human rights to attack the Reagan Central America policy." Abrams's fierce opposition to the Sandinistas and the FMLN only earned him their further enmity.

The charge that Abrams politicized his assessments was, on the whole, a hollow one. Usually, it came down to a dispute about two or three countries, out of more than 160. To the extent Abrams may have softened some criticism with a country like El Salvador, this was consistent with his philosophy, laid out in his human rights memo and established earlier by Kirkpatrick, namely that effective human rights work was a tireless balancing of backroom diplomacy and public recriminations. It was also consistent with his job as a public official—he was charged with working for his president, not engaging in noisy criticisms at odds with his own administration's policy.

And Abrams had a record to be proud of on human rights. He sought and eventually gained the removal of Jean-Claude Duvalier, known as Baby Doc, the merciless dictator in Haiti. He would support removing Ferdinand Marcos in the Philippines. He was every bit as tough with the right-wing dictatorships of Augusto Pinochet in Chile, Alfredo Stroessner in Paraguay, and Manuel Noriega in Panama, as he was with Communist tyrannies in Nicaragua, the Soviet Union, and East Germany. In the process, he angered his own conservative base, tangling with Jesse Helms, the powerful far-right Southern senator, who thought Abrams was too tough on America's friends. Even Peter Rodman, a former disciple of Henry Kissinger's and head of State's Policy Planning shop under Reagan, and a thoughtful conservative's conservative, worried about Abrams's human rights zeal. He once joked that Abrams was a "pinko." In more serious moments he cautioned Abrams about creating another Iran, pushing out pro-American dictators in return for something even worse. But, as Abrams continued in his job, Rodman changed his view.

Abrams was resolutely a Reaganaut, replete with sunny optimism, a stubborn defense of the democratic ideal, and a belief that the great battle of the Cold War was about the struggle between democracy and its enemies. At the core of his philosophy was the view that the best way to secure and improve human rights was not by judicial fiat, or vigorous human rights monitoring, though he supported both of these. His human rights paradigm was surprisingly bolder, more comprehensive, than those held by his detractors. Where they were concerned with individual cases, he spoke of "government structure." Human rights, he contended, was best guaranteed by democracy and fundamental political rights—regular elections at the ballot box, a thriving free press, bustling labor unions, and freedom of association.

He shared another view of Ronald Reagan's. "I start from the premise that the world is a dangerous place." Accordingly, he became an assiduous supporter of administration Central America policy, which, outside of the arms talks, was where the action and energy was.

And, when Abrams was attacked in the press, few charges went unresponded to. He wrote frequent op-ed articles and letters to the editor. "When the policy is controversial, you have to go out there and defend your views," he never tired of saying.

After five years in the human rights job, however, he felt he had done all he could. The learning curve had gone flat, and he wanted something new. In the spring of 1985, after making overtures for the top job at the

Agency for International Development if Peter McPherson left (he didn't), he set his sights on one of two ambassadorships: Taiwan or South Africa. He talked it over with Rachel, and they were ready to pack their bags if the offer came. He made inquiries.

Instead, that May, Shultz asked him to take over Motley's job. Shultz didn't even bother to interview Abrams, he just asked him. It was a bolt out of the blue, but Abrams didn't flinch.

For Abrams, it didn't require much mulling over. This was even better than an ambassadorship. He felt the five regional bureaus, Europe, Latin America, Africa, the Middle East, and Asia, were the "dukedoms," where the power, access, opportunity to be involved in substantive policy, and ability to advance one's career were. He immediately said yes.

The only bump in the road was when his old nemesis, Jesse Helms, held up his nomination, finally relenting that July. Thus the Latin American affairs slot had changed once more, but Abrams was poised to eclipse his predecessors. Shultz told the press that the feisty Abrams was "tough-minded," "smart," and has "good judgment." To be sure, he didn't have the mellifluous charm or bureaucratic savvy of a Richard Perle, he lacked the presence, eloquence, and star quality of Jeane Kirkpatrick, he was not a counterestablishment Wise Man, the soft-talking, lawyerly insider like Max Kampelman. But by every criteria, he had been strikingly successful thus far, and his full potential was still far from being realized.

At just thirty-eight, in his third position in State, he was breathtakingly young. But he had already earned serious plaudits as a good boss, an effective manager, a respectful listener with colleagues, tenaciously loyal, and principled. He could also be an engaging raconteur and had a zest for imitations, easily launching into a rendition of Henry Kissinger. Though the outside world thought of him as very Harvard, he was also remarkably unpretentious.

But he did have his handicaps. In a position that was normally occupied by soothing diplomats, he was anything but diplomatic. Moreover, he despised "schmooze lawyers and diplomats," which included much of the liberal Washington establishment. Where most of his colleagues held their tongues and softened their hard edges with the Hill, he drew sharp lines and told it like it was. Rather than cater to his determined political enemies, he confronted them. It was a risky style, at times making him sound shrill, like nothing more than an ardent partisan, when he would perhaps be better served by retreating, acting more like the establishment diplomats he had come to loathe. For many, his brashness was in part a function of age, but it was also a function of his temperament.

It was clear that just as he would bring a youthful gusto to his position, he would also forever be navigating between the shoals of his partisan adversaries, poised to strike. But Abrams was a doer. He had not come into public service just to sit quietly by. Whatever it took, he would do. If it meant skating precariously along the edges, he would be there. If it meant being a vulnerable spear carrier for the cause, so be it.

Once, when he was testifying on the Hill with Thomas Enders about the war in El Salvador in 1982, he asked Enders, "I'm happy to testify, but why isn't the undersecretary, or the secretary doing it?" Enders, an old Foreign Service hand, was well aware of the rules of the game, the quiet code of knowing when, during the heat of political battle, to stand in the glare of the public, and when to quietly recede into the background. With a lilt in his voice, the patrician Enders grinned, and then looked down at Abrams grimly and said, "Because it's a dirty little war and they don't want to touch it."

But, with the crosier of authority on Latin America passed to Abrams, that was exactly what he would now have to do.

CHAPTER 32

Elliott Abrams picked up his telephone. A deep baritone voice at the other end of the line said, "Mr. Abrams, this is the Diplomatic Security Bureau of the State Department." There was a pause.

Then the voice continued. "I'm calling to inform you that the group Witness for Peace has asked for a permit to hold a silent vigil in front of your house."

"That can't be," Abrams said. "They shouldn't be allowed to do that. It's my home. Don't give it to them."

"It's not our call. They went to the D.C. government. The permit is a done deal."

Abrams's face turned a hot red. My God, he thought. It's wrong. It was bad enough to be hounded by these so-called peace groups every day at work. They had no right to harass him at his home, and bring his children into a political grievance. He muttered, "It should be unlawful."

"Look, it may not be so bad. There are restrictions. They are forbidden by the permit to step on your property. They are not allowed to be disruptive. They have promised this will be a silent vigil."

"How many people?"

"Fifty, maybe seventy-five."

God, Abrams thought. He felt violated—none of this was much of a consolation. What could he do?

The voice continued. "We have a request. We would like you to go home early tomorrow to avoid having to cross a picket line to enter your house. That might be the best way to avoid an incident."

"What time?"

"To play it safe, about three o'clock."

The next day, Abrams pulled his car into the driveway of his house at 6367 31st Place at exactly three o'clock. The sun was shining, bright and distant, the way it usually does in late fall, before the first snow. He wondered about the neighbors. The neighborhood, fashionable Northwest D.C., was home to the well-off but not rich, speckled with lobbyists, lawyers, and government officials. The curb outside was typically lined with Saabs, Volvos, Hondas, a few BMWs. Stepping out of his car, he briefly gazed at the modest sweep of lawn in front of his house. There was 147 feet of frontage. It was flanked by a weathered hitching fence, giving the home a rustic feeling. Today, rather than a welcoming decoration, it would be an ominous barrier, standing between him and what he feared would be an unruly mob.

He then cast his eyes on his house, a broad red-brick facade, punctuated by a white doorway and rows of windows. Everything was so quiet, yet he felt a terrible unease.

By four, three diplomatic security cars were patrolling the block. Then they parked themselves visibly at strategic locations. Abrams felt a sense of momentary relief. These were his guys. He admired the precision with which they took their places.

Soon thereafter, three more cars pulled up, District of Columbia police cars.

Inside the house, his three kids, home from school, were playing quietly. Rachel was trying to put a good face on things, but he could see her mounting apprehension. Trying not to show distraction, he busied himself with work. His right leg jiggled up and down with nervous tension.

Then, for a brief moment, he wondered if the thing had been called off. Everything was so quiet.

At 5 P.M., more than fifty people suddenly massed at the sidewalk in front of his house, forming a wall between him and the rest of the world. Rachel hollered, "Elliott, come take a look. They're here."

Outside, the mob clustered around like linebackers eager to rush the opposing quarterback. Through a parted curtain, Abrams saw a zeal in their faces. Each of them carried a large wooden cross, creating a mobile cemetery. Emblazoned across the signs were different names, presumably of alleged victims of the wars in Central America.

"Baby killer!" one of the protesters shouted.

"Stop the killing in Central America!" another bellowed.

For a terrible moment, Abrams felt frozen, then flushed with anger. By now, neighbors had poured out of their houses to see what was going on. One laughed, later telling Elliott, "If they had brought a keg of beer, it would've been perfect." But to Abrams and his family, holed up like hostages in their own home, it felt ghastly.

Another neighbor was fuming at the indignity of the protest. She strode angrily over to the protesters, and screamed, "Don't you know there are children in that house? Leave them alone."

The scene tensed. Several of the protesters surrounded the woman in a half circle. She stood her ground, they stood theirs.

"There are children in there!" she repeated.

One female protester thrust her face into the neighbor's, and at the top of her lungs screamed, "Don't you know he's responsible for killing the children of Central America?"

Then, almost as quickly as it began, the fleeting standoff ended. Recognizing she couldn't reason with them, the neighbor slowly retreated to her lawn.

The protesters continued to chant, "Baby killer, baby killer!"

Some then began to lay their signs against his fence. Abrams felt a surge of anger. They were not supposed to do this. He had been promised. Moreover, they were supposed to be silent. Looking at the white wooden crosses symbolically angled against his fence, he felt as though it were a direct assault on him. Dozens of protesters were now walking in a circle in front of his home.

At one point, Abrams's five-year-old son, Joey, dashed to the windows. Pushing aside the blinds, he anxiously pressed his nose to the window. He looked shaken. "Why are they shouting all those horrible things about Daddy, Mom? What's going on?"

It was now dark, and the protesters had lit candles, illuminating the walkway in front of the house. One neighbor later said she felt the whole scene was eerie, like something out of the Deep South in the 1950s, not Washington, D.C., circa 1985. It was as though they were carrying little torches, circling like a Ku Klux Klan lynch mob. Rachel pulled Joey aside, and sat him down. What to say?

Rachel wasn't one to sugarcoat things, and gave it to her son in black and white. "Joey, the Communists are trying to take over Central America. Daddy is trying to help the president stop them. He wants the people to be free. These people want the Communists to win."

At seven, the crowd finally marched off. Abrams slumped into a soft, overstuffed chair. It was over.

The incident was a jarring experience for Abrams, leaving him with "a deep and profound distaste for the ideological left." He had gotten used to the slights, people who would not shake his hand, people who said to his wife, "You're so nice, how can you be married to a man like that?" He had gotten used to the people in his own temple who turned their backs to him as he passed, who made snide remarks, who disparaged him not because he wasn't an observant Jew, but because he was.

But slowly, as the street returned to a chill, dark calm, broken only by the occasional passing of a car, a new fear began to settle over Elliott Abrams. It was clear that the public debate in America had changed, taking on a rancorous, uncivil tone. Ideological opponents on the ideological left of the president didn't just think he, Abrams, was wrong in

pursuing the policies he did, or that they and he had a profoundly different vision of the world. No, Abrams now felt that they had concluded that
he was evil. And because they thought he was evil, they would and could
suspend all standards of conduct in their political behavior. That was
why they could invade his family like this.

He thought of the time when he, Rachel, and the children had been ac-
costed by opponents of Reagan's Central America policy as they sat in an
airport terminal. Rachel had to threaten to call the police. Then there
was the time when a throng of protesters had descended menacingly
upon his car, shouting, "It's him, it's Abrams." For the first moment in
his life, Elliott Abrams began to worry that if he were not careful the
people who disagreed with him could become an unruly mob—and a violent one.

NEVER WAS A policy more misunderstood than what Elliott Abrams was
trying to do at the State Department. In August 1985, Democrats in Congress, increasingly unnerved by Sandinista behavior, and embarrassed
by Daniel Ortega's trip to Moscow, were no longer willing to deny Reagan
support for the contra resistance. They were still not yet ready to authorize military aid, but they were willing to sign off on humanitarian aid—
food, clothing, medicine—and passed $27 million in nonlethal aid for the
resistance. The program would be distributed not by CIA, but by State,
which meant Abrams would oversee it.

After the vote for the $27 million, Shultz called Abrams into his office.
He told Abrams that the president was going to want to make a big request for military aid, so he needed to lay the groundwork now. Take
soundings on the Hill with our friends, Henry Hyde and Mickey Edwards
in the House, Richard Lugar and Sam Nunn in the Senate, he said,
adding, "Let's see if we can come up with a big chunk of change."

This was just what Abrams wanted to hear. For the past year, the contras had been languishing without support from the U.S. He was convinced that until they were again a viable military force, there could be
no resolution of the conflict. By logic, national security interests, and
ideology, the Sandinistas would continue to foment revolution beyond
their borders, destabilizing the isthmus right up to Mexico. Any treaty
signed with the Sandinistas would be useless without a means of enforc-
ing the negotiated settlement. For Abrams, this translated into the necessity of military support for the contras. They were the only way to
influence, and enforce, any diplomatic outcome.

Abrams had known from the moment he took the job that it would be a
battle. One of the first things he had done after being nominated was to

consult with his old friend Paul Wolfowitz, the assistant secretary for East Asian affairs. Tall, dark-haired, and soft-spoken, the Yale-educated Wolfowitz was a close friend of Richard Perle's and a seasoned government servant. Thoughtful and low key, he was a serious man to be taken seriously. Wolfowitz knew that it was a big change going from a functional bureau, like human rights, to a regional bureau, like Latin American affairs.

You need a good interagency process to work with the other parts of the executive branch involved in the region, he told Abrams. The left hand and the right hand need to be talking to each other. Abrams thought it was good advice, and he took it.

As it turned out, an interagency process was already in place. His predecessor, Tony Motley, had formed an ongoing working group. He changed its name several times and limited the group to as few as possible. He finally settled on calling it the RIG—Restricted Interagency Group. The group's core was Motley, Dewey Clarridge and Alan Fiers of the CIA, Lieutenant Oliver North of the NSC staff, and Nestor Sanchez of the Department of Defense. Indeed, it was the RIG that approved the ill-fated policy in 1984 to mine the Nicaraguan harbors, and sent it to Shultz for his review (Shultz listened and said simply, "Fine."). But whatever mishaps had occurred in the past, everyone agreed it was necessary to have a working interagency process. Abrams quickly continued the RIG meetings. They convened once a week, usually in his office. He was the chair.

At every meeting, one or two attendants represented the major institutional players: DoD, CIA, NSC, State, and the JCS. Sam Watson, of the vice president's shop, also often attended. As a matter of course, meetings were usually bigger than ten. In Abrams's shop alone, a number of his more energetic aides, from deputies to special assistants, repeatedly clamored to be included. They pleaded with Abrams that it was "necessary to do our work." Abrams could see everyone wanted to come and agreed with their logic. It *was* crucial for their work. They were included. Sometimes, though not quite as packed as Perle's interagency meetings, which busted at the seams, these meetings swelled to fifteen or twenty people.

At one point, Shultz asked Abrams to try to adhere to "a real RIG." He asked Abrams to keep it "really restricted." Abrams gave it a shot and his efforts lasted three weeks, before everyone again howled to be included. For all intents and purposes, the RIG was once again open.

Each week, any number of policy and implementation issues were discussed. What to do about Noriega in Panama? How to lean more on Chile? How to keep Haiti from going down the tubes? What should we do if Honduras is invaded? But the lion's share of attention was spent in dealing with the issues dear to the president's heart, Nicaragua and the contras. One day Abrams might ask, "What kinds of shipments are the Sandinistas getting, and what kind of weapons are they using?" The JCS would recommend appropriate responses for the contras. Another week he might want to examine the state of the "internal opposition" to the Sandinistas—Violeta Chamorro and the independent press, the unions, Cardinal Miguel Obando y Bravo and the church. "How can we help them?"

After the $27 million was authorized, the group oversaw the implementation of the program. Early on, the contras had requested wristwatches. On its face, it seemed like a reasonable request, and coordination of time was certainly crucial for a guerrilla group in the field. Abrams had no problem with this. Yet one RIG participant mused that Congress might deem watches a form of lethal aid. This debate, the participant added, paralleled discussions about some of the other covert programs that were nonlethal, like the aid to the non-Communist Cambodians. The group thrashed it out, and finally decided it was preposterous to consider watches lethal. But they also knew they were being watched like hawks by a highly sensitive Democratic Congress.

In this case, the exigencies of the Boland Amendment, not political logic, reigned. Abrams felt it was better to err on the side of safety, and regretfully decided to turn down the contras. If they got watches, it would have to be from somewhere else.

But of all the issues, one was consistently on the RIG agenda, and fought over, again and again. Democratizing the contras, or what Abrams called "giving them a serious face-lift." It brought Abrams into repeated conflict with an institution he trusted too much, and understood too little, the CIA.

IN HIS FIRST days, Abrams had tried to get a handle on the CIA as an institution. One of his young assistants, Bob Kagan, gave him Arthur Schlesinger's *A Thousand Days*. The book, about John F. Kennedy's fleeting tenure as president, was dog-eared and marked at all the pages in which the CIA played a role. Abrams paid particular attention to the stories about the CIA and air drops to the guerrillas on Cuba in the Bay of Pigs fiasco. The whole operation was cockamamy. It was also clear to him that the CIA was a culture deeply different from that of State, but just how different he had not yet learned. He put the book aside, convinced that his serious problems weren't with the Agency, but with the Congress. It would only be later that he came to realize they were with both.

Abrams's goal was to reform the contras, turn them from a purely guerrilla force to more of a democratic, politically astute organization, so that if they came to power, they could govern Nicaragua as a democracy. He envisaged the contras being led by prominent Nicaraguan politicians, social democrats and left-of-center figures who were broadly representative of the Nicaraguan people and would provide the contras with greater legitimacy in the eyes of the Congress. Reforming the contras would, he felt, not only help solve their festering image problem as former Somocistas, loyalists of the ousted Nicaraguan dictator, Anastasio Somoza, but at the same time would put in place the infrastructure for any new government that could emerge out of a political settlement.

This meant Abrams had to do several things. For one, former members of Somoza's National Guard would have to be squeezed out of the leadership (although contra critics vastly inflated the influence of the old National Guard on the contras—since 1983, the contras had been largely comprised of disaffected peasants with little political ideology). Second, the resistance would have to be more attentive to human rights violations and the rules of war. This was a problem. Third, they could not function just as a guerrilla operation, but needed a political program. He believed that the military wing of the resistance needed to be unified with a new civilian leadership—even if it had to be implanted, like a heart transplant. He contemplated big ideas, virtually unheard of for any guerrilla movement in the middle of a prolonged and dangerous civil war, including a contra political assembly and an internal human rights monitoring outfit within the contras, in addition to the full-blown political program. To most observers, these ambitious plans were certainly laudable, but much easier said than done.

But if this could be accomplished, Abrams reasoned, it would demonstrate that the administration was not looking to overthrow the Sandinistas on the battlefield, as liberals feared, but was pursuing a strategy of a workable negotiated peace and genuinely free elections, supporting the democratic center against the extremes of both the right and the left.

The more Abrams studied the contras and thought about the situation, the more he believed that these changes needed to be made. He told his young aides, Bob Kagan, Danny Wattenberg, and Daniel Fisk, smart second-generation neoconservatives—Kagan the son of a renowned Yale history professor, Donald Kagan, Wattenberg the son of notable neoconservative Ben Wattenberg, and Fisk a loyal idealist from the Oklahoma heartland—that the problem might be "that the contras were put together too soon." He added, "In 1981, the only large-scale anti-Sandinista opposition was made up of the conservatives and Somocistas. The liberals and moderates of Nicaragua hadn't yet seen the true nature of the Sandinistas." Late into the night, over pizza in the office, they often brainstormed over how to democratize and reform the contras.

Abrams wanted to meld disparate contra elements into a unified political structure, creating a new political leadership. The primary anti-Sandinista forces were in Honduras, called the Nicaraguan Democratic Force, or by their Spanish acronym, the FDN, led by Adolfo Calero and commanded in the field by Enrique Bermúdez. Together, they had been the backbone of the contras.

Calero was a Nicaraguan by birth, educated at a boarding school in the United States and Notre Dame University. He returned to Nicaragua, where he spent twenty-five years as the manager of a Coca-Cola bottling plant in Managua. He was among the first to oppose the Somoza regime and then its Sandinista successors, until, like so many others, he was forced out of Nicaragua in 1983. He joined the FDN, becoming one of its civilian leaders. A pragmatic businessman, down-to-earth, he also became a favorite of the CIA. On the ground itself, the forces were led by Bermúdez, a colonel in the Somoza National Guard and Somoza's former military attaché in Washington. Bermúdez was not one to be saddled with philosophical discussions about human rights. He was a traditional Latin American military officer. An able enough leader in the field, he was too easily labeled a Third World goon, too slow to curb abuses, not the man Abrams wanted heading the political wing of the resistance. Nor was Calero sufficient. The optics were bad. He was a patriot and an honest man, but was too cozy with the Agency.

But what recourse did Abrams have? He decided to include two other men in the leadership, Arturo Cruz and Alfonso Robelo. Robelo, a social democrat and a former businessman, had impeccable credentials. Not only was he a moderate, and acceptable to liberals, but along with Violeta Chamorro, had even been on the five-member national governing council with the Sandinistas, until he was forced out. He was now part of the contra opposition. For Abrams, Cruz also had perfect credentials. A moderate, an economist, he was more likely to be found teaching a graduate course at Harvard than camped out in the mountains opposing the Sandinistas. But after his brief bid for president in the stacked 1984 Nicaraguan election, he had joined one of the other contra factions, the Democratic Revolutionary Alliance, or ARDE in its Spanish acronym.

The plan Abrams now hatched was to unify the rival contra factions and create an entirely new leadership structure—comprised not just of Calero, but also of Cruz and Bermúdez. Contras with a human face. It would be called the United Nicaraguan Opposition, or UNO. To pull it off, Abrams had to convince another key player in the RIG: Alan Fiers.

But Alan Fiers, the head of the CIA's Central America Task Force, had other ideas. He had a war to run, men to feed, a Sandinista regime to bleed.

HOWEVER MUCH THEY may have been bound together, however much they may have shared a distaste for the Sandinistas and wanted to deliver a serious blow to the Soviets by defeating them in Nicaragua, it would have been tough to find two men more different than Elliott Abrams and Alan Fiers.

Abrams, a blunt-speaking intellectual, Jewish, with a slight frame, was of New York and Harvard; he grew up with images of Kennedy and the Democrats, had worked for Moynihan on the Hill, and was a convert to the Republicans.

By contrast, Fiers, a minister's son reared on a sense of duty in the small-town Midwest of the Eisenhower era, became a lineman playing both offense and defense for the legendary Woody Hayes at Ohio State. After pursuing a master's degree at Indiana University in the mid-1960s, at the height of the Cold War when young men were drawn to the battle against Communism, he joined the CIA, not on the analytic side, but the super-secret operative side, or covert actions.

As journalist Gerald Seib noted, Fiers quickly rose to become the consummate Cold War soldier, the American version of Le Carré's perfect spy. Under Hayes, the muscular, thick-necked, athletic Fiers had earned qualities that would serve him well in the CIA—toughness, fierce loyalty to authority, and an unyielding competitiveness. In the Operations Directorate, the shadowy part of the CIA that manages agents and runs covert operations, he was sent to Turkey, then Pakistan, and by the late 1970s rose to become CIA station chief in Saudi Arabia. He liked the big game of global espionage. Where other agents succumbed to the pressures of clandestine activity, alcoholism and drug use, the isolation that comes from not even being able to tell your neighbor or your best friends what you do for a living, Fiers was undaunted. For two decades, including with his neighbors in Washington, he maintained the fiction that he worked for the State Department.

In Saudi Arabia, he was increasingly sucked into what he termed the "paranoid" mind-set, of always watching and being watched, "on stage twenty-four hours a day." As a CIA agent in hostile environments overseas, Fiers was in the thick of it. It was a clubby and tight-knit world. It was also dangerous, and he would be forever haunted by the day when two of his closest friends, both agents, were killed by the massive car bomb in Beirut that exploded in front of the U.S. embassy in April of 1983. But he thrived in the labyrinth of the Middle East, developing a polished style, an uncanny ability to put his listeners at ease, and to tell them what they wanted to hear—whether or not he meant it. ("My job is to lie, cheat, and steal for the security of the United States," he once remarked.) He was down-to-earth and shrewd; he was also unusually flashy for a spy, but he was careful to save it for the right time and the right place. It made him a most formidable agent.

Like other CIA officers, he quietly fumed through the 1970s over what he perceived as a series of American humiliations: Vietnam, Angola, Afghanistan, Iran, Nicaragua. He never forgot what his teenage daughter, who was in Kabul, Afghanistan, when the Soviet-backed regime seized power in 1978, told him. "It drove her crazy. She was sitting in the compound looking over the walls into a house of Russians next door, and watching them sing and dance and celebrate what was happening," he would recount. He concluded that America had to assert itself abroad against the Soviets, and was a willing soldier in Ronald Reagan's vision of a resurgent America.

Bill Casey spotted him as a rising star in the early 1980s, drew him into the ranks of upper management, and the two developed a father-son relationship. "I'll do anything you ask me to do," Fiers told Casey. In 1984, Casey made him head of the CIA's Central America Task Force, and shortly thereafter invited him to lunch alone in the posh director's office, which was decorated with French Empire furniture, on the seventh floor of CIA headquarters. Casey said he wanted to discuss how important Fiers's job was.

"Alan, you know, the Soviet Union is tremendously overextended and they're vulnerable," Casey said. "If America challenges the Soviets at every turn and ultimately defeats them in one place, that will shatter the mythology, and it will all start to unravel.

"Nicaragua," Casey stressed, "is that place."

IN THE FALL of 1985, as the Sandinistas once again stepped up their military activities against the contras and the administration increased the pressure for more contra aid, Congress responded. The intelligence committees quietly broadened the definition of aid, allowing the contras to receive radios and transportation equipment, and "intelligence advice" for fighters in the field. The Central Intelligence Agency was given $13 million to carry out this task. The CIA was once again fully back in the loop.

IT SLOWLY DAWNED on Abrams that for all his authority as assistant secretary of state, he had no real buttons to push when it came to contra reform. The buttons he had went primarily to the boys at Langley. But because the CIA guys were the ones on site in the mountains of Honduras, training, feeding, equipping, and plotting the movements of the contra guerrilla army, their buttons stretched thousands of miles away, straight into the contra camps. This meant Abrams had to work through the Agency at every step of the way.

In October of 1985, he called Fiers to tell him he wanted to meet with Calero, Cruz, and Robelo. It was one of countless meetings. It didn't occur to him to ask how these things were done, just *that* they were done.

Several days later, he was in a hotel in Miami. A suite of rooms had been retained, and sure enough, Fiers produced the three resistance members. Food was ordered, and, over a working meal, Abrams made a big pitch as to why they had to unify. He also made a long and impassioned speech about "the need to respect human rights." Afterward, he felt the meeting had gone well, and significant progress had been made. Calero nodded in agreement. Fiers was also cooperative and genial. He said very little. It was Elliott's show.

Only much later did Abrams come to see how dependent he was on Fiers. "What impressed them more, my human rights exhortations," he recounted, "or the fact that it was Alan Fiers who paid for their plane tickets, bought their meals, produced a fancy set of hotel rooms, and produced me as well?" He saw that when Alan wanted to make something happen, it usually did.

How little Abrams even understood the Agency began to sink in with depressing certitude. In a meeting of the RIG, Abrams said he was upset with Calero. He felt Calero had to do more to work with Cruz and Robelo, and exercise more leadership in asserting the need to follow the rules of war in guerrilla operations, and in cracking the whip on human rights transgressions. But this was not the sort of issue to be thrashed out in the RIG, he felt. Better to deal with it one-on-one with Fiers. He believed, "Some things could only be settled by us in candid conversations."

He asked Fiers to stay behind and talk with him in private.

Abrams felt he and Fiers were largely singing off the same sheet of music, but sometimes the "tone" and "notes" were different. This was one of those occasions. Fiers, he believed rightly, had little time for his neo-conservative theorizing about democracy and human rights. Never was a successful guerrilla war waged that was encumbered with such niceties as Abrams was seeking to impose on the contras. Abrams was sympathetic to all these points—and they were valid. But "damn it," he felt "reform was absolutely necessary." And if Fiers thought Cruz and Robelo were nothing but "stuffed shirts, liberal windbags and politicians who knew nothing about living in the mountains for weeks and fighting a difficult war, then so be it."

"I've got problems with Calero's operation," Abrams said firmly. He insisted that contra human rights abusers be disciplined. Without making any commitment, Fiers said he understood.

Slightly buoyed, Abrams pressed on, detailing an objection he had with one of Fiers's men in Honduras, who wasn't doing enough to get the point across about the need for reform.

Fiers was a walking encyclopedia on the contras, the detailed geography they fought in, the hills, weather, roads, and every contra personality, both military and political. They talked about how to sort things out. But Abrams noticed that when talking about his own men, Fiers suddenly took on a different tone, real hush-hush, as though he were conspiring. He told Abrams not to worry, that he would work things out. As the conversation came to a close, Fiers rose to leave. When he was just about out the door, he turned around unexpectedly and said, "By the way, Elliott, this conversation never took place."

Abrams sat there in his seat for a minute, pondering the odd phrase he just heard. "Great," he thought, "it's just like in the movies."

This time, like so many other dealings with Fiers, he could not be sure of the outcome, no matter how hard he pressed.

As ABRAMS AND Fiers increasingly sparred in the RIG over contra reform, Abrams was himself drawn into the alien mind-set of the netherworld of covert operations. He saw that the CIA valued people "it could trust." Whereas assistant secretaries would come and go, the Agency would maintain long-established relationships for five, ten, fifteen years. As an institution, it was faithful and in turn prized faithful behavior. In Abrams's view, it preferred mercenaries, people on its payroll whom it could more easily control. His arguments about the need for left-of-center types like Cruz and Robelo were antithetical to the Agency culture. He wanted natural political leaders, educated people who could write policy papers and run a political party and a government. Fiers wanted natural military fighters, or, as one Agency operative put it, "animals who could do the job."

Abrams also encountered the frustration of never being able to fully pierce the veil of what the Agency really wanted, how much of what he asked it to do it really did, and when it was really resisting him or just posturing. As one Abrams aide, Dan Fisk, noted wearily, "Alan, like the other Agency guys, was very good at making you think he knows everything that's going on. But you never really knew what he knew."

But Abrams became more resourceful in checking up on the Agency, and in trying to manipulate it. He learned to use his own sources for information, and play the bureaucratic game with greater care. Once, he even colluded with Senator Bill Bradley of the Senate Intelligence Committee concerning a classified hearing about contra human rights practices. Abrams wanted to ensure that Marta Patricia Boltando, a twenty-nine-year-old tireless Nicaraguan human rights worker, would be made head of the contra commission to monitor human rights practices. She had a soft way about her, spoke with a quiet voice, and had a frail demeanor, but she was as tenacious in her human rights work as she was in being anti-Sandinista. Through his staff, Abrams primed the pump before the hearing to get Bradley to ask pointed questions about "whether Marta would be given operational control of human rights monitoring." Bradley, though a Democrat, was a contra supporter, which gave him standing with the administration, did lean on Fiers. The senator's pressure coalesced with Abrams's arguments in the RIG, and the plan worked.

Abrams also decided to visit the contra camps, one of a number of trips he would make. The more he saw on his own, the better prepared he was to take Fiers on. While he could rarely check on Fiers's actions directly, this enabled him to do what he called "triaging his information resources."

When one trip date arrived, Abrams had been sick in bed, suffering from an intestinal flu he had contracted while in Haiti. Though he had been subsisting only on tea and toast, he was determined to go. Abrams traveled by Gulfstream from Andrews Air Force to Tegucigalpa, the Honduran capital. After a quick country team briefing in the secure room of the embassy with the U.S. ambassador, he changed into casual clothes and then took a helicopter for the hour ride to one of the main contra camps in Honduras.

From the window, he looked down on the lush green countryside, then over pockets of poverty, thatched huts, broken-down rusting cars on front lawns, and mud homes. The vast countryside was, however, often beautiful. The chopper blazed its way over the serenity of a thick, verdant tropical forest. For the better part of forty minutes, often all he could see were tall trees, massed so closely that the ground below was completely obscured. Just as suddenly, the chopper emerged out of the thick forest, bursting into the wide-open space of the FDN camp, surrounded on all sides by a wall of trees. It was one of nature's hidden enclaves that would be an island of tranquillity in more normal times, but was now a contra base headquarters.

When Abrams emerged from the chopper, Enrique Bermúdez, wearing military fatigues, greeted him. The contra fighters were lined up, standing erect in military formation, some several thousand strong. Landing in the helicopter, he had seen them from above, looking like an army of miniature dolls.

They moved into the headquarters, a large open tent with benches and chairs, and maps, lists, and charts were promptly pulled out. Using a pointer at a large map on a makeshift easel, Bermúdez gave a careful briefing, detailing the contra capabilities, the status of the men, the military activities of the Sandinistas, and so on. It was a case for military assistance he could have made in his sleep.

Abrams then talked to the contra fighters themselves. Most of them were young, peasant kids, no more than twenty-one or twenty-two, who had come to hate the Sandinistas. For them, this was a war of liberation. Their faces were dark, their eyes hardened, and they were uncharacteristically marked by the rigors of war. Abrams had learned Spanish fluently as assistant secretary for human rights, and used it to make a rousing speech to the contras, once again in formation. This message was crafted to keep the spirits of the guerrilla forces high, until the U.S. could once again resume military aid.

"We will not abandon you," Abrams said from a rickety wooden dais. "America will stick by your side.

"We will be together until there is democracy in Nicaragua."

It was a pep talk for the resistance. They knew Abrams was one of their best friends in the U.S. government. At State, Abrams was dubbed "the contra commander in chief," and deep in the Honduran jungles he was eagerly embraced as a tried and trusted supporter of their cause.

As Abrams was boarding a small propeller plane that would take him back to Tegucigalpa, he barely noticed the American man innocuously mingling with contras. Clad in khaki, he had on aviator glasses, was trim and stood erect, smoothly fingering a cigarette between his thumb and forefinger. For a Caucasian, he was remarkable not for how he stood out, but for how he blended in with all the faces, even the sea of Latin ones. He was one of the CIA's men on the ground. He shook hands with Abrams, introducing himself like a figure out of *Casablanca*, and receded silently into the crowd to let Abrams run the show.

After the plane took off, he also departed, but by jeep, to call Fiers.

How'd it go? Fiers asked. Was he impressed with the men?

Fine, it went just fine. Elliott just loves this stuff.

BY THE END of the fall, Abrams had elbowed Fiers enough to get some results. Fiers showed he could be a constructive force when he wanted to be. With Agency prodding, Abrams was able to successfully unify the disparate elements of the contras and could announce that they had been recast into UNO. Their face was no longer that of the National Guard and the Somocistas, but of true democrats like Cruz and Robelo. Considering this was a guerrilla force smack in the middle of a civil war, with the U.S. as an uncertain patron, this was a significant achievement.

Twice, early on, the perpetually insecure Arturo Cruz threatened to quit, once because he was sick of fighting with Calero, the other because he was just sick of the war. Each time, Abrams gave him what he called "The Speech."

"If you quit," he told Cruz, "it will be terrible for your country. Your country and your people are depending on you. It is your patriotic duty." Each time, Cruz agreed to stay. (After the speech, Abrams knew that he had shoveled out a lot of hyperbole. "The things we do for our country," he quipped.)

Abrams's high energy infused a can-do spirit into his bureau, which was so highly charged, so out of character for the normally stodgy State Department, that its people became known as the "cowboys."

And, as 1986 opened, they were riding into a new battle. Shultz's early entreaty to Abrams to feel out the Hill for "a big chunk of change," had evolved into a formal request. The president was asking the Congress for $100 million in military aid for the contras.

The battleground had shifted from the jungles of Honduras to the Hill once more. But Abrams was a happy warrior. This was one of the best times of his life. Meeting with heads of state, traveling extensively on air force planes, helping formulate Central America policy, appearing on television talk shows. Every morning he woke up enthusiastic for work. As the administration's point man for the most controversial job in government, he felt like the luckiest man in the world.

At times, he could scarcely believe it. "I'm waiting for a safe to fall on my head," he told Rachel. She laughed in response.

Neither had any inkling then of how prophetic those words would soon prove to be.

CHAPTER 33

Elliott Abrams opened up 1986 with a political cannon shot.

He had a scant three months to help build a case for lethal-aid money for the contras. The $27 million was running out, and a vote for a new aid package was to be taken up by the House in March. Meanwhile, the Sandinistas had been flexing their muscles. Without warning, they had closed down the official radio station of the Roman Catholic Church. They forbade Cardinal Obando y Bravo from broadcasting his homilies because he refused to submit to censorship. And in a bit of fiery year-end bluster, Daniel Ortega had assailed the U.S. in his 1985 wrap-up message to Nicaragua. He declared the upcoming year, 1986, the "year of all the arms against the aggression of the Yankee invader."

Well, Abrams thought, he had a message of his own to deliver.

Abrams hated equivocation. Inviting Shirley Christian, one of the star Central America reporters for the New York Times into his office, he gave her an exclusive. Christian was a rare breed among reporters covering Latin America. A number were anti-Reagan and hostile to his Central America policy. But Christian, who had written a book about the Nicaraguan revolution, had, after painstaking research, come to the scathing conclusion that the Sandinistas were a systematically repressive regime and a dangerous Marxist state—just as the administration had said.

"There's been a change in attitudes on the Hill," Abrams told her. "Most everyone in Congress agrees the Sandinistas are bad guys." But, he hastened to add, "Some liberal Democrats just keep wishing the problem of the Sandinistas will go away, without the U.S. doing anything."

Christian asked what the alternatives were.

Abrams had been waiting for this question. There are really only three, he said. "Either we give the support that the Nicaraguan democratic opposition needs," or "there are two other ways to go."

He paused. "You can use American military force, which is the last thing we wish to do, or you can surrender, which is, I think, unacceptable not only to the administration, but to Congress."

If there was one thing members of Congress hated, it was being faced with clear-cut, up-or-down choices. The beauty of being a legislator was having the opportunity to endlessly criticize, and even make policy, while knowing final responsibility would fall on the shoulders of the president. But with a fiercely partisan Democratic Congress repeatedly combating the administration, Abrams had decided to take off the gloves.

In effect, he was saying that if the Congress blocked the president's aid request for the resistance, it would be responsible for the consequences—whether invasion, or the consolidation of a Communist regime. While Reagan repeatedly ruled out using American troops, Abrams knew Congress couldn't repeatedly invoke the specter of Vietnam, and then not believe that if pushed to the wall Reagan wouldn't consider the option.

It was a high-risk strategy of political confrontation. Within days, the first major response came not from the Hill, but from the press. The *New York Times* took the lead. The *Times* editorial board was particularly tough on Abrams. They wrote that while the Contadora talks, the hemispheric regional peace initiative started by Mexico, Panama, Colombia, and Venezuela, and the core four Central American countries, Costa Rica, El Salvador, Guatemala, and Honduras, and also Nicaragua, was all but dead ("a negotiated settlement seems remote"), U.S. policy's "proclaimed idealism is dishonored by its means," by which they meant military aid to the contras. Tom Wicker, the esteemed old-guard liberal *Times* columnist, called Abrams's actions "the oldest scare tactic in the book," while conceding that they just might work.

Meanwhile, the old Democratic bulls on the Hill, Tip O'Neill, Jim Wright, and Tom Foley, maintained an initial, and surprisingly studied, silence. Having been given a preview of administration thinking by Abrams, they were keeping their powder dry as they formulated their own strategy. However controversial his formulation, the blunt-talking Abrams had successfully made public the high-stakes decisions facing the nation, stimulating a charged debate, notable if not for its incivility on all sides, then at least for its intensity.

This time, however, Abrams was picking up influential allies in the public debate, no longer just from conservative groups, but from the political center as well. Suddenly, the tide seemed to have begun to turn.

ONE SEEMINGLY UNLIKELY ally was the venerable Washington publication *The New Republic*, begun by a cadre of intellectuals, including Herbert Croly, at the start of World War I. Known as *TNR* by its writers and friends, under the careful leadership of its editor (and Harvard professor) Marty Peretz, the magazine had begun in the late 1970s to shift in direction from a predictable magazine of considered liberalism to a stubbornly iconoclastic and at times impressively thoughtful neoconservative magazine. But no matter how much it may have been sympathetic to the Reagan foreign policy, it remained at its core a magazine oriented to the Democratic party and domestic liberalism.

For many longtime readers though, this shift on foreign policy signaled that the magazine had lost its moorings. They groused that it had become "a hopelessly right-wing rag," and wrote angry letters to Peretz canceling their subscriptions. Those on the right, who increasingly found in its pages a fresh voice for their policies, were often disappointed by TNR's stark domestic attacks on the administration. But by mid-decade, the magazine had established itself as the thunderclap of the political center, smack in the eye of public debate in the hitherto cloistered world of magazine opinion.

Each week, its blizzard of stories became for many in the establishment and counterestablishment alike a "must read." TNR's relevance came not just from its pointed articles, but from the fact that the editors, spanning the political spectrum, themselves seemed to mirror the national policy debate at large.

Peretz, who himself occasionally wrote powerful pieces for the magazine's pages, was wise enough to know a relentless strength of TNR was its ability to surprise the readers, to eschew the predictability that had dogged so many other liberal publications, now limping tepidly along like The Nation. Peretz was also determined that TNR would not suffer the same myopia on the right as was happening on the left.

On one end of the spectrum, TNR was ruled by Michael Kinsley and Hendrick Hertzberg, two dogmatic but feisty voices of liberalism. They embodied it all, the social values, the political commitment, the friendships of McGovernism and the New Left. On the other end of the spectrum were Fred Barnes, Morton Kondracke, and Charles Krauthammer. Barnes, a Republican, a journalist of the old school, dressed like a preppy and, pad and pen always in hand, cultivated sources like a sponge, skillfully producing inside stories about the buzz and battles of Washington policy making. Morton Kondracke, or Mort as his friends called him, was the quintessential CDM-Jackson Democrat. He became a tireless champion of the counterestablishment, defending not just the Reagan foreign policy, but also the ideas of budding moderate Democrats still clinging to their party, like Les Aspin and Sam Nunn, as well as Ben Wattenberg and his Democratic-CDM allies.

Krauthammer was a whole different story. His friends called him Charles. He too was a fierce Scoop Jackson Democrat (even though he never met the senator), but unlike Barnes and Kondracke, he was not a reporter. A psychiatrist by training and, like so many other *TNR* writers, Harvard-educated, Krauthammer was also a *Washington Post* columnist and a frequent contributor to *Time* magazine. For *TNR*, he wrote long essays, usually on foreign policy, but not exclusively. As time went by, Krauthammer lost much of his emotional attachment to the Democrats, and, along with the likes of George Will and Bill Safire, became one of the most ardent and thoughtful defenders of the Reagan foreign policy, sometimes even more so than the Reagan administration itself.

At *TNR*, Charles was considered so smart that, as one younger editor put it, "even when you disagree with him entirely, you always, always have to listen to him." Whether the topic was the nuclear freeze, SDI and nuclear strategy, the Central America debate, the future of the Democratic party, or social and domestic issues like AIDS, Jane Fonda, or the religion-and-politics controversy, Krauthammer wrote with a rare incisiveness and cutting edge that rang with conviction and lofty intellectual weight.

Astride in the liberal middle was the book review editor, Leon Wieseltier. Leon, tall and gangly, with his long mane of premature white hair, brown cowboy boots, and the bottle of whiskey that sat on his desk, gave the magazine an aura of eclectic chic.

All told, the magazine was an exciting and explosive mix, with journalistic gladiators arrayed from across the political spectrum. Given wide latitude by Peretz to do their own thing in tenured fiefdoms at *TNR*, every week they convened for a luncheon with a prominent political figure in the main conference room. In the charged 1980s, this weekly lunch developed into an intellectual "happening." Over the long meeting table with deli sandwiches and Cokes, *TNR* became a fountain of debate, in which the urgent issues of a tough-nosed foreign policy, social liberalism, and political parties were thrashed out.

One week, Elliott Abrams was the featured speaker. *TNR* had already shocked the liberal Washington establishment and dismayed left-wing Democrats by running hard-hitting articles from liberals (and former liberals) who felt betrayed by Sandinista thuggishness, repression, and its clear embrace of Marxism, including Bernie Aronson, Robert Leiken, and Penn Kemble, each of whom came to support aid to the contras. When John Kerry, a Massachusetts liberal Democrat and unwavering contra foe, attended one week, he was seated across from this cabal of contra supporters.

But, as the person on the front line of the debate in government, Abrams was bothered by the "one hand, on the other hand" makeup of the editors. He wanted clarity and clean lines, not debate. (A year later, stung by a cover story about a White House contra supply network run amok, he canceled his subscription. It was a statement about politics more than journalism. In the swirling eye of the storm over contra policy, Abrams was living chronically on the edge of a political battlefield. As he put it, the opposition "fights with every weapon it has," and "we need to fight equally hard.")

But Abrams remained well aware that TNR was an important ally in the fight for aid to the contras, less because it swayed the key congressional votes he desperately needed than because it affected the tone and climate of debate about Nicaragua policy, shifting the balance of power and isolating the liberals in a corner. Never was this more apparent than in a single essay written in mid-1985 by Charles Krauthammer.

A fact unknown to most of his readers is that Krauthammer, a prize-winning journalist with swarthy skin and dark brown eyes, is a paraplegic, confined to a wheelchair. At the tender age of twenty-two, the former ski champion dove off the springboard of an outdoor swimming pool and hit his head on the bottom, breaking his neck and injuring his spinal cord. For fourteen months, he struggled in hospitals, first to live, then to get out and get on with his life. His body may have been mangled badly, but not his spirit. Rather than allow the terrible accident to defeat him, he finished studying political theory at Oxford and then, remarkably, went through Harvard Medical School, going on to become a psychiatrist. The courageous Krauthhammer spoke of his paralysis with a startling understatement. "It's a nuisance," he would say, adding, "if you have it all the time, you learn to pick up."

Bored with psychiatry, he undertook a second career, politics. He became a speechwriter for Walter Mondale, until Michael Kinsley hired him as a writer at The New Republic. Moving around in his wheelchair, he worked like an enthusiastic graduate student, arriving at TNR at 10:30 in the morning and going well into the night.

In the mid-1980s, he had been reading Hans Morgenthau, the father of the political realist school who formed the basis of Richard Perle's philosophy years before. Krauthammer wanted to lay out a new theory, post-Morgenthau and post-realism, establishing a foundation for U.S. internationalism based on the sturdy twin pillars of national security and morality. In one striking and influential essay, he seized on a little noticed passage in Ronald Reagan's 1985 State of the Union address. "Truly new ideas—what Democrats lie awake at night dreaming of—are as risky as they are rare," he wrote in Time magazine. But this Reagan speech, he declared, contained such ideas.

In it, Krauthammer noted, Reagan proclaimed, "We must not break faith with those who are risking their lives on every continent from Afghanistan to Nicaragua to defy Soviet-supported aggression and secure rights which have been ours from birth. . . . Support for freedom fighters is self-defense." In turn, Krauthammer declared that *this* was the Reagan Doctrine: "overt and unabashed American support for anti-Communist revolution." Moving beyond Truman's containment, he asserted that the Reagan Doctrine established the "doctrinal foundation" for "armed resistance" to Communism, "whether foreign or indigenously imposed."

The Reagan Doctrine, as Krauthammer explained, sought nothing less than to directly challenge the Brezhnev Doctrine, which claimed that Soviet geopolitical gains of the 1970s from Cambodia to Afghanistan and Nicaragua were irreversible, or, as George Shultz later put it, "what's theirs is theirs, and what's ours is up for grabs." Krauthammer noted that the Cold War contest was too often fought solely on Western terrain. Yet the Reagan doctrine of support for anti-Communist rebels took on this asymmetry, declaring Soviet acquisitions at the periphery of their empire open to Western challenge. It established a dynamic equilibrium in the strategic equation between the U.S. and the Soviet Union—by not requiring resistance at every confrontation, but instead only at those of America's choosing, thus restoring the foreign policy initiative to the U.S. side.

Critics like the international relations scholar Robert Tucker feared this doctrine would dangerously overextend the U.S. Not so, Krauthammer replied in a follow-up essay in *TNR*. "It is, in fact, astonishingly cheap," he pointed out. Aid to the contras, he noted, was but $27 million the year before, and now an anticipated $100 million, "which amounts to three-hundredths of one percent of the defense budget." Moreover, he added, it confronts Soviet expansionism without risking any American lives, making it in economic and military terms "one of the most cost-effective tools of American foreign policy." In short, unlike Allen Dulles's failed policy of "rollback" of the 1950s, the Reagan Doctrine was neither toothless nor reckless.

It was also clear that the Reagan Doctrine had tapped into a new, inexorable wave of historical forces that governed the era. While liberal academic and political icons, from Harvard's Stanley Hoffman to Senator Christopher Dodd, had direly predicted a tide of leftist revolution in the Third World in the 1980s, the decade was marked instead by profound and heated struggles by popular rebellions against the brutalities of Soviet colonialism. Historical sentiment had now ineluctably shifted away from movements of "socialist popular liberation" to Western-aided, often democratic, forces.

In the tumultuous mid-1980s, the Reagan Doctrine was beginning to shake the Soviets' faith in the efficacy of their own system. Its pinch on the Soviets was considerable. They were spending $8 billion fighting the mujahadeen in Afghanistan, and pumping another billion a year into Sandinista Nicaragua (ten times what the administration was asking for the contras), plus up to $20 billion elsewhere abroad defending their gains.

Yet a final question remained. What about the legality of it all? What about morality? Once again, Krauthammer offered a response. Look, he said, "at the nature of the oppression" and the "purposes of fighting it." El Salvador was a fledgling democracy under attack by Marxist-Leninists. Nicaragua, a fledgling totalitarian state, was under attack by a mixture of forces, most of which were pledged to democracy and pluralism. In sum, whenever possible, support forces committed to democracy—which had also been the underlying principle and conclusion of Elliott Abrams's 1981 memo on human rights.

In short, as Krauthammer put it, in spirit and in practice, the Reagan Doctrine constituted a powerful threat to the Soviets.

Moreover, the doctrine was also clear. Few presidents were gifted with such skilled rhetoricians, in tune with the harmony and language of presidential pronouncements, as was Ronald Reagan. He picked the best speechwriters the White House and the nation had seen since JFK's Ted Sorensen, including Tony Dolan ("evil empire" and "campaign for democracy"), Peggy Noonan ("the contras are the moral equivalent of our Founding Fathers"), and chief speechwriter Ben Elliott. Each was a verbal artist, each a committed Reaganaut, each tapped into the underbelly of the Cold War, the notion that, more than steel and bullets, ideas could move mountains. In Noonan's case, she wrote with such feel and passion, and with such an ear for the music of Ronald Reagan, that her words regularly brought tears to those who heard her speeches.

So, by 1986, a remarkable thing had happened. The usually disparate worlds of theory and practice, lofty considerations of rhetoric and the dreary particulars of action, had converged in the administration, coming together into a neat package. Intellectually and practically, the U.S. had created a larger framework for conducting the Cold War. The time for agonizing over policy choices in the administration had ended. The arguments had been made, the rationale painfully and at length explicated, the lines drawn, liberals on one side of the ramparts, conservatives and neoconservatives on the other, with the moderates swaying cautiously in between.

In the stormy months of early 1986, and beyond, the race would be on for the contra votes, with the feisty, pugnacious Abrams leading the charge. The battleground? The House. His target? The moderates.

. . .

THAT SPRING, IN one of the many meetings of the House Democratic party leadership preceding the March vote on military aid to the contras, Tip O'Neill, Jim Wright, Tom Foley, and Democratic Campaign Committee chairman Tony Coelho were meeting in Tip's office. Staff members milled around, and the speaker's aides scurried in and out. Chairs were set up around the speaker's large desk, and Tip, leaning back in his leather swivel chair, was the center of all eyes.

Tip had been in the House for a quarter of a century. For years, he had been portrayed, often wrongly, as a liberal dogmatist, but in truth he had little in common with the issue-oriented ideologues of the New Left. His political style had catered to individual constituents, his was the politics of personal response. With his shock of white hair folded across his forehead, a gait like a whale with short legs, and a bulbous nose that lit up his jowly face like a neon sign, he had long remained stubbornly decent, rooted in the finest traditions of the House, embodying the noblest sentiments of liberalism. He stalked the institution like a constant friend, pumping out his hand to a young member, asking what he could do for the old guard, shuffling, joking, always helping someone out.

But he began somewhat to lose his way as speaker in the 1980s, succumbing to the raucous, ideologically determined tenor of the activist New Left dominating his party. He had never seen a political opponent like Reagan, so determined, so relentless. He was determined to defeat him.

O'Neill made it clear to the leadership gathered around him, and to his troops, that he, the speaker, cared *very* much about this issue of aid to the contras. Little more had to be said. This was a litmus test. Getting ahead in the House meant toeing the line on this issue. Crossing the line to vote with the Republicans meant crossing Tip.

A staffer on the House Foreign Affairs Committee, a staunch devotee to the quaint notion that "politics stops at the water's edge," sounded a dissenting note. "This," he said, "was not an issue to play politics with—was it right in view of the stakes?"

Jim Wright, the speaker-in-waiting, a former contra supporter from Texas, his eyebrows flaring, cracked a smile. Addressing the staffer directly, he asked, "What's wrong with a little politics?"

But there was another issue to be addressed. Tip and other House diehard liberals had rejected all kinds of aid to the contras. But with the political reality changing, they knew that some type of assistance was probably inevitable. Today, O'Neill's biggest problem was David McCurdy and his band of some thirty to forty moderate Democrats. O'Neill knew McCurdy and the moderates were feeling the heat for voting against the contras. Nothing hurt them more than going back home, to the conservative heartlands of the South or Midwest, where Republicans could say they were "soft on Communism," "undercutting the president's foreign policy," "tying down the hands of George Shultz." He also knew that beyond electoral politics, a number of them personally favored aid.

O'Neill made a decision. He wanted to defeat the administration on March 20. But he would offer McCurdy and his moderates another crack at voting for some kind of aid to the contras—down the road.

But for now, he sent out a message to the Democrats: no aid.

DAVID MCCURDY HAD positioned himself as one of the most influential brokers in the contra debate. The boyish-looking thirty-five-year-old rural Oklahoma Democrat was friendly to the administration on most issues of national security and avidly pro-defense. Soft-spoken and hardworking, he was a protégé and key ally of Les Aspin's on the Armed Services Committee. Far more straitlaced in demeanor than Aspin, and generally more conservative than the Wisconsin Democrat, McCurdy was often compared to another straitlaced moderate, Senator Sam Nunn.

To critics, he was ambitious to a fault, but to moderates, his defiant stand against orthodox Northeast liberalism in the House was a welcome breath of fresh air. Few doubted that McCurdy saw himself in the White House one day, and he had some twenty-five years to get there. He was a man on the move. Knowing that a Democrat could only get elected to the presidency if the party shifted to the center, a message Les Aspin was assiduously promoting, McCurdy organized moderates in the house as an alternative bloc to O'Neill and the liberals. He also had his sights on the Intelligence Committee chairmanship, smartly allying himself with Jim Wright, likely to be the next speaker.

Without having to think twice, McCurdy supported administration requests for anti-Communist rebels in Afghanistan, Cambodia, Angola, and Ethiopia. In truth, his philosophy, when removed from the procrustean shackles of his own party, would have revealed few differences on most issues between him and the Reaganauts—including Elliott Abrams.

But to rise in the party *and* in the House meant calibrating his every step with a surgeon's care. Move too far to the left, he would pay back home in Oklahoma. Move too far to the right, the liberal Democrats would cut him off at the knees. It was the curse of being a pro-defense Democrat in a weak-on-defense party.

In the debate over the $27 million in humanitarian aid for the contras, McCurdy sought assurances from the president that his policy was not "to overthrow the Sandinistas." Reagan sent a personal letter declaring that this was most certainly not his policy. The administration's policy, the letter said, was to pursue "a political solution" in Central America, not "military solutions." Support for the contras was support for the democratic center, designed to foster democracy and peace through dialogue and regional negotiations. Once given this assurance, McCurdy was instrumental in pulling a number of moderate Democrats to vote for the aid. Administration officials hoped he would do the same this time.

To ABRAMS, IT seemed he was spending more time with McCurdy than any other single individual. He counted at least ten instances that he personally went to McCurdy's office to talk about the administration's contra aid policy. He knew McCurdy was anything but soft on the Sandinistas, and was thoroughly convinced McCurdy would be the leader of the moderate Democrats voting with Reagan. With McCurdy's help, he smelled victory on March 20.

If McCurdy wanted to talk about human rights, Abrams discussed everything he was doing. If McCurdy needed up-to-date information about Sandinista repression, Abrams distilled the latest cable traffic coming into State, and immediately sent it his way. If McCurdy had ideas about how to shape the contra political program, or had ideas about the regional negotiations, he cocked his head to listen smartly, and relayed the suggestions to the secretary. If McCurdy wanted the assistant secretary to make a presentation to his moderate bloc of Democrats, Abrams trucked on over from Foggy Bottom, charts and statistics in hand, aides in tow.

"I truly believe these Democrats will vote their conscience and do what's right for the country's national security," Abrams told his staff that spring. But his attention to McCurdy was creating problems.

For one, the Republicans felt they were being shortchanged. They saw that Abrams was spending more time briefing McCurdy, Jim Slattery, Jim Cooper, and John Spratt than such Republican stalwarts and fervent contra supporters as Bob Michel, Henry Hyde, Dick Cheney, and Mickey Edwards. "Hell," one staffer even groused, "and George Shultz has the Democrats up to his seventh-floor retreat at State for cocktails, but not us guys who are doing the legwork in the party."

The slight wasn't intentional. But with a lot of work and a shortage of time before the vote, Abrams felt he had little alternative. In one of his many meetings with Democrats, he pulled Bill Richardson of New Mexico aside. "Bill, why are the Democrats so intense about this contra issue when it isn't even an electoral issue for members, except for perhaps ten in the whole country?"

Richardson smiled gravely, thinking that Abrams just didn't understand his own former party. He told it to Abrams straight. "It is a Democratic caucus issue, Elliott. We are looking for a way to beat Ronald Reagan and this is it. A number of the liberals, like David Bonior, are true believers. But look at Tony Coelho. You think he really cares? He doesn't. It's politics."

Abrams was stunned. But the full gravity of Richardson's message did not sink in. He still had faith in McCurdy and his swing group of moderates.

WELL BEFORE THE vote, Abrams was in Venezuela, talking with President Jaimie Lusinchi, briefing him on the upcoming vote. He wanted Venezuela's public support for the $100 million.

Lusinchi was aghast. He couldn't make such statements publicly, though he had no problem with aiding the contras. "You want $100 million? Fine, do $200 million. But why do you and your president have to make so many public speeches about it? It would be so much better to do it quietly."

At first surprised, Abrams explained the president couldn't do anything without going to Congress.

Well then why doesn't he just give the contras less money and not go to the Congress, like $20 million or so? Lusinchi asked sternly. That would be so much easier.

Abrams explained, "The way our system works, the president can't do anything without going to Congress. He doesn't have the ability to appropriate a single nickel."

Lusinchi flashed a broad smile. "That's amazing, I have more power than the president of the United States does."

AFTER ONE OF his March meetings with McCurdy, Abrams went to see Shultz to debrief him on the state of play. "I gave McCurdy an overview of our recent thinking and addressed his concerns," Abrams reported.

Shultz was stony-faced as usual, and gave Abrams a minor lesson in Washington political civics. "You don't understand what type of game McCurdy is playing," he said. "You move right, he'll move right, but you move left, he'll move left. His game is always to be just to the left of you."

Shultz paused. "Elliott, it's a waste of your time."

As Abrams left for his office, the words hung there. But he continued to believe that McCurdy would come around.

• • •

THE SUNDAY BEFORE the Thursday vote, Reagan went on national television to deliver an address from the Oval Office, asking for a positive verdict on the $100 million request. Looking serious and committed, he appealed for bipartisan support to send arms to the "freedom fighters," whom he compared to "the French resistance that fought the Nazis in World War II." Using charts, maps, and photographs, he devoted most of his address to describing Nicaragua's ties to the Soviets and their proxies, and explaining the stakes for American security interests. He made clear, "I am not talking about American troops," adding, "the democratic resistance is only asking America for supplies and support to save their own country from Communism." He closed with a touch of class, invoking Democrats who in earlier times had rallied with Republicans to combat Soviet influence, Scoop Jackson, John F. Kennedy, and Harry S. Truman. However classy it was to mention these Democrats, and it was, it was probably a mistake. The party had come a long way since the days of Truman, and even Jackson.

The Democratic response was delivered by Jim Sasser, a liberal Southern senator. He warned, "Let's not rush into a quagmire. We've done that before." He added that U.S. troops will ultimately be required if military aid is passed for the contras. O'Neill then made the rounds with the press, asserting defiantly that Reagan's remarks were "a declaration of war against one of the smallest, poorest nations in the hemisphere."

The intense thirty-hour House debate began on Wednesday. From the outset, it was emotional, with charges and countercharges roaring across the aisle, Democrats decrying the administration's tactics, comparing them to the "dark hour of fear" in the 1950s (O'Neill), Republicans charging that the U.S. must not "tolerate another Communist state in our hemisphere" (Cheney).

The vote was set for Thursday.

TUESDAY AND WEDNESDAY, the administration made some last-minute concessions to the Democratic moderates, including a promise of issuing an executive order determining that military assistance would be restricted until all diplomatic efforts had been exhausted.

For his part, a determined O'Neill pulled out all the stops. Inviting McCurdy and his bloc of swing voters into his office, he promised them a chance to offer an alternative "compromise package" within ninety days, most likely as soon as April. He left open the possibility that it could include military aid.

McCurdy did not call Abrams to tell him of his current thinking. Instead, he told the press that the presidential compromise "was still unacceptable."

All Thursday, Abrams had camped out in the office of the minority leader, Bob Michel, just off the House floor. Surprisingly, he did not have the whip count for votes, but was confident that the administration would win. He was geared up to celebrate. The mood was one of anxious hope.

Two hours before the vote, Shultz joined Abrams to lobby members, buttonholing Democrats and Republicans who were thought to be still open-minded on the vote. The secretary felt he could do two things: impress upon members why this was a major issue of national security, and two, address any lingering concerns. Mainly, he stressed how he could succeed in talks with the Sandinistas. "Look," he said sternly, "I'm an old labor negotiator. If you want me to negotiate with the Sandinistas, I have to have something to trade with. I have to go to their table to meet their force with my force."

Shultz was unusually impassioned with Tom Lantos, a liberal California Democrat but a thoughtful straightshooter. Lantos was a respected leader in the House on human rights. Midway into Shultz's speech, Lantos waved his hands to the secretary, calling on him to stop talking.

"I don't want to hear your speech. I know the arguments, and you are absolutely right. I don't need to be persuaded. The rationale is good, and the contras should get this aid. But if I vote for the contras there will be a primary challenge against me in the summer back at home. So I will be voting against aid."

A New York Democrat, James Scheuer, came in and also echoed the same argument. Watching this, Abrams felt his heart sink. He knew many Democrats were still fighting the Vietnam War, but he didn't realize the depths of how political the issue was.

Abrams settled down to watch the final vote after the emotional climax, when Bob Michel turned to his old friend and golfing partner O'Neill and said, "I love you, we're great friends, but I have to say you're wrong, you're wrong, you're wrong."

The bruising battle was soon over. The Democrats defeated the proposal by twelve votes, 222–210. The administration was a scant seven votes short. McCurdy voted with O'Neill.

Watching it on C-SPAN in Michel's office, Abrams was sitting with Alan Fiers and Oliver North. He felt bitter disappointment. When Fiers muttered a string of four-letter words, as well as "sons of bitches," he didn't voice any protest. He had a few choice epithets himself.

O'Neill had handed Reagan a stinging defeat, but the fight was far from over. "I'll be back," the glum president said, "until this battle is won."

.   .   .

AFTER THE VOTE, there was little time for recriminations. Reading the rejection of contra aid as a green light, the next evening 1,500 Sandinista soldiers swept into Honduran territory to attack a contra base camp. At Abrams's initial urgings "that the U.S. must show resolve and determination on this," the administration immediately airlifted Honduran troops into the border zone as a tangible symbol of American concern. It also rushed $20 million in additional military aid to Honduras. The invasion was yet one more embarrassment to the Democrats, who fumed that the Sandinistas were "incompetent Marxists." ("Would they be happier with competent Marxists?" Republicans rejoined.) Even if the Democrats had won the first round, the incursion was a stark reminder that the Democrats were on perpetually shaky ground, particularly if all hell broke loose in the region.

In a matter of days, the Sandinistas were also digging in their heels at the regional Contadora peace talks. Since 1983, the Contadora process, ambitiously aimed at attaining a regionwide solution to the diverse problems of Central America, had awkwardly progressed in fits and starts. In many ways, Contadora was to the many political and military problems of Latin America what the Geneva arms talks were to the U.S.-Soviet Cold War, a high-profile, albeit limited, forum to thrash out the issues of war and peace. Elaborate documents were urgently tabled and discussed, twenty-one-point plans were boiled down to four-point simultaneous objectives, and, like the arms talks, the thorny provisions of treaty verification, compliance, and enforcement continued to bedevil any successful regional settlement. And always, Sandinista Nicaragua remained a central concern: what to do about its support of guerrillas in El Salvador and its export of revolution, how to shrink its huge and imposing army, how to entice Soviet and Cuban advisers to leave Nicaragua, and, perhaps most important, how to bring Nicaragua into step with the new wave of democracy sweeping the rest of the region, and hold free and fair elections. In the spring of 1986, the Contadora talks were again floundering, as the Sandinistas defiantly refused to sign any document that required them to expel Soviet and Cuban advisers or to reduce the massive size of their military forces. This only further undercut the Democrats' arguments that a meaningful treaty could be secured without leverage.

But if Nicaragua's intransigence placed the administration on better footing for the next vote, they had an even more pressing problem. Democrats rigidly controlled all House floor votes, and refused to allow a Republican or administration alternative to be offered in the promised

April vote on contra aid. That meant the Republicans would have to wait until late June for another crack at military aid. In the meantime, the $27 million in humanitarian assistance from the year before had run out.

It was then that a fateful decision was made: to secure new funding from a third country to assist the contras, like a bridge loan, until Congress came around—that is, if it ever did.

CHAPTER 34

They're out of money, Shultz said dryly. The contras are not in great shape. Sitting at the long table in the White House Situation Room, Shultz minced no words.

He looked over to the president, and eyed the other officials meeting at the May 16 National Security Planning Group to formulate a strategy for assisting the contras. Abrams was seated behind Shultz in a staff chair.

In the press, the president was notorious for his ostensible lapses of attention at meetings. He doodled, made off-the-cuff comments, appeared to doze, and at times was generally uninterested. Some aides wondered how much he grasped the issues. Yet, like other senior officials, Abrams had come to notice, as Shultz certainly had, that the president usually knew exactly what he was doing, and was anything but a passive vessel for his staff. This was always evident in discussions on Central America policy. The president became forceful in his comments, deeply engaged in the intricacies of policy discussions, and when he deemed it necessary, radiated an unswerving commitment to his causes.

Shultz raised the question of soliciting funds from a third country. In two June NSPG meetings in 1984, when the issue of asking third countries to provide funding for the contras was raised, Shultz had snapped, "No games," adding, "going to third countries is very likely illegal." Shultz was in the minority then, and Weinberger, Casey, and Kirkpatrick had jumped all over him, while Reagan sat quietly by, saying nothing. Indeed, it was a recurring pattern for Shultz to be on the opposite side of Kirkpatrick and Weinberger. And after Kirkpatrick left, Shultz continued to scrap with Weinberger.

But on this day, almost two years later, Shultz was now the one bringing up the issues of solicitations.

Third-country solicitations, however questionable from the perspective of carrying out policy—and it was a deeply questionable device, raising constitutional issues about the Congress and the executive in policy making—were not illegal. Moreover, the political environment had changed.

In December of 1985, the intelligence committees explicitly put an amendment into their secret bill allowing the State Department to solicit humanitarian assistance from foreign countries. Based on this amendment, Section 105 as it was known, Abrams raised the idea with Shultz, who had agreed to take it up at the NSPG. The main proviso of Section 105 was that there could be no explicit quid pro quo. Like the Boland Amendments, this dodged hard questions. It was inevitable that any country helping out the U.S. would be buying the goodwill of the American president, just as American foreign aid bought the U.S. a measure of influence over its recipients. That was how the world worked.

No one argued with Shultz as he outlined a proposal for finding "bridge funds" to tide the contras over until they received a positive verdict in Congress. The figure of $10 million was raised. It was a round sum, and also was calibrated to the previous $27 million in humanitarian aid, which provided $3 million a month. Shultz reasoned that this funding would last for three months. Enough time to bridge the gap until the planned summer vote on new aid.

"Let's try it," the president said.

AFTER THE MEETING, Shultz asked Abrams to take care of things. He gave two hard instructions. "No bad actors," he emphasized, meaning no right-wing dictatorships. "And no aid recipients," that is, countries receiving U.S. foreign aid, because "it could appear that we had twisted their arms in some way."

Abrams quickly plunged into the task. His first step was to canvass the other regional assistant secretaries of state to ask if they knew of a country that fit the requirements—rich, amenable to U.S. concerns, not a recipient of American foreign aid.

The logical place was the oil-laden Middle East. Abrams sought out Richard Murphy, the assistant secretary for the Near East and South Asia. Murphy, a close-to-the-vest career foreign service officer, and an Arabist, virtually all but laughed at the proposition. "Central America is not on the map as far as Middle Eastern countries are concerned," he told Abrams. (Neither man knew at the time just how wrong Murphy was.)

Abrams persevered, speaking with Gaston Sigur, the assistant secretary for East Asian and Pacific affairs. Sigur had a brainstorm: Brunei. Brunei, a tiny enclave on the island of Borneo in the South China Sea, was a country roughly the size of Delaware, run like a private possession. Its ruler was Sultan Hassanal Bolkiah, listed in *The Guinness Book of World Records* as the richest man in the world. Once a British protectorate, it was occupied by the Japanese in World War II, and obtained its independence in 1984. The sultan was so rich that his air-conditioned palace contained 1,788 rooms, and cost over $400 million.

The sultan was also fiercely anti-Communist. Sigur and Abrams thought Brunei was perfect. Shultz was going to be visiting Brunei in early June on the way to a meeting of the Association of Southeast Asian Nations in Manila. They decided the secretary could raise the issue then, directly with the sultan.

But then a hitch arose. Sigur, who made the plane trip with Shultz, decided it was not "befitting" for the secretary to ask for money from a foreign head of state. They decided that the U.S. ambassador should make a direct approach to the Brunei foreign minister.

To Abrams's dismay, the U.S. ambassador indicated it would entail "considerable groundwork" of more than a month or two before there was a reasonable chance to get the money from the sultan. He proposed an early U.S.-Brunei meeting, and then pushed and pushed. Finally, after an exchange of several cables, a meeting was arranged for August 8, 1986, in London.

The sultan's people made a firm stipulation to the U.S. ambassador. They wanted everything to be held in the strictest of confidence. No one should know of their role. Shultz cabled back that "absolute secrecy" would be maintained. He also offered his word of thanks to Brunei, for "this endeavor which we believe has great importance for the overall security of the free world."

ALMOST NO ONE knew about the planned solicitation. It was so secret that whenever a cable came into the secretary's office, it was hand-delivered to Shultz. Abrams would then be called up to the seventh floor, where he would read it in Shultz's office. He would then hand it back, and it would immediately be secured in the secretary's safe. Regular State Department cables were distributed to roughly 1,100 people. Even a "no dis" cable, that is, no distribution, would be reproduced for dozens of people—all of the principals on the seventh floor, the undersecretaries, deputy secretaries, and their chief aides, and the assistant secretaries. No copies were made of the Brunei cables.

Only a handful of people knew anything. Shultz, his personal secretary and his top aides, Charles Hill and Mel Levitsky, the U.S. ambassador in Brunei, Abrams, and Gaston Sigur. Abrams told his staff nothing.

No decision had been made as to who would actually make the trip to London, Abrams or Sigur. As the assistant secretary for Asian affairs, Sigur was the likely candidate. But because the contra program was his direct issue, Abrams had questions about procedure.

In early June, he asked Hill, "What if the foreign minister just says, 'Okay, where do I send the money?' How would the money be transferred to the contras?" No one had thought about this. Money transfers and fund-raising were not standard fare for the State Department. Hill said, "You need a bank account. There are two people to talk to. Alan [Fiers] and Ollie [North]."

Abrams sought out Fiers. The wily Fiers laughed. "We do this all the time," he said. "We'll just open up a secret bank account for you." The next day, Fiers opened up an account in the Bahamas.

That same day, Abrams went to see North. North said that he could give him an account number on the spot. He opened a drawer in one of his massive file cabinets, riffled through some papers, and pulled out a folder. "Oh yes, this is right," he said.

It didn't occur to Abrams to ask North how he had a bank account, what it was for, or who could draw upon it. He figured North, like Fiers, knew what he was doing. He had no reason to think otherwise.

North called his secretary, Fawn Hall, into his office. Abrams looked at Hall. Blond, attractive, leggy, she was well known in government. She had been dating the son of the contra leader Arturo Cruz, and the two were quite an item. "Type this number on a blank card for Elliott," North barked, as he read it off.

Abrams looked at the card, smiled, folded it up, and stuffed it into his pocket. It was at Crédit Suisse, in Geneva. He now had not one account, but two, and didn't have the foggiest notion what his next step was.

Some days later, Abrams was on a flight to Los Angeles with Shultz and Charles Hill. He asked Hill about the two accounts. "Which should I use?"

"We're always fighting with the CIA about the contra program," Hill explained. Abrams certainly agreed with Hill on this. "And this was a State Department initiative," Hill added. "Why give the CIA greater authority?"

Abrams thought Hill, Shultz's right-hand man, was always so reasonable. Now was no exception.

Hill continued. "God knows what's actually in the CIA accounts, and what it's actually used for. This aid is for purely humanitarian purposes. We'll be able to monitor the spread of the money much more easily if it's in Ollie's account."

Abrams understood and agreed.

Ironically, when he had started as assistant secretary, an NSC staff aide, Constantine Menges, had warned Abrams about North, saying he couldn't be trusted. For Abrams, this was a common refrain. In his almost five years in government, Abrams frequently heard complaints like this about people. Sometimes it was a daily occurrence. In Menges's case, North had elbowed him out of the Latin America portfolio on the NSC. So Abrams chalked his warnings up to "personal motivation" and a "sour experience."

Then, almost a year earlier, Shultz had gotten a bad feeling about North, and told Abrams to "watch him." He wasn't specific, but Abrams caught the general point. He penned into a loose-leaf notebook, "Monitor Ollie." But North, whom he worked with regularly, always seemed to be pretty straightforward with him, following the bureaucratic lines of authority, and Shultz never followed up on his initial concern. Months later, Abrams had all but forgotten that he even should be concerned about North. He was also impressed with North's can-do spirit and his unwillingness to accept defeat. Whatever North's faults, he felt the two were singularly on the same side.

Evidently, Hill also thought the same thing, saying, "It's much cleaner to use Ollie's account. Let's do that."

"Right."

ON JUNE 16, Shultz learned from Bud McFarlane that President Reagan and the National Security Council had for some time quietly been raising money from Saudi Arabia and Taiwan. He further learned that Cap Weinberger and Admiral Bill Crowe of the joint chiefs knew, but he didn't. Shultz was irritated and angry. But he figured the train had already left the station. If he were out of the loop, he would stay out of the loop. If it all unraveled, it would be someone else's problem, not his.

All told, the Saudis kicked in some $32 million, and the Taiwanese $2 million. It was not illegal, but it certainly violated the spirit of the Boland Amendment—and was potential political dynamite in the already volatile executive-legislative relationship.

Shultz was faced with a decision. Should he tell Abrams, his point man managing the contra policy day to day, about these foreign donations? The contra issue was already controversial enough, Shultz reasoned, and, according to sources, he also thought, "once you tell one person, you might as well tell everyone." So, in the run-up to the vote for the $100 million in military aid for the contras, now slated for June 25, 1986, Shultz made the fateful decision to keep Abrams, his top aide on Latin American affairs, squarely in the dark.

BACK IN THE Congress, a number of Democrats were beginning to reevaluate their stance toward the contras. Moderate Senator Sam Nunn took the lead. Speaking before the hawkish Coalition for a Democratic Majority on April 17 in Washington, he warned, "The end of all aid for the contras would be a victory for the Sandinistas." In the March vote several weeks earlier, liberal Democrats had complained about the McCarthyite tactics of the Republicans, but Nunn was now saying virtually the same thing as the administration, albeit less confrontationally. It was no longer a message that the Democrats could lightly discount.

Nunn, who as much as any other politician knew how to position himself in the center of great debates confronting the country, put the issue starkly. "Central America is a great testing ground for our nation," he declared, "and also for the Democratic party."

One very influential member of Congress who carefully noted Nunn's remarks was Les Aspin, who was now reassessing his own stance toward military aid. For several months, one of his aides had been conducting comprehensive studies on "how to reverse Communist regimes." Now the report was in. "The problem with Communist regimes in the direct Soviet sphere of influence," Aspin read, "was that even if they weren't consolidated, the Brezhnev doctrine prevented them from evolving into a democracy." Aspin agreed with this. He knew it was the lesson of Czechoslovakia and Hungary.

"Communist regimes outside of the direct sphere of influence were different," the study continued. "Ironically, once they consolidate power in countries with little or no democratic background, traditions, or institutions, as with a Vietnam or North Korea, these regimes tend to be more dogmatically Marxist-Leninist. Reversing them was thus that much more difficult." This was both the "paradox and the opportunity," the paper said. "The opportunity for reversing Communist gains was in third world countries where the Soviets could not directly use overwhelming force, and where the regimes had not consolidated their influence over all aspects of the state." Unlike a North Korea, Nicaragua, the paper pointed out, was one such place. It was a refined conclusion that Aspin firmly agreed with.

In those spring months, Aspin was also briefed by Bob Leiken, Bernie Aronson, Bruce Cameron, and Penn Kemble, all Democratic party foreign policy activists and former liberals turned neoconservative, and pro-contra. Then, aided by Leiken and Aronson as trip guides, Aspin took a trip to Nicaragua to see things for himself. What he saw, he didn't like. Not one bit.

Aspin had already developed a theoretical foundation for supporting the contras. Now he had an eyewitness foundation, "kicking the tires," as he and his aides called it. It troubled him that the Sandinistas "were messing around dangerously in the U.S. hemisphere—not halfway across the world, but at *our* doorstep." For Aspin, it was a dangerous Soviet foothold. And while he harbored few romantic notions about the contras as enlightened democrats (he knew some were "thuggish goons," but he saw that most "were simply peasant fighters"), he agreed with the argument that it was terribly important for them to keep the pressure on the Sandinistas. He also felt that the seeds of the contra movement could ultimately hold promise for a democratic Nicaragua.

In this painstaking step-by-step process, Aspin came to the conclusion that the contras had to be supported. In his opinion, they were the "best hope" for facilitating true elections and regional peace talks.

One thing was certain. Aspin would be the most visible and influential convert to contra aid. He had no constituency for the aid, and had previously opposed it. He decided not to signal his intentions to the administration, which would only arouse the ire of the liberal House Democrats. Taking stock of the highly charged debate in his party, he stayed out of the fray of legislative maneuvering, and quietly went about his way. He was a vote Elliott Abrams never knew he had—and an extremely important one at that.

Another Democrat, Ike Skelton of Missouri, a tall, soft-spoken, and gangly legislator, who normally eschewed the limelight, decided to cosponsor the administration aid package with Republican Mickey Edwards. Skelton, whose long neck reminded others of a giraffe, was low key, self-effacing, and highly regarded by his moderate colleagues. His shift meant the administration would have cover to pick up some of the moderate votes it hoped for in March, but which had gone with McCurdy.

Skelton and Edwards's package called for $70 million in military aid, and $30 million in humanitarian aid, including funds specifically earmarked for contra human rights training and observance, and progress reports on the peace negotiations. The package had been worked out in advance with Abrams. In addition, $300 million in economic aid would be proposed for the surrounding Latin American democracies. In this sense, it was a very small-scale version of Kirkpatrick's Marshall Plan idea for Central America.

In the shifting political winds of the Democratic party, McCurdy was now on the other side, positioning himself as conservative, moderate, and liberal all at once. Ironically, once he decided he would not buck Tip O'Neill and the leadership, he was in the awkward position of angering all sides of the political spectrum, and earning the accolades of only a handful. *His* plan was, on paper, similar to the administration's, while differing in one big way. Military aid could be released *only* after a second congressional vote down the road. As a political reality, the package meant that military aid would never be approved. McCurdy's package had become an unwitting smoke screen for killing contra military aid.

It was now or never for the contras. In the days leading up to the vote, Reagan himself lobbied hard, and often. He canceled a vacation to his Santa Barbara ranch, made another national speech, twisted arms, and even called Democrats to ask for their votes. Reagan's personal intervention worked. In the end, fifty-one Democrats joined him, including five swing votes who had previously gone with McCurdy. In a stunning reversal, the vote was 221–209.

Shultz and Abrams had watched the vote with great intensity. Afterward, they were overjoyed. For them, it was a great victory. But actual aid still wouldn't be on its way until late October or November. The bill had to be approved in the Senate, and then be cleared through the conference committee, one of the arcane alleyways of the legislative process, a process O'Neill was in no hurry to speed up.

For Abrams, this made the Brunei solicitation all the more important, to keep something flowing to the contras, until the $100 million was actually dispersed.

THAT JUNE AND July, rumors began swirling that the White House was secretly directing a private aid network to arm the contras. Oliver North of the NSC was named at the center of the activities. The *Miami Herald* took the lead running the stories, and soon the *Washington Post*, the Associated Press, and even the more conservative *Washington Times* were reporting on the unfolding isolated fragments of what appeared to be a brazen, illegal, and wholly far-fetched story. Soon, television got into the act, doing its own scouting around, the first blast coming from the CBS program *West 57th.*

For many, what was so disturbing about these rumors was that military aid was purportedly involved, which would have been in stark defiance of the Boland Amendments, and the articles also talked about an "operational role" at the NSC. But around the administration and even among some Republicans on the Hill, a lot of people liked North, even if he was known for his excessive hyperbole and what many came to see was an unnerving pathological tendency to distort the truth. Abrams himself was well aware that few people questioned the actions of those in the White House. Acting in the name of the president, their calls got returned faster, their requests got more attention, their authority given greater weight.

Over at Foggy Bottom, Abrams was overwhelmed with things to do. There was the contra program, the Contadora negotiations, festering problems in Chile, Haiti, Argentina, and Panama. Many days were a jumble of activity, with no end in sight.

As this new story surfaced in the press, he took it with a grain of salt. Abrams knew that there was a private and legal effort to raise funds from wealthy citizens. He was twice asked to make pitches at fund-raisers. At one of them, in the Hay-Adams Hotel the previous January, Ronald Reagan himself stopped by. Abrams strongly supported this activity. He would have pitched in at more of these fund-raisers, but after the first two, his services were not requested again. One of the reasons: North didn't fully trust Abrams. He saw him as "Shultz's boy."

Abrams himself was subjected to repeated press attacks, and the reports were often politically inspired—and grossly inaccurate. That year the Democrats had gone on a witch-hunt concerning a delivery of boots to the contra army. Using a Government Accounting Office study, they cited evidence that not all of the boots had reached the contras. As the Democrats dramatically waved the study, they talked about the delivery as though it were nighttime takeout of Chinese food in Manhattan, and the courier hadn't shown up. In countless hearings and statements on the floor of the House, this report was replayed as evidence of perfidy and gross incompetence in the contra program, with little mention of the problems of arming, feeding, and clothing an army in wartime. The Democrats got weeks' worth of play out of what many serious observers considered a nonissue.

Why, Abrams thought, should it be any different when it came to the accusations about the White House? Besides, if anyone should have been troubled, it would certainly be George Shultz—but Shultz hadn't said a thing to him. Abrams dismissed the reports as yet more instances of innuendo, fodder for the Democrats, who were now losing and were increasingly grasping at straws.

It was raw political combat, pure and simple, and both sides were pulling out all the stops. Abrams wasn't going to sidetrack himself looking after someone else. He had a war to oversee—in Nicaragua, and in the Congress.

And he was particularly distracted as August rolled around. That week he was informed that he, not Gaston Sigur, would be making the trip to London. Shultz wanted it done fast, without tipping anyone off—meaning "in and out of London" the same day. It would entail a brutal overnight flight with little sleep. Elliott was only thirty-eight; Sigur was in his late fifties. Shultz felt it would be a far easier trip for Elliott, "a much younger man," to make.

· · ·

BY PRIOR ARRANGEMENT, the meeting would take place not during the work-week, but on a Saturday. That way, no one at State would ask, "Where's Elliott?"

Abrams was to check in at the Hilton. He would call the Brunei foreign minister, Pengiran Muda, who would be registered at the Dorchester. Muda cabled that it would be better for Abrams not to identify himself by his own name when he called. Soviet or British intelligence would surely pick up the call once he identified himself, ask what this was all about, and set off a chain reaction that could blow the secrecy of the arrangement.

Abrams cabled back that he would identify himself as "Mr. Kenil-worth." This was a touch of private humor. Kenilworth was the name of the street where his mother had grown up.

Thursday night after dinner, he talked about the mission with Rachel. A recurring dilemma in the Cold War was, do you tell your wife classified secrets? It was usually more effective not to keep things from your wife, and Abrams, like most other public servants, rarely did.

Aside from a change of clothes, there was little packing to do. Elliott would leave Friday night, arrive in London in the morning, stay as long as he needed to make his pitch, perhaps several hours, then return to Heathrow Airport and fly back by commercial airline. He would land in Washington late Saturday. It would be as though he never left. He would never be missed.

The plane arrangements were made by Abrams's personal secretary. No one else in his office knew. That Friday, as with every other day, his young aides Bob Kagan and Danny Wattenberg were buzzing in and out, bringing him papers and cables, updating him on the action in Congress, giving him the latest news from the field. At one point, the two were milling around in his office.

The question of weekend plans came up. Abrams tried to keep his cool. He didn't want to suggest that anything out of the ordinary was up. For a brief moment, he worried that they might know, that his cover had been blown.

Abrams shrugged his shoulders, and asked his aides: What do you have going on this weekend? They began talking, and he slowly let out a deep breath. It was clear they were checking up on the boss, as usual, but they didn't know a thing.

ON THE FLIGHT, Abrams mulled over what he would say. Before leaving, he had discussed it with Shultz, but he wanted to have everything right. He felt a little like a spy, like the man he so often sparred with, Alan Fiers. Abrams napped briefly, but was too anxious to really sleep.

Arriving in London at daylight, he stopped at customs, and was unrecognized. He immediately took a taxi to the Hilton. It was always customary when traveling in a foreign country to contact the embassy and pay a courtesy call on the ambassador. Not this time. He checked in under his own name, went to his room where he showered, shaved, nibbled on roasted peanuts from the room mini-bar, and then called Muda.

An aide, not the foreign minister, answered. "It's Mr. Kenilworth calling."

Abrams suggested he meet the minister at the Dorchester.

"No, he wants to meet with you in the lobby of a different hotel. At the Grosvenor House on Park Lane."

"Where to then?" Abrams asked.

"You'll be told at the time."

THE FOREIGN MINISTER suggested taking a walk in Hyde Park. "That way, eavesdropping would be difficult," he said.

The two strolled at a slow pace for fifteen minutes, while Abrams talked about the nature of his mission, U.S. policy in Central America, how strongly the president felt, the troubles with a difficult Congress. Mentioning the sum of $10 million, he emphasized that there was no quid pro quo, but Brunei would "have the gratitude of the secretary and the president for helping us out of the jam."

"Do you expect the money now?" the minister asked.

"No, we don't. We understand you will have to talk with the sultan."

"In any event, I don't make the decisions," the minister said. "I don't have access to the cash."

Abrams handed him a slip of paper that had the account number, name of bank and branch, telex number, and bank official to deal with. They shook hands and parted ways. The meeting was over. Abrams had no idea that North's secretary, Fawn Hall, had slipped up. She had accidentally transposed the first two numbers on the account. The money would never reach the contras.

The whole meeting had taken less than half an hour. An hour later, Abrams was back at Heathrow ready to board a flight home. He would be able to tell Shultz on Monday that the mission was a success. He had every reason to believe Brunei would provide the money.

LESS THAN TWO weeks later, on August 19, the U.S. embassy sent an "eyes only" cable to Shultz. When Abrams was summoned to the secretary's office, his heart beat with joy. The sultan had approved the deal. The money would be forthcoming. Remarkably enough, secrecy about the mission had held.

A series of delaying tactics had held up the $100 million in the Senate, but the tide had turned. Military aid would soon be flowing to the resistance—and the Congress was on the run. In Abrams's office, they often jokingly referred to their congressional tormentors as "the Cong." This time, though, the replay would be different.

But just as unexpectedly, fate would take a new twist, as a secret White House operation of almost nightmarish proportions would slowly unravel. Like being caught in a hot vat of sticky taffy, a wriggling Abrams would eventually be trapped in a confusing imbroglio, once more at the hand of his enemies. It began on what was otherwise a regular day, October 5, with a missing plane over the skies of Nicaragua.

AT 12:38 P.M., a C-123 Caribou plane, loaded with a thousand pounds of ammunition, jungle boots, and AK-47s, was shot down by a Sandinista surface-to-air missile over the skies of northern Nicaragua. It was on its sixtieth mission of resupplying the contras. This time, the plane's luck ran out. The pilot, co-pilot, and a seventeen-year-old Nicaraguan died on impact. Almost miraculously, the plane's fourth man, forty-five-year-old Eugene Hasenfus, "a kicker," who pushed the cargo out of the plane, survived.

Dazed, he wandered for twenty-four hours in the jungle, until the Sandinistas captured him the next day. They rifled through his muddy clothes, and found an identification card issued by the Salvadoran air force. It called him an "adviser." Late the following morning, Havana radio broadcast a report that a plane had been shot down over Nicaragua, and a crew member had been taken prisoner. Almost immediately, a call was placed from Felix Rodriguez in Miami to Samuel Watson of George Bush's staff in the VP's office. Rodriguez, a Cuban exile and former CIA operative, had been assisting Oliver North and the vice president's office on Central American issues since 1985. Soon, all of official Washington knew about the flight.

There was one pressing question. Was there any U.S. government connection with the flight?

A denial reflex took over in official administration circles. Stunned at first by the news, and the TV coverage of the Sandinistas parading a haggard Hasenfus in front of the cameras with his arms held behind his head, Abrams called around to the CIA, the NSC, and DoD. Was this a U.S. operation? Did we in any way pay for this flight? Did we facilitate it? Did we have any involvement?

With each call, he encountered confused officials and received the same answer: no. It was all categorical, and that's what he told Shultz. "The plane was hired by private people," he said, and "had no connection with the U.S. government at all."

Shultz's immediate reaction was not to disavow what Abrams had been told, and to affirm there was no official U.S. connection with the flight. The secretary immediately went forward with a rebuttal. In his first public statement, Abrams also referred to the private effort, which was legal, saying, "some very brave people" have been willing to bring matériel into Nicaragua, adding, "God bless them, if these people were involved in this effort, they were heroes." His concern now was not the operation, but the bodies of the slain men. Shortly thereafter, he called Oliver North to take care of the two dead pilots and ensure they were brought home. Reagan himself stepped forward on October 8, praising the efforts to arm the contras and comparing them to the Abraham Lincoln Brigade in the Spanish Civil War.

All sides of official Washington were in a fighting mood. The Democrats smelled a scandal—and blood. The press streamed after the Hasenfus story like piranha circling in bloody waters. And on the other side of the aisle, the administration went on the offensive to deny any government connection. The chief figure in limiting the damage was Elliott Abrams.

ABRAMS STEPPED FORWARD for the next two weeks, flatly denying any operational government involvement in the illegal resupply operation. He knew of none, and decided to say it loudly. North's name came up repeatedly, but this meant little to Abrams. He was not North's keeper (after one confrontation, North had denied skirting any laws to Abrams), or anyone else's for that matter. If there were questions to be asked, he saw that not as his role, but as the role of North's superiors, like National Security Adviser John Poindexter, the career navy man, who replaced Bud McFarlane in the NSC slot in December of 1985. Like other administration officials, Abrams personally supported the private groups helping out the contras (which the administration did know about). But as with the wristwatches, he had maintained a studious hands-off official policy, knowing that he would otherwise be implicated for facilitating the effort.

On October 9, an unshaven and clearly frightened Hasenfus gave a press conference from Managua. He declared that the CIA "did most of the coordination for the flights and oversaw all of our housing, transportation, also refueling and some flight plans." Hearing this on CNN, Abrams thought it was just incredible, off-the-wall stuff. There was no evidence of an illegal operation. Everyone he had talked to, everyone, had said there was no U.S. involvement. On one hand, he didn't want to know if there were a cover-up of something illegal. On the other, it just seemed, so, well, far out. Fiers had never once suggested an inkling of anything to him in all their meetings.

Over the following days, Abrams adopted the aggressive trial-lawyer defense mode. He was fed up with the press, and fed up with the Congress. For five and a half years, the Democrats had sought to defeat Reagan's Central America policy. Now that contra aid finally had passed, and was awaiting the president's signature, he felt the Democrats were using signs of scandal to bloody the administration. As reports appeared in the press suggesting that the administration had helped organize the supply mission, Abrams was so livid at the lack of hard evidence that he even called up senior editors, including at the *New York Times*, asking that his response to the stories be printed. "People are entitled to believe the government is constantly lying to them, but it isn't," he said angrily.

While signs of an impending scandal were increasingly unraveling, Abrams was undaunted. He was in a fighting, not a thinking, mode. Where other more cautious policy makers were watching their every step, Abrams plowed ahead as though nothing had changed. It was naive and foolish. When asked by Senator Kerry, at a Senate Foreign Relations Committee hearing, if the U.S. had played a role in helping out the private support network aiding the contras during the period of the Boland Amendments, he gave the same answer he gave Shultz: in effect, a categorical no. ("We stay away" from these people, he said.) The next day, he appeared on the Evans and Novak television show, once again giving a blanket denial of any U.S. involvement with the Hasenfus operation. "No government agencies, none," he said defiantly.

He was so forceful that Novak called it a "convincing performance."

Three days later, he appeared behind closed doors before the House Intelligence Committee. Alan Fiers and Clair George, the number three man at the CIA, were also testifying with him.

The question was raised if other governments were providing money to the contras. Abrams thought quickly about how to answer, and then said, "No." For several reasons, he decided on the spot not to mention the Brunei solicitation. First, the U.S. had pledged to Brunei that the contribution would be held in absolute secrecy. If he told Congress, it would surely leak, and find its way quickly into the press. Moreover, Shultz had not released him from his secrecy pledge. Second, the money had still not been deposited in the Geneva account, and Abrams had begun to doubt that it ever would. In the past weeks, he had asked North several times to check for the transfer, and in each instance was told, "No, it's not there." Very concerned, he sent a cable to Brunei about the $10 million, and was told, "these things take time." So, not only was the money not in the account—meaning he was technically correct in saying no government had helped the contras—but he had come to fear the money would never actually reach them.

And also, Abrams, watching his detractors on the other side of the raised horseshoe dais grilling him with hostile questions, saw no reason to help his congressional tormentors by offering up this information.

Again, he was asked about the Hasenfus affair. And again, he vehemently denied any involvement in the private contra resupply mission. Abrams felt he was in good company this time around. The denial was made with equal tenacity by Clair George. Clair George wasn't just anyone. As deputy director of operations, he was certainly in a position to know.

However, in George's and Fiers's cases, they did know something—that Abrams was way off the mark.

DURING THE EARLY days of the Boland Amendment in 1984, Alan Fiers, Clair George, and Oliver North were in a meeting convened by Bill Casey. Casey confronted North: "Ollie, are you operating in Central America?" North replied simply: "No, I am not." "Good. Keep it that way," Casey snapped.

Since 1982, Casey had visibly gone out of his way to impress upon his men the need to adhere to the Boland Amendment. So Fiers had little reason to doubt the veracity of this exchange until February of 1986, when he and an old CIA friend, another operative, went for a drink in Charley's Place, a watering hole nestled in the sleepy confines and rolling hills of rural Virginia. Suddenly, a whole new picture of U.S. activity in Latin America began to emerge.

They sat inconspicuously in a darkened corner as the agent confided to Fiers that the U.S., and the CIA, were involved in secret operations to help the contras. Wow, Fiers thought to himself, putting the pieces together. But Fiers had little incentive to tell anyone. He thought, who was he to blow the whistle on other guys in the Agency, let alone the director—that is, if he knew? Nor was it his place to rat on someone from the White House. The rules of the game, fealty, ruled that out.

Instead, he did what any good undercover agent does when given the dirt on a highly secret operation. He didn't ask questions or ruminate on hair-splitting nuances about the legal loopholes of congressional legislation. Analysts might lose sleep at night over such things, but not operatives. Fiers simply kept his mouth shut, watched, and waited.

The equation changed dramatically that summer. One day in August,

North confided to him that he was running a resupply network out of the White House. He also told him an uncanny story about the diversion of funds from the covert sale of arms to Iran, to the contras. Fiers played it cool, letting North feel he could be trusted, and could take him further into his confidence. It was one thing to be told about an operation from another agent on the inside, quite another to be told by someone from the outside. Elliott Abrams's name came up. Does he know? No. Are you going to tell him? No, he's Shultz's boy, he can't be trusted. That was fine with Fiers.

But Fiers decided he didn't want to be the only one with this information. He went to his superiors to tell them everything—to Clair George and another highly placed Agency operative.

The boys in the Agency hated the fact that North was involved. They considered him a rank amateur. He had no training in espionage, and had broken the cardinal rule of all good intelligence operations: never combine two covert operations. Yet they also knew the colonel was a favorite of Casey's. Fiers continued to lie low.

A few days after the Hasenfus plane went down, North once again reached out to Fiers, telling him that it was part of his resupply operation. Fiers was not surprised. It had all the earmarks of a bush-league operation, not a CIA one. Both men continued to keep Abrams in the dark.

In the following weeks, Fiers watched Abrams increasingly hang himself with his vociferous public defense—before the Hill, on television, to the print media. He didn't see it as his role to save Abrams from himself if the whole thing were to unravel. It was his ass on the line. He had been around long enough as a good bureaucrat, even if an undercover one, to know to stay out of harm's way—not to get too close to political or questionable legal activities. During the testimony on the 14th, Fiers again played it cool as Abrams ran his mouth.

Any member of the old establishment, whatever his political beliefs, would have told Abrams to back off, don't get too far out in front, don't expose yourself until all the facts are known. But this was not Abrams's way. Washington had also changed considerably, and was a far more partisan place. His instincts were those of a heated policy advocate, not a Washington bureaucratic insider. He thought he had the facts. He was locked in mortal combat with the Democrats, and he had a policy to oversee. It was a brazen strategy, characteristic of youth and perhaps inexperience, a combative style that members of Congress could get away with, but not most members of the executive branch. Abrams thought he was operating within the rules of the game on policy, unaware that they were changing beneath his feet even as he spoke.

Brash, smart, energetic Elliott Abrams was exposed and didn't even know it. However supportive he was of his president and the administration, politically, it was a fatal error.

A week after Abrams's testimony before the Hill, his Agency counterpart sought out Fiers in a panic. The whole covert affair was about to blow. It would soon be known that Hasenfus was not operating on his own. And the CIA inspector general was conducting an internal probe of CIA activities. There was nothing to be gained by anyone insisting there was no activity. Tracks had to be covered. It was time for Abrams to stand down.

Fiers knew Abrams was in the dark. But he couldn't let on that he had known, and had been lying for over nine months to Abrams. The next evening, Abrams's CIA counterpart told him that he and everyone at Langley had just learned the CIA might be involved in the Hasenfus affair. Abrams asked when they had found out. The operative responded, "Yesterday."

As Abrams heard this, a chill ran down his spine, like a thick piece of bond paper being slowly ripped in half. For two weeks, he had been telling the Hill, the media, the world one thing. But he had been duped. The Agency was involved.

Finally, he knew there was a lot he didn't know. He had to protect himself, the secretary, and the administration.

He called Charles Hill immediately. It was vital that he see the secretary to brief him on a new development. As early as possible.

Hill said he could meet the secretary at his 7 A.M. briefing. Abrams carefully counted the hours that he would have to wait.

CHAPTER 35

Richard Perle, sitting in his home study late at night, pushed his evening reading aside and stared at the flickering streetlights outside of his house. His home address was unlisted for fear of terrorists. He had lost track of how many foreign trips he had taken, how few weekends he had spent with Leslie and Jonathan, now six. It was one of those snug late-winter evenings, the kind of crisp air just before spring so conducive to appreciating one's good fortune. But here he skulked about in his study, walled in by books and files, overcome by uncharacteristic doubt.

This should have been the best time of his life, the moment he had been working for since arriving in Washington in 1969. He had come to embody the definition of the Reagan hard liner and was widely acknowl-edged as one of the most influential policy makers in the administration. To his backers, he had fought a lonely and heroic battle to resist the discredited logic of arms control and reject any giveaway deals with the "evil empire." He single-handedly inspired whole segments of Reagan supporters, conservative and neoconservative alike ("Please keep telling it like it is, there are some here who remain profoundly grateful for what you are doing," Ben Elliott, the chief presidential speechwriter, wrote to him in 1985).

His detractors saw him quite differently, implacably and appallingly opposed to arms agreements. In one telling exchange, British MP John Gilbert summed up Perle's situation perfectly; he penned a note to Perle about how Perle could do no right in the eyes of his liberal critics. Referring to Labour party leader Denis Healey, he wrote, "Healey appears to subscribe to the view that you are personally responsible for the 'arms race,' hunger in the third world, violence on television, and the inclement weather." Perle privately relished frustrating his opponents and appearing outrageous to them. Altogether, his future prospects were splendid. But he'd been in the doldrums throughout the barren winter months of 1986.

It wasn't government service that fed his doubts. He believed deeply that winning the Cold War was a noble and historic mission. He now saw his job as almost complete, nearly convinced that Reagan would not cut a deal with the Soviet Union that gave up SDI, and that his philosophy of negotiations might yet be vindicated with a successful INF accord. There was only so much *he* could do.

It was true that he remained an object of establishment condescension and criticism. But he was beating the establishment at its own game. His expertise in arms control was matched only by that of the seventy-nine-year-old Paul Nitze, the president's and Shultz's chief adviser on arms control, and even here, the once young protégé had outshone the mentor on the most critical occasions. (Indeed, for all of Nitze's obvious intelligence, on many major issues, like INF and SDI, he showed surprisingly poor judgment.)

Clearly, Perle would never neatly fit in with that old establishment crowd: he was anything but a tight-lipped, buttoned-down Yankee, driven by a Calvinist work ethic. Moreover, in a town where many are defined by their work and shaped by their job title, where they were always coming and going from a meeting, Perle stood out. He typified complexity in life and richness in spirit: a cauldron of emotions, slightly lazy and bohemian, anything but a workaholic, although zealously effective, someone who decided which meetings were worth attending, and avoided those that were not. He approached everything with a single-minded determination and a quiet but unremitting passion—winning the arms race, mastering the bureaucracy, preparing French cuisine, looking after his family.

The criticism was harsh, but he was able to keep his distance, and in refusing to personalize most of the attacks, however bitter and even untrue, he was able to distinguish between glancing blows and fatal wounds. "We love you for the enemies you make," one Massachusetts family wrote to him after a particularly scathing attack by liberal Massachusetts Democrat Ed Markey. Yet other, more open-minded politicians looked beyond Perle, the political opposition, to Perle, the public servant: "As ever, you were superb," Colorado Democrat Tim Wirth told him in 1986 after Perle helped him out with a favor. "I appreciate your willingness to help, and respect your resistance to politics."

But now, he felt his job might nearly be done. He had little yearning to join the establishment for its own sake, nor to stay in a position, however lofty, if his job were nearly complete. He thought of leaving government, seeing more of Jonathan, now starting school, and Leslie, of trying his hand at something new after nearly seventeen often blistering years in government service.

He also thought of writing a book, a novel about government based on his own experiences, changed only enough to make it publishable. It could be an insider's account, and could include his own rivalry with Rick Burt, who had since been made ambassador to West Germany, revealing policy making for what it was, replete with the machinations and misperceptions, the vanity and conceit, and the ignorance and pride that shaped government policy makers, the nonstop headaches and the behind-the-scenes migraines. He decided it could be called *Memorandum.* The idea seized him.

He began to do up an outline that he could eventually present to a publisher.

LATER THAT SPRING, in March, Perle had to contend with the less glamorous part of his job, having little to do with the high stakes of summits and arms control, the side the public never saw—the grunt work of job survival and maintenance. If Perle's enemies couldn't defeat him on policy grounds, they could get at him in other ways, prick him with innuendo in the press, go after his staff, leak irregularities to the Hill, turn the heat up on nonissues and make them major controversies, discrediting him in the process.

Actually, this part of the job was nonstop, but in 1986 it began to intensify, like a thousand cuts, or a slow drip drip drip of annoyances, making his idea for a novel—and retirement from government—an increasingly attractive option.

ON MARCH 12, Perle walked through the establishment gates of Harvard, past the neatly cropped lawns of Cambridge Common, to give a speech at the John F. Kennedy School of Government.

In the talk, Perle said the Soviets still had far more military power than they possibly needed for any conceivable defensive purpose. When asked about *glasnost* and *perestroika,* he said it was not in the West's interest to finance an acceleration of the Soviet economy if faster growth in the economy led to faster growth in the Soviet defense budget—and signs were that Gorbachev was still pouring precious rubles, 12 percent to 14 percent of the Soviet GNP, into the Soviet military.

And he ventured a bold prediction. If the U.S. held firm in its current policies, the Soviet economy and system would reduce the Soviet Union into a "less significant position."

The audience was impressed by Perle's low-key style and disarming charm, as well as his logic. One Harvard Business School professor, David Beatty, dazzled by the performance, later got in touch with Perle, exclaiming enthusiastically that Perle's views "were considerably more enlightening than the press and historical coverage that you usually receive."

EARLIER IN THE month, Perle had submitted a five-page outline of the novel he wanted to write, tentatively entitled *Memorandum*. It was to be an epistolary roman à clef consisting of memoranda circulated among the Defense Department, the State Department, and the White House. It would focus on a power struggle between assistant secretaries of state and defense. He had intended to meet with top editors at Simon and Schuster and Random House to discuss it.

Within weeks, Perle's book proposal had circulated around the leading New York publishing houses. On April 10, the bidding began in earnest, and it was reported in the "Style" section of the *Washington Post* that interest in Perle's book had topped $300,000. Richard Burt was asked to comment: "It sounds like exciting stuff. I would think a novel like the one you have described is well worth over a million dollars."

But not everyone was thrilled at the prospect of Perle's book. That morning, when Bob Bell, Senator Nunn's arms control aide, saw the "Style" piece, he immediately ran a copy into Nunn's office, querying whether this had the appearance of impropriety.

Nunn read Bell's memo and the article, and hit the roof. For some time, Perle and Nunn had been skirmishing over arms control policy, and this was a seemingly tangential issue. But this was precisely the right kind of issue Nunn could use to undermine Perle. That same night, Nunn sent a harshly worded letter—drafted earlier in the day by Bell—to President Reagan questioning Perle's efforts to sell the book proposal while serving as assistant secretary of defense. "One cannot have it both ways. One cannot claim that the published account is merely fiction while at the same time marketing the book as so authoritative and proximate to the locus of power in Washington as to be worth in excess of $300,000."

Nunn continued: "Perle must choose between remaining one of the principal architects of U.S. security policy or undertaking to become a best-selling novelist."

After sending the letter, Nunn promptly released it to the *Washington Post*. The next day, Perle was horrified to wake up to the headline: "Nunn Files Protest Over Perle Novel: Would-Be Author Denies Wrongdoing."

As one critic of Perle's remarked, "What you can't get on substance, you can get on process. Nunn zinged him with this one."

. . .

PERLE HAD TO explain himself quickly. The proposal had already been cleared with the Office of the General Counsel in the Defense Department. He didn't intend to write the book while in office, and he certainly wasn't going to receive any money until after he left government.

Then of course there was the thorny issue of other government memoirs, which told all—in nonfiction. Perle also pointed out that two of Nunn's colleagues on the Armed Services Committee, Senators William Cohen and Gary Hart, wrote a novel, *The Double Man.*

But Perle was on the defensive now. He called off the bidding war for his book, and by month's end terminated negotiations with publishers on his proposed novel for as long as he remained in office.

"Any impression that I would write a memoir that would violate the confidence and trust placed in me by the President and the Secretary of Defense is profoundly mistaken," he wrote in a statement released to the press. Perle added emphatically, "I have no intentions to leave government soon."

Perle was furious that Nunn didn't bother just to pick up the phone and ask him about the project. He had known Nunn since Nunn joined the Senate. Nunn was a disciple of Scoop Jackson's. But Nunn had clearly crossed a line here. He didn't give a wit about the book; he wanted to weaken Perle. This was a *policy* difference—and it was about politics. And with the fight over the ABM treaty interpretation still left unresolved, Nunn had taken off the gloves. Others were less charitable in their assessment. "It was more like Nunn stabbed Richard in the back," one of Perle's top aides said.

Unhampered by inner doubt, fired up, Perle was determined to tough it out.

AS IF THE heat for his book wasn't enough, Perle still had to contend with contentious policy disputes. One day in June, after a meeting on the SALT compliance issue, Nitze returned to the State Department and complained bitterly to Shultz: "Perle is getting impossible to deal with. The battles are Sisyphean."

But Shultz was unmoved by Nitze's panicked alarms. He increasingly had come to the view that Perle *was* willing to explore agreements with the Soviets, but that he set higher standards than other negotiators in the past, or many in his own department for that matter. For Perle, it wasn't the fact of an agreement per se that constituted a success but the content of the agreement. In Shultz's eyes, Perle had begun to emerge as one of the most reliable—and creative—thinkers on arms control.

FOR MONTHS, THROUGHOUT the spring and summer of 1986, U.S.-Soviet relations went from thaw to freeze, and the brave new experiment in openness and comity between the two countries and the two leaders was foundering on the shoals of continued mistrust, competition, and the nascent change in the Soviet Union. The date for the follow-up summit remained unresolved.

In mid-May, Soviet Foreign Minister Eduard Shevardnadze was scheduled to come to Washington to discuss plans for the upcoming summit. But on April 15, the Kremlin promptly canceled the trip after the U.S. bombed Libya in retaliation for a chilling Libyan-inspired terrorist attack in Europe that left several Americans dead. This was a tepid response, a continuing sign of the ailing state of the Soviet Union. In 1982, after Israel had demolished Syria's Soviet-supplied planes in screeching dogfights over the Bekaa Valley in Lebanon, the Soviets rushed extensive advanced weaponry to the Syrians, manned with Soviet personnel. This time, nothing.

But relations soured further. Toward the end of the month, Sweden, Denmark, and Finland picked up what were described as microscopic flecks, like a fine charcoal ash fanning the skies, indicating soaring levels of radiation. Days later, the nearly invisible particles descended over Eastern Europe, like a toxic snow. On April 28, a cryptic statement was released from Tass, the Soviet news agency, blandly announcing that "an accident had occurred" at the Chernobyl nuclear power plant.

Shultz relayed an urgent message to Gorbachev, offering humanitarian and technical assistance. There was no response.

Night after bitter night, the Soviets maintained a fierce news blackout, until some twenty separate countries were affected by the disaster. Finally, on May 14, Gorbachev emerged, looking gaunt and tired. He offered a more detailed explanation, only to abruptly fire off a philippic against the West for its "lies" and "distortions" of the severity of the event.

Even his most ardent supporters in the West were shocked by the callousness of Gorbachev's response, the duplicity and appalling unreliability of the Soviet regime. Eventually, 200,000 people, dazed and shocked by the disaster, were herded out of the range of Chernobyl, but only after prolonged exposure to the deadly radiation. They asked gut-wrenching questions in the aftermath of the tragedy. How could this be? What did this say about *glasnost*? Could Gorbachev be believed?

It was actually a far more subtle picture. Never in the past had the Soviets reported a disaster. But now, inexorably caged by modern technology, from high-tech satellites to a plethora of common ham radios beaming the initial reports about the accident back into the Soviet Union, Gorbachev had little choice. For days running, Soviet and East European citizens had heard about the immense catastrophe, not from their own leaders, but from the West.

If the incident felt like a vicious betrayal to Gorbachev supporters, for Perle it demonstrated one clear point: the Soviets did ruthlessly lie, they did imperil their own people, they did show a flagrant disregard for human life, young as well as old. Nor was this purely an academic argument, designed to score debating points against his opposition. He used it to help resuscitate the argument for ceasing to adhere to the SALT II limits, over which he had earlier been thwarted. This time, he was successful. On May 27, the president announced the U.S. would no longer live within the limits of the SALT II treaty.

The uproar was immediate. The Democrats in Congress, the NATO allies, and much of the media howled and shrieked, sharply criticizing the decision. Perle took it all in stride.

Later in the month, he ambled over to the *Washington Post* for a ninety-minute lunch with editors and defense reporters to explain the reasoning behind the decision. Overstuffed sandwiches were served, potato chips passed out, cans of Coke and bottled juice offered. But Perle was barely able to eat a bite. It wasn't a discussion; it was an ambush. "You're unreal," one reporter charged ("In the real world . . ." Perle explained); another critiqued, "Why not be more clever?" ("I don't know what you have in mind that's more clever," he fired back, wondering whatever had happened to the vaunted ethic of journalistic impartiality); a third asked, in an incredulous tone, "What *is* the problem with noncompliance?" (Reading the transcript later, a colleague of Perle's remarked: "Earth to editor, where have you been all this time?")

Perle had heard it all before, the same arguments, over and over and over again. He explained, "This is to make plain to the Soviets that when the president says he will not be bound by unilateral compliance, he means what he says. Historically, when the Soviets gained the impression that they are dealing with a weak American president, it is ultimately disastrous. Ronald Reagan means what he says."

It was a credible show. Perle was at the top of his game, and the nuance of his arguments reduced the sharpness of his critics' barbs. But he had no illusions about the outcome. He knew that at the *Post* he didn't change any minds—his staff never tired of reminding him that the reporters were too cynical. In a sense, that was okay, he felt. His working relationship with the press remained solid. And after all, if he couldn't change their minds, at least he did influence Soviet calculations—even in this era of summitry, the president could still be hard-nosed.

But it remained a fact that Perle privately took little delight in the SALT victory, despite the suggestions in the press. It gnawed at him that perhaps it was a minor victory, too little, too late, the finger in the dike. It didn't occur to him that, just then, it may have been all that was needed.

PERLE HAD NEVER been to the Soviet Union, though, as he had put it, he had "danced around the Russian bear from a number of strategic vantage points: the Norwegian border, the Chinese border, the Turkish border, the Finnish archipelago." His chance finally came that August, when the Kremlin proposed an "experts meeting," in which the two sides could get away from the repetitious monotony of the Geneva sessions and engage in a "free-for-all discussion." The U.S. accepted, and like a child drawn to a hot stove, Perle arrived in Moscow on August 11. Paul Nitze led the delegation, which was joined by senior U.S. negotiator Max Kampelman, and aides and advisers General Edward Rowny, Robert Linhard, Ronald Lehman, and Mike Glitman.

As the black limousines for the American delegation raced to the village of Mescherino, where the talks were to be held in a lavish guesthouse mysteriously tucked in a tranquil knot of woods south of Moscow, Perle saw barefooted children scampering about, young men fishing in a stream, creaky rustic wooden houses, and hunched villagers prodding cattle.

For his part, Kampelman was glad that Perle was part of the delegation. For some time he had been arguing that it was better to have Richard "inside the tent," where he could be enormously constructive, rather than outside the process, "where he would live up to the stereotype as an obstructionist." After an entreaty by Weinberger, Shultz included him.

For thirteen hours stretched over two days, the delegations engaged in quiet conversation behind the wind-blown curtains of the Foreign Ministry villa, in a town that was impervious to the outside world and even time itself. Taking breaks for meals of fine caviar, flaky smoked fish, thick black soup, and soft-boiled potatoes, washed down with Kvass, a dark, sour, slightly alcoholic beverage brewed from fermented barley, the two sides sought to lay groundwork for the eventual superpower summit. Perle argued on behalf of his zero ballistic missiles, and why it would be in the interest of the Soviet Union; the Soviets focused on SDI and the ABM treaty.

In the talks, Perle, not Nitze, was the one treated with extreme interest, almost like a celebrity. The Soviets were consumed with his simultaneous personal charm and anti-Communist hostility, and smothered him with warm words and respect.

"In his own way, he has been very helpful," said Victor Karpov. "Please come back," General Nikolai Chervov pleaded, adding, "I have a high regard for Mr. Perle, it is a challenge to deal with him." (No less than Eduard Shevardnadze later called Perle "the American heavy artillery," arguing that his ideas about ballistic missiles were more interesting than "Professor Nitze's.") For Perle, the Soviet entreaties vindicated his view that the way to deal with the Soviets was with toughness, consistency, and a clear eye.

In the evening, he prowled the streets of Moscow by himself, looking in vain for the famous Russian ice cream. The next day, the talks ended where they began, largely at a standstill. The date for a summit still had not been arranged.

But all was not lost. The Soviets gave further veiled hints that an INF deal could be in the offing. Moreover, a package was delivered to Perle before leaving. Affixed to General Chervov's engraved card ("with best wishes") were four tins of rare fresh Beluga caviar, Perle's favorite. He smiled impishly and later remarked to his colleagues: "We're realists; I think we understand each other."

BUT PERLE RETURNED to some sad news. One of his closest friends, Don Fortier, had died of cancer at the young age of thirty-nine. A high-ranking NSC aide, and widely regarded as a wonderful man, Fortier had been living on a government salary, and had little to leave to his pregnant wife. The funeral was held on September 9, and a shaken Perle had finally made his decision. Tired of the constant infighting, content in the notion that he had sufficiently left his imprint on the weighty arena of superpower arms control policy, with little more remaining to be done, and wanting to provide financially for his family, he decided to call it quits.

He soon let the word out.

But at first, he didn't take any concrete steps. Once again, the tug of events that this time began with a U.S.-Soviet espionage flap inextricably sucked him back into the fray.

For thirty-two days, from late August to the end of September, U.S.-Soviet relations increasingly soured. A single arrest, that of Soviet U.N. employee Gennadi Zakharov on charges of espionage by the FBI, unleashed a chain of incidents that would engulf both Reagan and Gorbachev in several weeks of high-stakes personal diplomacy. When the accused Soviet spy Zakharov was jailed in the Manhattan correctional center without bail, the Soviets swiftly retaliated by arresting an American, Moscow-based *U.S. News & World Report* correspondent Nick Daniloff, and holding him in a KGB prison. Daniloff was not a spy; instead, the arrest was a shrewd setup by the KGB. And from the start, the standoff had echoes of the bleak days of the Cold War in the 1950s. After weeks of a highly public battle of wills and strained behind-the-scenes negotiations, a complex deal was cut. Zakharov was released in exchanged for Daniloff and a leading Soviet dissident, Yuri Orlov.

Against this tense backdrop, however, came the surprise announcement of a new U.S.-Soviet meeting between Reagan and Gorbachev, proposed by the general secretary himself in a personal letter to the American president. The unexpected get-together would be a prelude for the full-fledged summit slated for later in the year. Gorbachev suggested two NATO capitals for the meeting, London or Reykjavik, Iceland. Reagan chose the ancient fishing port of Reykjavik.

The two sides formally agreed to the meeting on September 30, which left less than two weeks before they would come face-to-face on October 11–12.

As PREPARATIONS FOR the meeting in Iceland began to take shape, the eyes of the world were once again on the American president, Ronald Reagan. What did he have in mind for Reykjavik? How would he perform? In the clutch, was he a man of peace, or a man of strength? These were the urgent questions that now dominated the world.

But for the American people, there was never any secret to how they felt about Reagan. It was a remarkably intimate relationship, as though Reagan resided not simply in their hearts but in their homes. But if he was at once like the genial neighbor next door, and he was, Reagan was also a colossus, the man boldly rebuilding America's spirit and restoring its dominance in the world. He was fresh and buoyant, forceful and persuasive, and always inspiring. In word and in spirit, Ronald Reagan, this quintessentially American president, embodied the nation he led.

The axiom of the modern presidency had long been that presidents are surprisingly powerless, except for their power to persuade. Yet here, Reagan, like FDR and JFK before him, was able to forge and rally not just his administration, but the entire nation, literally lifting it by force of his own dominating presence and the sheer strength of his vision. He had the same effect abroad, with recalcitrant friends like NATO and with defiant foes like the Soviets or the Libyans. At his best, he was awe inspiring to watch.

But there is a second axiom about the presidency: invariably, every administration is a tireless reflection of its commander-in-chief. The suggestion that Reagan's effectiveness was due solely to the quality of his staff was not only simplistic but in truth explained very little. Staff, however capable, is never better than the man in the Oval Office, and the tone is always defined at the top, never the other way around. Here, the history of recent administrations is telling. Like himself, Truman's administration was tough-minded, down to earth, frequently unappreciated (without complaint), and remarkably effective; Eisenhower's was cautious and pragmatic, suffused with a military and Christian spirit; Kennedy's was again an extension of the man, filled with glitter, spirited and detached, and action-oriented; Johnson's was exhaustive, bighearted but ultimately flawed, run like the legislative calendar, one program after another, one update from the Vietnamese front after another, statistics here and facts there; Nixon's was conspiratorial yet often successful, shrewd yet paranoid, hard-headed and middle of the road; Ford's was like him, decent and a caretaker government; Carter's was moralistic yet actually quite cold, overly theoretical and often muddled, well-intentioned but mired in detail, frequently unable to act, and largely ineffective. And then there was Reagan, who like all presidents before him gave shape and direction to his administration and indelibly defined his presidency. Like FDR, it was revolutionary in spirit; like Truman, it was tough and visionary in difficult times, embraced old-fashioned common sense, and got the job done; like JFK, it was idealistic, energetic, and energizing; and like an earlier generation of presidents, it was, at the end of the day, inexorably rooted in the American dream of individual liberty and initiative, and the unshakable belief in American exceptionalism. In fact, Reagan was not like any single one of these presidents before him, but rather, in his own inexplicable way, often incorporated the best of each.

But inside the more liberal, cynical-minded establishment confines of Washington and New York, Reagan had to fight his critics every step of the way. Driven by hostility to his unabashed conservatism, countless magazine articles portrayed him as lazy and out of touch, academics scoffed at his reluctance to read every position paper and master the fine print of every policy detail (forgetting that while Jimmy Carter did this so well, it was of little help when it came to the actual job of governing), and a dismissive press quoted legions of think-tank experts and activists denouncing his work habits and policies.

So there it was: two diametrically opposed views constituting two parallel universes in the 1980s, intertwined like a rose and thorn wrapped in an uneasy, rancorous coexistence.

But what acounted for this difference, the stark gap between the American people and the establishment elites, the blue collar and office worker families of middle America and a cynical Washington press corps, the new counterestablishment and the denizens of Georgetown salons? To be sure, ideology accounted for most of it. Not only did Ronald Reagan want to dismantle the liberal establishment way of doing things and all that it cherished, but this former New Deal ADA Democrat also did not care about paying homage to the political and opinion barons of Washington. And this was an offense that aroused the ire of his critics.

But these differences exposed a vaster, more profound fault line, dividing an insular Washington and the world outside of the Beltway that was Reagan's domain.

One prominent reporter returning to Washington in the mid-1980s from gritty tours in the trenches of the Middle East and the Soviet Union had developed an almost hawkish enthusiasm for Reagan's foreign policy. But he quickly learned that his stateside colleagues, who gave immediate shape to the news and wrote the instant history, were unwilling to broker any diversity of opinion when it came to the president. Holding his outstretched hands an inch apart, the reporter said, "This was how much range of opinion we were allowed in the press. Zilch." But in their uniform hostility, many in the media often failed to do the basic prerequisite of their jobs, which was not to deliver opinions in the guise of news articles or to push their own agendas, but to report the facts and, more important, to understand the Reagan phenomenon. Although, in fairness, Reagan was no ordinary man and remained deceptively complex.

Indeed, even in exploring the many criticisms of Reagan—that Reagan was helpless without cue cards, impervious to facts, passive and out of touch, just a simple man who just happened to be lucky—one comes to a deeper understanding of this president, his style, his magic, and even his success.

While Reagan was portrayed as passive by his detractors (including some of his own staff, who never fully grasped how he operated), his senior aides like George Shultz and Cap Weinberger and others throughout the administration, who watched the president in action, saw that Reagan frequently knew far more than he let on. "He would have been a fool to do otherwise," Shultz would later note. Thus, when cabinet meetings and policy discussions at critical moments threatened to stall amid conflicting viewpoints and jumbled contradictory facts, Reagan could be surprisingly, and intimately, involved. With a modest smile, he would put up his hand and in a few short sentences pull everything together, summarize the disparate discussion, and make sense of the complicated issues bedeviling even the best of his advisers.

And when it was said that his views were simplistic, this took some examining. What exactly did that mean? Here again, usually not much. How quickly it was forgotten that all those bright experts and credentialed Ivy League advisers, like the Kennedy and Johnson men, who dismally ran the Vietnam War, and the Nixon and Carter teams, who toiled endlessly in Geneva to limit nuclear arms (but never did), and all the scholarly whiz kids, who concocted fanciful limited war theories and espoused esoteric footnotes of international law, had demonstrated a well-intentioned penchant for making things not just unnecessarily complicated, but of failing to boot. The fact was that both Reagan the man and Reagan the leader were utterly different. Where others were mired in footnotes, in governing, he immediately found the central text. He didn't look for complexities but verities, a point his establishment critics shockingly missed time and again.

Great leaders, like Truman or Churchill, are those who do not play to the crowd, but who choreograph the music of history. They do not crave consensus, but are willing to travel alone. Where others are most caught up in the difficulties of the moment, leaders, driven by bedrock core values, forge ahead. They elude easy definition. Frequently derided in their day, their successes are often not recognized until much later. This was Reagan's approach.

Leaders have but few confidantes, and even fewer friends. By the same token, they will often see things differently, and will dare and act on possibilities that others do not even dream of. Seizing the moment, they will do so no matter how much criticism they receive. So it was with Reagan. He knew who he was and what he wanted to do, and in the raw, partisan 1980s, he took on the inbred policy elite time and bitter time again.

SDI was of course one example, as was the zero option; talking tough to the Soviets was another, as was militarily contesting the Soviets in the third world; thinking the United States could—and should—defeat the communist world was yet another. For these stands, Reagan was derided. But it is well worth remembering that history is littered with naysayers, even great ones, who were later proven wrong. Thomas Edison once declared "alternative current is a waste of time"; two years before Pearl Harbor, Rear Admiral Clark exclaimed that ships could not be sunk by bombs; and no less than Albert Einstein, in 1933, wrote that nuclear energy would be "unobtainable."

But Reagan was a man of vison, seeing untold possibilities that others thought foolish, or dangerous, or unwise. However detached he may have sometimes appeared, and to be sure he often was passive, Reagan would nevertheless act on his central goals when it most mattered or when he had to. Early on in the administration, Shultz observed that behind Reagan's little quips and Hollywood homilies, and his remote and often joking veneer, everything the president did was "serious to the hilt." When the president was dissatisifed with the quality or direction of the advice he received, he had an uncanny ability to set aside position papers and get straight to the point that everyone else seemed to miss. He didn't gloat or condescend to his aides, like an LBJ or Carter; he just acted. And in doing so, Shultz noticed that Reagan repeatedly dominated major meetings, as with Anatoly Dobrynin or Andrei Gromyko, or NATO leaders, and later at the Geneva Summit, bolting from carefully prepared scripts in his tête-à-tête with Gorbachev. All this while making it look so effortless and simple, all this while so often being right.

So how to understand this outwardly simple but surprisingly complex man, Ronald Reagan? One answer lay with a little known and even less revealed incident from his past, told by Cap Weinberger. Years earlier, when Reagan was the California governor, he gave an outdoor bash for the Sacramento press corps and their families. It was a warm spring day, and everyone was jovial. That is, until a small child fell into the swimming pool and began to thrash in the water. Instantly, it was clear the child couldn't swim. But before any of the governor's aides or members of the press even moved their feet, a fully clothed Ronald Reagan sprinted across the lawn and dove into the pool, saving the child. Dripping wet, he delivered the child to the frightened and thankful parents, and then promptly said to the reporters, "I really hope none of you will write about this." Most of the press took him at his word, and never did.

And that was Ronald Reagan. There was a time to deliberate, and a time to act, a time to sit back quietly and a time to move quickly, and one had to know the difference.

George Shultz was fond of saying about his president, "If a man's been lucky all his life, it ain't luck." That others missed this didn't trouble Reagan, who had an unimaginably strong inner compass and powerful inner values, and who operated to a logic, rhythm, and instinct almost unfathomable to those who watched him in action, save for the eyes of history. But then there was Reykjavik. As the Iceland meeting approached, it was clear that all his instincts and judgments, however remarkable, would be tested as never before.

ICELAND'S GOVERNMENT HAD suggested that Reagan and Gorbachev meet in a local hotel, but the security teams of both powers quickly vetoed this idea, preferring an isolated structure that could be more easily guarded. Finally they selected a squat two-story building that sat on the bare Icelandic plains with a sweeping view scanning the edge of the North Atlantic at one angle, and a frosty bay at another.

Constructed at the turn of the century, the white clapboard house was called Hofdi House. It was built in a sturdy style characteristic of a phlegmatic land touching the Arctic Circle, hardened by a thousand-year struggle against the elements, fire, ice, driving rain. In a land where 55 percent of the people believed in elves, Hofdi House was said to be haunted by a female apparition. Hearing a cacophony of unexplained noises, an overly alarmed British ambassador evacuated the house in 1952.

After the summit announcement was made, the house's windows were quickly reinforced with steel, its furniture rearranged, the ornate porcelain chandelier with matching mirror brightly polished. But its most distinctive feature remained how the house stood, erect and balanced, unadorned yet steady. Even after years of relative neglect and pounding from the weather, its structure neither sagged nor buckled. Flanked by open barren spaces and gray skies, a steady drizzle and ubiquitous turbulence from the sea beyond, its thick coats of white paint and steel balusters and rails fitted together in an intricate meeting of pegs in holes, sealing the perimeter of the house, its proud façade rising timelessly against the world.

But inside, there was a curious spontaneity, hanging pictures crashed down from walls, doors creaked open and shut on their own volition, unexplained noises disturbed the night. It was a place where superstition drove away the meek, and, as lore would have it, where history could be made, and, as the history of the Cold War would have it, would be made.

CHAPTER 36

"Can you say summit?" Richard Perle said, half jokingly.

"Get out of here," Frank Gaffney responded.

"I just got the news. Reagan's meeting with Gorbachev October 11 to 12—one and a half days. Gorbachev proposed the meeting in a letter, and Reagan jumped at it. We've got to get ready."

"Is it really a summit?"

"Not exactly. It's officially billed as an informal prep meeting for a full-fledged Washington summit later in the year. Rumor has it that the Soviets could be ready to sign an agreement on INF. But you know how these things are. Anything can happen when heads of state get together."

Gaffney quickly got on the phone to a colleague. "Did you hear about Iceland? It's a bolt out of the blue."

"Yes," said the voice on the other end of the line. "I heard that Gorbachev meant to propose London or Ireland. His guys screwed up and proposed Iceland. It turns out that Gorbachev thinks Reykjavik is in Ireland.

"He still really doesn't know that much about the West, does he?"

AS THE HASTILY agreed to meeting started to take shape, the world quickly began to descend upon the tiny country of Iceland, and the small, quiet country did its best to accommodate the world. Not since Bobby Fischer toppled Boris Spassky with a king rook pawn had Iceland had so much activity, and that was nothing like this.

It was a jarring sight for the Icelanders, in a nation without an army, a navy, or a crime problem, to see throngs of agents securing the country. All five hundred city police officers joined the security battalions. Men in dark glasses, with walkie-talkies and shouldering long rifles, raced lock-step over rooftops throughout the city. In preparation for the invasion of two thousand press members, and Soviet and American diplomats, the tourist industry went into full swing: as the *Times*'s Maureen Dowd noted, Miss World, a stunning blonde and twenty-two-year-old nursery school teacher, was recalled home from a Far East trip to smile beautifully; horses galloped majestically around the center of town; stores were stocked with souvenirs as quickly as they could be churned out: sweaters with Reagan's and Gorbachev's names stitched in the map of Iceland, scarves with the Stars and Stripes on one side and the Hammer and Sickle on the other, and a book on the summit that was really a flask.

Meanwhile, the Russian advance men protested the presence of the large *Top Gun* movie poster across from the Hotel Saga, where part of their delegation was staying. It was taken down that Thursday.

The Americans rapidly took over a schoolhouse near Hofdi House, where they set up makeshift working offices for the staff. Cramped offices were created with crude dividers, phones installed on cheap office furniture desks, and filing cabinets brought in. Computers connected the workstations, and secure fax and phone lines were hastily added. But most prominent was not the changes, but the schoolhouse clock, with its 1950s flavor, its thick second hand that ticked loudly, displaying Reykjavik time.

Minutes away, the Soviets set up shop at the Reykjavik pier, where two large Soviet cruise ships trawled into the stark waters to serve as hotels and communication centers. In town, they erected a makeshift podium on the dance floor of the disco in the Saga, where they opened up their press center.

The Americans set up their press center across town, at the Loftleider Hotel.

At Hofdi House itself, the city paid the equivalent of $50,000 to hastily fix the plumbing, digging up large dirt ditches in the road behind the house. By the weekend, the job was complete. Iceland, which boasted one of the world's first parliaments, dating back to the tenth century, was ready for the superpower meeting.

IN WASHINGTON, THE official U.S. delegation was being finalized. Aside from the president, it would include George Shultz, Paul Nitze, Max Kampelman, John Poindexter, ACDA head Ken Adelman, and Ed Rowny, who, like Nitze, was a chief arms adviser to Shultz, plus a handful of core staff members, such as State Department assistant secretary Roz Ridgway. Richard Perle was going as the chief representative for the Pentagon.

As he waited to hear whether he too could go to Reykjavik to assist Perle, particularly in relaying any key developments to Weinberger,

Gaffney was getting impatient. For that matter, so was Perle. The State Department had significant control over the list of attendees, and was trying to block Gaffney from coming by keeping his name off the list.

Weinberger personally called Shultz about Gaffney twice, and finally State relented. As soon as he got permission, Perle told Gaffney. But there was a catch. State refused authorization to give Gaffney housing, saying that the hotels in Reykjavik were all booked up. The closest place was forty minutes south of Reykjavik, at the bachelor officers quarters for the Keflavik airfield.

They're trying to banish you to the boonies, Perle said. Gaffney was not happy. He didn't want to be left out of the action.

Perle told Gaffney he needed him there. Look, he said, you can sleep on the floor of my hotel room. We're going to be it—you and me, the Pentagon's lonely outpost in Iceland.

Gaffney wasn't wild about the arrangement, and feared a bait and switch by the State Department, being cut even further out of the loop. He asked Perle to speak with Roz Ridgway and secure an understanding that "he could participate as appropriate in the support activities." He only wanted to come if he were useful, and didn't want to leave his wife, Anne, and abandon the rest of his duties back home for five days simply to call Cap. Perle knew Frank would come. Frank was a loyal friend and colleague. He would be there; he always was.

What was unclear, however, was just what the "there" was. There was no agenda agreed to in advance; indeed, the two sides didn't even exchange lists of who would accompany the two leaders.

BACK AT HOME, even though there were expectations that the Soviets might be willing to sign up on an INF missile deal, liberal criticism for Reagan once again fiercely mounted. Raymond Garthoff, a Brookings Institution scholar, ridiculed the American proposal on INF missiles, saying that it was too much for the Soviets. He confidently predicted that it was "more than the traffic can bear." Jack Mendelsohn, deputy director of the liberal Arms Control Association, and a harsh critic of the administration, declared that the modified zero option proposal, which allowed each side to keep one hundred missiles, was "unrealistically low from the Soviet point of view." Michael Krepon, a former staffer to a Democratic congressman, now with the Carnegie Institute, was more pointed in his comments about Richard Perle's role: "The kind of agreements he has in mind, no Soviet leader can accept," adding, these guys in the administration are "doing some dangerous things."

On the other side of the political spectrum, Reagan also came under increasing criticism, from the conservative wing of his party. Representative Jack Kemp accused the administration of being seduced by "the allure of détente." Other conservatives decried the president's excessive eagerness to hold a summit meeting, prompting the president to respond, almost defensively, "I don't think I am going to be snowed into believing that the leopard is changing its spots."

UPON DEPARTURE, PRESIDENT Reagan downplayed expectations for the meeting with Gorbachev, and said in his remarks that it would essentially be "a private meeting between the two of us." He added, "We will not have large staffs with us, nor is it planned that we will sign substantive agreements."

The Soviets were a little less clear, and hinted that they had greater expectations. Upon arrival in Iceland, Gorbachev said he was prepared to "do all in my power to bring about reasonable compromises in my meeting with the president." In a Soviet briefing for the press in Iceland on the 9th, Yevgeny Primakov, the director of the Institute of World Economy and International Relations, set a slightly different tone, saying: "The Soviet Union believes the major task is to reach an agreement on cessation of the arms race." He added more ominously, "The agenda for this summit is wide open for discussion of any problems."

The weather was warmer than expected, forty degrees. But the city was soaked with a chilly drizzle, and even the U.S. participants conceded when they touched down in Iceland that a mood of uncertainty, even drama, lingered over the day-and-a-half meeting. It was slated to begin at 10:30 on Saturday, and end by noon the next day. Twenty-five and a half hours.

Once again, a total news blackout was in force.

PERLE HAD LEARNED the hard way from the Geneva summit. Food was eaten in fits and starts, and wasn't very good. So this time he brought his own stash: kosher salamis, cheese and crackers, canned pâté, rich chocolate brownies. Arriving at his hotel room, he was dismayed by the fact that he had no refrigerator or mini-bar. Outside his window he eyed the ring of rain-soaked armed security police dourly barricading the hotel from the rest of the world. What the hell, he thought, what's a little improvisation, as long as they don't shoot me. He opened his room window, and put his two salamis on the ledge to rest. It's plenty cold, he thought; they'll keep there.

. . .

From the start, at 10:15 on Saturday, nothing seemed to happen according to schedule. Gorbachev's motorcade arrived a few minutes late, and as he and Reagan shook hands on the steps of Hofdi House, Gorbachev visibly eyed his watch. His bearing was confident and boisterous. It was just minutes before 10:30.

The two delegations, after watching each other warily under the great chandelier, disappeared up the winding wooden stairs to the second floor. There, they withdrew into small staff rooms, while the two leaders met alone in an austere room downstairs.

Reagan and Gorbachev, with only interpreters present, took their seats by a small table. It was immediately clear that Gorbachev had something planned, that the meeting was not just purely a prep meeting and INF was far from the only thing he had in mind; he had brought with him a thick wad of folders, and announced that he had proposals to make "in every area of arms control." After general comments, Gorbachev, speaking briskly and confidently, suggested they call in their foreign ministers while he presented his arms initiatives.

After Shultz and Shevardnadze were seated, Gorbachev reached with his right hand into his deep folder and pulled out a sheaf of papers, and made a lengthy presentation. After an hour, he then handed Reagan a typed copy in English of what he had read, and an intricate set of instructions to be issued to their respective foreign ministers as the basis for the forthcoming summit.

The document was a series of concessions. Gorbachev accepted the 50 percent reduction scheme in heavy offensive missiles, thus harkening back to their earlier meeting in Geneva. He accepted major cuts in the Soviet heavy strategic missiles, an objective of U.S. policy ever since arms talks began in earnest under Richard Nixon and a particular concern to Reagan, and as the meeting wore on agreed to slash them by 50 percent. He accepted the U.S. INF proposal, saying it's "your own zero option of 1981," though he did not want to accept restrictions on mobile missiles in Asia. On ABM and SDI, he proposed a mandatory ten-year period of nonwithdrawal from the treaty, where he had earlier insisted upon a period of up to fifteen to twenty years.

Reagan listened attentively, and when it was his turn to react, he commented vigorously on each of the initiatives. On SDI, he stood firm, reiterating his July 25 letter to Gorbachev: "We are accused of wanting a first-strike capability, but we are proposing a treaty that would require elimination of ballistic missiles before a defense can be deployed: so a first strike would be impossible."

When time approached for a break, Gorbachev said earnestly: I hope you will study our proposals carefully.

We certainly will, the president responded.

The Americans then recessed to the claustrophobic bug-proof bubble in the American embassy to review the proposals, where they anxiously crammed around a tiny table, their knees knocking into one another.

THE MOOD WAS electric. As Shultz described Gorbachev's proposals, concession after concession, "gifts at our feet," everyone brimmed with excitement, eagerly hanging on Shultz's every word. Suddenly, there was a big whoosh and the door of the tiny bubble opened. In walked the president.

Everyone stood, and the president seemed taken aback by the commotion he had caused, craning his head around: "We could fill this thing with water and keep goldfish," he joked. He then added lightheartedly, with a bit of a swagger, "Why did Gorbachev have more papers than I did?"

Reagan then reconstructed the meeting for his advisers. "He's brought a whole lot of proposals but I'm afraid he's going after SDI."

Nitze was elated, calling it the best Soviet proposal in twenty-five years. Listening to this, Perle was convinced that the U.S. was in a position of strength. "By accepting the zero option in Europe," he said, "they have conceded a great deal to us although they could [still try to] shift missiles from Asia to Europe. But the principle of zero has been established."

Shultz then dispatched a team to help Reagan frame his responses for the afternoon session. The president agreed that a working group should meet that evening to review with the Soviets what had been accomplished during the day, and try to agree upon possible documents setting out progress.

PERLE CALLED GAFFNEY, and asked if he could bring him a salami from the room for lunch. Gaffney broke the news. The brisk winds had blown the salamis off the ledge, and as soon as they fell to the ground with a heavy thud, security guards rushed over and bayoneted the hapless meats until they were unrecognizable.

Perle thought to himself, Things get more amazing by the minute.

REAGAN AND GORBACHEV settled into their chairs in Hofdi House at 3:30 that afternoon, and locked horns once again. This time, Reagan was impassioned; while reading off note cards, he frequently looked up and improvised, speaking from the heart. He favored a new treaty that would supersede the old ABM pact, and committed the U.S. to sharing SDI technology. He compared SDI to gas masks during World War I. He again elaborated on his July 25 letter.

Gorbachev's temper began to flare.

"The ABM treaty must be strengthened, not scrapped." What about START? he asked.

We welcome your proposal, Reagan answered. Let's have a joint working party deal with the subject this evening.

And zero option for INF?

It must include missiles in Asia. This can also be dealt with in the working group.

The ABM treaty? Gorbachev's voice was rising.

Reagan paused briefly, and put the note cards aside. "I'm older than you are. When I was a boy, women and children could not be killed indiscriminately from the air. Wouldn't it be great if we could make the world as safe today as it was then?"

It was 5:45, and they had agreed on little. Gorbachev refused to budge; nor would Reagan yield. They referred the unresolved issues to a working group, to be convened that evening at eight. Reykjavik was no longer just a preparatory meeting. The working group meant that negotiations over far-sweeping ideas, more than had ever been discussed between the superpowers since the dawn of the Cold War, had begun.

THAT AFTERNOON, ON the second floor, the remaining officials shuffled their feet and milled around nervously. The two delegations were soon mingling informally. Russian officials, once virtually inaccessible to the many Americans, were all there, chatting informally with their American counterparts over black coffee, flaky pastry, and probing conversation. One Soviet stood out dramatically, Marshal Sergei Akhromeyev, the top military man in the Soviet Union. Small and compact, he joked that "I am the last of the Mohicans," explaining he was raised on the adventure tales of James Fenimore Cooper, and that he was the last active Russian commander who had fought the Nazis in World War II.

The Americans were puzzled as to why he was there, thinking Gorbachev brought him along to appease the military, thus avoiding a repeat of Geneva. The Soviet experts in the delegation confidently assured Shultz that Akhromeyev would not be a member of the working group that evening.

· · ·

BEYOND THE PROTECTIVE barriers around Hofdi House, the press anxiously milled around in an unbroken wall, jockeying for position. Rumors ran rampant when they heard that working groups had been formed. Speculation was immediate: an arms deal was in the works.

At Perle's hotel room, there was a stack of messages waiting for him. One was from Leslie; the rest were from reporters. They knew a blackout was in effect, but they tried anyway. Perle had not yet called Weinberger.

AS NIGHT BROKE, the American working group team returned to Hofdi House. As they greeted the Soviets, they were surprised with a curveball: Akhromeyev was leading the Soviet side. The American team was led by Nitze, who Perle felt was doing a first-rate job.

"I'm no diplomat, like you," Akhromeyev said. "I'm not a negotiator, like you. I'm a military man. Let's not repeat all the familiar arguments. Let's see how much progress we can make."

In demeanor, tone, and authority, the marshal was different from previous negotiators. It rapidly became clear that he was shrewd, clever, and spoke with authority. He did not have to consult with Gorbachev, but could make decisions right on the spot. He did most of the talking. When he didn't like what his colleagues, Georgi Arbatov, Valentin Falin, and Victor Karpov, said, he muscled them aside with panache, then innocently asked the Americans, "Now, where were we?"

The two teams wrestled until 2 A.M., when they recessed. Nitze was agitated, feeling that he didn't have enough authority to override objections raised by his colleagues, and feeling that real progress could be made. He, Perle, and Kampelman, along with other delegation members, NSC staffer Robert Linhard, Shultz aide Charles Hill, and ACDA assistant James Timbie then went to wake an already antsy Shultz, who, wearing pajamas, a heavy sweater, and a thick bathrobe, greeted them in his sitting room.

Nitze called Akhromeyev a first-class negotiator; "a good man in a bad system." Perle explained the problem with some of his proposals. Shultz agreed.

Nitze then looked expectantly at Shultz. What about my authority? his face said. "This is your working group and you're the boss," Shultz told him. "There's no rule of unanimity." In short, Nitze's word would be final.

Shultz then retired to sleep, but tossed and turned fitfully. He felt the U.S. had within its grasp a historic arms deal.

.   .   .

GAFFNEY WAS IN Perle's room. He had camped himself out on the floor, but could not sleep. He kept staring at the phone, and wondered what the hell was going on. He got up intermittently, stroked his beard, and paced.

THE WORKING GROUPS struggled, deep into the blackness of the night. At 5 A.M., the American delegation wanted to hand out a long document they had put together, but they needed to make copies of it first. But there was no copy machine. A Soviet aide presented them with carbon paper; the Americans shook their heads no, and instead called the American embassy. There was no copy machine there either. They borrowed the Soviet carbon paper.

At 6:15, they finally broke. The Soviets had made significant concessions, leading to the cherished 50 percent cut in offensive weapons (i.e., to equal outcomes), eagerly sought by the Americans. INF was still snagged over missiles in Asia, but this too seemed close. Nitze remarked, somewhat oddly, that he hadn't had "so much fun in years," and that this was more progress than had ever been made in arms control history.

Perle was running on adrenaline, that slightly hyperspace feeling, even more so than at Geneva. He personally did not share Nitze's enthusiasm for Akhromeyev. The marshal was not as rigid or staid as previous Soviet military men, and in this sense was refreshing. But he was not taken with his manner, which was gruff at times. Moreover, he could not forget that Akhromeyev was ultimately negotiating for the Soviets. He was not a friend, but an adversary. What mattered was not how they felt about each other, but the results of what they came up with. He felt no reason to celebrate the fact that the marshal was shrewd.

Back at the hotel, he marveled at all the phone messages. The press never gave up, and no doubt had moved on to wild speculation. He took a catnap for half an hour, then quickly debriefed an anxious Gaffney (who had not gotten much more sleep than he had), shaved, showered, and changed clothes, feasted on some of his remaining munchies, and ran back out to the lobby, where the limo was waiting. They reconvened again by nine.

THE WEATHER WAS ominous the next morning, and struck Shultz as like a rotating giant wheel, one spoke driving rain, another brilliant sunshine, then heavy rain, then white sunshine. There was one morning, four hours, left to Iceland.

At Hofdi House, the president bounded in, fresh and sparkling, ready to go for the next meeting. The rest of the delegation wandered around the sitting rooms upstairs, pacing nervously, making idle chitchat to work off anxiety, talking about the weather, the press, the food, how they couldn't wait to get back home, anything but the summit. But the president was deeply engaged.

Upon being briefed, the president was at first euphoric, commenting "that literally a miracle was taking place," so much agreement on so many issues. Shultz, normally sphinxlike, radiated ebullience, feeling that "stunning breakthroughs" had been made. There was an enormous sense of possibility hanging like a hard-earned gift, long delayed.

But the final session between Reagan and Gorbachev quickly soured. "What about INF, why is that unresolved?" Reagan asked testily.

Gorbachev chimed in heatedly, "What about SDI and the ABM treaty?"

The two got down to work now, poring over the issues. At one point, after a long pause, Gorbachev accepted the modified INF proposal, agreeing to cap Soviet missiles in Asia at one hundred, with the U.S. retaining the right to deploy one hundred in the U.S. Reagan looked at Shultz, the look of "Is this something I should sign off on?" The secretary leaned over and whispered: "We should keep after complete elimination, but this is a good deal." The president accepted. This was a major breakthrough.

Everything was now moving at a rapid clip and the two sides were no longer dealing in directives, but full-blown historic deals. One issue remained unresolved, however: SDI. Gorbachev then threw what Reagan called "the curve."

The general secretary now emphasized that there could be *no* cutbacks in offensive arms or INF without an agreement on SDI. It *must* be a package deal. This was the deal that the arms control groups, Nitze and others in the State Department, media critics, and many congressional Democrats had long been urging. Suddenly, Gorbachev had changed the rules of the deal: all progress hinged on SDI.

"No," Reagan pleaded, proposing that the two teams put together language detailing the progress on offensive arms and INF, and then turn over the remaining disagreement on space to the negotiators in Geneva. Reagan reached out to Gorbachev as best he could. But it was no go.

It was now Gorbachev's turn to say no. "We would be eating this porridge forever," he said.

The time had long since passed for both leaders to pack their bags and go home. It was 1:20, eighty minutes longer than was originally scheduled. The meeting was about to end, in a dismal deadlock, the most far-reaching arms reduction schemes on offensive and medium-range weapons virtually accepted, then, just as suddenly, held hostage by Gorbachev's stubborn insistence on tying everything to SDI.

Shultz had a look of disappointment on his face. Everything was so close, yet . . .

Gorbachev finally said, "We've accomplished nothing. Let's go home." But he was still sitting, and gave no sign of budging.

But what could now be done? The meeting was over, the two delegations on the second floor stared at their watches, shuffled their feet, contemplating the flight home. But downstairs, no one had reached for the door.

Reagan was not budging either. He did not feel finished. With just a bit more time . . .

Then it dawned on both Gorbachev and Reagan. They did not need permission from anyone to give it one more shot.

Reagan leaned forward, and looked intently at Gorbachev. Gorbachev, slightly slumped in his chair, stared at Reagan. The two exchanged a few testy words, but then made a dramatic decision.

One more round, let's give it one more shot.

Heads nodded, everyone felt more comfortable with this, their work was not complete. Both Shultz and Shevardnadze, sitting on the edge of their seats, heaved huge sighs of relief.

Reagan and Gorbachev would meet again at three. They directed Shultz and Shevardnadze, and their advisers, "to capture" the progress so far, and see if there was a way to square the circle on the thorny issue of missile defense.

All of a sudden, everything had changed, all the rules of superpower meetings had been thrown out the window. No longer was anything scripted or preplanned. It was phantasmagoric and high-stakes. The result of the ensuing hours would be anyone's guess, two leaders now improvising, making decisions that would affect the entire globe, as much on chemistry, personal feel, instinct and emotion, as on crafted policy. This was what it had come down to, an inexorable tug between conflicting poles, the vision of two men struggling against statements, their gut feel contesting cognitive logic, their wide-ranging dreams against bitter day-to-day realities of politics and survival.

Reagan and Gorbachev rose, exited separately into their limousines, and their motorcades sped off. The press was utterly mystified. They knew something had happened, but what? That answer would not be known until hours later.

GAFFNEY WAS COOLING his heels at his Pentagon cubbyhole in the makeshift offices where other staff from State, the Arms Control and Disarmament Agency, and the White House were busily mingling, sending and reading messages, waiting for word on the progress of the meeting. Gaffney's feeling was that if you can't play in the process, "you're for sure getting screwed." He was completely frustrated by being unable to participate. He wanted to help. He wanted information. He wanted to be able to tell Cap what was going on.

Like an animal looking for its prey, he paced past other cubbyholes, seeing if he could scout up any information.

"Have you heard anything?" Gaffney asked the guys from European Affairs of the State Department.

"No."

"Anything up?" he asked the Political-Military Affairs people from State.

"Haven't heard a thing."

Where was Perle? Perle hadn't called him; he hadn't left his meetings; had he left Hofdi House? Intellectually, he knew Perle was tied up. But where was he?

He repaired back to his cubby and contacted the Pentagon. No, he hadn't heard anything. Yes, of course he understood that Cap wants to know what's going on.

Click, he hung up, frustrated. He looked at the damned clock. Even the clock didn't seem to work. Someone swore that it looked like even the clock had stopped.

WHEN GAFFNEY HEARD there was going to be an afternoon session, he slumped in his chair. Holy shit, he thought to himself. This whole thing is surreal. What was going on?

AFTER THE MORNING session broke, the Soviets, in a blatant act, violated the press embargo and released a statement that the two sides were close to agreement on deep cuts in offensive weapons and an INF deal. That the two leaders would be meeting again in an hour, where as much as anything else the trust and good faith of these men would be crucial, did not stop this astounding breach.

Yet like everything else, this matter was dealt with through hasty improvisation. At Richard Perle's suggestion, Shultz ordered that the NATO allies and Japan be informed that an INF deal was in the works, so they didn't hear it first from the press or the Soviets.

Shultz gathered Perle, Kampelman, Poindexter, Nitze, Linhard, General John Moellering of the Joint Chiefs of Staff, and Ken Adelman around him. Everyone was suffering from an overdose of exhaustion, sleep deprivation, overwork, and high-strung nerves. "It's been a slugging match all the way between Gorbachev and the president. We're going to have one more round."

At two they were joined by the Soviet delegation, and seated themselves on opposite sides around a long wooden table.

Shultz tried to be constructive, emphasizing what they had agreed to. Shevardnadze was unusually cold and taunting, and cut him off.

"We have made all the concessions," he said fervently. "Now it is your turn. There is one issue before us. Everything depends upon agreement on how to handle SDI. Is the president prepared to agree on a period of time, ten years, when there will be no withdrawal from the ABM treaty and strict adherence to its terms?" Gorbachev, he said, "feels this very strongly." He thundered, "This is our bottom line."

As if sensing that he had crossed the line of civility, he pulled back, turned to Kampelman and queried, "You are a creative person, can't you think of something?" Then he stared at Nitze, "You are so experienced, can't you come up with something?"

He did not look over to Perle. But while he talked, at the end of the table Perle and Linhard were putting their heads together, whispering and busily scribbling on a long yellow pad, trying to formulate a possible solution. They stitched together a proposal that had been agreed to in principle the night before—50 percent reductions in offensive arms over five years—with the Soviet proposal for a ten-year adherence to the ABM treaty. During this second five years, they proposed to apply the zero ballistic missile idea from the July 25 letter. At the end of ten years, with all offensive ballistic missiles eliminated, each side would then be free to deploy defenses. (Perle thought to himself, "After all, if there are no first-strike offenses, then there is no reason to fear defenses. They also are a vital insurance policy against cheating or other nations that might acquire nukes. If the Soviets won't go for this, it will expose them as being disingenuous in their publicly stated opposition to SDI.")

After a few minutes, they finished their draft, and passed it down to Poindexter, then to Shultz. Heads nodded in assent. Shultz read it carefully, thinking: This is what Poindexter had discussed with the president last night, that a bold gesture was needed and the July 25 proposal is it. The president had not objected. Independently, Perle and Linhard had come up with this. He felt it was worth exploring.

He then passed it on to Nitze and Kampelman to get their views. They also asserted their agreement.

"You've seen some writing at this end of the table," Shultz announced to an anxious Soviet team. "This is an effort by some of us here to see if we can't break the impasse. I don't know how the president will react to it, but I would like to explore it with you."

He injected a bit of gallows humor. "I have no authority to present this, so if afterward you hear a loud noise pounding against the wall, you'll know that the president is knocking my head against the wall." But the mood was still very serious. Very.

He then read the proposal, which was no longer a concept, subject to a murky plan to be offered in five years as stipulated in the July 25 letter, but a real proposal, with a strict timetable and hard and fast deadline.

Shevardnadze, listening intently, turned his expressive eyes and mane of white hair toward his colleagues, and spoke quickly in Russian. He then said he doubted Gorbachev could accept it because of the right to deploy defenses after ten years. But, he added, it is worth considering.

It was the most sweeping proposal ever made between the superpowers, far outstripping even the events of the night before.

It was now 3:00 and the two leaders were arriving. The U.S. team filed out of the conference, and moved upstairs. The Soviets moved to the other side of the upper floor. Both delegations caucused with their leaders.

EVEN THOUGH EVERYTHING was breaking fast, Perle felt supremely confident. The issues were all familiar ones. The men assembled in this room had dealt with the intricacies of these proposals for months. Indeed, with a tenacity of purpose, they had been working toward these decisive moments all their professional lives. Perle thought the proposal being presented was based on ideas the Americans had already tabled. The Soviet arguments were all familiar ones—and were all expected. They're trying to restrain—and kill—SDI. Others, he knew, felt that these were not ideal working conditions. But, he thought, it was just a matter of pulling together material that reflected an ongoing process of negotiations. He did not think they were unprepared, though he knew this would be the rap from the press. More than that, he felt that the U.S. was in a strong position.

KAMPELMAN FELT OTHERWISE, that things were now moving too fast. His view was that ample progress, even unprecedented, had been made on INF and START, and there was no need to rush into something for which the U.S. delegation was not adequately prepared.

He was also irritated by the Soviet bait and switch. Gorbachev had deceived the Americans, he thought. He had given no indication beforehand that serious matters would be taken up in a true summit-like fashion, but this was exactly what had happened.

He was unhappy about the evening meeting. It had lasted too long and was held in the wrong part of the day. He worried about the effects of such all-nighters, with their tension, exhaustion, and potential for unclear thinking.

Long after Reykjavik, he would still think about that.

UPSTAIRS, THE PRESIDENT stood, so his delegation also stood, cluttering around him, right by a large ornate gold porcelain mirror, matching the chandelier overhead. Shultz briefed him on the proposal that he had just tentatively broached. Reagan liked it. It was an extension of his own ideas, and he saw it as a win-win situation. "He gets his precious ABM treaty, and we get all his ballistic missiles. And after that we can deploy SDI in space. Then it's a whole new ballgame."

Reagan then turned to Perle, and surprising the whole delegation, asked a highly detailed operational question. "Could the United States eliminate ballistic missiles that fast?" he asked. This was Reagan's uncanny instincts at work once again.

A knot formed in Perle's stomach, saying, get it right. "I think we can," Perle said, then explaining that the U.S. had other programs under way—stealth bomber and cruise missiles—that would not be affected by the drastic cutback being proposed.

After almost thirty minutes of discussion, Reagan was intrigued with this proposal on the lined yellow pad, which he later called, "the most sweeping and important arms reduction proposal in the history of the world." At 3:25 the two sides reconvened.

. . .

GORBACHEV COUNTERED REAGAN'S proposal. He wanted to eliminate all offensive missiles, not just ballistic missiles; he wanted to tighten the restrictions on SDI that would be imposed by the ABM treaty, specifically confining it to the laboratory, and not allowing for genuine testing; and he wanted the Soviets, in effect, to have a veto on space defense after the ten-year period.

Reagan suggested setting the ABM issue aside to be resolved in Geneva, or at the summit he would be hosting in Washington. But Gorbachev was adamant.

This will "kill SDI," Reagan said. "Who knows when the world will see another Hitler? We need to be able to defend ourselves."

Gorbachev barked back, "Then there will be no package."

An hour had gone by, and the bargaining had been unprecedented. But the two leaders were also intensely worked up. Shultz sought to cool tempers, and suggested another brief recess.

The Americans moved to a side room. The fate of this extraordinary meeting would be decided in the next few hours.

THE PRESIDENT FIRST looked at Perle. "Can we carry out research under the restraints the Soviets are proposing?"

Perle's mouth was dry; he felt short of breath. Reagan was asking him for a reason. If he said yes, it gave Reagan cover with the conservatives to confine SDI to the laboratory ("Richard Perle assured me . . ."); if he said no, he would be arguing against Shultz.

But his view was an unequivocal no. "Mr. President, we cannot conduct the research under the terms he's proposing. It will effectively kill SDI."

The president paused, and weighed this, and then turned to Nitze and Shultz. They both counseled him to accept the language proposed by Gorbachev, and suggested that they could worry about whether research could be conducted in the laboratory later.

Perle stared hard at Reagan. What was he going to do?

They next discussed the merits of destroying all missiles versus all ballistic missiles. The Soviets were dependent upon ballistic missiles more than the U.S., the aides explained. But if all nuclear weapons were eliminated, the Soviet Union would be left with a much larger conventional army, and America would not have a counterweight to a possible conventional threat. Reagan accepted this, and Perle and Linhard were sent off to redraft the American proposal, keeping the key U.S. concepts, but using some of Gorbachev's wording.

Every room in Hofdi House was occupied, so Perle and Linhard moved into a second-floor bathroom, put a board over the bathtub, knelt down and redrafted a new proposal on this makeshift desk.

GORBACHEV WAS IN a side room with Shevardnadze, Akhromeyev, and Bessmertnykh. He was frenetic, practically jumping out of his own skin. One minute he sat, another he paced wildly, then he moodily stared out the window at the sea, then he sat again. Finally, he said, bordering on hysteria: "Everything could be decided right now."

BEFORE THE FINAL session, even the president seemed clearly battle-scarred and worn down. He looked at the redrafted proposal, and waved it around. "Does anyone here think we're proposing this just to get an agreement?" There was stark silence, heads shaking, no, of course not, sir.

Intense and excited, Shultz, feeling that history was knocking, finally jumped in: "Let's not lose it, we've done some amazing things here."

Chief of Staff Don Regan suggested it might be necessary to stay in Reykjavik another night. Reagan grimaced hard. "Hell no, we're not spending another night here." One aide marveled at how decisive Reagan repeatedly was.

At 5:30, as the two delegations were about to return to the meeting room, Reagan grimaced, half in disgust, half in exhaustion, "Hell, he doesn't want to *set* up a summit, he wants to *have* one, right here."

Then, one unexpected turn led to another.

THE DOOR TO the side room barged open violently. It wasn't an American or a security guard, but Gorbachev. He neither knocked nor paused as he entered. He was ready to resume.

This scene left a profound impression on Kampelman. He thought of Gorbachev as a complicated man—what the political philosopher Sidney Hook once called an "event-making man"—who deserved credit for loosening the reins of the totalitarian Soviet system. But he also had a ruthless and tough side to him, a side Americans could ill afford to underestimate. At this moment, Gorbachev reminded him of Al Capone.

As Gorbachev and Reagan, and Shultz and Shevardnadze, left to meet once again, Kampelman was saddened. He felt the atmosphere was all wrong, that the morning meeting was too high-strung, emotions too frayed, their relations now strained.

· · ·

THE TWO MEN wrestled over the redrafted text once more. "What happened to the laboratory?" Gorbachev barked. "Why just eliminate ballistic missiles?"

After a lengthy discussion back and forth, the president finally said, leaning across the small dining room table, "It would be fine with me if we eliminated all nuclear weapons." Gorbachev excitedly responded, "We can do that. Let's eliminate them. We can eliminate them." This was Reagan's first concession, and a dramatic one. He had made the calculation to meet Gorbachev on some of his terms.

Shevardnadze stared out the window at the billowing clouds. Shultz said nothing at this enormous step Reagan had just taken. He felt that the president, overwhelmingly elected twice, had made no secret of his passionate antipathy toward nuclear weapons. This step, he felt, was the president's right, and most certainly his decision.

There was one major issue left: SDI. Gorbachev once again demanded that all research, development, and testing be confined to the laboratory. "I cannot do without the word 'laboratory,'" he told Reagan.

"I have promised the American people that I will not give up SDI. You're asking me to give up SDI.

"We are so close," Reagan continued, it is "a question of one word."

Gorbachev tipped his hand. "It's not a trivial thing, it is everything. I cannot carry back to Moscow an agreement that gives up this limitation of research and testing in the laboratory." Shultz thought to himself that Gorbachev came to Iceland prepared to make concessions only because of SDI, but he had also clearly agreed "to get the scalp of SDI.

The president tried a personal appeal, the ultimate and final offer of an elected American president: his word. "Just this one thing, for me." When that failed, he told Gorbachev, "I have a picture that after ten years you and I come to Iceland and bring the last two missiles in the world and we have the biggest damn party in celebration of it."

The two men sparred back and forth; every appeal was used, logic, politics, personal considerations. They were at this for almost ninety minutes. Finally, Gorbachev, with an air of resignation, sighed, "My conscience is clear before the president and his people. What had depended on him, I have done."

Everything was clearly winding up now. Gorbachev said, "It's 'laboratory' or good-bye."

Reagan feverishly scribbled a note, and pushed it over to Shultz. Written were the three words: "Am I wrong?" Shultz did not hesitate. He leaned forcefully over to Reagan and whispered, "No, you are right."

The two men began gathering their papers. Reagan snapped his briefing book closed and stood. His face was lined; he was visibly angry. Gorbachev rose too, and before they left the room, he tried to narrow the gap with the president just a bit more. "Pass on my regards to Nancy," he asked Reagan.

"HE'S OUT," BARKED a beefy Secret Service agent as the doors to the meeting room flung open downstairs. Upstairs, the American delegation rushed to grab their coats and briefcases, and they stampeded as fast as they could down the grand round wooden staircase. Spying Reagan's face just before he walked out of Hofdi House, Ken Adelman shouted to Max Kampelman, "There's no deal."

Reagan and Gorbachev ambled down the steps to their waiting cars. The sky was pitch black, but they were initially blinded by the hot white of assembled klieg lights, illuminating the outside.

Reagan looked unusually irate, and was. "I still feel we can find a deal."

"I don't know what else I could have done," Gorbachev replied.

"You could have said yes," the president said.

The two motorcades sped off. Iceland had come to an end.

RETURNING IN THE car to the U.S. ambassador's residence, Reagan and Shultz discussed what the secretary should tell the press. "There's no way to sugarcoat it," Shultz said.

"Okay," Reagan told his secretary. "Just go out there and tell them what happened."

BACK AT THE U.S. ambassador's residence, Reagan was exhausted. He climbed the stairs to his room to rest, and bumped into Perle, heading downstairs. "We sure tried," he said, shaking his head with disappointment.

Perle looked hard at the president. He was happy the U.S. had stood firm, but seeing Reagan's obvious disappointment, he also got swept up in the emotion of the moment, the lingering thought of "what could have been."

The American team sat around the dining room of the ambassador's residence. Coats were flung on the ground in the corner. Shultz was emotional, recapping the events to his team: Gorbachev wanted to gut SDI but the president wouldn't give in. "SDI was the engine driving the arms control process"; the president "was right" to hold. It was "a principled stance by a principled president." He had "never been prouder" to work for this president. As he recounted later, privately Shultz was still sorting out all his feelings. He was conscious that these final hours had been a great triumph. "Gorbachev had put all his cards on the table and, having done so, now couldn't take them back." It had been, he felt, "Reagan's summit." He was proud, the nation should be proud.

Then, in an emotion-filled instance, Shultz stood up and looked at his aides. He would have to rush off to give a press conference, but for a brief yet very long moment, he stood, while his aides, baggy-eyed, unshaven, like a shambling herd of men in rumpled suits, started clapping, and clapped and clapped and clapped.

AT THE ENSUING press conference in the crowded press center, Kampelman fought back tears as Shultz spoke. In a nearby room, Nitze met with journalists, his voice hoarse with exhaustion. "We tried, by God we tried, and we almost did it."

As Shultz spoke, he talked of "extremely important potential achievements," and a "deeply disappointed" president. Journalists listened more to his expression than his words. They felt a sense of grief was etched across the secretary's usually expressionless face.

The suspense and high expectations that had been building throughout the weekend exploded in a burst of public disappointment.

SHULTZ WAS ALWAYS conscious that appearance was as important as what is said. After the press conference, he later regretted not having taken more time first to collect himself and, in his own words, be "more bouncy."

GAFFNEY PICKED UP Perle to take him to the airport. He was stunned by what he saw. Perle looked like he had just survived a car wreck and escaped with his life; he had the "deer in the headlights look." Gaffney could not recall ever seeing Perle like this. He finally got his debriefing.

Perle was all emotions: relief, exhaustion, concern. "He's on an incredible jag," Gaffney thought. Perle told him about how fast everyone was playing with policies and principles, but it turned out all right. The president "did the right thing." Absolutely the right thing.

Gaffney looked over to Perle, barely visible in the blackness of the night. He was jittery and clearly still on an adrenaline rush.

· · ·

PERLE GOT ON the plane. Images of the last two days were swimming through his brain. The outcome was good. The Soviets had given way on the principle of 50 percent reductions, there was no taking that back. They had given way on the principle of an INF deal—the deal the critics had said they would *never* agree to—and there was no taking that back. And the president hadn't given away SDI. It was also clear that resistance to SDI was not due to Soviet fears of U.S. first-strike systems. Gorbachev would now know there was no way he could ply SDI away from Reagan. Not anymore.

Perle had been in the thick of it, in a moment that almost made unprecedented history. Reagan had sided with arms agreements *and* principles. Good arms agreements mattered. Bad ones should be walked away from. And, by word and deed, that was what Ronald Reagan had done.

Sure, he knew the press and the Democrats in Congress would howl, and say it was Ronald Reagan's "stubborn attachment to SDI" that blocked everything. They would never say it was Gorbachev, who refused to give on SDI, who blocked the enormous agreements.

Oh hell, so what else was new? Richard Perle was wearing the black hat again.

Like Shultz, Perle was proud, very proud, of the president. All in all, not bad work for a couple of days.

He leaned his head slightly against the window on the plane. He was god-awful hungry, but figured he would close his eyes for a minute. He hadn't really slept in forty hours. His muscles were suddenly weary.

Perle's eyes closed. The meal in front of him was still uneaten when he woke, his stomach grumbling, as the plane touched down near Washington, D.C.

WANE

As the Iceland summit ended, Les Aspin was munching reflexively on salted potato chips and hunched forward in his easy chair at home, momentarily glued to his twenty-five-inch screen. The picture of a grimacing Ronald Reagan, his controlled anger bubbling beneath the surface, and Mikhail Gorbachev, looking tense and drawn, walking together down the steps of Hofdi House, played again and again with hypnotic regularity on the network news. The shot had an almost dizzying, dreamlike quality that was matched only by the high-stakes-poker summit being waged in Iceland, all suggesting that this couldn't really be happening. Reagan and Gorbachev weren't really doing all that.

But it did happen. And it was happening.

The major network stations even interrupted Sunday afternoon football to carry Shultz's post-Reykjavik press conference live.

"Jeez," Aspin thought again. "What the hell went on there?"

As the first bits of news dribbled out, he had been startled. All ballistic missiles. All offensive missiles. Marshal Akhromeyev was there. An INF deal. An extra session. Richard Perle in a bathtub writing out a proposal to do away with all ballistic missiles. It foundered on SDI. Shultz, speaking to the press, looked grim and exhausted.

Before the weekend in Iceland closed, Aspin had already been on the phone to his senior staff, dialing one aide ten times until he got through.

"Jesus, are you watching?" he asked. "It gets wilder by the moment."

"I can't believe it. Nothing like this has ever happened," the aide replied.

"I want us to meet tomorrow in my office. Let's say around ten-thirty." Tomorrow was Yom Kippur, the holiest day of the Jewish year, and the aide was Jewish, but there was no doubt that he would attend. With Aspin, the country and the job came first. Service was everything.

To most of his Georgetown friends, his brainy think tank colleagues at the Center for Strategic and International Studies (CSIS) on K Street and at the Rand Corporation, his Wisconsin constituents, and even the press corps he wined and dined, the affable Aspin was not "Congressman," but "Les." To his closest friends, he was more boisterously called "Aspin." To most of the eighty-member staff on the Armed Services Committee, the highly professional and dedicated worker bees who fed him detailed information daily on every defense issue imaginable, he was the more respectful "Mr. Aspin." But these days, whatever he was called, he was, ultimately, "the chairman," the powerful head of the influential Armed Services Committee, and the most important voice in the Democratic party on defense and national security issues. It was, in those years, a pivotal position, and Aspin loved it.

But with every action, he was navigating through treacherous shoals: he was more conservative than many in his party, which he feared was becoming a captive of the political left and antidefense forces, and yet he was more liberal than the Reagan administration. As a result, his political base was often weak. He was far more loved and admired by national security intellectuals than he was by ideologically driven Democratic party pols or Reagan movement conservatives.

But in the raw and bitter decade of the 1980s, as the Democrats were passionately locked in virtual mortal combat with the Reagan administration over policy toward the Soviet Union, what Les Aspin said mattered.

Now, with Iceland over, it would be the chairman's turn to speak.

Working with sketchy evidence and analysis provided to him by the press reports and his staff, Aspin could carve out a pretty good sense of the bare outlines of what had transpired. He knew Reykjavik quickly devolved—or evolved—from a presummit prep meeting into the fastest, most far-reaching summit in history. In the final hours, an impromptu session was added, and Reagan and Gorbachev almost cut a deal—the largest reductions in nuclear arms ever seriously contemplated—a precarious, sweeping deal that could have changed the map of global politics virtually overnight. Nuclear deterrence, NATO, the Cold War rivalry, everything would look different. After years of wild rhetoric about arms control, now the U.S. had almost gotten it, he thought, in one big, practically indigestible chunk. But had anyone fully thought through the implications, he wondered.

Aspin leaned back reflectively, arched his eyebrows and thought: Now this was wild stuff.

There were big questions for him to address; what should he say about the summit? Should he be critical or supportive? What should his demeanor be? How should he play it?

The answer was, of course, that he needed more information. This was not a time to shoot from the hip. For the nation and the world, and for himself, too much was at stake.

. . .

BUT ASPIN HAD his own difficulties. He would be trapped in a swirling maelstrom of complicated and arguably incompatible considerations. There would be his statements as Aspin the nuclear strategist, nonpartisan, coldly rational, impartially asking, *What's the right policy for the country?* And then there would be the actions of Aspin the Democrat, a political creature, bound and potentially tethered to a liberal Democratic party caucus, which, however much it was to his left, had the power to oust him as chairman of the Armed Services Committee if it felt he were too cooperative with the administration.

And with the liberals already threatening to remove him as chairman, this drama too was playing out at this very moment.

So as Iceland was being assessed, Aspin was walking a fine line, involved in his own high-stakes game of political survival, of lofty national policy versus backroom, bareknuckle politics. Depending upon which way he played it, not only administration policy would be affected, perhaps not only the policy of hanging tough with the Soviet Union, but also whether he would be on a collision course with his own party from which there would be no retreat.

Thus far, he was willing to cater to some, but hardly all, of the anxieties and goals of the liberal Democratic caucus; but he could not bring himself to play the strident demagogue—a move some political observers had privately felt could prove fatal, and which, as Aspin prepared to sort out Iceland and the other great issues of the Cold War, he mightily resisted.

IF EVER A man were born and bred for the politics of national security, a remarkable union of two strains uneasily woven into each other, it was Les Aspin.

Born July 21, 1938, in Milwaukee, Les Aspin and his brother, James, were true children of the Midwest. His father, Les Sr., despite the lack of a college education, became a certified public accountant in a major Milwaukee accounting firm; his mother, Marie Orth Aspin, a product of a well-established Milwaukee family, dutifully raised her kids and later put her two years of law school to use as a legal secretary. The family lived in an Everyman's home: a classic red-brick, three-bedroom house along the well-cropped lawns in the well-to-do village of Shorewood on the outskirts of Milwaukee. There, they ate American cheese and baloney sandwiches on Sunbeam bread, and were reared on the familiar and comforting values of the Midwest.

But Aspin was not one to stand still. He quickly rose through the ranks of society, racking up impressive academic credentials: Phi Beta Kappa at Yale College, a master's in economics at Oxford (he wasn't a Rhodes Scholar, though the media frequently credited him with this credential), and a Ph.D. from the celebrated Economics Department at MIT. During the Vietnam War, he worked as an army captain in the Department of Defense for Alain Einthoven, a numbers-crunching systems analyst who, like Robert McNamara and the Whiz Kids of the day, believed the answers to national security needs came from bloodless and dispassionate analysis, not political logrolling or the subjective appeals of the military services.

The systems analysts were first and foremost analytic, seeking to bring order and reason out of chaos, breaking down complex problems in a multistep process, often applying mathematical models to arrive at ultralogical solutions. McNamara and Einthoven, analytic men from an analytic organization, were among the early dominant influences on the young Aspin, and Aspin was the willing student.

After he left the Defense Department, Aspin spent a relatively uninspired year as a professor at Wisconsin's Marquette University. However much of an intellectual he was, and he was, he was not content to toil quietly, out of sight, in a cramped junior faculty office. He wanted desperately to be a part of the real action and have more than a marginal impact on defense policy. In 1970 he ran for the first district congressional seat, opposing the Vietnam War, and won 61 percent of the vote. After his election, he quickly rose from the ranks of obscurity in Congress, one of just 435 representatives with little status and low visibility, and seized the initiative once again. He joined the House Armed Services Committee and began churning out well-timed and pungent Sunday press releases (ingeniously guaranteeing that the press, scouting for news from sleepy weekends, would likely use them), exposing egregious Pentagon expenditures. There was often a frivolous and some felt undignified component to his exposés, and he earned himself a reputation as a flamboyant gadfly. But within a short time span, he had made a name for himself.

As the 1980s broke, Aspin soon revealed that he was not the wild-eyed antidefense liberal his colleagues thought he was, but a more serious centrist thinker on national security. He hired crack staff, people from the best schools and with the brightest minds, and set them to work formulating long-term policy studies, not on issues simply of concern to his district, but to the nation at large. When the nuclear freeze became fashionable, he fidgeted endlessly about its gross inadequacies, always quick to point out that it was more symbolic than serious (privately, he was disdainful of it). Where fellow liberals went to great pains to dismiss Soviet perfidy and military aggressiveness, Aspin warned that the U.S. was underestimating the U.S.S.R.'s menacing actions. And in the early 1980s, instead of simply denouncing the controversial ten-warhead MX, he disappointed liberal colleagues and negotiated with President Reagan over it. Assembling a coalition of Republicans and moderate defense Democrats, the so-called gang of six, he supported a limited number of MXs in exchange for another smaller, mobile missile called the Midgetman, and for a commitment that the administration would seriously pursue arms reductions.

Throughout, he maintained an irreverent, even mischievous streak, never more amply demonstrated than when he once accused Tip O'Neill, the powerful House speaker, of being "in a fog" and a "beached whale."

By 1985, long since married and divorced, a confirmed workaholic, he had become a fixture on the Washington scene. Aspin frequented Georgetown dinner parties, hobnobbed with the power brokers over games of tennis at the bastion of the inner establishment, the St. Albans Tennis Club, and sailed at Lake Beulah in Wisconsin on his twenty-foot wooden boat, aptly named *Potomac Fever.* As a regular member of the defense policy elite, he discussed arcana of nuclear strategy in rarefied policy conferences and strategy sessions at Harvard and Aspen, Colorado. In many ways, he was never more at home than when discussing the abstractions of the nuclear priesthood, finely spinning eerie doomsday calculations of nuclear deterrence, arms control, and hypothetical nuclear war, employing such expressions as "exchange ratios," "counterforce targeting," "circular error probability," and "nuclear stability calculations."

Aspin remained a curious and likable enigma in Washington. While a politician, he was often ill at ease in dealing with other people, preferring intellectual debate to glad-handing and idle schmoozing. A bloodless, often seemingly detached animal, who rarely ever talked about himself, he had a heart of gold, displaying a keen loyalty and deep concern for his closest intimates.

He had none of the classic Washington swagger of men at the top. Though he had the credentials and power of the old establishment types, he had none of their bearing and mannerisms. A shambling bear of a man in rumpled suits and burly sweaters, bespectacled and balding with a shock of white hair folded across his head, he spoke not in the crisp syntax of a Yale grad, but in folksy colloquialisms of the boys in a Chicago bar (to his staff: "Let's scope it out"; to the dean of columnists, David Broder: "Ey, Broder, whatta ya know?"; to a girlfriend: "Come awn, let's play hooky"). He was not stiff and measured like the Episcopalian Yankee establishment, but gestured with his hands, even while he searched for the perfect scholarly footnote. He did not hold himself erect and primly well mannered like his colleagues, the blow-dried JFK look-alikes, Vietnam baby-boom-generation congressmen, but at hearings and meetings rubbed his face and eyes incessantly; and both on the Hill and about town, instead of waiting for people to rush to him, he would amble over to them, like a curious cub prowling in the woods, fold his arms and from his six-foot-two frame look down at them, often with a wide grin, "So whatta ya doin' these days?"

It was notable that for his personal office on the fourth floor of the House Cannon Office Building, he rejected the perks of a congressman, using instead the smaller, more cramped room usually inhabited by the representative's chief of staff, and ceding his far more spacious suite to provide his staff with additional space. Instead of the Washington ritual of signed pictures of Les Aspin with presidents and dignitaries framing the walls, in his office, dotted with piles of policy magazines and Xeroxed articles, what stood out most was a green chalkboard, heavily marked up with mathematical formulas of nuclear exchange ratios. Instead of relying on staff to explain everything to him, he read extensively and asked countless questions. He made comprehensive notes on memos with questions and ideas, supplemented by his thoughts written out on long yellow pads in thick black marker: "Let's discuss this."

Aspin, despite a near total devotion to his work, also liked to enjoy himself, amiably needling and joking, playfully twitting friends and associates (to Congressman Tim Wirth he bellowed, "Wirthless, whatta ya doin?"; to Gerry Studds, the gay and very patrician congressman from Massachusetts, he laughed in his finest Massachusetts faux accent, "Hey Gerry, what's up at Hah-vad Yah-d?"). He brought his rumply sheepdog, Junket, to work with him every day, and Junket, curled up at his feet, was included in all meetings. He would sneak out of his office to play tennis, often without telling his staff.

Political parties meant very little to him, and at one point, as Aspin's more centrist and Midwestern conservative tendencies revealed themselves, some of his political aides even feared he might become a Republican (it was not a justified fear at the time). They fretted that he seemed a little *too* comfortable with conservative Scoop Jackson Democrats, Jim Woolsey and Richard Perle among them, but also with Ben Wattenberg and others, and worried that he took what conservative commentators like George Will and Charles Krauthammer said *very* seriously.

Restless by mid-decade, Aspin bucked the seniority system and audaciously made his bid for Armed Services Committee chairman. The chairman of the conservative Armed Services Committee was the eighty-year-old Mel Price. Debilitated by arthritis, he was viewed as largely ineffectual, and to the right of the predominantly liberal House Democrats, particularly the post-Vietnam ones. Price had the backing of the party leadership, who hoped to protect the integrity of the seniority system. But Aspin shrewdly capitalized on the fiery sentiment of younger House Democrats, who craved a more energetic leadership, one more responsive to the wills of the liberal Democratic caucus (consisting of all the Democratic members of the House) than to the old ways of the conservative committee Southern Democrats. In a stunning defeat, and staving off an impassioned, last-second plea by Tip O'Neil to retain Price, Aspin successfully shouldered Price aside, hopped over five others his senior, and became the chairman.

And that is when the agenda of Les Aspin, the political moderate, deeply skeptical of Soviet aggressive power and imperial intentions, a believer that the Cold War was real, became clear.

He sought nothing less than to recast the Democratic party away from the leftward leanings that had gripped it since the McGovern candidacy, pulling it toward a more pro-defense, anti-Soviet stand that had once been the mainstay of hard-nosed, Cold War Democrats from Harry Truman to John Kennedy. To the extent that he was far more captivated by the arms control process than his friend Richard Perle (he was), less willing to throw dollars at the Pentagon than Cap Weinberger (he was), he would differ dramatically from the Republican administration. And while he did believe the Soviet Union was an evil empire (he did indeed), and that Communism did erect totalitarian, not authoritarian, regimes (here he agreed with Jeane Kirkpatrick), he felt less comfortable dealing in the world of these philosophical abstractions, and focused more on measurable tangibles, like military power. In this sense, he was as much like Kissinger, whom he read carefully, as like the neoconservatives.

But despite such differences, the tough-minded party he sought to create would prove to be dramatically different from the one that had now elected him chairman. His leadership was at first intoxicating, and soon everyone on the Cambridge–New Haven–D.C. axis was talking about Aspin's efforts: Aspin, the centrist white knight, would lead the soft-on-defense Democrats out of the wilderness at long last. It was a brave and bold adventure that, after a flourish, would come to an unceremonious crash shortly after the Reykjavik summit. But in typical Aspin style, it was a hell of a ride along the way. And, however difficult and sobering, enormously courageous.

IN MARCH OF 1985, the Coalition for a Democratic Majority gave Aspin its Henry M. Jackson Friend of Freedom Award. That CDM selected Aspin said something about the new chairman; that Aspin took his receipt of the award seriously also said something.

Before the evening award ceremony at the Hyatt Hotel on Capitol Hill, Aspin left work early and drove home alone. He had been fidgety all day. He was unhappy with the speech that had been drafted for him, and decided to work on it himself.

That night, as he gave his acceptance speech, he was unusually serious in his demeanor; gone were the joking and rambling delivery. The speech was vintage Aspin, from the head and from the heart. He warned about the twin dangers of our time, embodied by the symbols of Auschwitz and Hiroshima: Soviet totalitarianism and the threat of nuclear war.

Then he delivered the zinger. The Democrats could no longer be "the Dr. No of defense." It was a strong charge; Democrats were always for a strong defense, or so they said, but never seemed to find a weapons system they could support. Aspin said it was time for that to come to an end—which would be good for the party, and good for the nation.

Overnight, this speech became a sensation, and even liberal Democrats found themselves scrambling to show tangibly that they supported weapons, that they too *did* stand for a strong defense.

But in the wake of that speech, something else occurred. Liberals feared Aspin had become a neoconservative. This, however, was not quite true. Aspin's political ideology, firmly anti-Soviet, and his increasingly conservative instincts continued to be propelled by the instrumentalities of social science reasoning, hard statistics, and persuasive charts. Thus, his anti-Soviet animus was driven less by his inherent distaste for Communists, than by his fervent anti-aggression stance and his belief (supported by empirical evidence) that Communists were aggressive and repeatedly acted as the aggressors. It was a subtle and finely parsed distinction, but a distinction nonetheless. Yet, still, while Aspin was his own man intellectually, at this point his instinctive ideology was certainly far more neoconservative than liberal, closer to Richard Perle than Tip O'Neill.

His next public assault against the liberal wing of his party came later that year, when he led the House Democrats in their conference on the defense bill with the Senate. The House defense-spending budget was $292 billion; the Senate figure was $302 billion. Gone were Aspin's reflexive anti-Pentagon days. He allowed the Senate figure to prevail ("Look," he later said, shaking his head, his arms crossed, "we had to go with that; it was the right figure."). House liberals were immediately enraged at his insufficient zeal in cutting defense ("The average of 292 and

302 is not 302," complained Barney Frank, the liberal congressman from Massachusetts and an Aspin supporter).

He also continued to support a compromise on the MX, leading a number of liberals to claim that Aspin had stabbed them in the back, that in campaigning for chairman he promised to oppose the MX. Aspin denied this, chalking it up to a misunderstanding. But they were furious. And they paid little attention to the positive, concrete initiatives that Aspin undertook which made a genuine impact. He showed a steely determination to reform the military retirement system, and was a pioneer in shepherding military reform legislation through the House, over administration objections, to strengthen the chairman of the Joint Chiefs of Staff and to enhance how the four military services would train and fight together. To many, these were just the kinds of efforts and successes that both the Democratic party and the country needed. Still, to his liberal colleagues, Aspin was dangerously straying from the faith.

Privately, his liberal colleagues said they would stick with him; but they cautioned against losing sight of who put him there. It was a not-so-subtle warning: don't wander too far off the reservation.

YET THAT SUMMER and fall Aspin was looking beyond his splashy headlines on the legislative calendar to larger, thornier policy disputes that had heatedly divided the Democrats and the administration, and quietly set about tackling the bigger issue: devising a serious national security program for the Democrats.

Democrats had to be tough on the Soviet Union and their client Communist states, he felt, so he asked, "What should U.S. policy be, short- and long-term, toward the Soviet Union and other totalitarian regimes?" If Democrats weren't for SDI, then what did they support? He asked: "What is the attitude toward nuclear deterrence?"—e.g., SDI and nuclear modernization. Like an ostrich with its head in the sand, the Democrats instinctively shied away from the use of force, but, to Aspin, that was bad policy and bad politics, so he asked: "What is the attitude toward the use of power in defense of American interests?"—e.g., Grenada, Libya, regional conflicts.

Aspin further concluded that the bitter partisanship afflicting the country was affecting the ability of the U.S. to carry out its commitments. A consensus on these issues had to be developed. Philosophical underpinnings for American national security policy had to be agreed upon. He set to work on this too.

He charged his senior staff to study these issues.

Every Friday, in a combination academic seminar and moot court, they would sit down with cold sandwiches in cardboard carryout boxes, and iced tea and Coke, to go over dog-eared policy papers prepared for him, and he would spend hours relentlessly hammering away at new policy possibilities. The issues were big ones: "Can the Soviet Union peacefully evolve the way France and Germany have?"; "Pressuring Communist regimes to Retrench"; "The criteria and conditions for the use of force"; "Looking beyond deterrence." It was professor Aspin and politician Aspin as one and the same. Often, the meetings took on a bustling life of their own, and Aspin was loath to tear himself away from the seminar atmosphere. Once, when Weinberger was on the phone, Aspin slowly rose from his seat at the conference table, walked out of the meeting room, abruptly came back, sat down, then got up again, and finally yelled across the hall to his secretary that he would "call Cap back." He was in the middle of a thought and didn't want to lose it.

Soon, he and his aides branched out in the inquiry, meeting with an impressive roster of politicians, academics, and specialists, to thrash out answers to these great subjects of the Cold War.

Aspin lunched with noted Russian scholar and Smithsonian head, Jim Billington, at the Cosmos Club (Billington said modestly: "You're the chairman of the Armed Services Committee: what could I possibly tell you about the Soviet Union?" Aspin: "People too often confuse expertise in nuclear arms control with authority on the Russians; I've spent over ten years thinking about arms control, now I need to learn about the Russians"); he kicked around his ideas with political scientist Graham Allison over dinner at Nora's, a tony restaurant off Dupont Circle; he listened to Dan Yankelovich summarize stacks of polling data about American attitudes toward nuclear war and SDI. "Les," Yankelovich said, "Americans want to be strong vis-à-vis the Soviets, but they also want the U.S. to sit down and talk to them."

Later that season, Aspin dispatched aides to talk with Harvard professors Joseph Nye and Al Carnesale about their research on avoiding nuclear war, to grill the historian Paul Kennedy about historical precedents for the end of the Cold War, to talk to scientists in industry about new technologies that could be incorporated into modern warfare. The ideas started to come together, so he had staff write up a long conceptual paper on paths to end the Cold War and convened a conference of experts, Soviet experts, arms control experts, technology experts, and scholars to hone some of his ideas. But more than ideas were gelling. Aspin was also working to build a coalition to stand behind his ideas.

He had policy paper after policy paper written. Frustrated one day, he chucked a paper down on his desk and said sternly: "Look, the policy debate has to be very high. We have to get it right." Privately, though, he despaired that his party "could be impossible when it came to defense."

But the strategy paid off, and Aspin began to formulate a new basis for a Democratic party philosophy on defense. Personally skeptical of SDI, he recognized that to a large degree it captivated the public imagination. But he had his own embryonic alternative to SDI for the Democrats. The American people, he maintained, needed a "roadmap" to show a route away from nuclear disaster, although not a blueprint. He called it "Beyond Nuclear Deterrence," envisioning the use of long-range nonnuclear missiles, such as pinpoint accurate cruise missiles, for strategic missions, even pitting them against Soviet nuclear missiles, but also holding other targets at risk. It was a major doctrinal shift that he was considering, aided by the revolution in targeting and technology, and made all the more radical by the fact that these accurate weapons were, unlike nuclear weapons, readily usable. (In so doing, Aspin was foreshadowing the Gulf War, which employed new conventional technology in much the way he had laid out.)

At first, this use of conventional weapons for strategic and combat purposes was mightily resisted by some of his academic friends (Harvard's Al Carnesale, not just one smart guy but a great raconteur, who called himself the Great Kibitzer, kept telling the chairman, "Les, I'm just not sure you can have the confidence in the accuracy of this stuff"). Other more liberal members of his staff, invoking the experience of targeting during the Vietnam War, also urged Aspin to tone down his plans. But some did like the idea—hardheaded thinkers like Albert Wholstetter; technologists like Steve Lukasik and Jim Roche at Northrop; and Carl Builder at the Rand Corporation. So Aspin continued to move ahead, slowly working each angle, and rebutting the criticisms. This too was classic Aspin—Aspin the systems analyst, building his case block by block, step by step.

By the summer of 1986, his campaign to reform the Democratic party had shifted into high gear. He had been made head of the National Security Committee of the Democratic Policy Commission, the midterm body drafting the Democratic National Committee's party platform. The platform had reeked of being soft on defense since 1972; Aspin was determined to reverse this.

He moved quickly to get the Democratic National Committee to endorse his Midgetman missile ("It's no small feat when *this* party embraces a nuclear weapon," Aspin quipped); military reform ("So we can fight effectively"); and, in a sop to arms control, burnishing his party credentials, called for continued adherence to SALT II. In a keynote speech at a convention of Democrats in Washington that spring, he harshly attacked Reagan, not from the left, but from the right, for not spending a trillion defense dollars wisely, and for lacking a coherent strategy. The attack was carefully couched not to oppose the defense spending, as Democrats usually did, or the goals of Weinberger, which he largely shared.

Aspin also prevailed over party opposition, and urged the Democrats to move beyond the Vietnam syndrome and embrace symbols of freedom. He conceived of the John F. Kennedy Friend of Freedom Award, which the party gave in absentia to Poland's Lech Walesa at a gala Washington dinner on April 24, 1984, at the Omni Shoreham Hotel and sent to him in Gdansk. It read: "Tireless leader of Solidarity, man of Labor, organizer, whose fearless efforts to promote freedom of association for the Polish people have demonstrated that workers and their fundamental rights can never be separated." Aspin also even persuaded Paul Kirk, the chairman of the Democratic National Committee, to sign off on hanging the award in the new DNC offices (although the party later reneged).

When the final Aspin platform for the party was readied that September, after being held up for months by intraparty wrangling over its contents, it boldly echoed Ronald Reagan and called the Soviet Union "a totalitarian empire in the classic sense," and stated squarely that "the Soviet Union poses the greatest threat to world peace and freedom." It accused the Soviets of "cheating on arms control agreements," of "walking out of the Geneva talks," and of engaging in "posturing and polemics" instead of negotiating. This precipitated a vigorous fight. All previous Democratic party drafts had blamed not the Soviets, but Reagan. Aspin though felt this had been a gross contortion of logic and let the new formulation stand.

While avoiding specific positions on aid to the contras, El Salvador, and other regional conflicts, the new platform now noted many "political conflicts have a sizable military dimension," and called on the U.S. to "support movements in regional conflicts" fighting against the Soviet Union and its Marxist clients. Finally, it accused the Russians of brutality in Afghanistan and of "spreading totalitarianism in Central America, Africa, and Southeast Asia." And it said the Democratic party had to be prepared to support the use of force.

The document also staked out a rigorous middle ground on other traditional bread-and-butter party issues. But while realistically acknowledging that arms control couldn't resolve the "deep, ideological and enduring" U.S.-Soviet conflict, it also continued to endorse standard liberal priorities such as SALT II adherence, arms control, and testing the sincerity of the new generation of Soviet leadership.

Yet all told, it was a stunning reversal for the party. Some liberal party elders, the Black Caucus, and other scions of the left revolted. A furious

Andrew Young, Carter's U.N. ambassador and now mayor of Atlanta, even flew up to Washington to insist that changes be made. But Aspin stood his ground and the document was unaltered. When another, more liberal party draft was prepared by a Stephen Solarz–led task force of such party sages as Clark Clifford, Harry McPherson, Arthur Schlesinger, Stansfield Turner, and drafted by John F. Kennedy aide Ted Sorensen, it was simply included as a separate box in the final report, rather than allowing Aspin's language to be diluted—the usual practice in previous years.

The results were striking. For the first time since 1972, the heart and soul of the party had shifted, at least in the platform. No less than Theodore White, the great chronicler of modern American history, personally pored over a copy of the final draft, and gave it his enthusiastic endorsement. After talking to Aspin, White called up an Aspin aide and boomed, "At long last, this is exactly where the party ought to be; you tell Les to stand firm on this. It's superb." Aspin smiled when told. He felt he was right on track.

Meanwhile, the Republicans publicly and contemptuously complained in the press that the platform could have been written by Ronald Reagan. But this was precisely Aspin's point, because for once what Republicans weren't saying was this: that the Democrats were "weak on defense."

Despite grousing within the liberal Democratic party ranks, Aspin received high marks for his foreign policy vision and accolades across the political spectrum, from the steady bastion of liberalism, the *New York Times*, to the dynamic organ of thoughtful neoconservatism, *The New Republic*, to William Buckley's conservative *National Review*. E. J. Dionne, writing in the *Times*, termed the platform a "paradigm shift," and Morton Kondracke called it "tough, eloquent, and right." David Broder said, "It put the Democrats back on the right track," and George Will heaped praise upon the document. Suddenly, the small but growing moderate Les Aspin wing of the party was displaying a fresh and energetic voice in national security, less stridently partisan, often more serious and thoughtful; in effect, not only attempting to hit the administration from the right for what Aspin called being "not serious about defense," but also carving out far-reaching ideas for the country's foreign policy more generally.

ASPIN'S ATTEMPTS TO move the party to the center were not solely about politics, but were also a matter of conscience and a concern that American power and influence did matter. He felt the U.S. still had to develop a consensus on the ultimate post-Vietnam issue: the use of force. And it was this contentious issue that suddenly thrust him into the white-hot cauldron of domestic conflict, the debate over funding for the Nicaraguan rebels fighting the Communist Sandinista regime in Nicaragua.

Aspin, for some time, had been convinced that the Sandinistas had betrayed the incipient strains of democracy in Nicaragua, and were a menace to their democratic neighbors and a threat to U.S. interests. Short of sending in troops, Aspin generally came to feel that the U.S. should fund guerrilla movements seeking to stem Soviet power.

In June 1986, the issue of $100 million in aid came to a vote, and Aspin had still not publicly signaled his intentions one way or the other. One day, meeting with his staff, the sordid early beginnings of the contras—their training by the CIA and Argentinean generals—were raised. "That's not the issue," Aspin said. "The Sandinistas need to be pressured, *that's* the issue. That's why the contras need help."

In his assessments, Aspin came to agree with Reagan that the problem with Communist regimes, unlike with democracies, which he believed did not wage war on each other, was that they had no democratic check on their ability to make war. It was also important to pressure Soviet client regimes.

The day of the contra vote, Aspin was wandering around on the House floor and bumped into the garrulous Illinois Republican Henry Hyde. The two walked over onto the Republican side as the vote was tallied. To anyone watching at that moment, it was a symbolic walk. Unlike in 1984, this time Aspin voted to aid the contras, violating the ultimate litmus test of Democratic party orthodoxy. However sound a policy decision it may have been, and he felt deeply that it was, it was a big political gamble.

If Aspin succeeded, he would pave the way for moderate post-Vietnam Democrats. If he failed, he could be slapped down by colleagues trying to trip him up. Liberal colleagues watched in horror as Aspin joked with Republicans. They felt betrayed—again.

Virtually overnight, the vote unleashed a firestorm of criticism, and it was clear that, far from making room for other moderate Democrats, Aspin would now have to explain himself. His euphoria over bravely recasting the party was built on shifting sands, for even as he continued forward to strengthen the defense Democrats, events were under way that would foreclose his chance of leading the Democrats out of the wilderness and would also jeopardize his chairmanship.

Within weeks, the excruciating dilemma of Aspin's position became apparent. In mid-July, Marvin Leath, only the fourteenth-ranked Democrat on the Armed Services Committee, announced his intention to unseat

Aspin as chairman. A Texas conservative, Leath maintained that he was less capricious, more capable of garnering the trust of the liberal House caucus. He was quick to point out that as Aspin had moved to the right, he himself was moving to the left. That same week, Charles Bennett, a conservative Florida Democrat and the third-ranking member, announced his candidacy. Nicholas Mavroules, a Massachusetts liberal, also signaled a conditional intent to get into the running. Suddenly, Aspin had his hands full. A horse race was on.

Aspin was strangely calm about the whole affair. He didn't believe the caucus would seriously entertain deposing him, only that he was being sent a strong message. Yet he knew he had to moderate his move to the right and appease House liberals.

Before the Iceland summit, he vigorously supported a package of five so-called peace amendments to the defense bill, which would, among other things, compel the administration to abide by the unratified SALT II treaty and freeze funding for space-based missile defense. It was a feel-good package, cooked up by the liberal arms control groups and liberal members of Congress. To atone for his contra vote, Aspin ran with it, becoming their new champion.

Reagan strongly rebuffed Aspin and the other House members, declaring that such legislative restrictions would unilaterally "restrict our bargaining positions at the negotiating table" and "send a message to the Soviets" that what they can't get from the administration they can get "from the Congress later."

On the eve of the Iceland summit, the House Democrats, including Aspin, held a flurry of meetings with the White House. At the last moment, they caved, and withdrew the amendments. They were unwilling to face the legitimate charge that they had undermined the president in his negotiations, and forced him to bargain with one hand tied behind his back. Privately, Aspin agreed with the White House. But in this round, politics reigned. He acted dutifully in concert with powerful liberal members of the House. After months of straying from the liberal fold, he was now inching, though not yet sprinting, back.

THE DAY AFTER the Iceland summit, as Aspin drove to his office, the situation had reached equilibrium. He would moderate his conservative actions more in tune with the caucus. Soon enough, he could emerge again, stronger than ever, and, in time, continue nudging his party to the center.

Aspin held lengthy hearings in his committee on the summit during the cold months of November. Over three weeks, he brought Weinberger, Perle, Adelman, Bill Crowe, the chairman of the joint chiefs, and a host of other expert witnesses before him.

In a calculated show designed to keep himself in good graces with the caucus, he grilled, mocked, and even taunted ACDA head Ken Adelman, like a county prosecutor ripping apart a key defense witness. He was so tough on Adelman, one of the most genial, easygoing men in government, that even White House people were shocked—watching it on C-SPAN, one White House aide, no patsy herself, recoiled: "He's a really mean guy; he's a bully."

That day, Aspin was relentless. He chided the administration for not having its act together ("Did the administration offer to get rid of all strategic weapons, or all ballistic missiles, which is it?" he said incredulously. "Did you know Akhromeyev would be there? Well, why not? Why wasn't NATO consulted? What studies were conducted of such full-blown reductions?") The answers themselves were almost irrelevant; this was pure political theater.

But on the day when Richard Perle took his seat in the witness chair, the tone was dramatically different. The hearing was marked by good-natured sparring between the two men. After banging his gavel to open the hearing, he described Perle as "the only person in the administration who knows anything about arms control—the only question is, Is he for it or against it."

He went on in his opening statement, saying, "If the president can't bring home the bacon after six years in office, perhaps it is time for Congress to try its hand."

Perle smiled impishly, shifted forward in his chair, and read his opening statement, along with one quick improvisation: "An institution as adept as this one in the handling of pork could form up an awesome negotiating team for the purpose of securing the nation's bacon. The trouble is that you are rather better at giving it away than bringing it home, and that skill, so essential in politics, is hardly what we need in the management of national security policy."

Aspin was privately snickering at Perle's barbs. He liked jousting with Perle, respecting him as a keen and subtle thinker, even if they sometimes disagreed. Perle felt the same way about Aspin.

Perle continued, "I think you are unduly modest in suggesting that you have been waiting these six years before trying your hand. When it comes to arms control, the hand of the Congress has been deep in the pockets of the administration for as long as I can remember.

"Unfortunately that hand has been turned to drafting gratuitous resolutions expressing the sense of Congress when what we have needed all along has been a helpful hand in funding the military programs that are the subject of negotiation, and support for which is vital to their success. And while I don't wish to seem ungrateful, the help that you have given us as we sought to negotiate with the Soviet Union reminds me of Mark Twain's observation that "To do good work is noble. To urge others to do good work is even more noble—and it isn't very hard."

Perle added that he firmly rejected the characterization that the administration's conduct in Iceland was "slipshod." He also rejected Aspin's assertion that the administration should have been willing to trade SDI, as a bargaining chip, for deep arms concessions, the very kind that Reagan had turned down. Perle contested this bitterly. He said that view missed the point, and constituted a misreading of Gorbachev's failure to accept the zero ballistic missile proposal.

In the following days, however, Aspin made great hay in exposing differences in substance and emphasis within the administration over arms control issues. By year's end, the chairman felt his efforts had paid off, and that by backing liberal arms control positions, he had settled back into the good graces of the caucus.

THE VOTE ON his chairmanship was scheduled for January 7, 1987. It was a vote only on whether he would be retained. Only in the very unlikely event that he lost, would there then be a runoff for chairman on January 2. His political advisers informed him that he would be reinstated by a healthy margin of fifty votes. Not surprisingly, he was so confident that he felt free to schedule a hearing with Weinberger the following day. He fiddled with his squash schedule—maybe it would also be a good time to play a few games.

AT FIRST, ALL went as expected. The full caucus vote to retain all chairmen was by secret ballot. It was preceded by a vote of just the congressional leadership, the Steering and Policy Committee, recommending whether or not all chairmen should be kept. Aspin was given a surprisingly weak endorsement vote of 22–8; but it was still a green light. The chairman fidgeted nervously, looking around at his colleagues with a weak smile during the full vote. But he felt he was still a shoo-in.

After the final vote was taken, the tally was read. His colleagues had voted to dump him 130–124.

It was like one massive blow to the stomach.

Aspin momentarily slumped at hearing the news.

He was stunned, shaken and humbled by the vote of no confidence.

But he wasted no time in subjective analysis, and immediately huddled with his supporters on the floor of the House. They persuaded him to remain in the race and seek reelection as chairman at the January 2 meeting of the Democratic Caucus.

For several hours he skated around the floor of the House, keeping up the best face that he could, and buttonholed members. The vote "was a good device to send a message about dealing with other members of the House, and the message has been received," he intoned. In the grim predusk hours of that evening, after consulting with his top political advisers, he hustled over to his personal office to plot his comeback strategy. He closed the door to his inner office and did not emerge for hours. There were countless calculations he had to make. He had two weeks to campaign. But he had clearly been misled this time, and in view of the secret ballot that would decide his fate, there was no way to know which way the final tally would break. Some members had not been totally straight with him. Others had simply lied. That too was a problem.

But he was determined to give it his all.

THE NEXT MORNING, an edict was issued by the committee staff director to all professional staff, including Aspin's committee high command who were his personal appointees. The staff director warned that no communication should go out on committee stationery listing Aspin as chairman, because until the vote on the 22nd, "the committee doesn't have a chairman."

Now technically without a committee staff at his disposal, and no longer the chairman, Aspin was relying on his Wisconsin staff, and, most of all, on himself.

ASPIN LEFT THAT night looking wan and pale, even ghostly. With the mood of bitter confrontation deepening between him and his rivals, he briefly harbored private doubts and misgivings about his future, and the movement of centrist Democrats he had hoped to nurture appeared to be falling increasingly further from his grasp, even as it swept him closer and closer to the brink of personal disaster.

One comforting thought consumed him as he wrestled with sleep that night: he was a fighter.

He had two weeks to turn it around.

Suddenly, it had all changed.

Aspin had hoped to have the wiggle room in his own party to cooperate with the Republicans on the great issues of the Cold War, even as he fashioned his own alternative vision for the Democrats. No one was more qualified on national security issues to lead the Democrats than Aspin. But in a display of congressional furor, largely over ideology, his liberal colleagues had sent the unmistakable message that this was not to be. They were determined to wrest concessions from Reagan that, in two separate summits, Gorbachev himself had been unable to secure. If it meant the sacrifice of Les Aspin, indisputably one of the best and the brightest of the Democratic stars, and just as arguably one of the leading thinkers on national security in the country, then so be it.

The day after the first vote on the chairman, the race was on.

PERLE WATCHED THIS struggle with ill-disguised contempt. It was like fratricide, Democratic liberals eating one of their own, the best of their children. Never was there more vivid proof that their ideological agenda took precedence over good sense and a concern for a serious security policy than in their humbling of Aspin. It was a raucous and transparent political struggle, with Aspin, for all his talents, the unwitting pawn writhing painfully in the middle.

Perle felt Aspin should have known better. For years, he had seen the Democratic Caucus at work while he was on Scoop Jackson's staff in the Senate. It was ironic. Liberals talked about *him*, Perle, "never giving in, never, never, never." Well, if his credo were "so many Russians, so little time," their credo might as well be "so many conservatives, so little time."

Perle felt terrible for Aspin. He felt the whole incident was a disaster, not just for Aspin, not just for the Democratic party (though it surely was), but for the country at large. An effective national security policy can scarcely be maintained if one party is pro-defense and the other is hostile to defense. Yet that would be the message of Aspin's public whipping.

Privately, Perle was rooting for Aspin. Aspin was a friend, and also a serious policy thinker. But Perle had no illusions about the outcome. Whatever happened, things would not be the same. If Aspin's brief meteoric rise briefly gave him a patina like Scoop Jackson, and clearly established him as a candidate for the next generation of Wise Men, that would, like the fall of objects compelled by gravity itself, soon be reversed. Even meteors one day come crashing to the ground.

THE JOCKEYING FOR the chairmanship began immediately, and shaped up to be a boiling cauldron of intrigue and drama, involving countless clashes of ideology, but also of personality, style, and tradition. It rapidly became apparent that the winning strategy came down to one path: courting the House liberals.

Aspin's principal challenger, Marvin Leath, boldly drawled, "I killed the king, and I deserve the crown." Leath was no defense intellectual like Aspin, but a folksy former high school teacher and salesman. He had the support of the conservatives on the committee, aging barons like Sonny Montgomery, Bill Nichols, Samuel Stratton, and of course Mel Price. But he set about rapidly solidifying his support with House liberals as proof that he could be an honest broker, forging a consensus for the diverse strains of the party. It was thus critical that he picked up the vocal support of the freewheeling black liberal Ron Dellums, whose district included the University of California at Berkeley, the hotbed of numerous radical movements. With Dellums's support, Leath set about picking up the disaffected liberals in the House.

Despite profound political differences, Leath and Dellums, one white, one black, one relatively conservative, one ultraliberal, one a son of the Boll Weevil tradition, the other of the Black Panther tradition, had a genuinely strong friendship, which in the lexicon of House politics—where politics is often personal—counted for a great deal. "They became soul brothers," one colleague noted.

But Dellums, like other liberals, was impressed by another fact. On the Budget Committee, Leath had demonstrated a willingness to compromise, earning him widespread praise. He also turned his hawkish conservatism to his favor: "It would," he claimed, "make him an effective critic of President Reagan's defense policies." In short, Leath pleased Dellums. Moreover, Dellums was also a man of his word, who, politics aside, was actually a conservative when it came to tradition. More so than most of his reformist colleagues, he abided by the rites and rules of the House as an institution. Thus, his endorsement had a visceral resonance. Dellums intended to give the nominating speech for Leath on January 22.

Leath was the acknowledged front-runner. But as the four candidates, Leath, Aspin, Nicholas Mavroules, and Charles Bennett, scrambled to lobby colleagues, energetically tracking members down in their districts, on official trips to Africa, Central America, Jamaica, and Ireland, and even a lobbiest-sponsored golf tournament in Palm Springs, California, the race was coming down mainly to Leath and Aspin. Leath would have the support of the conservatives. With Mavroules and Bennett in the race, the liberals would be fractured in two or three directions.

By midweek, around January 13, predicting the winner appeared to be all but impossible. The vote would be secret, and the lowest vote-getter would be dropped after each ballot until one member had a majority. In the beginning, all three sides privately agreed that Leath would take the lead at first—and that three ballots would probably decide the winner.

Leath himself confidently predicted: "We are very close to the number we need for a first-vote victory—131, if all Democrats are present." For his part, Aspin set about denying Leath the early momentum, psychological or otherwise.

ASPIN'S CALCULATIONS WERE at least twofold. First, he had to address the "personality issue," the rap that he wasn't trustworthy, and was too prone to freelance political wheeling and dealing. If he could resolve this, then he would only have to persuade his colleagues on the ideological issue—where he would generally come down on matters of central concern to the caucus.

Aspin brought the same message over and over to his exasperated colleagues, supporters and critics alike. "There are a lot of things I need to do differently in dealing with people," he said. "No more MXs, no more unexplained change of heart on contras."

Aspin was told he couldn't just walk up to colleagues, fold his arms across his chest, look enraptured, and shake his head and say, "Uh huh, ah-hah, ah-hah."

"We think this means you're agreeing with us," one member said. "You have to be more clear in your intentions."

Aspin, shaking his head, exclaimed, "I know, I know."

Demonstrating contrition and remorse, he acknowledged his style was aloof and cocky. Give me another chance, he pleaded, I've learned my lesson. "I know I have to do better."

The look of remorse was on his face. The look had to be convincing. The eyes were earnest.

For everyone to see, Aspin was sincere, even contrite. Fighting for his political life, there was no other choice.

During this hectic week, closeting himself off in his office, surrounded only by his political lieutenants, political staff, and loyal congressmen, Aspin the policy maker became Aspin the juggernaut. He was no longer relying on his committee staff—who had miscounted his support by fifty votes—but on his personal advisers, roll-up-the-sleeves pols from his Wisconsin congressional staff. Deep into the night, with lists drawn up by these political aides, he made over a hundred calls to members, talking to them for as long as necessary. Sometimes he would call them twice. Trying to sort out the whole mess, he sought to impart the central message: "Give me another chance."

But there was another message that he carried to his rebellious colleagues. Despite a well-known conservatism, Leath had made impressive inroads with the liberals, even insisting he had shifted to the left. Aspin meant to blunt this.

An Aspin political aide explained, "The members have to see that you're one of them, and Leath is more conservative than they thought. We have to show that he is completely out of step with most House Democrats."

Aspin, gritting his teeth with iron determination, a scowling face few people, even those who have known him well, had ever seen, replied, "Let's do it."

ON JANUARY 19, the campaign shifted into high gear. Two of Aspin's key supporters, Matthew McHugh of New York and Don Edwards of California, circulated specifics of Leath's well-honed conservatism. It was a no-holds-barred attack on Leath's views.

"In eight years in the House," they proclaimed, Leath "has made a career of voting against his party." They included votes across the spectrum, not just on defense spending and arms control, but on civil rights, the environment, job training, education, women's issues (none of which had anything to do with the Armed Services Committee, but this was, after all, a full-scale political war for the hearts and minds of the liberals). The ineluctable impression the letter meant to convey was that Aspin was the only serious candidate whom liberals could reliably trust to head the committee.

Liberal members were delighted. All four candidates were singing off their sheet of music. "You've never heard such a chorus of commitments to arms reduction, procurement reforms, and no defense spending increases," Congressman Barney Frank said, excitedly echoing the views of the caucus.

In return for Aspin's newborn fealty to their causes, liberal arms control groups, groups with names like the Union of Concerned Scientists, the American Federation of Scientists, Sane/Freeze, and Women's Action for Nuclear Disarmament, were now lobbying members to vote for him.

But the groups themselves were hardly models of fealty or automatic Aspin supporters, and they still weren't taking any chances. In the final days, Women's Action for Nuclear Disarmament, a group that sported only two full-time staff people, warm in demeanor and likable, but neither of them experts in defense and national security issues, and three other activist groups circulated a questionnaire to the four candidates. The first nine questions dealt predictably with arms control issues, but not the tenth. The final question asked, "Will you oppose any new funding of the Nicaraguan contras?"

And what did the contras have to do with SDI? Nothing. But this was not a time of rationality, but of politics, not of "voting one's conscience," but of litmus tests. It was on this final question that Aspin paused. How could he go back on the vote he just cast in behalf of the Nicaraguan resistance? Would this expose him as being a flack in the pocket of a handful of liberal interest groups, the very groups whose power he had sought to diminish in his effort to move the party to the center? Would he be callously betraying a revolutionary movement he had only recently thrown his support behind?

But what choice was there?

On the questionnaire, Aspin answered that he had voted for aid to put military pressure on the Sandinistas, but that it was no longer needed. "I will not be supporting additional aid for the contras," he concluded.

And with that, the chairmanship fight had come full circle.

"WE'RE WORKING OUR heart out for Les," said one female arms control lobbyist after the questionnaires were returned. She was smiling from ear to ear. They had gotten everything they wanted.

But if the arms control lobbyists were ecstatic, this only annoyed some of the committee staffers who were Aspin appointees, anxiously awaiting the outcome of the chairmanship vote, upon which their jobs now depended. They remembered that only a few weeks earlier, these same groups were more than willing to throw Aspin overboard, like an overstuffed dog spitting out a chewed-up bone.

Later that day, Barney Frank announced: "To liberals, this is a great race, because everyone's running toward the liberal platform. The liberal agenda has become the mainstream agenda."

DURING THE FINAL week, one of David McCurdy's top aides popped in on the committee to talk with several Aspin staffers. McCurdy, tough-minded on national security, was the kind of moderate Democrat that Aspin had been cultivating in his months as chairman. Liberals might have wanted Aspin to be one of them, but moderates, like McCurdy, felt he *was* one of them. Now, the moderates feared they had been consigned to purgatory.

The McCurdy aide, tall with bushy hair and thick hands, was a committed moderate. He was from the Midwest, a devoted family man, and completely down-to-earth. Like his boss, he was dedicated to moving the party back to the center, to its Truman-Kennedy roots in foreign policy. He plunked himself into a chair, looking vaguely hysterical, like he had just seen a ghost.

"Have you seen this," he bellowed, waving a paper around.

It was the questionnaire.

"We've been working night and day for Aspin. Dave has done everything in his power to get him reelected. We have worked *our* hearts out for your guy. And the liberals [he said this with disgust], these, these groups [more disgust] say they are working for him. Hell, they're the ones who were trying to depose him."

Silence from the Aspin staff.

"Why, they, they're the Pac-Man of activist politics. They don't know anything about the issues. They don't care about the Soviets. They precook their analysis, and feed it to their liberal-l-l friends [with Midwestern emphasis] in the press. They gobble everything in their path, just to get another arms control deal, another administration concession, another airy-fairy declaration, whatever the price."

More silence.

The agitated aide was sweating now. "When was the last time they have ever supported anything in defense, or took any side that was not with the Soviets? We're not Reagan; we're moderate Democrats. But could you imagine *these* people running foreign policy? These are not our people and they will destroy us."

The stony faces of the Aspin aides, who couldn't believe how quickly everything had changed, registered little on the outside. But it felt like the end of a heroic adventure, their own little Camelot, the attempted resuscitation of the Democratic party, crashing to its death. Their heads hung sadly.

"Well, I'll tell you where the liberals have Aspin now, I can't even say chairman," replied one aide. He thrust his hand into the air, and made a squeezing motion with his fingers. "Right by the balls, that's where."

BEN WATTENBERG, THE neoconservative columnist, called Aspin on the phone. He told Aspin to hang tough, and that his friends were behind him. Aspin said, "Uh huh," and quickly hung up. He liked Wattenberg, but it was not clear that Wattenberg, a brainy intellectual and eternal optimist, dedicated to the triumph of hope over reality, fully understood just how determined the caucus was and how much he was hanging by a string.

Aspin also didn't want to signal that changes would have to be in the offing, that the brave, bold experiment would have to go into low gear. What could Wattenberg expect him to say? Aspin quickly shifted his attention to another call.

The vote was on January 22, just days away.

THE NIGHT BEFORE, Aspin's aides walked around quietly—actually, they nervously tiptoed, because everyone was on eggshells. A new chairman meant they would be out of work. They were not civil servants, but Aspin appointees. They served at the pleasure of the chairman, an honor. If Aspin were not reelected—still a very big if—so many things would be different. It would be the end of a brief, exciting era.

Some had started putting résumés together, but hadn't shown anyone; word could get out. Anything that looked like conceding defeat could in turn spell a loss for Aspin. Other aides had spent extra time cultivating the arms control groups, preparing to defect from Aspin if necessary. Meanwhile, the press was swarming around for gossip.

One longtime aide of Aspin's from his Wisconsin personal staff could not believe her eyes. Aspin had been a virtual machine, working night and day since the first vote. He nervously prowled in his office in between calls. When he spoke, it was as though he were muttering aloud. She couldn't remember the last time she ate a home-cooked meal—or, sitting in her cubicle, saw daylight.

THE CRITICISM SEEMED now to come from all sides. One respected and prominent Democrat, level-headed and pro-contra, was now in an unspoken rage. He asked if Aspin were going to sell out to the "totalitarianism of the left." The chairmanship, the perks, and private planes were not worth it. Aspin should *not* sell out, he said.

But this was voiced in the fever-pitched moment. Aspin had been truly brave. The criticism was misplaced. It was the caucus, not Aspin, that was the problem.

THE MORNING OF the vote was like a scene out of a *Dr. Zhivago*. A fierce blizzard swept through Washington, and members had to struggle through the city's unplowed streets. Most people didn't go to work in D.C. that day—except for the Democratic Caucus. Outside, it felt like pitch black night, punctuated with thick balls of white raining down, a day of sharp contrasts and impassioned oratory, of sin, redemption, astonishing grace.

Aspin was at work early. In his own, barely scrutable way, he was fidgety. That morning, a large profile on him by Sidney Blumenthal had appeared in the "Style" section of the *Washington Post*. Blumenthal, a deadly writer, a hit man for the left, had been a fierce critic of Aspin's since he had become chairman. His piece concluded that Aspin, "who would transform the party image of the Democratic party from weakness to strength," had been reduced to "the master of little, particularly his own fate." Aspin shrugged off the predictable commentary, and readied himself for the vote; he could not look weak, but must look confident, yet at the same time sincere.

He soon got the word. The vote had been put off for two hours. Members had been unable to make it through the snow. Special vans with four-wheel drive and chains were being sent out to pick up stranded members. The vote was on the verge of being canceled.

FINALLY, HOWEVER, THE contest began. The doors to the House chamber were ominously closed. A handful of staff members nervously paced at the edge of the chamber. The speeches, stirring oratory, were made, and the time came to vote.

The first ballot was a surprise. Instead of leading, Leath came in second. The vote was 96 for Aspin, 69 for Leath, 44 for Bennett, and 35 for Mavroules. Mavroules was out.

Aspin supporters clenched their fists and braced themselves for victory. Mavroules's liberal votes should swing to Aspin, even putting him over the top in the second try.

But the second vote did not follow the expected pattern. Leath picked up 22 votes; Aspin only 12. The second tally stood at Aspin 108, Leath 91, and Bennett 47.

This time, Bennett was out. But Aspin was again denied victory. He steadied himself. The vote was tough to gauge, but he still thought he had it. His emotions were corked.

Suddenly, three newcomers straggled in to vote, having only now just made it through the snow. It was not readily apparent if they were Aspin or Leath supporters. This was not necessarily good news; the vote chemistry was too volatile.

Two of Aspin's staff members eyed each other wearily. They were afraid to show emotion, one way or the other.

The next vote was taken, the count finally made: 114 for Leath, 115 for Leath, 116 for Leath . . . but then, just as quickly, the votes topped out. Aspin sprinted ahead, winning 133–116. For the first time in two weeks, he showed an unforced smile. Appearing relieved and ecstatic, he bounded wearily into the well of the House, his head bowed, his hands reaching out. He stood in the center of the sunken room, looking like a supplicant in the Roman Colosseum.

"I have learned my lesson," he said to the entire caucus, peering out through his glasses. "Things will be different now."

Leath immediately joined Aspin to make peace. "You'll never have to look over your shoulder, because I'll be in the harness right next to you."

One aide watching would later swear that the whole scene was an eerie confessional, that it almost looked like something out of a Stalinist show trial, or a grim scene in George Orwell's *1984*.

THE DOORS BURST open to the outside. Everyone was proclaiming victory for Aspin. *Everyone* was now an Aspin supporter—and always had been. It seemed nobody had voted for Leath, Mavroules, or Bennett.

In the stately hallway, a quickie verdict was rendered. Yes, this was about Aspin and his way of dealing with people. But it was foremost a battle of ideology. The contest for the chairmanship of the traditionally pro-defense House Armed Services Committee was viewed as one that liberals could not lose. Now they had the best of all worlds. They still had the brainy Aspin as their leader. But a warning shot had been fired. They could make the chairman—or break him. They felt that if he was not now one of theirs, they at least owned him when it counted.

EVEN AS THE Soviet Union was buckling under the weight of American pressure, ideological pressure, pressure in regional conflicts, pressure in the defense arena, the balance of power in the U.S. between the legislative branch and the executive, the hard-liners and the liberals, the establishment and counterestablishment was tilting dramatically. The

Reagan counterestablishment revolution, fired by energy and enthusiasm, which had so changed the world and gripped a city for six years, was now ebbing.

Rise was now wane, and the victory that would have been Aspin's— that of crafting a more muscular policy for his party, would now be denied. Nowhere was this more evident than in the retreat from the tough issues, not just on arms control and policy toward the Soviets, but in his vote cast a month later against aiding the same contras he had supported just months before.

That Aspin had demonstrated enormous guts in taking his party even as far as he had was apparent to any serious political observer. He was a good man wanting to do good, on the verge of statesmanship, but was ultimately trapped in a thick and inescapable partisan web, always juggling and synthesizing in a party that desperately needed him, but only wanted him under the right conditions. But the terms would not now be his own. Not yet, not at least for a while. In order to continue to be the chairman, Aspin had little choice but to make painful, difficult, and gut-wrenching compromises. To him, this meant not abandoning his long-term plans, but putting them into abeyance. Anyone who knew Aspin well, knew he would be back—eventually.

To be sure, it was a lesson for all Democrats, but it cut a larger swath in the rhythm of Washington policy making. What about the hard-liners, what role for them in a dawning period of liberal congressional ascendancy? Richard Perle for one, and Elliott Abrams for another, would both soon be up against a new order, with their own painful choices—at the hands not of the Soviets, but the Congress, and a less tough-minded order, that belonged not to Reagan movement hard-liners, but to a style of policy making that harked back to the centrist verities and staid philosophies of the establishment.

And as Aspin would have to bide his time and wait a decent interval before asserting himself again, a new voice would pick up the gauntlet, also seeking to move the party to the center, but only after reining in the administration. This voice would come from the other body of the Congress, the new chairman of the Senate Armed Services Committee, Sam Nunn of Georgia.

In an ensuing clash, this time Perle versus Nunn, the senator versus the assistant secretary, Congress versus the executive, Southern Democrat versus Reagan Democrat, only one man would be left standing.

CHAPTER 40

Elliott Abrams had spent a mostly sleepless night before he arrived in the dark early morning hours of October 24, 1986, for George Shultz's 7 A.M. briefing. He was still anxious when he took his seat with Charles Hill, Shultz's executive assistant, in the secretary's office. Over and over in his mind, Abrams heard the agency operative telling him the CIA had been involved in the Hasenfus flight, shot down over Nicaragua. Suddenly, everything that had been certain, everything that Abrams had said, seemed in a state of total collapse.

Trying to sound calm, Abrams explained that he "had been out there for two weeks as the administration point man," vehemently denying that the U.S. government, including the CIA, had *any* involvement in the Hasenfus mission. "I have been saying absolutely not," Abrams stressed.

But Abrams now explained he had been wrong, dead wrong. The CIA had misled them all, and had allowed Abrams to take the lead, and then watched as he slowly hanged himself. Abrams also feared that once the Hill found out, the Democrats would be up in arms. The press would crucify the administration. His own reputation could suffer. For the first time, he was openly worried that something truly illegal might have taken place.

"Ollie assures me he has talked to White House counsel and is not doing anything illegal," Abrams added. But he had his doubts.

Abrams felt damage control was necessary. He asked what he—and the department—should do now?

One of Shultz's more remarkable abilities as secretary was to maintain an air of composure. The greater the crisis, the more relaxed he seemed to become. Where others panicked, the secretary radiated calm. Rarely one to act in haste, Shultz was also a big believer in timing. There were times to lie low, and times to go forward. Where Abrams perpetually sought to solve problems through vigorous action, Shultz often was content to let issues slowly smolder, waiting to see if they would burn themselves out, or find resolution on their own.

A worried Abrams waited for his response. Long moments passed. Shultz, sitting calmly, a picture of repose, gave little hint that he felt a crisis was embroiling the administration.

He calmly told Abrams that the CIA inspector general was conducting an internal investigation of the issue. All the facts weren't in yet. Let's not be hasty, he counseled.

"In the meantime," Shultz said, "we should remain silent."

The meeting ended.

Abrams always followed a single rule: keep Shultz informed, receive authorization for all actions, give him his best advice, then follow his instructions. Shultz, in his quiet but firm way, had spoken loud and clear.

For now, the message was: sit tight.

ABRAMS ALSO HAD another concern. The money from Brunei still had not arrived in the Swiss bank account. Oliver North had been checking all fall, and each time the response was the same, nothing had been deposited. By the start of November, Abrams was convinced that the money "might never arrive."

He broke down and forwarded a top secret cable to the U.S. ambassador in Brunei, who in turn spoke to the sultan's people. The message he received was laconic but straightforward. The $10 million "had already been sent."

For Abrams, none of this added up. By late November, he had begun to think the money had been "embezzled." He drafted a tough cable to the Brunei government, suggesting that the money may have been taken, and that Brunei authorities should take steps to see who might have pocketed the $10 million. The draft cable sat in his office, awaiting final clearance from the secretary, when he went to the Hill for another round of testimony on contra policy on November 25.

He was anxious to get this cable out. But November 25 was to become one of the worst days in Elliott Abrams's career in government.

PROMPTLY, AT TWELVE noon, Ronald Reagan and Attorney General Edwin Meese held a tumultuous press conference on national television, to announce the remarkable story that arms had been sold to Iran and some of the proceeds had been diverted to the contras. Significantly understating the magnitude of the looming crisis, President Reagan spoke of "serious questions" raised by the Iran initiative. He announced that Admiral John Poindexter "had asked" to be relieved as national security adviser, and that Colonel Oliver North had already "been relieved of his duties."

Reagan then departed, leaving Meese to hold forth on the issue in greater depth with a hungry press corps.

Abrams listened aghast to the press conference as he prepared for his two o'clock testimony before the Senate Intelligence Committee. He was stunned. It was now clear that he had been played for "a fool" and "a chump," not just by Alan Fiers and the CIA, but also by Ollie North and the NSC. Yet Reagan and Meese had given only sketchy details, and it was unclear just what they knew. Everything was still murky, like a bad picture out of focus. Only slowly would details emerge about both initiatives, about who was involved, what actually happened, and what, if anything, was actually illegal.

Still knowing very little—in fact, Shultz had continued to keep him in the dark about the legal Saudi and Taiwanese contributions to the contras—Abrams continued to be an advocate for the administration's Nicaragua policy. He paid no heed to his own backside, even as the political winds of Washington were perilously shifting.

Abrams's advocacy included maintaining the secrecy pledge to Brunei.

In a meeting behind closed doors with the Senate Intelligence Committee, Bill Bradley asked him about government fund-raising activities.

To Abrams, testimony was just one of the arenas of ongoing political warfare between the Democrats and Republicans over Central America policy. Historically, executive branch officials had resisted fully disclosing information on national security affairs to the Congress. If members didn't ask exactly the right questions, they didn't get full disclosure in the answers. However constitutionally inappropriate it was to mislead Congress, examples of administration prevarication and obfuscation were commonplace in the annals of American history.

In the middle of the nineteenth century, President James Polk had falsely blamed Mexico for the onset of hostilities in the war of 1846, claiming that he had no desire to take any Mexican territory. The pattern was little different over a century later when, in 1958, Secretary of State John Foster Dulles baldly misled the House Foreign Affairs Committee about CIA assistance to antigovernment rebels in Indonesia. Later, in 1962, after the Cuban Missile Crisis, Defense Secretary Robert McNamara coolly prevaricated to Congress about the sensitive agreement struck between President Kennedy and Khrushchev over removing America's Jupiter missiles from Turkey as part of the deal to resolve the Cuban Missile Crisis. Two years later, under President Johnson, McNamara, his face ever confident, again misled Congress, this time about the actual events leading up to the 1964 Gulf of Tonkin incident, including the role of prior U.S. Navy and South Vietnamese ship attacks on North Vietnam. Outright lying became less accepted after the Nixon presidency, but the tendency to thrust and counterthrust, and to withhold and shade information from the Congress, continued in both the Carter and Reagan administrations.

Abrams was not a stickler when he came before the Congress. He saw his job as promoting his administration's policies. Courting the Congress would have been easy—and politically smart. A little stroking here, a little stroking there might have gone a long way. But it wasn't his way. He had contempt for the Democrats, hated their partisan maneuverings, and was determined to give away only as little as he had to.

So Abrams did what he had been doing for quite some time: by his own acknowledgment, he was evasive in hearings. He volunteered little beyond what he had to. On November 25, when asked about funds from foreign countries for the contras, he used the same formulation he had been using in the preceding months, including what he had said on October 14. In effect, none.

"We don't engage—I mean the State Department's function in this has not been to raise money, other than to raise it from Congress."

But, as that Tuesday came to a close, Abrams felt a churning in his stomach. Events were moving very fast now. By day's end, it was clear Washington was in the grip of a far-reaching political crisis. He felt his misleading testimony had been a "great mistake." Returning to the department, he asked Shultz for permission to break the secrecy pledge and tell the committee about the Brunei solicitation. Shultz said, "Fine, you probably should." Caught in the whirlwind of the burgeoning scandal, Abrams also never sent his cable to Brunei.

On December 8, Abrams went before the Senate Intelligence Committee a second time, at his personal request, "to set the record straight." He admitted ducking the issue and, in effect, misleading the committee. But with the Iran-contra scandal swelling, the senators were in no mood to be trifled with, and raked Abrams over the coals. The exchanges were testy. Senators were aware he had broken no laws, but they felt he had violated the essential spirit of give-and-take between the Congress and the administration. However much the two sides had sparred over Central America policy in the past, in the midst of a scandal, the rules of Washington conduct had changed, almost overnight.

As a political necessity in the Washington of Iran-contra, if Abrams needed to do one thing, it was not just to apologize, but also to show contrition, to freely admit that he had wronged the committees and place himself at their mercy. He didn't. Indeed, as one of his detractors put it, he showed "insufficient inspiration" in apologizing.

For the combative Abrams, it was a politically risky strategy. And, unwilling to adapt to the new rhythm seizing the capital, he would soon pay a terrible price.

OVER THE NEXT six months, well into 1987, Washington became a different city, pitting, as never before, liberal Democrats against conservative Republicans, the administration against the Congress, and executive branch colleagues against each other. To administration officials, rocked by the scandal, at times the city appeared barren, grim, and raw, like the charred remains of a wilderness burned by an uncontrollable fire. To congressional Democrats, and even to many Reagan supporters, it was appalling that a former marine colonel could run a private arms and foreign policy network out of the White House. Meanwhile, in news bureaus across the city, reporters smelled Pulitzers, and seized upon the story with unparalleled tenacity. As the blustery days of winter turned to spring and then into the hot summer months, the Iran-contra scandal held the capital in a viselike lock, engulfing anyone remotely related to the policies in its path. This included Elliott Abrams.

But in truth, the scandal was both less than its critics charged, and in some ways more.

For months on end, each day brought fresh, often astounding revelations. Sleazy retired government characters, shadowy Middle East arms merchants, opportunistic con men, and policy zealots were paraded as being at the epicenter and tentacles of a rogue policy. A special bipartisan Presidential Review Board, chaired by former Senator John Tower of Texas, and including such staunch pillars of rectitude as Brent Scowcroft and Edmund Muskie, was convened. While the president was absolved from wrongdoing, he was portrayed as out of touch with policies conducted in his name.

Critics charged that arms export control procedures were flouted, that the Boland Amendment was illegally circumvented, and that the alleged cover-up was not just a violation of law, but a gross abuse of power with constitutional implications. With each scintillating revelation, however tangential or large, there seemed to be no end to the web of deceit, foolishness, and rogue actions in the Iran-contra affair.

Yet amid the revelations, it was also clear that Iran-contra had mushroomed into a scandal in large part because a failed Iran policy had been egregiously linked with contra funding.

The secret arms sales to Iran, designed to foster a new strategic relationship with Iran as well as to release American hostages in Lebanon, were a highly debatable policy proposition. Reagan, the hard-liner, desperately wanted Americans held hostage by Iranian-backed Beirut-based terrorists to be released. Thus, he seemed to have succumbed to wishful thinking about a strategic opening with Iran. But in and of itself, the Iran policy was not criminally illegal. Another dubious proposition was the foreign solicitations for the contras, which were also legal, as were the private donations made by wealthy citizens (although Oliver North's official involvement—the full extent of which remained unknown—was to virtually all serious observers, deeply troubling). In the ensuing months, constitutional scholars and political columnists hotly debated the diversion, including loopholes in congressional statutes like the Boland Amendments and imprecise compromises inartfully crafted between the two branches of government.

Throughout 1987, the battle also broke down along partisan lines, further blurring where legal culpability and policy responsibility lay. Conservatives pointed out that a partisan Congress had ignored key issues of national security and dire exigencies of the Cold War before the altar of politics. In their view, Democrats displayed a "fanatical obsession" with halting aid to the contras rather than being willing to work with the administration to craft a policy aimed at fostering genuinely democratic elections in Nicaragua. In turn, Democrats pointed with alarm to a "cabal of zealots" like Oliver North who sought to take over key aspects of American foreign policy, and denounced the idea of a midlevel NSC official using the president's name and abusing the National Security Council without presidential sanction.

Yet at the core was a set of old disputes, in many ways notable less for perfidy, and more for the depressing regularity with which they reappeared in American foreign policy. Ultimately, one of the most troubling aspects of the affair was the conflict between timely management of foreign policy on the one hand, and constitutional accountability for policy makers in a two-party democratic system on the other. But the press, and the parties and players themselves, dealt less with these larger questions, and more with details, whipping up more smoke than fire, and giving continuous rise to guilt by association and innuendo. Even the joint House-Senate panel to investigate the arms transfer to Iran and the diversion of funds to the contras was marred by partisan warfare, too frequently degenerating into political theater rather than genuinely serious inquiry.

It was into the sticky hot center of this debate that Abrams fell. The Iran-contra scandal seemed so widespread, so bizarre, the debate was so intense, that each day brought the terror of a new headline, the anxiety of the latest congressional finding, the sting of the most recent incriminating rumor.

.   .   .

FOR WEEKS ON end, the scuttlebutt was that Abrams "had to know more than he was saying" because he chaired the RIG, and met regularly with Fiers and North. Privately, even most of Abrams's detractors on the Hill readily acknowledged that North had lied to Abrams, as he had to virtually everyone else. But publicly, every inconsistency between Abrams's statements and those of numerous other participants, however marginal, was held up as a possible example of Abrams's complicity in the whole sordid affair. He was now being roughed up regularly in the press and on the Hill. No one had accused him of doing anything illegal. Instead, it was just the ubiquitous suggestion that he had had to "know more." His nemesis, Senator Christopher Dodd, played the issue for all it was worth, seeking to implicate Abrams by association.

"We haven't heard from North, and apparently there was substantial contact there," he taunted. "Abrams has got some explaining to do. He's not out of the woods yet."

Privately, Abrams began to reevaluate his tenure in government. He loved his job, believed deeply in the cause, and was willing to fight the Democrats to the bitter end. But he now saw how naive he had been toward the CIA, how trusting he had been of people who had an agenda much different from his, and who made their living off of deception. He felt the same about North. Facing the first serious crisis of his life, the thirty-nine-year-old Abrams would eventually come to what he called "a sad but partial conclusion" that he should have been "more suspicious and less trusting of his colleagues."

After Abrams appeared before the Tower board, the left criticized him for misleading Congress, while on the right some conservative Hill staffers continued to voice their frustrations that Abrams had paid too much attention to reforming the contras, was too much a stickler for "democracy" and "human rights," and was unwilling to wage an all-out war against Communism.

Moreover, all throughout the spring, it was an open secret that congressional investigators were working tenaciously to find a link between him and Colonel North's secret arms network. The constant drip, drip in the press began to take its toll.

Where Abrams once spoke freely, almost always on the record with the press (unlike other senior administration members who invariably spoke as unnamed "senior officials"), he now shied away from reporters.

At home, he cringed when the phone rang, and his heart would race until the ringing stopped. He worried it was another reporter calling to torment him. Or another unsubstantiated accusation. He knew he could be killed not by wrongdoing, but by merely issuing a mountain of denials, implying there must be something there.

Turning on the nightly news became another exercise in personal terror, as night after night the lead story was Iran-contra.

In his State Department office, Abrams kept up an air of composure, and maintained a cheery, upbeat disposition, even as his staff worried when the next shoe would drop. He kept his bureau focused tightly on its work, and not on Iran-contra, never letting on that he was feeling the heat.

Abrams even continued to fight for the contras, sparring with Senator Dodd in a February 1987 hearing before the Senate Foreign Relations Committee, and trying to rein in Philip Habib, when he appeared too eager to cut a premature deal with the Sandinistas. After the release of the Tower Commission report, he put on a good face and scoffed that he "wasn't hit very hard." And when the *New York Times* published the headline "Tower Report Tarnishes the Luster of Abrams," with a flick of the hand he cheerily waved it aside, telling his staff to get to work.

But by the time he was about to appear before the Iran-contra committee in June, as the first administration witness, to many who knew Abrams well, he was a man deeply under siege.

APPEARING BEFORE THE Iran-contra committee for two days on Tuesday and Wednesday, June 3 and 4, Abrams was repeatedly grilled by the committee Democrats and committee lawyers. He did himself little good with the members by appearing defiant and unrepentant, an unapologetic champion of the contras.

The hearing covered mostly old ground, focusing on policy differences, and how Abrams had misled Congress about the Brunei money. He was chastised for not seeking out corruption more readily. Senator Howell Heflin asked him if he had something "to hide from the committee," and chided, "You see no evil, hear no evil, speak no evil, and inquire of no evil." Members suggested he could face legal penalties if he were shown to have deliberately deceived Congress during testimony on other matters. But throughout the two days of grueling testimony and questions, it quickly became apparent that Abrams was out of the loop for the central issues concerning the private contra resupply network and other aspects of the Iran-contra affair. George Mitchell, the influential Maine liberal, concluded after listening to Abrams that it was others who were guilty and who were content to "watch him twist in the wind."

Unlike his boss, George Shultz, who was deft at soothing irate congressional sensibilities, Abrams again showed that he was not a political animal. Congressman Jack Brooks, a fiery Texas Democrat, accused Abrams of lying, and lit into him for squandering his credibility. "I can only conclude after this that you are either extremely incompetent" or that "the administration had intentionally kept you in the dark on all these matters so that you can come down and blatantly mislead us, the secretary of state, and the American people on all the issues that we have been discussing."

Abrams was livid. Rachel, sitting in the audience, could barely contain her anger at the assault on her husband.

Brooks continued, "I am deeply troubled by it and wonder if you can survive as an assistant secretary of state."

This across-the-board attack was too much for Abrams, who fired back, "Fortunately, I guess, I have to say I don't work for you; I work for George Shultz and he seems to be pretty satisfied with the job that I have done for him. That makes me very happy and very proud."

As Abrams wrapped up his testimony, the issue came down less to an inquiry about Iran-contra and more to a struggle over raw political power. Even if Abrams weren't guilty of any illegalities, it had become an occasion to mar his name, and even pressure him out of government. To seasoned observers at the time, the intense questioning of Abrams was a "kind of marathon group therapy session" by Congress, in which they could finally "return some of the fire that Abrams inflicted on them during his many appearances."

The following day, the *New York Times* editorialized that Abrams had created so many problems not because he knew or didn't know about Iran-contra, but because he had held himself out as "being informed." While Abrams had dodged the Iran-contra bullet, he now faced a new threat, repeated calls for his resignation by the Democrats. Senate Majority Leader Mitchell said that he displayed an "arrogance that has been so typical of the administration," and "whatever credibility he had is gone, shot completely."

Indeed, far from abating, the storm surrounding Abrams continued. The issue was no longer Iran-contra, but that he had misled congressional committees about the Brunei solicitation. On June 12, 129 House Democrats sent a letter to Shultz, demanding Abrams's ouster. "We ask for the immediate resignation or replacement of Mr. Abrams as assistant secretary of state for inter-American affairs," the letter demanded.

On the Senate side, Chris Dodd declared that Abrams was an "unfit spokesman" for the administration, and that he would not be invited to testify before the committee. At one point, Abrams was even escorted out of a Foreign Relations Committee briefing by security guards, at the behest of grinning Democratic staffers.

The bleeding of Elliott Abrams was now a hemorrhage. Abrams's supporters feared he would fall victim to the classic Washington squeeze play. To cut their losses, officials would publicly praise Abrams while seeking to pressure him to resign.

It was up to George Shultz and Ronald Reagan to decide if the blows were fatal.

SHULTZ, EVER THE political realist, didn't hesitate for a minute. He knew that Abrams had acted with his sanction and blessing throughout this difficult period. He was doing the job the president wanted him to do. Abrams was not a loose cannon, but had kept him fully informed. And he was as deeply involved with the Brunei solicitation as Abrams, and in this sense, every bit as accountable for withholding the information from the Congress. He said he was "adamant, totally adamant" that Abrams stay on. Speaking with reporters from an economic summit in Venice, Italy, Shultz acknowledged that Abrams "had a rebuilding job" to do with the Congress, and that his feisty assistant secretary was "a combative person." But, he added, "he's a good man, and a patriotic man, and a tremendous public servant." Privately, Shultz maintained that he thought Abrams had done "an excellent job" and was "taking an awfully bad rap for Brunei."

The president gave his verdict in a closed-door meeting with Shultz. He told Shultz that he was "an admirer of Abrams," and expressed "his full support."

Within days, Abrams had become a cause célèbre of the conservative right. Jack Kemp declared he wouldn't allow Abrams to be a scapegoat and organized a letter-writing campaign on Abrams's behalf. His neoconservative friends also rallied to his defense. Ben Wattenberg, still speaking as a party Democrat, said that "if the Reagan people toss him overboard, they'd suffer major wounds." Charles Krauthammer said the Democrats were making a phony argument. He pointed out that if Congress were calling for Abrams's resignation over the $10 million solicitation, they should also be calling for Shultz's resignation. But, Krauthammer said, "there are no calls." Why? "They want to get rid of Abrams because for two years he rolled over them on contra policy and because, if they can force the administration to fire the chief architect of the policy, they will have revealed the administration's weakness on Central America."

In her syndicated op-ed column, Jeane Kirkpatrick joined Krauthammer in rallying to Abrams's defense. She knew the lynch mob against Abrams was, as much as anything else, part of a naked battle over the direction of American policy. "Abrams has become a symbol of Reagan's policy of support for the contras," she wrote. "The strongest opponents of that policy think Abrams should be fired for having implemented it with energy, determination, skill, dedication and considerable success." She also carefully embedded the defense of Abrams into a larger philosophical question, concerning the problematic workings of "divided government." She noted that the two parties were at each other's throats over politics and power, in proportions that the Founding Fathers could never have foreseen. The result of such partisan activity was to hamstring American foreign policy.

That summer, Abrams appeared before the Citizens for America, a conservative group, in Washington. He did not look like a broken man. He showed little of the battering he had taken. (His staff noted that he showed up every day for work at seven, "bright and enthusiastic as ever.") The question on everyone's mind was not his policy, they knew where he stood, but his personal plans. What was he going to do?

Abrams adjusted the microphone so all the guests in the auditorium could hear his announcement. Would he resign? was the question.

"No," Abrams said, "I have no plan of going anywhere."

ON NOVEMBER 18, 1987, the dust began to settle on the Iran-contra affair as the committee delivered its final report. It was informed by the Tower Commission report, four months of intense televised hearings on Iran-contra, 250 hours of public testimony under the hot lights of Congress, thousands and thousands of pages of private depositions behind closed doors, and the appearance of thirty-two public and private officials, including foreigners, delivering their testimony. The Democratically led committee delivered a scathing public indictment that talked of a "seriously flawed" policy process. But it was telling that eight of the eleven Republicans sharply denounced the "hysterical conclusions" of the majority report, further underscoring how thoroughly the affair had devolved into partisan quarreling.

The committee, however, had found no smoking gun. Not a shred of serious evidence was produced that President Reagan had known of or authorized the diversion of profits to the contras. Not unlike with Vietnam and Watergate, one lasting institutional effect of the affair was that withholding of information from the Congress was deemed a serious offense—and a potentially criminal one—signaling a dramatic shift in the balance of power between the two branches of government. But ironically, even though the root of the whole affair was ultimately found to lie in rogue actions of NSC officials, implementing policy without full discussion before the president and all the administration's principals, Congress made no attempt to legislate changes in the National Security Council structure or staff. This too was a revealing epilogue to the whole affair.

Abrams, though roughed up, had dodged the political bullet. As the holiday lights were lit throughout the capital, for Abrams, it was a period of introspection and reassessment. The conservatives had come to his defense, for which he would always be grateful. He had emerged from this episode not just a full-fledged conservative, which he had been for some time, but a full-fledged Republican. Conversely, he would never look at the Democrats, his former party, in quite the same way again. True enough, he could have sympathy and respect for moderate Democrats, those in the mold of Scoop Jackson. But overall, there was too much bad blood, too much hostility, too many ill-feelings toward those who he felt wanted to destroy him, his family, his reputation, attacking not just all he stood for in the realm of politics, but all he loved in life.

Few had posed as inviting a target for the Democrats as Abrams. His reputation had suffered on the Hill and in the press, and he had been through hell. But with his name finally cleared in Iran-contra, he could return unfettered to what he loved most: public service. What last bit of unfinished business in Iran-contra remained appeared to be no problem. The six-year, more than $50 million investigation by Lawrence Walsh, the independent counsel appointed to look into the criminal component of the affair, had commenced. But the independent counsel's office had informed Abrams that he was not a target of the investigation.

One day, in the halls of the State Department, Abrams bumped into Max Kampelman. Kampelman, now not only the chief arms control negotiator but also Shultz's new State Department counselor, had emerged as one of the secretary's most trusted advisers. He told Abrams flat out, "No one has done more important work in this building than you."

Abrams was able to muster a smile of thanks.

He was ready to get back to work.

IRONICALLY, DURING THESE months of turmoil in Washington, the contra forces, aided by the $100 million, were gaining strength so rapidly that only the slow speed of the American weapons resupply effort was limiting the growth of their recruitment. As never before, the contras were receiving significant amounts of logistical support, training, equipment, weapons, and political advice. And the balance of forces on the ground was not just related to sheer matériel. U.S. backing provided a psychological lift to the contras, a dramatic boost against the Sandinistas. And the Sandinistas were reeling from the pressure, which in turn resulted in greater political space for struggling democratic institutions inside Nicaragua.

Yet further significant military funding for the contras was effectively out of the question. Gun-shy and dispirited, the White House was unwilling to take on the Congress in another major battle over contra aid. For their part, emboldened Democrats in Congress were unwilling to appropriate such aid. At this juncture, the U.S. government once again stood divided.

Increasingly, Congress sought to initiate its own separate foreign policy in Central America. Senator Dodd's staff aides routinely met with Nicaraguan officials, refusing to consult with or debrief the U.S. ambassador in Nicaragua, as was customary.

Later, a minor scandal also erupted when National Security Agency intelligence intercepts picked up remarkable evidence of a congressional equivalent of Iran-contra. Democratic Senator Tom Harkin and Senate staffers traveled to Latin America, and conducted their own form of diplomacy. After meeting with the Sandinistas, Harkin sought to convince *La Prensa* publisher Violetta Chamorro to accept "limited press censorship." (And while he also counseled her that she could then "violate" the agreement, there were no provisions to protect Chamorro and *La Prensa* if the Sandinistas subsequently retaliated or cracked down, leaving many to question why Harkin was more solicitous of the Sandinista regime, which sought press repression, than of the publisher who sought to defy it.) In another instance, there were startling accounts of Dodd Senate aides coaching the Sandinistas on how to deal with the Americans.

Yet when administration officials brought this information to the congressional oversight committees, and then presented the repeated incidents to the intelligence committees, no investigations were launched. The Congress was unwilling to police itself. Abrams was outraged. He was equally disgusted by Congress's usurping of the executive branch's prerogative to conduct foreign policy. But he knew the administration had only a year left, and members of Congress had adopted, in their own words, "a live and let live attitude." The matter soon died down.

ADMINISTRATION WEAKNESS WAS never more evident than when new House Speaker Jim Wright publicly took the lead on a separate foreign policy initiative toward Nicaragua. He met with the Sandinistas, bullied the Honduran government, and encouraged a Costa Rican initiative that was opposed by the administration. It was too much even for the normally unflappable Shultz, who later wrote about Wright, "He could smile at you while he cut your throat."

At one point, in August of 1987, Shultz sought to cut a deal with Wright, hatching a joint congressional-executive peace plan, the so-called Wright-Reagan Plan. It allowed humanitarian assistance to flow to the contras, called for a cease-fire in the Nicaraguan war, linked an end of U.S. aid to the contras to an end of Soviet military support for the Sandinistas, and called for national reconciliation in Nicaragua.

To Shultz's chagrin, the next day, the five Central American presidents met in Guatemala and advocated a separate peace plan, which called for an immediate halt to insurgent forces, steps toward democratization and reconciliation, and an end to outside support for regional insurgencies. It ignored the matter of Soviet aid to the Sandinistas. It also watered down the democratization provision by leaving elections up to the constitution of each country. Shultz saw the plan as weak, as insufficiently democratic, and as sidestepping the issue of the Soviets. He rejected it.

Within a day, Wright had double-crossed Shultz, immediately renouncing the Wright-Reagan Plan and embracing the new Central American plan, named for Costa Rican President Oscar Arias. Yet all was not lost.

Abrams had always argued that peace would only come to Nicaragua after genuine and fair elections, and Congress, once it cut off military aid, openly signaled its agreement with this logic. On December 8, 1987, the House Democrats passed a resolution insisting the Sandinista regime reform itself to assure free and fair procedures in advance of any elections. It called for tough political and institutional changes, ones that Abrams's State Department could have written: freedom of expression, assembly, religion, and education; abolition of arbitrary police tribunals and practices; safe return of exiles; complete freedom of the press and open access to the airwaves; the right to strike; the right of independent labor unions to publish their own material; and Indian rights.

Meanwhile, amid the throes of conflict in Washington, the Nicaraguan contras did not disband or dwindle into stateless refugees. As the fighting slowed, and they watched their fate rest on a rash of diplomatic activity, their numbers did not diminish. Amazingly, they remained a military—and political—force to be reckoned with. Although they signed a sixty-day truce with the Sandinistas in March of 1988, it broke down within weeks as the Sandinistas cracked down on *La Prensa*, halted Radio Católica, and harassed the internal opposition.

But under continued pressure from the contras and the U.S., the Sandinistas remained unable to fully consolidate their power. Here lay the seeds of a possible democratic resolution. And even while the final outcome remained uncertain, most importantly, the Soviets had been denied a beachhead in Nicaragua, were thwarted in El Salvador, and what was once viewed as impossible by much of the left and the establishment was now called a common goal: that Nicaragua should not just be free of Soviet influence, but should enjoy the same benefits of democracy that were taking hold throughout the rest of Latin America.

FOR ABRAMS, HIS last year was a time of satisfaction. He had served longer than most officials in the administration. He continued to plod toward the goal he cherished most: establishing working democracies among all the Latin American countries. As Nicaragua receded from domestic conflict, even his adversaries came to a grudging recognition that if he were an ideologue, he was a passionate ideologue for democracy. Where Ronald Reagan had been the champion of a worldwide revolution for democracy, Abrams had been his happy gladiator in Latin America.

On Abrams's watch, he continued a number of efforts first begun as assistant secretary for human rights. He defended democratic Peru and Guatemala from serious coup attempts. He vigorously fought against the consolidation of a Communist dictatorship in Nicaragua, took on the existing Communist regime of Castro in Cuba, and worked to build the political center in embattled El Salvador. With equal vigor, he lashed out against the right-wing dictatorship of Augusto Pinochet in Chile, helping to force a plebiscite, pressured the dictatorial Stroessner regime in Paraguay, and called for removal of Latin America's chief thug, Panama's Manuel Noriega.

Among Abrams's other accomplishments was assisting Haiti to oust the oppressive dictator "Baby Doc," Jean-Claude Duvalier, and working to establish a new constitution and a viable electoral process for this poorest of poor nations in the Western Hemisphere.

He also offered forward-looking policies. To quell economic discontent in the region, he supported a big-hearted and open trade policy, the Caribbean Basin Initiative, to promote free trade between the poor countries of the Caribbean and the U.S., opening up American markets to cheap and bountiful Caribbean goods and textiles.

It was a record of which he could be proud, one that belied the stereotypes of him painted by his critics. He also had the unwavering loyalty of his staff. To the very end, young political appointees like a Danny Wattenberg, or Dan Fisk, or Bob Kagan, and even his senior deputies, Foreign Service officers like William Walker and Chris Arcos, merrily remained "Abrams's cowboys." And Abrams continued to display an intellectual honesty about his convictions, never shying away from a fight over principles.

In the final months of the Reagan administration, when other officials were worn out by the abrasions of government life and were looking toward a more comfortable position in private life, Abrams went out swinging for what he believed in.

IN ONE OF the first interagency meetings of his RIG, Abrams had advocated sending a tough message to General Manuel Noriega, the military strongman leading Panama, insisting "Panama had to democratize." Nestor Sanchez, the Pentagon representative and a former CIA official, argued strongly against this, saying that the Panamanians themselves weren't calling for democracy. In a comment reminiscent of Tony Motley, who had said about Nicaragua, "it was foolish to seek its democratization," Sanchez now said Abrams was like Don Quixote tilting at windmills. But Abrams was not deterred, and waited for further opportunities to press his point. One soon came.

In mid-1986, Noriega was implicated in drug trafficking. Without naming the general directly, Abrams took this occasion to warn that the U.S. would not tolerate such activity. Still toeing a careful line down the middle, he at first rejected early congressional calls for Noriega's resignation, but began to change his mind in mid-1987, when the Panamanian leader lifted a state of emergency long enough to permit some five thousand government-inspired protesters to attack the American embassy. Then, in February of 1988, the U.S. Justice Department caught many by surprise, including Abrams, and announced Noriega's indictment on charges of drug trafficking.

This provided Abrams with the opportunity he had been looking for. He publicly called on Noriega to step down, and plotted with Panamanian opposition leaders to remove him by force. He encouraged President Eric Arturo Delvalle to dismiss Noriega. But the strongman simply ignored the order, and extracted his revenge by engineering a Panamanian National Assembly vote to remove Delvalle. The vote was unanimous, and Delvalle was forced to flee, going underground.

As tensions rose, the Reagan administration's stiff economic sanctions against Panama inspired significant anti-Noriega sentiment in the countryside. This emboldened Abrams, who confidently predicted on national television that Noriega would soon be gone. But the sanctions weren't enough, and the general maintained the loyalty of his defense forces and was able to ride out the storm.

With Noriega more entrenched than ever, Abrams hatched a new, more drastic set of plans. He called for the U.S. military to abduct the general or provide a U.S. military base in Panama as a sanctuary for the Delvalle government. This quickly brought him into conflict with the chairman of the Joint Chiefs of Staff, Admiral William Crowe.

Abrams was widely recognized as the "engine" behind the anti-Noriega policy at State. "I've never heard anything come out of Shultz on Panama that I haven't heard Elliott say more articulately and brilliantly," one White House official noted. (In 1988, Shultz was consumed with the Middle East and the Soviet Union, and largely turned Panama policy over to Abrams, much as he did with Nicaragua policy. During this time, Abrams even chaired one of the NSPG meetings, almost unheard of for an assistant secretary of state.)

Noriega himself was also keenly aware that Abrams was his most assiduous opponent. A briefing paper for Noriega written by an American consultant, Joel McCleary, simply said: "Policy toward Panama is strongly shaped by Abrams. . . . He knows the human rights community and is sensitive to those issues. . . . He, more than any other individual in the U.S. government, has a world view that will make it impossible to ever have a sympathetic understanding of the Republic of Panama."

But for Crowe and the Pentagon, Abrams's arguments that Noriega must be removed at all costs as a matter of international credibility rang hollow. Distasteful as Noriega was, Crowe felt he wasn't endangering American lives, U.S. property, or regional security interests. He didn't buy Abrams's democracy argument, and considered Abrams a "dangerous ideologue pursuing a perilous policy." More than anything else, he was reluctant to have American soldiers drawn into battle by politicians who then might be unwilling to follow through.

The sixty-three-year-old Crowe was the very antithesis of Abrams. Where Abrams was a sharp lawyer with finely honed arguments, Crowe wore a rumpled professorial facade that masked a keen intellect. The tougher the scrape, the more he put on his Oklahoma "aw shucks" attitude, drawling to disarm his opponents. Where Abrams sought to use logic and argumentation, Crowe, despite his Ph.D. from Princeton, made himself out to be a good old boy, winning his adversaries over with self-effacing jokes. Crowe also had never felt very comfortable in the Reagan administration—the more liberal and establishment-minded Crowe was never in tune with Reagan's philosophy. Indeed, he was a frequent behind-the-scenes critic of the administration with the press—and he was a tough bureaucratic infighter. He was not adverse to pulling out all the stops and saying that as JCS chairman he felt, "the risks are too great for a military operation." Only a brave president would dare question such an appeal.

In a critical March 1988 meeting with the president, Crowe effectively blunted Abrams's arguments. He warned the president that U.S. basing rights would be endangered in all countries throughout the world. He also argued that fifty thousand Americans, including ten thousand American troops, would be threatened or taken hostage. Speaking a language that Reagan understood, he then maintained that Noriega's opposition was made up primarily of "well-off Panamanians." They didn't see much point in dying to oust Noriega, and why should the U.S., he said.

"Why should the good ol' boys from Peoria, Illinois, go down and die for people in Panama driving Mercedes?" he drawled, drawing an implicit comparison between the Panamanian opposition and the contras.

Abrams never disguised his contempt for Crowe's excessive caution, what he felt was an ill-guided, post-Vietnam hangover. He accused Crowe and the JCS of a lack of will. As he later said, "The problem was a failure of nerve of the JCS, not protection of Noriega. JCS wanted to know how we could defend bases from the Panamanian Defense Forces, which were like a Mississippi police force in the 1960s, vicious, corrupt, incompetent. They had never carried out a military operation."

Crowe fired back to friends that Abrams was "arrogant, still wet behind the ears." Crowe couldn't understand why Shultz had given him power that "exceeded his capability."

In another meeting about Abrams's plan to set up a military and political leadership in exile in jointly administered Panamanian territory, Shultz came to Abrams's defense. Crowe, along with new Defense Secretary Frank Carlucci, had created an atmosphere of panic about Abrams's plan. They insisted to the president that hostages would be taken, and "at least two brigades" of additional U.S. troops, six thousand men, would be needed to augment the ten thousand U.S. troops already on the ground. Shultz's face reddened with the ever-escalating troop estimates. He said he was a marine himself, and knew that much force wasn't needed to get rid of one small dictator.

But Crowe's arguments were powerful, and held sway.

Days later, the Pentagon leaked to reporters that Abrams was coming up with "harebrained schemes." In return, Abrams fired back that Crowe was fighting him with press disclosures. For weeks, the Abrams-Crowe spat held center stage. But in the end, Crowe and the Pentagon prevailed. Reagan, who had come around to the Abrams view that action had to be taken against Noriega, reluctantly bowed to his political advisers, who feared the effect of a military operation. The plans for forceful action were dropped.

Abrams then tried to plea-bargain with Noriega, proposing that the drug charges might be dropped if he were to agree to step down and leave the country, at least temporarily. A deal was worked out in May of 1988, but Noriega got cold feet and reneged. At this point, Abrams once again broadly hinted that the U.S. might have to resort to military force to oust the Panamanian dictator. In one of Washington's more curious scenes, the lion and the lamb lay down together, and Chris Dodd publicly joined Abrams in his advocacy of a tough policy to take on Noriega. But against the powerful opposition of the JCS, Abrams's policies would again be shot down by Crowe and his colleagues.

Abrams's argument would, however, eventually hold sway, in the next administration. Then, overruling opposition in the Pentagon, President George Bush would launch a major military operation, invading Panama and capturing Noriega—a variation of the "snatch operation" that Abrams had earlier proposed, and Crowe had labeled "harebrained."

As THE ADMINISTRATION drew to a close, it was a bittersweet time for Abrams. In so many ways, the past eight years had been a remarkable political journey, far afield from his youth when he stood out as prim and proper, establishment-oriented, racking up pristine credentials at Harvard, the London School of Economics, and Harvard Law. He had moved in impressive legal circles with Washington's ultimate insiders. But he had given up the cushy establishment life, eschewing financial security, prestige, and security for the combative arena of foreign policy.

Having stood at the center of two terms of unremitting conflict, he left the Reagan administration as one of the most defiant of the counter-establishment Reaganauts. For eight years, he had galvanized the attention of political Washington, the press corps, and his adversaries abroad—usually dictators. But at home, he never played the insider's game. As a result, he was perhaps as reviled by the establishment and the political left as any other senior Reagan official. The moderate country club wing of the Republican party also kept its distance from him. The one comfortable home that he now had was among the insurgent conservative counterestablishment, and the neoconservative movement that was one of its principal intellectual engines.

Had he softened his ways, or been a little less tenacious or committed to his cause, Abrams might have met with more acceptance. But that wasn't *his* way, as his boss, George Shultz, who stuck by him, recognized. But it was also unclear that such actions would have made a significant difference, not in the raw, hard-edged years of the Reagan era. When it came to Abrams, the hostility wasn't personal as much as political, although the two gradually became indistinguishable.

Ultimately, what consoled Abrams was his belief that public service in the Cold War was not about being liked, in some ways was not even about his own career, but was about a larger geopolitical struggle between the forces of freedom and those who opposed it. Where others looked after themselves, feathering their own nests, Abrams remained loyal to the president he served.

Yet, while the establishment Wise Men had been revered as much for their loyalty to the presidency as for the policies they crafted and stood for, in the 1980s the Washington political establishment turned the virtue of loyalty on its head. When it came to Ronald Reagan, the establishment found virtue in those officials who stood against the ideas of their president, who regularly leaked, and who sought to undermine him at every turn.

But, like the postwar generation, Abrams believed in loyalty, and, in the face of opposition, he believed in the policies he championed and implemented, which were now quelling the fires of the Cold War. Increasingly at every turn, the Soviets and their proxies were being checked and even reversed by the Reagan foreign policy. And Abrams's support for democracy, his determination to stand up against dictatorships on the right and the left, was being adopted by foreign policy thinkers across the political spectrum. His ideas were being validated, just not with any mention of his name.

When Reagan's term ended, Abrams chose to move to the Hudson Institute, a conservative think tank, where he hoped to continue to push for democracy in Nicaragua and the rest of Latin America. He left his State Department office, not with a heavy heart, but with his customary optimism.

Once in his new office, Abrams laid out a picture of himself with Scoop Jackson on one side of his desk, with Ronald Reagan and George Shultz on the other, and photos of Rachel and his kids, Jacob, Sarah, and Joey, in front of him. He was only forty years old, yet he had more high-level government service than most officials have in a lifetime, was a champion of the conservative movement, and had his whole life ahead of him. He could afford some downtime, to learn, to grow, to be with his family.

By his nature, his temperament, and his talent, he was destined for controversy, and almost surely for even bigger things in a future conservative administration. In the meantime, he represented a new strain in counterestablishment conservatism, a belief first and foremost in the little guy, like the ancient Chinese custom of releasing a caged bird and watching it take flight, soaring into the heavens unfettered by man's intrusion, its course determined exclusively by nature, its own will, and its own heart.

CHAPTER 41

Mikhail Gorbachev dismally failed, not once, but twice, to wrest SDI out of the hands of the Americans. The consequences were enormous. SDI prompted gnawing frustration, crippling disillusionment, and even mounting panic, not just among the military ranks, but among the leadership at large in the Soviet Union, reinforcing a frightful sense that history was inexorably passing them by. For the U.S., the ramifications were rapid and dramatic.

Far from slowing the crusade for reform in the Soviet Union, the administration's steadfast posture on INF and SDI, combined with a willingness to talk without preconditions, hastened Soviet reform and change at an almost dizzying pace. Weinberger's unremitting military buildup squeezed a Soviet economy that was going bust, as Shultz's open but tough negotiations further wore down Soviet will. Though it was not fully apparent at the time, these were the seeds of a triumph of epic proportions sprouting through the folds of history, signaling, however tentatively, the passing of one gray age, the Manichaean struggle of American democracy and Soviet Communism, and the dawning of a still undefined but brighter, more hopeful era. Suddenly, change was the watchword.

In this age where seemingly incompatible opposites were woven uneasily into each other, Reagan grafted with Gorbachev, SDI was pitted against *perestroika,* an American hard line tugged at Soviet *glasnost,* summitry wrestled with spontaneity, the impossible became possible. What was deemed nonnegotiable now became inevitable, what liberal critics once blithely dubbed the intransigence of the U.S. administration now seemed to yield one Soviet concession after another.

After Iceland, the first tangible crack in the Soviet armor came in late February 1987, when the Soviets briskly departed from their long-held stance about medium-range missiles in Europe. They announced that the INF missiles could be singled out from the rest of the arms talks, and that a "separate agreement could be concluded, and without delay." Later in the year, the Soviets further stunned the Americans, sending them private signals that they would withdraw their troops from Afghanistan.

Yet if the incipient and sweet smell of Cold War victory was in the air abroad, in Washington, a rather different, clammier environment reigned, and a new conflict was heating up. It was the gritty smell of domestic political warfare, of bitter partisanship and institutional maneuvering, of a fierce struggle between two men, Richard Perle and Sam Nunn. It would culminate in the end of one order, the Reagan hard-line counterestablishment, and the beginning of another, a less activist policy order, largely imposed by a Democratic Congress.

There was a price to the intense style of brinkmanship of the counterestablishment. It ran contrary to the rhythms and mores of the dominant liberal Washington establishment. In an awesome display of congressional muscle flexing, what the Soviets would fail to get at the bargaining table, Congress would seek to deliver through congressional action.

On one hand, like everyone else in the executive, Perle was weakened by the Iran-contra scandal that erupted in November of 1986, engulfing the entire apparatus of government. National Security Adviser John Poindexter was replaced by Frank Carlucci, and Howard Baker took over Donald Regan's job as White House chief of staff. Both were men of moderate to conservative leanings, but they were consummate Washington pragmatists, keenly attuned to the sentiments of the Hill and quick to embrace political compromise. Not unsurprisingly, upon settling in, they immediately formed an alliance with another moderate, George Shultz.

One other major change occurred. Shultz had made Max Kampelman the State Department counselor, elevating him to the lofty position of one of his "home office" senior advisers for all policy issues, a hat he now wore in conjunction with his arms negotiator's position.

But, despite Kampelman's promotion, the tide was changing. The Soviet empire was crumbling. But, so too, it seemed at home, was the counterestablishment revolution. Perle's days in the government were numbered.

At the moment, though, Perle's most immediate problems were elsewhere. The Democrats had recaptured the Senate, and a new Armed Services Committee chairman, looking to flex his committee might and considering a bid for president, decided to mount a new challenge to the earlier Perle-Sofaer reinterpretation of the 1972 ABM treaty between the U.S. and the Soviets. This would be the catalyst for the first sparks to fly.

What was perhaps surprising, even in the raw decade of the 1980s, where the political had often become personal, where the genteel ways of the establishment had since given way to open conflict in the policy-making arena, is just how *personal* it became.

WHAT MOST OF his admirers failed to grasp was that Sam Nunn had little love for the ABM treaty. In 1985, when the administration announced that it would embrace the broad interpretation of the treaty, which would allow for the full development of SDI, the senator privately was furious.

Nunn discussed it with his arms control aide, Bob Bell. He was no great supporter of the ABM treaty, he said, but he would not tolerate actions "that would curb the rights of the Senate." He felt Sofaer and Perle were unilaterally hijacking Senate prerogatives by their reinterpretation of the treaty. Even if they were right, the Senate should have been consulted. And *he* had not been consulted.

Instead, they had trampled on the Senate's treaty prerogatives.

Bell knew that if Nunn were zealous about one thing, it was the Senate. And it was in defense of the Senate, not anything else, that Nunn, in effect, told Bell that they should be prepared to do battle with the administration.

Bell also knew this battle would establish an important precedent. Power in the Senate flowed not from losing skirmishes, but from winning them. Lose one, and your power ebbs; win one, and it grows. Perception begets power, and power begets perception. This was one they had to win.

For the wearying first months of 1986, Nunn requested access to the entire ABM negotiating record that had formed the basis for the Perle-Sofaer decision. At first, the administration stonewalled and he got nowhere. The senator was livid that the administration was playing hardball with him, and continued to make a stink. Finally, that summer, Nunn prevailed; the entire record was turned over to the Hill for review. Access to the record was carefully restricted, given only to six Senate aides with top secret clearances; among them was Bob Bell.

The record could only be reviewed in S-407, the room where classified material was stored and where top secret conversations could take place without fear of being monitored by the Soviets.

Nunn sternly told Bell to "be an honest seeker of the truth," that the outcome "should not be preordained." But even at the start, Bell was skeptical of the reinterpretation.

"What Perle and Sofaer were saying seemed incredible," he later said. He just didn't believe that Gerard Smith and John Rhinelander, the chief

American negotiators of the 1972 treaty, both failed to explain their negotiation goals to the Senate and then misled the Senate about what was achieved. Moreover, Bell knew his boss was deeply unsettled by Perle and Sofaer's actions. If Perle and Sofaer had their agenda, then Bell knew that Nunn had his. Just as a lawyer serves his client, so a Senate staffer serves his boss.

Unlike Abraham Sofaer or Philip Kunsberg, the Pentagon lawyer who first reviewed the ABM record, Bell was not a lawyer, and had no legal training. He was a graduate of the Air Force Academy, with a master's in International Relations from Tufts's Fletcher School of Law and Diplomacy. Nonetheless, Nunn turned the assignment over to him. This in itself was not necessarily an issue. Bell was a seasoned aide; he knew arms control, had traveled widely with the Senate Observer Group, and could be counted on to do his job effectively. He also knew how to play hardball.

Once given his marching orders, Bell waded into the negotiating record what he called "big-time." For days on end, he lumbered over to S-407 and sifted through the piles of documents and cables. He was at first overwhelmed by the amount of material. "Oh my God," he thought, "this is a massive amount of material to digest." For the next five months, in between the blinding Senate schedule of defense bills and Senate floor action that could run from the early morning until midnight, and his other Senate duties, Bell spent his time studying the arcane instrumentalities of the negotiating record.

In 1981, when Bell was still working for the liberal Republican Senator Charles Percy, he had sent out feelers to Perle for a job with the new assistant secretary designate. Perle didn't bite, and Bell stayed in the Senate. But overall, Bell had enormous respect for Perle, just as Nunn had enormous respect for Scoop Jackson. He didn't know Sofaer, but within weeks, he had decided that Sofaer was a "brilliant genius." After five months, he revised his estimate: Sofaer was, he thought, a brilliant genius "who had grossly misinterpreted the record."

Late that fall, he concluded that there was not a basis for the broad interpretation, and wrote a lengthy draft report, running more than 250 pages, laying out his observations and conclusions for the senator. It was at this point that he was ready to take his inquiry to the next stage.

Bell consulted with Andy Effron, the short, balding legal counsel on the Armed Services Committee for Nunn. Effron was no expert in negotiations or arms control, but he was a lawyer and a trusted Nunn hand. But Effron did not look at the original negotiating record. Instead, he talked at great length with Bell, and read his report.

He concurred with Bell's findings, and thus provided Bell with what he regarded as independent confirmation.

Bell was now ready for the next step: bringing his conclusions to the senator.

What the senator said would now have all that much more impact, given two new developments: Nunn was no longer just the ranking member of the committee but its new chairman, and the new chairman was contemplating a bid for the presidency.

IN THE PENTAGON, both Perle and Gaffney felt a certain trepidation about Nunn's impending review. From their own experience, they knew that much of what senators believed and did was "staff-driven," and they had little reason to trust Bell to carry out an honest inquiry, free of political considerations. The word about town was that Nunn was eyeing a run at the presidency, which meant he would have to cater to the arms control liberals; otherwise, they would cut him down to size, much as they had done to Aspin. What finer way to endear himself to the liberal wing of the party than by becoming a champion of the ABM treaty, they thought. It was a twofer for Nunn, who could also claim to be fighting for the Senate in the same breath.

Bell never consulted with Perle, not once, even though Senate staff and executive branch official discussions were common. This was especially uncharacteristic for someone like a Sam Nunn, who traditionally prided himself on bipartisanship.

They braced themselves for an inevitable onslaught from Nunn, but they didn't know what shape or form it would take. Only that it would happen.

EVEN AT THIS stage, nerves were getting awfully frayed over the ABM controversy. One day in the fall, the Senate Arms Control Observer Group met with Abe Sofaer in S-407. In addition to his duties for Nunn, Bell also wore the hat of staffing the Arms Control Observer Group since its inception. He was thus close to senators on both sides of the aisle, reinforced by his earlier tenure with the Republican Charles Percy.

Republican senator from Alaska Ted Stevens said: "Judge, you know that Senator Nunn says you are wrong about the ABM treaty."

Sofaer angrily fired back: "His staff is lying to him." He looked over in Bell's direction and scowled.

Then, Stevens came to Bell's defense. "Wait a minute, Judge, that is not some amorphous staff you're talking about, that's Bob Bell. We've been working with him for years."

Exasperated, Sofaer stuck to his guns, and added that Bell had misread Scoop Jackson's role and views on the ABM treaty in 1972.

Bell thought to himself that Nunn had a real reverence for Scoop, and had taken his death awfully hard. He didn't agree with Sofaer.

So here they were, each vying to interpret what Scoop Jackson thought of the treaty. But it was not his place, nor was it his style, to speak up. Bell kept his mouth shut.

The meeting ended on a sour note. When Sofaer marched out, Bell knew the upcoming months would be a real scrap.

"Once it became known that I was the point man, it was a black mark against me to the true believers," Bell would remark.

What he didn't understand was that his problem would not just be with true believers, but with SDI advocates in general, those who believed immeasurable benefits could flow from even its partial success.

SOFAER WAS DEEPLY frustrated by Sam Nunn. Nunn was always nice to Sofaer in private, but didn't hesitate to rough him up in public or distort the facts. And it didn't stop with just Sam Nunn.

From sources on the Hill, Sofaer had heard that Bob Bell and other Senate staffers had met to devise a common Democratic party strategy for the ABM treaty. They concluded that the Democrats need not address the substance of what was actually agreed upon in the 1972 treaty. Instead, Sofaer was told, they had decided to focus on Sofaer personally—to question his morality, his credibility, his honesty. New to the ways of Washington, Sofaer, they decided, was a target ripe for the picking. The staffers reasoned that if they could destroy Sofaer's reputation, the broad interpretation would die a similar death. It was a classic Washington strategy—one that Sofaer was ill-prepared for.

If one thing mattered to Sofaer, it was his reputation. But this judge, who had impressed such luminaries as Mario Cuomo and George Shultz with his legal temperament and formidable scholarly intellect, felt virtually defenseless when it came to playing what he called "the vicious Washington game." He was not a seasoned politician, but a lawyer, not a rough-and-tumble Washington insider, like Richard Perle, but, in his own words, "a New York Jew who signed up with Reagan."

In the following weeks, Sofaer reeled as the Bell strategy was set in motion. The word was put out on the Hill and in the press that Sofaer "had deliberately falsified research." He was alternately called a "whore," accused of "giving a green light to mislead the Senate," and pegged with the accusation that "he played fast and loose with the facts."

Sofaer burned. He felt the substantive arguments of his critics ranged from poor knowledge of the facts to grotesque distortions and outright lies. The hard evidence, he believed, was overwhelmingly in his favor. The record was unmistakable. But no matter how much he sought to address his critics—answering their questions, sending them letters of clarification—it seemed to fall on deaf ears. Beyond the Hill and arms control groups, he singled out the *New York Times*'s editorial page for its rampant fervor. To Sofaer, the *Times,* far more than the *Washington Post,* was the most reckless with the facts. Increasingly, Sofaer felt his critics were driven by rabid ideology—an unwavering devotion to the theology of the arms control process—even as he harbored the hope that they could be reasoned with. But they couldn't. Here, the brilliant judge was naive.

Sofaer had felt an absolute duty to present Shultz and the president with an honest finding of the administration's options. He knew Shultz would have been content with a finding that the narrow interpretation was correct, and, in the face of the Senate pressure, he had even suggested that they abide by the narrow interpretation. But unlike Nitze, who so skillfully manipulated the media and carefully cultivated the arms control groups, Sofaer relied solely on facts and reputation. Neither was enough in partisan Washington. When asked about his accusers, a weary and embittered judge simply called them "disgusting."

WHEN NUNN MET with Bell and Andy Effron, he liked their ABM treaty review. Running over 250 pages, it had extensive legal footnotes that gave it a confident air of scholarly authority. But he didn't want to release it as a report. Instead, he wanted something more immediate, more dramatic—a speech. He often liked to release his major pronouncements in a speech. They had much more punch. The press would be more likely to cover it.

For the next five weeks, Bell worked to fold the report into a speech. Drafts were written and rewritten. All told, the speech was laid out not as one event, but three, to be delivered on consecutive days. Nunn alerted his Democratic party colleagues to his intentions, so they could coordinate supporting responses.

When the time came for him to deliver the speeches, Nunn asked his staff to do one final thing. "Inform the White House," he instructed. "You can now let them know this is coming."

But while the speech was in its final stages, Nunn's planned assault was threatened by a nascent compromise, cooked up not in Washington, but, of all places, in Geneva, and with all people, Kampelman and Perle.

FOR SOME TIME, Kampelman had been watching the brewing controversy over the ABM treaty with a mixture of disgust and horror. Like Paul

Nitze, he accepted the broad interpretation, and did not discount that, during the ratification debate over the treaty in 1972, American negotiators wrongly asserted the U.S. had achieved its aims, the so-called narrow interpretation. This was what they told the Senate and what the Senate ratified. And, Kampelman felt, the Soviets were correct at the time of the original treaty signing in 1972, when they maintained that the negotiated text of the treaty embodied the broad interpretation.

But also like Nitze, Kampelman felt that what was past was past, and he believed that the Pentagon and the White House were politically unwise in asserting the broad interpretation without having the support of the Congress. It was just leading the administration into an unnecessary confrontation with the Hill, and eroding what little consensus there was behind SDI. He did not accept Perle's view that necessary testing for SDI could not be carried out under the narrow interpretation.

Moreover, Kampelman felt a judicious compromise was possible. On Saturday morning, February 28, 1987, Nitze and Perle, who were on their way to Brussels, were in Geneva, as were members of the Senate Arms Control Observer Group, led by Claiborne Pell, the chairman of the Senate Foreign Relations Committee, and including Al Gore and two respected Republicans, Ted Stevens and Richard Lugar. Taken together, the group represented the array of opinions on SDI. Kampelman decided the time was ripe to forge a consensus, on the spot.

The group convened in the bubble of the U.S. mission, and Stevens gave an impassioned talk about how the congressional Democrats and the administration were on a dangerous collision course. Congress was poised to dramatically cut SDI funding; this would unilaterally do what Gorbachev had failed to do, and would surely undercut Kampelman in his negotiations.

After listening attentively, Kampelman heartily agreed. But he had a suggestion.

After a lengthy discussion, Kampelman proposed a deal. For a fixed period, "say a year and a half, Congress would fund SDI at a modest increase without a legislative fight or seeking to enshrine a strict interpretation of SDI in law. In return, the president would give assurances that the administration would not carry out SDI tests beyond the narrow interpretation for that same time period."

Heads nodded. Everyone liked it.

The senators signed off on the idea, and Gore even volunteered to call Nunn about delaying his three speeches for a couple of weeks while they tried to forge a compromise. To the surprise of many, but not of Kampelman, Perle also signed off on the compromise. They committed the deal to paper, and Kampelman quickly cabled the details to Shultz and Carlucci at the NSC. That afternoon, Kampelman and Stevens also called Howard Baker, the new White House chief of staff.

Kampelman thought the fix was in the works, but when he returned to Washington the following week, he was aghast to learn that the White House had not contacted Gore or Nunn about finalizing the details of the compromise. Something had gone awry. He immediately asked to see the president to reactivate the compromise.

Kampelman and Reagan met in the Oval Office. Weinberger and Howard Baker were also there. Kampelman explained it as a win-win situation. "SDI would not be compromised; there would be no fight with Congress; the negotiations would not be harmed; and the president would look like a statesman."

Reagan nodded his head in apparent agreement, although he didn't say anything. But then Weinberger launched into a vigorous dissent. "It was imperative," he said, "that the U.S. embrace the broad interpretation immediately." The administration would get the money from Congress, he insisted.

Listening to Weinberger, Kampelman was appalled. He thought to himself that Cap was misleading the president.

Still, Reagan agreed to the Kampelman plan. Kampelman left the meeting in a mood of self-satisfaction. A grand compromise had been struck.

But just as quickly, the deal all but fell apart. Some liberal senators complained that Gore and Pell struck too weak an agreement, and subsequently toughened their conditions for what would be an acceptable compromise. In turn, Weinberger spoke with the president after the meeting and convinced him that the compromise would do irreparable damage to the SDI program.

Sam Nunn told his staff he felt deceived. While the possibility of a compromise still remained a technical possibility, the stage was set for a confrontation. Nunn said he had little choice but to go forward. He was going to give his speeches on the floor of the Senate on March 11, 12, and 13.

IF EVER A man were destined to be a congressional institution, it was Sam Nunn, an ardent son of the South, a scion of a distinguished political legacy, a remarkable mix of unerring political instincts and a stolid sense of personal destiny. He quickly rose to become one of the capital's most powerful politicians.

Nunn came to Washington from the dusty roadways of Perry, Georgia, the same swath of land that, from the Southern perspective, had suffered the indignation of General Sherman's relentless march to the sea.

In the early 1700s, just east of Perry, Georgia had astonishingly rich soil, ideally suited to the Southern plantation system, replete with acres of gleaming bungalows and estates, lush lawns and picnic grounds. But it was also a land founded on the backs and the blood of slaves. Reconstruction after the Civil War was a trying period, marked by conflicting feelings of Northern-imposed guilt, a deep sense of Georgia history and destiny, and a burning attachment to the land. It took years for the state to prosper, and young Sam was conscious that astride imposing patches of proud white-columned homes was another part of the state, desolate tracts where the poorest residents lived in tar paper shacks ringed by thick swamps.

Nunn's grandfather was a proud Confederate veteran, and from an early age Sam was steeped in the Southern military tradition and seared with the consciousness that the South had been ignominiously beaten. His father, a stern man, was fifty when Sam was born. His great-uncle was the legendary Carl Vinson, first elected to the House in 1914, who served the country for half a century, as chair of the Naval Affairs and then the Armed Services Committee. Nunn's eventual Senate seat was held for four decades by another proud Georgian, Richard Russell, an austere bachelor, who rose to become chairman of the Armed Services Committee and a powerful member on issues of war and peace in the 1950s. Both Vinson and Russell ardently used their power to build a strong American military, even as they evinced caution about the use of force.

It was this legacy, rather than that of the anti-Vietnam activists, which Nunn brought to the Senate when he was elected in 1972.

In his early years, Nunn was the paragon of the conservative Southern Democrat, patiently attending to the unglamorous details of defense policy, and supporting the defense buildup tentatively started in 1979 and dramatically increased by Ronald Reagan. He was a young disciple of Scoop Jackson's, a strong believer in bipartisanship in foreign affairs, and, like Scoop, fervently opposed the SALT II treaty.

When Scoop died in 1983, Nunn was regarded as a natural heir to his legacy.

But Nunn was different. Where Scoop was completely unpretentious, Nunn was tight-lipped, button-downed, and often, but not always, humorless (though in private his humor was sometimes deadly); where Scoop viewed his staff as literally an extension of his family, Nunn was always "the Senator"; where Scoop never aspired to be accepted by the Georgetown dinner party elite and establishment media barons, Nunn cared what the *New York Times* and *Washington Post* said about him. And where Scoop was a big government social liberal and his political views were shaped by the haunting images of the Jewish Holocaust and a pilgrimage to the Buchenwald concentration camp just after World War II, Nunn remained a cautious and committed son of the South.

It was perhaps predictable that Nunn did not seize Scoop's mantle, but carved out *his* own identity, in *his* image, with *his* voice, in *his* region's mold and deeply conservative values. Whatever else could be said, Nunn was "the Senator," first, foremost, and, despite his own aspirations, perhaps always.

By the time Les Aspin had survived his near defeat at the hands of the caucus, Nunn had overtaken him as the leading Democratic voice on national security. Nunn was neither the freewheeling nor original thinker that Aspin was. Nor, for that matter, was he as bold as Aspin had been in his first two years as chairman. Nunn did not get out in front of issues, but, as his staff soon learned, he hung back while opposing sides "would pummel each other into submission," and then he would come in and shape a consensus in the middle.

It was expected that Nunn would be conservative; he was, after all, from Georgia. But when Nunn campaigned for other national Democrats, something Vinson and Russell never really did, including for liberals like an Alan Cranston, it was clear he harbored deeper ambitions, perhaps even commander in chief.

In the cold months of January and February of 1987, the new chairman shook up his staff and prepared for a presidential run. For a time, he even sought out a high-profile speechwriter who could given him a larger image on the national scene, someone who could boldly package his ideas. Internally, there were still burning questions about his candidacy, particularly on domestic issues. His new administrative assistant wryly noted the tension between his Georgia background and the exigencies of his party. "He still doesn't know which side of a civil rights march he should be on—for or against—and is still conflicted on abortion."

But even as he considered this run, observers noted another of Nunn's ambitions: acting as de facto secretary of defense from the secure confines of the Senate. He knew if he moved too far to the left, he would lose his credibility with the military as a leader on national security; if he ratified the administration's policies on everything, he would be relinquishing his and his committee's oversight prerogative and forgoing the good graces of his party. And the fact was, the senator insisted that on all major matters, *he* be consulted. This would give him the best of all worlds: the security of his Senate seat, casting him in the role of the white knight, conferring legitimacy to the liberal national Democratic party on defense policy, ensuring that his party and the administration alike came to him on matters of great importance. In short, like his great-uncle before him, and his predecessor, he was the quintessential senator, and an avid devotee of the Senate as a revered institution.

So in March, when Nunn prepared himself to take on the administration, sharply challenging its interpretation of the ABM treaty, the fight was more over the legitimate role of the Senate than the actual veracity of the reinterpretation itself.

It was also not a step he took lightly, nor was it a fight he was prepared to—or could afford to—lose.

CHAPTER 42

"The Senate has a crucial constitutional role in treaty making and thus has a direct interest in ensuring that treaties are accurately presented and faithfully upheld," Senator Nunn thundered, beginning his lengthy review of the ABM treaty dispute.

Nunn had finally waded down to the Senate floor, and, for three days running, held forth; standing upright and looking serious, he opined on the murky esoterica of treaty law and ratification.

"If the president can unilaterally change treaty obligations which were clearly understood and accepted by the Senate at the time it consented to ratification, it dramatically alters the Senate's constitutional role as a co-equal partner in this area."

He charged that Sofaer's work was based on a "complete and total misrepresentation" of critical parts of the historical record. The administration's analysis is, he said, "absurd," "illogical," "woefully inadequate," "ideologically driven," and "fundamentally flawed."

His concluding shot: if the administration persists in pressing its view, the reinterpretation "constitutes a fundamental constitutional challenge to the Senate as a whole."

The next day, March 12, while Nunn was still holding court, Richard Perle formally submitted his long-planned resignation to the president, "effective after an orderly transition in my office."

WITHIN WEEKS, any chance of an ABM compromise between the executive and the Congress rudely fell apart, and Nunn reinforced his powerful warning on May 5, when he pushed through an amendment in his committee that would prohibit funding for any SDI tests that would violate the traditional interpretation.

. . .

SITTING IN HIS office, Perle was disillusioned, even disgusted with Nunn, sometimes exploding at the mention of Nunn's name ("I have to deal with Sam Nunn *now*."). First, there had been the flap over the book; now this display over the ABM treaty.

"I think," he said, "that my view on this matter is more authoritative than Sam Nunn's, who wasn't there." Nunn's reference to the "rule of law" for the ABM treaty was empty, he added, and was "pure rhetoric." His motivation was purely political: "I don't think it's a very effective way to run for president," Perle said.

It irritated Perle that Nunn never bothered to call him once, to see if they could thrash it out. Nor did it escape his attention that Scoop had actively advanced Nunn's career, making him vice chairman on the Government Operations Committee, and "*I was all for it.*" In his eyes, Nunn was no Scoop Jackson; he was, however, bordering on becoming a partisan politician. He was "overrated."

"He didn't call me, not once," Perle said. As political as it was, it had become, he conceded, by Nunn's failure of courtesy to work with Perle, very personal.

Whatever Perle's political differences with Aspin, who had to bob and weave to the left far more than Nunn, their relationship remained professionally sturdy and personally warm. With Nunn, it was like ice.

The debate over the ABM treaty was, Perle felt, a phony debate. He was convinced that Gerard Smith, the head negotiator in 1972, had failed to secure the narrow interpretation with the Soviets, but nonetheless sold it that way to the Senate—misleading the legislators in the process. Yet this was not seriously explored by the Senate. Even Paul Nitze, who *was* a member of the delegation in 1972, agreed that the broad interpretation was correct. But to the Democratic Senate, it no longer mattered.

"It's becoming," Perle told colleagues, "springtime for arms control around here." With the Democrats mightily striking back, the arms control mafia was, he felt, getting its way.

Perle felt it was the right time to leave. In his mind, he had accomplished his three main policy objectives: he had helped keep the Reagan administration from concluding new agreements he deemed unsound, and from observing those he was against from the start. Moreover, with his zero option, he had set a standard for meaningful arms control, agreements that were more than cosmetic arms control blithely equated with peace, but that were militarily significant, verifiable, and balanced, and that genuinely restrained Soviet forces. Third, he had instituted policies restricting defense and technology transfer that put additional pressure on the Soviets.

The fact was he deplored the black hat–white hat view of the liberal establishment. Say you are for arms control, whatever the actual result, and you are a good guy; insist on holding out for real arms control, and look after U.S. security interests first, you are a bad guy.

He intended to join the American Enterprise Institute for Public Policy Research, one of Washington's most influential think tanks and home to such leading policy intellectuals as Jeane Kirkpatrick, Ben Wattenberg, Herb Simon, and Michael Novak; he also would remain an adviser to both Weinberger and Shultz, in addition to writing a monthly column on international affairs for the news magazine *U.S. News & World Report*. After more than fifteen years of a government salary, he could at last make money lecturing and consulting, and write the novel based on his own experiences. Finally, he could spend more time with his family, Leslie and Jonathan.

In his letter of resignation to the president, he exuded the same sense of confidence and acerbity that had marked his six years in government. "While much difficult negotiation lies ahead, I believe you will succeed where your detractors failed and that you will finally prove that those who appear most passionate for arms control are often the least competent to go out and negotiate for it."

Ironically, having announced his intention to leave, the steady paragon of the liberal establishment, the *New York Times*, suddenly paid Perle rare homage. Devoting a lead editorial to him, the editors acknowledged that he dominated administration arms control policy making for six years, and averred, "this 'Prince of Darkness' has shone brightly." Yet they couldn't help but add one last dig: "In undermining more than he built he pressed a useful caution to sometimes harmful extremes."

Perle took it all in stride. But before leaving, he wanted to pave the way for an orderly transition: arranging for his faithful deputy, Frank Gaffney, to succeed him, and facing his congressional accusers one more time, before upcoming Senate hearings on the ABM treaty.

FOR THREE DAYS in March and April, the Senate Foreign Relations and Judiciary Committees held rare joint hearings on the ABM treaty, convened by the two liberal Democratic chairmen, Joseph Biden of Delaware and Claiborne Pell of Rhode Island. The joint hearings had all the makings of a full-court press—the Democrats thought they could embarrass the administration, and were determined to push their momentum to the hilt.

On March 26, Sofaer and Perle were summoned to be among the witnesses to testify. The Democrats were waiting. Massachusetts liberal John Kerry repeated the same charge that Nunn had made—the administration was "precipitating a constitutional crisis" (although neither he nor Nunn fully spelled out just what that crisis really was). Biden, contemplating his own presidential bid, added his blistering commentary, accusing Sofaer of "unjustified politicization of the office."

Under this withering criticism ("I can't believe my ears," Biden, his eyes widening, even mocked sarcastically at one point), Sofaer recoiled. He defended his broad interpretation, but the body language and tone of this small, energetic man was defensive, which, to his critics, put the administration in a less than flattering light. Personally, Sofaer was outraged. He felt Biden and his staffer John Rich "played very fast and loose with the truth." He also felt Biden treated him not just like "a scoundrel," but as "less than a human being."

Perle thought to himself that Sofaer was new to the rough-and-tumble world of Senate politics, and little in private life could have prepared him for the harsh grilling he was now undergoing.

Perle, however, was no stranger to the ways of the Senate, nor was he intimidated by its tactics. He knew what members did and didn't respond to.

"I lived through the ratification record and I remember it well, indeed," he testified. "The thing that stands out most clearly is the paucity of discussion on the Senate floor about the issue that is now under discussion."

Senator Edward Kennedy interrupted, growling, "Not Scoop Jackson. Thirteen pages of questions on exotic systems in the record. Thirteen pages."

"Indeed," Perle shot back, "I wrote most of them."

"If I may continue," Perle said, concluding darkly, "this was not the Senate's finest hour."

Once more, both sides claimed Scoop Jackson's mantle to support their views. But in the end, Biden and Perle sparred inconclusively over Scoop Jackson's views of the ABM treaty, and why he ultimately voted for it.

Returning to his office that afternoon, Perle knew that the committee Democrats, following Nunn's lead, were stacking the deck. This was never more apparent than in late May, when the committee gave pride of place to William Sims, a disgruntled lawyer who quietly left government for private practice in Arizona, but who had worked briefly for Sofaer.

"Defense seemed to be in the driver's seat," Sims said, and the "deliberations" on the subject were "rushed." The result: the president was provided a "flawed decision memorandum."

Yet when pressed by Senator Arlen Specter, a Republican from Pennsylvania, Sims freely acknowledged that his perspective was as "a lowly staff attorney in the process," and that as the "youngest attorney" he could be "very wrong." Moreover, he added that he did feel "there was enough ambiguity in the negotiating record to leave room for the broad interpretation."

Sims gave the appearance of being fair and honest in his testimony, but he had his own arms control agenda. Moreover, his clarifications and qualifications went unreported. Instead, in Senate debate, he was held up as "exhibit A," proof of administration perfidy, duplicity, prevarication, and, by implication, of Perle's nefariousness.

PERLE LEFT GOVERNMENT in June. Two weeks later, he spoke at a meeting of the Council on Foreign Relations in New York. It was a bright and sunny day, and the stabs of light piercing through the elegant windows left a special glow in the mahogany-paneled Elihu Root Room as Perle spoke.

That day, history completed another turn. In 1978, Perle and Larry Smith, then both Senate aides, had squared off in a debate at the offices of *Time* magazine over SALT II. This time Perle was the sole speaker; Smith was in the audience. In the question-and-answer session, Perle was attacked repeatedly for his stubborn attachment to INF and SDI, and his excessive suspicion of the Soviet Union. Still, he was at his best, articulate, lively, displaying deft nuances on defense policy.

Larry Smith rose, looking slightly agitated, and added his voice to the fray. He intoned solemnly, "Richard, you and I have had many discussions and debates over the years about policy. But I want to talk politics."

Perle made a face, looking vaguely annoyed.

"Are you a Democrat or a Republican?"

The intent of the question was not immediately apparent. Was the wrong answer to say he was a Republican, and that he had abandoned his roots? Or that he was a Democrat, and he was a traitor to his party?

Perle smiled and thought of Scoop Jackson, whom he loved like a father. The answer was a no-brainer. "I'm a Scoop Jackson Democrat, and I hope the party produces someone like him to lead them again soon to the White House, someone courageous and smart, like a Bill Bradley, who supported the contras. That would be good for the party, and, I daresay, it could be good for the country."

FROM THAT SEPTEMBER through December, the Congress voted to prohibit testing of SDI components without its prior approval, thus codifying the narrow interpretation of the ABM treaty legislatively. SDI funding was also sharply reduced by a third. Cap Weinberger had since resigned, and was replaced by Frank Carlucci. Colin Powell was elevated to the head of the NSC. A new order was in power, one that would not have been appropriate to the exigencies of the Cold War just two years earlier, let alone six, but which now fit in with the tenor of the times, and with the current temperament of the president.

With Weinberger gone, Carlucci and Howard Baker, both pragmatists, quickly reached an accord with Nunn and the Congress—but on Congress's terms, not those of the administration. SDI would, in effect, be restricted to the traditional interpretation of the ABM treaty for one year—that is, until Reagan left office. It was labeled as a compromise, but it was far more, or more precisely, it was far less than that. As a practical matter, it was Congress imposing its will—and for all purposes served to deliver a slow death knell to SDI. On this issue, Sam Nunn, working with the liberal establishment, actually leading it, prevailed.

YET IN THE twilight of the Reagan era, Perle's hard-line views had paid off. The Soviets came to Washington for the third summit, in December of 1987, this time to sign the first ever nuclear arms reduction treaty, the INF zero option that was Perle's brainchild. Six years earlier, it was scoffed at by establishment experts and high-minded liberals as non-negotiable, and rashly dismissed as a public relations stunt. Now, on the day of the accord's signing, December 8, it had become the model for arms control negotiations, vindicating Perle's philosophy after two decades of wandering in the wilderness.

The Soviets also were set to leave Afghanistan, the most significant sign of the slow, inexorable ebb of the Soviet empire. And on SDI, the two sides agreed to disagree—or, in Max Kampelman's memorable phrase, "We decided to kick the can down the road."

Ailing at home, and needing respite abroad, the Soviets no longer had any leverage to curtail SDI, but it didn't much matter at this stage. SDI had brought the Soviets back to the bargaining table and kept them there. The technological wonders that it evoked were the central preoccupation of the Russians, the dominant symbol that their Marxist system could no longer compete with the combined military might and entrepreneurial system of the Americans.

The Soviets were in retreat.

No other major progress was made in arms control at this summit, but that too didn't much matter. Unable to continue unrestrained military competition with the U.S., the Soviets were quickly withdrawing on the international stage. The Soviet threat to the U.S. was receding, and peace seemed to be suddenly breaking out everywhere. This was not because the Soviets had fewer weapons, but because their economy could not support their military adventures, and their political system and international aims had become less confrontational, more focused on internal concerns than foreign conquest. An arms deal over strategic weapons was in fact secondary, far less important than the changes now taking place within the Soviet empire. For this reason, Perle opposed a rush to further arms treaties in offensive weapons negotiated against a tight deadline, not until they, like INF, truly served American interests. In the end, Reagan, acting on his instincts, would in effect follow his advice, and it would not be until the next administration that a START treaty would be signed.

For years, Perle had preached that arms control was a symbol, a metaphor for the larger state of U.S.-Soviet relations, a manifestation of the intense political rivalry between two adversarial camps. During the darkest days of the Cold War, he, like Reagan, felt the U.S. had to maintain a strong defense posture, forcing the Soviets to make the hard choices the West made on a day-to-day basis, deciding between guns and butter, and that if this competition were brutally prosecuted, pressing the ailing Soviet economy to face the contradictions of a Marxist economy and imperial expansion, it could one day crumble of its own weight. Now that moment was approaching. America, in Cap Weinberger's words, had "sent an unmistakable message of resolve under Reagan."

It was a sharp contrast to a decade earlier, when the ideas and ideals of America and the democratic West were in stark decline. Afghanistan, Central America, Africa, a failed SALT II treaty, increasing repression of human rights in the Soviet Union: the world back then was a jumble of escalating chaos and conflict. As George Shultz would lament, under Carter, "the U.S. was the Hamlet of nations."

But now, in 1987, discussion of democracy and human rights, raised at Geneva and codified at Reykjavik, was commonplace; the Soviets were suing for peace in regional conflicts; even the future monopoly of the Communist party itself within the Soviet Union seemed jeopardized. All this was a stark reminder of just what Reagan and his counterestablishment had achieved in only six years.

Both Weinberger and Shultz would later ascribe much of the same explanation for the historic change: confronted by the U.S. in every arena and on every issue for six years, the Soviet Union was literally imploding. Weinberger focused especially on the military buildup, SDI, and the European missile deployments. For his part, Shultz believed INF had been the turning point and then, finally, Reykjavik. Gorbachev later told him that it was Reagan's performance at Reykjavik and his insistence on keeping SDI that, once and for all, shifted the balance and led Gorbachev to decide that the time had come "to call it off."

Whatever the ultimate explanation, the Cold War was, after more than four decades, finally coming to a close.

Never was this more evident than on the third and final day of the summit, when Gorbachev brought his motorcade to a screeching halt, jumped out of his car at the corner of Connecticut Avenue and L Street, one of the capital's busiest intersections, pumped out his hand to astonished Americans and waved merrily to the crowd, like an old-fashioned American pol. Even the general secretary of the Communist party was emulating the rites and rituals of the American system.

PERLE HIMSELF LEFT government in the nick of time. It took the likes of a Richard Perle to help get Ronald Reagan to the remarkable changes in 1987, but it took the amazing instincts and far-reaching vision of Ronald Reagan to know exactly when to close the deal.

Having faithfully served his country through its most tense and trying era, from the aftermath of Afghanistan and Desert One to post-Reykjavik, Perle saw little need to stay on. He felt that government was about service and commitment to one's country and its ideals. The Cold War was not fully over, but the Soviets were weakened, perhaps fatally. No longer did the shadow of nuclear Armageddon hang daily over the heads of Americans; more than at any time in the past forty years, this had become somewhat more like normal times, before the onslaught of the Cold War. Perle's work was largely done, his legacy and its fruits largely in place.

Upon going to the American Enterprise Institute, Perle was a virtual hero to his admirers, an enigmatic legend to political watchers, and still the villainous "Prince of Darkness" to his detractors. He was the subject of numerous honors and awards, and he reveled in his newfound celebrity. But there was also an attempt by the liberal establishment to rewrite history, purge his ideas and contributions. In one telling and early example, Sidney Blumenthal of the *Washington Post*, having sought to savage Les Aspin on the morning of his critical chairmanship battle the year before, now wrote three articles on consecutive days in the influential "Style" section on Perle, reputed to be the longest series ever devoted to one individual.

But the series, like so many of the attacks on Perle throughout the years, was little more than a clever philippic, an ideological broadside against a caricature, lacking serious analysis. It was hardly suitable commentary on someone who history would boldly record was the stepfather of the first nuclear arms reduction treaty in history.

ONE DAY IN 1988, Perle went up to the Hill to testify before his old friend Les Aspin. Walking past the Capitol, he recalled a time when moral imperatives had seemed so clear and compelling, and he caught himself reminiscing about that era, when a sense of high purpose had swept him through the late 1960s, the early 1970s, and into the 1980s. His time in the Congress, with Scoop, one of the true quiet heroes of American history and of the Cold War, was filled with tightly knit friendships and old certitudes, a provocative reminder of some of the best years of his life.

But some of the clarity had changed with perspective. Henry Kissinger once predicted that his old nemesis, Richard Perle, would not succeed in the executive branch, but Kissinger was wrong. In turn, Perle understood much of what Kissinger had gone through in his tenure, including putting up with his and Scoop's steady stream of criticisms ("Henry just wanted it to stop" he later acknowledged). With the benefit of hindsight, Perle had come to appreciate Kissinger's own selfless and bold contributions to the nation, even as they had, and did, differ on a number of policy prescriptions such as détente, though not on the centrality of American security and the intrinsic worth of liberal democracy.

Once out of office, Perle still kept involved in the affairs of state. His political columns in *U.S. News* were widely read and quoted, George Shultz still called on him for advice, he was a regular attendant at policy conferences and the Defense Science Board, and he even advised one of the 1988 Republican presidential candidates, Jack Kemp.

But more and more, Perle spent time at home, with Leslie and Jonathan. There were not just his elegant dinner parties, but hot dogs and burgers at cookouts with friends, not just policy discussions about the twists and turns of the Cold War, but twisted ankles and rumpled clothes at soccer games for Jonathan, and beyond his summers in Provence, he continued to take the stream of Russian émigrés pouring out of the Soviet Union into his home, his heart, and his life.

PERLE WAS NEVER afflicted with Potomac Fever. But while his eventual return to government as a Democrat in a Republican administration was certain, and, for many, he remained a likely candidate for secretary of defense, his pursuits now turned inward—and outward.

One project had a special meaning to him, adding a huge addition to his home in the form of a study. His address and telephone number, long unlisted for fear of terrorists, were now readily accessible. The house itself was an architectural hybrid: a rebuilt bungalow in fashionable Chevy Chase, remodeled with honey-colored natural cedar shingles and expanded with a slightly postmodern style, employing motifs of the past, columns, window circles, and pediments, to fit into practical accoutrements of a modern home. The most spectacular part of the house was its world-class kitchen, with its double ovens, a large restaurant gas stove, set inside a space so expansive that it made the rest of the house look like an anteroom. It was framed by multimullioned windows that peered into the landscaped backyard.

But now, Perle added a massive study, itself the size of two rooms in a normal-sized house. Like the rest of the house, it self-consciously flowed from the kitchen, and was a product of the juncture of postmodern aesthetics and Yankee functionalism.

The study was entered via a revolving door from the kitchen. It was lined with bookshelves built into the east and west walls; then, an internal second-story balcony overlooking his desk area was attached to his master bedroom, organically linking the room with Leslie; and finally, an imposing twenty-five-foot cathedral ceiling was added, filling the study with openness and light. The study was then lined with books and decorated with personal mementos from trips around the world, many exotic and rare gifts from heads of state and defense ministers, but also including little handmade dolls evoking the musical *Fiddler on the Roof*, playfully arranged around the room. The floors were covered with richly pigmented rugs from Turkey and Iran.

When spring came, Perle hung a painting by an Egyptian Jew, which he had picked up quite by happenstance in Provence, to the left of his large country French desk by the eastern wall. The colors were a unique combination, muted yet fervent blues and soft greens, conveying serenity. It was the portrait of a thin woman sitting upright, her lips pursed impishly, her hair strung quietly into a ponytail, her hands gently folded on her lap. She sat serenely, staring out to the north, through an expanse of light-filled windows, openly looking out into the garden and the world, where eight-year-old Jonathan played, uninhibited, in full sight of his father on the first floor, his mother on the second.

EPILOGUE:

"Tear Down This Wall"

The Reagan era came to an end much the way it began: with a breathtaking revolution against an old and decrepit order.

Its formal end was not marked by the moment when Ronald Reagan gripped his wife's hand on a cold wintry afternoon in January of 1989, congratulated his successor, George Bush, gave one last wave, and bid farewell to return to his beloved California ranch. Rather, it came eleven months later, on November 9, 1989, the day when the Berlin Wall fell, symbolizing the toppling of brutal Communist regimes from Budapest to Prague and Cracow to Tbilisi, as the Cold War came to a stunning close, and a continent cheered.

But as word of the revolution seeped into the inner sanctums of the Washington establishment, the reaction was at first oddly restrained. No one had foreseen, let alone even dreamed of, such a remarkable event. The new Bush White House moved cautiously.

Discussions in the paneled chambers of the Harold Pratt House, the inner sanctum of the Council on Foreign Relations, were marked by a comparable temperance. It was a "set of events to be managed," most assembled concluded, the poetry of the moment almost completely lost amid the drone of the foreign policy technocracy.

For the prophets of détente and for die-hard doves, the event had a jarring, even uncomfortable, ring to it. The euphoria of the young people madly chipping away at the Berlin Wall, smashing its concrete, and dancing ecstatically on its crumbling remains, stood in stark contrast to those in the West who had for years preached coexistence with the Communist world, long sounding alarms at Reagan's tough talk against the Soviets, warning that it signaled another "menacing round in the escalating arms race."

But this was not what happened.

The reverberations of the collapse were almost without precedent. Not a single shot had been sounded. Instead, it was the sweet music of democracy that had lifted the Iron Curtain of Communist repression. A transformation of unbelievable proportions was taking place. The long hand of history had been reversed in one decade, and the dreary pessimism of the 1970s had given way to the democratic aspirations of burly dockworkers, avant-garde writers, former apparatchiks, and a legion of other heroes, who had silently braved the gulag, outlived the work prisons, outsmarted the secret police, and, blustery winter after winter, had never lost faith that, at some point, their destiny would once again be theirs.

Speaking from his stark, crudely paneled office in Gdansk, the framed symbol of Solidarity watching from the wall, Lech Walesa, clad in a short-sleeved white shirt, his beefy hands flying as he spoke, would boisterously tell how Ronald Reagan and his policies "gave strength and sustenance" to his people, and "helped defeat the Communists." The supporters of the Czech Velvet Revolution that produced Václav Havel, looking more like beatniks with corduroys and thick black glasses than slayers of the Red Army, would echo Solidarity, as would countless other dissident movements throughout Eastern Europe and the Soviet Union.

As the fading remnants of a decadent and evil order were being quickly swept away, the future was now theirs. And ultimately, even as they heaped much deserved credit on Ronald Reagan, so was the revolution.

Now on the outside, Reagan and his people were perhaps equally surprised by the suddenness of Communism's collapse. But it was an outcome that they had not just dreamed about, but also assiduously and deliberately worked toward since the start of his administration. Even in the quiet satisfaction of his final days, Reagan remained a staunch proponent of the worldwide democratic revolution he had proclaimed in 1982.

When in June 1987 the seventy-six-year-old Ronald Reagan stood erect at the Brandenburg Gate in Berlin, and challenged, "General Secretary Gorbachev, if you seek peace, if you seek prosperity . . . come here to this gate! Mr. Gorbachev, open this gate! Mr. Gorbachev, tear down this wall!" his detractors immediately wrote this off as another dangerous example of his "simplistic rhetoric of confrontation." They were wrong. In preaching the language of freedom, Ronald Reagan was seeking to keep in motion an unshakable chain of events and energies that would lead to the inexorable demise of the socialist system.

In May 1988, during his final summit with Gorbachev, in Moscow, Reagan praised the positive changes that Gorbachev had instituted, declaring the "evil empire" a relic of "another time, another era." But once again, the president, although physically less steady than he used to be, was unyielding in his insistence on greater individual freedom and more democracy. Speaking a language that he hoped would touch the atavistic stirrings of the Russian soul, Reagan quoted the Russian poet Pushkin to Gorbachev. In a reassuring but firm voice, he urged continued change, saying, "It's time my friend, it's time. The heart begs for peace, the days fly past. It's time, my friend, it's time."

Gorbachev had long since learned his lesson and knew better than to quarrel with Reagan. Since Reykjavik, he saw that what Reagan said, he meant. And he knew that Reagan was both a fighter *and* a peacemaker.

After strolling through Red Square, when formalities were again about to begin, and after the two men had the very last of their disagreements, over a communiqué, Gorbachev decided not to quibble with the president. The old rivalry between these two great leaders was now a friendship. The younger Soviet leader, who like Reagan was ready to take his own place in history, instead smiled, wrapped his right arm around Reagan in a warm clasp, and said of their last summit, "Mr. President, we had a great time."

Eighteen months later, with the quiet lighting of 100,000 candles in Wenceslas Square, the toppling of a wall, and the eventual counting of Russian ballot boxes, the Cold War had drawn to a close.

AMAZING HOW IT all came together. Explanations will be pored over and debated by historians for decades to come, but invariably they will say this: Under Ronald Reagan, everywhere the Soviets had turned, their pressure was met by U.S. counterpressure. Where the Soviets had supported Marxist-guerrilla movements, their imperial gains were checked and reversed by U.S.-backed anti-Communist groups; where they had blustered that "History is on our side," the U.S. rocked the very conceptual foundations of their empire with robust ideological warfare in defense of democracy; and where the Soviets had deployed their missiles, the U.S. refused to back down and firmly put its missiles into place. The INF deployment was the first crossroads at which a then precarious Cold War decisively turned. The Soviets were never again the same, although this was just the beginning. Eventually, when they could no longer compete, not militarily, not politically, not ideologically, not economically, in one last desperate attempt, Gorbachev sought to reverse the tide, at Reykjavik. He did not succeed. But this historic event at Iceland had its own epiphany. Rather than simply back the wounded bear into the corner, Reagan made it clear to Gorbachev that the U.S. stood not just for freedom, not simply for strength and principle, but also for peace. The Soviets saw the inevitable, and then took the only feasible door left open to them, and, in turn, they too chose peace, even at the price of dismantling themselves. And so it happened, the beginning of the end, and then the end itself.

SO THIS WOULD be the Cold War's epitaph: no less momentous than the Allied and American victories in World Wars I and II, America's winning of the Cold War liberated entire nations and freed ordinary individuals from tyranny. And Ronald Reagan and his administration won it without sacrificing battalion upon battalion of bright, young lives, without dotting any continent with freshly dug American graves. It was a marvelous thing, and rightly a time for celebration, both of the promise and possibility of democracy, and of the complex magic of what the writer Mark Helprin once called "an infinitely expansive universe."

YET AMIDST THE astonishment of one old order being replaced overseas, at home, another old order had once again reestablished itself. Ronald Reagan's counterestablishment was not welcome in President George Bush's administration. Bush filled his ranks primarily with Eastern establishment Republicans, who shared little of the optimism, the can-do spirit, or the sense of destiny that had galvanized the counterestablishment.

After eight years of gripping the capital and the world, after fighting and winning the Cold War, Reaganism and the counterestablishment were not just relegated to the back bench, they weren't even members of the team.

On issue after issue after issue, Bush, like Reagan before him, would confront a bitterly partisan Congress. But there was a huge difference. Reagan was a big-tent man, standing less for partisanship and more for his philosophy of smaller government, greater individual freedom, and a dominant American leadership role in the world. Shining stars in his administration were not just men like George Shultz or Cap Weinberger, but could be Democrats, like a Jeane Kirkpatrick or a Richard Perle. His most cherished policies, like human rights or Central America, could fall into the hands of a Max Kampelman, the consummate hard-line negotiator, or an Elliott Abrams, a dedicated and tenacious defender of the Reagan Doctrine. Reagan's was an administration founded on principle, not political party, and was dedicated less to getting along than to getting the job done.

Bush was different. A skilled and extraordinarily decent public servant, and a most seasoned foreign policy pro of the old school, he did remain a partisan—but as a quintessential member of the Washington establishment, he was also a ready compromiser with Congress. If Bush wanted one thing—though he rarely got it—it was to cooperate with the Democratic barons on the Hill, and there was little place for the counter-establishment's intense style of policy making in the more refined, more upper-crust Bush administration. (The most notable exception was Bush's defense secretary, Dick Cheney, the calm, measured Wyoming congressman. He was gutsy and extraordinarily capable, a man of leadership, sound common sense and a clear head, and a true Reaganaut. Another exception was Defense Undersecretary Paul Wolfowitz.)

Shunned by the Bush people, damned by the Democrats, the counter-establishment had to be content to make their voices heard from their think tank warrens, on the op-ed pages, and in policy conferences around Washington. For the most part, after eight years of being in the spotlight, they quietly receded into the background, as though biding their time.

ALL HIS LIFE, Max Kampelman, a pacifist turned hawk, a lawyer turned diplomat, had been a tireless warrior for peace. No issue had consumed him more. And, in leaving the Reagan administration, Kampelman managed, as he so often did, to float above the furor, his name intact. Even his enemies paid homage to his considerable contributions to public service.

He was also, after years in the law, a wealthy man. Living in his large, comfortable Victorian mansion, he could have been content in blissful retirement, spending more time with his wife, Maggie, doing laps in his pool, attending Washington's many social functions as a guest of honor, bouncing his grandchildren on his knees. But retirement from government only led to a whirlwind of further activity. Despite having suffered a heart attack in 1987, Kampelman remained strangely ageless. He returned to his old law firm, with the honorific status "of counsel." He spent most of his time working on the numerous boards on which he served, shaping the emerging political debate, writing his memoirs, and continuing his quest to make a difference.

In 1989, he assumed the post as chairman of Freedom House, a preeminent private group that monitored the progress of liberal democracy around the world. With a sense of satisfaction, Kampelman noted in 1990 that the spread of democracy, fragile, often embryonic, had nevertheless seized hold from Asia to Latin America and "far outnumbered any other political system around the world." To Kampelman, it was a rich legacy of the Reagan era.

But Kampelman was not immune to the continuing tug of public service. When George Bush's secretary of state, James Baker, asked him to remain engaged in the newly democratizing Eastern Europe, he cheerily said yes. In so doing, Kampelman was serving his fourth president. In 1990, and again in 1991, he led American government delegations to conferences that further reviewed and built upon the provisions of the Helsinki Accords, over which he had presided in Madrid in the 1980s. For Kampelman, these conferences, designed to perpetuate the concept of democracy and the rule of law, were a "thrilling contrast" to the earlier difficult meetings in Madrid that had spanned the better part of four years during the Cold War's tensest moments.

But, in 1992, Kampelman would feel another tug, older than his record of service, and still, after all these years, strong. He was drawn back to the Democrats. Kampelman had never changed parties, although he remained deeply troubled by the Democratic left, disgusted by its "disdain about our own system." He inveighed against its resistance to "the realities of the Communist failure" and worried about a party that was "anti-anti-Communist" at a time when the whole Communist world was seeking to overthrow the shackles of Marxism-Leninism, although he found the party's hostility toward national defense, as well as the new liberalism's aversion to patriotic values, appalling, and feared that the Democrats might have lost their qualifications to govern in international affairs.

Yet, sitting in his office, a lawyer's office filled with beautiful antique chairs of deep green leather, after years of being out of partisan politics, Kampelman was focused on the 1992 presidential campaign.

For the better part of two decades, the neoconservative counterestablishment had been held together by enduring friendships, deeply shared views about the Soviet Union, and shared service fighting the Cold War. Once the Soviet Union formally dismantled itself in 1991, however, cracks over domestic policy that had once lain beneath the surface began to appear. And as the George Bush–Bill Clinton campaign swung into high gear, they could no longer be papered over.

Max Kampelman was drawn to Bill Clinton.

Clinton glibly reeled off facts and figures about the domestic state of the country, and seemed to sound the music of empathy for an America portrayed as adrift at home. And for those who listened hard enough, he claimed to be and often talked like a "new Democrat," a misnomer that, in truth, really meant an old-style Coalition for a Democratic Majority Democrat: tough on defense, preaching hard work and equal opportunity, pro-business, playing by the rules. For those Democrats who in their hearts still clung to the notion that their party would one day move to the center, Bill Clinton seemed to be their man. Clinton was also pro-

Israel, thus setting himself apart from many in the Bush administration. And he had even headed the Democratic Leadership Council, the group of moderate Democrats that had formed in the mid-1980s, after many in CDM's ranks had joined the Reagan administration.

Two former executive directors of the Coalition for a Democratic Majority, Penn Kemble and Josh Muravchik, stalwart opponents of McGovernism, signed on to support Clinton's campaign. Washington lawyer Peter Rosenblatt spoke on Clinton's behalf. So did Les Aspin's old buddy, as well as one of Carter's harshest critics, Jim Woolsey, who had also led two CDM task forces on defense. Another moderate, Congressman David McCurdy, beseeched Democrats to support his "fellow moderate" Bill Clinton. Ben Wattenberg cast his lot with Clinton too. Declaring that Clinton "talks the talk," he asked, "will he now walk the walk?" But the ebullient former CDM chairman nonetheless gave his endorsement.

Then Max Kampelman's longtime friend Richard Schifter weighed in. Schifter, also one of Jeane Kirkpatrick's closest friends, had been brought into the Reagan administration by Kirkpatrick. He was one of the co-founders of CDM, and a fierce opponent of McGovern. A soft-spoken, hard-line anti-Communist, Schifter managed to stay on in the Bush administration as assistant secretary of state for human rights, eventually resigning over a policy difference concerning Bush's "heavy-handed treatment" of Israel. Having served under both Reagan and Bush gave him some gravitas in the foreign policy community. So when he declared that Clinton was a "Hubert Humphrey Democrat," and, after meetings with top campaign foreign policy adviser Anthony Lake, when he stated that "the old differences no longer were relevant" and "we all stand for democracy now," Schifter sent a strong signal to the troops that Clinton was okay.

It was a great error in judgment.

Lake, a dove and committed multilateralist, was the man who had once bragged about keeping Kirkpatrick out of the Carter administration. He was also one of the harshest critics of Reagan's foreign policy, and a leading foreign policy guru for the liberal left. But he was the heir apparent to the national security adviser's slot under a President Bill Clinton. Which meant what he said mattered. Which also meant that what Schifter said about Lake—and Clinton—mattered too.

Schifter harbored the hope that other neoconservative heavyweights would join him. He thought the high priest of counterestablishment theology, Jeane Kirkpatrick, could be convinced to endorse Clinton, even musing, "She'd make a wonderful ambassador to France under Clinton." He remarked that perhaps Richard Perle would also become part of the Clinton team. In the campaign's waning stretch, Schifter even worked with Lake to prepare a joint op-ed for the *New York Times*. But, in what would in hindsight become a key bit of symbolism, their joint op-ed was never published.

CLINTON LOOKED LIKE a sure winner in the final weeks of the campaign, but Kampelman remained publicly silent about where he stood. He offered the view that Schifter may be "a bit naive" about Lake, but he also felt that perhaps Lake and other liberal Democrats might have become less Pollyannaish about America's muscular role in the world because, as Kampelman put it, "ambitious people change." If Clinton was a new-style Democrat, he allowed for the fact that the people Clinton would hire could become "new Democrats too."

In his office confines, Kampelman had been weighing a number of concerns. He had his severe doubts about the Democrats. But, to Kampelman, not the bipartisan negotiator of the Reagan era but the instinctive Democrat, the problems of a crumbling domestic infrastructure, social decay, and crime seemed to cry out more for liberal answers. In the end, the patrician Bush left him cold; he was taken by his old ties—and perhaps his old dreams—of the Democratic party and surprisingly broke with the other Reagan neoconservatives. Just weeks shy of the election, he declared that he would "vote for Clinton."

CLINTON WON, AND the hard-line foreign policy Democrats who, hope against hope, broke ranks to support the Arkansas governor, waited; but, for nearly all, the call to service never came. Indeed, in a repeat of the Carter presidency, conservative and tough-minded voices were shunted aside. Cyrus Vance's former deputy, Warren Christopher, became secretary of state. *Time* magazine's virulently anti-Reagan columnist Strobe Talbott (whose foreign policy predictions had repeatedly been proved wrong), was picked to oversee Clinton's Russia policy. Tony Lake took the NSC post. And the signal went out: counterestablishmentarians, conservatives, and most certainly Republicans were not welcome. Of the CDM Clinton supporters, only Penn Kemble initially received a post, as a deputy director in the United States Information Agency. The Democrats' bright light on defense, Les Aspin, would become secretary of defense, but he would be forced out in less than a year. Jim Woolsey was named head of the CIA. He was gone in two years. While far less experienced people were offered top spots in the new administration, Dick Schifter drifted in limbo for over a year, until finally being offered a quiet post in the White House with the NSC, under Tony Lake.

From the start, a hapless Clinton administration lurched from debacle to disaster, worlds apart from the Bush administration, let alone the Reagan administration.

Watching from the sidelines, Kampelman, as always, took a larger view. He had never lost faith in his own country or questioned the fundamental assumption that the U.S. had a dominant world role to play. He had never succumbed to cynicism. Throughout his career, he had maintained a sense of graciousness, always the gentleman. That did not change.

Nearing his seventy-fifth birthday, he looked thinner, his voice crackled with a hint of frailty, his elfish frame seemed somehow smaller. Age was one tyrant he could not fend off forever. Again, he promised a true retirement. In the meantime, his mind was as sharp as ever; but he began to look at the world less through the peering eyes of a discerning policy maker, more as a happy grandfather who had lived a full life, and could sit back to marvel at the changes gripping the globe over the last fifty years. This Wise Man of the counterestablishment, now at home in the complexity of life, watched the rapidly evolving world about him with a sense of awe and fascination, pondering its mysteries. "The world of politics," he said reflectively, is "catching up with the world of science and technology."

By THE SUMMER of 1991, Elliott Abrams had happily settled into a new routine as a private citizen. Though he rarely received credit for his efforts in the popular press, the democratic revolution that he fought for so laboriously, not just from Chile to Panama, but in Nicaragua as well as El Salvador, had taken hold in Latin America.

He didn't make his way back to the corridors of establishment Washington very often, but in the spring of 1990 he attended a meeting on human rights in the Senate. Emerging from the elevator, he ambled slowly through the long corridors of the Rayburn Senate Office Building, looked up at the high ceilings, and flashed a smile of nostalgic satisfaction, as if tasting a fine red wine that had just been uncorked and deciding that he liked it. Almost inaudibly, he reminisced, "Those were the days," as if contemplating the old certitudes that first drew him into public service.

For the irascible, energetic, three-time assistant secretary, it was in these marble hallways where his remarkable personal odyssey had begun. As a Democrat, with Scoop Jackson and Pat Moynihan. Under Reagan, whatever differences he had with the Democrats, however much he himself had evolved politically, he still maintained a certain reverence for the institution of the Senate, though not for the partisanship of the Democrats.

In the summer of 1991, while the bustling downtown lawyers and lobbyists had wound down for their summer retreats in North Carolina and Martha's Vineyard, Abrams was hard at work on a book about American foreign policy. George Bush had proclaimed a New World Order but had difficulty defining it. He was an able manager, had shown true guts with Desert Storm, but, unlike Reagan, was woefully bereft of vision. Others would have to provide it. What were the principles to guide an internationalist America in the post–Cold War world? What were the instruments at America's disposal? What obligations did the U.S. have? How much could it afford to undertake? When he wasn't out giving speeches, lunching over cooked meat and plantains with the Salvadoran or Honduran ambassadors, or speaking on behalf of conservative or Jewish causes, it was questions like this that Abrams tangled with as he set out to write his book.

Still astonishingly youthful, he wore none of the pomp and formality that often accompanied the new policy elite of Washington's many assistant secretaries. He was completely approachable. But in his own way, he was a paradox. In government, when given the facts, Abrams made decisions quickly. It was the style of a man comfortable with his judgment, not of an intellectual befuddled by a problem's many angles. Indecision made him antsy. He liked action.

But Abrams also saw himself as an intellectual. Indeed, in contrast to his public persona, at times his demeanor was like that of a student, a man who loved learning. Where many authors struggle through the tedium of research and writing, he genuinely liked the challenge of reading densely packed academic tomes or classic treatises on American history for his own book preparation. This too was trademark Elliott Abrams, always enthusiastic, optimistic, and intellectually curious.

That August, he gathered his wife and children into the family car for a week's vacation at a rented house on the Delaware shore. Reading the newspapers, a shiver went down his spine. He was disturbed by an increasing pattern of suggestion and rumor that he was under investigation by Lawrence Walsh, the Iran-contra independent prosecutor. To Abrams, it didn't make sense. After the hearings, he was cleared of any wrongdoing. He had apologized for misleading the Congress, and even George Shultz had written to the Senate to explain—and defend—his actions. The three times he was interviewed by Walsh's people, they assured him he was not a target of criminal prosecution, including at the last meeting three years earlier, in 1988.

But within weeks, Abrams would suddenly be plunged into the fight of his life. Walsh's office indicated they were going to prosecute him for "false testimony" before the Congress—meaning his testimony about Brunei as well as his failure to discuss Oliver North's involvement in the private fund-raising effort.

To Abrams, this just stank. It smacked of nothing more than criminalizing foreign policy differences and the actions of overzealous, young prosecutors looking to put a feather in their cap and enhance their own careers. Nor was the fact lost on him that because Oliver North had just gotten off scot-free—his conviction was tossed out of court on appeal—Walsh, now on his fifth year, and having spent more than $50 million, desperately needed other indictments. Abrams would be one of them.

But Walsh was accountable to no one but himself, and Abrams was powerless to stop him. Meeting with his lawyer, it became brutally clear that Abrams was at the mercy of the independent counsel. Abrams wanted to fight, but the strain that would place on his family would be enormous. The legal fees would certainly bankrupt him. For his own sanity, and for the health of his family, he had to put an end to it all. In one emotionally charged October day, he and Rachel decided that they had cried and fought too long. Enough, he thought. He agreed to plead to the counsel's charges.

On October, 10, he pled guilty to two counts of "withholding information" from Congress, a violation of the United States Code, Section 192, Title 2. On Friday, November 15, 1991, Abrams rose in the courtroom to be sentenced. The day began with auspicious portents. It was an Indian summer day, sunny and radiating. The judge could have fined Abrams $100,000. Instead, Judge Aubrey Robinson suspended Abrams's sentence, placed him on two years' probation, and fined him nothing, except for the required $50 in court costs. "I'm not suggesting your life needs rehabilitating," the judge stressed. Leaning his frame down gently, he gave Abrams only one hundred hours of community service, saying, "There are those, especially in your practice, who could gain from your experience." The judge had signaled he didn't think much of the charges, and it was as much of a vindication as Abrams could have hoped for.

Hugging his crying wife and then his lawyers, a drained Abrams, looking thinner and a little peaked, collected himself and walked out of the courtroom. He and his wife now had their lives back.

On Christmas Eve of 1992, one of the final chapters in Iran-contra closed. President George Bush issued a presidential pardon for five members of the Reagan administration, including Elliott Abrams.

. . .

FOR ABRAMS, THERE was a tinge of bitterness that President Reagan hadn't stood by some of the men who had so faithfully carried out the president's policies, but he was deeply proud of his work for Ronald Reagan and remained a committed warrior for the Reagan philosophy. "It was a movement victory," Abrams described. "The neoconservatives have become part of our own establishment." And as was his wont, Abrams was again relentlessly focusing on the future.

Abrams, the old Reagan veteran, was still a young man. On the outs with establishment Bush Republicans, on the outs with the new Clinton White House, the proud neoconservative fixed his sights on the prospect of conservatism. With pride, he could tick off the budding talent among the new counterestablishment, particularly the feisty young House Republican Turks, with equal alacrity as he could the accomplishments of the Reagan foreign policy team.

As the Clinton White House stumbled in one area after another, Abrams was not surprised. To Abrams, there was no clarity of vision in this administration. He saw a sea of old Carterites: Tony Lake, Warren Christopher, and even Jimmy Carter himself, globe-trotting seemingly everywhere from North Korea to Haiti, trying to clean up one mess after another left by Clinton's weak foreign policy team and his own stumbling stewardship. For Abrams, it was history repeating itself. Carter had made a hash of American leadership in his tenure, and now Clinton, surrounded by many of the same people, "compromising" and "weak," was doing it again.

But in his many speeches and writings, Abrams preferred to devote less of his time to scorn for an amateurish crowd in the Clinton administration and more time to the emerging conservative movement, a new wave of Reaganism. Not dedicated to upholding an old order, not founded on big government or the heavy hand of regulation, Abrams felt this defiant band of Young Turks was a whole new breed. They wanted to build a new order, guided by the principle of individual freedom, and by the entrepreneurial energies and decent instincts of all Americans. To be sure, Abrams was an integral figure in this movement. And for Elliott Abrams, this new generation of Reagan followers were *his* type of Republicans. And their optimism was where he wanted to be.

IN HER HEART and spirit, Jeane Kirkpatrick remained foremost a teacher and scholar. A decade out of government service, she insisted her "biggest challenge is understanding and figuring out the problems of the world." It is a carefully crafted scholar's phrase, of the old school, of someone who looks deeply for—and reveres—the truth.

At a time when conservatives hailed her with encomiums, and amid

the rumblings of a worldwide democratic revolution she helped precipi-
tate, she remained decidedly indifferent to the talk show appearances,
the fame, the influence. Unlike so many of the new professional foreign
policy elite, she served at the request of a president, not at the call of ambition or grasping opportunism. As the mantle of the presidency passed
from Reagan to Bush to Clinton, Kirkpatrick's greatest measure of satisfaction continued to come from an old Aristotelian pursuit, teaching.
From her endowed chair at Georgetown University, she covered such
topics as the "Philosophical Foundations of Capitalism," to seminars on
"French Politics and Government," "The Critics of Utopia," and "Culture,
Democracy, and Politics."

History will remember her for other things: her successful work for
Ronald Reagan, her penetrating essays on world affairs, her writings on
political parties. But it was ultimately the lure of books, the smile of an
enlightened student, the pride of supervising a well-crafted dissertation,
and the sense of sending young people out into the world, more informed
and more inquisitive, perhaps more civic-minded in an age of cynicism,
which rewarded her. At day's end, Kirkpatrick, the ambassador and cabinet member, was again a scholar, devoting herself to the life of the mind,
giving of her time and of her years of expertise as a careful and generous
guide.

OUT OF GOVERNMENT was not though, for Kirkpatrick, out of history. Galvanized by the slaughter in Bosnia and appalled by American indecision
and false posturing, she co-founded the Action Council on the Balkans,
a bipartisan group of distinguished Americans, to speak out against the
atrocities and to pressure the United States into action. Earlier on,
under Bush, she had joined with Margaret Thatcher and George Shultz
in calling for a tough Western response. In so doing, she once again
placed herself squarely in the midst of a moral fight, acting on principle
and belief.

And, as the decade of the 1990s unfolded, Kirkpatrick's own historical
journey continued. The onetime sympathetic socialist came to see the
greatest accomplishments of the Reagan administration, aside from its
monumental foreign policy victories in winning the Cold War, as "deregu-
lation, decommunization, and decentralization."

She chuckled at analysts who lumped George Bush together with
Ronald Reagan, when in fact, in her view, Bush was closer to Bill Clinton. In the waning desperate days of the Bush campaign in 1992, she
privately predicted that Jim Baker, hailed as a savior by the press, would
be unable to salvage the sinking Bush campaign. He was, she noted

wearily, not a man of ideas, or someone in touch with the American people, or a conceptualizer. He was an establishment fixer, a deal-maker. He would be no more successful in helping Bush capture the imagination of the American people than he had been as secretary of state in laying out a strategic vision for the world. As was so often the case, the perceptive Kirkpatrick was right. A fact too often forgotten, Kirkpatrick began not as a foreign policy expert, but as a student of American politics.

Finding Bush uninspiring, she nonetheless did not support Clinton the way her old friends Max Kampelman, Richard Schifter, and Ben Wattenberg did. Two years later, she would muse: how could such smart people have supported Clinton?

To her, it was also remarkable how many Democrats and most of the establishment media still scarcely understood Ronald Reagan and what he stood for. She saw the 1994 election and Republican resurgence in the Congress as a continuation of the Reagan movement, a clarion call on the domestic front for what the counterestablishment championed in foreign policy. It was also an election that marked, for Kirkpatrick, "the second defeat of George McGovern, as well as the third election of Ronald Reagan." She cited a book of Reagan's speeches, not primarily from his years as president, but from 1961–1982, called *A Time for Choosing*. Her finger pointed lightly. "His philosophy is all set out there," she said. "The rest is history."

KIRKPATRICK WAS A reluctant leader, if ever there was one, in an energetic intellectual movement. Were it not for George McGovern, she almost surely never would have plunged so deeply into her efforts with CDM to reform the Democratic party. Had Jimmy Carter been a better commander in chief, she might never have written her seminal essay, "Dictatorships and Double Standards." Had Ronald Reagan not personally charmed her and appealed to her civic obligation to assist the country in a time of dire need, she never would have served as U.N. ambassador. And had the Democratic party not veered so alarmingly far off the spectrum and away from its once noble roots, she never would have delivered her "Blame America First" speech at the Republican Convention.

Twice, she could have made a credible bid for the highest offices in the land, especially in 1988, but also in 1992. She surely could have received serious support for the presidency—many conservatives were pleading with her to run. In 1988, a number of insiders felt the vice presidency was all but hers for the asking. Republicans also wanted to run her for the U.S. Senate in Maryland. Each time, for this all too private woman in the bustling vortex of public life, the answer was no. She was already consumed with meetings in New York, conferences at the American Enterprise Institute, her regular schedule of book writing, her op-ed column, speaking engagements before Republican groups and corporations, teaching and advising.

Transcending her prickly battles in the rough-and-tumble bureaucratic struggles while at the United Nations, she had been a key architect of not just the policies that transformed the Soviet Union and ended the Cold War, but the democracy movement as a whole. With adversaries and allies alike, she never lost her gracious qualities, her wry sense of humor, or her old-fashioned values and common sense.

Through dint of her sweeping intellect and insights, Kirkpatrick, a woman who had pioneered the way for women in the national security arena, had become one of the central philosophers of modern conservatism and one of the preeminent leaders of the counterestablishment. Yet this event-making woman, who spent the better part of her life considering the forces that sway nations and the systems that give rise to war and peace, adamantly said that nothing was so precious to her as her late husband, her children, and her home. She remained ever a woman of class and style.

THE END OF the Cold War gave rise to a burst of enthusiasm about possibilities throughout the globe. Liberals and conservatives alike looked to a time that could end the scourge of xenophobic nationalism, the threat of the bomb, even the end of Third World hunger and sickness. As Communist dictatorships shrank to a handful, it was even possible to dream now of an end to war. In Nicaragua, free elections had swept the Sandinistas from office. Across the globe, democracy was taking hold.

But then, on August 2, 1990, Iraq's dictator, Saddam Hussein, moved his troops on the oil-rich country of Kuwait, declaring it Iraq's "nineteenth province."

As George Bush resolutely concluded that military action against Iraq was the only viable alternative, Richard Perle was no longer content to wait in the wings and jumped into the fray. He agreed with Bush that too much was at stake, that the U.S. had to lead an effort to dislodge Iraq from Kuwait, with war if necessary. It was unthinkable to Perle that the U.S. could idly stand by while Iraq seized a sizable chunk of the world's oil riches; committed a flagrant act of aggression against a sovereign nation; urgently moved to develop its nuclear weapon; and threatened the security of Israel, moderate Arab regimes, and quite literally the globe. He thought it was dangerous escapism to think that sanctions could work against the Iraqi dictator.

For weeks on end, Perle was a whirlwind of activity. It was reminiscent of his days as a staff assistant for the Committee to Maintain a Prudent Defense Policy in 1967, fighting over the ABM system. He testified before Congress, wrote op-ed pieces, rallied associates to the cause, and made phone call after phone call lobbying senators and staff to stand firm against Saddam.

Perle saved his most stinging comments for his old nemesis, Sam Nunn, who was opposing the president, mustering the votes to defeat a resolution authorizing war, and demanding that the U.S. rely on sanctions to dislodge Iraq. Once again, Perle and Nunn were dramatically on opposite sides of the fence.

To stem the tide, Perle and Anne Lewis, a Democratic party liberal consultant, assembled a bipartisan committee of foreign policy experts, political officials, and members of Congress to support the use of force against Iraq. His old friends Kirkpatrick and Kampelman were part of the committee. Perle's bipartisan group made a difference. It helped sway the climate of opinion in official Washington, and it gave much needed support to two Democrats who bravely broke ranks with their party to bolster the president: Les Aspin and Stephen Solarz.

As politicians inexorably tied to their party, Aspin and Solarz were never fully members of the counterestablishment. But, by their actions and evolving instincts, they ultimately formed a quasi-counterestablishment outpost among the elected Democratic ranks.

Aspin and Solarz chose this defining period of the post–Cold War period to stake out their independence from their party's reigning liberal orthodoxy on foreign policy. In both men's cases, it was a bold move.

The congressional vote on a resolution authorizing the use of force was scheduled for January 13, 1991—a Saturday, to go into Sunday if necessary. Aspin lined up behind the resolution. His endorsement, couched in analytic phrases, was a high-risk strategy. If Bush lost the vote, Aspin's stature among the Democrats, carefully built up in the previous three years—and his chairmanship—would plummet for a second time. There would be no third chance.

This was never more clear than when George Mitchell, the powerful Senate majority leader, looking irritated, strode onto the floor of the Senate. Without using Aspin's name, Mitchell ridiculed his contentions as "dangerous" and "irresponsible." But Aspin had acted quickly and decisively, placing principle over partisanship, as he had done earlier in the Reagan era. In doing so, his was an act of courage. And, after long being shackled by the myriad contradictions of his party, he had not just earned a place as a great House legislator, but had solidified his position as one of the nation's more serious and respected leaders in national security.

Aspin was not alone. Another prominent Democrat had directly taken on Nunn: Stephen Solarz.

A quarter of a century earlier, a boyish-looking Solarz came to Washington as an anti–Vietnam War Democrat. Like Aspin, since the mid-1980s, the brainy Solarz had sought to move the party to the center on foreign policy. The attempt failed, and by 1989, when he authored the groundbreaking peace plan for the war-torn land of Cambodia, he was on the outs with his party's leadership. And when the Democrats raised the specter, once again, that war in the Gulf was "another Vietnam," Solarz was undaunted. He shot back that the appropriate analogy was not Southeast Asia, but World War II. The worst legacy of Vietnam, he hastened to add, would be if the U.S. were paralyzed from acting when it most needed to act.

On a gray Monday late in the fall of 1990, the Democratic caucus, the leadership, and committee heads met behind closed doors to debate a unified policy for the party. More than two hundred members attended. Solarz went to make his case.

The meeting started out on a low note. As it had been doing for months, the leadership argued for sanctions. Nunn's shadow loomed over the discussion. There was no dissent. Everyone agreed. No one spoke up to the contrary.

No one.

Standing in the room, Solarz was stunned. To him, the members had suspended their judgment and their common sense at the twin altars of Sam Nunn and Vietnam paralysis. Solarz broke the silence. He declared that "the moral and security stakes" couldn't be more "compelling" or "clearer." If the U.S. wasn't willing to use force on this issue, he asked, when would it ever be willing to defend its interests?

There was a prolonged hush in the room. The faces of sanction supporters reddened with anger. No one stood up in support of Solarz. After the meeting, members filed out quietly, unable to believe the spectacle they had witnessed. It was inevitable that Solarz's effort would be read as a direct affront to Nunn. A number of members used the same words to describe Solarz standing up to the Georgia senator: "gutsy—and quite possibly suicidal."

But if Solarz was one thing, it was gutsy. More than just thoughtful, he could also be deeply principled. The defiant Brooklyn Democrat stood his ground, joined Perle's group, and eloquently spoke out on why force was necessary. (Perle privately worried that the party would unleash its fury at Solarz, which it eventually did do.)

During that tense and drawn final weekend leading up to the congressional vote, Solarz sat in a large room with Republicans and a handful of moderate Democrats, and was the key drafter of the resolution authoriz-ing President Bush to go to war. When the resolution was introduced on January 13, he was its principal sponsor. Pounding his right fist into his open left hand, he was its most articulate defender during the debate.

Over 70 percent of the Democrats voted against the resolution, but enough voted with Solarz to give it a narrow margin of victory.

The Gulf War ended in a matter of days. Aggression had been pun-ished. Kuwait was liberated, and Saddam Hussein was locked up like a caged animal in his own country under harsh conditions imposed by the victorious coalition. It had been an impressive show of diplomacy com-bined with force, leaving the U.S. as the world's remaining—and sole—superpower.

But, ironically, for Solarz it was a time of some ambivalence. At fifty, no longer in the mainstream of his party, Solarz was left to ponder what his future held. He had nurtured the hope that one day he would be sec-retary of state in a Democratic administration. It was a post he had surely earned; and he was, by his extensive experience and sheer exper-tise in global affairs, well suited for it. By every measure, his career thus far had been remarkable in its own right, and his future remained even more promising.

But when the Democrats captured the White House in 1992, like Richard Perle and Jeane Kirkpatrick in the Carter administration, Solarz was passed over and left to quietly watch from the sidelines as mediocre men and women struggled through one policy mishap after another.

ON A WARM fall day in September of 1992, Richard Perle was lounging in the lush backyard of his house, dressed in khaki pants and an open shirt, wearing Topsiders without socks. Perle was never one to wear his feelings on his sleeve, but this day, deep circles ringed his eyes; his voice was even softer than normal, the undertow of his mood was one of deep introspection, even gloom. An old colleague and a dear friend of many years, Seymour "Sy" Weiss, had just passed away. Most of official Wash-ington was scurrying about, obsessed with the presidential campaign; by contrast, Perle was consumed with the job he had been given upon hear-ing the news of Sy's passing: to coordinate efforts for the funeral.

It was a measure of Perle, the man, that when his friends were in need or trouble, he would drop everything to come to their aid. He didn't ask questions or stop to calculate whether it was good or bad for him. He acted. His adversaries always mistook his uncanny savvy in bureau-cratic intrigues, his relentless ability to press his policies to successful conclusion, his lack of self-doubt in the tensest of crises, for a certain ruthlessness. Never was a well-crafted political myth more off the mark. Perle had a big heart and a generous spirit.

David McCurdy had just called him. Would Richard sign up with the other moderates to support candidate Clinton? Perle's endorsement would be an immediate story. Perle demurred, out of serious doubts over Clinton and many of his Carter-era advisers, and out of loyalty to Bush's defense secretary, Dick Cheney. "I've never been much on parties," Perle sighed. "It seems to me that there ought to come a time when one gets beyond that sort of thing."

Indeed, for Perle the only remaining tie to the Democratic party was not the present, but the past. "I would be a Republican today if it weren't for the memory of Scoop. That's the only reason I haven't changed my registration."

LOYALTY. ALL HIS life, Perle prized loyalty, to principles, to colleagues, to friends. Where other officials were scampering to watch their own back-sides in government, more often than not, he was helping his colleagues protect themselves. He had little tolerance for heedless politicians or unprincipled social climbers, greedily clawing their way in the policy world at the expense of others. Like Kirkpatrick, for this most intense of policy makers, his was the view that public service remained a special calling.

When President Bill Clinton, after a series of foreign policy flounderings and mishaps, from a desire to slash defense budgets too quickly, to re-peated efforts in military "social engineering" and a disastrous exercise in "nation building" in Somalia, made a scapegoat of his defense secretary, Les Aspin, and publicly sacked him, Perle was again moved by loyalty. He thought the whole incident was disgusting, down to a White House leak of Aspin's replacement within hours of his resignation, and said so, writing a piece in the *Washington Post* magnanimously praising Aspin.

Perle kept busy. He wrote his memoirs in a thinly veiled novel called *Hardline*, a book marked as much by its insider humor as a characteris-tic punch. With a wry smile, he found it ironic that a consulting project brought him to the former Soviet Union, where he was helping the Rus-sians privatize their military-industrial complex. And, just as he was drawn in by the Gulf War, Perle followed his instincts and fastened on another source of evil, the wanton aggression in Bosnia.

Ever since he first began working for Scoop Jackson, Perle regarded evil political systems and wanton aggression as the snake lurking in the garden, the ultimate threat to peace and security. Others fixated on an elusive quest for stability between the U.S. and the Soviet Union, dangerously ignoring deep-seated moral differences between democracy and Soviet Communism. But Perle never lost sight of the fact that it was the ruthless imperialist impulses of an expansionist regime that tempted the peace, not the weapons themselves.

So it was in Bosnia. There, Serb nationalists were dismembering the predominantly Muslim state of Bosnia, in full glare of the civilized world. For three years running, carnage reigned. With the U.S. on the sidelines, indifferent diplomats callously imposed a one-sided arms embargo on the Bosnians, exchanged meaningless NATO communiqués, and passed hollow U.N. resolutions, while Bosnia was ruthlessly shelled and destroyed. For more than two-and-a-half years, Bill Clinton effectively subordinated American policy to the preferences of the French, British, and Germans, refused to lift the arms embargo so that the Bosnian government could defend itself, and failed to engage in meaningful air strikes that might give pause to the murderous Serbian forces. The administration hid behind the foil of the need for multilateral actions, including U.N. peacekeepers who couldn't keep the peace.

For Perle, world leadership was about setting priorities and making distinctions. Bosnia, he felt, was an important American interest. "The U.S. must show that we will react to blatant aggression," he maintained.

But now, after years of carping and complaining, Perle's critics held the reins of authority. No longer faced with the awesome specter of inflaming the Cold War, for months their actions were nonetheless characterized by a strange mix of timidity and paralysis, with inflated rhetoric but little concrete action. Despite Clinton's campaign pledges, they dithered while half of Bosnia's inhabitants were uprooted or killed. To many, like Perle, their failure to intervene early on, when the opportunity was there and American leadership would have made the greatest difference, was a stunning contrast with the Reagan era's Cold War foresight and boldness. Whatever the final outcome of the tragic Balkan conflict, it could not erase the damage done during the administration's prolonged waffling and empty posturing. And here, the contrast between the indecision of the Clinton administration, the multilateralists, and the decisiveness of Ronald Reagan and his administration, the visionaries who had won the Cold War, could not have been more apparent.

SINCE THE DAYS of the Wise Men, few in the postwar era had put their stamp as firmly on the Cold War policies that eventually brought the U.S.-Soviet conflict to a grinding halt as had Richard Perle. A master of the intricacies of complicated weapons policies and arms control, he saw

American leadership and international security in bold but pragmatic, conceptual terms. Others preferred to duck the horrors of international life. Perle took them on.

Belatedly, if not begrudgingly, his adversaries came to see that he was a far more nuanced thinker and policy maker than they had recognized. As for his future, Perle's name was inevitably mentioned as a secretary of defense in a Republican administration.

In the meantime, the paternalistic roles in his life had reversed. The earlier disciple of such masters of nuclear theology and global geopolitics as Albert Wohlstetter, Paul Nitze, Scoop Jackson, and Cap Weinberger had become the mentor to young policy makers scattered throughout Washington. Every spring, many flocked to an annual barbecue that Perle held with his two old friends Stephen Bryen and the policy intellectual Michael Ledeen. Neoconservatives like Ben Wattenberg were regulars, as were friends like Frank Gaffney and Doug Feith. Policy heavyweights like former Reagan-Bush official Paul Wolfowitz and former Kissinger and Shultz aide Peter Rodman also came, as did political guru Bill Kristol and *Washingtonian* magazine publisher Phil Merrill. It was virtually a shadow government in waiting.

But the annual family picnic was notable for another reason. It was a warm gathering of old friends.

Kids batted around the softball on the green grass, Russian émigrés new to the country munched on humus and pita chips, and, whether camped out on benches or strolling about, everyone chatted incessantly. If Perle was insistent on one thing, it was that everyone eat. Wearing a big chef's hat and an apron stained with grease, Perle flipped enormous hamburgers and hot dogs, while he and Leslie waved people over to the salads, watermelon, desserts, and other more exotic dishes brought by the guests.

Perle had survived the labyrinth of the Senate and the Pentagon over two decades, was a key figure at the two decisive summits in the mid-1980s, authored what would become the first nuclear arms reduction treaty in history, fearlessly tangled with Henry Kissinger and Sam Nunn, and pushed for policies that eventually brought down the Soviet empire. But he believed true excellence could not come from doing a job at any price, but from being willing to defy orthodoxy, to be contrary, to fight for what was right, and even to lose one's job. The commandment was unorthodox: loyalty over ambition, excellence over bureaucratic survival, results over process. And, in his own case, in overworked Washington, family first.

It was perhaps a telling metaphor that he never seemed more intense or happy than on those afternoons when he was raking the hot barbecue coals, calibrating the sizzle, flipping his hamburgers, and browning the hot dogs.

AND THEN THERE WERE the secretaries, George Shultz, the diplomat, and Caspar Weinberger, the warrior. As the decade of the 1990s neared its midpoint, both men continued to probe the great philosophical questions of the Cold War. What happened? How? Why? George Shultz's memoirs, comprehensive and engaging, had been written, but he still had much to say. Shultz scoffed at those who suggested that the Cold War's outcome was preordained or was the result of inevitable Soviet weakness. "Utter nonsense," he replied. To Shultz, like Weinberger, the Cold War had been a life-or-death struggle, a fierce contest between two radically different political systems, with the final outcome uncertain. Before Ronald Reagan, he noted, the U.S. "was in terrible shape: psychologically, militarily, economically." And, he would firmly remind others, in 1980 and for most of the decade, the Soviets "had a very profound military machine."

From his perch back home in California, there remained little doubt in Shultz's mind that the U.S. actions in the Reagan era—"standing firm in Central America and Afghanistan," "leading the NATO alliance," "getting the American people to think realistically about the Soviet [empire]," "supporting democracy worldwide," "the U.S. military buildup," and, "most of all the INF deployment" and the two key summits at "Geneva and Reykjavik"—created the environment that led the Soviets to implode and the U.S. to win the Cold War. However tumultuous a time it was, these years left a record of which he was personally proud.

Indeed, with each passing year, Shultz's own stature as a statesman continued to grow. Ever a consummate pragmatist, and not an effusive man, like other leading Reaganauts, he too was gripped by the human drama of Bosnia and the appallingly weak American response. Now on the outside, he was surprisingly blunt in his assessment of America's conduct of world affairs under Clinton. These are amateurish people, he pointed out, whom he saw as "products of the Vietnam era," and "almost anti-U.S." in their orientation. Not a man prone to overstatement or hyperbole, the former secretary watched events in Washington with a mounting sense of dread, worrying about the steady erosion of American leadership and failure to shape the emerging post–Cold War world. He believed, as well, that America needed SDI. Shultz, however, took solace in the 1994 elections, seeing, like Kirkpatrick, the Republican congressional victory as a continuation at home of what Ronald Reagan had accomplished abroad.

Back in the peaceful confines of northern California, where he maintained two offices, one in the repose of the Hoover Institution near Stanford and the other among the gleaming glass towers of the San Francisco skyline, Shultz's own contributions were not in doubt. He had understood well that strength and diplomacy must go hand in hand; "my theme song," he later noted. He had operated with a steady nerve in some of history's most perilous moments. But the former secretary was quick to assign ultimate credit to Ronald Reagan. "To me," Shultz said directly, "Ronald Reagan was a great leader."

Asked if he would hold Reagan up as a model of historic world leadership, and for future U.S. presidents, he repeated one of his favorite stories, a telling homily about knowledge versus wisdom. He spoke of a newly tenured MIT professor who since the first grade "knew everything but *realized* nothing." Reagan, Shultz said quite simply, accomplished so much, not just because he knew things, but because, like other great leaders, he "knew them instinctively and in his gut." In short, his answer was an unequivocal yes.

As for Cap Weinberger, his memoirs also finished, he continued to be equally active. He left government in 1987 to become chairman of *Forbes* magazine, in which he wrote a trenchant weekly "Commentary" column about international affairs, defense, and politics. And, in print and in person, he was as no-nonsense and straightforward as ever. From his small light-filled corner office in downtown Washington, he could be as critical of the dogmas of the official D.C. establishment now as when he was defense secretary. Like Shultz, he too was distressed by the Clinton administration's stewardship of foreign policy. He worried about the defense budget and still was pressing for the U.S. to develop strategic defenses. Similarly, he held great hope for the new conservative revolution that had captured the Congress in 1994.

Where Shultz was the diplomatic arm of the Reagan team, taking the more optimistic view of the Soviet Union's ability to change, Weinberger was the vigilant defense arm, more pessimistic, cautioning against early overconfidence. In truth, the two men were so effective, not just because they were enormously able spokesmen for their respective viewpoints, but because both so effectively played the roles Ronald Reagan had assigned to them, with the ultimate decision about policy always being the president's.

Outside of the president himself, more than any other single individual, Weinberger had relentlessly pushed to rebuild America's military might, sending an unshakable message to America's adversaries and allies alike about the will of this country (as Shultz himself would later point out). Successful in pushing the Soviets, it was not always easy going at home. He faced blistering domestic attacks from his establishment critics and fought back angrily as the Iran-contra special prosecutor sought to cloud his name. But Weinberger emerged unscathed.

He remained remarkably unaffected by the criticisms he had faced when in office, laughing them off with a wry wave of his hand. Like others in the Reagan administration, he was a man with a remarkable inner compass and a strong sense of self. It had served him well in difficult times. And like Shultz, Weinberger would also take his rightful place as having presided over policies that helped undo the Soviet Union.

But, like Shultz, for Weinberger there was more. Since his youthful days in California, Weinberger had always admired Ronald Reagan, a man who "lit up a room when he walked in." Sitting back in his chair, Caspar Weinberger now modestly but firmly pointed his finger to make clear: Reagan had been the engine driving the events that shook the globe. Ultimately, in weighing the great moments that had preserved democracy and changed the globe, Weinberger assigned the final credit to one man, his president, Ronald Reagan.

IN 1994 AND 1995, as the liberal Washington establishment floundered aimlessly and cast about seeking to find its way, and as a Republican revolution swept the Congress and the new, vibrant, conservative counterestablishment savored its power, there was but one man whose mantle all sides would reach for (only time would tell if they could truly claim it), and but one true figure at the movement's head, leaving a far-reaching legacy based on verities of an earlier age, their qualities timeless as ever: Ronald Reagan, who never lost faith in the value of rugged individualism and the inherent goodness of the American people.

The former Democrat was the bête noire of liberals; university intellectuals ridiculed him; the establishment never understood him; the Democratic Congress fought him tooth-and-nail; and Washington culture never took to him. They wondered how a man could be president who took naps, sometimes got his talking points wrong, freely delegated authority, allowed his staff to quarrel, and didn't plow into the details of position papers. On all these counts, Reagan would certainly have to plead guilty.

But this carping missed the central point of Ronald Reagan's greatness. Where a Richard Nixon or in his own way even a Jimmy Carter desperately wanted to fit in with the Washington elites, it never interested Reagan. He did not come to Washington to meld into the entrenched elite culture but to create his own whole new culture. It was not just his presidency, but his movement—and the people's. Ronald Reagan came from the center of the country, and it was his country that he carried at his core. He spoke the commonsense language of its towns and its everyday citizens. His life was the very definition of the dream that any child from any background can grow up to become America's president.

In office, Reagan had a self-assured style. He refused to get bogged down in unnecessary clutter, he stuck to his fundamental beliefs, he didn't compromise lightly, he inspired the allies as well as individual citizens the world over, and he was effective with Congress. His inner reserve of optimism was quintessentially American.

Yet, while critics erroneously deride his "simplicity" and his "faults," Ronald Reagan remains inordinately complex and his policies unusually nuanced. He had the guts of a Harry Truman, the rousing charisma and far-reaching vision of an FDR, a brain trust of intellectuals who more than rivaled that of JFK. He could work with a hostile Congress: where LBJ bullied members, Reagan charmed them. In foreign policy, he knew when to use strength and when to extend a hand to an enemy. He did not want America to retreat to the safety of the oceans; he wanted to remake the world.

Always, Reagan carried with him a faith in the greatness of his nation. But, for all this, Reagan was a humble man. After his final summit with Gorbachev, he modestly joked, he felt as though he had "dropped in to a grand historical moment." Yet this moment, like so many others, was in many ways of his making.

Reagan's victory changed the course of history. By the fearful year of 1980, the country had lost faith in itself, its ideals, its underpinnings. It cannot be forgotten how day in and day out, for over four decades, the lives of all Americans, and indeed the world, were consumed with one central, overarching issue, the Soviets and the Cold War. In Eastern Europe, half a continent was enslaved; for its part, the free world lived uneasily in a time shaped by images of mushroom clouds, fallout shelters, and children ducking under school desks in mock drills. Every other issue, from such crucial matters as domestic race relations to the health of the economy, was inevitably and inexorably dwarfed by the most urgent of all concerns, peace and war. Had the Cold War been resolved differently, or not at all, as was entirely posible given the state of the world in the 1970s, history would have had a much uglier, more unimaginable face. Yet Reagan and his people, men and women like George Shultz, Cap Weinberger, Jeane Kirkpatrick, Richard Perle, Max Kampelman, and Elliott Abrams, changed that.

Despite repeated criticism from the legions inside Washington, they forced a reticent nation not simply to face up to its global obligations in the tensest of times, but also to its historic commitment to democracy. True, they did not win the Cold War solely on their own. It was also a victory for those brave, nameless people who, generation after generation, struggled against Communism in Eastern Europe, in the Soviet Union, and in conflicts stretching from Asia to Africa to the Americas. Mikhail Gorbachev and Boris Yelstin, who came to realize that further conflict was futile, also will find their way onto the register of history. And Margaret Thatcher, the British prime minister, was an indispensable ally, a brave leader helping keep NATO's knees firm where they otherwise might have buckled. But, ultimately, the vision and the triumph decisively belong to Reagan and his counterestablishment.

RONALD REAGAN, THIS larger-than-life man, who embodied at his very core the human aspirations of Americans in every era, will be remembered by history as one of America's greatest presidents and his administration as one of the most historic. It will be commonplace to mention his name in the same breath as those of Washington, Lincoln, FDR, Truman, and Kennedy. And just as FDR and Kennedy inspired generations of Democrats, so Reagan's legacy will inspire generations of conservatives. It has in fact already done so.

Ironically, today, Ronald Reagan the conservative now looms as one of the twentieth century's great revolutionaries. In championing a movement away from statism, bureaucracy, and centralization, toward individual freedom, entrepreneurship, and democracy, he propounded a vision rooted in this country's heritage, one that appeals to the grandest hopes of Americans, not to their fears; to their confidence, not to their doubts. It is a vision, at once powerful and profound, that has increasingly found roots around the world.

And it was the loyal members of Ronald Reagan's administration, the counterestablishment, empowered by a shared sense of duty and common philosophy, who found the will to change the world. They took over at a fearful time when the globe was mercilessly divided between East and West, frequently hovering at the brink, and Soviet power, not democracy, was on the rise. In the end, they preserved the West from totalitarianism and aggression and quite literally ushered in a new world, restoring the possibility of freedom and dignity throughout the globe.

Like all men and women, they had their weaknesses, but their common strengths were considerable, their achievements truly extraordinary. By fate, hard work, and solid determination, they rose to the immense task of leaving perhaps the finest legacy to the nation: bequeathing a period of relative global tranquillity, freed of the chronic threat of nuclear war, a time when liberty could flourish, a once tentative America no longer at risk.

ACKNOWLEDGMENTS

For most authors, writing a book is a thoroughly personal venture. This book is no exception. At the same time, a work of this magnitude has immeasurably benefited from a reservoir of friends, colleagues, and contacts, in formal and informal ways. They span the political spectrum in fields ranging from government, politics, journalism, academia, business, and labor. If these acknowledgments are too long, I ask the reader's forbearance. In its own way, every debt is special, and merits a word of its own.

From the outset, as anyone who reads through these pages will immediately recognize, I am deeply indebted to a number of my principal subjects, Richard Perle, Jeane Kirkpatrick, Elliott Abrams, and Max Kampelman. Each graciously spent countless hours and numerous sessions with me over a three-year time span—including formal tape recorded sessions that lasted for up to six hours at a stretch, in less formal and extended talks over food and drink, in repeated phone calls to fill holes and check facts. In particular, Richard Perle gave me unfettered access to a veritable treasure: his personal papers, scrapbooks, and diaries. Jeane Kirkpatrick and Elliott Abrams were also helpful with personal papers. Each of these four figures has withstood intense public scrutiny, yet I frequently pushed them beyond the bounds of even today's microscope of public discourse—asking deeply personal questions about feelings as well as policies and personal actions, about the impact of public life in the Reagan years (and before) on them personally and professionally, as well as on their families, and to reconstruct and discuss events in as much vivid detail as possible.

In short, I asked them to open up their lives to me with a candor rarely seen in public life, and on some thirty-five occasions they did this with grace and magnanimity, for which I am most grateful. No one asked for— or received—the right to see the manuscript before publication, or any measure of editorial control. Given the scope and size of this project, I must ask their understanding for any inaccuracies, however small.

I also want to thank George Shultz and Caspar Weinberger for taking time out from their busy schedules to share their thoughts and recollections.

Special thanks to Richard Norton Smith, Director of the Ronald Reagan Library, who in the final stages of my book shared his fascinating insights into President Reagan and his presidency with me.

For help in collecting photographs, I want to thank the staffs of the Ronald Reagan Library (especially Steve Branch) and the Henry M. Jackson Foundation. Michelle van Gilder in Richard Perle's office, always of good cheer and good ideas, was also a great help in this and countless other ways, as were Mary Purdy and Barbara Tiplady in Jeane Kirkpatrick's office, and Sharon Dardine in Max Kampelman's office. Elliott Abrams was kind enough to pore through his personal files, as was Jeane Kirkpatrick. My thanks also to Rinelda Bliss Walters of the Center for Security Policy. Eric Chenoweth of the Institute for Democracy in Eastern Europe provided useful assistance. Also helpful were Lauren Ariker Korman of the Department of Defense, and Kim Simpson of the President's Foreign Intelligence Oversight Board.

Throughout the course of my writing, valuable archival research assistance was provided by the National Defense University Library, the Sterling Memorial Library at Yale, the Firestone Library at Princeton, the Library of Congress, the University of Maryland libraries, and the Historian's Office at the U.S. State Department. I was also helped by access to the Coalition for a Democratic Majority's files. My thanks to the embassies of: Great Britain, Brunei, France, Germany, Israel, and Saudi Arabia for assisting me with queries.

This book is the product of four years of work, and I have benefited immeasurably from the selfless help of many good and talented people and fine organizations. To start, the Lynde and Harry Bradley Foundation helped support this project with a most generous multi-year grant. I especially want to thank Bradley's Hillel Fradkin and Daniel Schmidt for their encouragement and steady assistance. In 1990–1991, the National Defense University and its NDU foundation appointed me their first senior research fellow, and NDU was a congenial setting from which to start this project. My thanks to Al Bernstein, General Mike O'Connell, and Colonel Tom Gallagher at NDU. Subsequently, I have been a senior fellow and adjunct professor at the University of Maryland School of Public Affairs and its Center for International Security Studies at Maryland. It's a marvelous place, and I especially want to thank my colleagues and friends Michael Nacht and Mac Destler, both deservedly respected scholars and deeply insightful students of public policy, for making Maryland an enriching and comfortable home for me to write my book. I could not have had a more accommodating setting.

At critical junctures in the preparation of this book, a number of writers, all good friends, some tennis partners, offered me jewels of advice about the often grueling process of writing and publication. They include authors Jerry and Leona Schecter, David Ignatius of the *Washington Post,* David Kusnet, and Michael Barone, of *U.S. News & World Report* who has a rare gift in that everything he says is interesting. At the book's outset, James Grady gave me crucial nuggets of advice.

In writing this book, and over the years, I have benefited immeasurably from the wisdom, observations, and friendship of a number of people: Paul Gigot, the *Wall Street Journal* columnist, and one of this nation's most penetrating thinkers on politics and conservatism, as well as a good-natured and warm friend; previously at the *Journal,* Tim Ferguson saw fit to publish me with regularity, but usually only after long meals and extended talk, in which he taught me more about conservatism and libertarianism than I ever let on; and Peggy Noonan, who is even better than her reputation, and is in tune with the music of America as much as anyone I know.

There is my old friend who first introduced me to Washington: Ben Wattenberg, a great American and one of the capital's more fascinating thinkers and inveterate optimists.

I have many debts to scholars in the academic world: at Yale, my friends and former teachers Joe LaPalombara, Dave Mayhew, Bruce Russett, and Brad Westerfield; also Stephen Smith and Joseph Hamburg; Emeritus Professor Geoffrey Goodwin, my former tutor at the London School of Economics and Political Science; and my colleagues at Maryland, who at one point or another shared many a stimulating idea with me: Tom Schelling, George Quester, Townsend Hoopes, Stansfield Turner, Bill Galston, Audrey Kurth Cronin, Steve Fetter, and Doug Besharov. Fran Burwell, executive director of the Center for International Security Studies at Maryland, was always there not just with administrative help, but a stream of suggestions; Carola Weil was always encouraging; Ivo Daalder was enthusiastic in sharing his chronologies and books. My thanks also to Harvey Mansfield of Harvard, Dick Fenno of Rochester, Donald Kagan of Yale, and especially Jim Kurth of Swarthmore, each of whom in a single meal or extended discussion(s) invariably gave me much to ponder; the late Paul Seabury, with whom I earlier on discussed the issues in this book over many a coffee; and Amos Perlmutter.

Steve Solarz, a good friend and truly great public servant, whom I had the pleasure of working with on Southeast Asia policy, has been a constant source of inspiration and thoughtful insights.

Others have been a help in numerous ways: Jim Billington, the Librarian of Congress and formerly of the Wilson Center, has in the past been a marvelous tutor about the Soviet Union and Russia; Charles Krauthammer, who packs more into stimulating lunches than virtually anyone; George Weigel, president of the Ethics and Public Policy Center; Doug Johnston, my old colleague, friend, and COO of the Center for Strategic and International Studies; the ever-helpful Frank Gaffney and Doug Feith; John Woodworth, who always gave freely of his time and knowledge; Al From and Will Marshall of the DLC and Progressive Policy Institute; Penn Kemble, formerly of Freedom House; Peter Rosenblatt, my old friend; the late Mike Rashish, a wise, funny, and dear man; and the late Tom Kahn of the AFL-CIO, who left a legacy of which he and labor could be proud. I also had the privilege to have two in-depth conversations with Theodore White before his death, which have time and again proven to be intellectually invaluable for a number of issues in this book.

Other individuals in one manner or another shared their thoughts at length: Ken Adelman, a modern-day Renaissance man; Gene Rostow, who drew me into public life when I was still an undergraduate and wet-behind-the-ears columnist at Yale; former Representatives Dave McCurdy and Beverly Byron; Jim Thompson of the Rand Corporation, who first taught me arms control; at the American Enterprise Institute: Mark Falcoff, Suzanne Garment, Michael Ledeen, Michael Novak, and Joshua Muravchik; at the Center for Strategic and International Studies: Bill Taylor, Fred Iklé, Robert Kupperman, Brad Roberts, Stephen Sestanovich, and Gerit Gong. Also Peter Rodman, Philip Merrill, Samuel Lewis, Richard Soloman, Jud Sommer, Daniel Yankelovich, Morry Amitay, Howard Kore, Benjamin "Bibi" Netanyahu, Senator John McCain, Soviet scholar William Wohlforth, Karl Jackson, Bob Andrews, Peter Watson, Richard Schifter, Al Santoli, Mona Charen, Dan Fisk, Peter Flory, Frank Gregorsky, Tod Lindberg, Michael Humphries, Mark Werksman, Mort Kondracke, Cord Meyer, Fred Kempe, Abe Sofaer, Ben Elliott, Alton Frye, and Peter Collier.

For the past three years, I have taught a graduate seminar in foreign policy at the University of Maryland's School of Public Affairs. I must confess to these students that I have learned every bit as much as I have taught. This past year, I have been a visiting professor of international politics at the George Washington University, where my graduate and undergraduate students have provided similar stimulation. My thanks as well to all my colleagues there, especially Lee Sigelman and Henry Nau.

In all, over two hundred interviews were conducted for this book, many of which are listed in the bibliography and source notes. I am deeply indebted to each and every one of these people. While I spent considerable time with decision makers at the highest levels, I also spent lengthy amounts of time with policy makers in the second, third, and fourth tiers of government, as well as with congressional staff, foreign diplomats, journalists, and members of the intelligence world, who were invaluable in corroborating information, sharing their recollections, piecing together the events and the play. Some people were interviewed as many as a dozen times; a number were kind enough to share extensive private papers with me, or to point me in the direction where I could find information I needed. Understandably, a number of people spoke with me on the condition that they not be identified as sources. Those who were in a position to be named or who provided keen insights in more casual conversation are listed in the source section. But for both those named and those who must remain anonymous, my gratitude is immense.

I owe a special debt of gratitude to Bill Maynes, editor of *Foreign Policy*, who encouraged me in 1988 to write about the neoconservatives and their enormous influence, and "how they should declare victory." I at first balked at the assignment, thinking it too tough and much too extensive. He pressed, and I then made excuses, and when that didn't work, I stalled. Yet Bill, a most intelligent and thorough editor, insisted, and I relented. The article I wrote for him attracted broad attention, but in writing the piece I had the feeling that I had only just started; and, in no small measure, it was an early formulation for this book. Bill Maynes remains one of the most thoughtful, principled theoreticians of a liberal foreign policy, and his journal one of the very best. It is a measure of this man and his intellectual integrity that he asked me to write the piece.

Throughout the writing of this book, three good friends of great character and loyalty were always there, with ideas, a sympathetic ear, provocative thoughts, or a warm meal or movie: my wonderful and dear, dear friend and political sparring partner from Yale, now at the AFL-CIO, Burnie Bond, along with Peter Berkowitz, a former classmate and a government professor at Harvard. Aside from the countless hours of encouragement, steady stream of ideas, and tremendous moral support, they were both extremely helpful when it came to the difficult task of actually naming my book. For Burnie, especially, who also read, proofed (carefully), and commented on the final manuscript, thanks is nowhere near enough. Also, Jim Denton, one of the quiet giants of Washington, who runs the National Forum Foundation, an organization doing marvelous work building democracy, offered to set up interviews in Eastern Europe and has been a great help to me in more ways than can be enumerated here.

My thanks as well to Jack and Nina Pomerantz for the great stories and meals at Eppes Essen in New Jersey. To Vaneeta Acson and Howard Streicher and to Chuck and Susan Freed for respite from writing. To Sara Brzowsky at *Parade,* for friendship and respite from life inside the Beltway. And the folks at Spring Creek in Jackson, Wyoming, and Bishop's Lodge in Santa Fe, where I holed up to write and edit.

For research assistance, I especially want to thank Sonia Park, who was extremely diligent and thorough in plowing through and collecting sheer mountains of material. She was invaluable. Randy Wells and Kevin Stone also provided key help at other intervals.

I am deeply indebted to Pam Bernstein, my first agent at the William Morris Agency, whose continuous enthusiasm, unwavering encouragement, and common sense convinced me that the time had come to write a book rather than stay in government. She helped make this book happen. When she left William Morris, I was fortunate to hook up with Michael Carlisle, also at William Morris, and his ever helpful assistant, Arnold Kim. Michael is a most gifted agent who knows writers and their unique needs, and is a voice of optimism and good counsel. He is also a good friend.

At Simon and Schuster, this book was treated with great importance, and I am thankful for that. I especially want to thank Bob Asahina, my editor, for his encouragement, ever thoughtful advice, and indefatigable patience. From the outset, he saw a need for this book, and helped give it shape. His reputation for vision in publishing is richly deserved, and an author could not ask for more. From the top down, Simon and Schuster has a great team of professionals who have paid special attention to this project, including Sarah Pinckney and Melissa Roberts, who have my continuing gratitude for their always good-natured assistance, suggestions, and answers. In the publicity department, Victoria Meyer is simply terrific. In the legal department, Neira Weisel was most helpful and thorough. And, finally, I very much want to thank Florence Falkow, and my superb copy editor, Fred Chase. Their painstaking review of the manuscript has helped make it a far better book.

I owe an enormous debt to Les Aspin, a remarkable man who had a great impact on me. For twelve years, Les was a boss, a close and dear friend, a cherished and caring mentor, a witness at my wedding, and my tennis partner twice a week. A wise and thorough teacher of national security and defense matters, he also taught me much about intellectual discipline and rigor, while always sharing his thoughts, advice, and encouragement—at times, I felt he was more excited about this book than I was. Les was one of America's great, bipartisan public servants, an important legislator, a man of greater conviction and moral courage than he has been given credit for, and a truly serious public policy intellectual. His time here was far too short, and his death has created not just a great void in my life, but in the life of the nation.

Above all, there is family, which has my endless gratitude and love. My uncle and aunt, Norman and Elaine Winik, generously shared their compassionate hearts and their enthusiasm for the value of knowledge and political discussion. My in-laws, Jim and Lark Wallwork, carefully read the manuscript and offered numerous useful edits and suggestions, and also supplied a continuous stream of ideas and a generous dose of warm encouragement, support, and counsel. My father, Herb, and mother, Lynn, selflessly encouraged and supported my ongoing education, and grounded me not just with love, but with a healthy appreciation of common sense. In the best sense of the word, they are the wonderfully good citizens of America who believe in hard work and play by the rules.

Finally, my greatest debt is to my wife, Lyric Wallwork Winik. She helped in every way in this book, from its conception to conclusion. A brilliant thinker, a person of remarkable moral clarity, and a most accomplished writer, on a number of occasions during the writing and editing, she selflessly took time off from her own extremely busy schedule of cover stories to assist for weeks and weekends on end. While her contributions are too extensive to catalogue (they are), she helped with everything from research, to repeated brainstorming, to the kind of comprehensive editing and careful fine-tuning that is every author's dream. There is not a part of this book that does not in some way bear her imprint, and her assistance and moral support were invaluable. Indeed, without her, I'm not sure I could have completed this project. But even more valuable are Lyric's love and smile. She is the most special person I know and the love of my life. So for this and an infinite number of other reasons, this book is dedicated to her.

NOTE ON SOURCES AND BIBLIOGRAPHY

This book, some four years in the making, is a product of more than two hundred interviews, extensive access to private papers, classified memoranda, reports, and memos of conversation (memcons), cables, and private notes, as well as scholarly research. It is buttressed by my own government service and intimate experience in the political and policy world.

Early on in this project, I set about reading and rereading the massive literature on the Cold War, focusing especially on the period of détente and then the Reagan years. In addition to overall U.S.-Soviet relations, I covered in detail the specific areas of arms control and defense; human rights and the Helsinki Process; the growing tumult in Eastern Europe, notably Poland; the United Nations; and regional conflicts (particularly Central America, Afghanistan, and the Middle East). I also reviewed the literature on the immediate postwar period of American foreign policy, decision making, Vietnam, and histories of the Cold War, from its inception through the major crises of the 1950s and 1960s. Finally, I examined the work on the establishment and the changing nature of politics and political parties in America from the 1960s through the 1980s.

With the diligent help of my research assistants, I then exhaustively combed through articles from major magazines and newspapers from the mid to late 1970s to the end of the 1980s. I also consulted the dominant academic journals for these same years. Finally, a number of key participants from the Reagan era have since written their memoirs. I read each of these accounts thoroughly, and frequently found the writers' often in-depth efforts to recount their recollections and thoughts illuminating.

While this array of written sources was often valuable in conveying a feel for how events were viewed at the time, and how major debates were perceived, I also had invaluable access to the personal papers of key policy makers, as well as staff members at mid and lower levels in the government, and others who were directly and intimately involved in American foreign policy. A number of government sources, civilian, military, and intelligence, provided me with private documents, which included personal notations, meeting records, contemporaneous hand-written notes, private letters, transcripts, schedules, chronologies, drafts, and other information that was extremely useful in depicting specific events and the play behind them. Frequently, I had papers or documents from several sources that dealt with the same incident or issue, each set of which acted as a check upon the other.

Finally, in addition to this voluminous written record, I also conducted extensive interviews, many lasting several hours, and in a few cases as long as six hours. In addition to the book's central figures, dozens of key participants were interviewed many times, and often graciously allowed me to revisit the same issue or incident to seek further details and information. Many also allowed me to tape our conversations; otherwise I took detailed notes. In a few instances, what began as a short, informal conversation ultimately evolved into a freewheeling interview, or provided important insights. I spoke both with foes of the Reagan administration as well as friends, and the adversaries were drawn from the ranks of congressional staff, interest group activists, academic and think tank experts, and officials in the bureaucracy.

Throughout the process, a substantial number of the people interviewed requested that their comments be used off the record, without direct attribution. I agreed to honor that request. Many still hold government positions. Others wanted such a stipulation in order to speak frankly about incidents and public figures and to provide me with papers. Just as it is important to maintain integrity in the research process, that in turn demands respecting the wishes of unnamed sources—without which this book might not have been possible. However, no portion of this book is based solely on the account of an unnamed source speaking off the record.

In most cases, for any event, description, episode, or analysis, there is in fact no one single source, but multiple sources or complementary information that I culled from different individuals, documents, and other accounts, and then carefully triangulated. Too often, the formal written record alone is misleading or has gaps; or sometimes the still nascent historical and scholarly literature is overly narrow or contains a key inaccuracy. And policy participants themselves, while their recollections as a rule are extremely strong and detailed, can still suffer from a limited vantage point, their own desire to shape history, or, on occasion, faulty memory. For this reason, in my reconstruction of events and analysis, I went to great pains to cross-check my information and sources as carefully as possible.

Wherever possible, I have sought to preserve the language that the participants themselves used, as well as their emotions and attitudes.

When dialogue is in quotations, and is not drawn from journals, notes, or source accounts, it is based on the confident recollection of at least one participant. Quotation marks are not used when sources were unable to recall precise wording with clarity. Moreover, classified material was not directly used, unless it has, in some fashion or another, become part of the public domain.

As is always the case in this sort of endeavor, the historian and the writer must sift through the thicket of material, seek the most reliable source, weigh the most credible evidence, and ultimately make informed judgments about the flow of events or analysis. This is particularly important when there are contradictions in the way different sources, written and oral, recount an event, which is not uncommon.

For the benefit of future scholars and the public, arrangements have been made to deposit my notes, transcripts, documents, and tape recordings of interviews in the Manuscript and Archive division of the Sterling Memorial Library at Yale University. The files will be opened in forty-five years.

Finally, in addition to these sources, primary and secondary, I had the benefit of my own personal experience, which provided me with additional expertise on many of the issues covered. For three years, from 1985 to 1988, I was a senior aide on the House Armed Services Committee to the chairman, Les Aspin, with a broad portfolio working on arms control issues, U.S.-Soviet relations, and regional conflicts. (I later advised Aspin when he was defense secretary.) Subsequently, I served as a senior staffer designated to the Senate Foreign Relations Committee, dealing with foreign policy issues from Asia to Europe to the Middle East, as well as human rights and international organizations. In this position, I accompanied Senate delegations to four continents and played a significant role in drafting the blueprint for what would eventually become the Perm Five U.N. Peace Accords for Cambodia. In between, I was also deputy director of the first blue ribbon Base Closure and Realignment Commission.

Throughout these years, I traveled widely around the world, and met more than two dozen heads of state, and countless more defense and foreign ministers. When not in government or on the Hill, I had the luxury of reflecting on a number of these issues in research settings at the Center for Strategic and International Studies and the National Defense University, both in Washington, and the Center for Strategic and International Studies at the University of Maryland.

Finally, in the 1980s, I was also closely involved in the internal debates over the Democratic party's position on national security issues, including authoring the Democratic Policy Commission's 1986 midterm foreign policy report.

Thus, for many of the issues discussed in the preceding pages, in one manner or another, I either participated in the great debates, had expertise in an issue, or was able to watch events unfold from a front-row seat. This was absolutely vital to me in researching my book, particularly in helping to make sense both of the material culled from interviews and private papers, as well as the extensive record, unclassified and classified.

It is worth mentioning that a number of the conceptions that I began with were vastly different from the conclusions I arrived at four years later. For instance, as I plowed through the evidence, some people whom I thought of as large figures grew smaller; in turn, others grew larger. The same can be said about the decisive historical events of this period. Here again, with the benefit of some historical distance, I was often surprised by what I found. The decisive INF deployment in 1983, the critical evil empire speech, and the triumphant American breakthrough and Ronald Reagan's key performance at the Reykjavik summit are but three of numerous examples. To the extent that the story here runs contrary to the dominant initial journalistic accounts, in good measure it is precisely for these reasons.

Ultimately, however, the craft of history is an inherently human activity, in part because history itself is an inherently human drama.

This book is the history of an era, a dramatic saga that shifts from one view and vantage point to another, from the calculus and passions of a single individual to the overall dynamics and activity of large government organizations and political systems, covering a range of issues. Conveying this vast, remarkable story, and conveying it well, is and has always been my overarching goal.

INTERVIEWS

Elliott Abrams
Rachel Abrams
Morris Amitay
Les Aspin
Judy Bardacke
Michael Barone
Walter Beach
Robert Bell
Robert Bernstein
Barry Blechman
Burnie Bond
Stephen Bryen
Richard Bush
Beverly Byron
Bruce Cameron
Mike Chapman
Eric Chenoweth
Eliot Cohen
William Colby

Lloyd Cutler
Midge Decter
Jim Denton
Mac Destler
Richard Eaton
Amos Eiron
Mark Falcoff
Douglas Feith
Clarice Feldman
Howard Feldman
Louis Finch
Daniel Fisk
Peter Flory
Paul Friedenberg
Alton Frye
Frank Gaffney
Suzanne Garment
Woody Goldberg
John Hawes

Charles Henkin
William Hoehn
Pat Holt
Charles Horner
Michael Humphries
Norville Jones
Robert Kagan
Tom Kahn
Max Kampelman
Steven Kelman
Jeane J. Kirkpatrick
Michael Kraft
Charles Krauthammer
Michael Krepon
Joseph Kruzel
David Kusnet
Michael Ledeen
Robert Leiken
Michael Lind
George Lister
Cord Meyer
Joshua Muravchik
Michael Nacht
Lyn Nofziger
Ralph Nurenberger
Spencer Oliver
Thomas Parker
Steve Patterson
Leslie Perle
Richard Perle
Amos Perlmutter
Alan Platt
Norman Podhoretz
Austin Ranney
Mike Rashish
Otto Reich
Rozanne Ridgway
Peter Rodman

Peter Rosenblatt
Eugene Rostow
James Schaefer
Richard Schifter
George Schneiter
Paul Seabury
John Sears
George Shultz
Walter Slocombe
Larry Smith
Abraham Sofaer
Stephen Solarz
Charles Stevenson
David Sullivan
Stansfield Turner
Lech Walesa*
Jude Wanniski
Harvey Waterman
Peter Watson
Sam Watson
Ben Wattenberg
Daniel Wattenberg
Caspar Weinberger
Seymour Weiss
Mark Werksman
Peter Wilson
William Wohlforth
Thomas Woodrow
John Woodworth
R. James Woolsey
Abby Ziffren
Warren Zimmermann
James Ziron
Bud Zumwalt

(*August 21, 1989, group meeting in Gdansk, Poland)

Primary Bibliography

In addition to the Selected Bibliography, I would like to cite five books that were of very special assistance to me in a number of ways: David Halberstam, *The Best and the Brightest,* New York: Random House, 1972, the first book of a genre that set a standard for writing about an era and American foreign policy; Walter Isaacson and Evan Thomas, *The Wise Men: Six Friends and the World They Made,* New York: Simon & Schuster, 1986, a fantastic and richly written book about six men of the postwar establishment, but more important, about the larger theme of how America rebuilt the world after World War II; Don Oberdorfer, *The Turn: From the Cold War to a New Era, the United States and the Soviet Union, 1983–1990,* New York: Poseidon Press, 1991, a thoroughly written and most helpful account of many key events of the final years in the cold war; and also Strobe Talbott, *Deadly Gambits: The Reagan Administration and the Stalemate in Nuclear Arms Control,* New York: Alfred A. Knopf, 1984, which is laden with information, including behind-the-scenes action. Finally, J. Anthony Lukas, *Common Ground: A Turbulent Decade in the Lives of Three Families,* New York: Alfred A. Knopf, 1985, an absolutely marvelous and insightful piece of work. The story of three families and the busing controversy in Boston, it has nothing to do with the Cold War; but as much as any other book, this intelligent work served as a guiding inspiration for how to capture both a big subject and a prolonged period of time, and for the inextricable interplay of people and large events.

Also especially useful to me in preparing this work were:

Books:

Abrams, Elliott. *Undue Process: A Story of How Political Differences Are Turned into Crimes.* New York: The Free Press, 1993.

Adelman, Kenneth. *The Great Universal Embrace: Arms Summitry, A Skeptic's Account.* New York: Simon & Schuster, 1989.

Arnson, Cynthia J. *Crossroads, Congress, the President, and Central America, 1976–1993.* University Park: Pennsylvania State University Press, 1993.

Barone, Michael. *Our Country: The Shaping of America from Roosevelt to Reagan.* New York: The Free Press, 1990.

Beckwith, Charles, and Donald Knox. *Delta Force.* New York: Harcourt Brace Jovanovich, 1983.

Cannon, Lou. *President Reagan: The Role of a Lifetime.* New York: Simon & Schuster, 1991.

Cohen, William S., and George J. Mitchell. *Men of Zeal: A Candid Inside Story of the Iran-Contra Hearings.* New York: Viking, 1988.

Dionne, Jr., E. J. *Why Americans Hate Politics.* New York: Simon & Schuster, 1992.

Draper, Theodore. *A Very Thin Line: The Iran-Contra Affairs.* New York: Simon & Schuster, 1991.

Gerson, Allan. *The Kirkpatrick Mission: Diplomacy Without Apology, America at the United Nations, 1981–1985.* New York: The Free Press, 1991.

Glynn, Patrick. *Closing Pandora's Box: Arms Races, Arms Control, and the History of the Cold War.* New York: Basic Books, 1992.

Houck, Davis W., and Amos Kiewe, eds. *Actor, Ideologue, Politician: The Public Speeches of Ronald Reagan.* Westport, CT: Greenwood Press, 1993.

Kampelman, Max M. *Entering New Worlds: The Memoirs of a Private Man in Public Life.* New York: HarperCollins, 1991.

Korey, William. *The Promises We Keep: Human Rights, the Helsinki Process, and American Foreign Policy.* New York: St. Martin's, 1993.

Perle, Richard. *Hardline.* New York: Random House, 1992.

Persico, Joseph E. *Casey: The Lives and Secrets of William J. Casey, from the OSS to the CIA.* New York: Viking, 1990.

Reagan, Ronald W. *An American Life: The Autobiography.* New York: Simon & Schuster, 1990.

———. *A Time for Choosing, The Speeches of Ronald Reagan, 1961–1982.* Chicago: Regnery Gateway, 1983.

Rodman, Peter W. *More Precious Than Peace: The Cold War and the Struggle for the Third World.* New York: Charles Scribner's Sons, 1994.

Shultz, George P. *Triumph and Turmoil: My Years as Secretary of State.* New York: Charles Scribner's Sons, 1993.

Weinberger, Caspar W. *Fighting for Peace: Seven Critical Years in the Pentagon.* New York: Warner Books, 1990.

White, Theodore H. *America in Search of Itself: The Making of the President, 1956–1980*. New York: Harper & Row, 1982.

Woodward, Bob. *Veil: The Secret Wars of the CIA, 1981–1987*. New York: Simon & Schuster, 1987.

Articles:

Bernstein, Richard. "The U.N. versus the U.S." *New York Times Magazine* (January 22, 1984).

Blumenthal, Sidney. "Richard Perle." Three-article series in "Style," *Washington Post*, November 23–25, 1987.

Conaway, James. "Jeane Kirkpatrick: Reagan's 'Heroine' at the U.N." *Washington Post Magazine* (November 1, 1981).

Grove, Lloyd. "Elliott Abrams." Two-article series in "Style," *Washington Post*, January 13–14, 1987.

Kaiser, Robert G. "Senate Staffer Richard Perle: Behind the Scenes Power Over Arms Policy." In "Outlook," *Washington Post*, June 26, 1977.

Krauthammer, Charles. "The Reagan Doctrine." *Time* (April 1, 1985).

Rosellini, Lynn. "Richard Perle and the Inside Battle Against SALT." In "Portfolio," *Washington Star*, May 21, 1979.

Rosen, Jane. "The Kirkpatrick Factor." *New York Times Magazine* (April 28, 1985).

Wallach, Janet. "Richard Perle: So Many Soviets, So Little Time." *Washington Post Magazine* (April 13, 1986).

Wattenberg, Ben. "It's Time to Stop America's Retreat." *New York Times Magazine* (July 22 1979).

Winik, Jay. "The Neoconservative Reconstruction." *Foreign Policy* (Winter 1988/89).

Newspapers and Journals

The New York Times
Los Angeles Times
The Boston Globe
The National Journal
The New Republic
Commentary
Dissent
Foreign Policy
The National Interest
The Washington Quarterly
The Washington Post

The Times (London)
The Washington Star
The Washington Times
Congressional Quarterly
The Economist
The Atlantic Monthly
Foreign Affairs
National Review
International Security
Current Biography

SELECTED BIBLIOGRAPHY

Books

Acheson, Dean. *A Democrat Looks at His Party*. New York: Harper & Brothers, 1955.

———. *Morning and Noon*. Boston: Houghton Mifflin, 1965.

———. *Present at the Creation*. New York: W.W. Norton, 1969.

———. *Sketches from Life of Men I Have Known*. New York: Harper & Brothers, 1961.

Adelman, Kenneth. *The Defense Revolution: Strategy for the Brave New World*. San Francisco: ICS Press, 1990.

————. *National Security in the 1980s: From Weakness to Strength*. Edited by W. Scott Thompson. San Francisco: ICS Press, 1980.

Alexeyev, Ludmilla. *Soviet Dissent: Contemporary Movements for National, Religious, and Human Rights*. Middletown, CT: Wesleyan University Press, 1985.

Allison, Graham T. *Essence of Decision: Explaining the Cuba Missile Crisis*. Boston: Little, Brown, 1971.

————. Albert Carnesale, and Joseph S. Nye, Jr. *Hawks, Doves, and Owls: An Agenda for Avoiding Nuclear War*. New York: W.W. Norton, 1985.

Alsop, Stewart. *The Center: People and Power in Political Washington*. New York: Harper, 1968.

Ambrose, Stephen E. *Eisenhower: The President*. New York: Simon & Schuster, 1984.

————. *Rise to Globalism: American Foreign Policy Since 1950*. New York: Penguin, 1993.

Americas Watch. *Human Rights in El Salvador on the Eve of Elections*. Washington: Americas Watch, 1988.

Amnesty International. *El Salvador: "Death Squads"—A Government Strategy*. London: Amnesty International Publications, 1988.

————. *Guatemala: The Human Rights Record*. London: Amnesty International Publications, 1987.

————. *Honduras: Civilian Authority—Military Power: Human Rights Violations in the 1980s*. London: Amnesty International Publications, 1988.

Amstatz, J. Bruce. *Afghanistan: The First Five Years of Soviet Occupation*. Washington: NDU Press, 1986.

Anderson, Thomas P. *Politics in Central America*. New York: Praeger, 1988.

Andrew, Christopher, and Oleg Gordievsky. *KGB: The Inside Story*. New York: HarperCollins, 1990.

Arendt, Hannah. *The Origins of Totalitarianism*. New York: Harcourt Brace & World, 1968.

Arms Control Association. *Star Wars Quotes*. Washington: Arms Control Association, 1986.

Arnold, Anthony. *Afghanistan: The Soviet Union in Perspective*. Stanford, CA: Hoover Institution Press, 1985.

Atwood, William. *The Twilight Struggle*. New York: Harper & Row, 1987.

Ball, George. *The Past Has Another Pattern*. New York: W.W. Norton, 1982.

Baloyra, Enrique A. *El Salvador in Transition*. Chapel Hill: University of North Carolina Press, 1982.

Barnet, Richard, and Ronald Muller. *Global Reach*. New York: Simon & Schuster, 1974.

Barret, Laurence I. *Gambling with History: Reagan in the White House*. New York: Penguin, 1984.

Barron, John. *KGB: The Secret Work of Soviet Agents*. London: Corgi Reprint, 1975.

Bell, Coral. *The Reagan Paradox: American Foreign Policy in the 1980s*. New Brunswick, NJ: Rutgers University Press, 1989.

Belli, Humberto. *Nicaragua: Christians Under Fire.* San José, Costa Rica: Instituto Puebla, 1984.

Bellow, Saul. *To Jerusalem and Back.* New York: Viking, 1976.

Berman, Larry. *Looking Back on the Reagan Presidency.* Baltimore: Johns Hopkins University Press, 1990.

Beschloss, Michael R. *The Crisis Years: Kennedy and Khrushchev, 1960–1963.* New York: Edward Burlingame Books, 1991.

Betts, Richard K. *Nuclear Blackmail and Nuclear Balance.* Washington: Brookings Institution, 1987.

Bird, Kai. *The Chairman, John McCloy: The Making of the American Establishment.* New York: Simon & Schuster, 1992.

Blachman, Morris J., William M. Leogrande, and Kenneth Sharpe, eds. *Confronting Revolution: Security Through Diplomacy in Central America.* New York: Pantheon, 1986.

Blair, Bruce G. *Strategic Command and Control: Redefining the Nuclear Threat.* Washington: Brookings Institution, 1985.

Blechman, Barry, and Stephen Kaplin. *Force Without War.* Washington: Brookings Institution, 1978.

Bloed, Arie, ed. *From Helsinki to Vienna: Basic Documents of the Helsinki Process.* Dordrecht, Netherlands: Martinus Nijhoff, 1990.

Bloom, Alexander. *Prodigal Sons.* New York: Oxford University Press, 1986.

Blumenthal, Sidney. *The Rise of the Counter-Establishment.* New York: Harper & Row, 1986.

Bohlen, Charles. *The Transformation of American Foreign Policy.* New York: W.W. Norton, 1969.

———. *Witness to History.* New York: W.W. Norton, 1973.

Bonner, Raymond. *Weakness and Deceit.* New York: Times Books, 1984.

Bonosky, Phillip. *Washington's Secret War Against Afghanistan.* New York: International Publishers, 1985.

Booth, John A. *The End and the Beginning: The Nicaraguan Revolution.* Boulder: Westview Press, 1985.

Bowles, Chester. *Promises to Keep: My Years in Public Life, 1941–1969.* New York: Harper, 1971.

Bradsher, Henry S. *Afghanistan and the Soviet Union.* Durham, NC: Duke University Press, 1985.

Brinkley, David. *Washington Goes to War.* New York: Alfred A. Knopf, 1988.

Broder, David. *Changing of the Guard: Power and Leadership in America.* New York: Penguin Books, 1981.

Brodie, Bernard. *Strategy in the Missile Age.* Princeton: Princeton University Press, 1965.

Brown, Cynthia, ed. *With Friends Like These: The Americas Watch Report on Human Rights and U.S. Policy in Latin America.* New York: Pantheon, 1985.

Brumberg, Abraham, ed. *Poland: Genesis of a Revolution.* New York: Vintage, 1983.

Brzezinski, Zbigniew. *Between Two Ages.* New York: Viking, 1971.

———. *Power and Principle.* New York: Farrar, Straus & Giroux, 1983.

Buckley, William F., Jr. *United Nations Journal.* New York: G.P. Putnam's Sons, 1974.

Bundy, McGeorge. *Danger and Survival.* New York: Random House, 1988.

Burns, Bradford. *At War in Nicaragua: The Reagan Doctrine and the Politics of Nostalgia.* New York: Harper & Row, 1987.

Burns, James MacGregor. *Leadership.* New York: Harper & Row, 1978.

Callahan, David. *Dangerous Capabilities: Paul Nitze and the Cold War.* New York: HarperCollins, 1990.

Canfield, Cass. *Up and Down and Around.* New York: Harper & Row, 1971.

Cannon, Lou. *Reagan.* New York: Perigee Books, 1982.

Carothers, Tom H. *In the Name of Democracy: United States Policy Toward Latin America in the Reagan Years.* Berkeley: University of California Press, 1991.

Carter, Jimmy. *Keeping Faith.* New York: Bantam, 1982.

———. *The Presidential Campaign, 1976,* Volume 1, Parts 1 and 2. Washington: Government Printing Office, 1978.

———. *Public Papers of the Presidents of the United States: 1977.* Washington: Government Printing Office, 1978.

Chace, James. *Endless War: How We Got Involved in Central America—And What Can Be Done.* New York: Vintage, 1984.

Chafe, William H. *The Unfinished Journey: America Since World War II.* New York: Oxford University Press, 1991.

Chays, Abram, and Jerome Weisner, eds. *ABM: An Evaluation of the Decision to Deploy an Antiballistic Missile System.* New York: Harper & Row, 1969.

Child, Jack, ed. *Conflict in Central America: Approaches to Peace and Security.* New York: St. Martin's, 1984.

Christian, Shirley. *Nicaragua: Revolution in the Family.* New York: Random House, 1985.

Churba, Joseph. *The American Retreat: The Reagan Foreign and Defense Policy.* Chicago: Regnery Gateway, 1984.

Churchill, Winston. *Hinge of Fate.* Boston: Houghton Mifflin, 1948.

———. *Triumph and Tragedy.* Boston: Houghton Mifflin, 1950.

Cimbala, Stephen J., ed. *The Reagan Defense Program: An Interim Assessment.* Wilmington: Scholarly Resources, 1986.

Cirincione, Joseph, ed. *Central America and the Western Alliance.* New York: Holmes & Meier, 1985.

Clark, Ronald W. *The Greatest Power on Earth: The International Race for Nuclear Supremacy.* New York: Harper & Row, 1980.

Clifford, Clark, with Richard Holbrooke. *Counsel to the President.* New York: Random House, 1991.

Cohen, Warren I. *Dean Rusk.* Totowa, NJ: Cooper Square Publishers, 1980.

Cole, Paul M., and William J. Taylor, eds. *The Nuclear Freeze Debate: Arms Control Issues for the 1980s.* Boulder: Westview Press, 1983.

Coleman, Kenneth M., and George C. Herring, eds. *The Central American Crisis.* Wilmington: Scholarly Resources, 1985.

Collier, Peter, and David Horowitz. *Destructive Generation: Second Thoughts About the 60's.* New York: Summit Books, 1989.

Collins, Joseph J. *The Soviet Invasion of Afghanistan: A Study in the Use of Force in Soviet Foreign Policy.* Lexington, MA: Lexington Books, 1986.

Corson, William R., Susan B. Trento, and Joseph J. Trento. *Widows: Four American Spies, the Wives They Left Behind, and the KGB's Crippling of American Intelligence.* New York: Crown, 1989.

Crabb, Cecil Van Meter. *Presidents and Foreign Policy Making: From FDR to Reagan.* Baton Rouge: Louisiana State University Press, 1986.

Cuthbertson, Ian M. *Redefining the CSCE: Challenges and Opportunities in the New Europe.* New York: Institute for East-West Studies, 1992.

Dahl, Robert A. *Polyarchy: Participation and Opposition.* New Haven: Yale University Press, 1971.

Dallek, Robert. *The American Style of Foreign Policy.* New York: Alfred A. Knopf, 1983.

———. *Ronald Reagan: The Politics of Symbolism.* Cambridge: Harvard University Press, 1984.

Dallin, Alexander. *Black Box: KAL 007 and the Superpowers.* Berkeley: University of California Press, 1984.

Dallin, Alexander, and Gail W. Lapidus, eds. *The Soviet System in Crisis.* Boulder: Westview Press, 1991.

David, Charles Philippe. *Foreign Policy Failure in the White House: Reappraising the Fall of the Shah of Iran and the Iran-Contra Affair.* Lanham, MD: University Press of America, 1993.

Davis, Lynn Etheridge. *The Cold War Begins.* Princeton: Princeton University Press, 1974.

Deaver, Michael, and Mickey Herskowitz. *Behind the Scenes: In Which the Author Talks About Ronald Reagan and Nancy Reagan . . . and Himself.* New York: William Morrow, 1987.

Destler, I. M., Leslie Gelb, and Anthony Lake. *Our Own Worst Enemy.* New York: Simon & Schuster, 1984.

Diamond, Larry, Juan J. Linz, and Seymour Martin Lipset, eds. *Democracy in Developing Countries,* Volume 4: *Latin America.* Boulder: Lynne Riener, 1989.

Dickey, Christopher. *With the Contras: A Reporter in the Wilds of Nicaragua.* New York: Simon & Schuster, 1985.

Diggins, John P. *The Rise and Fall of the American Left.* New York: W.W. Norton, 1992.

Dinges, John. *Our Man in Panama: How General Noriega Used the United States— And Made Millions in Drugs and Arms.* New York: Random House, 1990.

Diskin, Martin. *Trouble in Our Backyard: Central America and the United States in the Eighties.* New York: Pantheon, 1983.

Djilas, Milovan. *Conversations with Stalin.* London: Pelican, 1969.

———. *Rise and Fall.* New York: Harcourt Brace Jovanovich, 1985.

Doder, Dusko, and Louise Branson. *Gorbachev: Heretic in the Kremlin.* New York: Viking Penguin, 1990.

Donovan, Hedley. *Roosevelt to Reagan: A Reporter's Encounters with Nine Presidents.* New York: Harper & Row, 1985.

Dorrien, Gary. *The Neoconservative Mind.* Philadelphia: Temple University Press, 1993.

Dorsey, Gary L. *Beyond the United Nations: Changing Discourse in International Politics and Law.* Lanham, MD: University Press of America, 1986.

Draper, Theodore. *Present History.* New York: Random House, 1983.

Drell, Sidney D. *The Reagan Strategic Defense Initiative: A Technical, Political, and Arms Control Assessment.* Cambridge, MA: Ballinger, 1985.

Drew, Elizabeth. *Washington Journal: 1973–1974.* New York: Random House, 1975.

Dumbrell, John. *The Carter Presidency: A Reevaluation.* New York: St. Martin's, 1993.

Dunkerly, James. *The Long War: Dictatorship and Revolution in El Salvador.* London: Junction Books, 1982.

Dupree, Louis. *Afghanistan, 1980: The World Turned Upside Down.* Hanover, NH: American Universities Field Staff, 1980.

Ehrman, John. *Neoconservatism: Intellectuals and Foreign Affairs, 1945–1994.* New Haven: Yale University Press, 1994.

Fagen, Richard R. *Forging Peace: The Challenge of Central America.* New York: Basil Blackwell, 1987.

Fagen, Richard R., and Olga Pellicer. *The Future of Central America: Policy Choices for the U.S. and Mexico.* Stanford, CA: Stanford University Press, 1983.

Falcoff, Mark, and Robert Royal. *The Continuing Crisis: U.S. Policy in Central America and the Caribbean.* Washington: Ethics and Public Policy Center, 1987.

Farr, Grant M., and John G Merriam, eds. *Afghan Resistance: The Politics of Survival.* Boulder: Westview Press, 1987.

Findling, John E. *Close Neighbors, Distant Friends: United States—Central American Relations.* New York: Greenwood Press, 1987.

Fleeing Their Homeland: A Report on the Testimony of Nicaraguan Refugees to Conditions in Their Country and the Reasons for Their Flight. New York: The Puebla Institute, April 1987.

Ford, Daniel F. *Beyond the Freeze: The Road to Nuclear Sanity.* Boston: Beacon Press, 1982.

Ford, Gerald. *A Time to Heal.* New York: Harper & Row, 1979.

Fosdick, Dorothy, ed. *Henry M. Jackson and World Affairs: Selected Speeches.* Seattle: University of Washington Press, 1990.

Fossedal, Gregory A. *The Democratic Imperative.* New York: Basic Books, 1989.

Freedman, Lawrence. *The Evolution of Nuclear Strategy.* New York: St. Martin's Press, 1983.

Freeman, John. *Security and the CSCE Process: The Stockholm Conference and Beyond.* New York: St. Martin's, 1991.

Fry, Alton. *A Responsible Congress: The Politics of National Security.* New York: McGraw-Hill, 1975.

Gaddis, John Lewis. *Containing the Soviet Union: A Critique of U.S. Policy.* Edited by Terry L. Diebel and John Lewis Gaddis. Washington: Pergamon, 1987.

———. *The Long Peace: Inquiries into the History of the Cold War.* New York: Oxford University Press, 1987.

———. *Russia, the Soviet Union, and the United States: An Interpretive History.* New York: Wiley, 1978.

———. *Strategies of Containment.* New York: Oxford University Press, 1982.

———. *The United States and the End of the Cold War: Implications, Reconsiderations, Provocations.* New York: Oxford University Press, 1992.

Garfinkle, Adam M. *The Politics of the Nuclear Freeze.* Philadelphia: Foreign Policy Research Institute, 1984.

Garthoff, Raymond L. *Détente and Confrontation: American-Soviet Relations from Nixon to Reagan.* Washington: Brookings Institution, 1985.

———. *The Great Transition: American-Soviet Relations and the End of the Cold War.* Washington: Brookings Institution, 1994.

———. *Policy Versus the Law: The Reinterpretation of the ABM Treaty.* Washington: Brookings Institution, 1987.

Gelb, Leslie, and Richard K. Betts. *The Irony of Vietnam: The System Worked.* Washington: Brookings Institution, 1979.

Gellman, Barton. *Contending with Kennan: Towards a Philosophy of American Power.* New York: Praeger, 1985.

George, Alexander, and Richard Smoke. *Deterrence in American Foreign Policy.* New York: Columbia University Press, 1974.

Gilbert, Martin. *Shcharansky: Hero of Our Time.* New York: Viking, 1986.

Gilmore, William C. *The Grenada Intervention.* New York: Facts on File, 1984.

Goodwin, Richard. *Remembering America: A Voice from the Sixties.* Boston: Little, Brown, 1988.

Gorbachev, Mikhail. *Perestroika.* New York: Harper & Row, 1987.

Greenstein, Fred, ed. *The Reagan Presidency: An Early Assessment.* Baltimore: Johns Hopkins University Press, 1983.

Gromyko, Andrei. *Memoirs.* Translated by Harold Shukman. New York: Doubleday, 1989.

Gutman, Roy. *Banana Diplomacy: The Making of American Policy in Nicaragua, 1981–1987.* New York: Simon & Schuster, 1988.

Gwertzman, Bernard, and Michael Kaufman, eds. *The Collapse of Communism.* New York: Random House, 1990.

Haas, Ernst B. *Why We Still Need the United Nations: The Collective Management of International Conflict, 1945–1984.* Berkeley: University of California Press, 1986.

Hahn, Walter F., ed. *Central America and the Reagan Doctrine.* Lanham, MD: University Press of America, 1987.

Haig, Alexander. *Caveat: Realism, Reagan, and Foreign Policy.* New York: Macmillan, 1984.

———. *Inner Circles: How America Changed the World, A Memoir.* New York: Warner Books, 1992.

Halberstam, David. *The Powers That Be.* New York: Alfred A. Knopf, 1979.

Halle, Louis. *The Cold War as History.* New York: Harper & Row, 1967.

Halperin, Morton H. *Nuclear Fallacy: Dispelling the Myth of Nuclear Strategy.* New York: Harper & Row, 1987.

Harriman, Averell. *America and Russia in a Changing World.* New York: Doubleday, 1971.

Hartung, William D. *The Economic Consequences of a Nuclear Freeze.* New York: Council on Economic Priorities, 1984.

Harvcy, Mose L. *Soviet Combat Troops in Cuba: Implications of the Carter Solution for the USSR.* Washington: Advanced International Studies Institute, 1979.

Head, Richard, Frisco Short, and Robert McFarlane. *Crisis Resolution: Presidential Decision Making in the Mayaguez and Korean Confrontations.* Boulder: Westview Press, 1978.

Heraclides, Alexis. *Helsinki II and Its Aftermath: The Making of the CSCE into an International Organization.* New York: Pinter Publishers, 1993.

Herf, Jeffrey. *War by Other Means: Soviet Power, West German Resistance, and the Battle of the Euromissiles.* New York: The Free Press, 1991.

Herken, Gregg. *Counsels of War.* New York: Alfred A. Knopf, 1985.

Hersh, Seymour M. *The Price of Power: Kissinger in the Nixon White House.* New York: Summit Books, 1983.

———. *"The Target Is Destroyed": What Really Happened to Flight 007 and What America Knew About It.* New York: Random House, 1986.

Hilsman, Roger. *To Move a Nation: The Politics of Foreign Policy in the Administration of John F. Kennedy.* New York: Doubleday, 1967.

Hoffman, Stanley. *Dead Ends.* Cambridge, MA: Ballinger, 1983.

———. *Primacy or World Order.* New York: McGraw-Hill, 1978.

Hogan, J. Michael. *The Nuclear Freeze Campaign: Rhetoric and Foreign Policy in the Telepolitical Age.* East Lansing: Michigan State University Press, 1994.

Hollander, Paul. *Political Pilgrims.* New York: Oxford University Press, 1981.

Holloway, David. *The Soviet Union and the Arms Race.* New Haven: Yale University Press, 1983.

Hook, Sidney. *Marxism and Beyond.* Totowa, NJ: Rowman and Littlefield, 1983.

———. *Out of Step.* New York: Harper & Row, 1987.

Hoopes, Townsend. *The Devil and John Foster Dulles.* Boston: Little, Brown, 1973.

———. *The Limits of Intervention.* New York: David McKay, 1969.

Hulme, Derick L. *The Political Olympics: Moscow, Afghanistan, and the 1980 U.S. Boycott.* New York: Praeger, 1990.

Hyland, William G. *The Cold War Is Over.* New York: Random House, 1990.

———. *Mortal Rivals: Superpower Relations from Nixon to Reagan.* New York: Random House, 1987.

Hyman, Anthony. *Afghanistan Under Soviet Domination, 1964–1981.* New York: St. Martin's, 1982.

Iklé, Fred Charles. *Every War Must End.* New York: Columbia University Press, 1971.

Isaacson, Walter. *Kissinger.* New York: Simon & Schuster, 1992.

Johnson, Paul. *Modern Times: The World from the Twenties to the Eighties*. New York: Harper Perennial, 1985.

Jungk, Robert. *Brighter than a Thousand Suns: A Personal History of the Atomic Scientists*. San Diego: Harcourt Brace Jovanovich, 1958.

Kaiser, Robert. *Cold Winter, Cold War*. New York: Stein & Day, 1974.

———. *Why Gorbachev Happened: His Triumphs and His Failure*. New York: Simon & Schuster, 1991.

Kalb, Marvin, and Elie Abel. *Roots of Involvement: The United States in Asia, 1948–1971*. New York: W.W. Norton, 1971.

Kalugin, Oleg. *The First Directorate: My 32 Years in Intelligence and Espionage Against the West*. New York: St. Martin's, 1994.

Kampelman, Max M. *Three Years at the East-West Divide*. New York: Freedom House, 1983.

Kaplan, Fred M. *The Wizards of Armageddon*. New York: Simon & Schuster, 1983.

Karnow, Stanley. *Vietnam*. New York: Viking, 1983.

Kearns, Doris. *Lyndon Johnson and the American Dream*. New York: Harper & Row, 1976.

Kempe, Frederick. *Divorcing the Dictator: America's Bungled Affair with Noriega*. New York: G.P. Putnam's Sons, 1990.

Kennan, George F. *The Cloud of Danger: Current Realities of American Foreign Policy*. Boston: Little, Brown, 1977.

———. *Memoirs, 1950–1963*. Boston: Little, Brown, 1972.

———. *The Nuclear Delusion*. New York: Pantheon, 1982.

Kirkpatrick, Jeane J. *Dictatorships and Double Standards: Rationalism and Reason in Politics*. New York: Simon & Schuster, 1982.

———. *Dismantling the Parties*. Washington: American Enterprise Institute, 1978.

———. *Leader and Vanguard: A Study of Peronist Argentina*. Cambridge: Massachusetts Institute of Technology, 1971.

———. *Legitimacy and Force*, Volume 1. New Brunswick, NJ: Transaction, 1988.

———. *The New Presidential Elite: Men and Women in National Politics*. New York: Russell Sage, 1976.

———. *Political Woman*. New York: Basic Books, 1974.

———. *The Reagan Phenomenon, and Other Speeches on Foreign Policy*. Washington: American Enterprise Institute for Public Policy Research, 1981.

———. *The Strategy of Deception: A Study in World-Wide Communist Tactics*. New York: Farrar, Straus, 1963.

———. *The United States and the World: Setting Limits*. Washington: American Enterprise Institute, 1986.

———. *The Withering Away of the Totalitarian State—And Other Surprises*. Washington: American Enterprise Institute, 1986.

Kirkpatrick, Jeane J., and Allan Gerson, "The Reagan Doctrine, Human Rights, and International Law." In *Might v. Right*. New York: Council on Foreign Relations, 1989.

Kissinger, Henry. *For the Record*. Boston: Little, Brown, 1981.

———. *Diplomacy*. New York: Simon & Schuster, 1994.

———. *Observations*. Boston: Little, Brown, 1985.

———. *The White House Years*. Boston: Little, Brown, 1979.

———. *Years of Upheaval*. Boston: Little, Brown, 1982.

Klehr, Harvey, John Earl Haynes, and Fridrikh Lgorevich Firsov. *The Secret World of American Communism*. New Haven: Yale University Press, 1995.

Korey, William. *Glasnost and Soviet Anti-Semitism*. New York: American Jewish Committee, 1991.

———. *Human Rights and the Helsinki Accord*. New York: Foreign Policy Association, 1983.

———. *The Promises We Keep: Human Rights, the Helsinki Process, and American Foreign Policy*. New York: St. Martin's, 1993.

———. *The Soviet Cage: Anti-Semitism in Russia*. New York: Viking, 1973.

Kornbluh, Peter, and Malcome Byrne, eds. *The Iran-Contra Scandal: The Declassified History*. New York: New Press, 1993.

Kraft, Joseph. *Profiles in Power: A Washington Insight*. New York: New American Library, 1966.

Kristol, Irving. *On the Democratic Idea in America*. New York: Harper & Row, 1972.

———. *Reflections of a Neoconservative*. New York: Basic Books, 1976.

Kuttner, Robert. *The Life of the Party: Democratic Prospects in 1988 and Beyond*. New York: Penguin Books, 1988.

Laber, Jeri. *A Nation Is Dying: Afghanistan Under the Soviets*. Evanston, IL: Northwestern University Press, 1988.

LaFeber, Walter. *America, Russia, and the Cold War, 1945–1992*. New York: McGraw-Hill, 1993.

———. *The American Age: United States Foreign Policy at Home and Abroad Since 1750*. New York: W.W. Norton, 1989.

———. *Inevitable Revolutions: The United States and Central America*. New York: W.W. Norton, 1984.

———. *The Panama Canal: The Crisis in Historical Perspective*. New York: Oxford University Press, 1989.

Lake, Anthony. *Somoza Falling*. Boston: Houghton Mifflin, 1989.

———. *Third World Radical Regimes: U.S. Policy Under Carter and Reagan*. New York: Foreign Policy Association, 1985.

Lawyers Committee for Human Rights. *From the Ashes: A Report on the Efforts to Rebuild El Salvador's System of Justice*. New York: Lawyers Committee for Human Rights, 1987.

———. *Underwriting Injustice: AID and El Salvador's Judicial Reform Program*. New York: Lawyers Committee for Human Rights, 1989.

Lebow, Richard Ned. *Between Peace and War: The Nature of International Crisis*. Baltimore: Johns Hopkins University Press, 1981.

Ledeen, Michael A. *Perilous Statecraft: An Insider's Account of the Iran-Contra Affair*. New York: Charles Scribner's Sons, 1988.

Leiken, Robert S., ed. *Central America: Anatomy of Conflict*. New York: Pergamon, 1984.

Leuchtenburg, William. *In the Shadow of FDR: From Harry Truman to Ronald Reagan*. Ithaca, NY: Cornell University Press, 1983.

Linz, Juan J. *The Breakdown of Democratic Regimes: Crisis, Breakdown, and Reequilibriation*. Baltimore: Johns Hopkins University Press, 1978.

Lippmann, Walter. *The Cold War*. New York: Harper & Brothers, 1947.

Lowenthal, Abraham F., ed. *Exporting Democracy: The United States and Latin America*. Baltimore: Johns Hopkins University Press, 1991.

―――. *Partners in Conflict*. Baltimore: Johns Hopkins University Press, 1988.

Mandelbaum, Michael. *The Nuclear Question: The United States and Nuclear Weapons, 1946–1976*. Cambridge: Cambridge University Press, 1979.

Marchetti, Victor, and John Marks. *The CIA and the Cult of Intelligence*. New York: Dell, 1975.

Marshall, Jonathan. *The Iran-Contra Connection: Secret Teams and Covert Operations in the Reagan Era*. Boston: South End Press, 1987.

May, Ernest. *American Cold War Strategy: Interpreting NSC 68*. Boston: Bedford Books, 1993.

―――. *The American Foreign Policy*. New York: G. Braziller, 1963.

―――. *Lessons of the Past*. New York: Oxford University Press, 1973.

Mayer, Jane, and Doyle McManus. *Landslide: The Unmaking of a President, 1984–1988*. Boston: Houghton Mifflin, 1988.

McCloy, John. *The Challenge to American Foreign Policy*. Cambridge: Harvard University Press, 1969.

McCullough, David. *Truman*. New York: Simon & Schuster, 1992.

McDougall, Walter A. . . . *The Heavens and the Earth: A Political History of the Space Age*. New York: Basic Books, 1985.

McGwire, Michael. *Military Objectives in Soviet Foreign Policy*. Washington: Brookings Institution, 1987.

McFarlane, Robert C. *Special Trust*. New York: Cadell & Davies, 1994.

McMahan, Jeff. *Reagan and the World: Imperial Policy in the New Cold War*. New York: Monthly Review Press, 1985.

McMichael, Scott R. *Stumbling Bear: Soviet Military Performance in Afghanistan*. Washington: Brassey's, 1991.

McNamara, Robert S. *Blundering into Disaster*. New York: Pantheon, 1986.

McNeil, Frank. *War and Peace in Central America*. New York: Charles Scribner's Sons, 1988.

McPherson, Harry. *A Political Education*. Boston: Atlantic-Little, Brown, 1971.

Menges, Constantine. *Inside the National Security Council: The True Story of the Making and Unmaking of Reagan's Foreign Policy*. New York: Simon & Schuster, 1988.

―――. *The Twilight Struggle*. Washington: American Enterprise Institute, 1990.

Meyer, David S. *A Winter of Discontent: The Nuclear Freeze and American Politics*. New York: Praeger, 1990.

Moens, Alexander. *Foreign Policy Under Carter: Testing Multiple Advocacy Decision Making*. Boulder: Westview Press, 1990.

Monks, Alfred L. *The Soviet Intervention in Afghanistan.* Washington: American Enterprise Institute for Public Policy Research, 1981.

Moore, John Norton. *Law and the Grenada Mission.* Charlotte, NC: Center for Law and National Security, 1984.

Morganthau, Hans J. *Politics Among Nations: The Struggle for Power and Peace.* New York: Alfred A. Knopf, 1967.

Morris, Edmund. *The Rise of Theodore Roosevelt.* New York: Coward, McCann & Geoghegan, 1979.

Morris, Roger. *Uncertain Greatness: Henry Kissinger and American Foreign Policy.* New York: Harper & Row, 1977.

Motley, Langhorne. "Letting Off Steam." In *Authoritarian Regimes in Transition,* edited by Hans Binnendijk. Washington: Foreign Service Institute, 1987.

Mower, A. Glenn. *Human Rights and American Foreign Policy: The Carter and Reagan Experiences.* New York: Greenwood Press, 1987.

Moynihan, Daniel P., with Suzanne Weaver. *A Dangerous Place.* Boston: Little, Brown, 1978.

Muravchik, Joshua. *Exporting Democracy.* Washington: American Enterprise Institute, 1991.

——. *The Uncertain Crusade: Jimmy Carter and the Dilemmas of Human Rights Policy.* Lanham, MD: Hamilton Press, 1986.

Nash, George H. *The Conservative Intellectual Movement in America Since 1945.* New York: Basic Books, 1976.

National Resources Defense Council. *Nuclear Weapons Data Book.* Cambridge, MA: Ballinger, 1984.

Neustadt, Richard. *Presidential Power and the Modern Presidents: The Politics of Leadership from Roosevelt to Reagan.* New York: The Free Press, 1990.

Neustadt, Richard, and Ernest May. *Thinking in Time: The Uses of History for Decision Makers.* New York: The Free Press, 1986.

Newhouse, John. *Cold Dawn: The Story of SALT.* New York: Holt, Rinehart & Winston, 1973.

——. *War and Peace in the Nuclear Age.* New York: Alfred A. Knopf, 1989.

Nicaragua, Civil Liberties, and the Central American Peace Plan. New York: The Puebla Institute, January 1988.

Nitze, Paul. *From Hiroshima to Glasnost.* New York: Grove Weidenfeld, 1989.

Nixon, Richard M. *Leaders.* New York: Warner Books, 1982.

——. *The Memoirs of Richard Nixon.* New York: Grosset & Dunlap, 1978.

——. *Public Papers of the Presidents of the United States: 1973.* Washington: Government Printing Office, 1975.

——. *Six Crises.* New York: Doubleday, 1962.

Noonan, Peggy. *What I Saw at the Revolution.* New York: Random House, 1990.

North, Oliver, with William Novak. *Under Fire: An American Story.* New York: Harper-Paperbacks, 1991.

Nye, Joseph S., Jr. *Bound to Lead: The Changing Nature of American Power.* New York: Basic Books, 1990.

————. *Nuclear Ethics.* New York: The Free Press, 1986.

O'Keefe, Bernard J. *Nuclear Hostages.* Boston: Houghton Mifflin, 1983.

Orlov, Yuri. *Dangerous Thoughts: Memoirs of a Russian Life.* New York: William Morrow, 1991.

Osgood, Robert E. *NATO: The Entangling Alliance.* Chicago: University of Chicago Press, 1962.

Oye, Kenneth A., Donald Rothchild, and Robert J. Leiber, eds. *Eagle Entangled: U.S. Foreign Policy in a Complex World.* New York: Longman, 1979.

————. *Eagle Resurgent.* Boston: Little, Brown, 1987.

Pastor, Robert. *Condemned to Repetition: The United States and Nicaragua.* Princeton: Princeton University Press, 1987.

Payne, Anthony, Paul Sutton, and Tony Thorndike. *Grenada: Revolution and Invasion.* New York: St. Martin's, 1984.

Payne, Keith B. *Nuclear Deterrence in U.S.-Soviet Relations.* Boulder: Westview Press, 1982.

Payne, Keith B., and Colin S. Gray, eds. *The Nuclear Freeze Controversy.* Lanham, MD: University Press of America, 1984.

Penkovsky, Oleg. *The Penkovsky Papers.* New York: Ballantine, 1977.

Pipes, Richard. *Survival Is Not Enough.* New York: Simon & Schuster, 1984.

Podhoretz, John. *Hell of a Ride.* New York: Simon & Schuster, 1993.

Podhoretz, Norman. *Breaking Ranks.* New York: Harper & Row, 1979.

————. *Making It.* New York: Random House, 1967.

————. *Why We Were in Vietnam.* New York: Simon & Schuster, 1982.

Porter, Bruce, D. *The USSR in the Third World Conflicts.* Cambridge: Cambridge University Press, 1984.

Powers, Thomas. *The Man Who Kept Secrets: Richard Helms and the CIA.* New York: Alfred A. Knopf, 1979.

————. *Thinking About the Next War.* New York: Alfred A. Knopf, 1982.

Pringle, Peter, and James Spigelman. *The Nuclear Barons.* New York: Holt, Rinehart & Winston, 1981.

Reagan, Ronald. *Final Reports: Personal Reflections on Politics and History in Our Time.* New York: Doubleday, 1984.

————. *Public Papers of the Presidents of the United States: 1981.* Washington: Government Printing Office, 1982.

————. *Public Papers of the Presidents of the United States: 1982,* Volume 1. Washington: Government Printing Office, 1983.

Regan, Donald. *For the Record: From Wall Street to Washington.* San Diego: Harcourt Brace Jovanovich, 1988.

Revel, Jean-François. *Democracy Against Itself: The Future of the Democratic Impulse.* New York: The Free Press, 1993.

————. *The Flight from the Truth: The Reign of Deceit in the Age of Information.* New York: Random House, 1991.

————. *How Democracies Perish.* New York: Doubleday, 1984.

————. *The Totalitarian Temptation.* New York: Harper & Row, 1979.

Roberts, Adam, and Benedict Kingsbury, eds. *United Nations, Divided World*. New York: Clarendon Press, 1988.

Rosenau, James N. *The United Nations in a Turbulent World*. Boulder: Lynne Rienner, 1992.

Rosenbaum, Herbert D., and Alexej Ugrinsky, eds. *Jimmy Carter: Foreign Policy and Post-Presidential Years*. Westport, CT: Greenwood Press, 1994.

Rostow, Eugene V. *Peace in the Balance*. New York: Simon & Schuster, 1972.

Roverc, Richard H. *The American Establishment and Other Reports, Opinions, and Speculations*. New York: Harcourt, Brace & World, 1962.

———. *Arrivals and Departures: A Journalist's Memoirs*. New York: Macmillan, 1976.

Rowen, Henry S., and Charles Wolfe, Jr., eds. *The Future of the Soviet Empire*. New York: Institute for Contemporary Studies/St. Martin's, 1987.

Rubin, Barry. *Paved with Good Intentions*. New York: Oxford University Press, 1980.

Rusk, Dean, with Richard Rusk. *As I Saw It*. New York: W.W. Norton, 1990.

Sakharov, Andrei. *Memoirs*. Translated by Richard Lourie. New York: Alfred A. Knopf, 1990.

Sanders, Jerry W. *Peddlers of Crisis: The Committee on the Present Danger and the Politics of Containment*. Boston: South End Press, 1983.

Sarin, O.L. *The Afghan Syndrome: The Soviet Union's Vietnam*. Novato, CA: Presidio, 1993.

Scheer, Robert. *With Enough Shovels: Reagan, Bush, and Nuclear War*. New York: Random House, 1982.

Schelling, Thomas C., and Morton Halperin. *Strategy and Arms Control*. New York: Twentieth Century Fund, 1961.

Schiff, Zeev. *Israel's Lebanon War*. New York: Simon & Schuster, 1984.

Schulz, Donald E., and Douglas H. Graham. *Revolution and Counter-revolution in Central America and the Caribbean*. Boulder: Westview Press, 1984.

Schulzinger, Robert D. *The Wise Men of Foreign Affairs: The History of the Council on Foreign Relations*. New York: Columbia University Press, 1984.

Schwartz, David N. *NATO's Nuclear Dilemmas*. Washington: Brookings Institution, 1983.

Schweizer, Peter. *Victory: The Reagan Administration's Secret Strategy That Hastened the Collapse of the Soviet Union*. New York: Atlantic Monthly Press, 1994.

Secord, Richard V. *Honored and Betrayed: Irangate, Covert Affairs, and the Secret War in Laos*. New York: Wiley, 1992.

Sharansky, Natan. *Fear No Evil*. New York: Random House, 1989.

Sharnik, John. *Inside the Cold War: An Oral History*. New York: Arbor House, 1987.

Shevardnadze, Eduard A. *The Future Belongs to Freedom*. New York: The Free Press, 1991.

Shevchenko, Arkady. *Breaking with Moscow*. New York: Alfred A. Knopf, 1985.

Smith, Gerard. *Doubletalk: The Story of SALT I*. New York: Doubleday, 1980.

Smith, Hedrick. *The Power Game: How Washington Works*. New York: Random House, 1988.

Snepp, Frank. *Decent Interval*. New York: Random House, 1977.

Sohn, Louis B. *The CSCE and the Turbulent New Europe.* Washington: Friedrich-Naumann, 1993.

Speakes, Larry. *Speaking Out.* New York: Charles Scribner's Sons, 1988.

Spector, Leonard S. *Going Nuclear: The Spread of Nuclear Weapons, 1986–1987.* Boston: Ballinger, 1987.

———. *Nuclear Proliferation Today: The Spread of Nuclear Weapons, 1984.* New York: Vintage, 1984.

Spengler, Oswald. *The Decline of the West.* New York: Alfred A. Knopf, 1928.

Steele, David. *The Reform of the United Nations.* Wolfeboro, NH: Croom Helm, 1987.

Steinfels, Peter. *The Neoconservatives.* New York: Simon & Schuster, 1983.

Szulc, Tad. *The Illusion of Peace: Foreign Policy in the Nixon Years.* New York: Viking, 1978.

Talbott, Strobe. *Endgame: The Inside Story of SALT II.* New York: Harper & Row, 1979.

———. *The Master of the Game: Paul Nitze and the Nuclear Peace.* New York: Alfred A. Knopf, 1988.

———. *The Russians and Reagan.* New York: Vintage, 1984.

Taylor, Charles, II, ed. *Alerting America.* Washington: Pergamon-Brassey's, 1984.

Thatcher, Margaret. *The Downing Street Years.* New York: HarperCollins, 1993.

The Chronology: The Documented Day-by-Day Account of the Secret Military Assistance to Iran and the Contras. New York: Warner Books, 1987.

Thompson, Kenneth, ed. *Foreign Policy in the Reagan Presidency: Nine Intimate Perspectives.* Lanham, MD: University Press of America, 1993.

Timerman, Jacobo. *Prisoner Without a Name, Cell Without a Number.* New York: Alfred A. Knopf, 1981.

Tower, John G. *Consequences: A Personal and Political Memoir.* Boston: Little, Brown, 1991.

Trager, Oliver, ed. *The Iran-Contra Arms Scandal: Foreign Policy Disaster.* New York: Facts on File, 1988.

Tucker, Robert W. *Nuclear Debate: Difference and the Lapse of Faith.* New York: Holmes & Meir, 1985.

———. *The Purposes of American Power: An Essay on National Security.* New York: Praeger, 1981.

Tucker, Robert W., et al. *SDI and U.S. Foreign Policy.* Boulder: Westview Press, 1987.

Turner, Robert F. *Nicaragua v. United States: A Look at the Facts.* Washington: Pergamon-Brassey's, 1987.

Turner, Stansfield. *Secrecy and Democracy.* Boston: Houghton Mifflin, 1985.

Truman, Harry. *Years of Decisions.* New York: Doubleday, 1955.

———. *Years of Trial and Hope.* New York: Doubleday, 1956.

Ulam, Adam. *Expansion and Coexistence.* New York: Praeger, 1968.

———. *The Rivals: America and Russia Since World War II.* New York: Viking, 1971.

United States Congress, House Select Committee to Investigate Covert Arms Transactions with Iran. *Report of the Congressional Committees Investigating the Iran Contra Affair: With Minority Views.* New York: Times Books, 1988.

Urban, Mark. *War in Afghanistan.* New York: St. Martin's, 1990.

U.S. Foreign Policy: The Reagan Imprint. Washington: Congressional Quarterly, 1986.

Valenta, Jiri, and Esperanza Duran, eds. *Conflict in Nicaragua: A Multidimensional Perspective.* Boston: Allen & Unwin, 1987.

Valladares, Armando. *Against All Hope.* New York: Alfred A. Knopf, 1987.

Vance, Cyrus. *Hard Choices.* New York: Simon & Schuster, 1983.

Van Slyck, Philip. *Strategies for the 1980s: Lessons of Cuba, Vietnam, and Afghanistan.* Westport, CT: Greenwood Press, 1981.

Walker, Martin. *The Cold War: A History.* New York: Henry Holt, 1993.

Waller, Douglas C. *Congress and the Nuclear Freeze: An Inside Look at the Politics of a Mass Movement.* Amherst: University of Massachusetts University Press, 1987.

Walsh, Laurence E. *Iran-Contra: The Final Report.* New York: Times Books, 1994.

Washington Office on Latin America. *Elusive Justice: The U.S. Administration of the Justice Program in Latin America.* Washington: Washington Office on Latin America, 1990.

———. *Police Aid and Political Will.* Washington: Washington Office on Latin America, 1987

———. *U.S. Electoral Assistance and Democratic Development: Chile, Nicaragua and Panama.* Washington: Washington Office on Latin America, 1987.

Wattenberg, Ben J. *The Good News Is the Bad News Is Wrong.* New York: Simon & Schuster, 1984.

———. *The Real America.* New York: Doubleday, 1974.

Weisberger, Bernard. *Cold War, Cold Peace.* New York: American Heritage, 1985.

Weiss, Thomas George. *The United Nations and Changing World Politics.* Boulder: Westview Press, 1994.

White, Richard Alan. *The Morass: United States Intervention in Central America.* New York: Harper & Row, 1984.

White, Theodore H. *In Search of History.* New York: Harper & Row, 1982.

Wiarda, Howard J. *In Search of Policy: The United States and Latin America.* Washington: American Enterprise Institute, 1984.

Will, George F. *Restoration: Congress, Term Limits and the Recovery of Deliberative Democracy.* New York: The Free Press, 1992.

Wills, Garry. *Certain Trumpets: The Call of Leaders.* New York: Simon & Schuster, 1994.

———. *Reagan's America.* Garden City, NY: Doubleday, 1987.

Wirls, Daniel. *The Politics of Defense in the Reagan Era.* Ithaca, NY: Cornell University Press, 1992.

Wohlstetter, Albert J., Fred S. Hoffmann, and Henry S. Rowen. *Selection and Use of Strategic Air Bases.* Rand Report 66. Santa Monica, CA: Rand Corporation, 1954.

Woodward, Bob. *The Commanders.* New York: Simon & Schuster, 1991.

———. *The Final Days.* New York: Simon & Schuster, 1976.

Wyman, David S. *The Abandonment of the Jews: America and the Holocaust, 1941–1945.* New York: Pantheon, 1984.

York, Herbert. *Race to Oblivion: A Participant's View of the Arms Race.* New York: Simon & Schuster, 1970.

Zuckerman, Solly. *Nuclear Illusion and Reality.* New York: Viking, 1982.

Zumwalt, Elmo, Jr. *On Watch.* New York: Quadrangle, 1976.

Articles
Abrams, Elliott. "Why America Must Lead." *National Interest* (Summer 1992).

"America Now: A Failure of Nerve?" A symposium. *Commentary* (July 1975).

Andersen, Martin E. "The Military Obstacle to Latin Democracy." *Foreign Policy* (Winter 1988/89).

Bagley, Bruce M. "Contadora: The Failure of Democracy." *Journal of Interamerican Studies and World Affairs* (Fall 1986).

Ball, Desmond. "Targeting for Strategic Deterrence." *Adelphi Papers*, No. 185 (Summer 1983), International Institute for Strategic Studies, London.

Baloyra, Enrique A. "Dilemmas of Political Transition in El Salvador." *Journal of International Affairs* (Winter 1985).

———. "The Seven Plagues of El Salvador." *Current History* (December 1987).

Bundy, McGeorge, George F. Kennan, Robert S. McNamara, and Gerard Smith. "Nuclear Weapons and the Atlantic Alliance." *Foreign Affairs* (Spring 1982).

Colburn, Forrest D. "Embattled Nicaragua." *Current History* (December 1987).

Collier, Peter, and David Horowitz. "Another 'Low Dishonest Decade on the Left.'" *Commentary* (January 1987).

Danner, Mark. "Beyond the Mountains." *The New Yorker* (November 27, December 4, and December 11, 1989).

Decter, Midge. "What Is a Liberal—Who Is a Conservative?" *Commentary* (September 1976).

Diamond, Larry. "Beyond Authoritarianism and Totalitarianism: Strategies for Democratization." *The Washington Quarterly* (Winter 1989).

Dillon, Sam. "Dateline El Salvador: Crisis Renewed." *Foreign Policy* (Winter 1988/89).

Duffy, Gloria. "Administration Redefines Soviet Violations." *Bulletin of Atomic Scientists* (February 1986).

Fagen, Richard R. "The Carter Administration and Latin America: Business as Usual?" *Foreign Affairs: America and the World* (1978).

Fairbanks, Charles, Jr. "Gorbachev's Cultural Revolution." *Commentary* (August 1980).

Farer, Tom J. "Manage the Revolution?" *Foreign Policy* (Fall 1983).

Fauriol, Georges. "The Shadows of Latin American Affairs." *Foreign Affairs: America and the World* (1989/90).

Finger, Semour Maxwell. "The Reagan-Kirkpatrick Policies and the United Nations." *Foreign Affairs* (Winter 1983/84).

Fukuyama, Francis. "The End of History?" *National Interest* (Summer 1989).

Fulbright, J. William. "The Fatal Arrogance of Power." *New York Times Magazine* (May 18, 1966).

Gaddis, John Lewis, and Paul Nitze. "NSC-68 and the Soviet Threat Reconsidered." *International Security* (Spring 1980).

Gershman, Carl. "The Rise and Fall of the New Foreign Policy Establishment." *Commentary* (July 1980).

———. "Selling Them the Rope." *Commentary* (April 1979).

———. "The World According to Andrew Young." *Commentary* (August 1978).

Geyelin, Philip. "The Reagan Crisis." *Foreign Affairs: America and the World* (1986).

Goldblat, Jozef. "Charges of Treaty Violations." *Bulletin of Atomic Scientists* (May 1984).

Harries, Owen. "The Cold War and the Intellectuals." *Commentary* (October 1991).

Hodgsen, Geofrey. "The Establishment." *Foreign Policy* (Spring 1973).

Hough, Jerry F. "Gorbachev's Strategy." *Foreign Affairs* (Fall 1985).

Ignatius, David. "Arms Wrestling: Deployment of Missiles Is Big Reagan Victory, but Problems Remain." *Wall Street Journal,* December 2, 1983.

Jacoby, Tamar. "The Reagan Turnaround on Human Rights." *Foreign Affairs* (Summer 1986).

Kaiser, Karl, George Leber, Alois Mertes, and Franz-Josef Schulze. "Nuclear Weapons and the Preservation of Peace." *Foreign Affairs* (Summer 1982).

Kemble, Penn. "The Democrats After 1968." *Commentary* (January 1969).

———. "Who Needs the Liberals." *Commentary* (October 1970).

Kemble, Penn, and Joshua Muravchik. "The New Politics and the Democrats." *Commentary* (December 1972).

Kennan, George F. "Morality and Foreign Policy." *Foreign Affairs* (Winter 1985/86).

———. "On Nuclear War." *New York Review of Books* (January 21, 1982).

Kirkpatrick, Jeane J. "Dictatorships and Double Standards." *Commentary* (November 1979).

———. "To Die in Sarajevo." *Policy Review* (Fall 1992).

———. "The Revolt of the Masses." *Commentary* (February 1973).

———. "U.S. Security and Latin America." *Commentary* (January 1981).

Kirkpatrick, Jeane J., and George Urban. "American Foreign Policy in a Cold Climate: A Long Conversation." *Encounter* (November 1983).

Korey, William. "The PLO's Conquest of the U.N." *Midstream* (November 1979).

Kraemer, Sven S. "The Krasnoyarsk Saga." *Strategic Review* (Winter 1980).

Krauthammer, Charles. "Morality and the Reagan Doctrine." *New Republic* (September 8, 1986).

———. "The Multilateral Fallacy." *New Republic* (December 9, 1985).

———. "The Price of Power." *New Republic* (February 9, 1987).

———. "The Unipolar Moment." *Foreign Affairs: America and the World* (1990/91).

Kristol, Irving. "American Intellectuals and Foreign Policy." *Foreign Affairs* (July 1967).

———. "We Can't Resign as 'Policeman of the World.'" *New York Times Magazine* (May 12, 1968).

Laqueur, Walter. "Containment for the 80s." *Commentary* (October 1980).

———. "The Gathering Storm." *Commentary* (August 1974).

———. "The World of the 70s." *Commentary* (August 1972).

Lehmann-Haupt, Christopher. "Books of the Times: Dictatorship and Double Standards," *New York Times,* July 6, 1982.

LeMoyne, James. "El Salvador's Forgotten War." *Foreign Affairs* (Summer 1989).

———. "Testifying to Torture." *New York Times Magazine* (June 5, 1988).

Lewis, Flora. "Alarm Bells in the West." *Foreign Affairs: America and the World* (1981).

Lipset, Semour Martin. "Neoconservativism: Myth and Reality." *Society* (July-August 1988).

Lowenthal, Abraham F. "CBI: Misplaced Emphasis." *Foreign Policy* (Summer 1982).

Lukas, J. Anthony. "The Council on Foreign Relations." *New York Times Magazine* (November 21, 1971).

Luttwak, Edward. "The Strange Case of George F. Kennan: From Containment to Isolationism." *Commentary* (November 1977).

Mandelbaum, Michael. "The Luck of the President." *Foreign Affairs: America and the World* (1985/86).

Millet, Richard. "The Politics of Violence: Guatemala and El Salvador." *Current History* (Fall 1981).

———. "The United States and Latin America." *Current History* (February 1984).

Millman, Joel. "El Salvador's Army: A Force Unto Itself." *New York Times Magazine* (December 10, 1989).

Morgenthau, Hans J. "Senator Fulbright's New Foreign Policy." *Commentary* (May 1964).

Moynihan, Daniel Patrick. "Joining the Jackals: The U.S. at the U.N., 1977–1980." *Commentary* (February 1981).

———. "The United States in Opposition." *Commentary* (March 1975).

"The Neoconservatives and the Reagan Administration." Christopher Bright, guest ed. In *World Affairs* (Fall 1990).

Nitze, Paul. "Deterring Our Deterrent." *Foreign Policy* (Winter 1976/77).

———. "The Strategic Balance: Between Hope and Skepticism." *Foreign Policy* (Winter 1974/75).

Novak, Michael. "Needing Niebuhr Again." *Commentary* (September 1972).

Nye, Joseph S., Jr. "Can America Manage Its Soviet Policy?" *Foreign Affairs* (Spring 1984).

———. "Farewell to Arms Control?" *Foreign Affairs* (Fall 1986).

Parry, Robert, and Peter Kornbluh. "Iran-Contra's Untold Story." *Foreign Policy* (Fall 1988).

Perry, William. "In Search of a Latin America Policy: The Elusive Quest." *Washington Quarterly* (Spring 1990).

Podhoretz, Norman. "Liberal Anti-Communism Revisited." *Commentary* (September 1967).

————. "Making the World Safe for Communism." *Commentary* (February 1976).

————. "The Neoconservative Anguish Over Reagan's Foreign Policy." *New York Times Magazine* (May 2, 1982).

————. "The New American Majority." *Commentary* (January 1981).

————. "The Reagan Road to Détente." *Foreign Affairs: America and The World* (1984).

Powers, Thomas. "Choosing a Strategy for World War III." *Atlantic Monthly* (November 1982).

————. "Is Nuclear War Impossible?" *The Atlantic* (November 1984).

————. "What Is It About? Neither Superpower Can Explain a Competition That Threatens Mutual Annihilation." *The Atlantic* (January 1984).

Rasky, Susan F. "The Jackson Democrats, Updated." *New York Times*, August 27, 1987.

Robinson, Linda. "Dwindling Options in Panama." *Foreign Affairs* (Winter 1988/89).

————. "Peace in Central America?" *Foreign Affairs: America and the World* (1987/88).

Rostow, Eugene. "The Case Against SALT II." *Commentary* (February 1979).

Rowen, Henry S. "Living with a Sick Bear." *National Interest* (Winter 1986).

Sagan, Scott D. "Nuclear Alerts and Crisis Management." *International Security* (Spring 1985).

Schelling, Thomas C. "What Went Wrong with Arms Control?" *Foreign Affairs* (Winter 1985/86).

Schifter, Richard, and Thomas Sowell. "Have the Democrats Really Changed?" *Commentary* (September 1992).

Seabury, Paul, and Patrick Glynn. "Kennan: Historian as Fatalist." *The National Interest* (Winter 1985/86).

Seib, Gerald, and David Rogers. "A Spy's World." *The Wall Street Journal*, October 7, 1991.

Serafino, Nina. "Dateline Managua: Defining Democracy." *Foreign Policy* (Spring 1988).

Smith, Wayne. "Lies About Nicaragua." *Foreign Policy* (Summer 1987).

Talbott, Strobe. "U.S.-Soviet Relations: From Bad to Worse." *Foreign Affairs: America and the World* (1979).

Tucker, Robert W. "America in Decline: The Foreign Policy of 'Maturity.'" *Foreign Affairs: America and the World* (1979).

————. "Exemplar or Crusader?" *National Interest* (Fall 1986).

————. "Reagan's Foreign Policy." *Foreign Affairs: America and the World* (1988/89).

————. "Realism and the New Consensus." *National Interest* (Winter 1992/93).

Warnke, Paul C. "Apes on a Treadmill." *Foreign Policy* (Spring 1975).

Wilson, James Q. "Neoconservatism: Pro and Con." *Partisan Review* (1980).

Wohlstetter, Albert. "The Delicate Balance of Terror." *Foreign Affairs* 37 (January 1959).

————. "How to Confuse Ourselves." *Foreign Policy* (Fall 1975).

———. "Is There a Strategic Arms Race?" *Foreign Policy* (Summer 1974).

———. "Rivals, But No 'Race.'" *Foreign Policy* (Fall 1974).

Zakaria, Fareed. "Is Realism Finished?" *National Interest* (Winter 1992/93).

Reports

Agency for International Development. Annual Reports of Section 116(e) Human Rights Programs.

National Endowment for Democracy. Annual Reports (1984–1989).

Report of the National Bipartisan Commission on Central America. Washington: Government Printing Office, January 1984.

U.S. Arms Control and Disarmament Agency. *Soviet Propaganda Campaign Against NATO.* Washington: Government Printing Office, 1983.

U.S. Congress. *Report on the Congressional Committees Investigating the Iran-Contra Affair.* 100th Congress, 1st Session. S. Report. No. 100, H Report. No 100-433. Washington: Government Printing Office, 1987.

U.S. Congress. House of Representatives. Committee on Foreign Affairs and Subcommittee on International Operations. *Hearings and Markup on Authorizing Appropriations for Fiscal Years 1984–85 for the Department of State, the U.S. Information Agency, the Board for International Broadcasting, the Inter-American Foundation, the Asia Foundation, to Establish the National Endowment for Democracy.* Washington: Government Printing Office, 1984.

U.S. Department of Defense. *Soviet Military Power 1982, 1983, 1984, 1985.* Washington: Government Printing Office, 1982, 1983, 1984, 1985.

U.S. Department of State. *American Foreign Policy Current Documents 1981, 1982, 1983, 1984, 1985, 1986, 1987, 1988.* Washington: U.S. Department of State, 1984–1989.

———. *Country Reports on Human Rights* (1981–1989).

U.S. Department of State, and U.S. Department of Defense. *The Grenada Documents: An Overview and Selection.* Washington: U.S. Department of State and U.S. Department of Defense, 1984.

U.S. Department of the Treasury. "The Latin American Debt Problem," Office of the Assistant Secretary, International Affairs, Department of the Treasury, November 13, 1984. In *Dealing with the Debt Problem of Latin America.* Proceedings of a Conference, Joint Economic Committee Print, 98th Congress, 2d Session. S. Report. 98-284. Washington: Government Printing Office, 1985.

U.S. General Accounting Office. *Central America: Impact of U.S. Assistance in the 1980s.* Washington: General Accounting Office, 1989.

———. *Events Leading to the Establishment of the National Endowment for Democracy. Report to Senator Malcolm Wallop.* Washington: General Accounting Office. July 6, 1984.

U.S. Library of Congress. Congressional Research Service. *El Salvador, 1979–1989: A Briefing Book on U.S. Aid and the Situation in El Salvador.* Washington: Congressional Research Service, April 28, 1989.

Woldman, Joel M. *The National Endowment for Democracy.* Washington: Congressional Research Service Issue Brief (April 2, 1987).

NATIONAL UNIVERSITY
LIBRARY   SAN DIEGO

PHOTO CREDITS

1: Courtesy of the Henry M. Jackson Library
2: Private Collection
3, 7, 11, 12, 22: Courtesy of the private collection of Jeane J. Kirkpatrick
4, 19, 21: Courtesy of the private collection of Richard Perle
5, 15: Courtesy of the private collection of Max M. Kampelman
6, 24, 25: Courtesy of the Institute for Democracy in Eastern Europe
8, 10, 16, 17, 18, 26: Courtesy of the Ronald Reagan Library
9: Courtesy of the American Friends Service Committee
13, 14, 23: Courtesy of the private collection of Elliott Abrams
20: Private collection of Lauren Ariker